Simon & Schuster's

SUPER CROSSWORD BOOK #8

Simon & Schuster's SUPER CROSSWORD BOOK #8

EDITED BY

EUGENE T. MALESKA

and

JOHN M. SAMSON

GALLERY BOOKS

New York London Toronto Sydney New Delhi

Gallery Books
An Imprint of Simon & Schuster, Inc.
1230 Avenue of the Americas
New York, NY 10020

This Gallery Books trade paperback edition April 2019

Gallery Books and colophon are registered trademarks of Simon & Schuster, Inc.

For information about special discounts for bulk purchases, please contact Simon & Schuster Special Sales at 1-866-506-1949 or business@simonandschuster.com.

The Simon & Schuster Speakers Bureau can bring authors to your live event. For more information or to book an event, contact the Simon & Schuster Speakers Bureau at 1-866-248-3049 or visit our website at www.simonspeakers.com.

The puzzles in this book were previously published in Simon & Schuster Crossword Puzzle Book Series 147,148,149,150 and 152.

Designed by Helen Barrow

Manufactured in the United States of America

39 40

ISBN 978-0-671-89709-3

FOREWORD

Attention, puzzle solvers! You have in hand one of the finest collections of crosswords gathered together in one volume. These 225 superb challenges have been selected from out-of-print books in the legendary Simon & Schuster series, all reviewed and updated for today's fans.

The variety ranges from crosswords featuring sports, history, literature, and geography to those focusing on movies, television, music, cooking, and more—all created with wit and sparkle, guaranteed to fill hours and hours with entertainment and knowledge.

So, dig in anywhere! The reward: enormous pleasure for the crossword aficionado.

THE PUBLISHER

P.S. The puzzles designated as winning the "Margaret" award—in honor of Margaret Farrar who helped launch crosswords as a national pastime—were chosen by the editors as the best in the original books from which this collection is drawn.

COMPLETE ANSWERS ARE AT THE BACK.

For the convience of solvers who find it awkward to work crosswords in a thick book, the pages are perforated along the spine edge. This makes for easy removal of a single leaf. If you prefer not to remove pages, open the book at several different places and press down gently from top to bottom in the middle. This will help the book lie flat.

1

FROM THE RANKS by James R. Burns
You won't find any brassy answers below, although 41 Across certainly wore a brass hat.

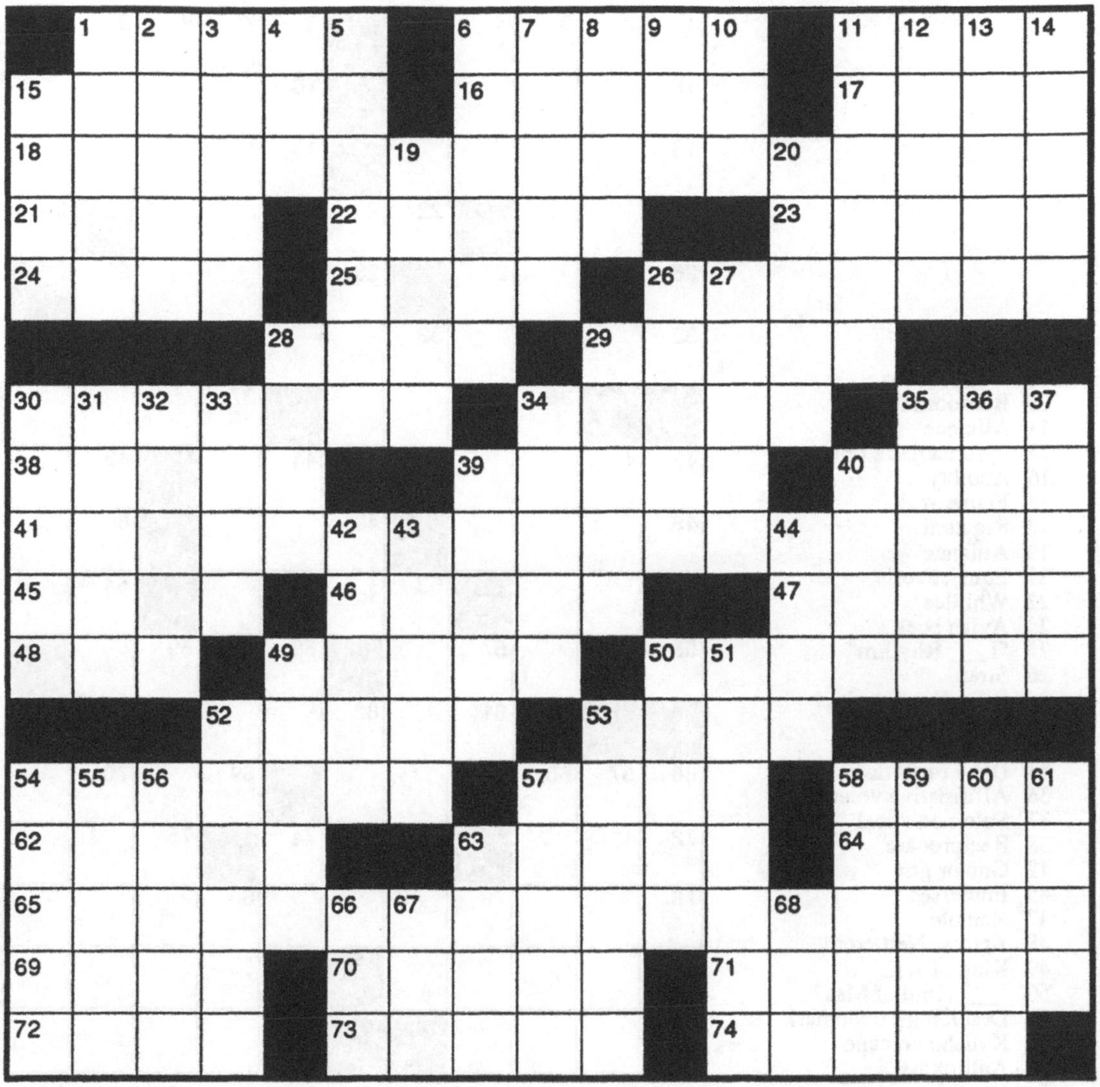

ACROSS

1 Code name
6 Fireplace
11 Joker
15 Tilt, to a tar
16 Steamer
17 Ripening agent
18 PFC's undertaking?
21 Noted film critic
22 "The Cloister and the Hearth" author
23 Functions
24 Brokerage order
25 Osprey relatives
26 Protective charms
28 Maui garlands
29 Coasts
30 Deep-six (with "of")
34 Prize
35 Fair Deal init.
38 Square-dance group
39 Filth
40 Roster
41 Napoleon I
45 First-rate
46 Come about
47 Of sound
48 Score's score: Abbr.
49 Athens attractions
50 Configuration
52 "Rouen Cathedral" painter
53 Urania, for one
54 Renegings
57 Plimsoll ___
58 Job
62 Proves legally
63 Lets up
64 Ceremonial act
65 Bill Gannon's partner
69 Language of Cork
70 Truncheon
71 Playful mammals
72 Shepherd-Turpin gun
73 Copycats
74 Woodwinds

DOWN

1 Dancer Champion
2 Bay window
3 Make merry
4 "The Cruel ___"
5 Admittances
6 Gathers grain
7 Barks
8 Part of A.M.
9 Place for swingers?
10 Slip up
11 Noels
12 Spry
13 Adjust the alarm anew
14 Kind of rehearsal
15 Accts.
19 Unearthly
20 Bluenose
26 Where Crockett fell
27 Cadence
28 Commune near Milan
29 Pizza portion
30 Bats
31 Blood of the gods
32 Path
33 Buddies
34 Fourth Estate
35 Nomadic tribe
36 One of a flight
37 Claw
39 Catch the sun
40 Laugher
42 Mock
43 Gives it a go
44 Paste of parties
49 Awaken
50 Baby food
51 Invites trouble (with "it")
52 Morning, in Mannheim
53 Shriners
54 Attorney's clients
55 Apparent
56 Deep shade of blue
57 John André's rank
58 Bromidic
59 Lent a hand
60 Rating symbols
61 West and Sugarloaf
63 Diminutive ending
66 Legal-eagle org.
67 Drop off
68 Map abbr.

2 BLOC PARTY by Martha J. DeWitt

Here's a relatively easy one from our South Carolina wordsmith. The clue at 3 Down should prove familiar by puzzle's end.

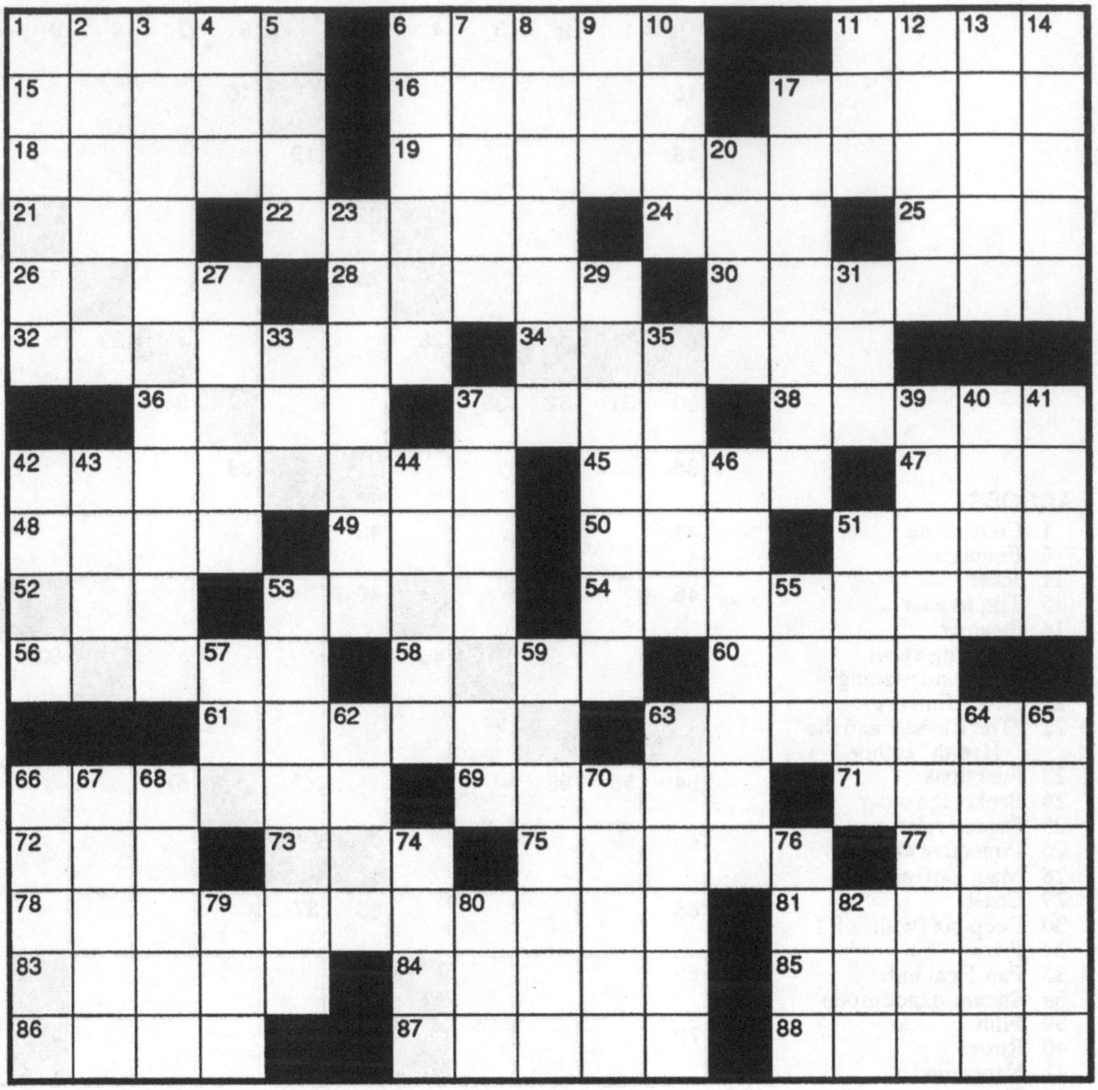

ACROSS

1 Heat and Jazz
6 Ballroom dance
11 Alliance
15 Pyromaniac's crime
16 Audibly
17 Framework
18 Rigatoni
19 Alliance
21 Equal: Prefix
22 Whittles
24 Avian beak
25 "I ___ Rhythm"
26 Strait
28 West German river
30 Foreigners
32 Languished
34 Did a turfy task
36 Affirmative voters
37 Solomon's seal
38 Reciprocate
42 Gnu or goa
45 Immerses
47 Remote
48 Actress Nettleton
49 Kind of sch.
50 "___ Kind of Man"
51 Don King's trademark
52 Kyushu volcano
53 Antitoxins
54 Dentist
56 Meaning
58 For men only
60 After fan or junk
61 Hidden
63 Brother or sister
66 Agree
69 Churchill ___
71 Liang
72 Quid ___ quo
73 Gershwin
75 Reliable
77 Congou, e.g.
78 Alliance
81 Icebox forays
83 "Love ___ the Ruins"
84 Mountain ridge
85 Tiki and Zemi
86 Latvian
87 Teredo, e.g.
88 Scrawny: Var.

DOWN

1 Recording
2 Gum ___
3 Alliance
4 Witty comeback
5 Pushover
6 Hallowed
7 Agalloch
8 Most relaxed
9 Dine
10 Djibouti's gulf
11 Cash of the court
12 Verona's river
13 Sing
14 Omar's products
17 Wirers
20 Study
23 Scary
27 "Flowers for Algernon" author
29 Menace to motorists
31 Chemical suffix
33 Either: Lat.
35 Freeze-___ coffee
37 Quieted
39 Alliance
40 Von Opel produced these
41 Jog
42 Woe is me!
43 Margin of loss
44 By itself
46 Warranty
51 Listing
53 Emitting
55 Apprehend
57 "Sioux City ___"
59 Further
62 Withered
63 Rooftop rifleman
64 Bodkin
65 Vitreous
66 Horrify
67 Fair stall: Scot.
68 French landscapist
70 Pen
74 Graceful horse
76 Little bit
79 Turner's ntwk.
80 Seatless sign
82 Fuss

3 MACEDOINE by Patterson Pepple

Patterson tells us he cooked up this little beauty without using a cookbook, but we suspect a salad chef gave him his title.

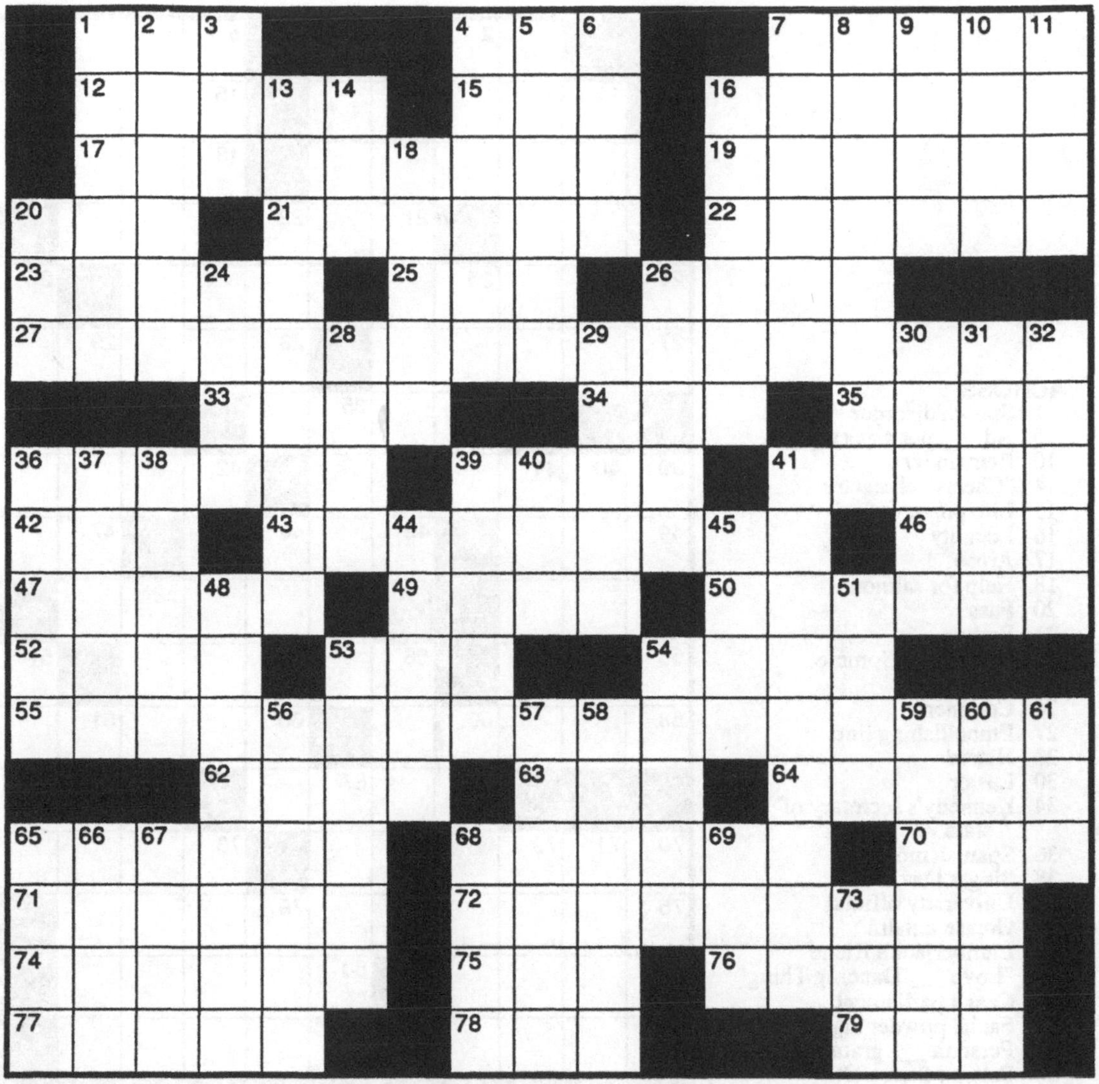

ACROSS

1 Devour
4 Gross!
7 Below-par car
12 Libel
15 Prefix for conservative
16 Desuetude
17 Helen O'Connell hit
19 Cause a riot
20 O.E.D.'s cousin
21 Responds
22 Raised
23 Soprano Mitchell
25 ___ volente
26 Milk-fed animal
27 Recompense
33 Hammer end
34 Table scrap
35 Mah-jongg piece
36 Lipped jug
39 Incursion
41 Jeopardy
42 Org. concerned with 18 Down
43 Altruistic
46 Twice LIII
47 Antiseptic
49 "___ Above All," 1942 film
50 Distinction
52 Cut of beef
53 Mauna ___
54 Festive
55 Suffer a setback
62 Grandson of Jacob
63 Nickname
64 Postpone
65 Mountain in E Turkey
68 Mosaic piece
70 Wisc. neighbor
71 Eminent scholar
72 Hand grenade
74 Stubbornly old-fashioned
75 Circle part
76 Redo a sheepshank
77 Actress Adorée
78 Curling target
79 ___ Juan

DOWN

1 O.T. book
2 Tinder
3 ___-gallon hat
4 Peace Prize Nobelist: 1965
5 Hindu
6 Weeds
7 Hereditary
8 Increase rapidly
9 Sierra Club founder
10 Bone: Comb. form
11 Require
13 "___ mind by owing owes not": Milton
14 Female ruff
16 Most urgent
18 Cellar gas
20 Memorable Landon
24 Asiatic palm
26 "Falstaff" composer
28 Sighted
29 "___ ands or buts!"
30 John ___ Society
31 Source of oil
32 Ignited anew
36 Does a top job
37 ". . . it must first fill ___": Bacon
38 Halves of a diameter
39 Renovate
40 4th caliph of Islam
41 "Too Late the ___": Paton
44 After home or bed
45 Leaf through
48 "Sweethearts ___," Lombardo hit
51 Garb for Dracula
53 Perplexing
54 Hollywood "king"
56 Suburb of L.A.
57 Look up to
58 Subtle quality
59 Hermione's attendant: Shak.
60 Heckart of the stage
61 Shipping abbr.
65 Tatar or Tuva: Abbr.
66 Appraise
67 Bard's river
68 Lovers' quarrel
69 Gob
73 Two make a qt.

4

SH! SH! by William Canine
Mr. Canine would like to dedicate this puzzle to all librarians.

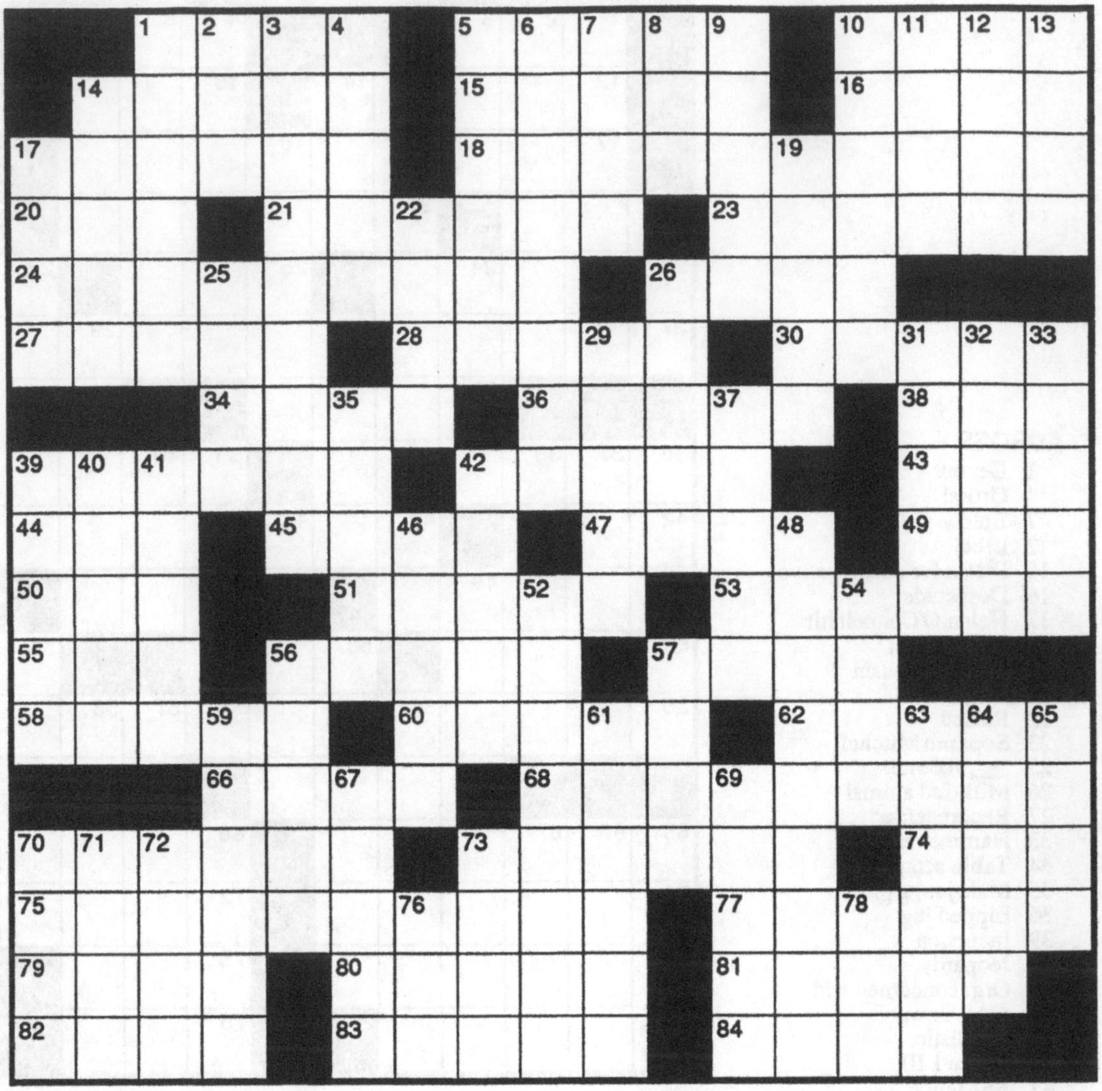

ACROSS
1 Speech disorder
5 Ad ___ per aspera
10 Remainder
14 "Cheers" character
15 Life preserver
16 Locality
17 Arose
18 Help for salmon
20 Fuss
21 Parlors
23 City on the Somme
24 Painting
26 Continent
27 Embellishing line
28 Hatred
30 Luster
34 Kennedy's secretary of state
36 Spanish month
38 Singer Davis
39 University official
42 Grease a palm
43 Lumberjack's friend
44 "Love ___ Dancing Thing"
45 Czar's parliament
47 Facial powder ingredient
49 Persona ___ grata
50 Pelican State coll.
51 Possibly
53 Poisonous gas
55 Cask
56 Carousal
57 Elizabethan coin
58 Put into action
60 Diving bird
62 Lengthy tales
66 Jason's craft
68 Literary device
70 Incarnation
73 City, to Juan
74 ___ Lanka
75 Low-paying job
77 Variety of apple
79 Throb
80 Spread
81 Like Yale's halls
82 Ludwig's 76 Down
83 Pastries
84 Exploit

DOWN
1 "The Hurricane" star
2 Anger
3 It's used for buying influence
4 Tropical fruit
5 Furnish
6 More stealthy
7 Chuck
8 Encouraging shout
9 Much put-upon Titan
10 Tire type
11 Earth, to Goethe
12 Observed
13 Water dogs
14 Organizing group
17 Jitneys
19 Pal, in Durango
22 Regard
25 Beget
26 Protozoan
29 Fuse
31 Muscat man
32 Alfred the Great, e.g.
33 Prospect
35 Baffle
37 Pass on
39 Austrian poet: 1875-1926
40 Antique auto
41 Assess
42 Moonstruck wolf
46 "Lost Horizon" actress
48 Sub's escape
52 Most brawny
54 Plank
56 Kind of vote
57 Decipher
59 TV anchor
61 Says suddenly (with "out")
63 Panted
64 Pungent
65 Rind
67 Implant
69 Savory
70 Bede of fiction
71 Smoking, e.g.
72 Tennis name
73 Singe
76 Moon mare
78 "Trivial Pursuit" piece

5

SUNNY SIDE UP by Eli Wesoff

If you think Eli's theme is about eggs, the yolk's on you. Fittingly, this puzzle was sent to us from Miami Beach.

ACROSS

1 Comedienne Peggy
5 Start of Montana's motto
8 Sault ___ Marie
11 Murray Schisgal play
14 Manet and Monet
16 Pinna part
18 White ants
19 Warm-water tuna
21 Vidalia ___
22 Milky, to Pierre
24 Tsar's command
25 Voice of Top Cat
26 Leg. claims
27 "___ the stick!"
28 Bonehead
31 First Hebrew letter
33 Ann-Margret movie: 1970
36 Observe
38 Temporary
43 Silk maker
44 Jacob's father: Ger.
45 "The Secret of My Success" star
46 Voiced
48 Deface
50 Popular when sun-dried
51 Stir up
52 Tendon
54 OTS grads
55 Andrew and N.C.
56 Spindrift on the Seine
57 Spy agcy. of WW II
58 Ancient Levite
60 A Guthrie
62 Truman's birthplace
66 "___ That Jazz"
67 Longed
71 Spenser's Emerald Isle
72 Connection
75 Useful
76 Noted drillers
78 Butter sub: Var.
80 "If folly grow romantic, I must ___": Pope
81 Sauciness
82 Satellite launched Dec. 7, 1966
83 Rock group
84 Clam genus
85 Kukui, for one

DOWN

1 "The Elder" and "The Younger"
2 "___ we a pair?"
3 Stripe
4 Magus and Legree
5 Polo Grounds star
6 Rod's partner
7 Greek peak
8 World's Fair site, 1962
9 "Honor Thy Father" author
10 "Tarzan of the Apes" auth.
11 English philosopher: 1632-1704
12 "Das Boot" setting
13 Left-hand page
15 Kelly classic
17 Pop song of 1928, à la "Pagliacci"
20 Twilight time, to Keats
23 Put on a happy face
29 Hostess with the ___
30 School org.
32 Famed French chemist
33 Stitch anew
34 Agent
35 Kind of pie
37 Reddy's "___ Woman"
39 Cap for Angus
40 Aviator Balbo
41 Shakespeare's seines
42 Insensitive
47 River islet
49 Arched bone
53 Marksman's org.
56 Recruits
59 Designer Carnegie
61 Eighth of a circle
62 Top
63 Tortilla's cousin
64 ___ Work (rock group)
65 Naysayers
68 Personnel personage
69 Beethoven's "Für ___"
70 Congested
73 Shiite leader
74 ___ a soul
77 Porker's place
79 G.E. acquisition

6 ALPHABET SOUP by James E. Hinish

Our skilled constructor from Arlington has managed to include every letter of the alphabet within the puzzle — not once, but *twice*. Hats off to Mr. H.!

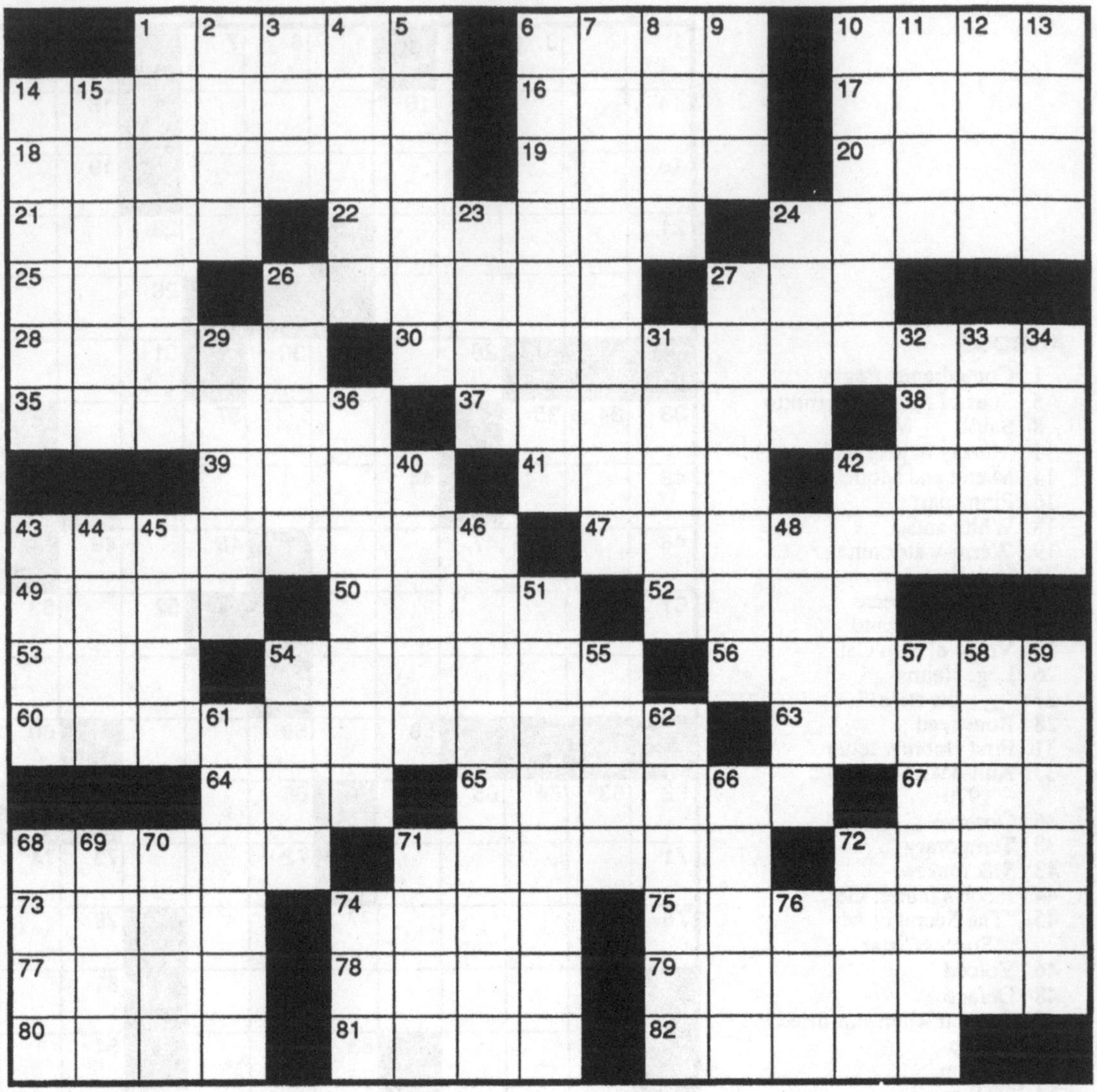

ACROSS

1 Four-wheel-drive vehicles
6 Veep's boss
10 Frenzied
14 Even-handedly
16 Madness
17 Sub shop
18 Cow-town crook
19 Analogous
20 Outlook
21 Silver's supper
22 Gideons' gifts
24 Mutable spirits
25 Part of TNT
26 Latin epic poem
27 Rocky peak
28 "___ happen here"
30 Fear of foreign things
35 Liszt's piano teacher
37 River in Wales and England
38 Agnus ___
39 Portuguese navigator
41 Indian of Sonora
42 Booty
43 Succession
47 Lowlifes
49 ___-bargain
50 Andy of comics
52 Battle site of 1944
53 Northumberland river
54 The "109" was famous
56 "The Magnificent ___": O. W. Holmes
60 Apprehension
63 Jean, John and Deborah
64 Suffix for shogun
65 Inborn
67 Chatter
68 Mouse who danced with Kelly
71 Inducement
72 Transept's projection
73 "And ___ we go!"
74 Destructive agent
75 Extremely nervous
77 Teller's partner
78 Discordant
79 Souped-up roadsters
80 Grand ___
81 "Laughing Cavalier" painter
82 "___ a Million"

DOWN

1 Fairness
2 Diner sign
3 Addition
4 USNA frosh
5 Shepherd's pipe
6 Pecan candies
7 ___ the coals (scolded)
8 Protection
9 ___ Buddhism
10 14 Across, e.g.
11 Chow ___
12 Oil: Comb. form variant
13 Chinese gooseberry
14 Like Henry Miller works
15 Commonest of all minerals
23 Four-winged insects
24 Thug
26 Andrea McArdle role
27 Frugal
29 "Per ___ ad astra" (RAF motto)
31 Persian fairies
32 Notion
33 Kind of confidence
34 Peevish fit
36 Chungking's river
40 Diver's gear
42 Disposed (to)
43 Dispute
44 Her, to Henri
45 Egyptian city on the Nile
46 Moving
48 Screwball
51 Ashcan School members
54 "Town Without ___," 1961 hit
55 Tennille or Basil
57 Where Superman was born
58 Wiped out
59 Osar
61 Voice box
62 Pueblo neighbor
66 Badger, in Barcelona
68 Poirot's inspector friend
69 Washbasin jug
70 Kashmiri queen
71 Goya subject
72 Abruzzi commune
74 Word of contempt
76 Suffix for 57 Down

7 SPORTS FIGURES by Robert Sturges

You won't find any hall-of-famers below; what you *will* find is a pleasant pastime.

ACROSS

1 Werewolf features
6 Hotel of 59th Street
11 Tot
16 African witchcraft
17 Like some seals
18 College in Loudonville
19 BASEBALL TEAM
22 Coterie
23 Pier
24 Numbers game
25 Famed Giant
26 Sunday supplement
28 Fancy marble
31 Glaring
34 Little and Travalena
36 Mount Ida site
38 Final notice
39 Like some gourmands
40 Stages
41 Cockney's abyss
42 Command to the helm
43 Ball-___ hammer
44 HOCKEY TEAM
49 Sandy tract: Brit.
50 Legal damages
51 Like Father William
53 Boaters on the Cam
56 Does a mechanic's job
57 Muse of history
58 Word with garde
59 Rustic's tuber
60 Porgy relative
61 L-XXXVI
62 Literary Nobelist
63 Input
64 Organic compound
67 Near island
69 Motel or theater sign
72 POLO TEAM
77 Palmer or Nuvo
78 Perfume ingredient
79 Sailor's delight
80 Cordwood measure
81 Gaggle members
82 Programmer's button

DOWN

1 Conductor Lukas
2 Akin to Bram
3 Following
4 Channel
5 Blade holder
6 Closely confined
7 Mongolian monk
8 Actress Meyers
9 Buddhist sect
10 Night-school students
11 Type of prof.
12 Provincial legislature
13 Dedicates
14 French article
15 Peter played by Martin
20 Tolkien tree
21 Canadian-U.S. canals
25 Hannover-to-Berlin direction
26 Refund
27 Coin of Norway
29 Gobbled up
30 Unseld or Westrum
31 Farmer's friend
32 Talented
33 Lunar valley
34 "A rag, ___ , a hank . . ."
35 Trendy wave
36 Kings in the kitchen
37 Rajah's mate
39 Starts the bidding
40 Cutworms, e.g.
42 Prevent, as an accident
43 Less polluted
45 Original sin site
46 "___ of your business!"
47 Grand slam
48 Director Kazan
52 Suffix for star
53 Kiss of peace, once
54 Egg: Comb. form
55 Shirley's friend
56 Bit
57 Shout
59 Boring
60 Jester's scepter
62 Pike: Scot.
63 Part of E.S.T.
65 Use a swizzle stick
66 King salmon
67 Bustlings about
68 Prefix for thon
69 HR or SO
70 Dream in Dijon
71 Lulu
72 Ol' Blue Eyes' monogram
73 Scrap
74 Between C and B on a typewriter
75 Fury
76 Craving

8 PRESIDENTIAL PERFORMERS by Albert J. Klaus

104 Across performed at the White House in 1988, but we don't think Albert's title alludes to that memorable gala.

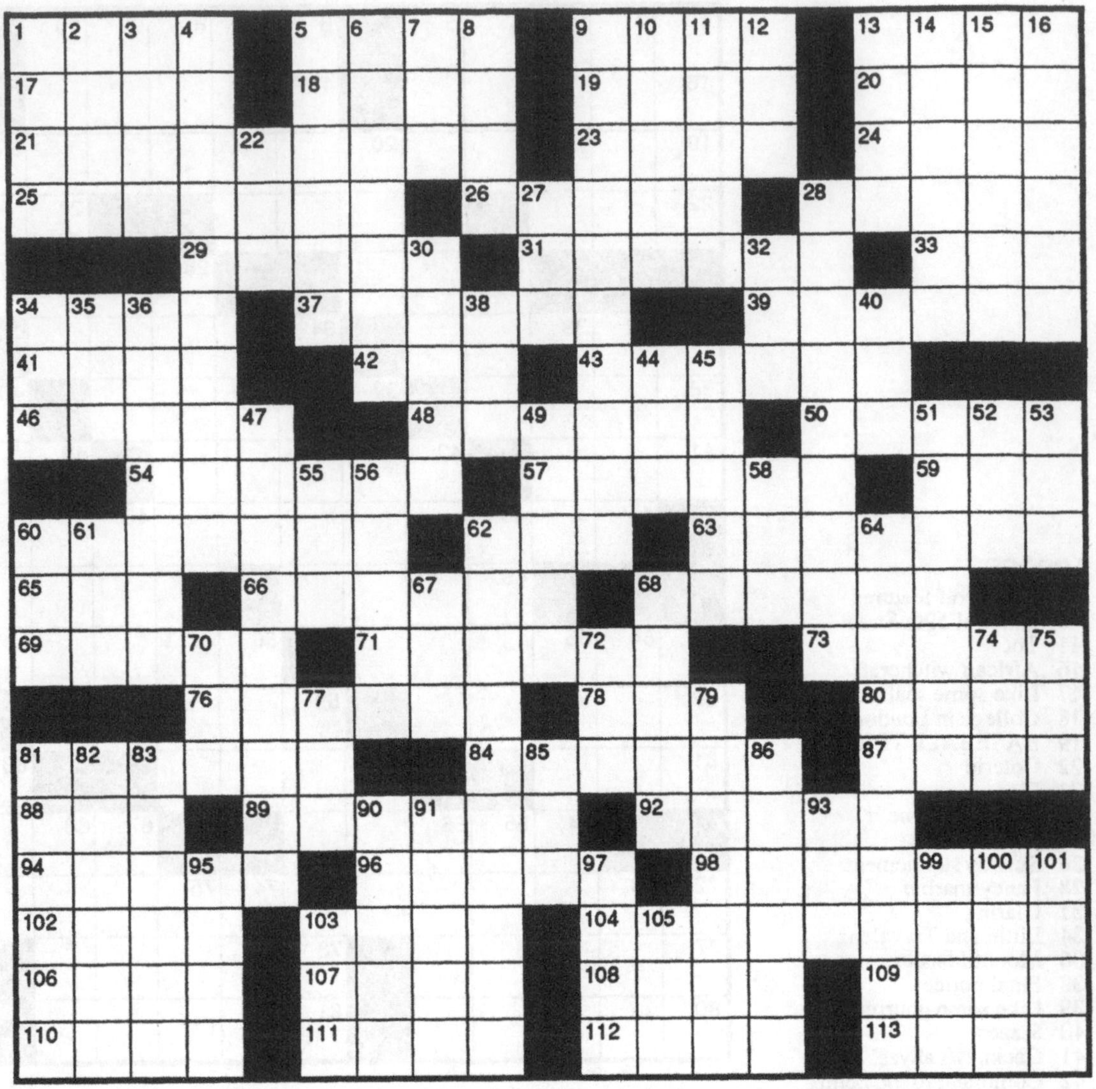

ACROSS

1 After street or heat
5 Bullfighter's cloak
9 Acerbic
13 Stain
17 Melody
18 Office of the President
19 Proboscis
20 Saxhorn relative
21 "Topper" star
23 Kind of blue
24 Suburb of Paris
25 Periodic-table member
26 Earthy pigment
28 T. Jefferson's birth month
29 U.S. Special Forces unit
31 Hurry
33 "I"
34 Assists
37 Three-wheeled vehicle
39 Jacob's ___
41 Box-spring support
42 ___-pitch softball
43 Teachable
46 Actress in "Anastasia"
48 Embellish
50 Stared
54 Diamond dealings
57 Punctually
59 Eggs
60 Aussie's willy-willy
62 Wasn't worth a ___
63 Treated badly
65 Computer memory
66 Take the tarp out
68 Race at Belmont
69 In the back
71 Prayer
73 He played Agent 86
76 Fast gait
78 Relative
80 Bavarian river
81 ___ Garden, London
84 Sagacity
87 Moors
88 Jackie's second
89 ___ of Capricorn
92 Overact
94 Uproars
96 Raft wood
98 Whisper
102 Lacquered metalware
103 ___ ex machina
104 She played Edith Bunker's cousin
106 Ardor
107 Christiania now
108 Mr. Dithers, e.g.
109 Sargasso Sea migrants
110 Remainder
111 Average
112 Hill dwellers
113 Cancel

DOWN

1 Chantilly or Cluny
2 Russian sea
3 Bog
4 Wages are their concern
5 Wind instrument
6 Archetypes
7 Spider
8 ___-relievo (high relief)
9 Actress in "Holiday"
10 Coconut fibers
11 Cay
12 Irish Sea feeder
13 ___-loss order
14 Felinely gave thanks
15 Accommodate
16 "Butterfield 8" actress
22 Capture
27 Half a dance
28 Insensibility to pain
30 A musical Davis
32 Part of R.E.O.
34 Bat wood
35 Dockers' org.
36 Kind of drama
38 Swindle
40 Goddess, to Gaius
44 Witchy mo.
45 Bonzo, for one
47 Permeating substances
49 Disturbs
51 ___-stamp bikini
52 Name that means "life"
53 Father
55 Secluded room
56 Flynn of filmdom
58 Russian commune of yore
60 Singer's syllable
61 Kind of cry or club
62 He played Geraldine Jones
64 How Marciano retired
67 Mountain: Comb. form
68 Derisive
70 Ripen
72 Alan Ladd film: 1946
74 Troops
75 B.M.O.C.s
77 Epist.
79 Rodomontade
81 "Wonder Woman" actress
82 Brightly-colored bird
83 Flower and instrument
85 Suffix for hero
86 Swamp
90 Like Humpty Dumpty
91 Flutist Robison
93 Thrice, to a pharmacist
95 Loose-fitting dress
97 Aramaic for "father"
99 Fare-___-well
100 Peace Nobelist: 1945
101 Irish
103 Comic DeLuise
105 Many, many years

9 "JERSEY JUICE" by Gary L. Schmunk

Here's an easy puzzle that should get you off to a good start.

ACROSS

1 Speedy
6 Rip-off operation
10 Fungus spore sacs
14 Sky-blue
15 TV sitcom
16 Potato
17 Soda fountain treats
19 Beget
20 One, in Soissons
21 Compassion
22 Suppresses a riot
24 Sunday discourses
26 Exploded
27 Baseballer Mel
28 Paul Bunyan, e.g.
31 Door's side-posts
34 "___ of Call," Ibert opus
35 Dockers' union: Abbr.
36 Sheep genus
37 Cosmetic item
38 Lash
39 ___ soda
40 Catcher in the Rhine?
41 Phony
42 Norwegian ___ (dog breed)
44 Mink or sable
45 Munich munch
46 Treasure State
50 SW European peninsula
52 Irrational number
53 ___ Alamos
54 A South African
55 Dale Evans's horse on "The Roy Rogers Show"
58 On a wing ___ prayer
59 Café au ___
60 Growing outward
61 Optimistic
62 Is human
63 Plied with potions

DOWN

1 Branch
2 Kind of dye
3 A baby, for one
4 Annoy
5 Tyrants
6 ERA and RBI
7 Forming crusts or lumps
8 Tool for 28 Across
9 Repeat someone's words incorrectly
10 Estimate
11 Don't cry over this!
12 Squiggle or spiral
13 January 13, e.g.
18 Suggestion
23 Indian beans
25 Unruly throngs
26 Danish comedian-pianist
28 Injury
29 Lotion ingredient
30 Hungarian hero
31 San ___, Capital of Costa Rica
32 Grandparental
33 Latex-bearing plants
34 Aim
37 Like some beer bottles
38 Ord or Dix
40 Fern spores
41 The ___ Years War
43 Cry of joy
44 Fairway cry
46 Mongrels
47 Otherwise called
48 "North Dallas Forty" star
49 Queried
50 Construction item
51 Cher's ex
52 Rouse
56 Former Mideast alliance: Abbr.
57 L-P connection

10 ACHIEVEMENTS by Betty Jorgensen

We know *you* will get a kick out of 74 Across.

ACROSS

1 Computer input
5 Thud
10 Catchall abbr.
13 Excited
14 City on the Red River
15 Trade
17 Rare achievement
20 Kind of trick in the NHL
21 One of a Latin trio
22 Hwys.
23 English article
26 Arizona tribe
28 Stat. for Hershiser
29 Quarry
30 Individual achievement
35 Applaud
38 Green shot for Green
39 Ex-pitcher Maglie
40 Razorbacks
41 French pantomimist
42 Cooled
46 "___ little teapot . . ."
47 Celebrating an achievement
49 Mineral
50 Veil
52 Attention-getter
53 Hawaiian wind
54 First U.S. regulatory agcy.
55 Newspaper notice
56 Prevent
57 Bow achievement
62 Hurt
63 Consumed
64 Lease
66 Robert ___ Frost
67 Market
69 Lift at Aspen
71 See 24 Down
74 Your achievement?
78 Orgy cry
79 Book part
80 Cruising
81 Wheat beard
82 Not live
83 Kind of job

DOWN

1 Panache
2 Ottoman VIP
3 Hound's-___ check
4 Past
5 Burmese deer
6 Humorous sound
7 Some, to Caesar
8 Gram molecule: Var.
9 Character for 41 Across
10 Serf
11 Deuces
12 "I ___ do anything . . ."
16 Dish of the lab
18 Nocturnal mammal
19 Type of type: Abbr.
24 Part of H.I.M.
25 Private ___
27 Files Chapter 11
28 Admirable
29 Cloy
31 " . . . to fetch ___ of . . ."
32 Skirt for Farrell
33 Composer Jones
34 Dog
35 Smart
36 Ecce ___!
37 Actor Richard
41 Smidgen
42 Huntley and Atkins
43 Joe Orton play
44 Piscivorous eagle
45 Precious
47 Virginia ___ (VPI)
48 Singer Collins
51 Homophone of sight
53 Sharp
55 Survive
56 Tinters
57 Prince of Broadway
58 Hot diamonds
59 "We hold ___ truths . . ."
60 Bundle
61 Wiped clean
65 Friend of 59 Down
67 Snail-like
68 Just
69 Stumble
70 Os
72 Angers
73 Neighbor of Neb.
75 Eggs
76 I.R.S. employee
77 Handful of cotton

11 TRIBUTE TO INGRID by Norman Wizer

A top constructor pays honor to Sweden's most gifted actress.

ACROSS

1 Bridge coup
5 Certain female fowl
11 Tennis star
15 Subway gate
16 "The Last ___ of Beau Geste"
17 "___ the Roof," Nyro hit
18 Bergman film of 1969
20 Split
21 Open-mouthed
22 Mrs. in español
23 Papal capes
25 Female ruff
26 Anagram of one
28 Org. for I.M. Pei
30 Cockney's nether world
31 Best in "Intermezzo"
33 Bergman film of 1944
36 Apron part
39 Vault
41 Swiss river
42 Lennon's Plastic ___ Band
43 Host
46 Muse of astronomy
49 Pol. union of 1958-61
50 Mauna ___
51 Bergman film of 1948
54 Mariner's reading
55 Cattle genus
56 Holy Saturday follower
57 Honeysuckle relative
59 ___ pro nobis
60 Bit's $12\frac{1}{2}$: Abbr.
61 Porky
64 Silky flytrap
65 Bergman film of 1964
68 Clefts
72 Sheltered side
74 "___ Men," DeVito film
75 Haggard novel
77 Ultra
78 Bleachers
81 ___ rule
83 Held the floor
85 Trace
86 Bergman film of 1978
89 Erst
90 ___ in Excelsis Deo
91 Pokeys
92 ___ and tear
93 Mason's secretary
94 Counting-out word

DOWN

1 Orchestrated
2 Growth on a rock
3 Canadian prov.
4 Belgian river
5 Evidence: Abbr.
6 Kingklip and lamper
7 Without scruples
8 Sandwich Islands now
9 Enlarge
10 Pianist Peter
11 Otic
12 Bergman film of 1945
13 Sharpen
14 Extremities
15 Fright
19 Cheap cigar
24 Goes back over
27 Hall-of-Famer Lajoie
29 Guam's capital
32 Pilot or pitcher
34 Sort of pilot
35 It had 1,750 Broadway performances
37 Lacking substance
38 Shipworm
40 Turned down
43 Kind of grease?
44 Lone Ranger portrayer
45 Bergman film of 1943
47 Caviar
48 Bushy coiffures
52 Pledge
53 Sense of humor, e.g.
58 Tibia locale
62 Encore
63 Cultural values
66 Traveler
67 Make certain
69 Achieve
70 Richard Wilbur's art
71 Fountain floats
73 Door sign
76 Jagged
78 "The Last Picture ___"
79 Antler branch
80 Slumps
82 Pierre's gal-pal
84 Before, to Brutus
87 In the preceding mo.
88 Turner of history

12 ESSENTIALLY SEQUENTIAL by Gale Dean

Note the careful placement of each main entry in this clever count-up creation.

ACROSS

1 Type of watch or computer
7 Where Seaver gained fame
11 Surf sight
15 Lady in Madrid
16 Singer Billy ___
17 Thunderstruck
18 Long-haired hunting dog
19 Top of the line
21 What diaskeuasts do
22 On the move
23 Wed
24 Clock part
27 Coarse and savage
28 Sixties' college org.
29 Spoken
30 Sculptor Lorado ___
31 Pierce
32 Barnyard animals
34 Busy one?
37 Malt grain
40 Non-aligned nations
42 Zone
43 Immerse
44 Leaning-tower city
45 Independence Day
48 Regard highly
50 Lowell gal
51 Urges a felon on
52 At times they're wild
53 Leave out
54 Story start
55 High spot
58 Lively wit
61 Odd-man out
64 Pseudonym of a sort
65 Piebald
66 "Vissi d' ___," Puccini aria
67 ESP
69 Printing errors
71 ___ Sedgwick, tragic heiress
72 Eve or Toni
73 Blew in squalls
74 Act
75 Housekeeper's concern
76 "Do unto ___ . . ."

DOWN

1 Appraise
2 Required
3 Silly tricks
4 Bingo-like game
5 Pay dirt
6 Needlefish
7 Heir
8 Slayer of John the Baptist
9 "___ of Eden": Steinbeck
10 Hill dweller
11 Waldorf salad bit
12 Expect
13 Roman hearth goddess
14 Motorized flop
16 Carrion
20 Deadline of sorts
22 Seventh king of Israel
25 Memo
26 Strong cart
27 Musical group
30 Trunk item
31 Homophone for sleigh
32 Closes
33 Genie's gift
34 Soft French cheese
35 Lord High Everything ___ in "The Mikado"
36 Town in Holland
37 Mexican peninsula, for short
38 Jack-in-the-pulpit, e.g.
39 Depend
40 Civil wrong
41 Chooses
43 Twosome in music
46 Starve
47 R.I.P. notice
48 Anagram for ache
49 Goulash
52 Atop of
53 Spoke in a grand manner
54 Frequently
55 Oxygenate
56 Varsity member's award
57 Implores
58 Abated
59 Playground device
60 Fairy
61 Discovers
62 Map within a map
63 Severe
65 Land of Lima
68 Unhappy
69 Monogram of Anna Christie's creator
70 Boring routine

13 HOT STUFF! by Harold Counts

This aptly named puzzle from Kentucky is a perfect one to warm up with.

ACROSS

1 Mr. Dillon
5 Basketballer
10 Border on
14 Arthur the racketeer?
15 Type of orange
16 Relate
19 Pullover
21 Panic
22 Inasmuch as
23 "Paper Moon" star
25 Terra ___
26 Confiscate
28 Knotted
30 Competed
31 Diocese
32 "Battle Cry" author
34 Drunk or wealthy
36 Part of a twin bill
38 Ron Ely role
41 No-no: Var.
44 ___ boy!
45 Partner of wide
46 Grand ___ Opry
47 Beast
49 Chinese city
51 Fencing with bamboo
53 Make public
54 Fib
56 Counterweight
58 Actor Stockwell
59 NYC skater
61 Sound system
63 Hails
66 Catbird ___
67 Hubbub
70 Russian river
72 Twofold
74 Mortified
76 Sagas
78 Explode
80 Lift up
81 Respite
83 Quickly: Slang
85 Cross out
86 Accustom
87 Hardy heroine
88 Gaelic
89 Vex
90 This: Sp.

DOWN

1 Plebeians
2 ___ as an owl
3 From that time
4 Blackbeard
5 Romaine
6 Wild guess, with 35 Down
7 Win
8 White heron
9 Like some prices
10 Guile
11 Complaint
12 Against the current
13 Equatorial region
17 Eternal City
18 Conventional: Abbr.
20 Prepare to drive
24 Papal name
27 Length x width
29 Info
33 City SSW of Montpellier
35 See 6 Down
36 Gone fishing
37 Crude boats
39 "The Four Seasons" star
40 Night light
41 Lift at Aspen
42 Met solo
43 Town of W North Carolina
45 Carnival performers
48 Robert ___
50 Diner sign
52 Tokyo of old
55 Hot
57 Periods
60 National park in NW Montana
62 A Kennedy
64 Vat
65 Helmet of yore
67 Astounds
68 Hate
69 Texas city
70 Pee-wee Herman, e.g.
71 Sword
73 "Mule Train" singer
75 Winged
77 TVs
79 Jaeger
82 Charge
84 Nectar collector

14

KID'S PARTY by D. J. DeChristopher
D. J. says he was listening to "Send in the Clowns" when the idea for this puzzle came to him.

ACROSS
1 Hemingway
5 Challenged
10 Racket
14 Over the hill
15 Declaim
16 Ms. Bombeck
17 Party refreshments
20 Peeper
21 Image: Var.
22 Backslide
23 Jacob's son: Douay
24 Kind of mat
26 In a numbing way
28 Stuff
29 Norm
32 Yellowish hue
33 Twitter
34 Cry of discovery
35 Hang around
36 X, for one
37 Splotch
38 Dine
39 Warm as ___
40 Cads
41 Peer Gynt's mom
42 Wander
43 Goatee
44 Numbered way
46 Rancor
47 Airborne
49 Kind of stitch
50 Portray
53 Party game, with 5 Down
57 ___ fixe
58 Dipper
59 Solar disk
60 Part of NAACP
61 Antiquated
62 "Alone" author

DOWN
1 Stride
2 Absent
3 Jab
4 Stout relative
5 See 53 Across
6 Fervor
7 Weather word
8 And so on: Abbr.
9 Billy ___ Williams
10 Ice pinnacle
11 Party decorations
12 Amo, ___, amat
13 Dennis's auntie
18 Corridor
19 Vise
23 Breezy
24 Publish
25 Shortening
26 Metrical stress
27 Adults at this party
28 Pursue
30 Grab ___!
31 Drat!
32 Greek peak
33 Hanker for
36 Kick
37 Bladdernose
39 Veracity
40 Greeting
43 Ingredient of 4 Down
45 Frequently
46 Culpability
47 Western Samoa capital
48 Covers
49 Cushions
50 ABA mem.
51 "Moonstruck" star
52 Incline
54 Nightmarish street
55 Greek letter
56 Collar

15

WIMBLEDON WINNERS by Arthur Palmer
Arthur pays tribute to the winners of an event which began in 1877 and is played annually at the All-England Tennis and Croquet Club.

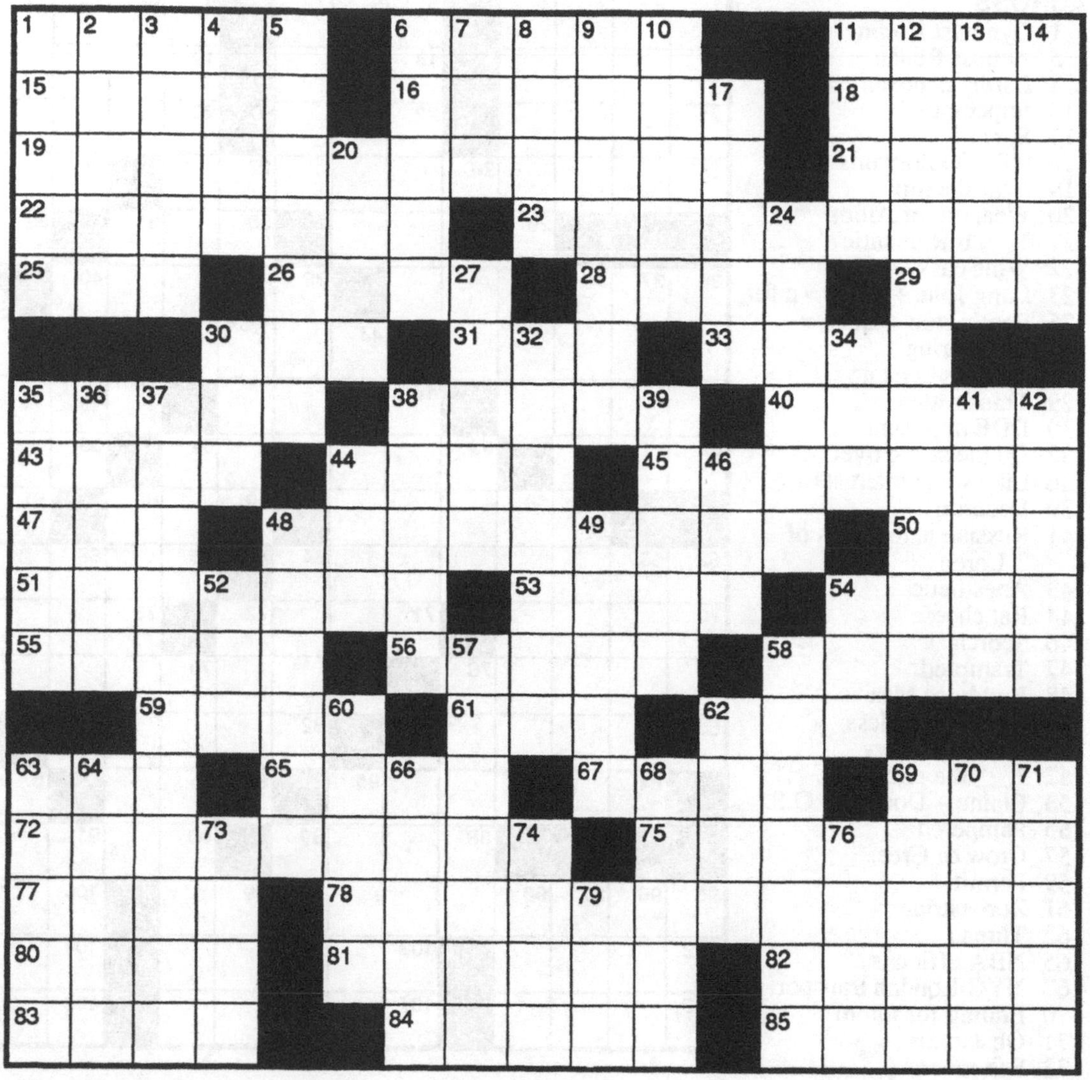

ACROSS

1 Packs away
6 Beetle genus
11 Cartoonist Addams
15 Silent
16 One-celled animal
18 Mother of Castor
19 A Wimbledon winner of 1958
21 Part of BTU
22 More precipitous
23 A Wimbledon winner of 1934
25 ". . . robins in ___ hair"
26 Desist
28 Juvenal's journey
29 Suffix for cash
30 Law, in Lourdes
31 ___ Saud
33 Pusher's foe
35 Kind of sentence
38 Chancy machines
40 Deary
43 Alpine goat
44 Lion-speak
45 Needlepoint lace
47 Tibetan gazelle
48 A Wimbledon winner of 1949
50 Hurry
51 "Two-ton Tony" of boxing
53 Streetcar of London
54 Soccer great
55 Office worker
56 Fortune card
58 Misanthrope
59 ___ for thought
61 Suffix for Martin
62 Persian, for one
63 Spring mo.
65 Insect stage
67 Town on the Zuider Zee
69 "Now we ___ six": Milne
72 A Wimbledon winner of 1972
75 Clothed in a certain fur
77 Coin for Pedro
78 A Wimbledon winner of 1983
80 Irritated
81 Like some TVs
82 Remainder, in Rouen
83 ". . . at the deep heart's ___": Yeats
84 Familiar Stein words
85 Charger

DOWN

1 Hide
2 "A ___ of Honey"
3 Earthy color
4 Trickery
5 Julian, to Yoko
6 Holy: Comb. form
7 Caesar's "I love"
8 Bungle
9 Publish anew
10 Red as ___
11 Lead for Poirot
12 A Wimbledon winner of 1927
13 C'est-___ (that is to say)
14 Woodland deity
17 Eve or Elizabeth
20 Abominable Snowman
24 Loquacious one
27 "For Whom the Bell Tolls" character
30 Smoked salmon
32 A Wimbledon winner of 1924
34 Director Howard
35 A Wimbledon winner of 1939
36 Sub of WW II
37 A Wimbledon winner of 1960
38 "___ that it do singe yourself": Shak.
39 Classmate of Nasser
41 Transparent linen
42 Express contempt
44 Sales slip: Abbr.
46 Moonmobile
48 Pries
49 Uneven
52 Wine prefix
54 A Nixon
57 It's only ___ of time
58 Olympians throw these
60 Unloads
62 Sandburg
63 Savory jelly
64 Feather: Comb. form
66 Michelangelo masterpiece
68 "Moll Flanders" author
69 Pernod ingredient
70 René's revenue
71 Two-___ sword
73 Knob
74 Hoagy
76 "___ a man with seven wives"
79 In medias ___

16 NEW MATH by Wilson McBeath

Don't be *nonplussed* by the title; Wilson's arithmetic is not the kind currently being taught in schools.

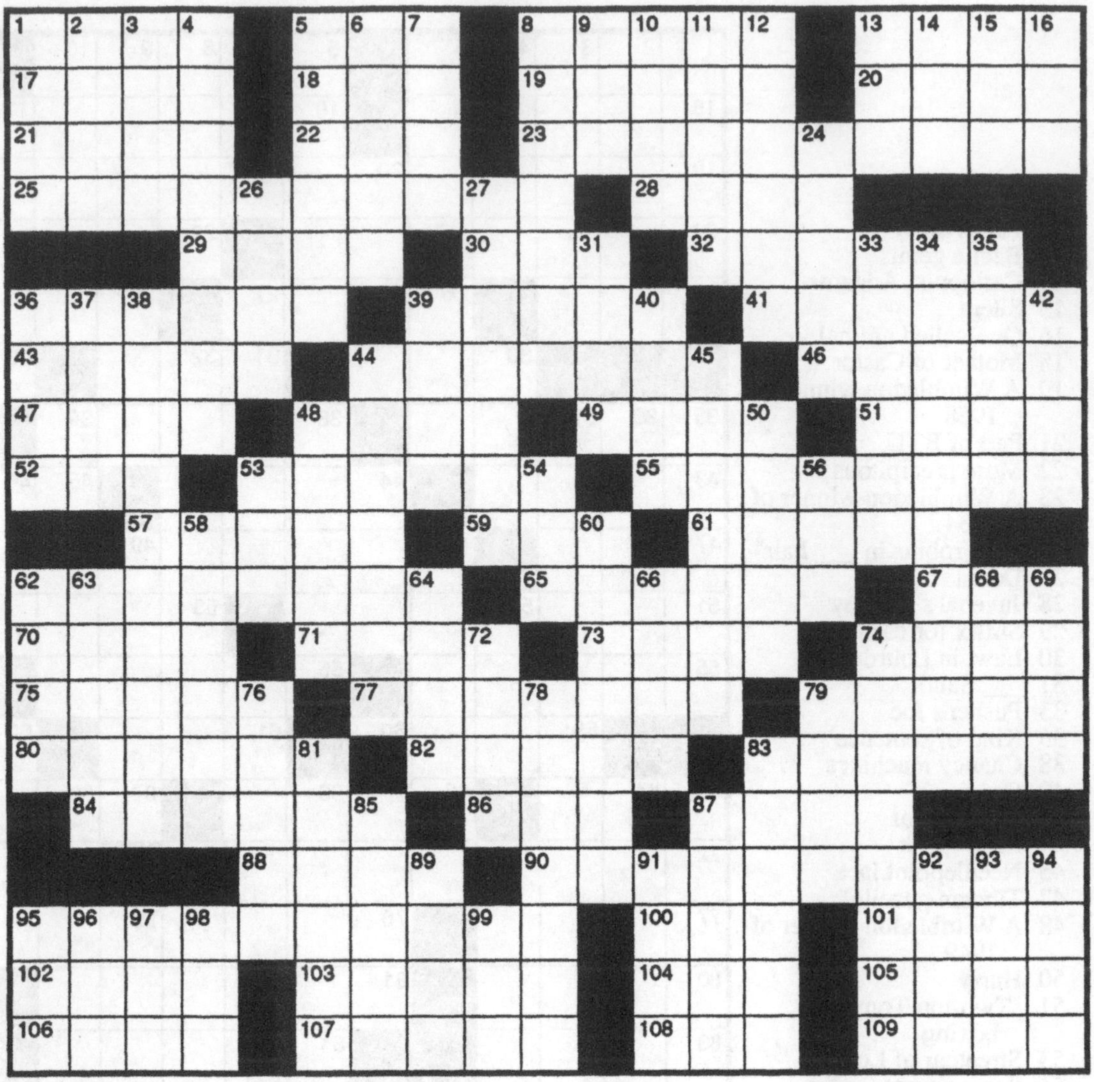

ACROSS

1 Gymnast Korbut
5 Actress Rehan
8 Earthy deposits
13 Impetuous
17 Spree
18 907.20 kilograms
19 Near the hip
20 Weapon for Athos
21 "___ It Romantic?"
22 Wine cask
23 Long John + Redd = a fur
25 Remington + Lucy = a bearing
28 Late-night name
29 Transmitted
30 DDE opponent
32 Do the scene over
36 Like some interests
39 Decorous
41 Russian namesakes of Loren
43 Anesthetic
44 Rat cheese
46 Scorch
47 Trampled
48 Buddy or Max
49 Discord goddess
51 Folklore heavy
52 "___ the ramparts . . ."
53 Elaine + Doris = S.O.S.
55 Pampered
57 Crow or Cree
59 Permit
61 Zoroastrian
62 Thread
65 NBA officials
67 NYC-London transport
70 Ending for idiom
71 Obstacle
73 Sea rovers
74 Quaker pronoun
75 Mastic
77 Authorizes
79 Palmists
80 Removed a ship's upper deck
82 Athenian saint
83 Horse and soap followers
84 Isthmus
86 Forget-me-___
87 Suffix for thermo
88 Abound
90 Oliver + Dinah = 1987 surfing film
95 Orville + Learned = reliable assistant
100 Half a bray
101 Messenger of the gods
102 Merit
103 Weird
104 Suffix for chariot
105 NBA team
106 Big bird
107 Takes five
108 ___ gratia artis
109 Merriment

DOWN

1 Cornelia ___ Skinner
2 "The ___ Chord": Sullivan
3 Left
4 Certified
5 Be present
6 Emulate Thomas
7 Held of the stage
8 Deceive
9 Clay, today
10 Brook
11 Tennis great
12 Pancrama parts
13 Ump's partner
14 GI's address
15 Vital statistic
16 Spell
24 Newspaper sections
26 Lascivious look
27 Kind of pass
31 Phase
33 Negatively charged atoms
34 Alan + Eddie = a bird
35 Tidal bore
36 Kill a bill
37 Raison d'___
38 Martin + Franz = a small roll
39 Molt
40 Indian timber trees
42 Rank players
44 Hot condiment
45 Tearers
48 Newborns
50 Flies high
53 Arabic letter
54 Thus far
56 Endings for debt
58 More risqué
60 Hold ___ (own)
62 "M*A*S*H" actor
63 Virginia willows
64 Strong flavor
66 Murray and West
68 Evening, in Bari
69 Dick's Trueheart
72 Profit
74 Kind of ring for baby
76 "___ the Southern Moon": Herbert
78 What gentlemen prefer?
79 Baden-Baden and Bad Nauheim
81 What Oprah Winfrey was
83 Not us
85 Happy sound
87 Guide
89 Bellona's brother
91 Mother of Hades
92 City on the Oka
93 Formal observance
94 Abstract being
95 Minute
96 Zodiac animal
97 Choler
98 Wildebeest
99 Insect egg

17 POTPOURRI by Elaine George

Here's an easy puzzle to fire up your gray matter.

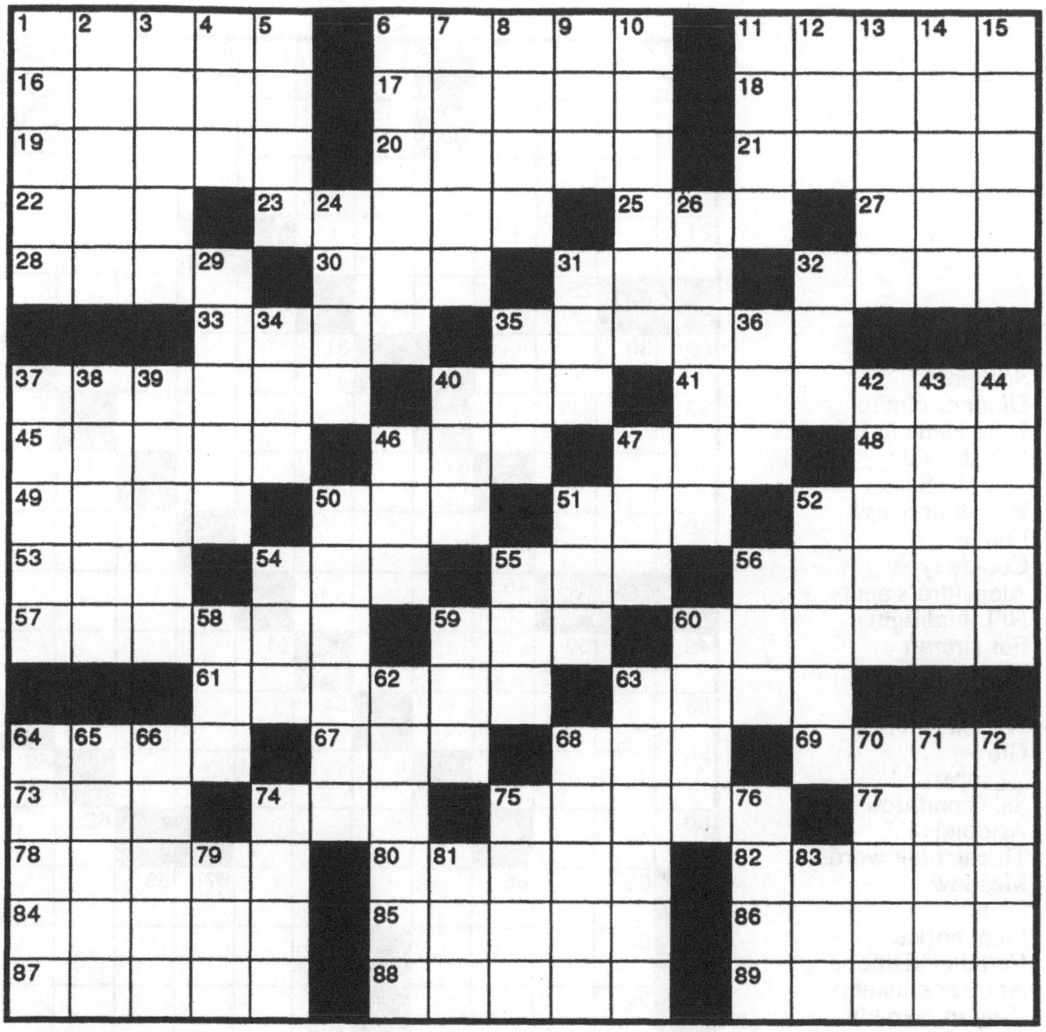

ACROSS

1 Surplus
6 Make amends
11 City NNE of Joplin
16 Street sign
17 Colonial newscaster
18 Residence
19 Bandage material
20 Tenth U.S. president
21 Relish
22 Bleach
23 Impudent
25 Liable
27 Important period
28 Existence
30 Humdrum routine
31 Lennon's widow
32 Paradise
33 Silly one
35 Meat dish
37 Ill-tempered
40 Stick out
41 Yens
45 Island dances
46 Watch chain
47 Springsteen's "Born in the ___"
48 Spanish cheer
49 Pretentiously sophisticated
50 Gang
51 Kind of can or tray
52 ___ *la Douce*
53 Golf norm
54 Hoodoo
55 Lamb's mom
56 Below
57 Scheduled
59 Indisposed
60 Directs
61 Strong veggies
63 Mime
64 Rebuff
67 Biblical boat
68 Federal project of '33
69 Stumble
73 ___ Pan Alley
74 Also
75 Match site
77 Bustle
78 California baseball player
80 Live coal
82 Rescues
84 Ruckus
85 Parts
86 Doublefold
87 Recumbent
88 Stockholm native
89 Music mistress

DOWN

1 American bird
2 Hospital pics
3 Corrects
4 Rosalind's nickname
5 Inspires with reverential fear
6 Misbehaves
7 Rendezvous
8 Greasy
9 Bess Truman, ___ Wallace
10 Wandering
11 Endure
12 Legal org.
13 Changed one's address
14 Idolize
15 Showed (a film) once more
24 Legion
26 Burnish
29 Thesis
31 Not at home
32 And the like: Abbr.
34 "___ no big deal!"
35 Novice reporter
36 JFK listing
37 Ranchers' leggings
38 Opposite of urban
39 Extreme
40 Position
42 Swarm
43 ___ *Gantry*: S. Lewis book
44 Scorches
46 Michael J. of films
47 Purpose
50 Highway divider
51 Leatherworker's tool
52 Sluggish
54 Leghorn, e.g.
55 Rides in Chi
56 Western Indian
58 Outdo
59 ___ Spots, of music
60 Bridge
62 Commands
63 Reluctant
64 Imprint
65 A baseball hit
66 ___-Saxon
68 Cornered
70 Untangle
71 Faultless
72 Puts in the mail
74 Downwind
75 Competent
76 Venomous snakes
79 Even, to poets
81 Trim the lawn
83 "The Greatest"

18 PASS THE SOY by Rhoda Kraus

Rhoda says "Chopsticks" is her favorite song and "Wok With Yan" her favorite show.

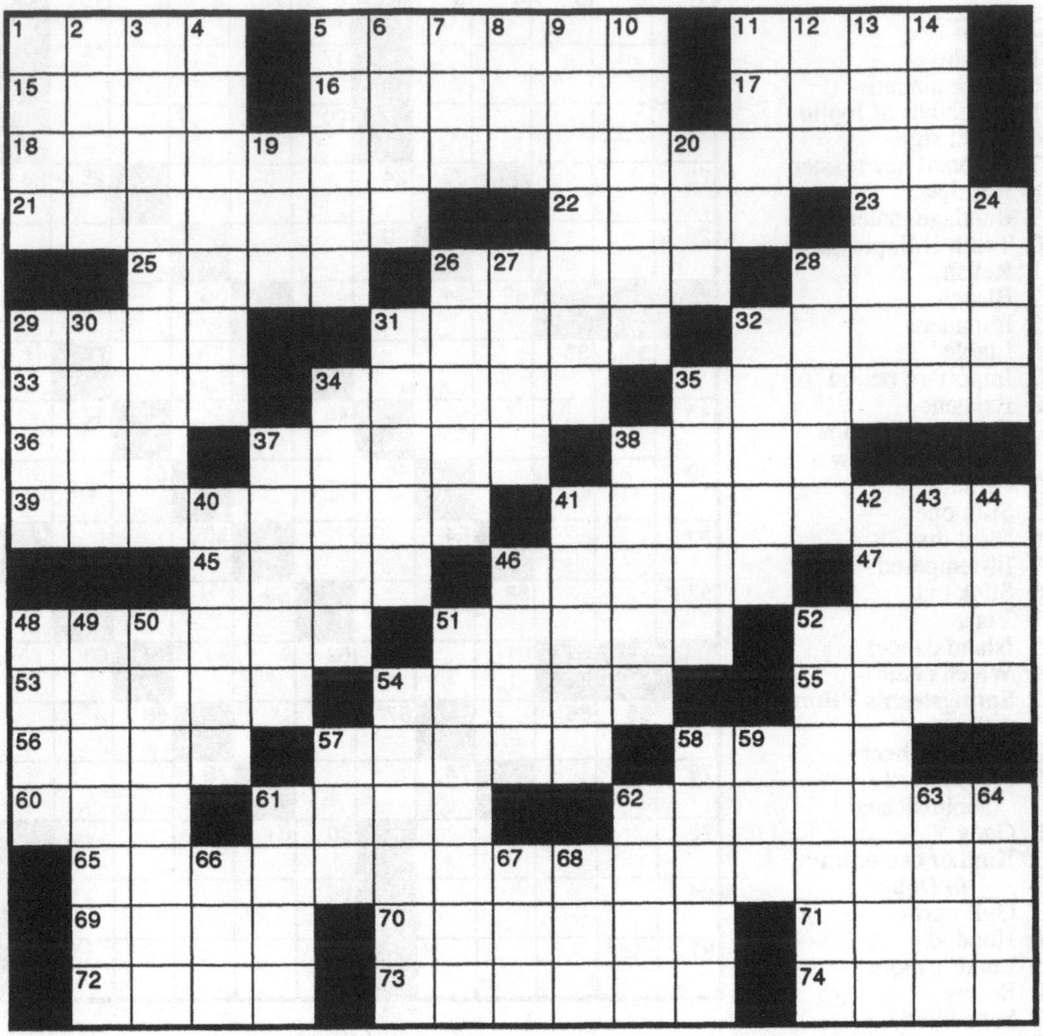

ACROSS

1 Buddies
5 Scattered
11 Dinar or dinero
15 Lake name in HOMES
16 "O, that this ___ solid . . .": Shak.
17 British princess
18 Entrée
21 Cookie type
22 Alejandro's aunts
23 NFL highlights
25 For aircraft
26 Timer
28 Festive
29 Wagon
31 Glow
32 ___ apart
33 Sale condition
34 Astounds
35 Threatening words
36 Meadow
37 Gape
38 Final notice
39 Certain cuisine
41 Another cuisine
45 King of comedy
46 Selected
47 Prefix for suppose
48 Equality
51 Actress MacMahon
52 House built on ___
53 Second son and namesakes
54 Unaccompanied
55 Expensive wood
56 Manhattanite's addr.
57 Low-cuts
58 Vocalist Vikki
60 Dir.
61 Hawaiian harbor
62 Egg-roll fillings
65 Entrée
69 James ___ Jones
70 ___ it (card game)
71 Jacob's brother
72 Shot of the NHL
73 Feared fly
74 Eyelid woe

DOWN

1 Booty
2 Buck ending
3 Book keeper
4 Six-line stanzas
5 Pool member
6 Ripped
7 Mythical bird
8 Letter from Greece
9 Soup dumplings
10 Observe
11 Fires: Sl.
12 Poor rating
13 Establish
14 Kentucky Derby winner, 1956
19 Wild goat
20 Live tree
24 MS. associate
26 Agitate
27 Wrinkle
28 "Pride ___ before a fall"
29 Serene
30 On the deep
31 Blot
32 Cost
34 Maverick
35 Overly overweight
37 Gobs
38 Atmospheric layer
40 Newspaper
41 Islanders pad these
42 First
43 Zone
44 Violin part
46 Hoof sound
48 Calls it a "bomb"
49 Yawning gulfs
50 Urban ___
51 Ellipsoid nuts
52 Hash marks
54 Café ___
57 Kind of bull
58 Waterfall
59 Timetable abbr.
61 Aid
62 Cries
63 Beseech
64 Twist: Obs. sp.
66 Period
67 John or Jane
68 Coal dust: Dial. var.

19

LOOK SHARP by Norma Steinberg
Hone your solving skills on this Golden Gater's keen construction.

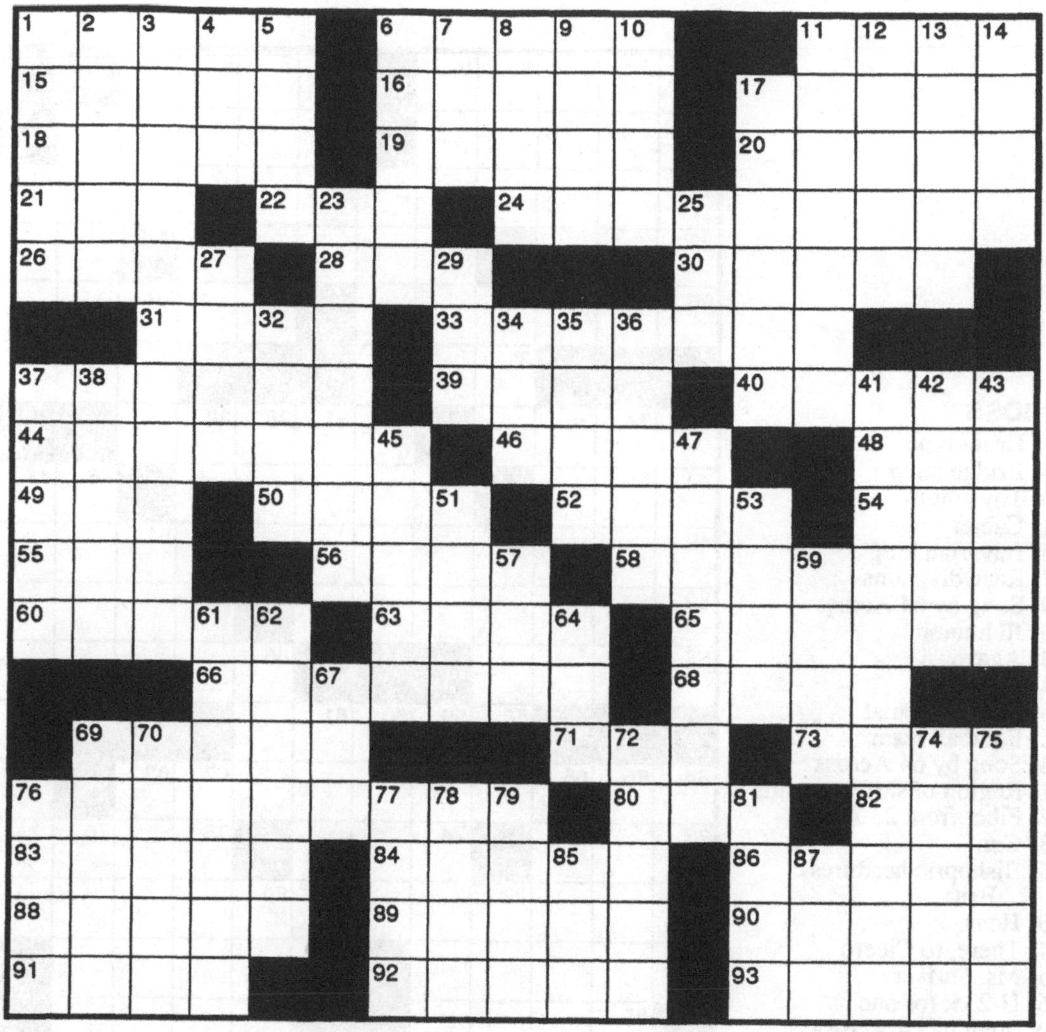

ACROSS

1 Actress Normand
6 Heathen
11 After roll or close
15 Dwight's opponent
16 San Antonio attraction
17 Western show
18 Closes in on
19 *Queen Christina* star
20 Jordanian capital
21 ___ Ironsides
22 Get a serve past
24 Fabric of Wall Street
26 Iamb and trochee
28 Keats poem, sometimes
30 Les ___ Unis
31 Harvest
33 Nudged
37 Thick as thieves
39 U.S. Surgeon General of the eighties
40 Scenery
44 Nag
46 Lobster traps
48 One for Pierre
49 Motel
50 Submerged
52 Lulus
54 Half a fly
55 Compass reading
56 Hop ___!
58 Wooed
60 Cultivates
63 Amorphous mass
65 Features
66 Like, wow!
68 Forked-tail avian
69 Hindu wraparounds
71 Actor Vigoda
73 Coop finds
76 Robert E. Lee's alma mater
80 Sts.
82 Stat. for Tanana
83 Sally Bowles' ex-roomie
84 Friend of Gandhi
86 Burdened
88 Change for the better
89 Liberates
90 Exhorted
91 Pro ___
92 Pizzazz
93 Assembles

DOWN

1 ___ *La Mancha*
2 An Astaire
3 Harrison Ford film
4 Jug lug
5 Actress Eilbacher
6 Summoned
7 Fla. neighbor
8 Robin Williams role
9 Prefix for dextrous
10 Twelve, half the time
11 Buddy
12 Own up to
13 ___ and bounds
14 Sole
17 Snitched
23 Mimic
25 Ply the needle
27 Interim worker
29 Mouse-sighting cry
32 Iowa city
34 Cut off
35 Betty of cartoons
36 ___ nerve
37 Boss
38 Hair rinse
41 Vanguard
42 Beginning
43 Rex and Willis
45 Door closers
47 Saw
51 2.2 pounds
53 Certain
57 Cruise, for one
59 Steak order
61 Ms. Navratilova
62 Filched
64 "___ Clown"
67 That, to Juan
69 Actress Diamond
70 Advantage
72 Graze
74 Welcome
75 *The ___ of Iwo Jima*
76 Attire
77 Data
78 Stepson of Claudius
79 Oates title
81 Urban eyesore
85 Salesperson
87 "Where ___ You?"

20 YOU'RE THE TOP by K. H. Wetherbee

K. H. has chosen his title from a song by 64 Across. We couldn't agree more with his selection!

ACROSS

1 Drum type
6 Bridge coup
10 Toy ammo
14 Cabler
15 Bavarian king
17 Race divisions
19 Song by 64 Across
22 Ill humor
23 Agave
24 Cont.
25 Dundee denial
26 Football team
28 Song by 64 Across
31 Region of shifting sands
32 Fiber from 23 Across
33 Con
36 Bishopric headdress: Brit.
40 Hoax
44 There, to Cicero
45 Ms. Shriver
46 U-235, for one
49 Song by 64 Across
52 Feline
53 Former Houston WHA team
54 Angelico or Lippo Lippi
55 Siouan Indian
56 Comprehend
57 Imprecation
58 *Otello* composer
62 Spider
64 Composer of over 800 songs
69 One who anoints: Arch.
73 Bauxite, e.g.
74 Nuptial words
75 Hold sway
77 Point of no return
78 Song by 64 Across
82 E Swedish town
83 Eat into
84 Coward and Harrison
85 Signet
86 Length x width
87 Concur

DOWN

1 Purloin
2 Actor Bruce
3 Mountain spur
4 Soak flax
5 Felt pad, e.g.
6 Emulates Killy
7 Slow train
8 Tarsus
9 *Winterset* hero
10 Beethoven's 9th, e.g.
11 Troops of WW I
12 Golfer Stewart
13 Greek porticos
16 Surmise
18 Tallow
20 Tristan's rival
21 Cluster
27 Victory sign
29 Foulard
30 Basket, in Barcelona
33 Dance hall
34 *Das Boot* setting
35 Bean or pony
37 "Dies ___"
38 Stannum
39 *M*A*S*H* character
41 Former Teamsters head
42 Disjunct
43 Borneo town
45 Avril follower
46 Cash followers
47 Obstruction
48 CIA forerunner
50 Denizen of 71 Down
51 Indeed
56 Shoo!, in Dogpatch
57 *A Chorus Line* song
59 Like *The Iliad*
60 Jockeyed
61 Hum
63 Roman goddess of annual crops
64 Coconut husk fiber
65 Killer whales
66 Sierra ___
67 Goof
68 *The Cloister and the Hearth* author
70 Hen
71 French school
72 Employ again
76 Virginia willow
79 Three R's org.
80 Song syllable
81 Yule drink

21 FOUR FOOLERS by Rhoda Kraus

Watch out for wordplay in the eleven-letter entries.

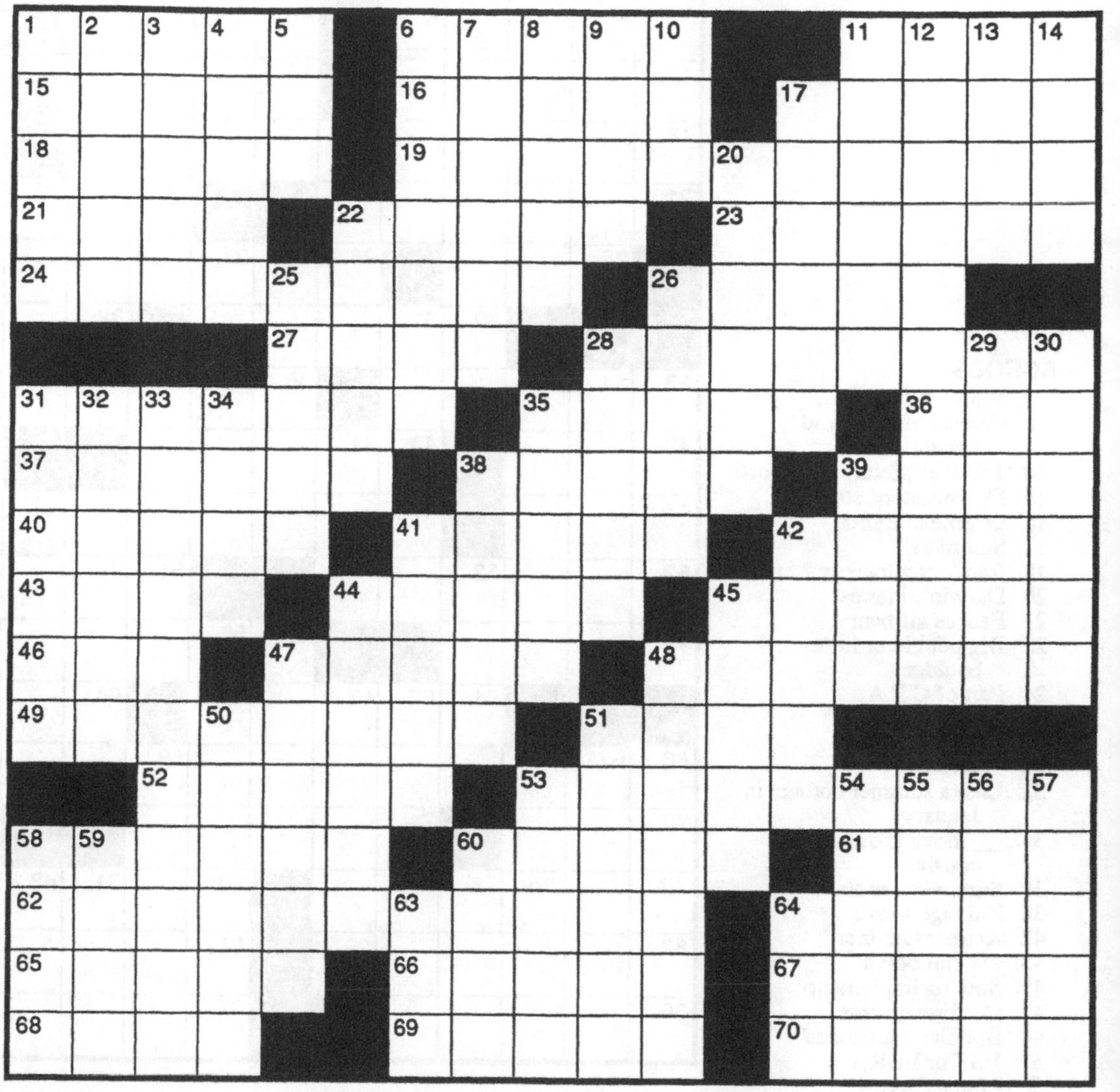

ACROSS

1 Bedded blossom
6 Home on the range?
11 Cicatrix
15 Oblong vestment
16 Raise spirits
17 Mexican painter, Frida ___
18 Barcelona girls
19 Circumscribed movement?
21 Stravinsky
22 Push back
23 Peaks
24 Fellow members
26 Predecessor of febrero
27 Crones
28 Serene
31 Flattering publicity
35 Hazards to shipping
36 Collection of sayings, etc.
37 Gluck products
38 Prove false
39 One of Cleopatra's servants
40 Worships
41 Irritate
42 Snatches
43 Carry
44 Hampton ___, Va.
45 Risk
46 Int. group organized at Bogota: 1948
47 Sign on a diner door
48 Procrastinator
49 Pops the question
51 ___ Van Kull
52 Eugene ___, the traveler's guide
53 Military groups
58 Biker
60 Modeled
61 Gear for a knight
62 Parts of James Joyce's garden?
64 City on the Ganges
65 Carts
66 Poet Stephen Vincent ___
67 Representative
68 "The ___ the limit"
69 Editorial instructions
70 Broadway awards

DOWN

1 Sudden terror
2 Friend of 18 Across
3 Thin fabric
4 Cold-weather item
5 Affirmative
6 Extrasensory perception force
7 Marries on the run
8 Strides of sorts
9 And others: Lat.
10 Slippery one
11 Literary device
12 Stylish one of the desert (with "The")?
13 Medicinal plant
14 The Reagans, senior and junior
17 Legal tender in Kiev: Var. sp.
20 Take charge
22 Raises
25 Ratite birds
26 Hair-raising
28 Skins
29 Helpless
30 Actress Louise
31 Beverage can opener?
32 Commotion
33 Examples of the potter's art?
34 Mimic David
35 Parts of a rosary
38 Churlish children
39 "___ La Douce"
41 One whose outlook is hopeless
42 Causes anger
44 Suck up
45 Icy
47 "___ Lady's Book" (first woman's magazine)
48 Gets rid of
50 Bergen and Adler
51 Fate
53 "Lorna ___"
54 Mature insect
55 Like a popular porridge
56 Simpleton
57 Slim boards
58 Military orders: Abbr.
59 War of the Roses faction
60 Blake or Burns
63 Dieter's abbr.
64 "___ and Mike," Tracy-Hepburn film

22

GUESSING GAME by Jeanne Wilson
You'll have fun trying to predict what outrageous pun is coming up next in this whacky Wilson creation.

ACROSS

1 White heron
6 Celeste of stage and screen
10 Transfer picture, for short
15 Downeasters' state
16 Overhead light?
17 Salt marsh
18 Rainy racetrack in May?
20 Darwin's interest
21 Fauces ailment
22 Big pebble or little boulder
24 Part of C.P.A.
25 Bo, to Dudley
26 Forty free-falls?
30 Welcome
32 Like a summer cottage in January
33 ___ nova (samba's cousin)
36 Surveyors' spots
38 Zhivago's love
42 Actress Gardner
43 Puccini opera
45 Sowing implement
47 Old French coin
48 Bobbies' barbecues?
51 HST or FDR, e.g.
52 Mama Cass ___
54 Director Lubitsch
55 Chin chaser?
56 Blips
57 Leonardo's town
59 Goofed
61 "___ lovely as a tree"
64 Part of U.S. Congress
66 Rooster's sore throat?
70 Certain bank savings: Abbr.
73 Accelerate the eng.
74 Writer Madame de ___
75 Galahad's mother
78 Georges ___ ("Roumanian Rhapsody")
80 Salome as a NY specialty?
83 Actress Meryl
84 Epic poetry
85 Montreal subway
86 Coin-flip call in Cannes
87 Pillow pretense?
88 Tiny nails

DOWN

1 Poet Lazarus
2 Like Ichabod Crane
3 Hogback
4 Finis, finis, finis
5 'Twixt twelve and twenty
6 Towel word
7 Eccentric
8 "Though last not ___" (Spenser)
9 Spring period
10 "___ Thou Now O Soul" (Whitman poem)
11 Wallach or Whitney
12 Cheroot
13 "Have ___ day"
14 Picador's weapon
17 Lays
19 Sprint
23 Burden
27 Nobel novelist Hermann ___
28 City on the Mohawk
29 War correspondent Ernie
31 Hoffman in "Midnight Cowboy"
33 Established
34 Convex molding
35 ___ Ste. Marie
37 Occupied, as a seat
39 Viper
40 Della from Detroit
41 Toting a gun
44 Baseball's Mel
45 Rds.' relatives
46 Kefauver
49 Prom flower family: Comb. form
50 CIO, e.g.
53 "All at once ___ a crowd": Wordsworth
57 Star in Lyra
58 Puts up a roadblock
60 Chair refurbisher
62 Twelfth zodiac sign
63 "___ of Old Smokey" (1951 song)
65 Kind of car
66 Part of a mountain or wave
67 Revenue, in Rouen
68 Not concealed
69 First Hebrew letter
71 Judicial assertions
72 Bergen's Mortimer ___
76 Symbol of meekness
77 God of love
79 Bishop's domain
81 Mauna ___, Hawaiian volcano
82 Doctrine

23 SKEWED COMPASS by Judith Perry

Beware! Our Vermont puzzler's purpose is to misdirect you.

ACROSS

1 Tied
5 Afternoon repasts
9 Landing boat, for short
12 Alpha's antithesis
17 Wash
18 Branchlike structures
19 Resident of: Suffix
20 Paddock females
21 Russian city on the Oka
22 Munich's river
23 Hr. segment
24 Yellow fever transmitter
25 Puccini heroine?
29 Ingest
30 European mountain chain
31 Cather heroine
32 Orkney fisherman's hut
33 Primps
34 Winter vehicle
38 Site of ancient sculpted heads?
42 Dactyl preceder
43 Quechuan
44 Parisian "white stuff"
45 Inept typist's activity
47 Biblical region
48 "A poem lovely as ___" (Kilmer)
49 Long-running Broadway musical
50 Michener locale?
52 Stream between Manhattan and Long Island?
57 Possessive pronoun
58 Social class
59 A 1492 vessel
60 What April brings
64 Poker play
65 Herb or male name
66 Potency
67 Annual Fifth Avenue bash?
69 Mimics
70 Motionlessness
72 Legal stipulation
73 Enter en masse
75 Italian wine city
76 Advanced degs.
79 T. Roosevelt's history?
84 Baseball great
85 Greek letter
86 Beehive State
87 Magic inscription
88 Sonata movements
89 Musical dir. to slow down
90 Bristle
91 Done
92 Hammett's detective
93 Opposite NNW
94 Waste allowance
95 Withered

DOWN

1 Funeral oration
2 Miscellany
3 Turn inside out
4 Mistress of Charles II
5 Flirt
6 Military students?
7 Indian nursemaids
8 Beget
9 Citrus-flavored solvent
10 Formally stiff
11 Achilles had one
12 Muscat is their capital
13 Life vests?
14 Wagnerian role
15 Turns right
16 Aide: Abbr.
26 Like S. Woodworth's bucket
27 Car barn
28 Naval off.
32 Onset
33 Practices
35 Garland
36 Sea bird
37 Track
38 German physicist
39 Inside (pref.)
40 Deface
41 You will be, in Paris
42 Young salmon
45 California or Oregon?
46 Ceremony
48 Assyrian war god
49 Author of "Peter Camenzind"
51 Markham subject
52 Remains in readiness
53 Finnish lake
54 Travel voucher
55 Author Bagnold
56 Respiratory sound
58 Outer cover
60 Mineral spring
61 School dance
62 Be indebted
63 Dirty Harry?
64 Permeate with a plant substance
65 Musical Count
67 N.A. deer
68 Topi
70 "Dombey and ___" (Dickens)
71 Coloring agents
74 Dishwasher cycle
75 Miller's "___ the Fall"
76 Purplish
77 Film and TV personality
78 Unit of volume
79 Makes lace
80 Celestial instrument
81 Silkworm
82 Evict
83 A friend of Antony

24 ON THE DISTAFF SIDE by Arthur Palmer

From the Wolverine State comes this no-nonsense delight. It's full of interesting clues and empty of esoterica.

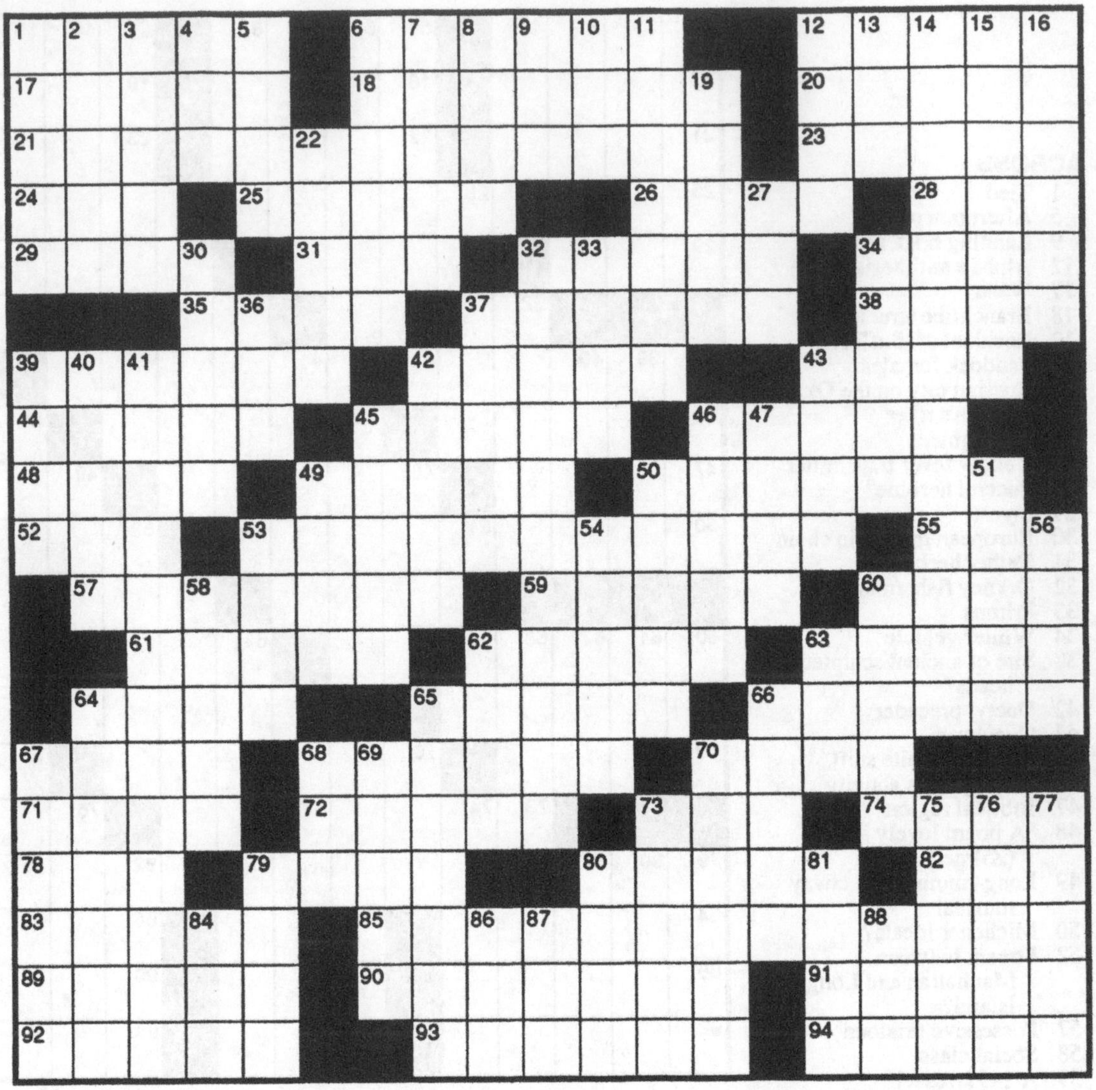

ACROSS

1 Argot
6 Inclines
12 Backslide
17 Trunk in a trunk
18 Rampart part
20 Be in store for
21 Willingly
23 Basketry fiber
24 Before, once
25 Dickinson or Post
26 Browning's "My ___ Duchess"
28 Short homily: Abbr.
29 "Farmer in the ___"
31 French wheat
32 Caesura
34 City on the Rhine
35 Crew members
37 On ___ knee
38 Formerly
39 Y.A. of q.b. fame
42 Clear the slate
43 Speck
44 Declaim
45 Delusion's partner
46 Silken sound
48 Libertine
49 Smithy sight
50 Moved effortlessly
52 Juillet's season
53 Red drinks
55 Word from Scrooge
57 Tidal river
59 "The ___ afoot": Shak.
60 Windmill blade
61 Thick-headed
62 Hen
63 A transfer design
64 Eur. or N.A.
65 Kind of eclipse
66 Drudged
67 Sounds from a rookery
68 ". . . but few are ___"
70 Creditor's claim
71 Lucky Lindy's wife
72 Peter and Paul
73 Opponent
74 Leisure
78 Metro stop: Abbr.
79 Duke's building
80 "The Art of Living" author
82 "___ the season to . . ."
83 Squaw's shelter
85 Code signals
89 Singer from Detroit
90 Perfume
91 TV-exec Arledge
92 Exasperate
93 Camped out
94 Man without a country

DOWN

1 Used a crosscut
2 River at Nantes
3 Russian collective
4 Kind of degree
5 Security
6 Victor's reward
7 Dipper
8 Wild revelry
9 Duffer's hope
10 Radon-concerned org.
11 Isolate
12 Café additive
13 Shucks' pals
14 Congratulates
15 They say it's golden
16 Forever, old style
19 What ecdysiasts and hairdressers do
22 Shaded in tone
27 But: Lat.
30 Soprano Lehmann
32 Heavenly entrance
33 Handle, to Henri
34 Promote vigorously
36 Companion of cakes
37 Pigtail
39 Sped
40 Burned up
41 Deflates
42 Messenger
43 ___ the boat
45 Sound from Rip
46 More tender
47 Roads
49 Word for Yorick
50 Ship of the desert
51 Mother of Perseus
53 Sacrifice at Shea
54 Guatemala tribesman
56 Anna who married Ziegfeld
58 Flexed
60 "César Cascabel" author
62 Forfeit
63 "Meet John ___ " 1941 film
64 Snack bar
65 Highest
66 Manipulate
67 Caesar's camps
68 Naval noncom.
69 Swarm
70 Like some dice
73 Yegg's customer
75 Dramatist Fugard
76 City of C Italy
77 Eat, to Ludwig
79 Ruminant animal
80 Throb
81 Make worthy of
84 Suffix for Stengel
86 Half a fly
87 Indonesian coin
88 He played Det. Yemana

25

STEPJOKE by Louis Sabin
The quip in this puzzle drops down like a staircase from left to right.

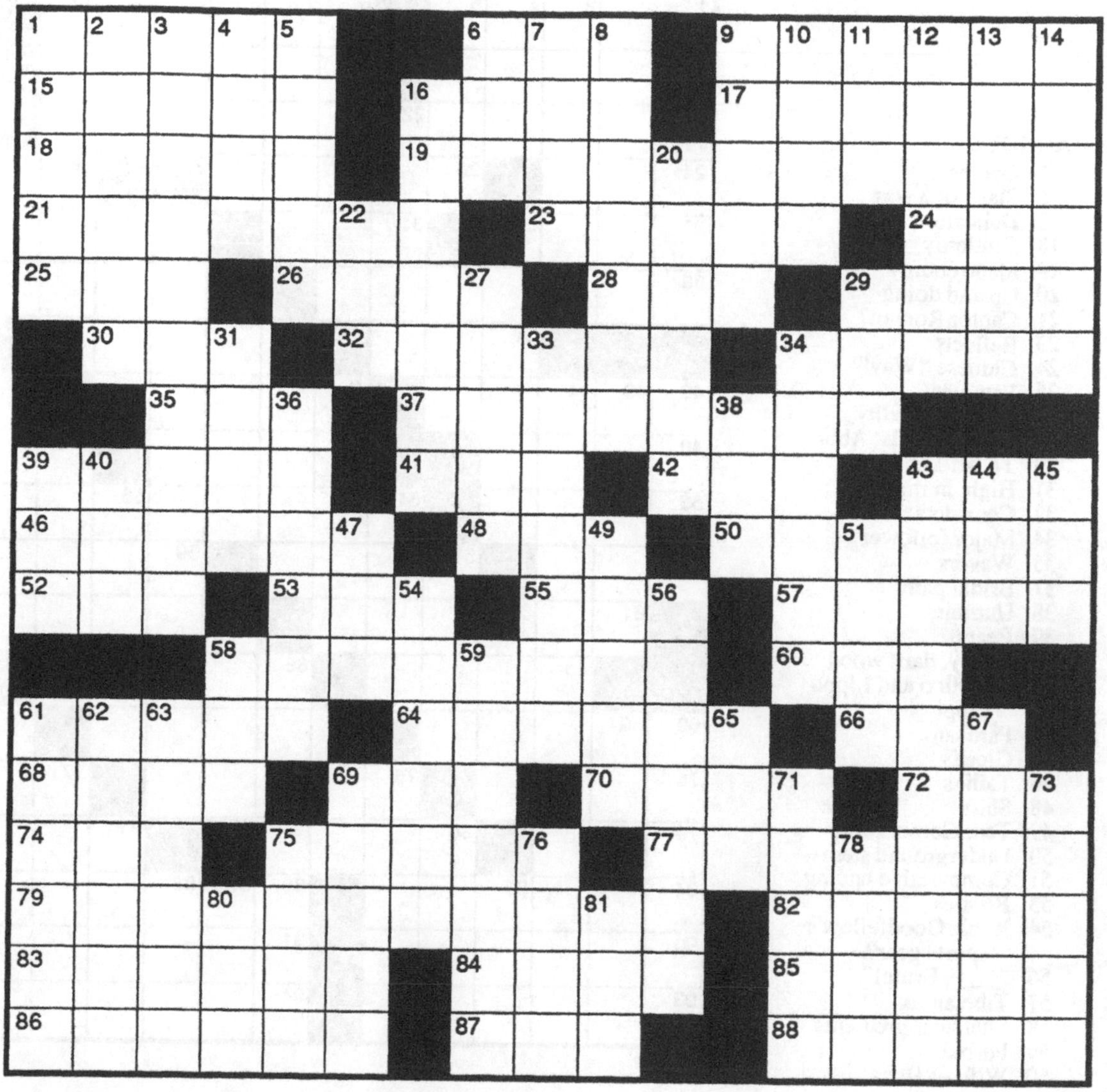

ACROSS
1 **Start of an eight-word "Stepjoke" ending at 89 Across**
6 Custer's 7th, e.g.
9 Amuse
15 Winged
16 Gold: Comb. form
17 Classroom item
18 Indonesian island
19 Theatre section
21 Take to court
23 Holiday events
24 Aries
25 Drivers' org.
26 **"Stepjoke": Part III**
28 Energy
29 Batty
30 Hardware item
32 Weak
34 Oar
35 Toss
37 Soviet transportation: Var.
39 Irish port
41 Supplement
42 Spade of whodunits
43 ___ de la Cité
46 Lessee
48 **"Stepjoke": Part V**
50 Actor Greene, et al.
52 Agreement
53 Fox-trot move
55 Na Na preceder
57 Sunday sections, for short
58 Kind of rifle
60 Leftover in the grate
61 Man or woman
64 "I'm nobody! Who ___ ?" (Dickinson)
66 Grasp
68 About
69 Globe
70 **"Stepjoke": Part VII**
72 Aggregate
74 Caesar's 201
75 Spring bloom
77 Java's sister island
79 Big 8 member
82 Slip
83 Protective body
84 Cry of old
85 Jumped
86 Singer and former shortstop
86 Rainbow element
88 **End of the "Stepjoke"**

DOWN
1 Londoner's dashboard
2 Mexican president (1946-52)
3 Canvas covers
4 Printer's dir.
5 **"Stepjoke": Part II**
6 Lowlife
7 War god
8 Face to face
9 Nero's ten
10 Blue flag
11 River near Nice
12 Legal deed
13 Fasten anew, in a way
14 Oscillation
16 Appendices
20 Some mags
22 Actress Alicia
27 **"Stepjoke": Part IV**
29 ___ Alamos
31 Forum wear
33 "___ Mignon" (Balzac)
34 Shark's sometime companion
36 Insured
38 Baron follower
39 Pigs' digs
40 Inventor DeForest
43 "Turkey ___ ," 1834 song
44 Zodiac sign
45 Curve
47 Pencil part
49 **"Stepjoke": Part VI**
51 Flagmaker
54 Words of wisdom, perhaps
56 Stirred up
58 Arikara
59 Judge
61 Squabble
62 If
63 Erstwhile frog
65 Ordinarily: Abbr.
67 Mother of Minos
69 Ejects
71 **"Stepjoke": Part VIII**
73 Borgnine's Oscar role
75 Biblical weed
76 Trainbearer
78 Kind of code
80 May-Day
81 Little one

26

ECHOIC by Arthur S. Verdesca

Our Jersey jester sounds off sonorously and makes interesting reverberations.

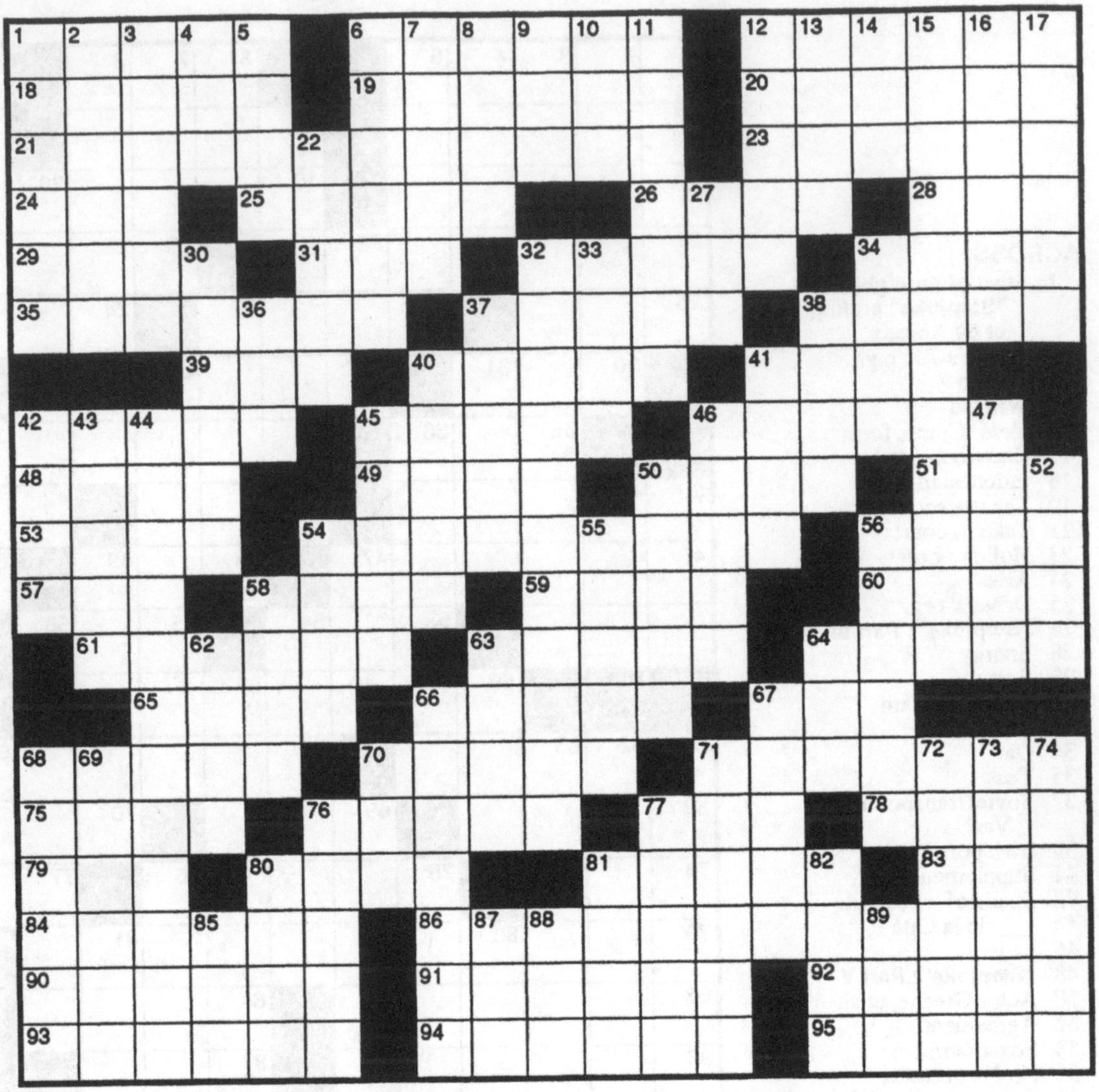

ACROSS

1 Oodles
6 Slave of a sort
12 Delicate
18 Fautleroy
19 Idaho county
20 Up and doing
21 Captor Roman?
23 Reflects
24 Chinese "Way"
25 Fatigues
26 Unit of heredity
28 Time periods: Abbr.
29 To be: Lat.
31 High, in music
32 Considers
34 Major follower
35 Wavers
37 Bridal path
38 Humble
39 Bears
40 Heavy, dark wood
41 Angelico and Lippo Lippi
42 Partisan
45 Glorify
46 Tallies
48 Shift
49 Ten: Comb. form
50 Underground stem
51 Comparative ending
53 Bristles
54 Robin Goodfellow's sports gear?
56 "___ , Brute!"
57 Tibetan ox
58 Shellac ingredients
59 Forbid
60 Wife of Boaz
61 Actress Signoret
63 Eyelashes
64 Loom bar
65 Hotbed
66 Kicks
67 Altos or Gatos preceder
68 Gravy dipper
70 Types of exams
71 Optimistic
75 Border on
76 Regional flora and fauna
77 Brain membrane
78 Film spool
79 Samovar
80 Dash
81 Report
83 Latin mouths
84 Foyt and Unser
86 Small village prince?
90 Saws
91 Where Mark Twain is burried
92 Channel
93 A spouse in Sevilla
94 Right-hand pages
95 Hard puzzle

DOWN

1 Sonnet section
2 Wrinkle
3 Melodic
4 Gro. divided by 12
5 Pivot
6 Renditions by singers
7 "Cooking has become ___": Burton
8 Escorts
9 Sonny's sibling
10 Nabokov novel
11 Primarily
12 Distresses
13 Summit
14 R.R. stop
15 Stingy like Andronicus?
16 Turns inside out
17 Tenant
22 Constructs
27 Flock member
30 Early anesthetics
32 Twelfth Nighter's instrument?
33 "But as it ___ , it ain't": Carroll
34 Israeli statesman
36 Musical ability
37 Taken ___ (surprised)
38 Jack-in-the-pulpit
40 Pres., V.P., etc.
41 Confluence
42 Lodge
43 Early Missouri tribe
44 Doughnut-loving Scottish king?
45 Bring out
46 Reddish-yellow brown
47 Uno e sei
50 Dermis
52 German river
54 Yearn (for)
55 Hurls snowballs at
56 Utensil on a pencil
58 Be outdone in a contest
62 Blend (into)
63 Outer garment
64 Aurora, to Aristotle
66 Fellow member of a lodge
67 Reluctant
68 Namesakes of Petrarch's beloved
69 Scrape off
70 Unctuous speech, figuratively
71 Lassos
72 Greek wind god
73 Cylindrical and tapered
74 Click beetle
76 ___ nova (dance)
77 Wing: Comb. form
80 Rabbit or Fox preceder
81 Fissure
82 O.K. Corral lawman
85 Self-esteem
87 English festival
88 Cato's 2100
89 Bovine call

27

YOU CAN BET ON IT! by Dale Burgener
An odds-on favorite to amuse and bemuse!

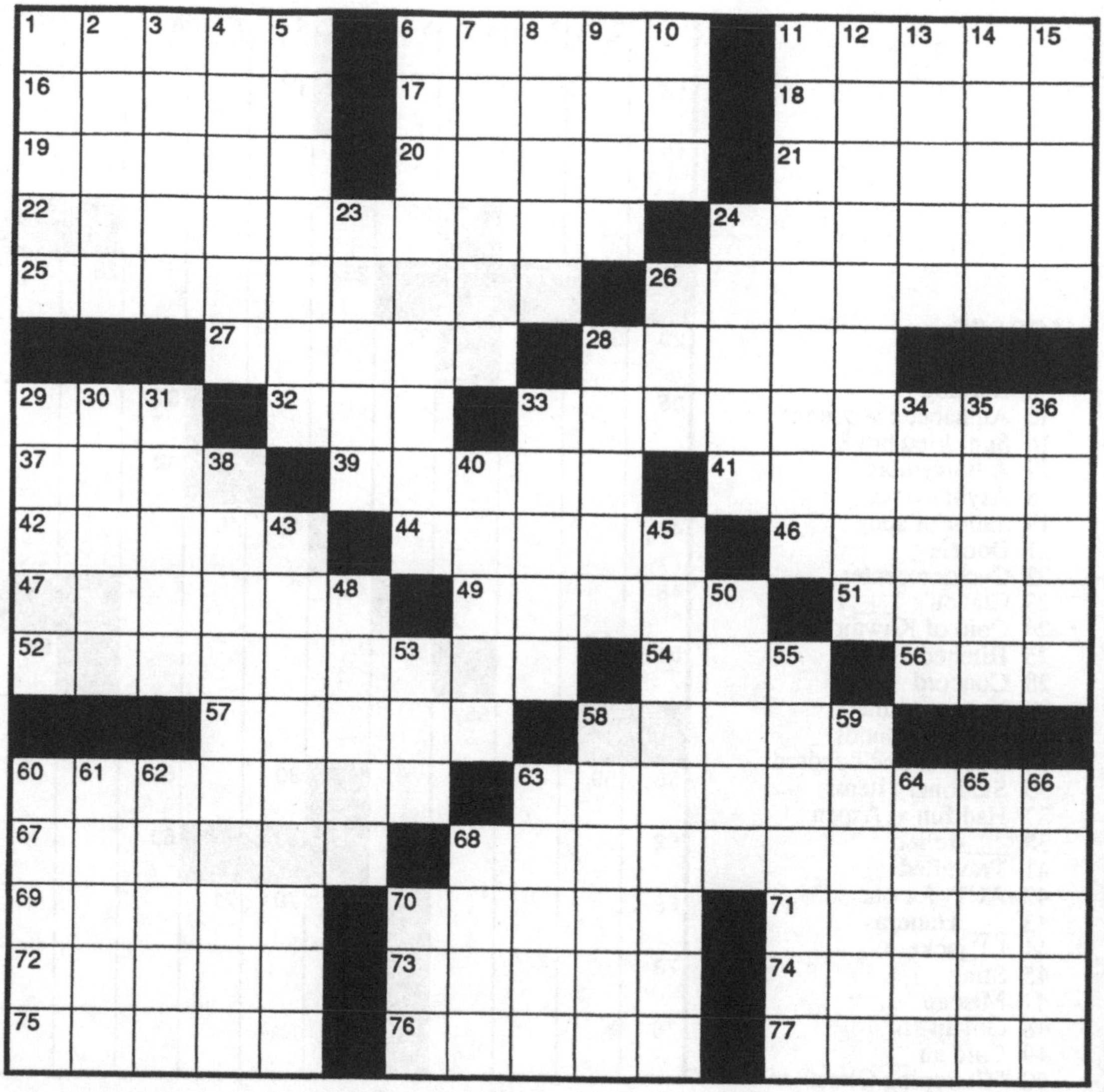

ACROSS

1 Wrinkly paper
6 Redowa or hora
11 Raps
16 Spiral
17 New Guinea
18 R2D2, e.g.
19 Doddering
20 Box elders
21 Fanon
22 Roulette bet
24 Outcault's Brown
25 Blackjack
26 Tahiti's capital
27 Twilled fabric
28 Norse gods
29 Police alert
32 Student of Rembrandt
33 Removed gunk
37 Per ___ (by the day)
39 Hot wine drink
41 Hall with lots of slots
42 Praise
44 Organ giver
46 Paine's "Common ___"
47 Spinets
49 Drive back
51 Stanch
52 Pyrex vessels
54 Part of C.I.A.
56 Pacino and Jolson
57 Lab burners
58 Devastation
60 Theft
63 Loner's game
67 Infamous cow owner
68 Eddie Felson gambled on these
69 Lemon or lime: Comb. form
70 Split fifty-fifty
71 Contaminate
72 White poplar
73 Young moray
74 Pump up
75 Stretch vehicles
76 Equals
77 More lucid

DOWN

1 Outline map
2 Begin again
3 Slur over a syllable
4 Texan lagniappes
5 Exercised
6 Conversed
7 Esoteric
8 Nephew's sister
9 It was once a worry
10 Danny's two
11 They really rake it in
12 Handicaps
13 Subside
14 For rent
15 Cubic meter
23 Lord of poetry
24 Iraqi port
26 Round ___ in a square . . .
28 Fabulous author
29 Skilled
30 Puckish sprite
31 Letters from Greece
33 Saharan drifts
34 Mr. Kringle
35 Car of 1959
36 Judges
38 Where the jet-set bet
40 Skirt inserts
43 Games with jackpots
45 They bring starters back
48 Radiant
50 Third Biblical bk.
53 Reddish-brown
55 Writes music
58 President from Iowa
59 Secret doctrine
60 Townie
61 Out
62 Desert shrub
63 Demystify
64 Of Troy
65 André's annuity
66 Sodium benzoate, e.g.
68 Enclosure
70 In the know

28 HOME ON THE GRANGE by Arthur Palmer

Can you guess what *home* Mr. Palmer is alluding to before solving 19 Across?

ACROSS

1 Savory
6 Burning
12 Alphabetic sequence
16 Sun-dried brick
17 A Barrymore
18 Asyut's river
19 Sailor of song
21 Doozie
22 Cyclone center
23 Clavell's "___ House"
24 Coin of Kuwait
25 Hitched
28 Concord
29 New socialite
32 Pastoral sounds
33 Body of one hundred
35 Stationery items
37 Had fun at Aspen
38 ___-relief
41 Travailed
42 ACT, for one
43 ___ Hatteras
44 LP jacket
45 Sting
47 Miscue
48 Got an "A"
49 Café au ___
50 "Galloping Ghost" of football
51 Compensation
52 "Home On the Grange," e.g.
53 Snack bar
54 Victory ___
56 Equal
57 Diocese
58 "Mighty Lak ___"
60 Mother of Dionysus
62 Perch
63 Official under Nero
65 It's often pierced
68 Advantage
69 Dickens novel
73 Joust
74 Shrewd
75 "Secrets" author
76 Chemical suffixes
77 "Children of a ___ God," 1986 film
78 Bathrobe material

DOWN

1 Savvy
2 An apple ___ . . .
3 Ponder (with "over")
4 ___ Saud
5 Actor Stockwell
6 "___ before, Love . . . ": Browning
7 "The Bank Dick" star
8 Like the oak leaf
9 Black cuckoo
10 Singer Tillis
11 Building wing
12 Smear with lotion
13 "It's In The Bag" actress
14 Soccer shoe
15 Seaport NW of Belfast
20 Poltroon
24 Pair
26 Gravelly ridge
27 Religious naturalist
29 Brahman's loose fold of skin
30 Beethoven's 3rd
31 His horse was Spark Plug
32 Schooner contents
34 Profit
36 Timetable, for short
37 Big Brother
39 Farthest point
40 Part of H.S.M.
43 Suffix for pluto
45 Surfeits
46 Tigger's creator
47 Sea bird
49 Top
50 In a plucky way
52 Waste allowance
53 Bullet size
55 Resources
56 Staid
58 Alpine ridge
59 "Age of Bronze" sculptor
61 Cartes du jour
64 Whilom
65 River of Hesse
66 "Happy Feet" composer
67 Bank (on)
69 Dance, in Dijon
70 Peer Gynt's mom
71 Certain NFL linemen: Abbr.
72 Mormon State tribe

29

OLD WEST SOBRIQUETS by Dorothy Elliott
Who was really who in the rootin', tootin' and shootin' days? Find out below!

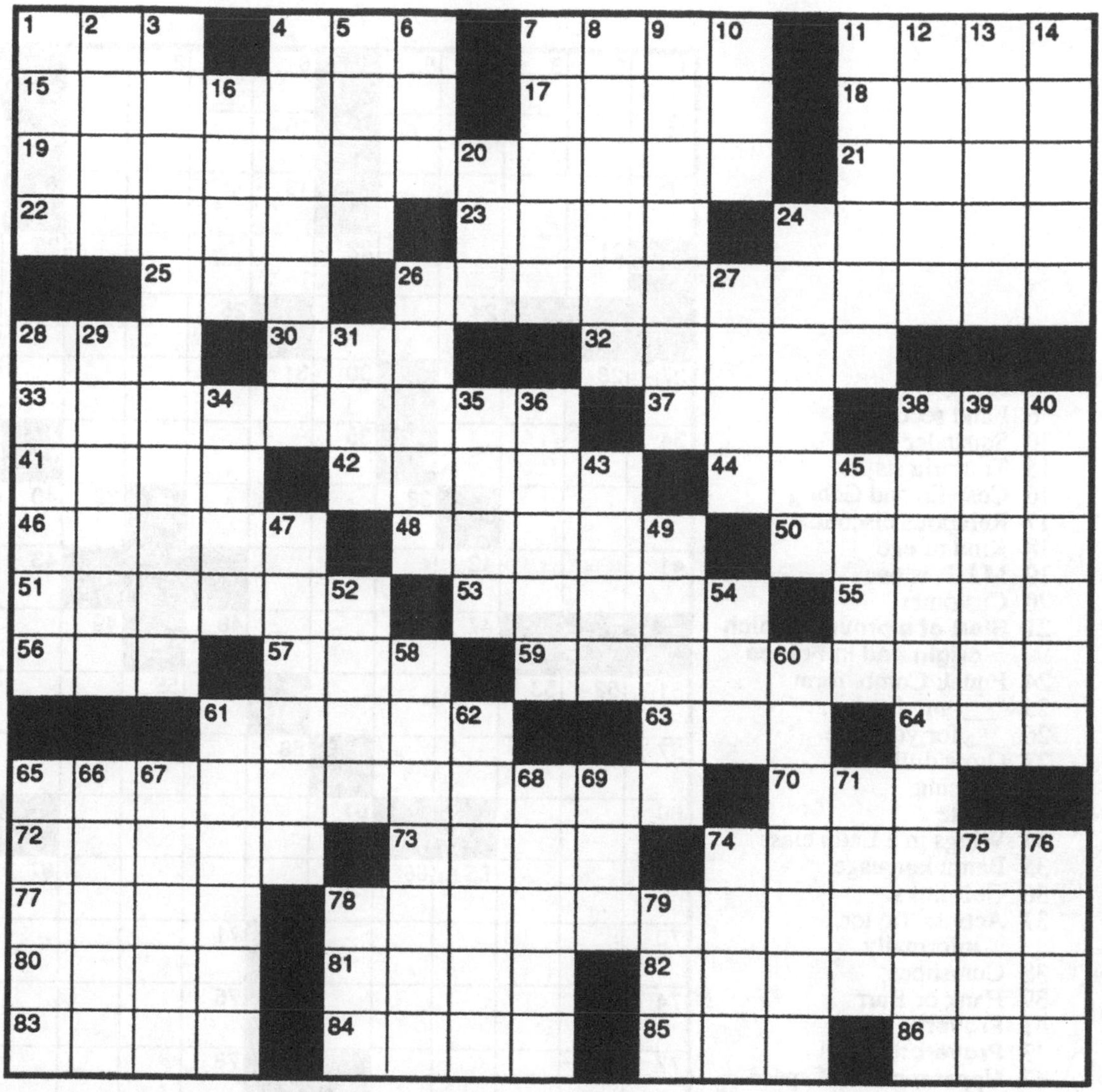

ACROSS

1 Little lie
4 John Henry Holliday
7 Rainy day rarities?
11 Aquarium
15 Where to visit London Bridge
17 Hearing: Comb. form
18 Hautboy
19 Martha J. Canary
21 Barrooms in Blarney
22 "___ not in Gath . . . "
23 Pained reaction
24 With 65 Down, Myra B. Shirley
25 Hankering
26 Phoebe A. Mozee
28 Tub
30 Four qts.
32 Actress Lindley
33 Aida was one
37 Gat
38 London's Big ___
41 Coaster
42 Restrain
44 UN General Assembly president: 1949
46 ___ powder (scram)
48 Jazz style
50 British homesteads
51 Afghans, Pekingese, et al.
53 Transparent linen
55 "He makes no friend who never made ___": Tennyson
56 Inc., in Inverness
57 "___ De-Lovely" (Cole Porter)
59 Charles E. Boles
61 Arabian VIP
63 One of the Clantons
64 Ancient card game
65 Harry Longabaugh
70 Prefix with classic
72 Oregon or Santa Fe
73 Secular
74 Gloomy
77 "Play It ___ Lays," 1972 film
78 Robert LeRoy Parker
80 Hit review
81 Alaskan island or strait
82 "Sweets to the sweet" recipient
83 Marsh growth
84 Trueheart of the comics
85 Org. founded by Juliette Low
86 Israel's main airport

DOWN

1 Fiction's antithesis
2 "Dies ___" (hymn)
3 W. H. Bonney
4 Sunday in Sonora
5 Step ___ (hurry up)
6 Dinah of "Alice in Wonderland"
7 Creole's cookery cousin
8 Tropical member of the pea family
9 "Horse Fair" painter
10 Hale into court
11 Capital of "The Wheat State"
12 Like ___ in a china shop
13 Peer
14 "One Flew Over the Cuckoo's Nest" author
16 Middleweight champ of the 40's
20 Hither's partner
24 Ex-Mme. Vadim
26 Out on ___ (in a precarious spot)
27 Scent
28 Certain virgin of yore
29 Finally
31 Gelada or pongo
34 Brainstorm
35 Harbor a fugitive
36 Mogul
38 W. F. Cody
39 Marine base in California
40 Keep one's ___ the grindstone
43 Disturb
45 Ruth's homeland
47 Kind of magnetism
49 Tartan
52 Star of "Nana": 1934
54 German theologian, opponent of Luther
58 Cloister
60 City on Lake Michigan
61 Blue-penciled
62 Vaqueros' gear
65 See 24 Across
66 Major et Minor
67 Gullible
68 Punts
69 "___ dien" (motto of Prince of Wales)
71 Scotch Gaelic
74 Cartographer's output
75 Word element meaning "personal"
76 Couple
78 Bartholomew Masterson
79 Gear tooth

30 GALLIC GEM by Eli Wesoff

This proverb from France is a shining example of the art of transposing phrases.

ACROSS

1 Gorge
6 Land section
10 Squander
15 Trattoria staple
16 Costello and Gehrig
17 Religious discourse
18 Kind of ego
19 M.I.T. is one
20 Customer
21 **Start of a proverb which originated in France**
24 Equal: Comb. form
25 "___ my heart . . ."
26 ___ for your life
27 Grow dull
30 Pressing
32 Salute
34 Wings in a Latin class
35 Bantu language
36 Golf links
37 Actress Taylor, informally
38 Gumshoes
39 Hank or Burr
41 **Proverb: Part II**
43 **Proverb: Part III**
47 Upper regions of space
49 Toppers in Ayr
50 Notable time span
51 Jolson's river
54 Computer ancestors
56 Draft
57 Pirogue
58 Opposed to written
59 Imitated
60 ___ Urt, Kazak plateau
61 Swiss canton's former name
62 Feel pain
64 **End of proverb**
70 Solutions used in a darkroom
71 College on the Thames
72 ___ Gay, famous B-29
74 Madness
75 Ireland, to Douglas Hyde
76 Histrion
77 Doomed eagle flier of mythology
78 Kind of bomb or sheet
79 Deviated

DOWN

1 He figures in Apr.
2 Time division in football
3 Regarding
4 Unfruitful
5 Trading centers
6 Part of et al.
7 Places in another's care
8 Stole livestock
9 Its capital is Tallinn: Var.
10 Gusher
11 Saharan
12 Vilifier
13 Glossolalia is the gift of ___
14 ___ cordiale
17 Dundee native
22 "___ Cream in My Coffee," 1928 song
23 Superlative ending
27 ___ Alto, California
28 Alphabet opener in Oman
29 Shiftless
31 Dress trim
32 Flubs
33 Litter peewee
36 Person listed on 48 Down
38 Kind of pupil
40 "___ in the Crowd," 1957 film
42 Comb. form denoting wine
44 Kennel protest
45 Dies ___
46 Pluck
48 Police blotter's relative
49 ___ ride (liquidate a mobster)
51 Butt preceder
52 Complete failure
53 TV appurtenance
55 Cravat's sporty relative
56 Villain portrayer in "Shane"
58 Posed
61 Like a phone in use
63 Perfect
65 Bring forth young of sheep
66 Cousin of a beluga
67 Incomparable person
68 "I've ___ Feeling I'm Falling," 1929 song
69 College in N.C.
73 Self-defense is one

31

THIS AND THAT by Rita Yelle
An old-fashioned delight with new-fashioned clues. We particularly enjoyed 70 and 104 Down.

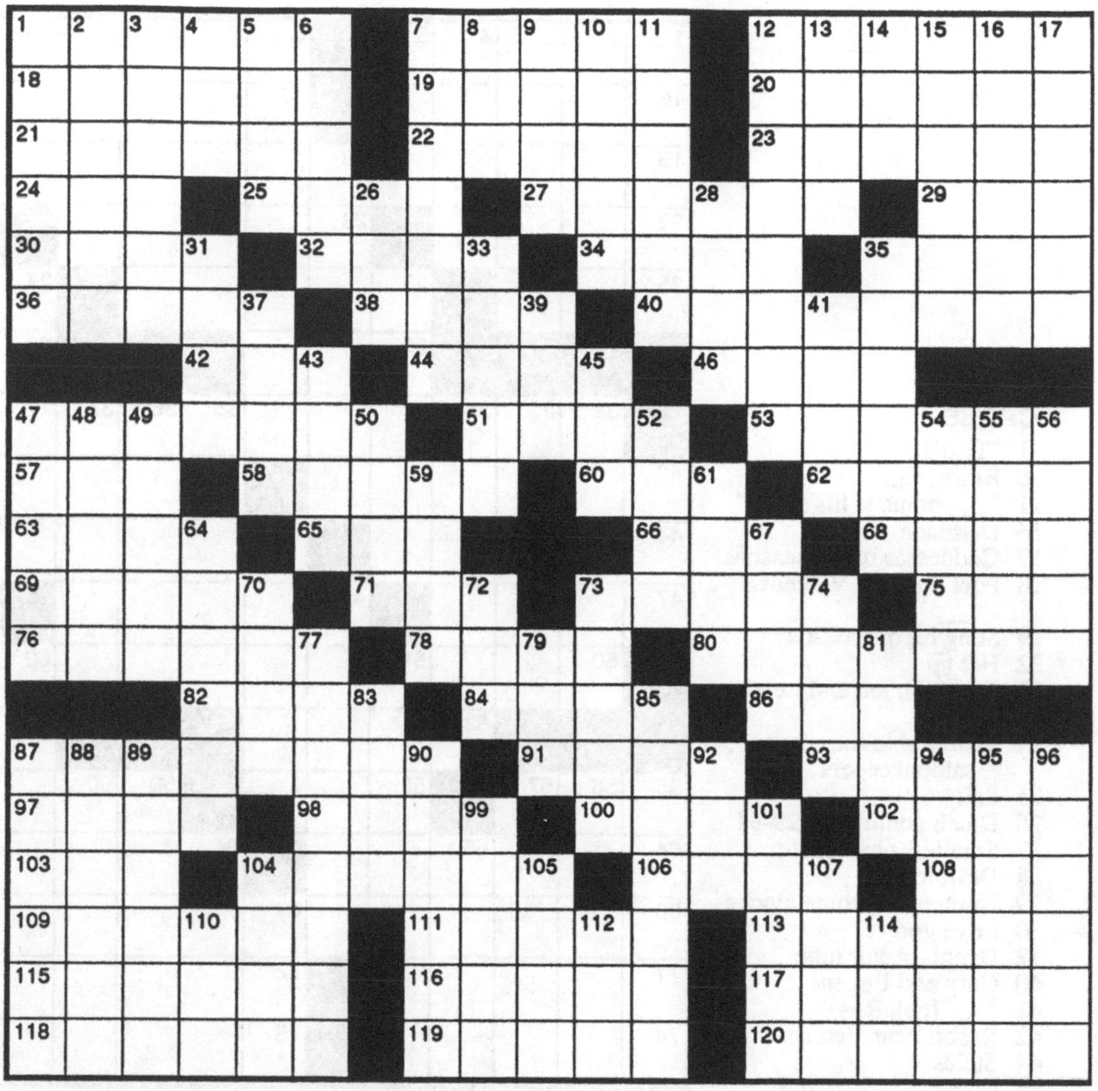

ACROSS

1 Tickled
7 NE Brazil port
12 Flotilla relative
18 Break a promise
19 Omit a vowel
20 Pater ___
21 Usher anew
22 Persian prophet: 216-276
23 Maneuver
24 Increase (with "out")
25 Strike out
27 E. B. White's Charlotte, e.g.
29 Turkish official
30 Smack
32 Grating sound
34 Actor Rip
35 Discovery
36 Part of MTM
38 Parsley's cousin
40 Balderdash
42 Cartoonist Gardner
44 Spoke
46 Brace
47 Parcel
51 Tide type
53 Elf
57 Hematite, e.g.
58 ___ larceny
60 Aries
62 Passover feast
63 Patch
65 Julie Andrews film: 1981
66 Chin
68 Kind of gas
69 Penetrate
71 Nothing
73 Areca
75 Chemical suffix
76 Snaps back
78 Tender
80 Fastened with a gun
82 Diner sign
84 Crux
86 Sicken
87 Bounce, to a banker
91 Judge
93 Stallone film: 1986
97 Charter
98 Spring bloomer
100 H.S. math course
102 Young voter
103 Model Carol
104 Fastidious
106 Gang
108 Steep ravine: Var.
109 Small tower
111 Halter
113 City in central Kansas
115 Divine revelation
116 Sign up
117 Kind of agent
118 Canceled a debt
119 Staggers
120 Roman chariots

DOWN

1 Collar
2 Humbly
3 Open
4 Glimpse
5 Mild oath
6 Prevent
7 Vengeance goddess
8 ___ king
9 Coats with Sn
10 Expert
11 Wound
12 Aerials
13 Leonine sound
14 M.I.T. degree
15 Achieve
16 Condescends
17 Pinball place
26 Stripling
28 Fall
31 Jaunty
33 Seedling
35 Rabbit hunter
37 Harvest
39 Whopper
41 Small drinks
43 "Rock of ___"
45 Stuntman Robinson
47 Apples and pears
48 Sporty dome
49 Coppers
50 Jacket type
52 Call by name
54 A perfect ten
55 Pester
56 Misreckoned
59 Long-billed wader
61 Wilander of tennis
64 Maroon
67 Beet genus
70 Peruse or perused
72 Roleo need
73 Assail
74 Secular
77 Striped
79 Dispose (of)
81 Garden spot
83 Wraparound of Bombay
85 Male falcons
87 Cicero, e.g.
88 Velvetlike fabric
89 Catch
90 One in a circle
92 Russian commune
94 Soon, in Scotland
95 Checked
96 History
99 "Wall Street" director
101 Beau ___
104 Where Genoa isn't a city
105 Long ago
107 Conflicts
110 G.E. acquisition
112 G in the key of C
114 Part of UNLV

32 FIDDLING WITH TUNES by Mary M. Murdoch

Mary has cast a *spell* over some pop songs—all the better to puzzle you. But she's letter perfect!

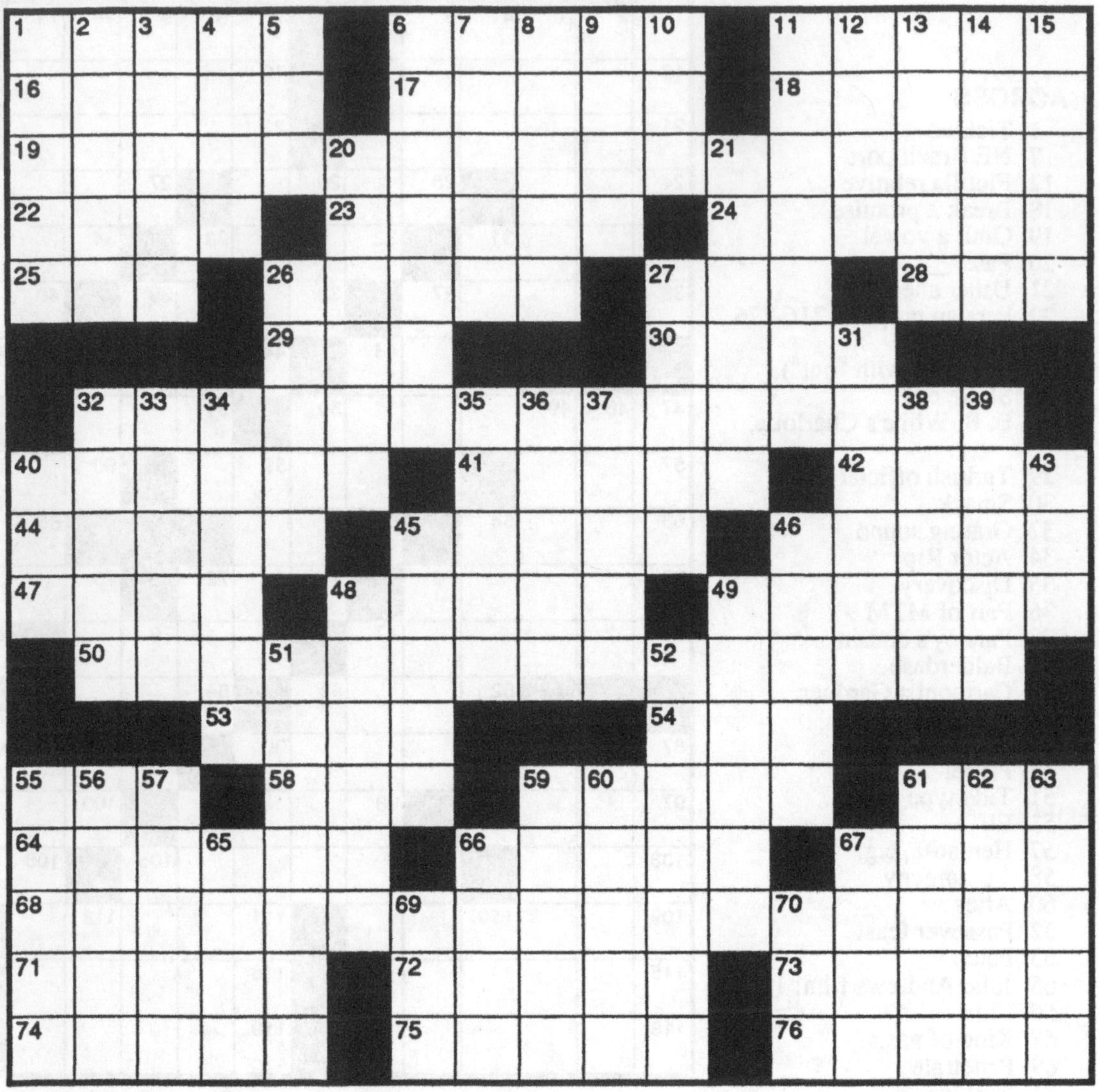

ACROSS

1 "That's ___"
6 Rinse, e.g.
11 "___ home is his castle"
16 Dissuade
17 Goddesses of the seasons
18 Poet Stephen Vincent ___
19 Song hit of the '20s
22 Het up
23 What Carson and Leno do
24 Memorable foe of saloonkeepers
25 Salt
26 Dutch admiral: 1629-91
27 Smallest physical pt.
28 Draft letters
29 Numeral on some clocks
30 Love god
32 Dennis-Adair tune
40 Gary and Eugene
41 "___ Irish Rose"
42 Resort near Venice
44 Steles
45 Coeur d' ___, Idaho
46 Deck with finery
47 Auk genus
48 Liberal; wide
49 Hidden
50 Isham Jones-Cris Kahn tune
53 Glut
54 Horse-and-carriage
55 P.I. tree
58 Parisian party
59 Wrong
61 Oleo holder
64 ___ Conquest of 1066
66 Divided
67 ___ en scène
68 Elvis hit
71 "Maria ___," old song
72 Wipe out
73 Corners
74 Office furniture
75 Packaged
76 Part of HST

DOWN

1 Let in
2 Comedienne Anne
3 Else
4 Instrument type
5 Vetch
6 Antelope
7 Capp family name
8 Brittle
9 Alley
10 Medical scan, for short
11 Favorite son of David
12 Drink's partner
13 Those against
14 Verne's captain, et al.
15 British guns
20 Sulla's foe
21 Enspheres
26 Mah-jongg pieces
27 Free-for-all
31 Quartz and agate
32 Designer Smith
33 "___ Depends on You," old song
34 Defames
35 Kite's weapon
36 Construction piece
37 ___ hop
38 Hyderabad ruler
39 Ideal spots
40 R. E. Lee's cause
43 Song from "A Chorus Line"
45 Gazelle
46 Leavings
48 Gas type
49 Best: Comb. form
51 Beach sights
52 Went with the current
55 "The Lady ___," old song
56 Relative of roulette
57 Roman ruins site in France
59 Silk fabrics
60 Former Attorney General, Edwin ___
61 Kind of lily or moth
62 Conduct
63 Seamstress Ross
65 Friar
66 Actress Witherspoon
67 Star in Cetus
69 Dry
70 To the ___ degree

33

MOB SCENE by William Lutwiniak
Here's still another opus from our Maryland master of words. He says that he created this puzzle after a visit to the Big Apple.

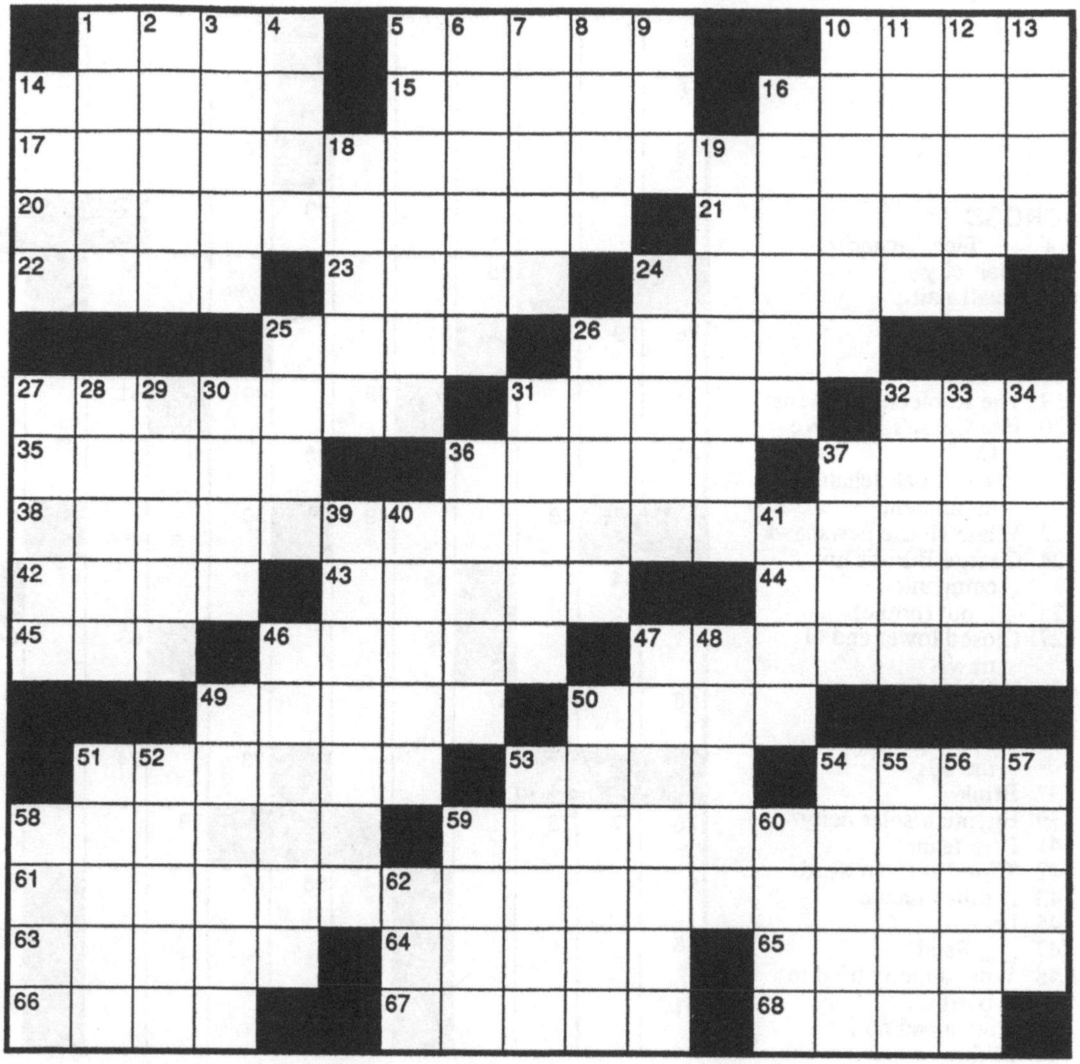

ACROSS

1 U.S. naturalist/explorer
5 Monte ___
10 Esth or Lett
14 Papal seal
15 Trackless expanse
16 He played Gene Krupa in 1959
17 Faultless person sometimes victimized by the mob
20 Farcical imitations
21 Stringencies
22 Made strips
23 Cat's-paw
24 Big Poison and Little Poison of baseball
25 "Yesterday" composer: 1933
26 Cries out
27 Sullivan's confrere
31 Paper mat
32 Concha
35 Peregrine
36 Car-wash step
37 "___ Do Is Dream of You," 1934 song
38 Noontime problem in a big city
42 He lived for 905 years
43 Like the Poconos
44 Forgo
45 ___ Plaines, Ill.
46 Developers' interests
47 She played Olivia Walton
49 Spoilage
50 Hollywood's Lamarr
51 T-bone and rump
53 End of Caesar's report
54 ___ precedent
58 Cabal's output
59 Part of a N.Y.C. crowd
61 Member of 38 Across; he's often interviewed
63 Lower Saxony seaport
64 Chilean export
65 A.F. reconnaissance satellite
66 Blue dye
67 Coast Guard group
68 Borscht base

DOWN

1 He wrote as Saki
2 Of an armbone
3 "___ Lucy"
4 Regatta, e.g.
5 Twist
6 What the track crowd likes
7 Insurgent
8 Minstrel's repertoire
9 Switch readings
10 Carousals
11 Phrase of choice
12 Looks lasciviously
13 Rocky peaks
14 Deck post
16 On the whole
18 A component of liquor
19 Fishing boat
24 Belt site
25 Rosewall and Venturi
26 Like Robert Burns's lass
27 Opened wide
28 A Mandrell sister
29 Ocean-liner pools
30 Honey bunch
31 Tunes in
32 Puckish; fey
33 Extant
34 Prepared potatoes in a certain way
36 William Bendix TV role
37 Off yonder
39 What some plots do
40 Tushingham and Hayworth
41 Absent
46 Mariner
47 Roués
48 What a diaskeuast does
49 Judged
50 Up more
51 Dolt or jerk, Yiddish style
52 Bara of the silents
53 Streak of color, to a zoologist
54 Durable cloth
55 Shoe width for Big Foot?
56 Robert ___ Jones of golfing fame
57 Nick and Nora's terrier
58 Vexed state
59 Impertinent one
60 Try, briefly
62 Electees

34 WHO'S NEWS? by Arnold Moss

The creator of this straightforward puzzle also appeared in the film mentioned in the 76 Across clue. Is that news to you?

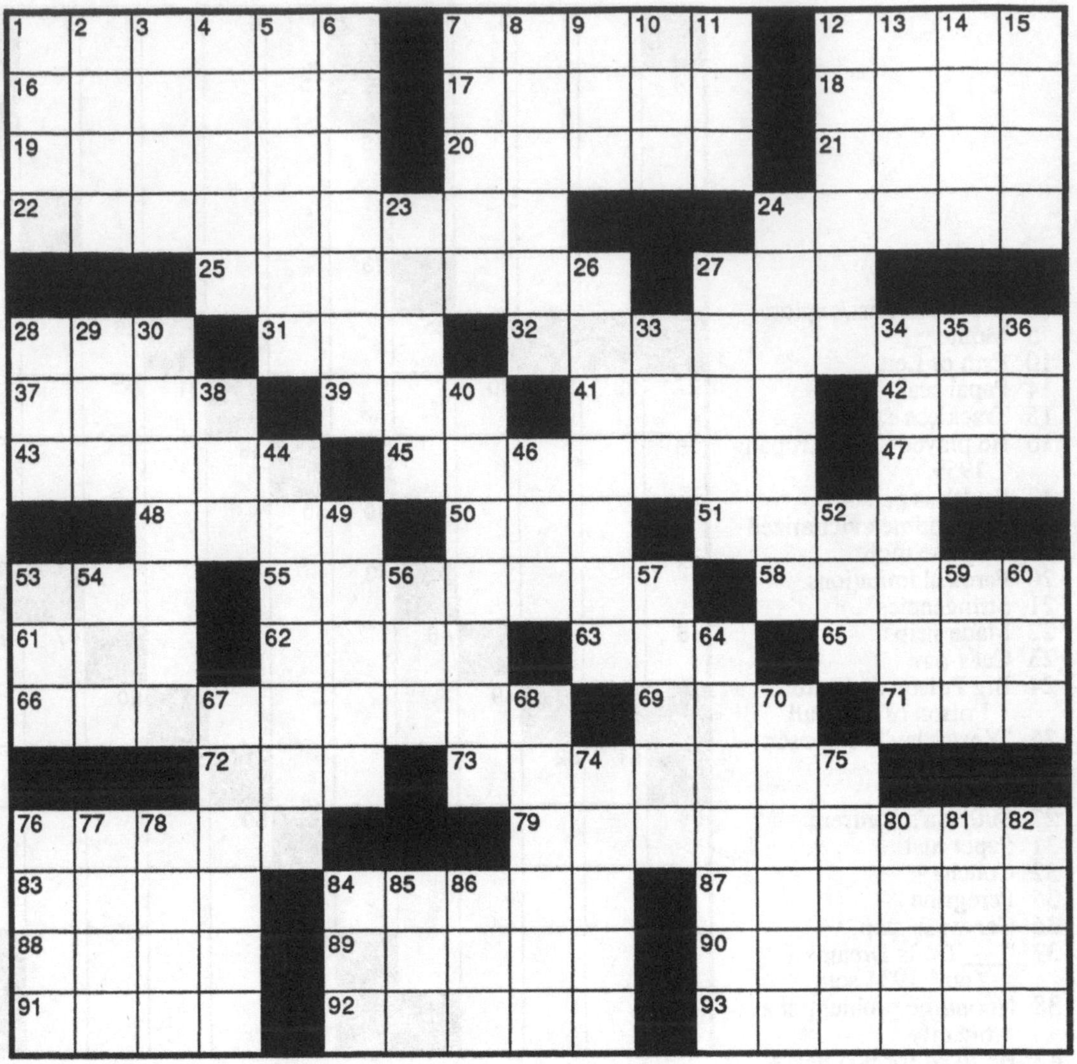

ACROSS

1 ___ face (shame)
7 Utah city
12 Small nail
16 Shrewd
17 Artless
18 Profuse
19 The Rubicon, to Caesar
20 Ilka Chase's "___ We Cry"
21 Site of Shah Jehan's monument
22 White House newshawk
24 George Burns's hot companion
25 ___ out (broke)
27 Closed lower end of trawl
28 WW I group
31 Killer whale
32 Famed sportscaster of the 30s
37 Brink
39 Egyptian solar deity
41 Polo team
42 Thumbs-down word
43 Antilles native
45 Feeler
47 ___ Saud
48 What Antony tried to borrow
50 Give a bad notice
51 Midge
53 An L.A. athlete
55 King of Spain: 1886–1931
58 Boswell sisters, et al.
61 Abbr. used at 71 Across
62 Stainers' containers
63 Kind of trip
65 Carlsbad or Mammoth
66 Network anchor
69 Filipino terrorist
71 So. Cal. airport
72 Koch and Asner
73 Surgical instrument: Var.
76 Actress in"Viva Zapata"
79 Network anchor
83 Chemical compound used in plastics
84 Nero Wolfe's creator
87 African antelope
88 Watch part
89 Legislative body in Paris
90 Pursued a food regimen
91 Joan Sutherland, e.g.
92 Kind of mate
93 Pressure

DOWN

1 CA flame fighters: Abbr.
2 Peace Prize locale
3 Petrify
4 Shrub or singer
5 Verdi opera
6 Mudguards
7 Hamburger garnish
8 Fish-eating sea bird
9 Dip bait lightly
10 Actress Arden
11 S. Foster's "Old Uncle___"
12 Whoopi's hair-do features
13 Actress Diana from Doncaster
14 Former radio performers' union
15 "___ Brutus," Barrie play
23 French actor/dramatist Guitry
24 Au ___ (up to date)
26 D.C. department was slated for Tower in 1989
27 Network newsperson
28 Network for anchor Peter Jennings
29 Christian or Olympian
30 Member of 1 Down
33 Russian river
34 Approve concisely
35 Pinch
36 Female: Comb. form
38 "Angela ___," 1928 song
40 Like "Candid Camera" shots
44 Braggadocio
46 Whip
49 Laths
52 Swing of a pendulum
53 Magritte's "The ___ Model"
54 One ___ time
56 Nautical six ft.
57 Old Irish script
59 Nero's breakfast?
60 Dr. Ruth's subject
64 Makes a better offer
67 Entertain
68 Religious formality
70 Miss Piggy's amour
74 Soprano Lehman or Lenya
75 Rodeo participant
76 TV commentator
77 Domingo specialty
78 Twenty quires
80 Smith or Jackson
81 Malt brews
82 Handfuls of cotton
84 Draft org.
85 ___ offensive (1968)
86 ". . . sat ___ wall"

35 ROMANESQUE by Jeffrey A. Mercer

Latin lovers will like this little teaser. Pax, amor et felicitas!

ACROSS

1 Word in a palindrome
6 Kind of rain
10 One of Yale's gifts to the White House
14 Warning to Juan
15 Location
16 Woody's son
17 Latin liturgical phrase
20 Dir. London to Dublin
21 Hawaiian royalty
22 Explosive stuff
23 Black Sea port
25 Give up
28 Fertility goddess
31 Stumble
33 Trade for cash
35 Type of hygienist
38 ___ even keel
40 Prefix with conservative
41 Byron's "before"
42 ___ consensu (by common consent)
44 Ab ___ (from the beginning)
45 Sibling nickname
46 Lamb
47 Barrel parts
49 Scottish goblet
51 Hindu fire god
53 Like Tonto's pal
54 Riga native
56 Summer headwear
59 Alias, for short
61 Word on an octagonal sign
62 "___ longa . . . "
65 Horace quote re the golden mean
70 Vidal
71 Snare or bass
72 Atoll
73 Golf or tennis event
74 Virgil's was "idem"
75 City on the Aire

DOWN

1 Produced
2 Stratford-on-___
3 Small coin
4 "___ Lay Dying": Faulkner
5 Single-celled organism
6 Lend a hand
7 Cicero's equivalent of "Ich bin ein Berliner"
8 Japanese statesman
9 Liability
10 Samples
11 Rainbow
12 Kin of la grippe
13 "___ Jones" Fielding novel
18 Rubber tree
19 "Murder, ___"
23 Bone: Comb. form
24 Japanese aborigine
26 Afresh, to Fabius
27 Cricket crew
28 That is, to Seneca
29 Soap opera, e.g.
30 Existing, to Ovid
32 Cook's collection
34 Lax
36 Suit topper
37 Entertainer Falana
39 Word with pick or wit
43 Soviet fighter planes
48 Ht.
50 Flower part
52 By and by
55 Stat for Spinks
57 Pet name
58 It has thirty days
60 Totals
62 Competent
63 Was remorseful
64 Jet-set jets
65 Alter ___
66 Bribe
67 Uno, due, ___
68 Sister of Ima Hogg?
69 Suffix with Siam

36

WRITING MATERIAL by Elaine George

Once you have solved 21 Across, the echoes that crop up later should put you into high gear.

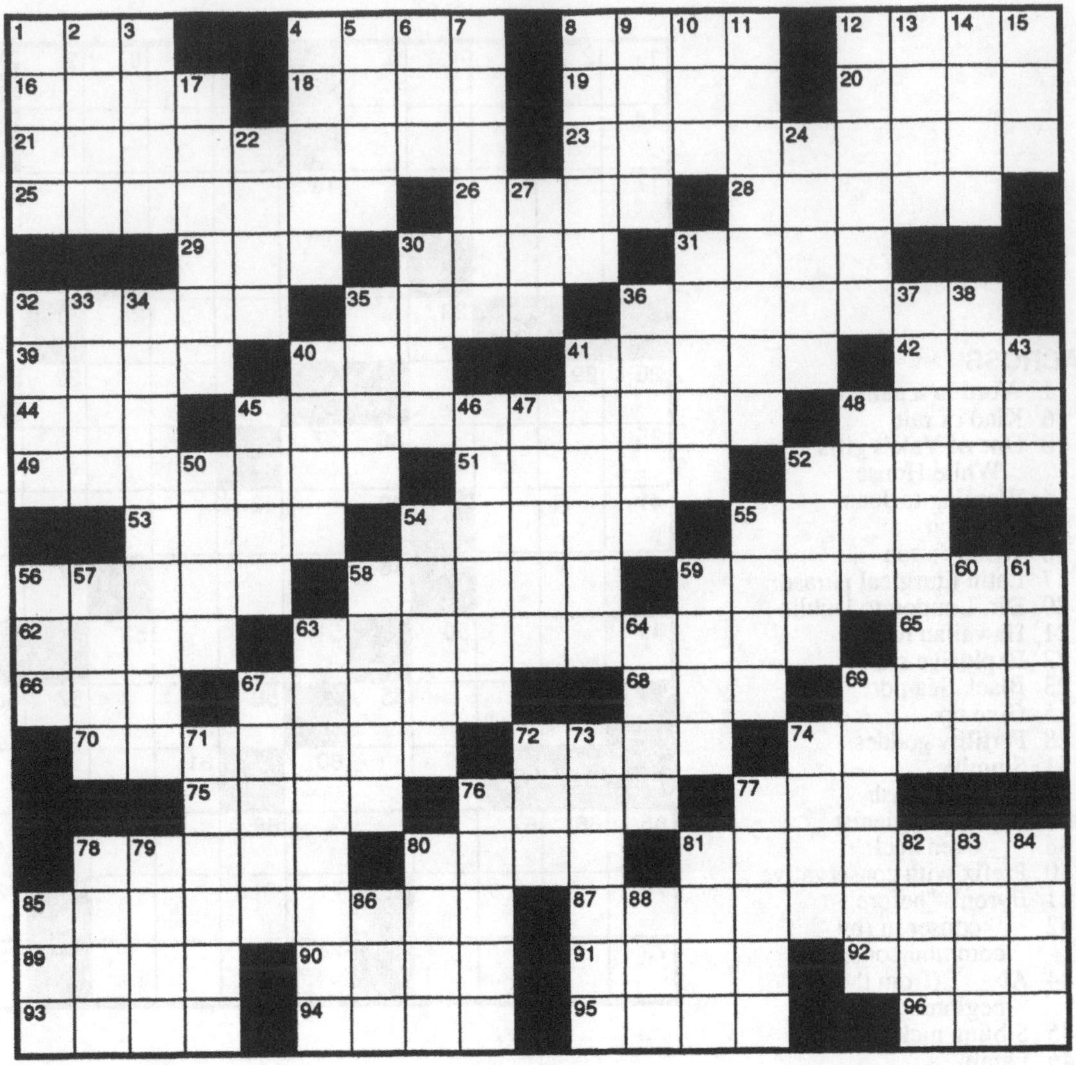

ACROSS

1 Dunk doughnuts
4 Lhasa priest
8 Dixie's Crimson Tide
12 Phooey!
16 Exhale
18 Generous
19 Askew
20 Wan
21 Clerical chore
23 Vacation spots
25 Entertained
26 Simba
28 Fortification
29 Sun. talk
30 Seabird
31 Noah's messenger
32 Headlands
35 Duty
36 A gear on a car
39 Type of exam
40 Flight on a shuttle
41 Heliacal
42 Important period
44 General's pinup
45 Blotter for spilled milk
48 Formerly of Uganda
49 "Jacks or better," in poker
51 Propelled a scull
52 Your birthday, e.g.
53 Burma or Tobacco
54 Despised
55 Singing brothers
56 V.M.I. student
58 Fleshy fruits
59 Lived
62 Brouhahas
63 Weak nation that talks big
65 Tokyo of yore
66 Elec. unit
67 Begat
68 Thersitical fellow
69 Lock-up
70 On a bias
72 Cannonballed
74 Upbeats, in music
75 Guns, to Capone
76 Pandowdies
77 Govt. ecology group
78 Water wheel
80 The best
81 Retaliates
85 State of being even
87 Weirs
89 Weird lake?
90 Bird coop
91 Largest dam in Germany
92 Slash
93 Does sums
94 Oklahoma city
95 Scoot here and there
96 High rides, for short

DOWN

1 The ninth mo.
2 Persian poet
3 Calumet
4 Demote
5 Location for two peas
6 Sea, in France
7 Leg joints
8 Salty meat
9 Thicke, of TV
10 Parent's nickname
11 Endorsement
12 An L.A. football player
13 One of Boomer's predecessors
14 Not now
15 NBC is one
17 Raise a nap
22 Hwys.
24 Break off
27 Irritate
30 VCR requisite
31 Removed from a galley
32 Perry, the singer
33 Daniel ___ Moi, Kenyan statesman
34 Girl's toy
35 The best
36 Propelled a gig
37 Half-years at college
38 "___ Go Bragh"
40 Difficult
41 Most hurtful
43 Colony denizen
45 Fuel from fens
46 Meandered
47 Spud
48 St. crossers
50 Anagram or homophone for nose
52 Moslem noble
54 Had great expectations
55 Canned
56 Hudson or DeSoto
57 Summer drinks
58 Peels
59 Major Hoople's exclamation
60 An Adams who married a Kovacs
61 "Reservoir ___"
63 The widow's mite
64 Chills
67 Symbol of slowness
69 Stigmatizes
71 Jibes
72 Trangress
73 Looked through a peephole
74 Mimic
76 Sat for
77 Chrissy, of tennis
78 Blockhead
79 Roman poet
80 Italian wine center
81 Declare
82 Nor'easter
83 Jannings of films
84 Giant jets
85 Author of "The Brave Bulls"
86 Ages and ages
88 "Apple cider" gal

37

OATER by Christopher Sherwood
The subject is wild and woolly, but this smooth puzzle can be solved with 65 Down.

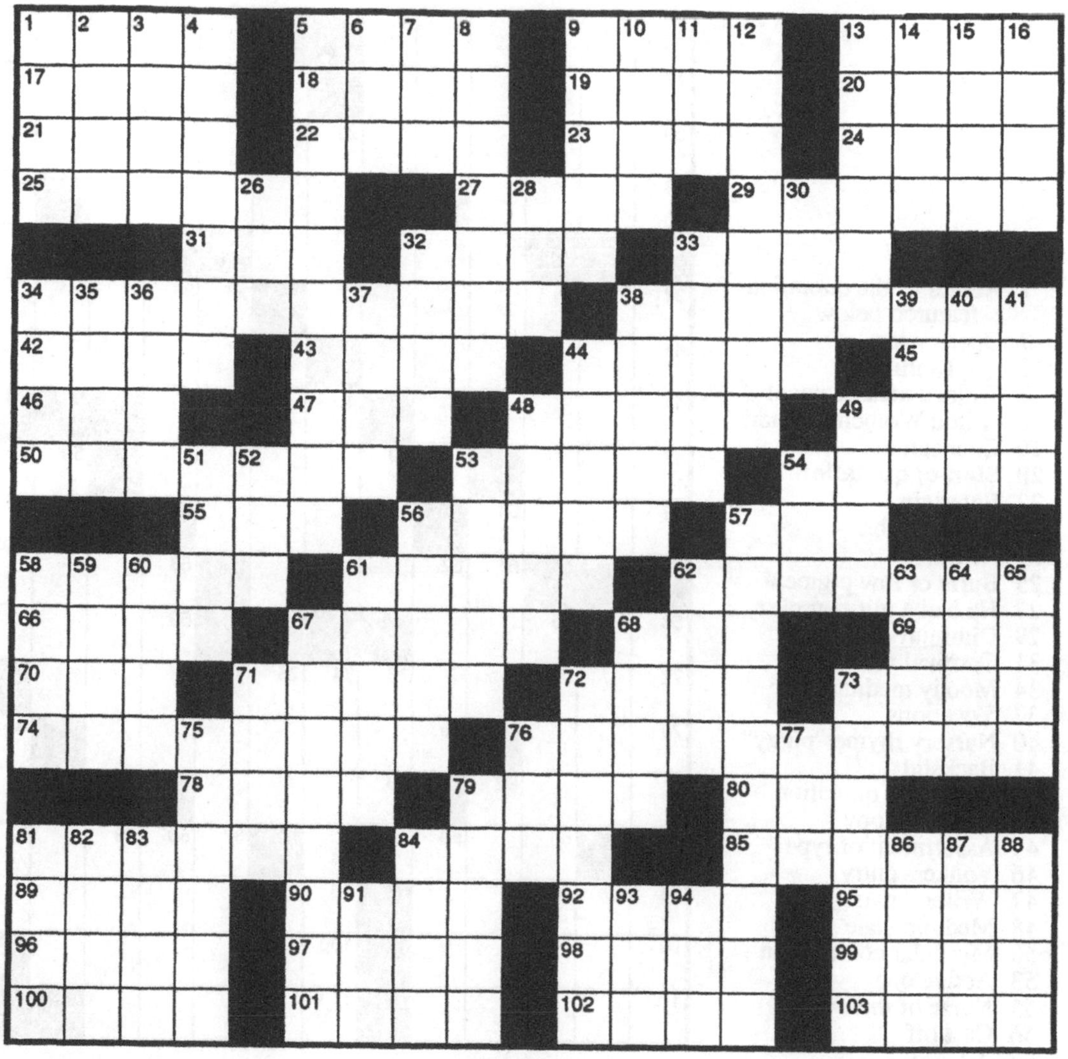

ACROSS

1 Disparities
5 Film crew member
9 Knighted actor Guinness
13 Holiday hideaways
17 Emulate Maxwell Perkins
18 Zeus's consort
19 Signal receiver of a sort
20 Uncouth fellow
21 Tiny critter
22 Baltic tributary
23 Basilica part
24 Sax variety
25 Virginia, Georgia, and the like
27 Middle East staples
29 Word with jack or jacket
31 Game, ___, match
32 Windmill component
33 One like John Wayne
34 Conestoga caravan
38 Vehicle for James Arness
42 North Carolina college
43 Give the boot
44 Greene of "Bonanza"
45 Football stat
46 Greek letter
47 Drenched
48 What Scarlett O'Hara was
49 "Moon Mullins" character
50 Western desperado family
53 Agreements
54 Famous Trojan captive
55 Mad. Ave. concerns
56 Childhood taunt
57 Half a sawbuck
58 Five-and-dime, e.g.
61 "Vita Nuova" author
62 Log-cabin kin
66 Seraph's adjunct
67 Setting for many a western
68 Former Bruin great
69 Amtrak's Canadian cousin
70 Tool for Bunyan
71 Galahad's garb
72 Champagne term
73 Cribbage markers
74 Gary Cooper classic
76 Little Big Horn strategist
78 Sometime soon
79 Mustang offspring
80 Convent resident
81 Convertible: Slang
84 TV detective Peter ___
85 Pastoral passages
89 Water vessel
90 Psyche's beloved
92 Part of the day
95 Ring event
96 Sea eagle
97 Laser beams
98 Rapier's cousin
99 Stare amorously
100 ___ in the wool
101 Be tipsy
102 Antelope playmates, in a song
103 Cry of anguish or surprise

DOWN

1 Tourmaline and onyx
2 Prospector's work entrance
3 Century plant
4 Cowboy's chapeau
5 Sights in the modern West
6 "___ River Valley"
7 Wrath
8 Fancy dessert
9 Hackneyed saying
10 Facial feature
11 Suffix with host
12 TV role for Clint Walker
13 Skier's downhill race
14 Canvass
15 Reo or Stutz
16 Put away
26 Suffix with velvet
28 Stagecoach stop
30 Language of Eire
32 Like the American West
33 What a pitcher does
34 Garden interloper
35 Wasatch ski resort
36 Netkeeper's domain
37 Regrets
38 Kin of gee
39 Girasol
40 Comedian Danny
41 School Shelley attended
44 Legal paper
48 Defeats in a gunfight
49 English county
51 Edible root
52 "___ to Billy Joe"
53 Iraqi coin
54 SRO show
56 Ivanhoe, e.g.
57 Sutter follower
58 Former Teheran ruler
59 Jitney relative
60 Haute couture's Cassini
61 DePaul U athlete
62 Santa ___, island in the Pacific
63 Declare
64 Jazzmen's jobs
65 Relaxation
67 Long Knives, to Sitting Bull
68 Examination variant
71 ___ Domini
72 TV series for Chuck Connors
73 Child's lap tune
75 Heinous emotion
76 Leavenworth resident
77 Paul Newman film
79 Persnickety
81 College in Oregon
82 Skewed
83 Kelly or Autry
84 Great name in the Prado
86 Lincoln Center seat
87 Calm interlude
88 "___ right up!"
91 Adjective for a rookie
93 What epigones do
94 Like a leprechaun

38

RIGHT BITE by Richard Silvestri

The quotation below ends as follows: "as distinguished from the Liberal who wishes to replace them with others."

ACROSS

1 Author of the quotation featured below
7 Opens wide
12 ___ Domingo
17 Tailor's measurement
18 "Little Women" author
19 Connection
20 **Start of quotation**
22 Entertain
23 Silver: Abbr.
24 Required
25 Burnt or raw pigment
27 He had a gilt complex
29 Diminutive suffix
31 Carnival prize
34 Moody meditator
37 Vocations
40 Nursery rhyme "piggy"
41 Backslid
42 Subject of quotation
44 Prepares copy
45 Assortment of type
46 Yonkers entry
47 Writer Anaïs ___
48 Medium state
50 Muscular contraction
53 Active one
55 Nurse of the Orient
56 Cast off
57 A tense
61 Many a time
63 Zoo laughers
65 Book by Nabokov
66 Kind of wave
69 ___ uproar (aroused, as a crowd)
70 Stephen or Hart
72 **Middle of quotation**
77 Brandishes
78 Grown-up elver
79 Dear to the heart
80 Method of production
81 ___ ex machina
83 Concept
84 Set straight
85 Disdain
87 Shrew's relative
90 Dies ___
94 Partner of error
96 **End of quotation**
99 Not a soul
100 Spring deposit
101 Matter excreted
102 Scout's rider
103 Something to see
104 Contests for cowboys

DOWN

1 Partiality
2 MIT or RPI
3 Punta del ___, Uruguay
4 Last in line
5 Persian or Siamese
6 Altered a text
7 In good spirits
8 Skin woe
9 Pulverizes
10 Biblical verb ending
11 Not so lean
12 Dirk thrust
13 Directed
14 Needing a psychiatrist
15 ". . . ___ of thee"
16 United
18 Iowa college town
21 Brand
26 Griffin of talk shows
28 I.e., in full
30 Links item
32 Nothing for Borg
33 Villainous gaze
34 Make whiskey
35 Crystal set
36 Conjecture
37 Spiral shell
38 Stud fee, of sorts
39 Enervates
42 Name before Doyle
43 Pack down lightly
45 Renown
49 Plague carrier
50 Straw bundle
51 Keystone State founder
52 Actress Rehan
54 Reddish horse
56 Church council
58 Allan-___ of Robin Hood tales
59 White ___, National Monument in N. Mex.
60 Part of a switch
62 Lack of muscle tone
63 Flog severely
64 Descendant
66 Deadlocked
67 Words of comprehension
68 Mistaken conviction
71 Took in
73 Begin's predecessor
74 Age
75 Preacher of baseball
76 Forte of the Artful Dodger
77 Old laundry device
80 Blueprint
82 In short supply
84 Moslem nobleman
86 Ersatz butter
88 Baltic native
89 Proof word
91 Respond to reveille
92 Lowest female voice
93 Those, in Pamplona: Fem.
94 Explosive
95 Aussie animal
97 Top of the dial
98 Caesar's favorite pronoun

39

HIGH-PROTEIN DIET by Arthur Verdesca, M.D.
This really isn't Dr. V's idea of a square meal—just a clever way to conceal six sources of protein within a square. Find all six and remember to say 33D the next time you see him.

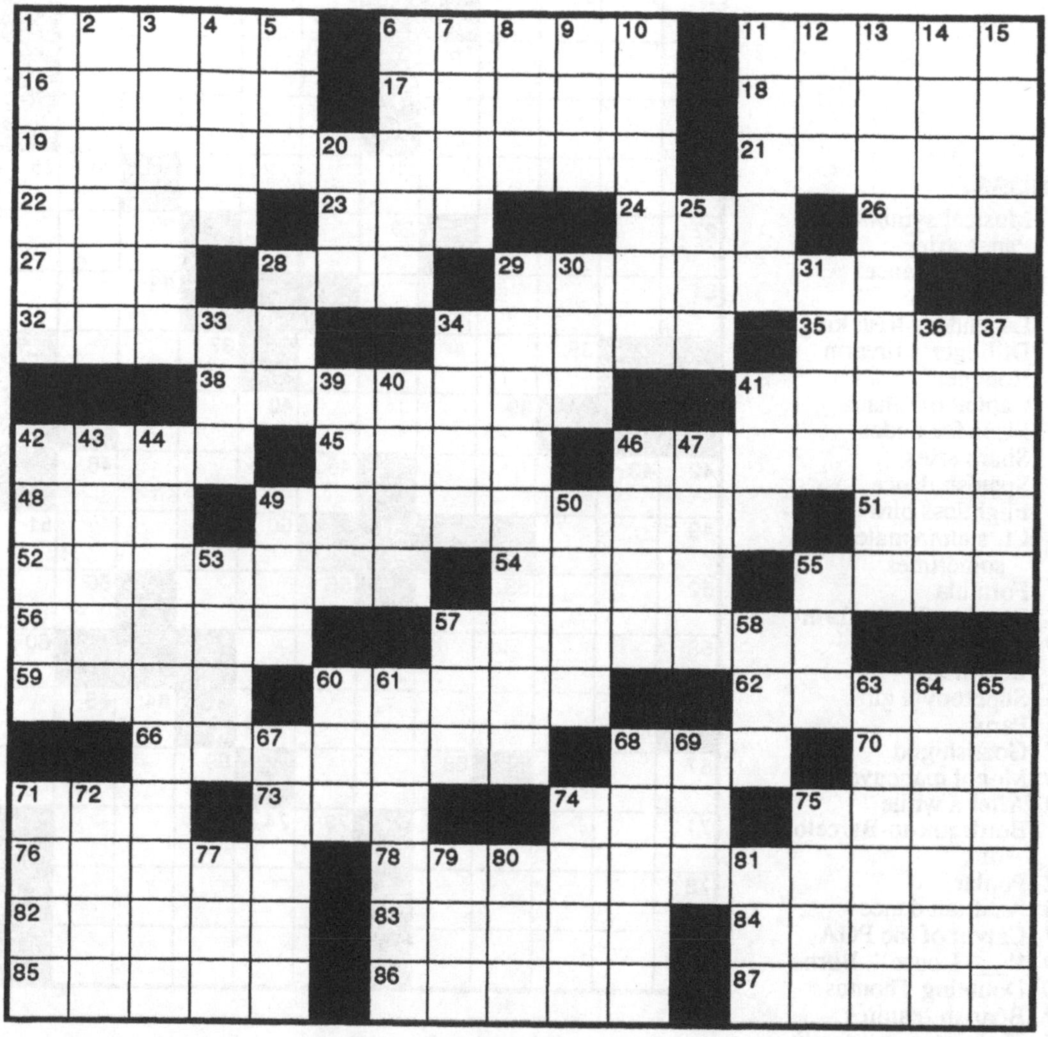

ACROSS

1 Ladies of Spain
6 Iowa or Kentucky county
11 Glutted
16 Beethoven's "Für ___"
17 Marshy inlet
18 Munster county
19 Wide-angle camera attachment
21 Exhausted
22 Feed the kitty
23 Yalie
24 Dine
26 Largo or West
27 So-so grade
28 Employ
29 Roman magistrate
32 Snorri stories
34 Give the ___ (contradict)
35 Bandleader Columbo
38 Correspondence
41 Strong point
42 Craving
45 Laban's daughter
46 Struck
48 Japanese drama
49 Tower of London warder
51 Brainy test
52 Leading
54 Fruity drinks
55 Jane of fiction
56 Nitrogenous compounds
57 Unyielding
59 Hardy heroine
60 Michaelmas daisy
62 Rival in *The Rivals*
66 Emulated Houdini
68 Doll type
70 Heady drink
71 Rainbow
73 Indian astrologer
74 Female bear
75 Scrutinize
76 Terminate
78 Side whiskers
82 Creates
83 Pixies
84 Mother ___
85 Pick out
86 Don Adams role
87 Units of loudness

DOWN

1 Mar
2 Trued
3 Fogged
4 Noted netman
5 Archdiocese
6 White poplar
7 *The Persistence of Memory* artist
8 Parliamentary vote
9 Free electron
10 Apple or potato
11 Flower stalk
12 ___ *the Way*
13 Gobble?
14 Cat Nation tribe
15 Disown
20 Brother of 8 Down
25 ET's vehicle
28 CNO's concern
29 Stubborn
30 King of Spain
31 Dundee, to friends
33 What to say to a doctor
34 Idle
36 Manage
37 Papyrus' family
39 Sheltered
40 Sly look
41 Partner of wide
42 Data for processing
43 ___ del Greco, Italy
44 Leg art
46 Bow structure
47 City near Phoenix
49 Twice
50 After Shebat
53 Bernstein opus
55 List abbr.
57 Corroded
58 Distanced horse
60 Drivers' org.
61 Foams
63 Cacomistle relative
64 Slip by
65 Touch and taste
67 Cockscomb
68 Perch
69 Barley beard
71 Peak
72 Actual
74 Young follower
75 Beat it!
77 Wine adjective
79 Birthplace of Einstein
80 Org. created in 1933
81 Metric abbr.

40 INTERNATIONAL AFFAIR by Kevin Boyle

There's a party below at the UN and you're invited. Kevin has taken *steps* to guarantee everyone a good time.

ACROSS

1 Musical symbol
5 Panel strip
10 King of France: 987–996
15 Legendary Irish king
17 Dillinger's firearm
18 Bouquet
19 Capital of Ghana
20 Place for dudes
21 Sharp cries
22 Spanish dance
24 Flightless bird
26 Lt.'s alma mater, sometimes
27 Formula
28 Recent: Comb. form
29 Descendant
31 Beer mug
33 Superboy's girl
35 Parts
37 Goatish god
38 Mogul maneuverer
39 After a while
41 Bordeaux-to-Barcelona dir.
42 Poplar
45 Austrian dance
47 Calvin of the PGA
49 "___ Louse": Burns
50 Doubting Thomas
52 Boarish features
55 Hydromassage facility
56 Kind of salami
58 Green liqueur
60 Aromatic herb
63 Withdrew
64 Bronze ___
66 Admittedly
67 Agent
68 ___ Dolorosa
69 German folk dance
71 "___ when it was not": Dickinson
73 City in the Nile delta
75 Helped
76 Peculate
77 Pelts
78 It flows to the Rhone
79 Yellow-fever mosquito
80 Arabian princes
81 Gaelic

DOWN

1 Restricts
2 Place
3 In ordinary language: Fr.
4 Basque dance
5 Carousal
6 Duke's eighty-eight
7 Musical Horne
8 CPA's record
9 Conference site of 1943
10 Black ducks
11 "We ___ the World"
12 Polish dance
13 Syndrome felt by parents
14 Red A.P.
16 Hayburner
23 Not rented
25 My, to Mimi
29 Ex-goalie Jacques
30 Wapiti
32 Dash
34 Superiority, in Selkirk
36 Stitch
37 Bohemian dance
40 Abraded
42 "___ Troll": Heine
43 Flirtatious young woman
44 French dance
46 Demographic abbr.
47 Fir-lined?
48 Scottish dance, abroad
51 Snicker
53 Pochette
54 Whines
55 Retract a claw
57 Widely separated
59 Numerical prefix
61 Commands
62 Carolina river
64 Change
65 Mirror
67 Hindu sentiment
69 "___ Love Her": Beatles
70 After April in Paris
72 Homophone of 70 Down
74 Objective

41 EXPLANATIONS FOR CITATIONS by Gayle Dean

Squeezed into this little diagram is a ten-word statement by the Sage of Concord. Nice work, Gayle!

ACROSS

1 African country
5 "We ___ Overcome"
10 Zodiacal sign
14 Hawaiian dance
15 Porch in Oahu
16 Nimbus
17 Dry
18 Taxpayer's dread
19 Eager
20 Hijack
21 **Start of an Emerson quotation**
23 Range item
25 Lip
26 ___ *Town*: Wilder
27 Linen thread
29 *Crusade in Europe* author's nickname
32 On one's toes
35 Coagulate
36 Articulate TV equine
37 **Quotation: Part II**
40 Lake or canal
41 Rat or sack follower
42 Bother
43 Mo. after Nov.
44 Panther color in movies
45 Youth org.
46 Betty's predecessor
47 Egg cases
51 **Quotation: Part III**
56 **Quotation: Part IV**
57 Horse color
58 **End of the quotation**
59 Seed covering
60 Analogous
61 Racer Al or Bobby
62 Gambling town
63 Like a busybody
64 Foyer
65 Nervous

DOWN

1 Broils
2 Memorable impresario
3 Cover story?
4 Pop
5 David, to Goliath
6 Hang around
7 Peruvian Indian
8 Secular
9 Intellectuals
10 Fissure
11 Musician Shankar
12 Landed
13 Kind of shop or language
21 Popeye's rival
22 Ice hockey team
24 Actor Peter in "Casablanca"
27 Sudden, light blow
28 Tennis score
29 Pahlavi once ruled here
30 Casino game
31 Whirlpool
32 In one's bunk
33 Apollo's instrument
34 Homeric work
35 Highlands group
36 Asian talking bird
38 Review
39 Sample
44 ___ *Joey*
45 New York City street
46 Price of your "thoughts"
47 Aquatic mammal
48 Having handles, as a pitcher
49 Hold fast
50 Combined metals
51 Breakfast food
52 Beatle widow's first name
53 Platform
54 Craig Stevens' detective
55 Innkeeper
59 Common verb

42

CHILLY RECEPTION by Bert Rosenfield
Don't be put off by the title. We're sure you'll warm up to Bert's clever construction!

ACROSS

1 A cappella offering
5 Yesteryear
9 Slackened
15 Jubilation
17 Strauss opera
18 Point-locating numbers
20 OSS successor
21 Top número
22 Calligraphy line
24 Point in an orbit
27 Legal synopses
30 Bell the cat
31 ___ noire
32 ___ gestae (things done)
33 British actor Moody
35 Grazing ground
36 Kind of triangle
38 Keflavik native
41 Smoker's hazard
42 "So that's how it is!"
43 Santander snooze
44 Got some sack time
46 "Blue Danube," for one
48 Fits of fever
52 Firenze square
54 Hallow or velvet ending
56 Blue Eagle letters
57 Dressing-room application
60 Stop sign, e.g.
62 Bird next to a jay?
63 Sense of pitch
64 Pull a face
65 Funny Foxx
66 GI grub
68 Easter wear
71 Estate
72 Trattoria serving
74 Atmospheric prefix
75 ___ to be tied
76 "Keep ___": 1924 slogan
83 Tickled
84 Making a comeback
85 Wyoming mountains
86 Orenburg's river
87 Former frosh

DOWN

1 Start of the school yr.
2 Containing element number 8
3 Not any, legally
4 Montana's national park
5 Agouti's cousin
6 Enero to Diciembre
7 Burnishes
8 City NE of Rome
9 Faulkner's ___ *Lay Dying*
10 Proscription
11 Unhappiness, vocalized
12 Lugged
13 May birthstone
14 Brando film: 1954
16 Speaker of Cooperstown
19 Anonymous Jane
23 Dread
24 Joins in with
25 "He loves me" indicator
26 About 1.31 cubic yards
27 Low, on the thermometer
28 Poker variant
29 Peruvian coins
32 Bowl bellow
34 Afloat
37 Call-board item
38 Religion founded in 622
39 Townsman
40 Scrawny horse
45 Not needing a stamp: Abbr.
47 Nitrogenous: combining form
49 Felix of *The Odd Couple*
50 Wear away
51 ___ *of Iwo Jima*
53 Descendant of Ishmael
55 Hosp. printout
57 Summer place
58 Two-base ball game
59 Pliant
61 Ankle-high overshoes
64 "Blues in the Night" lyricist
67 Hearty brew
69 ___ "King" Cole
70 First prime minister of India
71 Has the miseries
73 To boot
75 Bluegrass baby
77 Scalp bump
78 Bartender's demands
79 Three ___ match
80 ___ volente
81 Econ. yardstick
82 Biblical verb ending

43 AS THE SAYING GOES . . . IN REVERSE by Walter Covell

Here's an unusual idea, well executed by Rhode Island's top wordsmith.

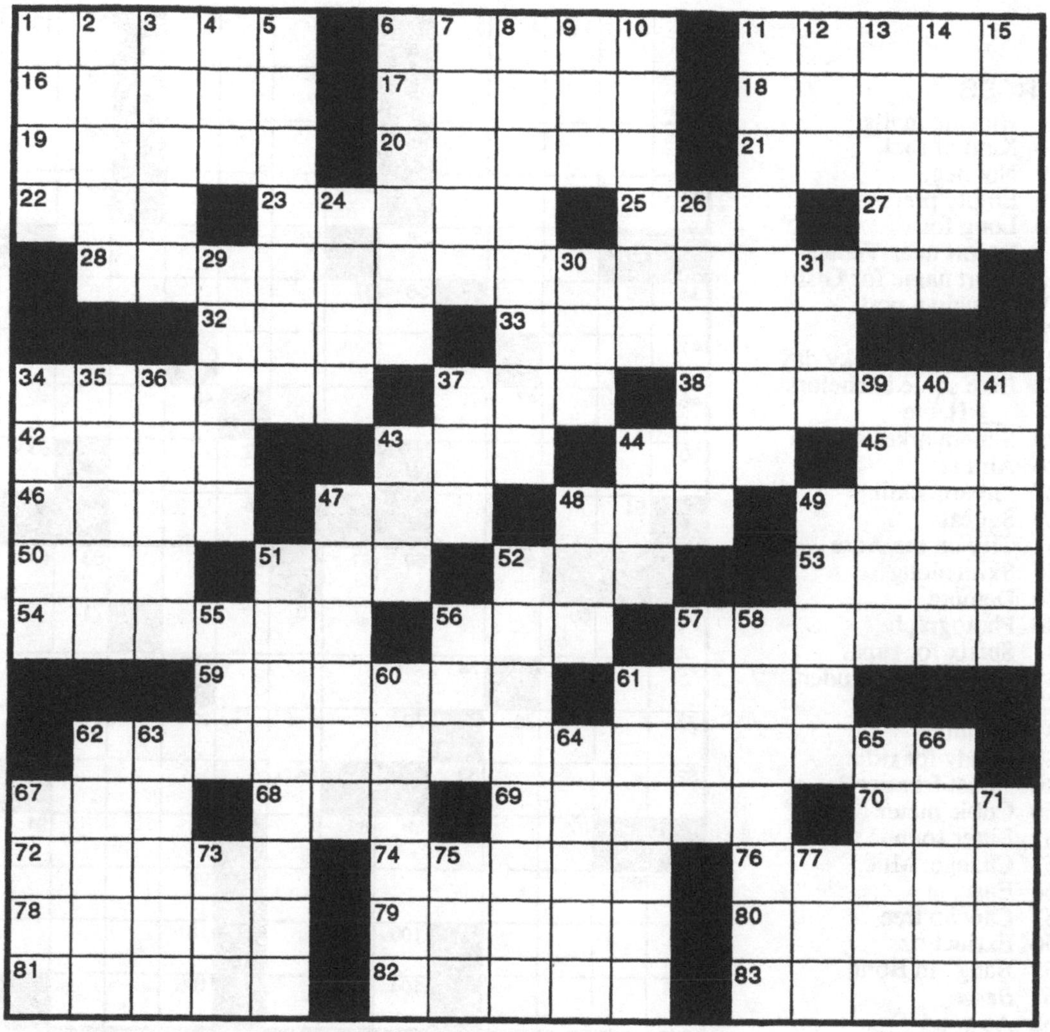

ACROSS

1 ___-hot
6 Hipbone neighbors
11 ___-pale
16 Maxim
17 Praying figure
18 Paperboy's circuit
19 Blend gradually
20 Chiastolite
21 Photographer Adams
22 L.A. or Phila.
23 Imbibed
25 Tennis stroke
27 ___-slippery
28 ___-phony
32 British composer
33 Merited
34 Loath
37 Deg. at RPI
38 Diva's style
42 Tiber town
43 Their, in Troyes
44 Parts of qts.
45 ___-clear
46 Frost
47 ___-straight
48 ___-easy
49 Lily
50 Bull, the fiddler
51 Operated
52 Israel tribe
53 Culture medium
54 ___-mad
56 Tune
57 Secures the door again
59 Tin and lead
61 Maine city
62 ___-hot
67 Cry of disgust
68 Resembling: Suffix
69 Inclined
70 Chemist's milieu
72 Think
74 Overlord
76 Courtroom excuse
78 Cranial cavity
79 Find
80 Thrift practitioner
81 Treaty town
82 Stitched
83 Cede

DOWN

1 Products of Virginia and Poland
2 Skillful
3 *Star Wars* villain, ___ Vader
4 ___-bald
5 Sowers
6 Hair dressing
7 Heavens: Comb. form
8 Describing some gowns
9 Be a vol.
10 Pertaining to an erect slab
11 Seizers
12 Judge's title: Abbr.
13 European water bird
14 Kind of plate
15 Apple-splitter
24 Clair or Coty
26 Rococo
29 Peep show
30 Varnish ingredient
31 Despot Amin
34 ___-straight
35 Sheer fabric
36 Ant of yore
37 ___-busy
39 Last
40 ___-sweet
41 Scents
43 ___-ugly
44 ___-neat
47 French revolutionary
48 Equal footing
49 Clog
51 Thinnest
52 Refuse permission
55 Medical org.
56 Tennis word for a tie
57 ___-right
58 Bliss
60 Warns
61 Was merciful to
62 Rhino relative
63 Pule
64 Thread a block
65 Martini garnish
66 Tag
67 ___-deaf
71 ___-free
73 Hebrew letter
75 Suffix with press or fail
77 Chou en ___

44 ON LOCATION by Eli Wesoff

Eli's clever title *does* apply to his theme, although movie buffs may feel they've been a little flimflammed.

ACROSS

1 Hits the malls
6 Kind of sack
9 Not neg.
12 Empty pretense
16 Long for
17 Resort near Venice
18 Short name for Gish
19 Hawaiian port
20 Coeur d'___
21 Caesar's unlucky day
22 Like some bachelors
24 ___ Haute
25 Supermarket section
26 Aim at
27 Firearm caliber
29 Squeals
31 City on the Aare
34 Skim along
36 Demote
40 Photograph
41 Suffix for super
42 Texas A&M student
43 Inactive
45 Wrath
46 Ready for riding
48 "Last frontier"
50 Cubic meter
51 Litter sounds
53 Change: Mus.
54 Ensnare
55 Caucho tree
56 Extinct ox
59 Bang! in Bonn
62 *Beau* ___
65 As good ___
67 Guiding force
71 Mounted attendant
73 *Barney Miller* actor
74 Camp David Accords personage
75 "___ Thee make my column read": Don Marquis
76 Greek letter
77 Charles' pet
79 Born loser
81 City near Albany
82 Marine mammal
84 Actress Blackman
85 New Haven team
87 Home of the Green Wave
90 Mild oath
92 Record
95 Disney employee
97 Homophone of dues
98 Carry ___ (sing on key)
99 Blessing
100 Ramon's rah
101 Dill, old style
102 City on the Meuse
103 ___ St. Vincent Millay
104 Launch site
105 Suffix for saw
106 Amorous meeting

DOWN

1 Begone!
2 Green sight
3 Weigh down
4 Tarkington novel
5 Guide
6 Pass a car poorly
7 Sweet girl of song
8 Nurse's Rx function
9 Agreeable
10 Flatters
11 Fall
12 Draft horses
13 Ireland
14 Only
15 Berg of baseball
17 Cover
23 Male cat
28 Advantage
30 Acts the grouch
32 Drugbuster
33 Sword
34 Sound of steam
35 Latex layers
37 Old Irish alphabet: Var.
38 Per ___
39 Light brown
42 Beery aceta
44 Firth
47 Hang
48 Little hooter
49 Zoroastrian
52 Should
57 One in the wings
58 Tend
60 Spare tire
61 Canine name
63 Excellent
64 Prefix for dollar
66 "King Kong" actress
67 Vidi, in English
68 Tidbit
69 Memo
70 Collected
72 Days, to Heinz
75 Coca of comedy
78 Graduate
80 ___ *at a Time*
81 Colorist
83 High note
86 Minimum
88 Sleep like ___
89 Lopez theme song
91 Spring-ahead abbr.
93 Alfonso's queen, et al.
94 Budget item
95 The Rail-Splitter
96 Cain's land

45 LITERARY LICENSE by Arthur S. Verdesca

Small changes in titles can lead to great fun, as you will see.

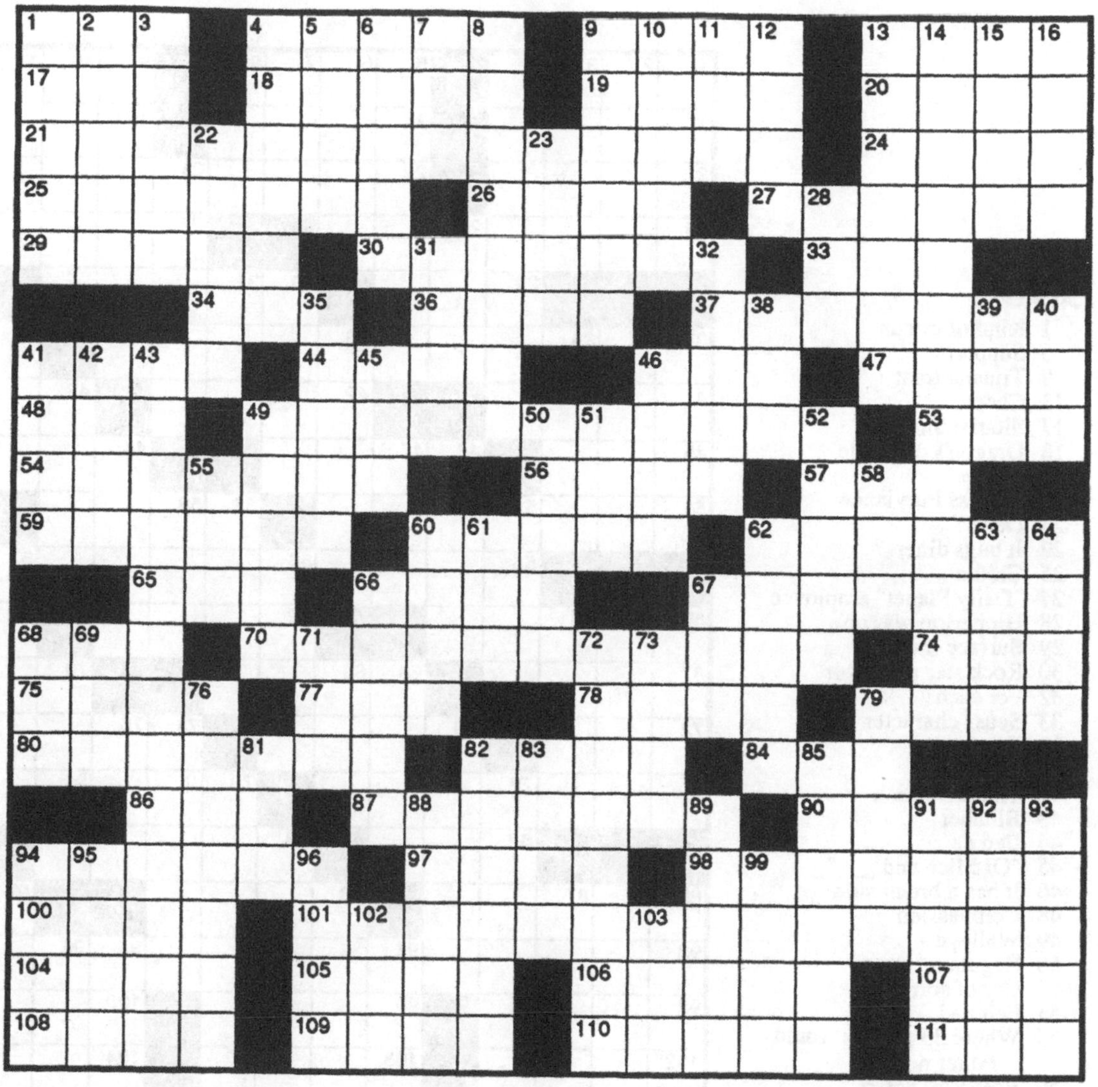

ACROSS

1 Little lie
4 Stock
9 Down with, in Dijon
13 On the horizon
17 Boswell's "Life," e.g.
18 Kind of eclipse
19 Mulberry bark cloth
20 Chinese: Comb. form
21 With "The," H. James's rewrite of Shakespeare?
24 Division word
25 Bent like a bow
26 Plod through mud
27 Basked
29 Hear
30 Abridgements
33 Contend
34 Coral or Red
36 Thrust against a wall
37 Controversy
41 Salinger heroine
44 Match
46 It precedes Virgo
47 M. Antony's request
48 Lillie or Arthur
49 Tolstoy's novel of rabbit amity?
53 ___ Dinh Diem of Viet Nam
54 Mild Irish oath
56 Final notice, for short
57 Taxing gp.
59 Ghost or angel
60 Roman age
62 Draws out
65 Fire
66 Grayish yellow
67 Polished
68 Wrong
70 With "The," J. F. Cooper's machinist?
74 Hawaiian acacia
75 Beet or radish
77 Uno, due, ___
78 Composer Wilder
79 Settle
80 Conservative
82 Word on a Biblical wall
84 Skater Babilonia
86 D.C. org. sponsoring opera, sculpture, etc.
87 Brandy-based cocktail
90 Apia's land
94 Where benedicts are made
97 Miss Piggy's "mine"
98 Pasches
100 Castle trench
101 With "A," Hemingway mendicant's adieu?
104 Thirties migrant
105 Cupid
106 Riser's place
107 Nectar collector
108 Cordial; benevolent
109 Amerind memorials
110 Secret meeting
111 Tate offering

DOWN

1 Decisive, in a way
2 Accrue
3 Hannibal's father
4 Mercury theater actor
5 Cluster
6 Prefix with mural
7 American cousin of olé
8 Problem for overworked execs
9 Informal afternoon reception
10 Cleopatra's boat
11 Gorilla
12 Proverbs
13 Obstinate or silly
14 Joyce's Irish pastry?
15 Price for a poker hand
16 Land area unit
22 Clara Barton was one
23 Disparaging remark
28 Grape
31 Dubai bigwig
32 Drudgery
35 Independently
38 Legendary bird
39 Opposite of sml.
40 Inner: Prefix
41 Lessens
42 Amphibious jeep
43 With "The," Mann's tribute to Trevi?
45 Constellation or screwpine
46 Flower garlands
49 Extort
50 Still abed
51 Kegler's org.
52 Sea duck
55 Old English coin
58 Toupee, colloquially
60 Port of importance in the Crusades
61 Forage plant
62 Exclusive
63 A grandson of Adam
64 Photocopy
66 Brings home the bacon
67 Witness
68 Globe
69 ___ yong, Chinese omelet
71 DDE's command
72 Most mountainous
73 Toward shelter, at sea
76 Picked up the tab
79 Lariat
81 Tribunal
82 Marceau, et al.
83 Sufficient, to FitzGerald
85 Classify
88 Seer's card
89 Shift
91 Ice cream-fruit concoction
92 Abalone
93 Valuable quality
94 In a frenzy
95 Norse god of discord
96 Tunisian seaport
99 Sweetsop
102 Candlenut tree
103 Pt. of the alphabet

46

THE IN-GROUP by Gayle Dean
Solvers are invited to see what members of the curious clique below have in common. Despite the title, Gayle always does an out-and-out job!

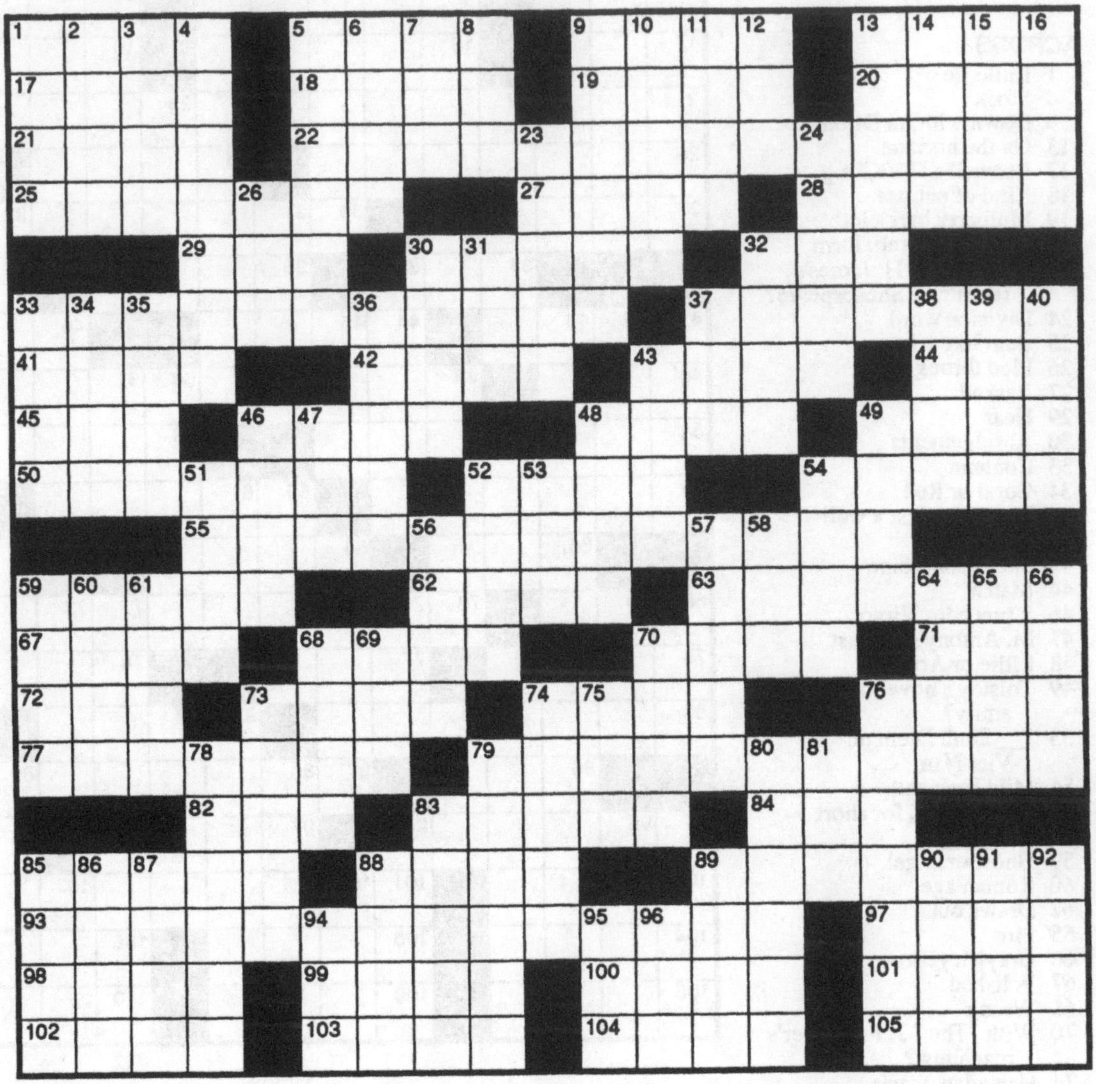

ACROSS

1 Kind of circus
5 Support
9 Tijuana treat
13 Cheer
17 Sitarist Shankar
18 Dragon's domicile
19 Verve
20 Actress Purviance
21 Done
22 It bugs diners?
25 Clothe
27 "Daily Planet" employee
28 Hipparion was one
29 Surface measure
30 Rock star and actor
32 For each
33 Seuss character
37 Feign
41 Seed cover
42 Thunderstruck
43 Blubber
44 Eau de ___
45 "Of Mice and ___"
46 It has a broad side
48 Compassion
49 Walleye
50 Regulars
52 Cry of sorrow
54 Felt bad
55 Where 33 Across would rather not be?
59 Poet Verhaeren
62 Spouse
63 Incarnation of Vishnu
67 Belt
68 Brink
70 "Two Years Before the Mast" author
71 Charged particle
72 Legendary avian
73 Beta is its genus
74 "___ of Fools"
76 Thin opening
77 Stuck
79 Porky wearing a bonnet?
82 Flaw
83 Stumbles
84 It has a strophe
85 Keepsake
88 After drop or place
89 Supplements
93 Ornithologist's sure thing?
97 Gloomy
98 Pelican State's "Kingfish"
99 Part
100 Rosacea
101 Cheese of crosswords
102 Homophone of seed
103 Water jug
104 Arizona-Nevada lake
105 Swear by with"on"

DOWN

1 ___ in the throat
2 Pumice
3 Always
4 Kind of stamp
5 Holst subject
6 Slew
7 Grease
8 Snoop
9 Lessee
10 "Drums ___ the Mohawk"
11 Split rattan
12 "A Chorus Line" number
13 Vacation spot
14 Smell
15 Burden
16 Record
23 Greek epic
24 Corriedale, e.g.
26 Suffix for west
30 Stitched
31 Definite article
32 Quarry
33 Fremont or Granada
34 See 67 Across
35 Color
36 Severe
37 Favorite
38 Like Mr. Scratch
39 Victory deity
40 Feat
43 Long for
46 Porterhouse part
47 Ergate
48 Messenger
49 Cobblers
51 Stir up
52 Cal Trask's father
53 Escapee from Sodom
54 Rock group
56 Discharge
57 Giraffe's kin
58 Tea server
59 Poet Pound
60 "___ Indigo"
61 Move like a snail
64 Hawaiian port
65 Remote spot
66 Feed the kitty
68 Lager
69 "The ___ Pony"
70 Lodgings
73 Stigma
74 Volleyball smash
75 Haunch
76 Trooper's target
78 Surface
79 Sagittarius
80 Silently approved
81 Tack on
83 Appellation
85 Fragrant powder
86 A woodwind
87 Type
88 Perceive
89 Poet Akhmatova
90 Knot
91 Twofold
92 Salvation ___
94 Rancor
95 Prosciutto
96 Pilot or pitcher

47

CRISSCROSS by Nancy Nicholson Joline
One of the definitions for the title of this fine puzzle is "having crossing lines." Keep it in mind and take it literally!

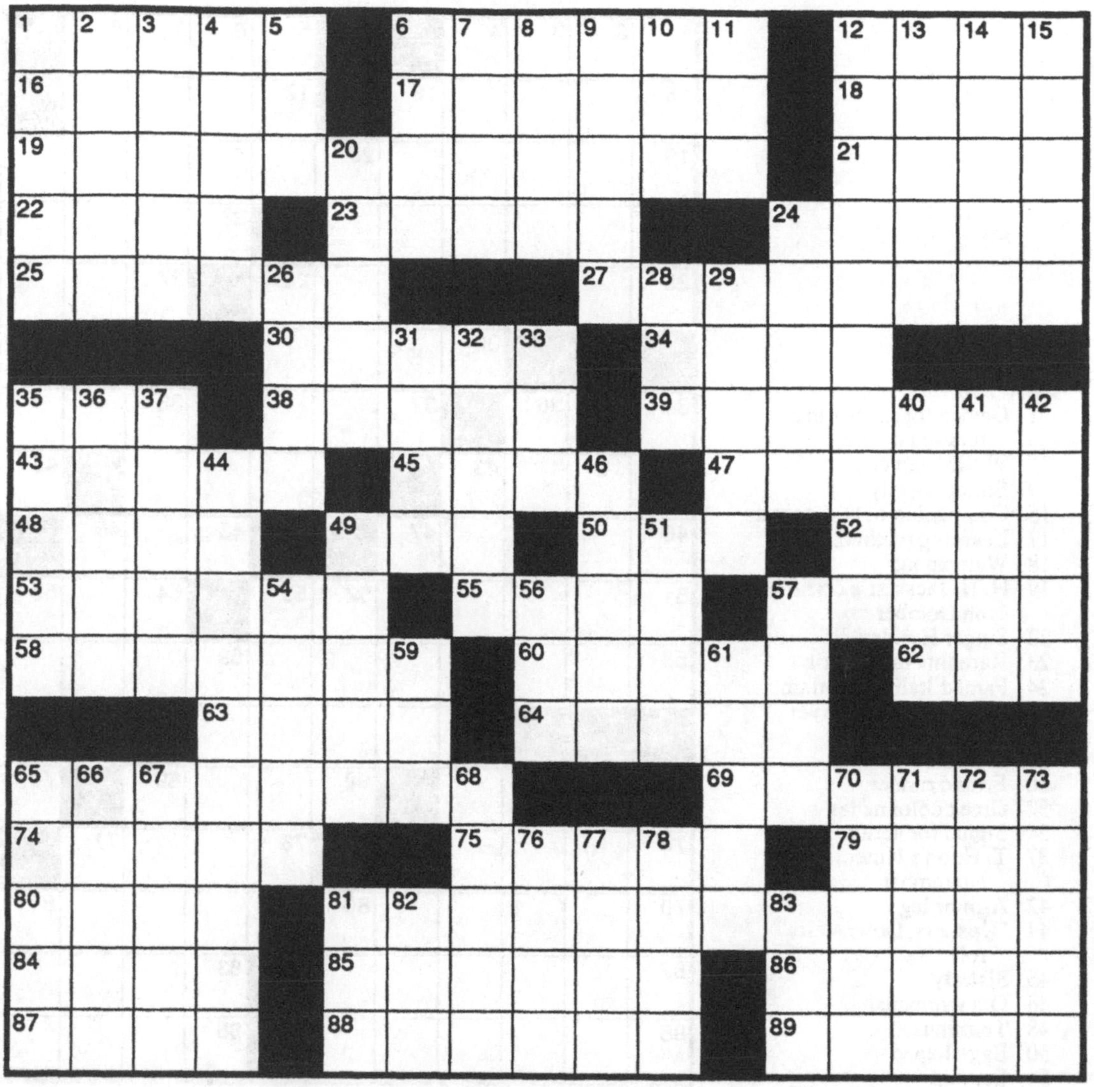

ACROSS

1 Majorca's chief city
6 Alfred Gerald Caplin, to readers
12 Telephone pole feature
16 Dialect
17 "Annie ___"
18 Dies ___
19 London street
21 Glacial snow field
22 Word with dial or muscle
23 Port north of Naples
24 "___ of God," B'way hit
25 Justice Antonin
27 Take up residence anew
30 Maori ancestral images
34 Track event
35 Outstanding one
38 Some cocktails
39 Short operatic number
43 Material for a model plane
45 Kind of bun
47 Bowers
48 Pro's opposite
49 Lincoln's or Gray's ___, London
50 Scrooge word
52 Egyptian sacred bull
53 Kid in "The Kid"
55 This is on the track
57 Loon's kin
58 John ___ Galbraith, economist
60 Hilo hello
62 Legal matter
63 Fairy tale baddie
64 Humeri neighbors
65 Toughs
69 Tex-Mex food items
74 Les ___-Unis
75 Guiding beliefs of a group
79 Sister of Zeus
80 Kind of chair or crime
81 Bogart film, 1942
84 "I cannot tell ___"
85 Lab vessel
86 Change
87 "Chariots of Fire" star
88 Emits
89 "La Marseillaise" composer, Rouget de ___

DOWN

1 People of ancient Scotland
2 Like some committees
3 Rain forest vine
4 "Sons and Lovers" family name
5 Pierre's pal
6 Pond plant
7 Sport once an Indian game
8 Brusque
9 Loud
10 Actress Zadora
11 Foot: Comb. form
12 Tennyson poem
13 "___ You Glad You're You?"
14 "Bolero" composer
15 Beleaguered attorney general under Reagan
20 Marsh of mystery books
24 Race of Norse gods
26 "___ boy!"
28 Author-counselor LeShan
29 Abraham's wife
31 Bowie of baseball
32 German decoration
33 Fast flyer
35 How one is sometimes taken
36 Pirogue
37 Singer John
40 He fails to x the bar
41 Arikara or Cree, e.g.
42 Kiangs
44 De Mille epic (with "The")
46 Finch family member
49 Prefix with city or mural
51 Ages upon ages
54 Auspices
56 Sigma follower
57 Greek earth goddess
59 Female lobster
61 Medieval merchant guild
65 Building once in disrepair
66 Useful
67 "Oliver Twist" heavy
68 Scottish tartan patterns
70 Kind of powder or sauce
71 Hoists
72 Large bay window
73 ___ Coeur, Paris church
76 Rodgers and Hart's "___ Swell"
77 "It Can't Happen ___"
78 Chooses
81 Jackie's second
82 Lines on a lover's letter
83 "East of Eden" youth

48 WRITER'S MONTHLY REPORTS by Judith Perry

Seasonal statements, mainly by poets, have been culled by our intrepid puzzler from Vermont.

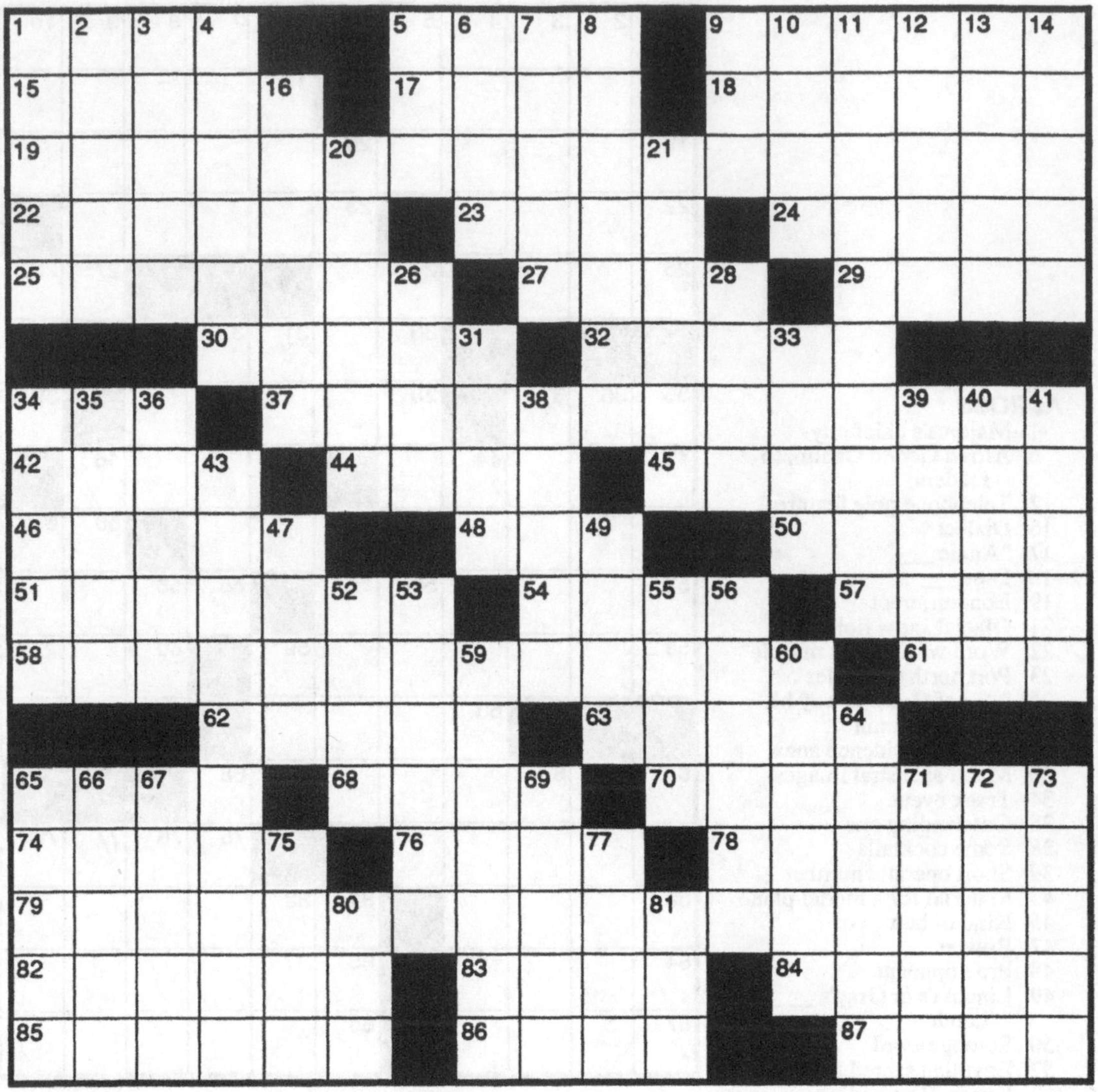

ACROSS

1 Device for measuring rotational speed
5 W Siberian city
9 Ethiopian city
15 Companion of D'Artagnan
17 Learning method
18 Waterspout
19 H. H. Jackson's comment on October
22 Singer Holiday
23 Karenina or Christie
24 Famed Italian fountain
25 An Ivy League player
27 Assay
29 Exploits
30 Errand runner
32 Greek colonnades
34 Signal for action
37 T. Hood's lament about November
42 Arm or leg
44 "Upstairs, Downstairs" role
45 Sisterly
46 Old womanish
48 Terminus
50 Egg-shaped
51 Banded
54 Toward the mouth
57 Actress Adams
58 R. Browning's comment about August
61 Otolaryngology initials
62 Artist Matisse
63 Antitank guns
65 Mercantile transaction
68 Melody
70 Temporary expedient
74 Style
76 Inlets
78 Upsweep, e.g.
79 What June resumes, according to E. Dickinson
82 Collection of rabbinic writings
83 Inert gas
84 Muttonfish
85 Veers from course
86 Speedy aircraft
87 Actor Talbot

DOWN

1 Domestic cat
2 Roman courtyards
3 What a September gale brought to O. W. Holmes
4 Revolver of Wild West origin
5 Sphere
6 Ocean sunfish
7 Dwarf
8 Sharpest
9 A vital statistic
10 Legislative membership
11 April in England, to A. Noyes
12 Residue
13 Superman portrayer
14 Part of an architectural molding
16 Israeli politician Peres
20 "___ Two": Youmans song
21 Squanders
26 Burial site of Moses
28 Barcelona bull
31 Ploy
33 Soul brother's hairdo
34 Fastening
35 Range of the Rockies
36 Eastern bigwigs
38 Purport
39 Turkish decree
40 Dine at home
41 Bane of winter
43 J. R. Lowell's adjective for May
47 Assurance
49 Kind of pan
52 Wine casks
53 Mistakes
55 Sale term
56 Demises
59 Wings
60 Ermines in summer
64 Helical
65 Glaswegians
66 Moslem supreme being
67 Soup scoop
69 Yawns
71 S. V. Benet's description of spring in the city
72 "Let's Make ___," TV game show
73 Search party
75 Disparaging remark
77 Injection
80 Orthodontist's deg.
81 Office holders

49 GRAY-MATTER MATTER by John R. Prosser

A cerebral creation from a thoughtful and talented Baltimore constructor.

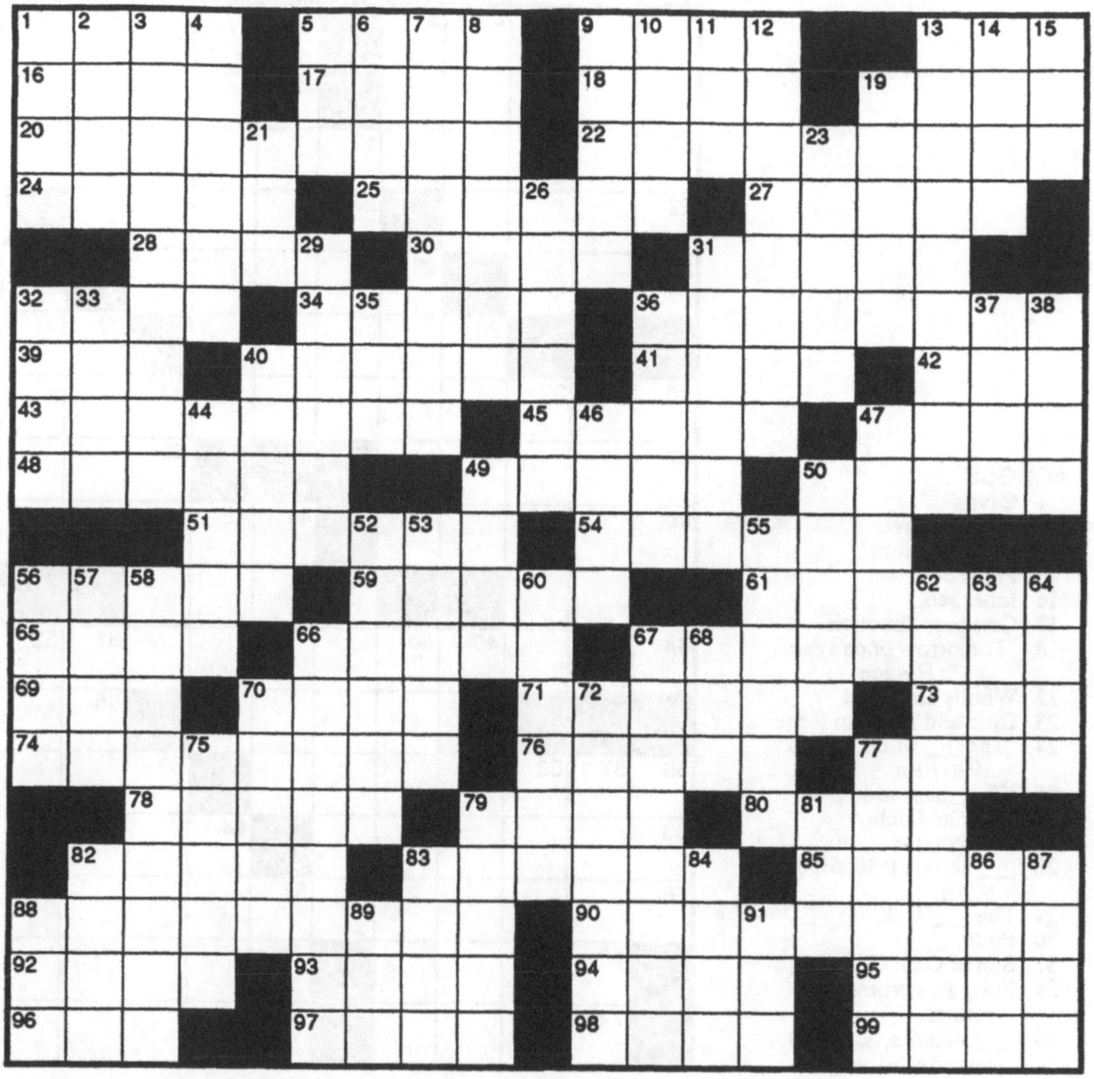

ACROSS

1 Set of signals
5 Train
9 Moneypenny's friend
13 Half a farewell
16 Deep blue hue
17 Sunday excursion
18 Cosmetics case
19 Greek group
20 Dogmatic teacher
22 Geniuses
24 Blab
25 Snippets
27 IBM's motto
28 One-___ sale
30 Egyptian cobras
31 Father of phonography
32 Fondles
34 At one's disposal
36 Is tipped off
39 Eurotas, formerly
40 ___ the dogs (deteriorated)
41 Give it the ___-over
42 Yoko
43 Son of Sophroniscus
45 Tom Thumbish
47 Skirt of tulle
48 Postulate
49 Desist
50 Coach
51 Having feet
54 Study unit
56 Zodiac sign
59 Henri's city
61 Tarzan, e.g.
65 Kind of poem
66 Birthplace of Alexander the Great
67 Sway
69 Kind of meal
70 Dog in "High Sierra"
71 Stone pillars
73 Tsk!
74 Make-believe
76 Before saw or store
77 Bellicose god
78 Attorney's "demise"
79 ___ Marian
80 Starchy rootstock
82 Tablet: Comb. form
83 She played Peggy Sue
85 Org. for high IQs
88 Instructor
90 Walking encyclopedia
92 Duncan's lake
93 ___ apparent
94 Novelist Morante
95 Self-images
96 Repeatedly
97 George Bush's alma mater
98 Whiskeys
99 Utah's flower

DOWN

1 Creator of Upper Slobbovia
2 Lulu
3 Science of teaching
4 Heartens
5 Tway or Strange
6 Tampers with
7 Broadens
8 Squints
9 Electronic sounds
10 Elevator name
11 Sister
12 Entertain
13 Publishes
14 Bronx Bomber
15 Endings for owl
19 Simulate
21 O.T. book
23 Thitherward
26 Place next to
29 Whistled
31 Styles
32 City on the Arno
33 Physical love
35 Wind dir.
36 Unbound
37 Being: Comb. form
38 Polo team number
40 Hoyle's expertise
44 Coin of Calcutta
46 In the pink
47 Radio receiver part
49 Big-house room
50 Pith helmet
52 Reluctant
53 Diacritical mark
55 Pundit
56 Sleep like ___
57 Din
58 Brainpower
60 East Indian sailor
62 Womanly guardianship
63 Flu symptom
64 Garden State team
66 Universal wisdom
67 In a sluggish manner
68 Whitney
70 Warlessness
72 Rodin statue (after "The")
75 "___ Your Children," 1970 hit
77 Alpine ridges
79 Razor-billed auk
81 Pal, in Paris
82 J. Moriarty, e.g.
83 Plug away
84 "Me and My Shadow" lyricist
86 Plod
87 Ditto
88 Mideast org.
89 Sri Lankan export
91 Existed

50 BON VOYAGE! by Avery P. Bromfield

Sometimes you'll be in deep water, but you should reach port safely.

ACROSS

1 Cavils
6 Kind of wave
11 Mets' stadium
15 Papal cape
16 Inner self
17 Compass direction
18 "Tomorrow once again ___": Horace
22 Wholly absorbed
23 Ohio and Iowa, to Rene
24 "The ___ of Dr. Mudd": 1980 film
25 What mos. add up to
26 Ahoy and belay
27 Consecrates
28 ___ bells: (1:30, 5:30 or 9:30)
29 The ___ Jack
30 Pinta, ___
37 Son of Gad: Gen. 46:16
38 Forecast favored by farmers
39 ___ Vickers, S. Lewis heroine
40 Noisy gull
41 English fish baskets
43 Suburb of Minneapolis
45 Suffix with serpent
46 Of the dawn
47 Great U.S. hurdler
48 Fast ships of 1830-50
54 Let loose from a corral
55 Piquant
56 Fairer
59 Quotidian
60 Housman's "A Shropshire ___"
63 Superficial layer
64 Furze
65 Toadfish
66 Wagner opera: 1843
69 Polynesian supernatural being
70 University in Texas
71 Betel palm
72 ___-poly (rotund)
73 Expunge
74 Fails to be indefatigable

DOWN

1 Seashell
2 Cousin of abaft
3 Coarse files
4 Municipal map
5 ___ whale (rorqual)
6 Blabbed
7 Takes a breath
8 Eats sparingly
9 Andy's friend
10 Genève is one
11 "You must have plenty of ___ . . .": Melville
12 "Iron ___ velvet glove": Carlyle
13 To eat, in Bonn
14 Corroded
19 Ascertain; hear
20 Long-lasting
21 Hirt and Jolson
26 Lawn or wing follower
27 Pros' opponents
28 Yarn
29 Single
30 SW Afr. diamond desert
31 "Faerie Queene" maiden in peril
32 Stair post
33 Benzene, e.g.
34 Poker play
35 ___ sanctum
36 "What ___ am I!" Hamlet
41 Swain
42 Be gainfully employed
43 Vacant
44 Fatuous
46 Control; dominion
49 Melodious
50 "___ there lies no plenty; then come kiss me, sweet and twenty": Shak.
51 Hungarian music or dance
52 Spare time
53 Cay
56 Nominal mil. commander
57 "The Merry Widow" composer
58 ___ a customer
59 Doctrine
60 Debussy opus
61 Fast; speedily
62 Spanish ladies
64 Growl
65 Title of respect in India
67 ___ de France
68 Kind of boat

51 FAMILY MATTER by Eli Wesoff

Our Miami Beach puzzler says the clues found below are pretty direct and solving should be relatively easy.

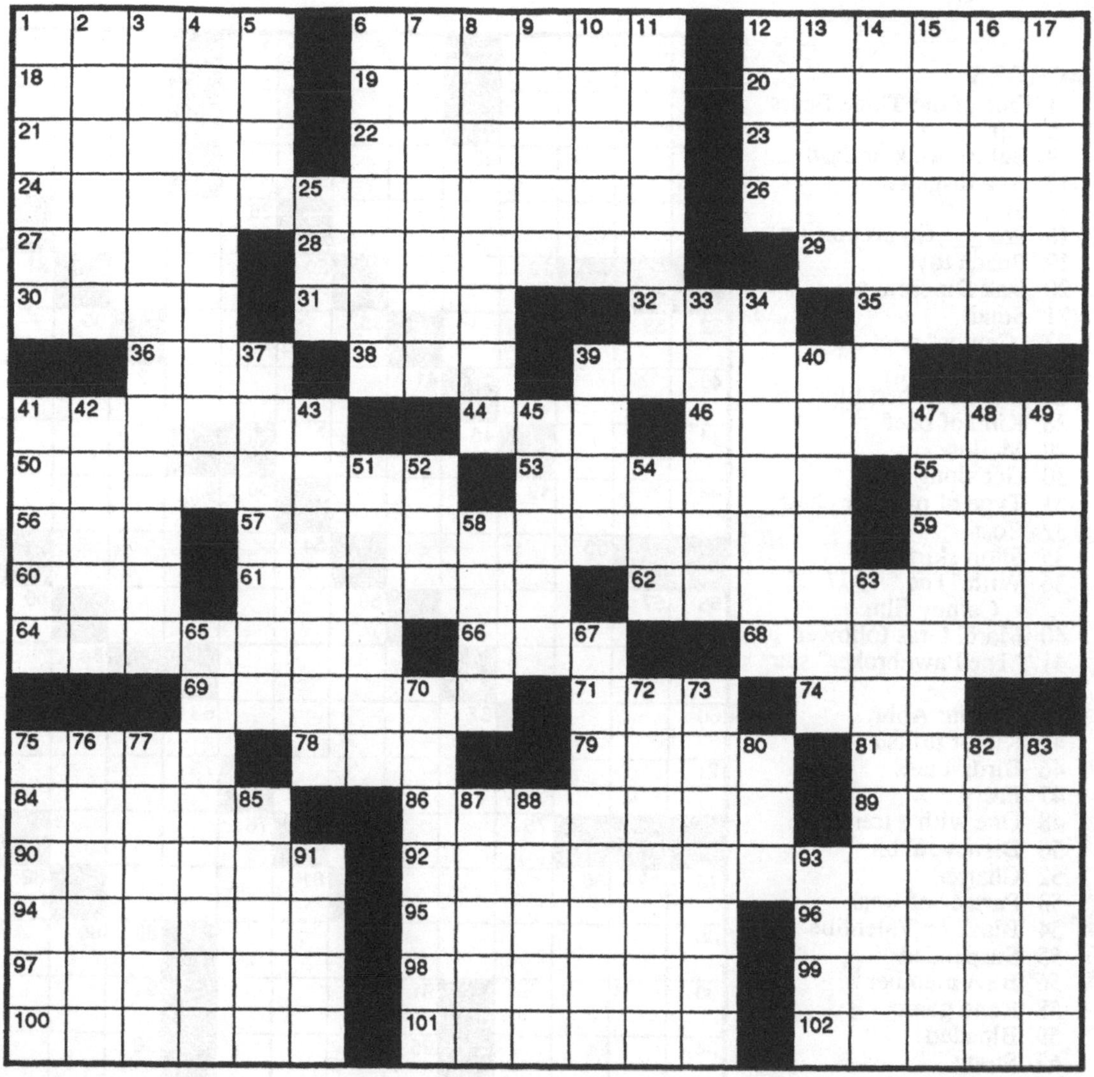

ACROSS

1 Rathbone
6 Pie à ___
12 Antics
18 Skirt type
19 Disintegrates
20 Kind of crab
21 Boxer's assets
22 Palmer and Aardvark
23 Interstice
24 Paternal one
26 Flower part
27 Notion, in Nancy
28 The Flintstones, e.g.
29 Actress Verdugo
30 Lille is its capital
31 Maturing agent
32 Jazz devotee
35 Advantage
36 Hack
38 Dutch commune
39 Beach S of Palm Beach
41 He flew with waxen wings
44 Sandra ___ O'Connor
46 Photographer
50 Sniper, usually
53 Prized
55 Origin: Suffix
56 Rainy mo.
57 Garland-Rooney film: 1939
59 Fourth Arabic letter
60 "But for the grace of God ___"
61 Muslim decrees
62 Change moorage
64 "No ___ rich quickly if he is honest": Menander
66 Dawn goddess
68 No more, ___
69 Hibernating
71 King Hezekiah's mother
74 Conflict
75 Irish islands
78 Long for: Abbr.
79 MIT degree
81 Big house
84 Bobby of tennis
86 "___ of Scandal": Loren film
89 And ___ bed
90 "___ Fideles"
92 Edward VIII and George VI
94 Resort near Nice
95 "Tiger Lilies" poet
96 Actor Toomey
97 Notch
98 Mr. Bones
99 Bet on ___ thing
100 Gazes
101 Traveler and Rosinante
102 Running brook

DOWN

1 Arctic bay
2 Ally, to Juan
3 Dreiser title
4 "Dancing ___," 1949 film
5 ___ majesty
6 Foliage
7 Achieved success
8 Hawked
9 Detestation
10 Plow pioneer
11 Extract
12 Bloke
13 Lofty home
14 Graceland family
15 Hammed it up
16 Causing vexation
17 Stone monuments
25 Famed NYC building
33 Fascination
34 Arborist
37 Guardsmen attire
39 Cannon of films
40 ". . . came both mist ___": Coleridge
41 Insect stage
42 Tasty rooster
43 ___ attired (chic)
45 Dispatch boat
47 Native language
48 A Musketeer
49 Closes in
51 Belittler
52 Mr. Buntline
54 White-handed gibbon
58 Ooze
63 Most stylish
65 Hood
67 "___, Next Year," 1978 film
70 Makes possible
72 Remain in the vanguard
73 New doctors
75 See 48 Down
76 Cheerful
77 Program
80 Baseballer Babe's monogram
82 Sobriquet for Clara Bow
83 Seasonal Pacific current
85 "Wall Street" director
87 Wild goose
88 Typeface
91 Tolkien trees
93 Long-tailed apes

52 MADE-TO-MEASURE by Norma Steinberg

From San Francisco comes Norma's latest creation—tailor-made for those solvers who enjoy witty clues and a clever theme.

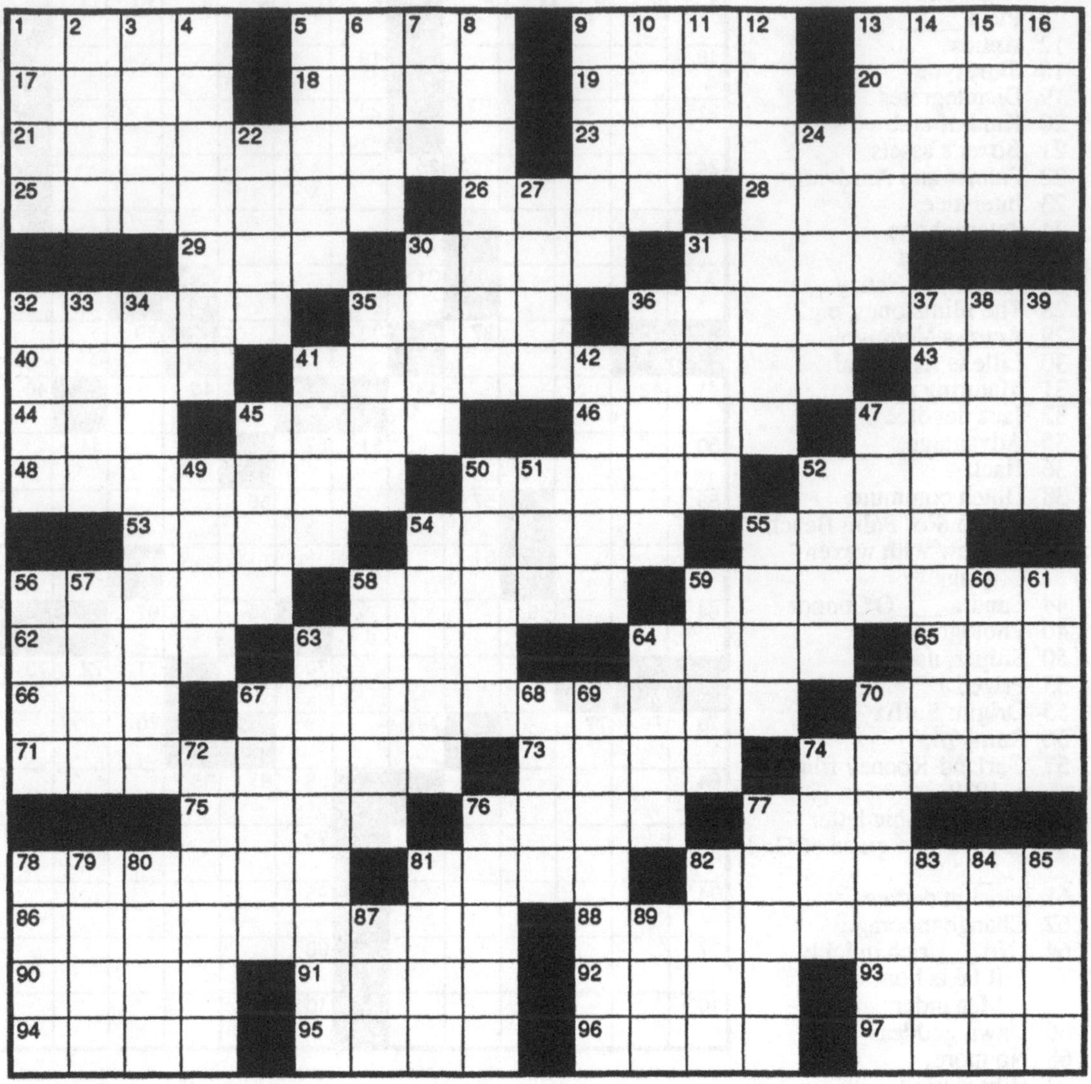

ACROSS

1 One of the Three Bears
5 Sip
9 Before stick or dash
13 At a distance
17 Skip
18 Pro ___ (in proportion)
19 Beach toy
20 Isak Dinesen, e.g.
21 Small
23 "Cantos" poet
25 Etch
26 Frank Herbert title
28 Kind of beef
29 Mellow
30 Get along
31 Type of party or chair
32 Cost
35 Short skirt
36 With "The," 1977 Carney film
40 Mardi Gras follower
41 "The Pawnbroker" star
43 Eggs
44 Within: Abbr.
45 Kin of jujitsu
46 Birds' class
47 Fat
48 One with a trainer
50 Disney rabbit
52 Charred
53 Partner of wear
54 Black or Valentine
55 Suspended
56 BSA member
58 Reno game
59 Blended
62 Stony
63 Had on
64 Natchez-to-Mobile direction
65 ___ rule
66 Supply with weapons
67 Jazz trumpeter
70 Peter or Nicholas
71 Madness
73 Article
74 Chief deckhand
75 Bad day for Caesar
76 Witticisms
77 Dandy
78 Buffed
81 Stripped
82 "Being There" star
86 Baseball-mitt oil
88 Soldier of 1776
90 Cajole
91 Ex
92 Nudge
93 Indian god
94 Better than fair
95 Scan
96 Bills
97 Gait

DOWN

1 Vatican VIP
2 Gemayel of Lebanon
3 ___-Pong
4 Draw
5 Ambition
6 Demolish
7 Broke a fast
8 Infuriates
9 Exhaust
10 Relax
11 Atmosphere
12 Appeases
13 Decorates
14 "Afternoon of a ___"
15 Mrs. Shakespeare
16 Foxx
22 Aromatic herb
24 Might
27 Kind of pricing
30 Canine name
31 Heady beverage
32 Entreaty
33 Lease
34 Geometrid caterpillars
35 Style
36 Animate
37 Kind of figure
38 Microwave
39 SI unit of power
41 Wife of Boaz
42 Like a beaver
45 Josh
47 Warbled
49 Praise
50 Roués
51 Below Wash.
52 Rye disease
54 Inchon locale
55 Sibilant sound
56 Former Iranian ruler
57 Grant
58 Greek city-state
59 Injure
60 Son of Isaac
61 Shoot!
63 ___ sound
64 Holiday times
67 Ecbatana natives
68 Fashion name
69 Have a go at
70 Like some bathing suits
72 Tinged
74 Take off in a hurry
76 Paired
77 Vendettas
78 Cozy
79 Sub
80 Othello's lieutenant
81 ___ Raton
82 Haughty one
83 Utter
84 Great review
85 Cinch
87 Primary number
89 Form of savings

53 POSSESSIONS by Stanley B. Whitten

Stanley's wit 'n' skill have produced a peerless puzzle for solvers' enjoyment.

ACROSS

1 Immediately, for short
5 Seaweed derivative
9 Computer input
13 Give off
17 Chanteuse Horne
18 ___ Grande, city in Arizona
19 ___ patriae
20 Billionth: Comb. form
21 "Too Close for Comfort" star's evening?
23 Pop singer's auto?
25 Incident
26 Mai ___ (rum drink)
28 Heraldic term for "proceeding"
29 Betelgeuse, e.g.
30 Pastry
33 Delaware seaport
34 Conglomerate's initials
36 Pinna
37 French miss: Abbr.
39 Hall of Fame pitcher's summons?
44 Depside and glyceride
49 Columbus campus initials
50 Coup d'___
51 Major or Minor preceder
53 Part of Q.E.D.
54 Con Ed, et al.
55 G.O.P. adherent
56 Aircraft shelter
58 City on the Tiber
59 Boulders
61 Searching device
63 Lutelike instrument
64 Dies ___
65 Truth
66 Greek letter
68 March 15, in Italy
69 Rejoice musically
70 Tailor a tale
71 Baby's bed
72 Presidential nickname
73 Squabble
75 British actor's stick?
79 Home of Gannon College
81 Garment border
82 Peruvian money
83 Slip through, nautically
87 Essences
90 Catches forty winks
93 Changed
95 Lawyers' org.
96 Prevailing weather condition
99 English philosopher's fastener?
101 English character actor's song?
103 Copied
104 In pain
105 Actor Andrews
106 Dickens heroine
107 Towel word
108 Ireland, poetically
109 Proofreader's word
110 Golf-bag items

DOWN

1 Der ___ (Adenauer)
2 Oozes
3 "___ came to pass . . . "
4 City in New Jersey
5 Sharp and biting
6 Securities
7 Bat wood
8 Run-down building
9 A king of Hebrews
10 Pierre's friend
11 "___ a Mockingbird"
12 Refuges
13 Follow
14 S.A. parrot
15 Foolish
16 Wrongful acts
22 Certain strong winds
24 British ___
27 Invisible emanation
31 Assay
32 Become visible
35 French head
38 Shakespearean king
39 Somewhat bitter
40 Oregon seaport
41 Florence natives
42 Slipped
43 Sack material
45 Garr of "Tootsie"
46 Amatory items
47 Period of fasting
48 Barren
52 Existentialist of note
56 West end of Hispaniola
57 Pismire
60 Small barrels
62 Black Sea peninsula
63 Pertaining to a certain speed
65 Change direction
67 Has the flu
71 Arrived
74 Looks salaciously
76 Minnow relative
77 Ushers in
78 Noisy
80 Enclosed, as a pool
83 Indian prince
84 Run away secretly
85 Clear sky
86 Peddles
88 Captured
89 Tea cake
91 "Gay ___"
92 Long scarf
94 Otherwise
97 Prospective atty.'s exam
98 Building extensions
100 Dernier ___ (latest fashion)
102 Corrode

54 BY THE NUMBERS by L. M. Rheingold

L. M. says he constructed this one on a periodic table. We believe him!

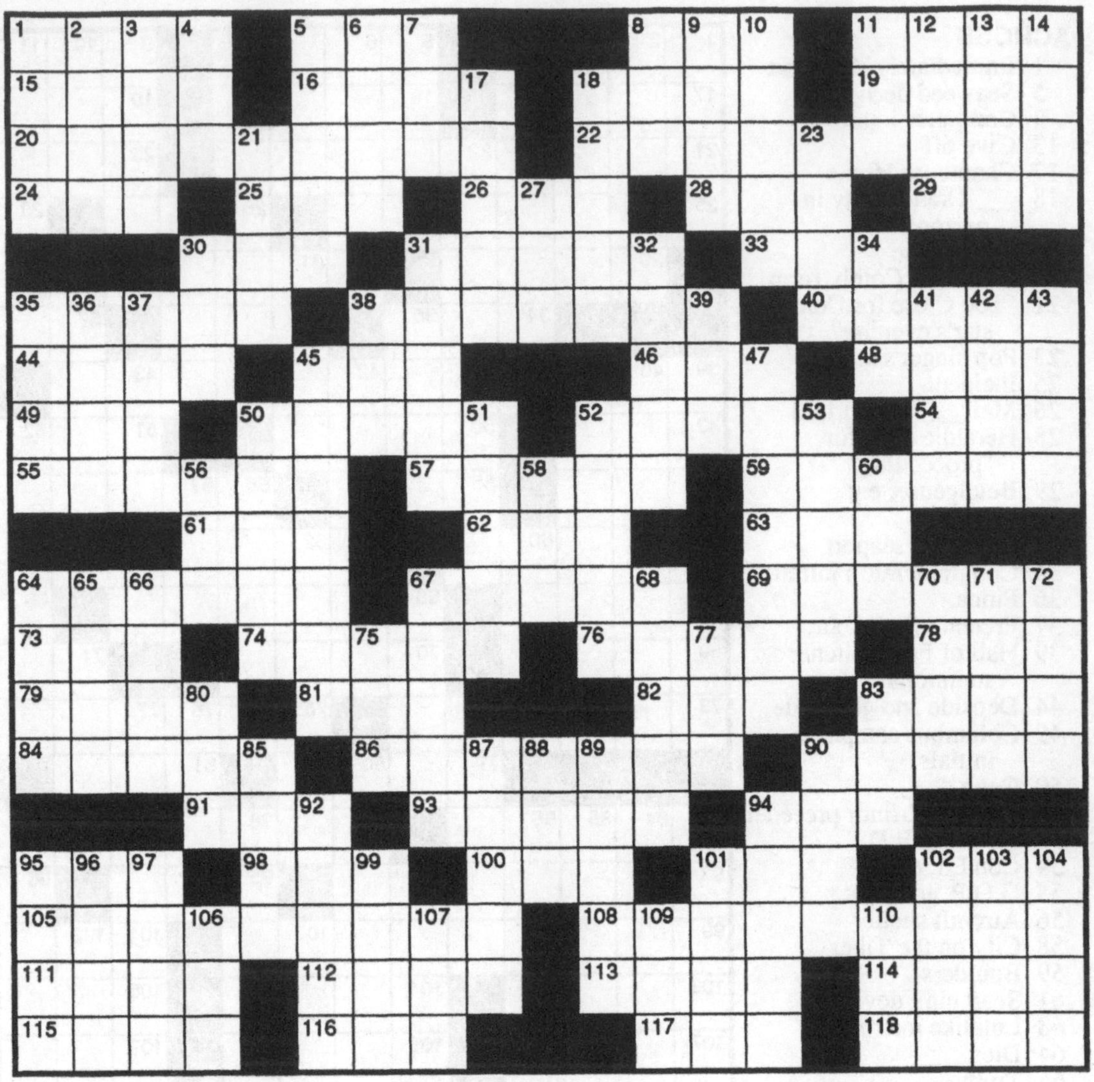

ACROSS

1 Grimm monster
5 Totem pole
8 Crowd
11 Trail
15 Trepan, e.g.
16 Sword
18 Remedy
19 Rio Branco's state
20 Basic
22 Atomic number 95
24 Append
25 Cattle genus
26 Jug's lug
28 Fleur-de-___: Var.
29 Part of D.O.D.
30 Heavy weight
31 Concur
33 Kind of service
35 Atomic number 5
38 Atomic number 36
40 Rooms, in Reynose
44 Help a crook
45 Objective
46 Turf
48 Crèche figures
49 L. ___ Hubbard
50 Passion
52 Quotes
54 Red fighter
55 What 62 Across and 97 Down are
57 Fortification
59 Atomic number 6
61 Rubber tree
62 Atomic number 50
63 Part of the Moluccas
64 Atomic number 8
67 Atomic number 18
69 Attractive one
73 Tax shelter for some
74 Part of TNT
76 Oread
78 She reigned in Spain
79 Orange-red gem
81 Lynx
82 ___ Gatos
83 Seed cover
84 Peepers
86 Atomic number 14
90 Ammonia compound
91 Thither
93 Noted violinist: 1891-1967
94 Choler
95 Cuckoo
98 ___ Passos
100 Vernal mo.
101 Record
102 Sharp turn
105 Atomic number 32
108 Atomic number 94
111 Nets' target
112 Old Testament book
113 Yemen capital
114 Pilaster
115 Sheridan and Miller
116 Two fins
117 It's a relief?
118 A. Smith's concern

DOWN

1 Great Barrier Reef
2 Atomic number 79
3 Like caviar
4 "Pears from an ___": Cervantes
5 Atomic number 54
6 Small flats
7 Most popular beverage
8 Flower, for short
9 City on the Oka
10 Aquamarine
11 Moccasin
12 Amino ___
13 Factual
14 Sisal
17 Pensive poem
18 Blue-pencil mark
21 Bard's "black"
23 Wife of Osiris
27 Dada founder
30 Toddler
31 Kay's defense
32 Cosmetic dye
34 Actress Dawber
35 Malty yeast
36 Hautboy
37 Tore
38 Tease
39 "___ As a Stranger"
41 Elia
42 Exchange premium
43 Billboard
45 Atomic number 33
47 Departs suddenly
50 Green Mountain boy
51 Prefix for rocket
52 Standard
53 ___ Lawrence College
56 Aestival mo. in N. A.
58 Gibe
60 Drugget
64 Seine tributary
65 Picture of health
66 Agile
67 Musical Shaw
68 Synthetic fiber
70 Italian saint
71 Sooner city
72 Story
75 Pile, to Pierre
77 Burmese language
80 Martini adjective
83 Simone's soul
85 Pop
87 Beast of burden
88 Brat
89 Cavils
90 Jason's craft
92 Ensemble of three trios
94 Particles
95 Moslem VIP
96 Atomic number 10
97 Atomic number 26
99 5, 6, or 6X
101 Large moth
102 Atomic number 30
103 Cord or Crosley
104 Fed
106 UK solons
107 Amphora
109 Beaker's home
110 Caledonian denial

55 TITLE TAMPERING by Bernard Meren

What's in the altered name of a musical, a song or a movie? Beware! You may develop a twisted mind.

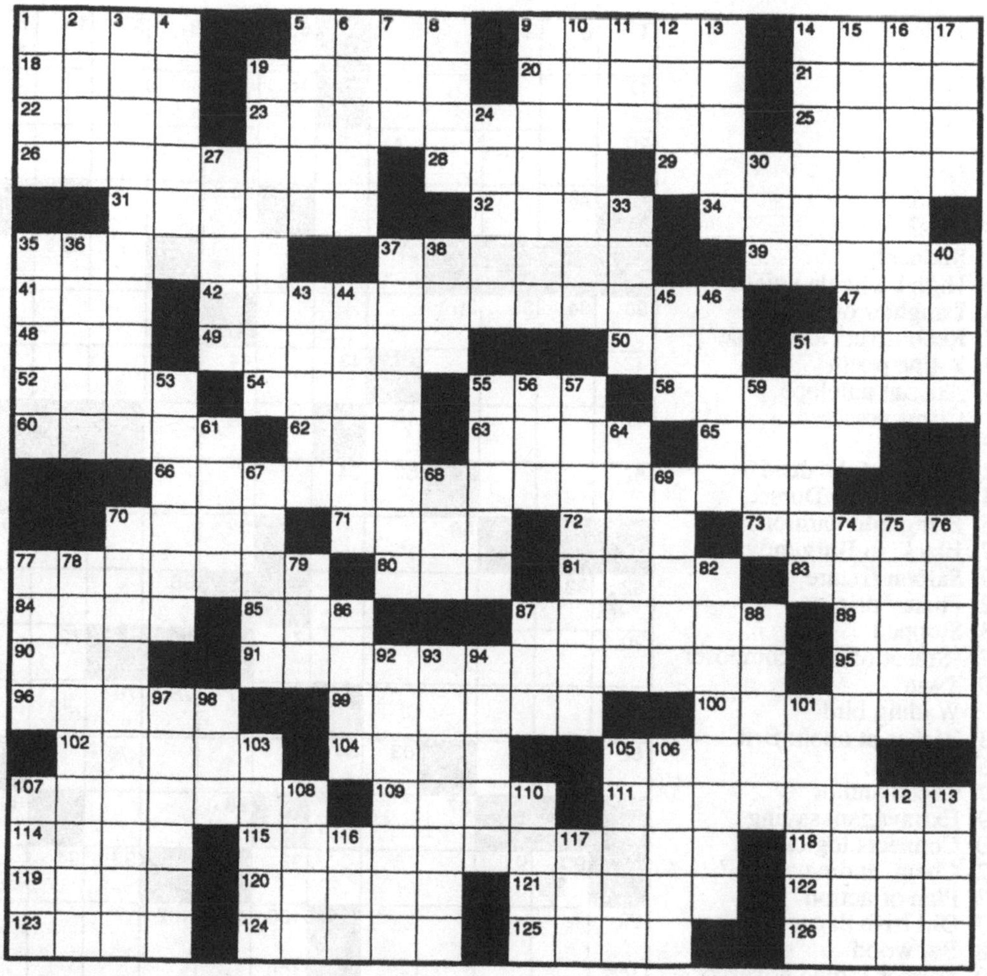

ACROSS

1 Little Sheba's creator
5 B–G connection
9 Big spender on a bender
14 Thor's father
18 European blackbird
19 Villein
20 Martinique peak
21 Yearn
22 "___ of Him who form'd the whole": Byron
23 Golfer's glad greeting after sinking an incredible putt?
25 "___ take arms . . . ": Hamlet
26 Gila and the incredible hulk
28 Stone
29 ___ up (get wise)
31 Pet name
32 Oversupply
34 A butterfly
35 Shrubby California herb
37 Old town media
39 Josh or Ella
41 Start of Montana's motto
42 Gershwin's catch of the day?
47 Pioneer in the electronic ind.
48 Coll. basketball tournament
49 Items in an uxor's closet
50 Farm power org.
51 Barracks furnishings
52 Antelope's range playmate
54 Set of matched horses
55 Sitcom about an alien
58 All together
60 Greece, to the Greeks
62 "___ tu," Verdi aria
63 Spoiled girl in a song
65 Rocky hills
66 Porter's declaration to a lowbrow?
70 Monk's hood
71 Sucker header
72 Early Nebraskan
73 Amiens is its capital
77 Read rapidly
80 Jet follower
81 Levee
83 Russian refusal
84 Dutch painter Frans ___
85 Turner or Hentoff
87 Like some partners
89 Managed
90 Wright wing
91 Play dedicated to Prince Albert?
95 Critic Huxtable
96 Woman's loose garment
99 Engaged in a scam
100 Kukla's pal and Hardy
102 Miter
104 Carnelian's cousin
105 Lawes was one
107 Interwoven
109 Napoleon and Wellington
111 Broke open a closed container
114 Noyes play
115 Youmans's song about a crowded table?
118 Not any in Dogpatch
119 Said Louis, "L'___ c'est moi"
120 Belief
121 Pathway to wedded bliss
122 Il Duce's daughter
123 Attic township
124 WW I planes
125 Plexus
126 Pitcher Nolan ___

DOWN

1 Muslim priest
2 Pianist Peter
3 Garbo vehicle: one for the road?
4 French President's residence
5 Darling, in Dijon
6 Edible seaweed
7 Schubert's "The ___ King"
8 B'way bomb
9 ___ the beans (told a secret)
10 Agitate
11 Antiquated
12 Former Brazilian coins
13 Pours
14 Portuguese wine city
15 Ranger unit: twelve times more despicable
16 Affects each other
17 Inert gaseous element
19 Open-ended cigars
24 Former Israeli P.M.
27 They cover all bases on rainy days
30 Indian mulberry
33 Ivan was one
35 Schnitzler's "La ___"
36 Bay window
37 Aluminum silicates
38 Comedienne Charlotte
40 Siegfried's schnozzle
43 Pollster Elmo
44 Fierce looks
45 Bishopric
46 André or Amaro
51 Fremont's scout
53 Synthetic fabrics
55 On one's toes
56 Tennis ploy
57 What 81 Across prevents
59 May honorifics
61 Seeded
64 Gaul invader in 451
67 Fraud chaser
68 Half a laugh
69 Keepsake
70 First words to the first woman?
74 Meteorological substitution: Thompson for Doolittle?
75 Victor at Gettysburg
76 Lab burners
77 "___ Funny That Way"
78 Mark off with gradations, as a thermometer
79 Dit's partner
82 Beneficiary of an assigned check or note
86 Weems and Husing
87 One-hundredth of a riel, in Cambodia
88 Diacritical mark
92 Drank
93 Extirpates
94 Duck
97 Emulate Earhart
98 ___ Rover (children's game)
101 Not "quoit" a ringer
103 Riga natives
105 Deli delicacy, not as bad as it sounds
106 Anoint, once
107 Engendered
108 Profound
110 Kindergartner's reward
112 Wagnerian goddess
113 Cannon from Tacoma
116 It follows Santa, in El Salvador
117 Hasten

56 GEM OF AN IDEA by Walter Covell

From Barrington, Rhode Island, comes this arty-crafty challenger. It's as *arty* as it is *crafty*. This one is rated "H" for HARD.

ACROSS

1 Silence!
6 High La Scala voices
13 Daughter of Eurytus
17 Reconstruct a bowline
18 8-line poem
19 African antelope
20 Citrus preserve
22 Custom
23 Abode of the dead
24 45 inches in Dorset
25 Bring into harmony
27 Black, in Burgundy
29 Saloon fixture
32 Foamy drink
33 Stopped
37 "Stabat Mater" composer
39 Twin
42 Wading bird
43 Wakes at noon: Brit.
45 Implore
47 Czech author
49 Extravagant saying
50 Connects logically
52 Chem. ending
53 Plan of action
57 Old Irish daggers
58 Bat wood
59 Former Indian governor
61 Roman bronze
62 Mystic interpretation of Hebrew scripture
65 Mozart's rival
67 South American deer
70 Determines bearings
72 Unusual
73 Biblical possessive pronoun
75 Foot bones
76 Debtors
81 Architectural pier
82 Signed up: Abbr.
83 Theater gallery
85 7-digit figure
87 Stir-fry vessel
88 "___ Kapital"
89 Ankles
90 Hilkiah's son: Jeremiah 29:3
93 Sin
95 School
99 Fish-dish garnish
100 Deterrents
105 Modules
106 Fragile
107 Ham it up
108 Deep cut
109 Wool fabrics
110 Swedish philanthropist

DOWN

1 Angel's lucky sign
2 Towel marking
3 Western state
4 Trigonometric ratio
5 Predominance of a kind
6 Pass. ship
7 Abalone shell
8 Concerning a brain membrane
9 Kind of desk
10 According to
11 Rorem or Sparks
12 Sweet spire
13 Go out
14 Scottish seaport
15 Theater section
16 Barely manage (with "out")
19 Amicability: Ger.
21 Medicinal plants
26 Chinese boat people
28 Sluggard
30 Fool
31 Greek letter
33 Tandem
34 Israeli politician
35 Period of existence
36 Inquire
37 Lassos
38 Rel. of Ltd.
39 Part II, the Talmud
40 Tied
41 Not as much
44 Dash
46 Arikaras
48 U.S./Canadian Indians
51 Eskers
54 The one there
55 Arab's robe
56 Study of jewels
58 War god
60 Tarry
62 English assembly before 1066
63 Galway Bay islands
64 Twist in Glasgow
66 Swelling
67 Zodiac sign
68 Do ___ others. . . .
69 Spare
71 Musical note
74 Henry V, to Falstaff
77 A–E connection
78 Mauna ___
79 Bugs
80 Trees of a region
84 Alias
86 Vassals
87 Livid
89 Verily
90 Zaire town
91 "I Want It Now" author
92 Manual: Abbr.
94 Surf sound
96 Detective Williams
97 Social pretender
98 Feminine ending
99 Machine projection
101 Anger
102 Letter opener
103 Legal matter
104 Cannes condiment

57 SWITCH POSITIONS by Shirley Soloway

Although Ed Asner is pretty popular among puzzlers, most solvers may be hard put to answer 45 Across. (Perhaps 106 Across can explain why.)

ACROSS

1 Pablo's love
5 Jet type
9 Blackthorn
13 Grandy or Allen
17 Additional
18 Tan
19 Spat
20 Popular fashion
21 Without charge
23 Not working
25 Most of N Africa
26 Rent one's pad
28 Collect
29 Widgeon or willet
31 Get the point
32 Nimbus
34 Not worth a ___
37 Craw
39 Skier's paradise
41 Snoozes
45 Asner sitcom first telecast 3/15/85
48 Trash-bag securer
50 Fashion name
51 Muck's mate
52 Corn porridge
53 Suffix for differ
54 Confused
56 Pee-wee Herman, e.g.
58 Generous giving
60 Above priors
63 Wave
65 Kind of jaw
68 Uniformed group
70 Type of kitchen
74 From ___ Z
75 French head
77 *The Making of an American* author
79 Finished
80 American humorist
82 Undecided
85 Rounds
86 Color-coded
88 Ball balancer
89 In the dumps
90 Bedouin garments
92 Speed: Abbr.
94 Apothecary weight
96 Once 1st Lady of Moscow
99 Dissertation
102 Trails
106 Where 45 Across ended up
108 Traveling
110 First or second
111 "___ Around": Beach Boys
112 Church section
113 Civil-rights leader Baker
114 Walked over
115 Costner's 1987 role
116 Breadth
117 Request

DOWN

1 Andy's buddy
2 Actress Freeman
3 Straight: Comb. form
4 Therapy, for short
5 *A Small Town in Germany* author
6 Old French coin
7 Sandy's sounds
8 Chaka Khan's group
9 Boas
10 Existence
11 Bizarre
12 Newt
13 Exploring general
14 Hindu ruler: Var.
15 What shrinks shrink?
16 Cotillion girls
22 Novelist Remarque
24 Cartoonist Foster
27 Lab vessel
30 Baylor building
33 Critter
34 Faro card
35 Make the best ___
36 Weather balloons, to some
38 ___ *Your Wagon*
40 Barnum and 109
42 Fits to ___
43 Holds fast
44 TVs
46 Pick up the tab
47 *Falcon* ___
49 Drinking bout
55 Helps
57 Plumber's concern
59 Classify
61 ___ leg! (Thespian phrase)
62 In the limelight
64 Leaves out
65 Jaffe's *Lost Horizon* role
66 Scintilla
67 Average
69 Wears away
71 Suffixes for simple
72 Peruvian tribesman
73 Require
76 Tarzan actor
78 Cote
81 Drank to
83 Worldly, long ago
84 SOS signal
87 Turns outward
91 Nonsense!
93 Service club founded in 1917
95 Pimlico females
96 Part of RLS
97 At a distance
98 In the event
100 Shakes a leg
101 Fastener
103 "The Oxbow" painter
104 Cabbage variety
105 Rapid City loc.
107 Cologne article
109 FDR project

58 SHOE-IN by Norman Wizer

Norman says you don't have to be an Oxford graduate to figure out his theme.

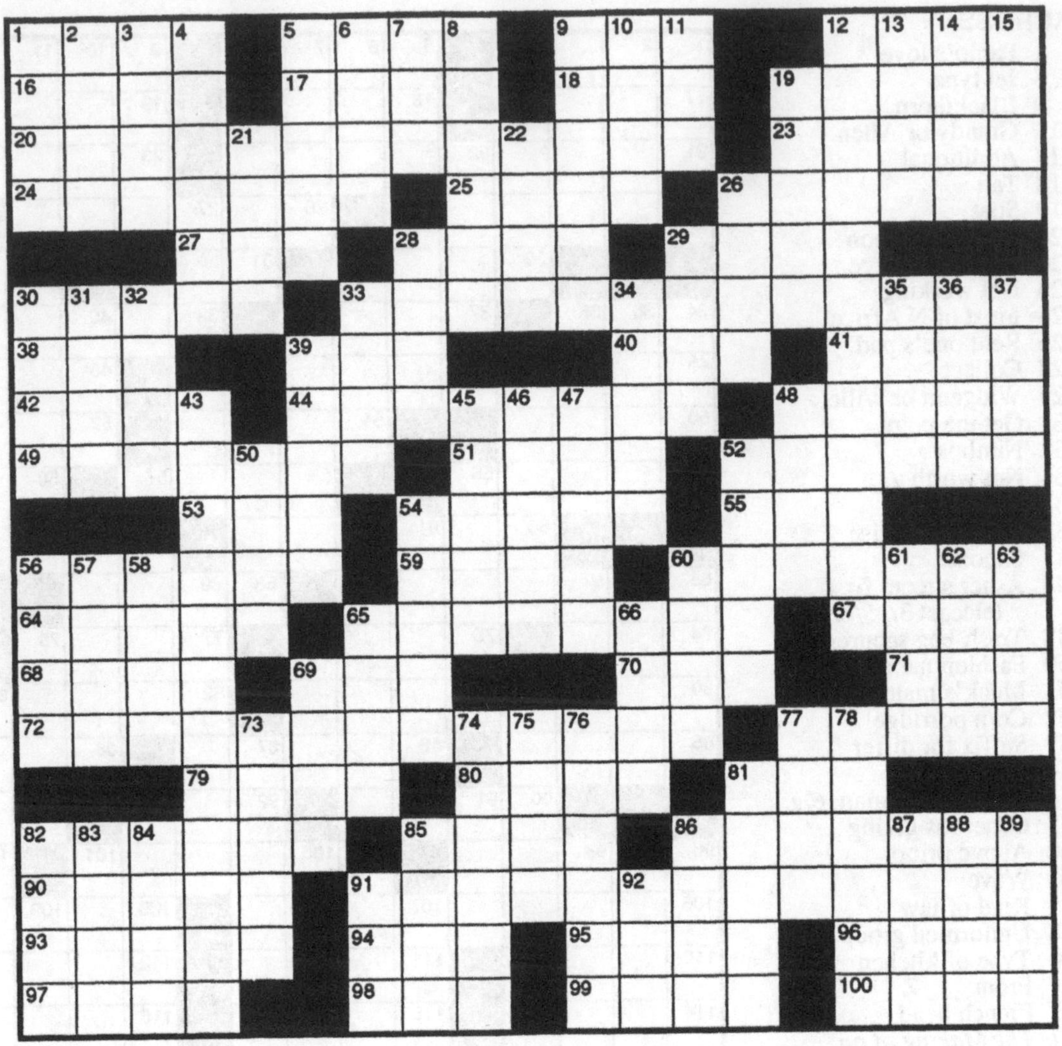

ACROSS

1 Eagled a par-3 hole
5 Alum.
9 Youth org.
12 Supplicate
16 Birdhouse
17 Steak order
18 In medias ___
19 Mentally-sound river?
20 Whimsically exaggerated
23 Rigatoni
24 Played the lead
25 Mare fare
26 Kind of tape
27 Pronoun for Hans
28 Norse deity
29 Of that kind
30 Source of the phoenix
33 Fitzgerald novel
38 Rubber tree
39 Part of TNT
40 Marker
41 Wide-mouthed jar
42 Canvas
44 Parris Island, for one
48 Bear
49 Ornamental veneer
51 Vinic prefix
52 Embellish
53 Comparative suffix
54 Suitor
55 Est. worth
56 Certain rays
59 Cuban coin
60 Entrance
64 Immigrant
65 Electro-magnetic coil
67 Congestive sound
68 Ultimate
69 Product of 36 Down
70 Sugary suffix
71 Sun god
72 Paris memorial
77 Stave off
79 Earth goddess
80 *Gil* ___
81 Twitch
82 Gaucho's milieu
85 Dispatched
86 Cultivated land
90 Approximately
91 Very strict
93 Feather
94 Noted architect
95 Yuletide
96 ___ *the Woods:* Sondheim
97 Emulate Tom
98 Caduceus org.
99 *Graf* ___
100 Paper measure

DOWN

1 Biblical book
2 Sluggish bird
3 Lab burner
4 Nth, for one
5 See 9 Down
6 Attack
7 Scottish alder
8 Solve a cipher
9 Elopers' destination of old, with 5 Down
10 Bishoprics
11 Query
12 Deep-dish treat
13 Put on the line
14 Part of a.m.
15 *The* ___ *of Living Dangerously*
19 Hot
21 *Trinity* author
22 Welcome
26 Nobelist bishop
28 Buckeye State
29 Knob on an organ
30 Plymouth or Hudson
31 Croatian
32 Present!
33 Ilium
34 One of the Disciples
35 Potpourri
36 Ransom Eli ___
37 MacTavish denials
39 Ski lifts
43 Get things started
45 It's often thrown in
46 Desist's companion
47 Charged particle
48 Amo, amas, ___
50 List
52 Dodge
54 Track
56 Festive occasion
57 Winged
58 Catchall abbr.
60 *Way Down East* star
61 Yellow jacket
62 Lily's cousin
63 Vociferate
65 Bristle
66 Sorry!
69 Address abbrs.
73 Speak pompously
74 Spain locale
75 It's next to the radius
76 Morning prayer
77 Small brook
78 Dessert
81 Championship
82 Joseph late of Broadway
83 Palindrome starter
84 Pout
85 Bow
86 Thyself
87 Teenage problem
88 ___ horse!
89 Esau
91 Evian or Bad Ems
92 Elephant org.

59 QUIPS AND QUOTES by Arthur W. Palmer

This mixture of puns and poetic allusions should increase the admirers in Art's army.

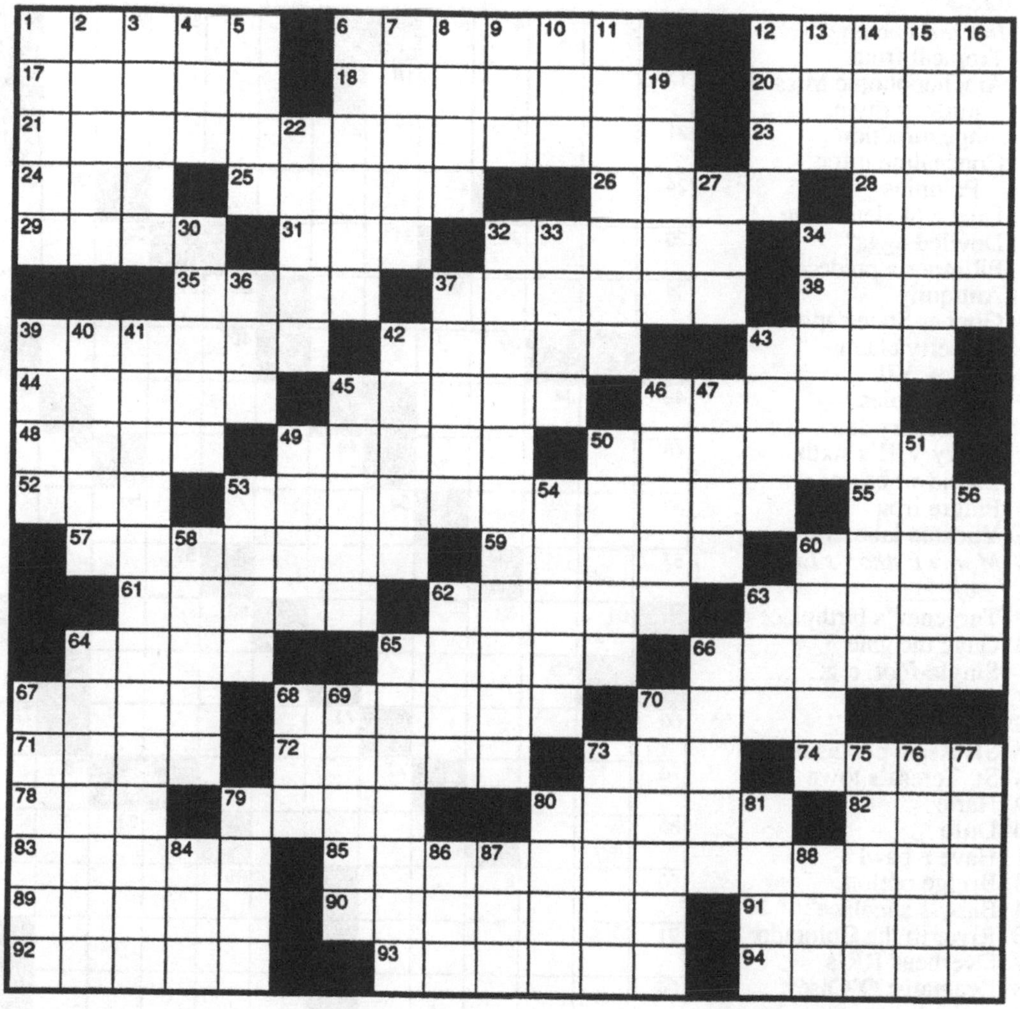

ACROSS

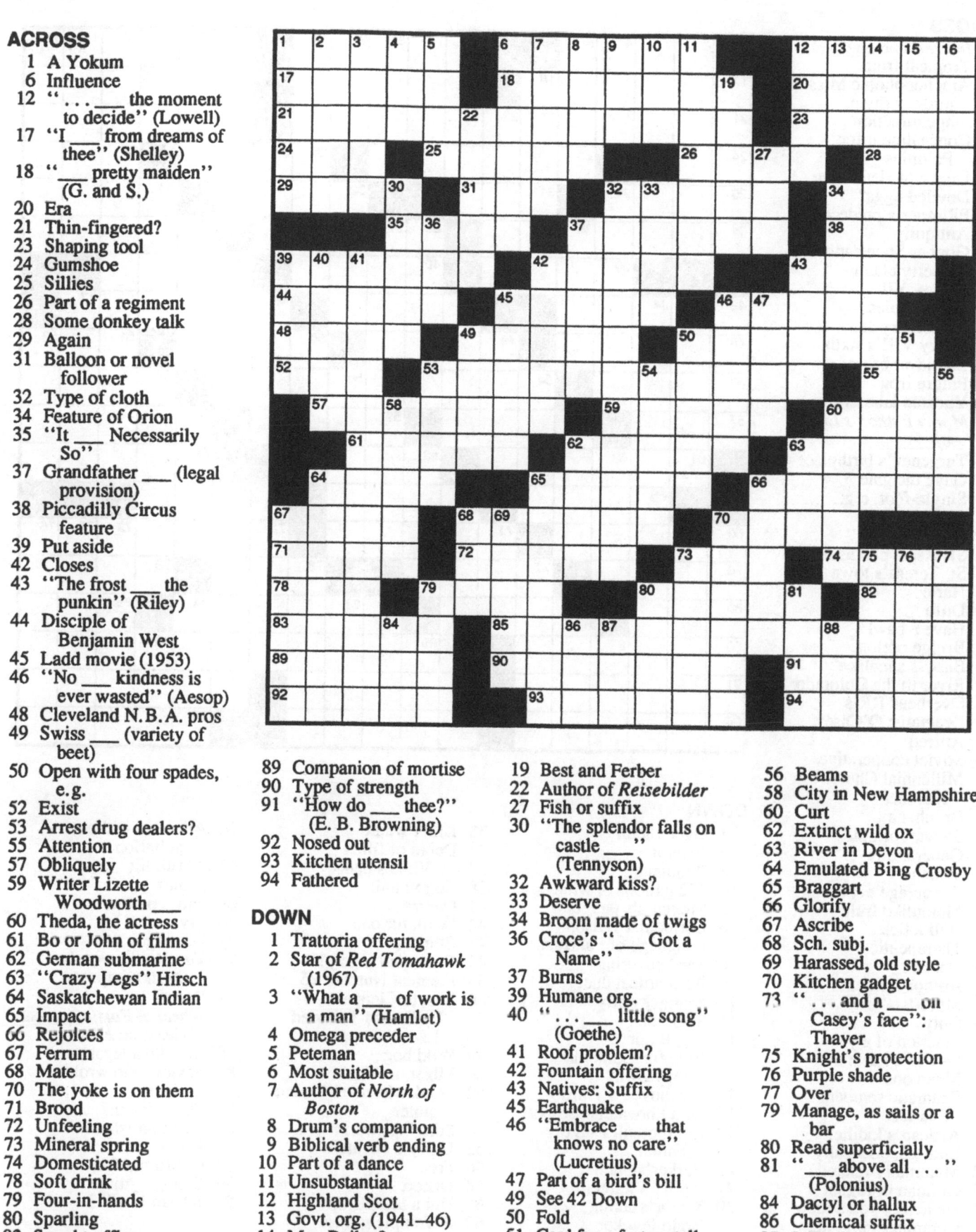

1 A Yokum
6 Influence
12 "... ___ the moment to decide" (Lowell)
17 "I ___ from dreams of thee" (Shelley)
18 "___ pretty maiden" (G. and S.)
20 Era
21 Thin-fingered?
23 Shaping tool
24 Gumshoe
25 Sillies
26 Part of a regiment
28 Some donkey talk
29 Again
31 Balloon or novel follower
32 Type of cloth
34 Feature of Orion
35 "It ___ Necessarily So"
37 Grandfather ___ (legal provision)
38 Piccadilly Circus feature
39 Put aside
42 Closes
43 "The frost ___ the punkin" (Riley)
44 Disciple of Benjamin West
45 Ladd movie (1953)
46 "No ___ kindness is ever wasted" (Aesop)
48 Cleveland N.B.A. pros
49 Swiss ___ (variety of beet)
50 Open with four spades, e.g.
52 Exist
53 Arrest drug dealers?
55 Attention
57 Obliquely
59 Writer Lizette Woodworth ___
60 Theda, the actress
61 Bo or John of films
62 German submarine
63 "Crazy Legs" Hirsch
64 Saskatchewan Indian
65 Impact
66 Rejoices
67 Ferrum
68 Mate
70 The yoke is on them
71 Brood
72 Unfeeling
73 Mineral spring
74 Domesticated
78 Soft drink
79 Four-in-hands
80 Sparling
82 Sought office
83 Combine
85 Mired twig?
89 Companion of mortise
90 Type of strength
91 "How do ___ thee?" (E. B. Browning)
92 Nosed out
93 Kitchen utensil
94 Fathered

DOWN

1 Trattoria offering
2 Star of *Red Tomahawk* (1967)
3 "What a ___ of work is a man" (Hamlet)
4 Omega preceder
5 Peteman
6 Most suitable
7 Author of *North of Boston*
8 Drum's companion
9 Biblical verb ending
10 Part of a dance
11 Unsubstantial
12 Highland Scot
13 Govt. org. (1941–46)
14 Mrs. Bailey?
15 Flight formation
16 Bridal shower gift
19 Best and Ferber
22 Author of *Reisebilder*
27 Fish or suffix
30 "The splendor falls on castle ___" (Tennyson)
32 Awkward kiss?
33 Deserve
34 Broom made of twigs
36 Croce's "___ Got a Name"
37 Burns
39 Humane org.
40 "... ___ little song" (Goethe)
41 Roof problem?
42 Fountain offering
43 Natives: Suffix
45 Earthquake
46 "Embrace ___ that knows no care" (Lucretius)
47 Part of a bird's bill
49 See 42 Down
50 Fold
51 Card for a fortuneteller
53 Disclose
54 Sierra ___ in Africa
56 Beams
58 City in New Hampshire
60 Curt
62 Extinct wild ox
63 River in Devon
64 Emulated Bing Crosby
65 Braggart
66 Glorify
67 Ascribe
68 Sch. subj.
69 Harassed, old style
70 Kitchen gadget
73 "... and a ___ on Casey's face": Thayer
75 Knight's protection
76 Purple shade
77 Over
79 Manage, as sails or a bar
80 Read superficially
81 "___ above all ..." (Polonius)
84 Dactyl or hallux
86 Chemical suffix
87 J. Davis's org.
88 Yalie

60

"YOU CAN SAY THAT AGAIN!" by Gloria Evans
Our terrific Texan gives you an illustration of the art of iteration. It should earn your admiration!

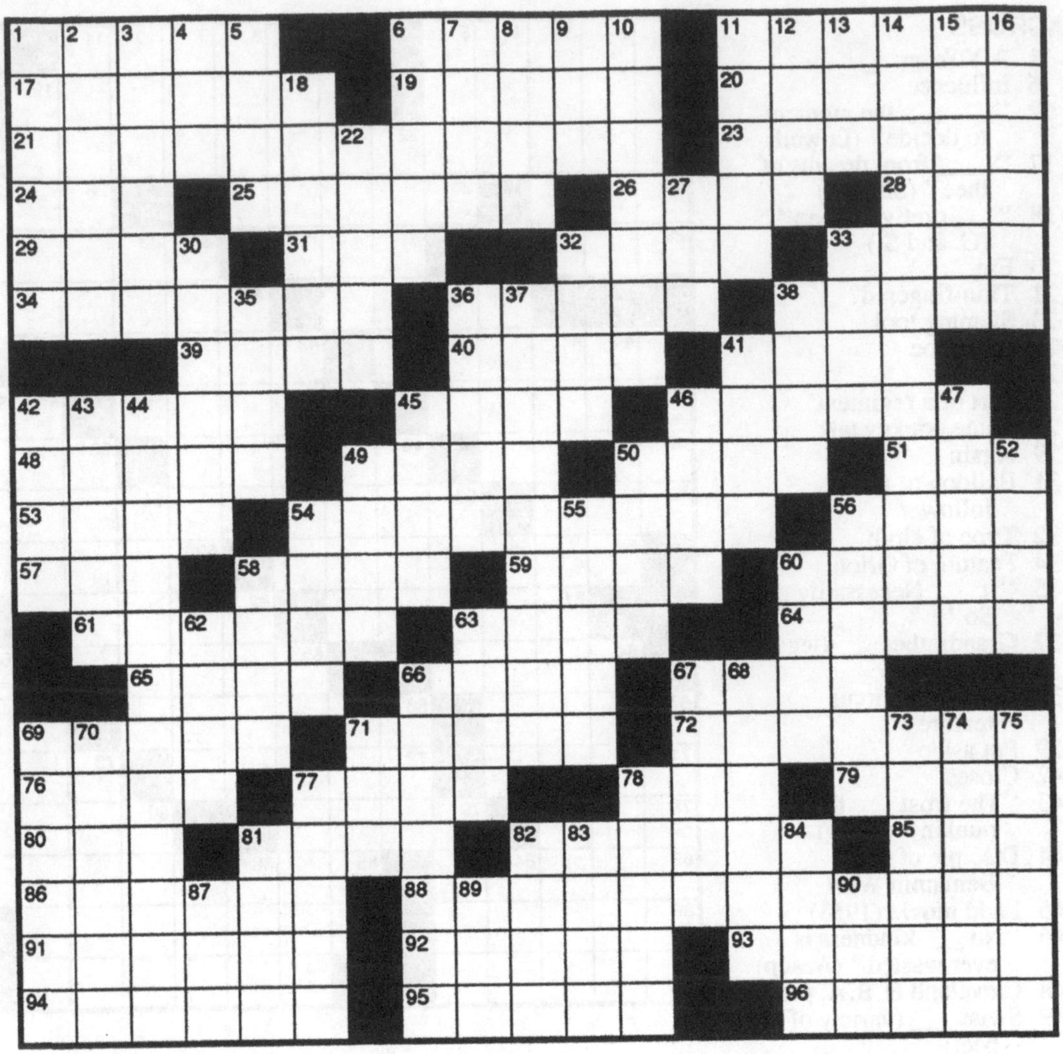

ACROSS

1 *Inferno* name
6 Tropical fruit
11 Arachnophobic Miss of nursery rhyme
17 Stage direction
19 Concealment for Polonius
20 Queen of sleuthdom
21 Deviled eggs?
23 Fillmore's predecessor
24 Antiquity
25 Gopher State capital
26 Property claim
28 XXI ÷ VII
29 Pub potables
31 Canterbury can
32 Henry VIII's sixth
33 Medieval brocade
34 Future frog
36 Yucatan laborers
38 *Monty Python's Life of* ___
39 Turgenev's birthplace
40 Gave the gate
41 Single-foot, e.g.
42 Stand-up guy
45 "___ Rhythm"
46 SE Asian peninsula
48 St. Teresa's town
49 Harte
50 Ditto
51 Have a bawl
53 Bridge option
54 Baby's shoelace?
56 River to the Colorado
57 Overhead RR's
58 Dramatist O'Casey
59 Attired
60 Soviet cooperative
61 Millennial Church member
63 Brouhaha
64 Stewart of golf
65 Generations
66 Voucher
67 Encourage evildoing
69 Melonlike fruit
71 Half a tick
72 Therapeutic
76 Declare
77 Author Hunter
78 Motorists' org.
79 Only
80 Fraction of a yen
81 One of a Latin trio
82 Mean one
85 Dramatic segment
86 "Scarface"
88 African's kiddie?
91 Endless, poetically
92 Maternally related
93 Dolman or raglan
94 He leaves you a loan
95 Computer input item
96 Potent beam

DOWN

1 Overwhelm
2 Armpit
3 Requisite
4 252 gallons of wine
5 Montana's targets
6 Cartoonist Wilson
7 Language of Pakistan
8 Seed covering
9 Anatomical duct
10 Kentucky city
11 39.37 in.
12 ___ Bator
13 Role for Goldblum
14 Happytown?
15 Beethoven's Third
16 Of a Phoenician seaport
18 Pro football Hall of Famer
22 Barker's pitch
27 April 15 letters
30 Victor's taking
32 Erato invoker
33 La Scala solo
35 Killer whale
36 Debra of films
37 St. Vitus's dance?
38 Cotton unit
41 Quarry
42 Horn, for one
43 Ellipses
44 Cockeyed pigsty?
45 Element Number 26
46 Iras, to Cleopatra
47 "Lydia, the Tattooed Lady" composer
49 Wild hog
50 Mizar or Algol
52 Frank Merriwell's alma mater
54 Stinging swarm
55 Duffy's clientele
56 Free
58 Distort
60 Did a takeoff on
62 A Temple spouse
63 Barking place?
66 Attended without invitation
67 At full tilt
68 Brutes
69 Part's partner
70 Fly
71 Dam agcy.
73 *Van Hunks and the Devil* composer
74 Recess
75 *Wheel of Fortune* guess
77 Mideast potentate
78 Revoke a legacy
81 Sexton who wrote poetry
82 Photo finish?
83 Aleutian island
84 Knell
87 California fort
89 Stop ___ dime
90 Jetsam in 1773

61 SOME CHANGES MADE by Betty Jorgensen

The theme of this puzzle is 25 Across—a word we've never seen in a puzzle before!

ACROSS

1 Lay an egg
5 Jet-set transports
9 Glove-compartment resident
12 Where not to go to
16 Love god
17 Be acquainted with
18 Seine aits
20 Scat lady
21 A Turner
22 Hebrides island
23 Of sound mind
24 Perjured oneself
25 Puzzle theme
29 Corny
30 601 to Cato
31 Misstep
32 Broke
36 Ike's command
38 Moslem religion
43 Show up
44 25 Across in "Cinderella"
48 Rosary segment
49 Wax: Comb. form
50 Bowl sound
51 ___ boy!
52 Low bows
56 Attach to
58 25 Across in a phone booth
63 Uproar, in Liverpool
64 Senator Kennedy, to Pablo
65 Salt tree
66 Murderer of Osiris
68 Genetic letters
69 Org. for S&L's
73 25 Across in a fairy tale
77 Most talented
79 Easy to use
80 CCP former in 1921
81 Quotations
83 Prefix for practice
86 Acronym for a blimp
88 Does some gardening
89 25 Across in a laboratory
97 Faithful
98 Eye part
99 Not yet final
100 Upon my word!
101 Healthy
102 Start of Scotland's motto
103 Actress Merkel, et al.
104 Hilo honker
105 Pitcher
106 ___ Juan
107 ___ majesty
108 Mardi ___

DOWN

1 Estonian
2 Persian poet
3 ___ Lisa
4 Ramified
5 Dragonfly
6 Pries
7 Chinese secret society
8 Turf
9 Square pegs in round holes
10 Jai ___
11 Peter's ___
12 Where cold cuts are hot
13 Mélange
14 Valley
15 Kind of iron
19 Char
26 Room in a casa
27 Wine cooler
28 Crowd, to lovers
32 Hack
33 Imitate
34 Vichy, e.g.
35 Gallagher's vaudeville partner
37 "___ the land of the free"
39 Fishing boat
40 Supple
41 London suburb
42 Intended
45 Wax eloquent
46 Brooke Shields film
47 Bag at Fenway
49 Red wine
52 Socko sign
53 Divert
54 Up-to-date
55 Old Italian gold coin
57 Ring dec.
58 Boat: Comb. form
59 Extreme
60 *A Fish Called Wanda* star
61 Correct copy
62 *Tootsie* star
67 Mix or Hanks
69 Roofing material
70 Winter mo.
71 Suffix for real
72 Small change
74 Flower cluster
75 Attacks
76 Roast, in Rouen
77 Spray, in Suffolk
78 Remus Rabbit
82 Zulu's relatives
84 Related
85 Instruments in Plato's day
87 Make void
89 Tie
90 One is golden
91 Scoff (at)
92 Peruvian city
93 Fork feature
94 River to the North Sea
95 Portrayer of Jose Jimenez
96 Ogles
97 Start of many a title

62 JUST FOR LAUGHS by Evelyn Benshoof

You'll never feel cross nor down in Evelyn's world of Across and Down.

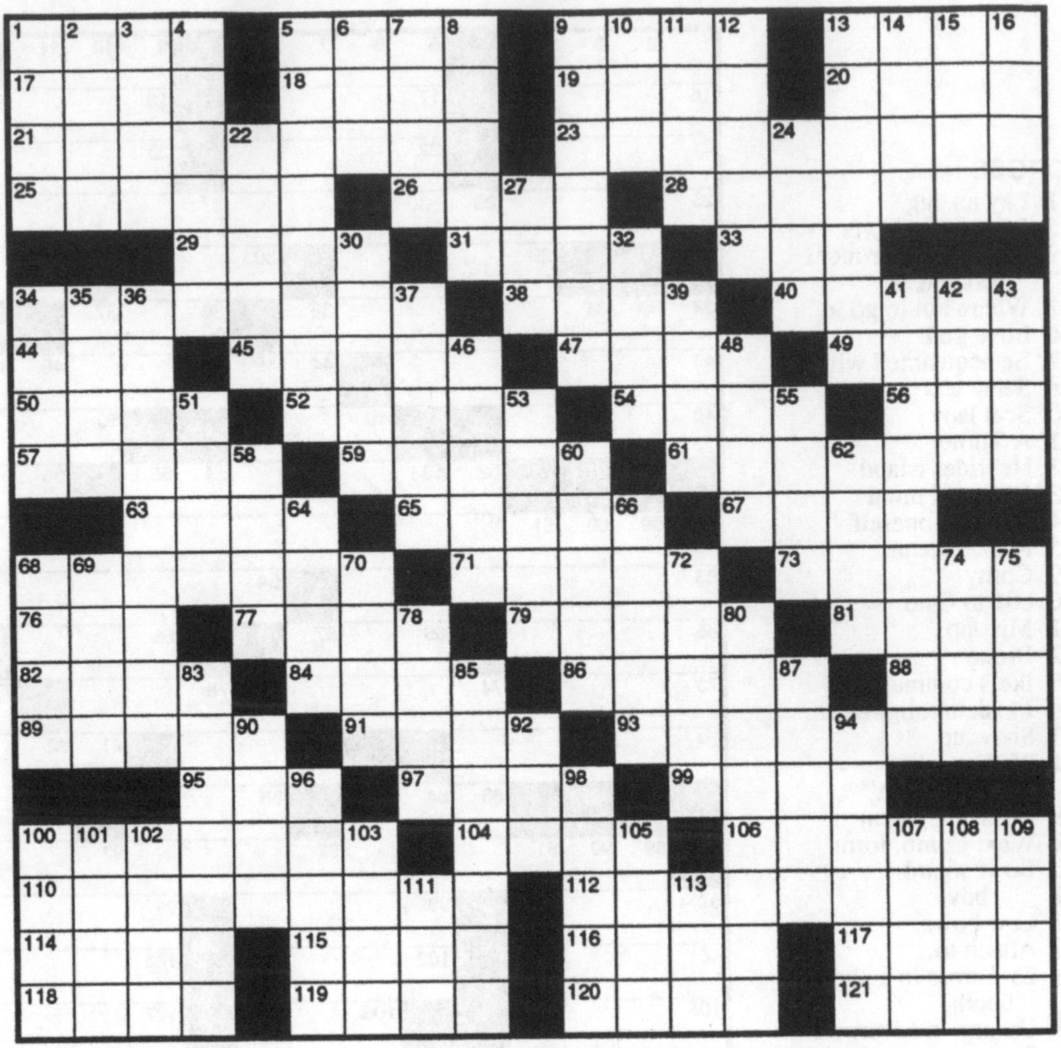

ACROSS

1 Cape
5 Fish of ponds
9 Cape Town loc.
13 Intrepid
17 Express
18 Farrago
19 Islands off New Guinea
20 Olympic sport implement
21 Zinger
23 Buffoon
25 Cause to err
26 Patroness of the Argonauts
28 *Jeux* composer
29 "Once ___ a midnight . . ."
31 ___ avis
33 Homophone of air
34 Influenced
38 Skirt style
40 Award for Geena Davis
44 Musical syllable
45 Playwright Mamet
47 Bottle part
49 Biblical pronoun
50 Hebrew month
52 Give a ___ (assist)
54 Humorous Jay
56 Jet-stream dir.
57 Indemnify
59 Shred
61 Contrived
63 Cookie
65 Lukewarm
67 Papilloma
68 Participated as a visitor
71 What a caddie replaces
73 Fine paper
76 *Love Story* composer
77 Clod
79 Recluse
81 Confident
82 Tolkien baddies
84 Conduct
86 Galsworthy novel
88 Reason for overtime
89 Oriental duck
91 Coin of Carrara
93 Halted a hearing
95 Queen of dreams
97 Catch
99 Card game for three
100 Slipped by
104 Active one
106 Syracuse U symbol
110 Jocular
112 Musical comedy of 1964
114 Lulu
115 Italian saint
116 Actress McClurg
117 Organic compound
118 N.L. team
119 ___ and bear it
120 Organ stop
121 Genoan magistrate

DOWN

1 Eft
2 Mideast chieftain
3 Porkfish
4 Escalate
5 Bodily
6 ___ king
7 Trump is this
8 Stud ___
9 Arid
10 Parseghian
11 *Stagecoach* director
12 Confederate gen.
13 Legacy
14 *Bloom County* character
15 Floral wear
16 Disavow
22 Blindfolded archer
24 Spanish river
27 Butt
30 "___ Can Say Goodbye"
32 Jump named after Paulsen
34 Danube feeder
35 Knot
36 Benny Hill's forte
37 Number
39 On the rocks
41 Old-as-the-hills jokes
42 Excellent
43 Regretted
46 Bamboozled
48 "I ___ him when . . ."
51 Reigning Hindu
53 Center of 62 Down
55 Kiwi-shaped
58 Yin's partner
60 Whirl or wheel
62 Eye part
64 Game with sticks
66 Sponsor
68 Mud
69 Lake of Thun feeder
70 Coward
72 Idiot boxes: Abbr.
74 Mercyhurst College site
75 Urgency
78 Piggin
80 Computed
83 Smirks
85 Injects irrelevant material
87 Like Niobe
90 Boss Tweed's attacker
92 Spanish year
94 Put on 112 Across
96 Person
98 Postpone
100 ___ effort
101 In the fast ___
102 Got a 100
103 Ending for evil
105 Brusque
107 Barcelona boy
108 Drink on the drink
109 Parisian pronoun
111 Swiss canton
113 German for 30 Down

63 ANAGRAMS by Elaine George

By George, here's a different kind of challenge! If you're good at transposing letters, this should be a cup of *eat* or *ate*.

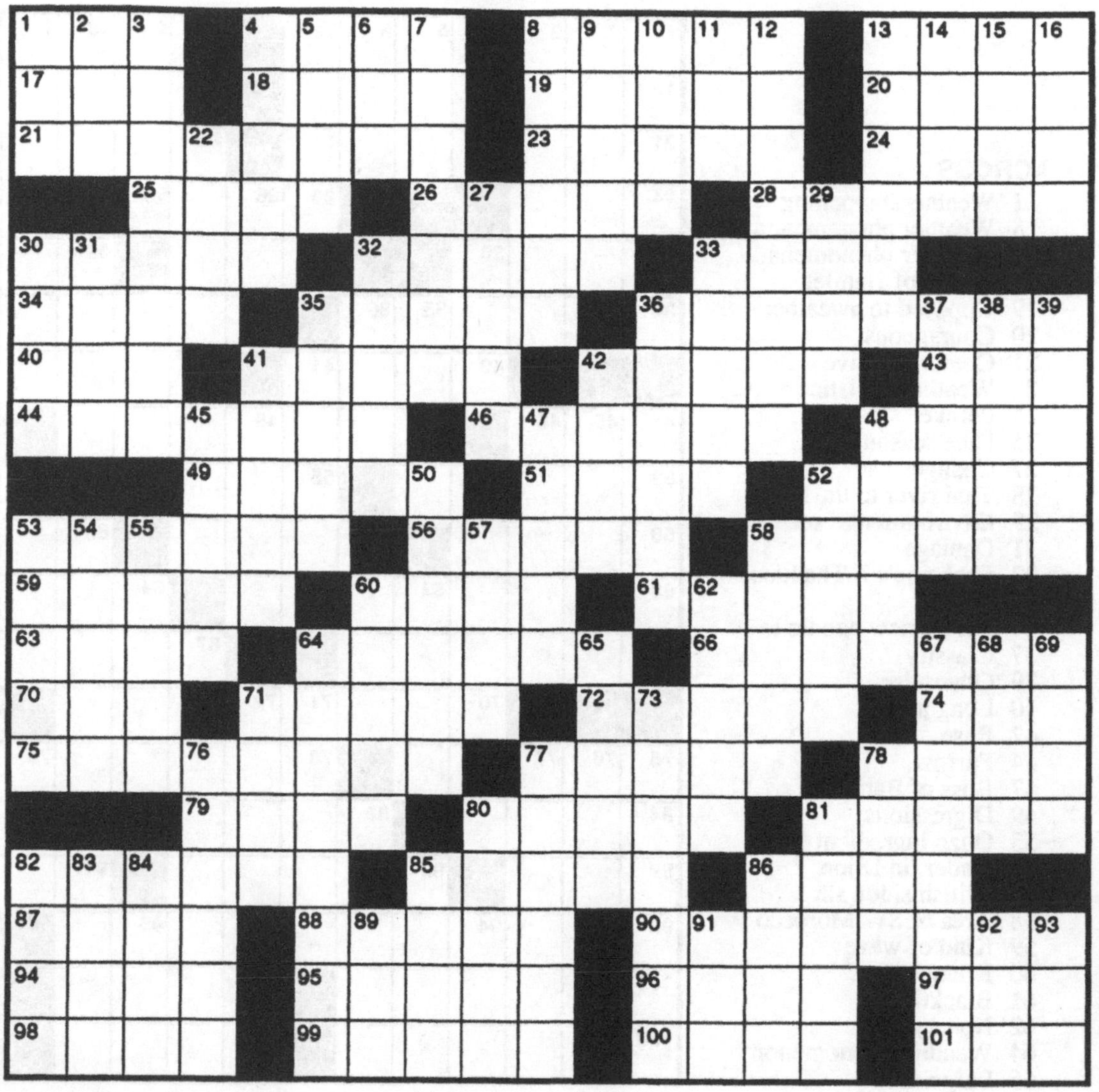

ACROSS

1 Pixie
4 An anagram for hoes
8 Crouch down
13 ___ paste (poi)
17 "Briny deep"
18 Anagram for rent
19 Wipe out
20 An anagram for lane
21 Meadows
23 Hardship
24 Pleasant
25 An anagram for note
26 Combine
28 An anagram for stream
30 Anagram for false
32 Inclined
33 Country furniture wood
34 Acreage
35 Ridge
36 Rodent-catchers
40 Rosary bead
41 Racket
42 Wickiup
43 Take a chair
44 Polliwog
46 Steam baths
48 An anagram for soil
49 An anagram for stale
51 Became larger
52 An anagram for Snead
53 Pablo, the cellist
56 Twist
58 Chargers
59 Searches
60 Experience
61 Make very happy
63 Summer coolers
64 Kicked the football
66 Bestowed
70 Gentleman's title
71 Anagram for start
72 Vagabond
74 Anagram for 40 Across
75 Unassumingly
77 Contended successfully
78 Zane, the author
79 Anagram for vast
80 Tunnels of sorts
81 Throbs
82 Hold in awe
85 An anagram for snare
86 An anagram for pass
87 Kiln
88 Circular
90 Object of dislike
94 Greatest
95 Anagram for runes
96 Slant
97 By way of
98 An anagram for pest
99 An anagram for reset
100 Moray and electric
101 British town

DOWN

1 Sixth-sense
2 Anagram for ale
3 Secured
4 Dazes
5 Not there
6 Anagram for roe
7 Guarantees
8 Dash
9 Entirely
10 Persuade
11 Since
12 Nasty ants
13 An anagram for enters
14 Anagram for tail
15 An anagram for care
16 An anagram for Reno
22 Symbol of ugliness
27 Snoops around
29 An anagram for neat
30 Apartment
31 St. Helens' output
32 An anagram for spier
33 Hawaiian fruit
35 Soft drinks
36 Break a promise
37 Notwithstanding
38 ___ up (heaped)
39 Glacial direction
41 Christmas songs
42 Anagram for runt
45 Land maps
47 Limber
48 Curl the lip
50 Score
52 Anagram for Tatar
53 Deep cleft
54 VCR sound, e.g.
55 Anagram for rends
57 Anagram for rest
58 Anagram for wades
60 Rolls up and binds
62 An anagram for valse
64 Diagrams
65 Hum
67 Scornful
68 Tie score
69 Calendar numbers
71 An anagram for rats
73 Manage
76 Incidents
77 Ash
78 Anagram for gasp
80 An anagram for names
81 Anagram for strap
82 Anagram for prom
83 Cry at a Greek orgy
84 Anagram for vets
85 An anagram for ruse
86 Vend
89 Ump's call
91 Contend
92 Lubricate
93 Anagram for any

64

SLIGHTLY WEATHERED by Walter Covell

An unusual theme and clever clues are just two elements of a good puzzle. Several more *elements* can be found below.

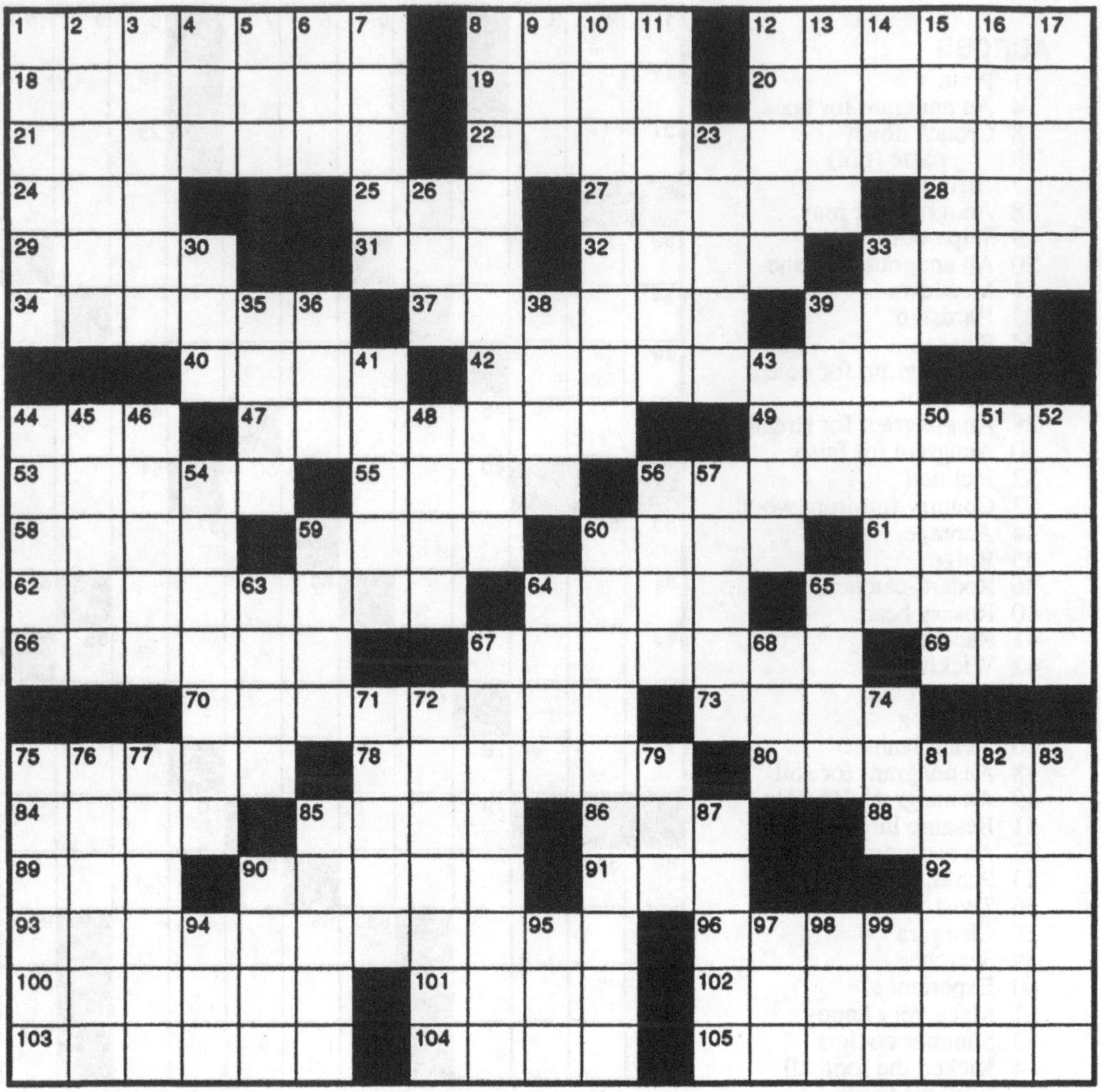

ACROSS

1 Weather happening
8 Weather phenomenon
12 Weather phenomena
18 Friend of Hamlet
19 Opposed to aweather
20 Courageous
21 Comprehensive
22 Weather statistic
24 Peruke
25 Nice season
27 Change
28 Thai river to the Ping
29 Environmental sci.
31 Damage
32 Grahame's J. Thaddeus
33 Brink
34 Give a new handle to
37 Classify
39 Otherwise
40 Long ago
42 Base
44 Furrow
47 Boss of Bari
49 Digressions
53 Ouzo ingredient
55 Under, in Dijon
56 British sidewalk
58 Area of SW Morocco
59 Kind of wave
60 Brumes
61 Blackthorn
62 Nonary
64 Weather phenomenon
65 Large net
66 Austrian province
67 Least believable
69 Commercial jet
70 Cheese dishes
73 Couples
75 Attacked
78 Of stone
80 UAR president, 1958-1970
84 Beehive State tribe
85 Ten: Prefix
86 Strike out
88 Spun a web
89 Former power agcy.
90 Street urchin
91 ___ Red apple
92 Serbian city
93 Reason logically
96 Unrestrained
100 On land
101 Roman way
102 Londoner's protection
103 Okays
104 Beats the bidder
105 Kicked off

DOWN

1 Weather phenomenon
2 Beginner
3 Trail of fame
4 Conflict
5 Call ___ day
6 Naught
7 Yiddish robot
8 Weather phenomenon
9 O'Neill play
10 Roundworm
11 Lament
12 Particle
13 Rip
14 Scrap
15 Ammo
16 Fata morgana
17 ___ of the crime
23 States in Saint-Malo
26 Chinese pagoda
30 Song
33 Conic section
35 Dawdle
36 Memorable time
38 Meaning in Marseilles
39 ___ Orange, NJ
41 Ford flop
43 Resort of New Mexico
44 Drizzles
45 Not qualified
46 Cheap and shiny
48 Yellow brick, for one
50 Some Prado paintings
51 Collars or jackets
52 Kind of lightning
54 Mountains or mackerels
56 Thwart
57 Eyed
59 Kind of frost
60 Forgers
63 Edict
64 "What ___ God wrought!"
65 Plato's colonnade
67 A salt of H_2TiO_3
68 Fair-weather sight
71 Varnish resin
72 Brief beachwear
74 Dir. of 8 Across, perhaps
75 Cheer
76 Military stance
77 Extinctions
79 Bounder
81 Voiced
82 Prove
83 Took it easy
85 Minnow relatives
87 Balms
90 Triangular piece of land
94 Hawaiian hawks
95 Hue holiday
97 At the age of: Abbr.
98 Sculptor's deg.
99 According to

65

PRESIDENTIAL NAME GAME by Peter G. Snow
Was Cary a descendant of Ulysses? Was Marilyn related to James? Get ready for a "Snow" job.

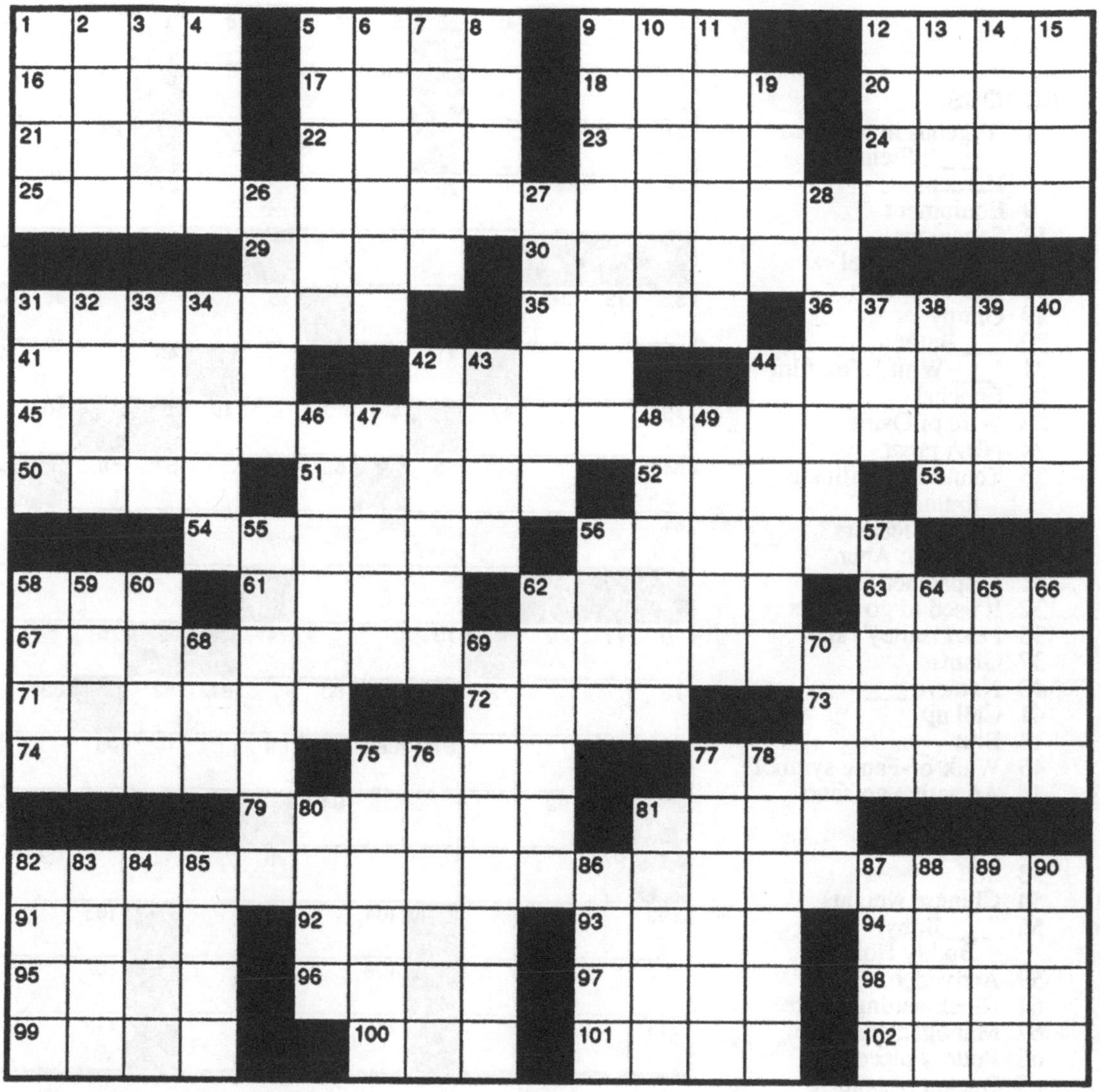

ACROSS

1 Reno machine
5 Engrossed
9 Police bul.
12 Cloche and miter
16 Tibetan monk
17 Site of a famous mausoleum
18 Wheat husk
20 Jai ___
21 Affirm
22 Jog
23 Father
24 Cousin of parsley
25 Kin of 17th president?
29 Rubber trees
30 Bear-like
31 Timid ones
35 Attractive and diminutive
36 Welcome sights on the Gobi
41 Tree or resort
42 Platform
44 Refined or suave
45 Kin of 6th president?
50 Bristle
51 Actress Anderson and namesakes
52 Otherwise
53 Cousin of a Ph.D.
54 Pacific
56 Sardou play
58 Draft org.
61 Author Kingsley ___
62 I or u, e.g.
63 Equal
67 Kin of 7th president?
71 Dialects
72 Very dark
73 Irregular
74 Seine tributary
75 Competent
77 Junior and senior
79 Give a new appellation
81 Wild hog
82 Kin of 12th president?
91 Elderly
92 Congregational response
93 Con
94 Operatic highlight
95 "The Way We ___," Streisand hit
96 Sediment
97 Rural structure
98 Hazard
99 Scene homonym
100 Tee predecessor
101 Dross or refuse
102 Minus

DOWN

1 Croat or Bulgar
2 Vesuvius output
3 Augur
4 Neighbor of Twelve Oaks
5 Baby's toy
6 Jibes
7 Airplane noses
8 Bye-bye in Britain
9 Recondite
10 Clergyman
11 "Little Minister" author
12 Pilgrimage of a sort
13 Albanian president
14 Bath powder base
15 Hit the ___ (parachute)
19 Inert element
26 Feeling remorse
27 Name of three Vatican heads
28 Put in a new request
31 Loses muscle tone
32 Words of understanding
33 Card pip
34 Caravansary
37 Presidential nickname
38 Infamous marquis
39 Geraint's mate
40 Spore
42 A pastry
43 Type of acid
44 As yet not purchased
46 Components of ink and varnish
47 Type of boom
48 Margin of a sort
49 John, of the Plymouth Colony
55 Bulls or elks perhaps
56 Tribe, e.g.
57 Mimics
58 Glance through
59 Actress Thompson
60 Recipe instruction
62 Give a superficially attractive appearance
64 Slaughter, of the Gas House Gang
65 Old language
66 Bread and whiskey
68 Very long time
69 Illnesses
70 Listened to
75 Rootlessness
76 Impracticable schemes
77 Sandinista foe
78 Freight
80 You were: Lat.
81 Hackneyed
82 Shark movie
83 Writer or former Met
84 Nothing more than
85 Anthony or Barbara
86 Selects
87 Monroe or Weaver of sports
88 ___ Smith, O'Neill hero
89 Overlook
90 Director Gene ___

66 WELL-SEASONED by James Burns

Mr. Burns tells us he was listening to four violin concerti by Vivaldi when the idea for this puzzle came to him.

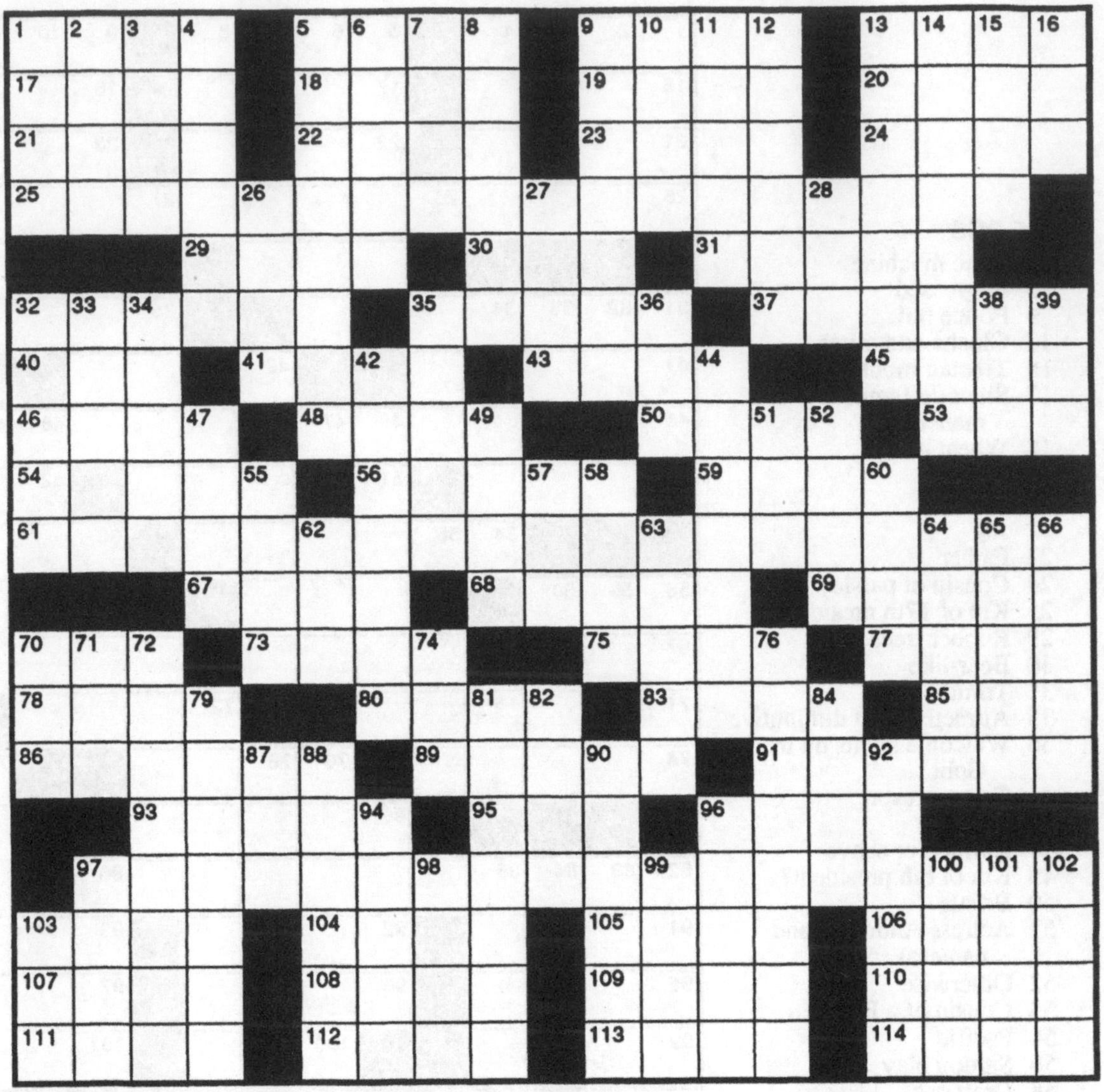

ACROSS

1 "Pigeons in the grass ___": Stein
5 Hardens
9 Equipment
13 Sagacious
17 Latvian capital
18 Show concern
19 Gimpy
20 ___ Bator
21 "___ Wolf," Fox film
22 Epochal
23 Wife of Osiris
24 NBA great
25 Tennessee Williams drama
29 Muslim leaders
30 Founded: Abbr.
31 Dispatched
32 It used to go farther
35 Pearl Bailey's sign
37 Giants
40 Numero ___
41 Call up
43 Brat
45 Walk-of-Fame symbol
46 An active volcano
48 Earthen pot
50 Pinball term
53 Self
54 Chinese weights
56 "___ Baby," Buddy Holly hit
59 Arrivederci
61 Clock-setting adage
67 Mahogany relative
68 Pottery piece
69 Bucket of bolts
70 Joke
73 Bireme, e.g.
75 Heath
77 Murphy or Robertson
78 Singer Guthrie
80 Pith
83 Shot up
85 Actress Caldwell
86 Elevenses' treats
89 Portable shelters
91 Kitchen buzzers
93 Respond
95 "___ Maria"
96 Trig function
97 What Chamonix hosted in 1924
103 Oxford, e.g.
104 Unless: Latin
105 Coveted position at Indy
106 Virginia of 1587
107 Markers
108 Misfortunes
109 Advance
110 Neglect
111 Brenner, for one
112 British dolt
113 Formerly, formerly
114 Wear's partner

DOWN

1 Skills
2 Stead
3 Long in the tooth
4 Hippy footwear
5 Synopsis
6 Warren and Monroe
7 Cafeteria item
8 Bearish investor
9 Catch the light
10 Orient
11 Not in proper order
12 Consequence
13 Knuckles under
14 Estrange
15 Actress in "Tootsie"
16 Wrap up
26 Minced oath
27 Sale condition
28 Michelle's merry month
32 Pairs
33 Readily available
34 Recluse
35 God of 29 Across
36 Pose
38 Hayburner
39 Near-sellout sign
42 Annual publication
44 Corrida participant
47 Came to rest
49 "The ___ have it!"
51 "___ Liza Jane"
52 Adjective for a julep
55 Muckamuck
57 Word from Ebenezer
58 Wax-covered cheese
60 Inventor Hussey
62 Infantile word
63 Aristophanes' "The___"
64 Dumfound
65 "The ___ Purple"
66 Mini revelation
70 Dental anesthetic
71 Electric ___ welding
72 Delightful
74 Moppet
76 Reserved
79 Unity
81 No dreamer
82 Deadly sin
84 Hockey position
87 "___ to Win" Haas
88 Picturesque
90 Owls' college
92 What Runnymede is
94 Avian sound
96 Eppie's Marner
97 Command to Dobbin
98 Christiania now
99 ___-boy sandwich
100 "I Remember ___"
101 Greek Discordia
102 Inventor Boyden
103 Dram

67 PAVING THE WAY by Harold Counts

Harold would like to dedicate this puzzle to John Loudon McAdam.

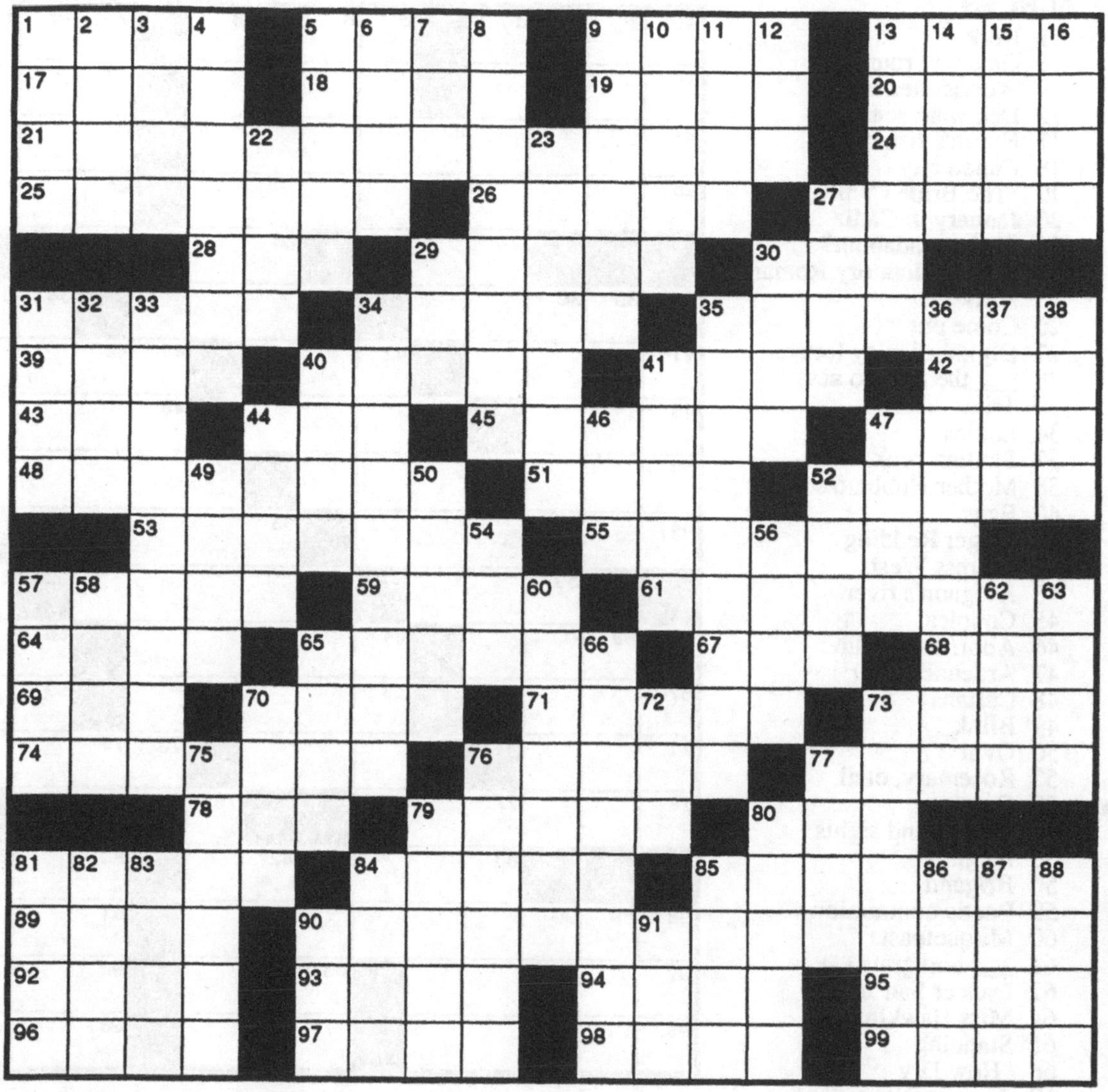

ACROSS

1 Eternal City: Ital.
5 Attend Groton
9 British experts
13 New Mexican art colony
17 Tarzan's friends
18 Hideaway
19 Part of Q.E.F.
20 Crooner Vallee
21 Exorbitant charge
24 School founded in 1440
25 Marine route
26 Tipsters
27 Germ cell
28 SAT relative
29 Penned
30 Actress Alicia
31 Avian fertilizer
34 Ushers
35 Rapid ___
39 Rarin' to go
40 Inasmuch as
41 Suffix for town
42 Prefix for angle
43 Spanish-1 verb
44 ___ of roses
45 Male peregrine
47 Test type
48 Transitions
51 Kind
52 Press ___
53 Add as a bonus
55 Marvel
57 Runner Sydney
59 Zone
61 Sad
64 Lamb
65 Vacuums
67 Middle note
68 ___-Magnon
69 Outdo
70 Home of the Blue Devils
71 Ladder rung
73 Marsh bird
74 Sonnet stanzas
76 Metrodome team
77 Succinct
78 Charlotte of TV
79 A Curtis
80 Little shaver
81 Swimming-pool part
84 Feline sounds
85 Brazilian rubber tree
89 Notion
90 Sets out
92 Came down
93 Weaken
94 Robert of the C.S.A.
95 Sooner town
96 Count (on)
97 Dies ___
98 Network of fibers
99 Retreats

DOWN

1 Bowl sounds
2 Early Howard role
3 Million: Comb. form
4 Site of Randolph-Macon College
5 Gromwell, for one
6 Wide-mouthed Martha
7 Norse healing goddess
8 Draw out
9 Openings
10 Mountain crest
11 Londoner's public houses
12 Swine confines
13 Rock-boring tool
14 Tin lizzie
15 Stench
16 Auld lang ___
22 Baylor University site
23 Baby shoes
27 Picnic, in a sense
29 O.E. runic letter
30 Seed covering
31 Catch one's breath
32 Eye part
33 Runways
34 Sale sites
35 "___ of My Tears," Johnny Rivers hit
36 Vehicle with a cowcatcher
37 Ahvaz locale
38 Slope
40 Utah's flower
41 Paper money of yore
44 In the buff
46 Gypsy boy
47 Girl watch
49 Home of 57 Down
50 Yes or no follower
52 Long for
54 Three-R's org.
56 Suited to ___
57 Amazing team
58 ___ vera
60 "Jeopardy" questions
62 Rainbow
63 Porter from Indiana
65 ___ as a button
66 Old maid
70 "___ Abby"
72 Poor rating
73 Put out to pasture
75 Ghent's claim to fame
76 Cylindrical
77 Sped
79 Friend of Fran and Ollie
80 Snicker
81 Ananias
82 Pointless
83 Young or Sedaka
84 Part of a full house
85 Let it stand!
86 Zilch
87 Improve
88 Affixes
90 Ghana native
91 "This ___ House," 1954 hit

68 NAMELY SPEAKING by Norma Steinberg

We promise there'll be plenty of chuckles once you get a *handle* on Norma's unusual theme.

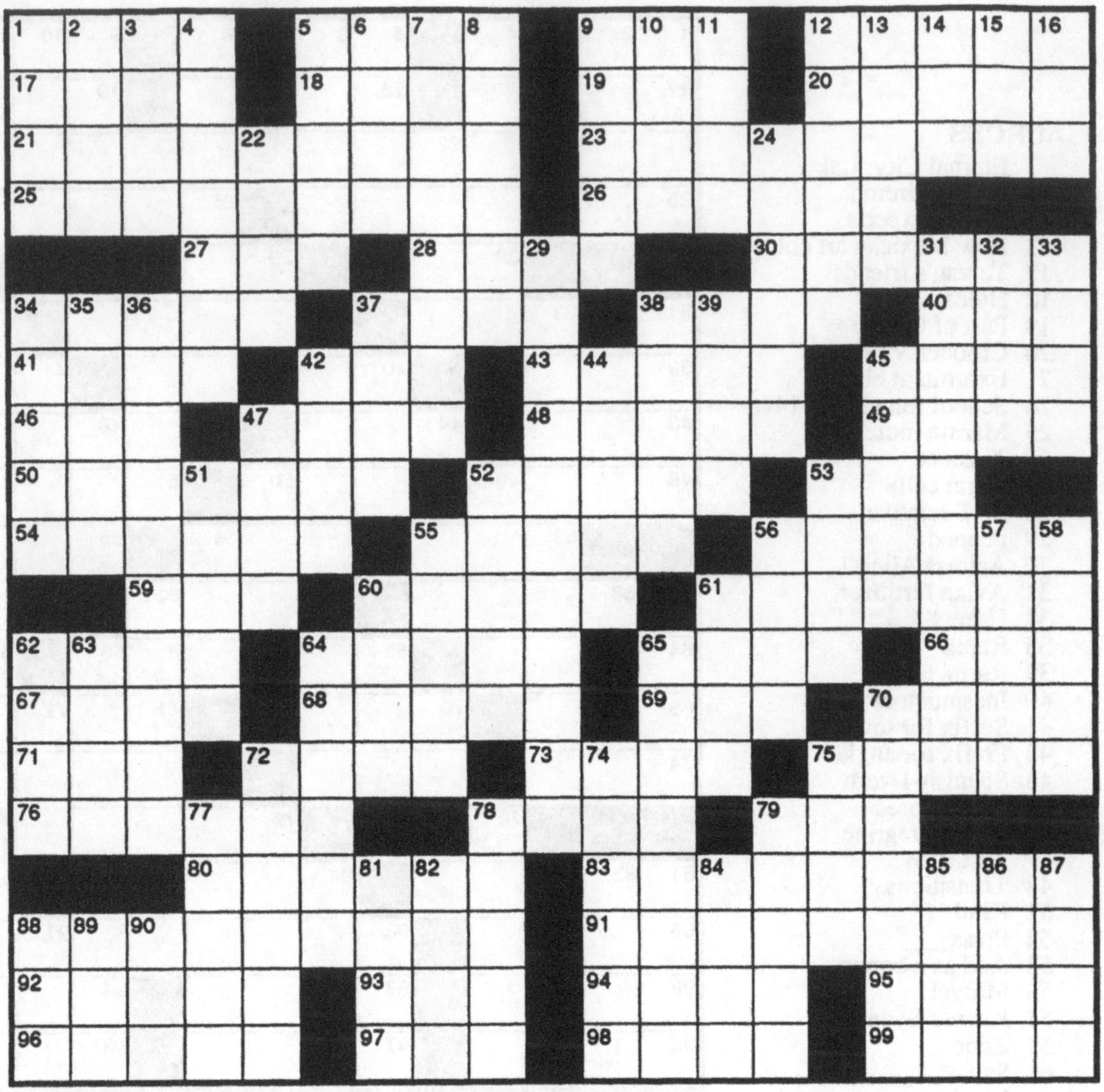

ACROSS

1 Dork
5 Go a few rounds
9 Woodcutter Baba
12 Delaware senator
17 Huron's sister
18 Cuneo city
19 "The Bride Came ___"
20 January in Cádiz
21 She's a gadabout?
23 He's a salutatory Roman?
25 Arils
26 Come out
27 Digital-display letters
28 ___ the time to act
30 Trite
34 Ladies
37 Sicilian peak
38 Mother Hubbard's quest
40 Eggs
41 Singer Redding
42 Actress West
43 Avignon's river
45 Couples
46 Abbr. on a radio
47 Ardennes river
48 Caftans
49 Blink
50 Oval
52 Rosemary, et al.
53 Quiche
54 Playground sights
55 Bright
56 Brigand
59 Poetic contraction
60 Milquetoasts
61 ___ non grata
62 Dancer San Juan
64 Miss Hawkins
65 Standing
66 "How Dry ___"
67 Actress Diana
68 Myers' Broom ___
69 Finale
70 "___ of the Thousand Days"
71 Variations ___ theme
72 Mound
73 "I ___ Stop Loving You"
75 Tattered Tom's creator
76 Stick around
78 Air: Comb. form
79 Neat's-foot ___
80 Assembles
83 Respond maniacally
88 He's good for nothing?
91 He's a New Orleans reveler?
92 Ms. Lauder
93 Minute unit of length
94 ___ time (never)
95 Jane Austen novel
96 Adolescents
97 Porcine place
98 Observed
99 Wayne ___, self-help author

DOWN

1 Makes a blouse
2 Dies ___
3 Grumpy's workplace
4 Hawks
5 Diet fare
6 Extra
7 Missing one
8 Snitches
9 Throbs
10 Rich soil
11 Stay in neutral
12 Snoopy, e.g.
13 "___ a hug!"
14 ___ Moines
15 Stat. for Hershiser
16 Computer gate
22 Serves well
24 Hags
29 He has a dual nature?
31 He wants encouragement?
32 Stratford's river
33 Chore
34 Non-belligerents
35 Bikini, e.g.
36 She's a lightweight?
37 Poise
38 He's a London policeman?
39 Singles
42 Fall short
44 Cornets
45 World Series winners: 1987
47 Sign on a door
51 Think-tank products
52 Moist
53 "MacArthur ___," Harris hit
55 Edge up to
56 Warp
57 Asinine
58 Circus star
60 Keen
61 Gasp
62 Stench
63 Solitary
64 Japanese religion
65 Redo
70 Declared without proof
72 Shards
74 Fragrances
75 Breezy
77 Gray
78 Fittingly
79 "Loot" playwright
81 Totals
82 Kind of pricing
84 Sea bird
85 Black, gold, gray team
86 It ___ to pass
87 Nicholas or Peter
88 After taxes
89 Sugar suffix
90 Noshed

69 "MIRROR, MIRROR . . ." by Joe Clonick

Joe says: "With a little reflection, you should enjoy this one."

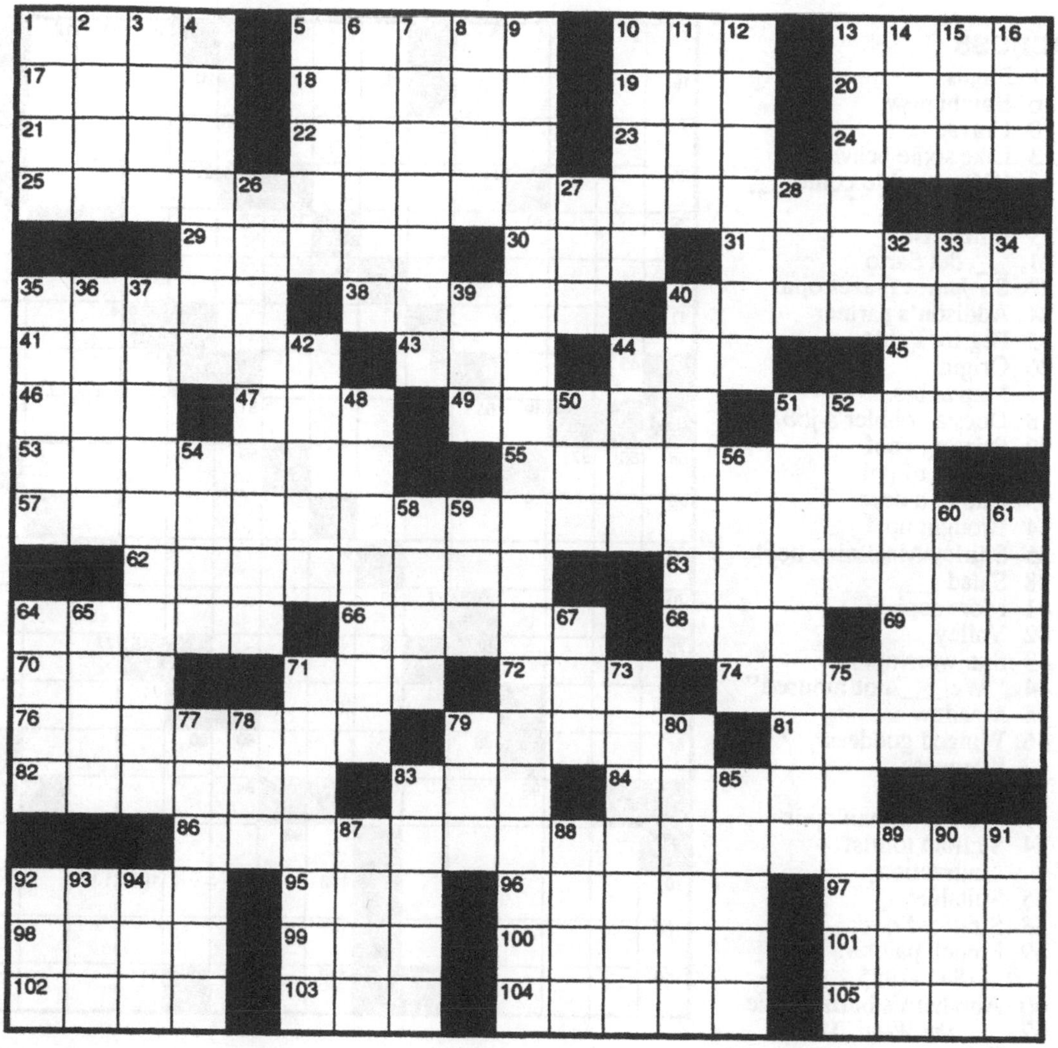

ACROSS

1 Loam or marl
5 Rustic home
10 Bethlehem's had no vacancy
13 Octagonal directive
17 Exile isle
18 On the market
19 Comment from the kine
20 It "placed" in a fabled race
21 Hebrew letter
22 CLI quintupled
23 Northern diving bird
24 Give a leg up to a hood
25 Embarrassed aviator of 1938
29 Most of us have or have had 32
30 Ovine mom
31 Man is one
35 Skewers
38 A raw deal, in seafood?
40 Mugs or chops
41 Beliefs
43 Hit sign
44 Footlike part
45 Livy's lang.
46 Jolson and Jarreau
47 Life-saving technique
49 Bucephalus or Trigger
51 L.A. air-quality hazards
53 Zipper or snap
55 Told a story
57 Justification for reciprocal action
62 Ho Chi Minh's one-time minions
63 Assess
64 Microwaves, e.g.
66 Former Red Sox pitching great Luis ___
68 Rickenbacker or von Richthofen
69 Blend
70 Skin blemish
71 Shad ___
72 A Gershwin
74 Swift antelope
76 Cryptographer
79 B-H connection
81 Unaccented parts of musical measures
82 Double-duty couch
83 Cupid's title
84 Ipso ___
86 Undergoes a negative change of fortune
92 The Censor
95 Former Rep. O'Neill
96 It sounds ap-peal-ing
97 Cat or buffalo follower
98 The Bard's river
99 Past
100 Rails
101 Earth goddess
102 Composer of *Lulu* and *Wozzeck*
103 Maritime deserter?
104 Orgs.
105 Clean a pipe

DOWN

1 O'Casey or Penn
2 Spanish pot
3 "___ mortality": Shak.
4 French pirate, Jean ___
5 Training group
6 Stylish neckwear
7 Eponymous god of drunken revelry
8 Poorly
9 Descriptive of Jacob's ladder
10 Likeness
11 It may be proper
12 Hiawatha's wise counselor
13 Ancestors of the oboe
14 Filing aid
15 Mesabi's is iron
16 Favorite
26 Spas often offer these
27 W.W. was Pres. during this
28 Ethiopian prince
32 *The Drunkard* et al.
33 Berlin's "He's ___ Picker"
34 WW II craft
35 Actor Keach
36 Alexander the Great's birthplace
37 Fiscal ruin
39 Fourth-yr. students
40 Character actress Lila
42 Diagonal spar
44 City in Illinois or Indiana
48 Nuclear-power device
50 Consume
51 Deadlock
52 List of available options for computer users
54 Whirl
56 Primitive computers
58 Pâté de ___ gras
59 Snow, to a Glaswegian
60 Serviceable
61 Where the Pedernales flows
64 Was in debt
65 ___ cava
67 Three, in Torino
71 Soviet symbol
73 Dalliances
75 Suggest; volunteer
77 Rectangle whose adjacent sides are of unequal length
78 Venus or Minerva: Lat.
79 Mounted army det.
80 Meter reader
83 Where to find "The Yankee Clipper"
85 Salad green
87 Latvian port
88 Greek letters
89 Last word heard by certain of the condemned?
90 Govt. meat stamp
91 Pretense
92 Bandleader Calloway
93 "Hail" to Caesar
94 Rocky peak

70 HIGHLY HORTICULTURAL by Jeanette Brill

Solve Jeanette's puzzle and discover what Shirley MacLaine has in common with Walt Whitman, Edna Ferber, Maxwell Anderson, and Pearl Buck.

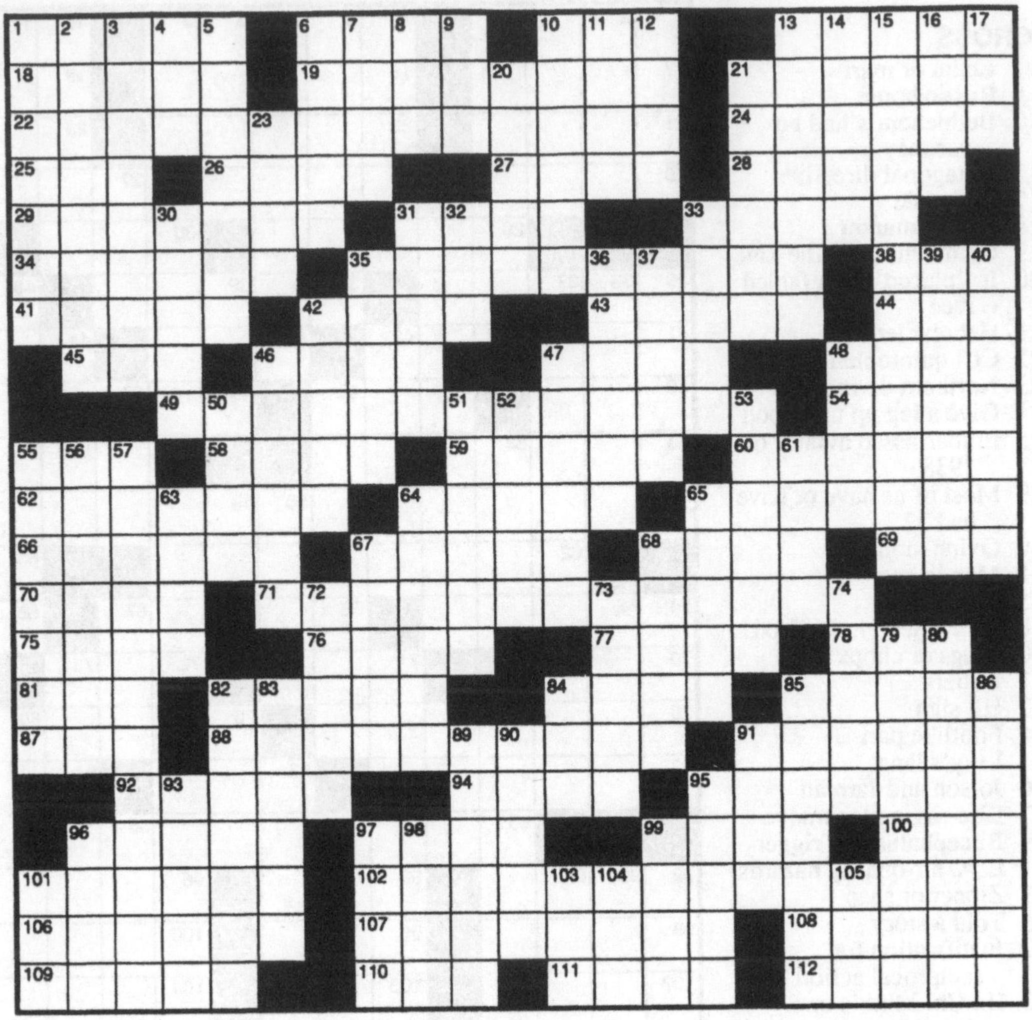

ACROSS

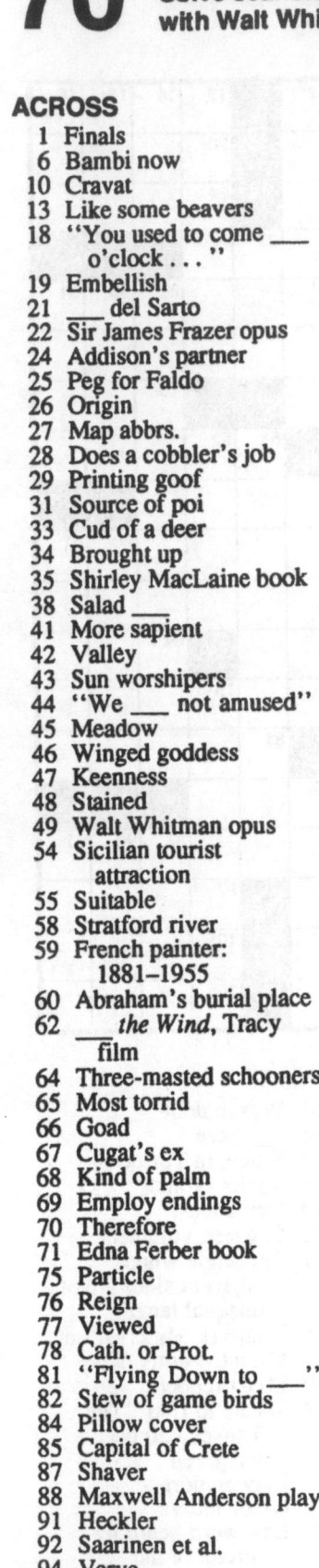

1 Finals
6 Bambi now
10 Cravat
13 Like some beavers
18 "You used to come ___ o'clock . . ."
19 Embellish
21 ___ del Sarto
22 Sir James Frazer opus
24 Addison's partner
25 Peg for Faldo
26 Origin
27 Map abbrs.
28 Does a cobbler's job
29 Printing goof
31 Source of poi
33 Cud of a deer
34 Brought up
35 Shirley MacLaine book
38 Salad ___
41 More sapient
42 Valley
43 Sun worshipers
44 "We ___ not amused"
45 Meadow
46 Winged goddess
47 Keenness
48 Stained
49 Walt Whitman opus
54 Sicilian tourist attraction
55 Suitable
58 Stratford river
59 French painter: 1881–1955
60 Abraham's burial place
62 ___ *the Wind*, Tracy film
64 Three-masted schooners
65 Most torrid
66 Goad
67 Cugat's ex
68 Kind of palm
69 Employ endings
70 Therefore
71 Edna Ferber book
75 Particle
76 Reign
77 Viewed
78 Cath. or Prot.
81 "Flying Down to ___"
82 Stew of game birds
84 Pillow cover
85 Capital of Crete
87 Shaver
88 Maxwell Anderson play
91 Heckler
92 Saarinen et al.
94 Verve
95 Campers
96 Less ruddy
97 ___ girl!
99 Sweet wine
100 Heinrich's "never"
101 Gluts
102 Enid Bagnold work
106 Manor
107 Alas!
108 Concise
109 Annealing ovens
110 Part of IRS
111 Cellist Ma
112 Aids (a felon)

DOWN

1 Rags
2 Celestial
3 Travel accommodations for the "huddled masses"
4 Two-year-old doe
5 Noisy horse
6 Gomorrah's neighbor
7 Weight allowance
8 Sothern belle
9 Rap
10 German
11 *Picnic* playwright
12 O.E. letters
13 Buries
14 Actress Jergens
15 Louis Bromfield novel, with *The*
16 Morays
17 Comical Charlotte
20 Historic castle of Havana
21 Take for granted
23 Forte: Mus.
30 Of a region
31 Marsh reeds
32 Consumed
33 Midway sights
35 "The Old ___ Bucket"
36 Gide and Agassi
37 Hoosier senator
39 Gritty
40 Russian emmets?
42 Piece of turf
46 Fleets
47 Holiday drink
48 Obligation
50 Below marquis
51 Chemical salt
52 Iron: Comb. form
53 Clavell title
55 Painting or sculpture
56 Torpor
57 Pearl Buck book
61 Collar or jacket
63 Esau
64 Comedy Muse
65 Seraglio
67 Mouse's meal
68 Lieu
72 Where Van Gogh painted
73 Pallid
74 Poisonous snake
79 Double ___
80 Most suspicious
82 Wall and Fleet
83 "My kingdom for ___"
84 Multitude
85 Bach specialty
86 Leblanc's Lupin, et al.
89 Emulate 86 Down
90 Loose
91 *Wozzeck* composer
93 "Pomp and Circumstance" composer
95 Ginza locale
96 Sit
97 Hun king
98 Word of comparison
99 Gambol
101 Set
103 Kind of fever
104 Stir
105 Mister: Yiddish

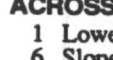

71 NEVER BORED! by Sidney L. Robbins

Whether you're world-weary or word-weary, you'll enjoy solving the puzzle below. Sidney always avoids ho-hum clues and tiresome themes.

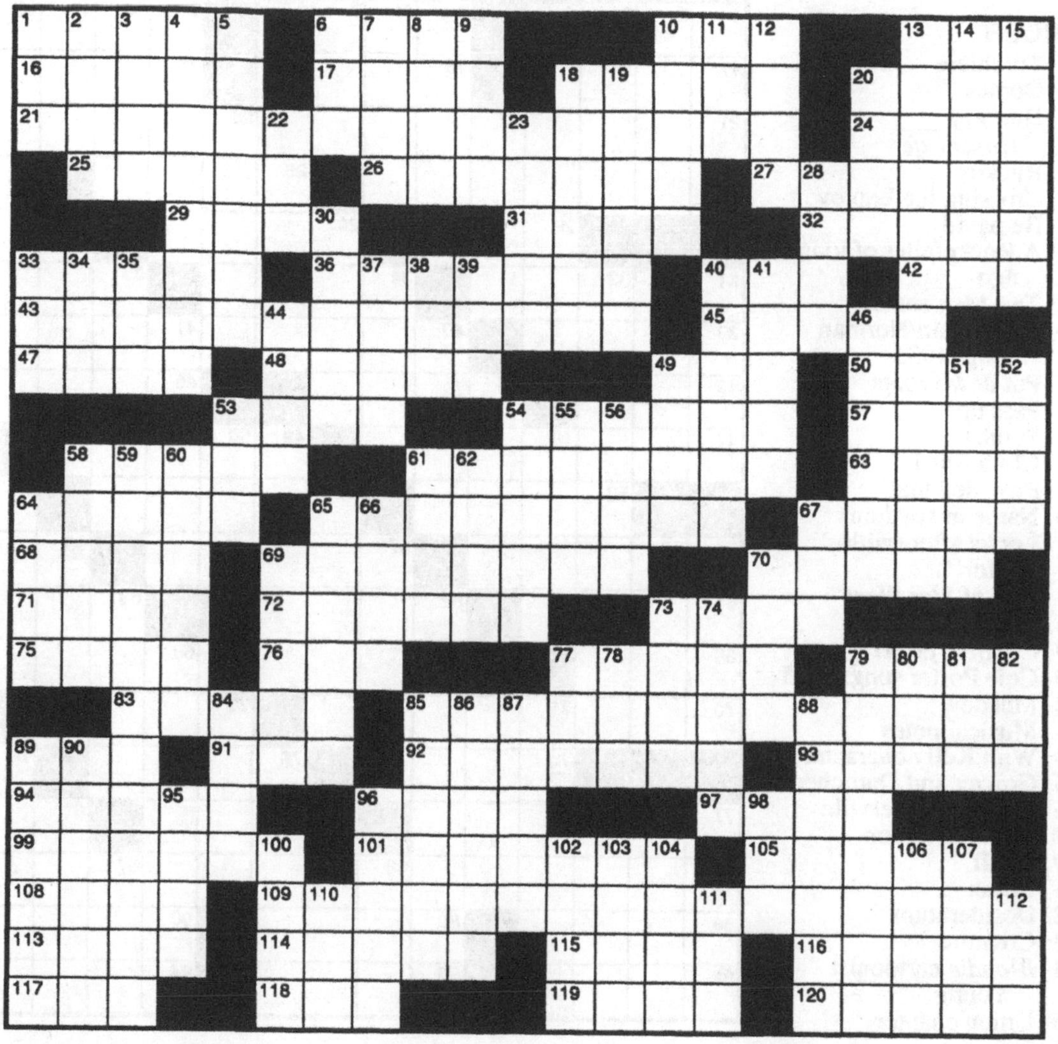

ACROSS

1 Lower
6 Slope
10 Illuminated
13 Uncooked
16 Olive-green fabric
17 Skin-cream ingredient
18 *Wall Street* director
20 Nat King or Old King
21 They get out the vote
24 Take it very easy
25 Combos
26 Wheel-rim parts
27 Embarrassed
29 Mars: Comb. form
31 Writer Wiesel
32 Reflection
33 I. W. and Walter
36 Include
40 Blocker or Marino
42 Sparks or Beatty
43 Certain exams
45 Assisted
47 Lenient
48 Polynesian of Timaru
49 Brit. mail org.
50 Capable
53 Diminish
54 Native of Columbus
57 Kind of food
58 *The Wild Duck* playwright
61 Heaven
63 Makes leather
64 Nose
65 Atlantic City sight
67 Combine
68 Add ___ of butter
69 Water holders
70 Cruciverbalists cross them
71 Encircle
72 Hard crust of skin
73 Strikebreaker
75 Notorious Marquis
76 Feasted
77 Escalator clauses
79 Beer ingredient
83 Overweight
85 Quarantine imposers
89 Landon
91 Walk down the aisle
92 Install
93 Err
94 Woodworking machine
96 Let stand
97 "The Man" of baseball
99 Poison
101 Athina Onassis, e.g.
105 Map in a map
108 Richard Roberts' dad
109 Learning group
113 Suffix for Christmas
114 Raft wood
115 Snare
116 Dance
117 Peg for Hoch
118 Sault ___ Marie
119 H. H. Munro
120 Keep your ___ the ball

DOWN

1 White robe
2 Shoe of a sort
3 Heb. month
4 How soaps are shown
5 Approve
6 Actor Vallone
7 Hebrew letter
8 Spy
9 Pare
10 Wanton
11 Hotel
12 Hardy girl
13 Bed and breakfast
14 Imply
15 Fused
18 Impassive
19 Connections
20 Bivalve
22 Chem. suffix
23 Pure
28 Female deer
30 Pacific
33 Royal-flush member
34 Constrictor
35 High ways
37 Slender woodwind
38 Neither's companion
39 Sparoid fish
40 Patterned silk or linen fabric
41 River to the Oise
44 Fed
46 Kind of bonnet or seal
49 Disturb
51 What pulmonates have
52 Otherwise
53 Anti-prohibitionist
54 Law partner
55 Goldie of the silver screen
56 Lupino and Cantor
58 Mehta's homeland once
59 Business boosters
60 Certain teenager
61 Lane
62 Region
64 Droops
65 Thrashed
66 Third of thrice
67 Crowd
69 Desist
70 Scrub
73 Place for a slug
74 Bistros
77 Computer terminal
78 Harem room
79 Chief support
80 Smith and Capone
81 Pal of Inc.
82 Shortened conj.
84 Pitcher
85 Chewers
86 Syracuse's lake
87 Jetsons' dog
88 Flow out
89 "Little Men" author
90 Sweet Annie
95 American hero of 1776
96 Laminated rock
98 Spasm
100 Declines
102 Newts
103 Antitoxins
104 Pierre loc.
106 One to Von Hindenberg
107 Ghana's neighbor
110 Kind of meal
111 Wire service
112 Negative prefix

72

SYNCOPATED SONGS by William Lutwiniak
We suspect that our Maryland master-puzzler dreamed up this one while playing cassettes and consuming alphabet soup.

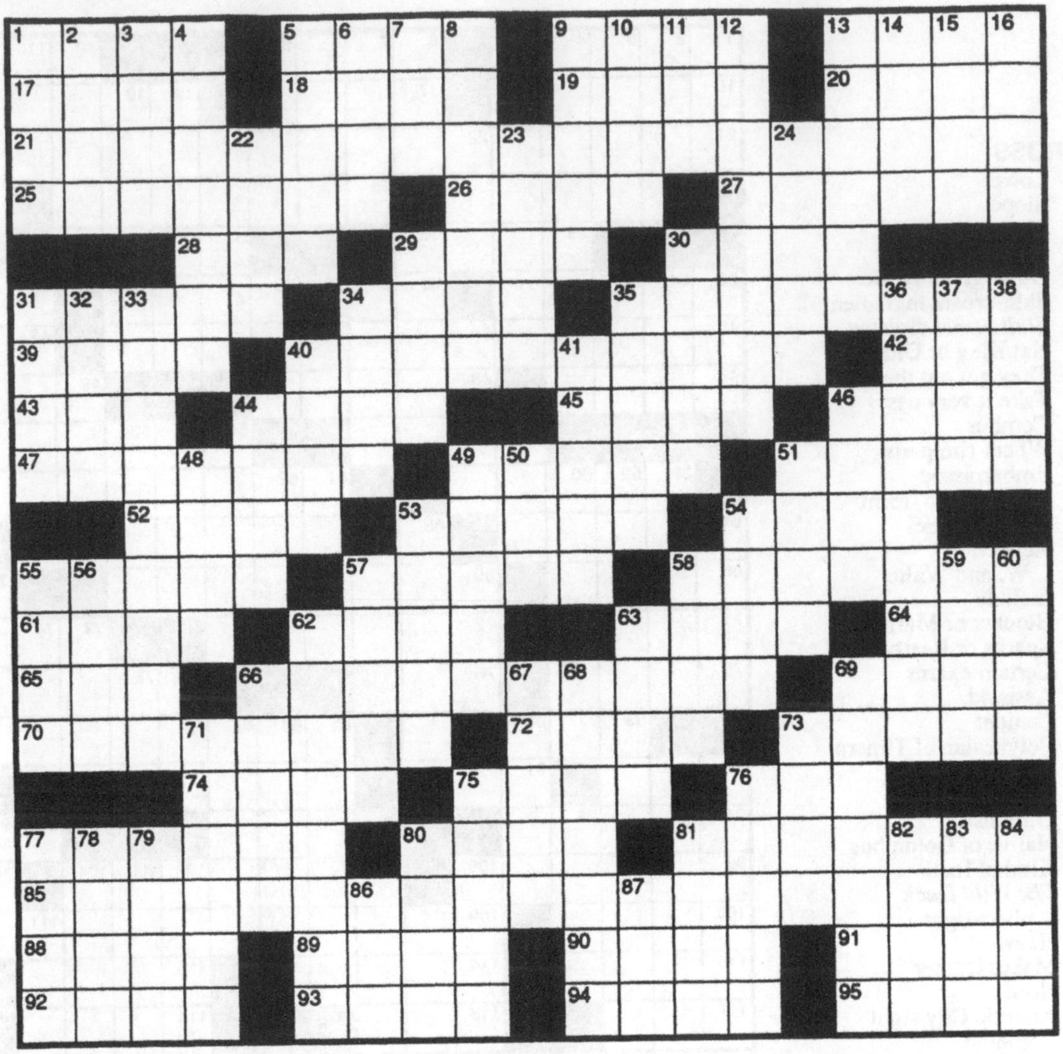

ACROSS
1 Torchière
5 Oodles
9 *Diary of ___ Housewife*
13 Ruckus
17 Crossing the Laptev
18 Be pavid
19 A Rockefeller of long ago
20 Tex-Mex snack
21 Kahal/Fain/Norman song: 1931
25 Put down roots
26 Pass up
27 Scrubs
28 Cloth finish
29 Provided that
30 Name in spydom
31 Looks after (with "for")
34 Han of *Star Wars*
35 Potter's field
39 Creative effort
40 Cole Porter song: 1935
42 Meadow
43 Musical notes
44 Walt Kelly character
45 Gorcey and Durocher
46 Actor Summerville
47 Neptune's prop
49 Quaff
51 Co-ax
52 Desideratum
53 Creature
54 *Blondie* cartoonist Young
55 Union chapter
57 Jargon
58 Netmen on ice
61 Kick off
62 Odium
63 Commotion
64 Tweak
65 Patriotic org.
66 Blackwell/Presley song: 1956
69 Scarebabe
70 "The signs of ___" (St. Matthew)
72 Transudation
73 Aligned
74 Ever so long
75 Highland hillside
76 Jet-engine housing
77 Noted Roman jurist
80 Electrified particles
81 Former president of Chile
85 Kahn/Brown song: 1940
88 "Nana" star
89 Functions
90 Pizzazz
91 Actress Anderson
92 Party VIP
93 Like Felix Unger
94 Scoot
95 Dixmude's river

DOWN
1 Capitol output
2 Name in Wimbledon lore
3 Come across
4 Lingerie item
5 Out to get
6 Prized part
7 Cerris or durmast
8 Organ device
9 Chasm
10 Playwright Hart
11 ___ Dhabi, eastern land
12 Light, two-wheeled vehicles
13 Flow
14 Ciao
15 Likeness
16 Goes bad
22 ___ du Vent
23 Tabby's word
24 Mountains of Asia
29 NYC section
30 Forget-___
31 Indianapolis athlete
32 On ___ with (as good as)
33 Wayne Walker song: 1957
34 Army NCO
35 B-H fill-in
36 Kahal/Fain song: 1938
37 Provide overhead
38 Consubstantial
40 "___ Cassius has a lean . . ."
41 Grassy plain in S America
44 Strip off
46 Jib
48 *East of Eden* star
49 Star in Cygnus
50 Horse and carriage
51 Wight
53 Deck posts
54 Coke source
55 Forfeited
56 Brightly-colored fish
57 Kegler's milieu
58 Jollity
59 Shamrock-land
60 Hotfooted it
62 Unpretentious
63 Detonator
66 Unearth
67 Horn
68 Cooked, as chestnuts
69 Neat
71 Star quality
73 Blabbed
75 Leg up
76 Mill
77 Propel
78 Respecting
79 Salt Lake City team
80 Start of a patent
81 In the offing
82 Modernists
83 Jutlander
84 Dubai VIP
86 Chi-Richmond dir.
87 Pay chaser

73 SOBRIQUETS by James R. Burns

One of the Bay State's best puzzlers has assembled all sorts of nicknames for your pleasure.

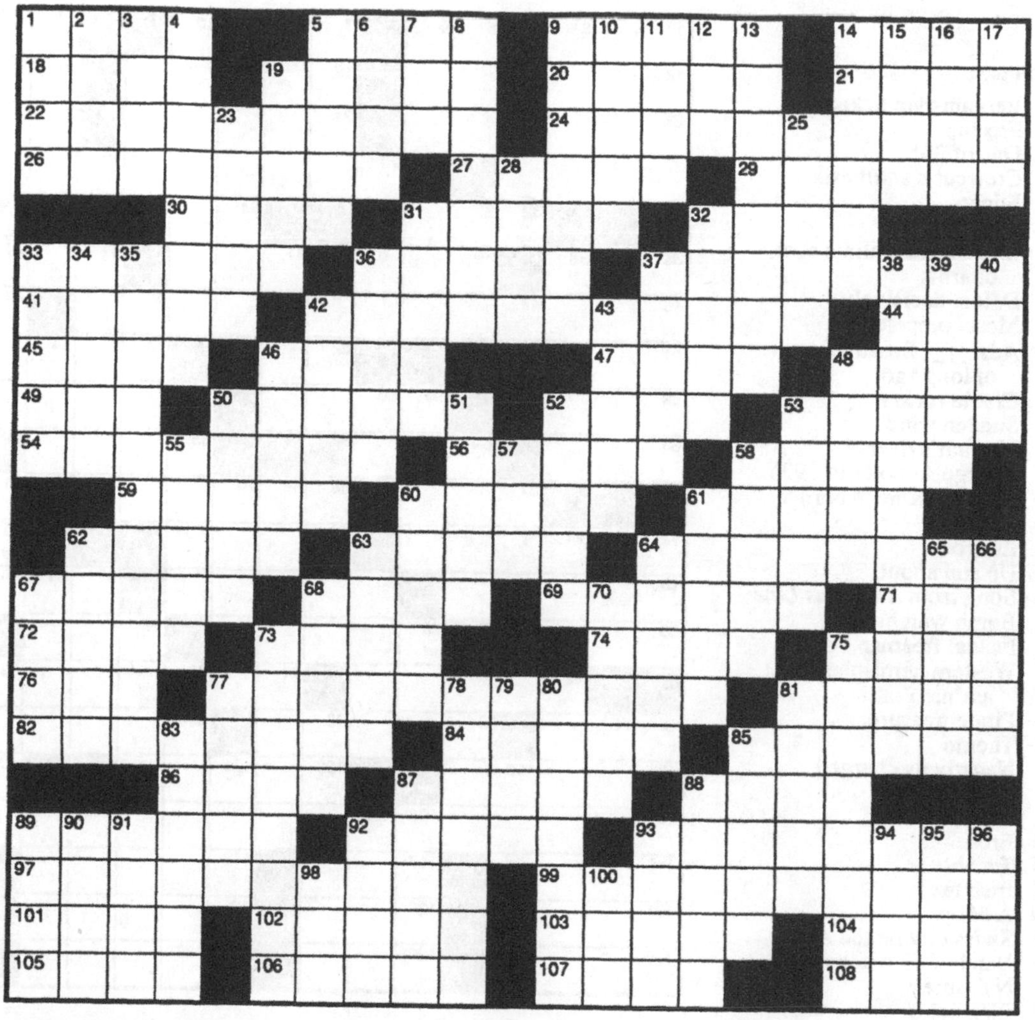

ACROSS

1 Israeli premier: 1969–1974
5 Inclined way
9 Mention (with "to")
14 *Moonstruck* Oscar winner
18 Celtic language
19 Setting for *Rain*
20 Typewriter type style
21 First-class
22 Characterization of Hollywood
24 Nickname of US general Stilwell
26 Colonize or become established
27 Southwest New York city
29 Innumerable
30 Actor Ray
31 Bandies words (with)
32 Author-Nobelist Wiesel
33 Pan-fries
36 Healing ointments
37 Like the runt of a litter
41 Airs
42 Characterization of postwar generation
44 "Long March" leader
45 Bright lights
46 Rhode Island's senior senator
47 Cub Scout groups
48 Breton, for instance
49 Four qts.
50 Two or three pointer
52 Forward
53 What grumpy ones are out of
54 Ennobles
56 Undisguised
58 Incursion
59 Like a healthy dog's nose
60 Homes for shoats
61 Type of golf competition
62 Fatuous
63 Bundle
64 Pertaining to armorial bearings
67 Does a haying job
68 Shed weight
69 Turns one's nose up at
71 Win ___ walk
72 Tritons
73 Painful cry
74 San ___ Obispo, California
75 D-day vessels
76 Maui garland
77 Nickname for an early Rolls-Royce
81 Thin slice
82 Bridges of a sort
84 Obliterate
85 Threadlike cotton pieces
86 Slippery ones
87 Rachis
88 Part of the "handwriting on the wall"
89 Nonacid
92 Results (from)
93 Hash houses
97 Characterization of a Western
99 Epithet for Satan
101 Exchange premium
102 Actor Bruce
103 *A ___ of Sundays*: Updike book
104 Zhivago's beloved
105 Navy petty officer
106 Hornswoggles
107 Watering spots
108 "Other side of the tracks," often

DOWN

1 They play at Shea
2 Tribe whose name means "Long Tail"
3 "___ It Romantic?": 1932 song
4 Paraphrases
5 Proportion
6 Egyptian deity
7 Haystack
8 Complete suit of armor
9 Lefthand book page: Var.
10 Elijah in the New Testament
11 Sawyer's pal
12 It follows printemps
13 First stringers
14 OPEC, for instance
15 Nickname of a motel chain
16 Chemical organic compound
17 Subject of *Reds*
19 Pungs or luges
23 Plural French pronoun
25 Purple dyes
28 Symbol of meekness
31 Much coveted fur
32 Correct
33 Put on
34 Pertaining to hearing
35 Cognomen for the first TV superstar
36 Pitching faults
37 Small food fish
38 Affectionate term for Ireland
39 Brackish
40 Moppets
42 Troubled
43 Perfumes
46 Fall guy
48 Kind of reef or snake
50 Dips out
51 Pagan image
52 Gripes
53 Fountain orders
55 Short-tailed rodents
57 By way of
58 Seedless plants
60 Stand out
61 Deserve
62 TV's Morley
63 Croats and Slovenes
64 Theater audience
65 Bury
66 Plaster models
67 Karate award
68 Does a cobbling job
70 Glenn of films
73 *Marco ___*: O'Neill play
75 Britain's Gladstone and followers
77 Stone pillar
78 Abrogates
79 Unrelenting
80 Holmes and Watson often hailed these
81 More elegant
83 Add spice to
85 Command to Fido
87 Scatter about
88 Tall Ships features
89 Ishmael's skipper
90 Corporate symbol
91 Actor Kristofferson
92 Kind of lily
93 Poet Millay
94 Printing type: Abbr.
95 Shade of brown
96 Counterfeit
98 Defeat at wrestling
100 Cut off

74 A NUMBER OF NUMBERS by Irene Smullyan

Every cardinal number from 1 to 10 is hidden below—and then some! It adds up to a remarkable effort.

ACROSS

1 Bargain-rate ticket
7 Freebie
11 One of 365
14 Crewcut's antithesis
18 Flight
19 The first
21 Bird on Australia's coat of arms
22 Defeat decisively
23 Most competent
24 Ada ___, Broadway star of long ago
25 Cradle rocker
26 Sudden wind
27 Munich's river
28 George Abbott hit: 1935
32 Chinese-Korean border river
34 Lustrous
35 Up and about
36 Song from *A Chrous Line*
39 Bomb weight unit
42 Feudal freeman
45 Western hemisphere ass'n.
46 Pirate treasure
49 Theme
51 Negatively charged particle
52 Gov't subsidy
53 Erose
55 Terrible
58 Irish tax
59 A Marx
61 Swiss city on the Aar
62 Band of 13 witches
63 NY time
64 Pine pal
65 Member of the House of Lords
66 Nutritious tubers
67 Offering on Mt. Sinai
72 Spent
75 Cult god of ancient Israel
76 Sign of the Zodiac
77 Lard
80 Floppy
81 Expenses
82 African fox
84 Cold Adriatic wind
85 Defile
86 Prefix for more than two
87 Doctors' org.
88 Cause of a sore tummy, often
89 Blacksnake
91 Short gig
95 Gratuity
97 Mountain nymph
99 Artists' oil
100 Secular
101 ___ Gay (Hiroshima, Aug. 8, 1945)
103 Portuguese ladies
105 Envelop
107 Disorganized
112 Tabula ___
116 Pocket bread
117 Hiatus
118 Essence
119 Passageway to Hades
121 One-tenth of an ephah
122 Creative skill
123 St. ___ in the Leewards
124 Joggers' kin
125 Salts
126 Prof. degree
127 "___ la vie!"
128 Combining form used with "year" or "week"

DOWN

1 Worshipper in a wat
2 Spun materials
3 Dakota Indian: Abbr.
4 Ablaze
5 Bitter vetch
6 Toys or noise
7 Immature salmon
8 On the sheltered side
9 Nasal bone
10 Embarrassing
11 Passé: Fr.
12 Fourteenth king of Judah
13 City on the Colorado River
14 Hundred-eyed monster
15 Tea time, for some
16 Where Muscovites live
17 Aquatic carnivores
20 Dill of the Bible
29 Author of *Les Misérables*
30 Blinked
31 MP's injunction
33 Verily
36 Fast
37 Dressed to the ___
38 Rational believer, such as Paine
40 At a distance
41 Linden tree
43 Portent
44 Reagan or Hubbard
47 Variety of lettuce
48 Wife of Menelaus
50 Adored ones
54 Time in office
56 Fabric for ties
57 Two make an em
59 Cattle, to Cowper
60 Curved line
61 Semiprecious stones
62 Third century author
64 Grand party
66 Dirk of yore
67 Edison contemporary
68 Ancient Greek coin
69 Extinct mammal
70 Morning prayer
71 Bx. transit
72 Gnome
73 Egg-___-yong
74 Cronyn-Tandy hit; (with *The*)
77 Pivotal
78 Scene of action
79 Dilatory
81 Salt or smoke
82 Former dictator of Uganda
83 Loses muscle tone
84 Short-order favorite
86 *La* ___, Debussy composition
87 Cordial
88 Pharm. monitor
90 Blandish
92 Flexible
93 Chopped down
94 With succinctness
95 Souchong receptacle
96 Artery lining
98 Fits
102 They need good memories
104 U.S. state where Peggy Lee was born
106 Private schools for short
108 Major Hoople's expletive
109 Chalcedony
110 Tuns
111 Formerly, formerly
113 Encourage, as a criminal
114 Word of assent
115 Pol. subdivision of former USSR
120 Caviar

75 FRENCH BRED by Lois Sidway

A notable Gallic gathering is assembled below. We're sure you'll say, "Tres bien, Lois!"

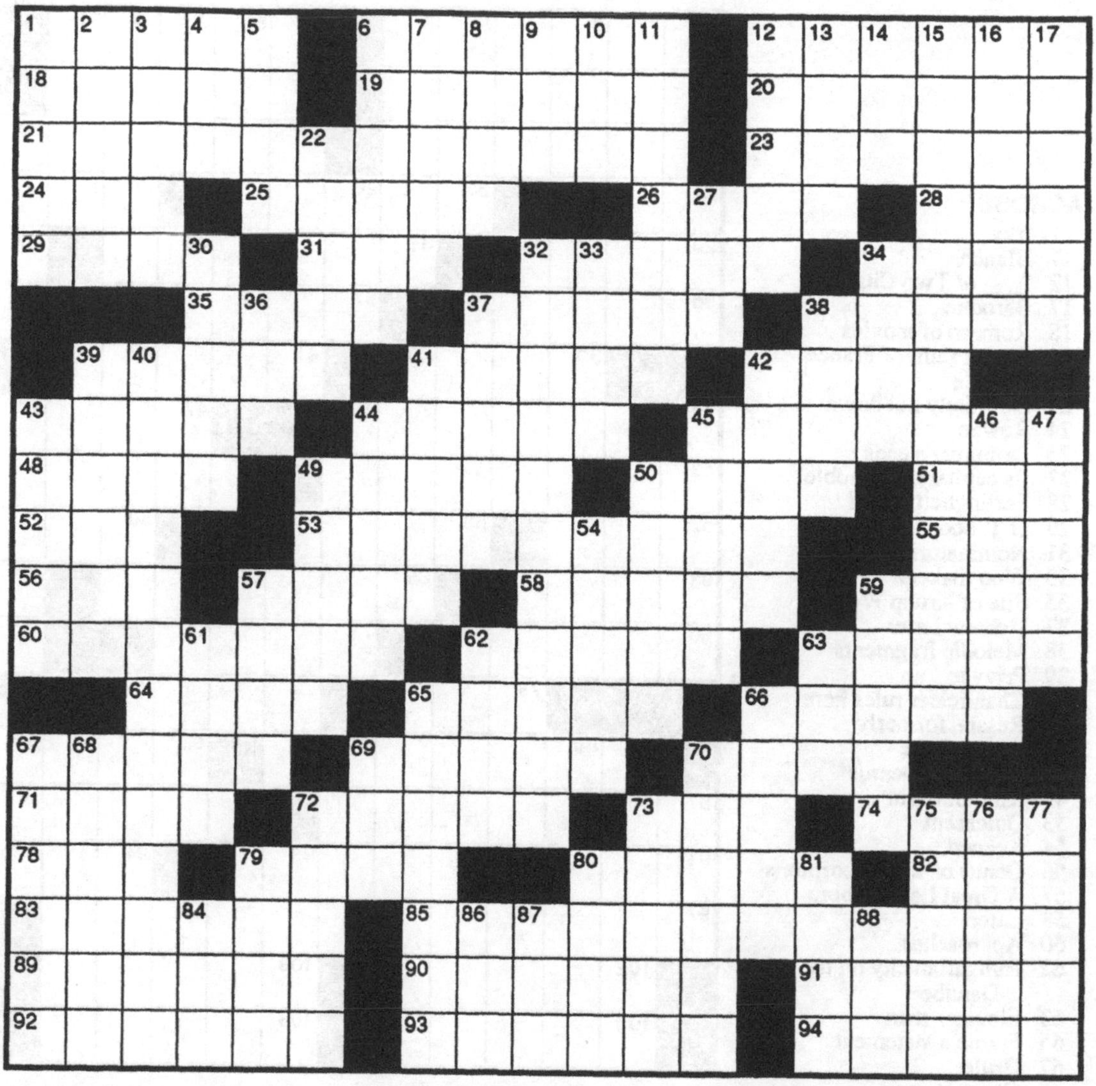

ACROSS

1 Henry ___ Lodge
6 Tarkington lad
12 ___ over (discussed at length)
18 God, to Fahd
19 Ebb
20 Stick
21 "Bolero" composer
23 Singer-actress Durbin
24 Foe of the Kiowa
25 Capital of Bulgaria
26 Atop
28 Incarnadine
29 Mtg.
31 Neck shape
32 Joshua or Ella
34 City on the Arno
35 Row
37 French painter of men and machines
38 "Ouch! That ___!"
39 Chic
41 Snooped
42 Quasimodo's creator
43 Some Kentucky babes
44 Arthur Conan ___
45 Pause in a line of verse
48 Purchasing power in 34 Across
49 An Iranian religion
50 Fuddy-duddy
51 Patriotic org.
52 Curve
53 Paul Muni portrayed this French hero
55 Alistair of filmdom
56 Golly!
57 "___ a Kick Out of You"
58 Burgundy, e.g.
59 Chilean coin
60 Popular dessert base
62 N California county
63 Aptitude
64 Appearance
65 Donkey
66 Wernher von ___ of NASA fame
67 Enchant
69 Sycophant's phrase
70 "Cheese!" product
71 Outside: Fr.
72 The ___ the moon
73 "Bali ___"
74 Pillow cover
78 Company closing
79 Crosby's roadshows co-star
80 Film family name
82 Historic period
83 Ogle lasciviously
85 "The Kiss" is his creation
89 O.T. prophet
90 A Wild West merchant
91 Assistants
92 Short and chunky
93 What every dog will have
94 Unexcited and bored

DOWN

1 Algerian-born existentialist
2 Having wings
3 Jazz style
4 Paddle's cousin
5 "Now hear ___!"
6 Opt for
7 Unearthly
8 Univ. sports watchdog
9 Gun one's engine
10 Lyric poem
11 Flooded
12 Wore
13 Arabian Sea gulf
14 ___ Na Na, entertainment group
15 Paris customs official who turned primitive
16 Actor Borgnine
17 ___ a doornail
22 Long for enviously
27 Norm, for Greg Norman
30 No longer fresh
32 Thank heaven for this French actress
33 Pointed arch
34 Wrinkle-faced little dogs
36 U.S. revenue agency
37 Supportive
38 "Kingfish"
39 Evening affair
40 Silent star of the French stage
41 Describing a fine pitching game
42 Viking of the comics
43 Actress Fannie
44 Leipzig ladies
45 "Mission: Impossible" has one
46 Dried grape
47 Knight suit
49 Initiate
50 Case for loose papers
54 Masked hero of fiction
57 News bit
59 Schemes
61 Tunes
62 Conductor Riccardo
63 Part of TGIF
65 Under
66 Zsa Zsa, often
67 Tex-Mex recipes
68 Really!
69 Cartographer's creation
70 Lancaster role
72 What cedar chests shouldn't be
73 Contemporary of 89 Across
75 Hopper of Hollywood
76 Zodiacal sign
77 Parsonage
79 Maya calendar year
80 Bugs's adversary, Elmer ___
81 Yamani, for one
84 Tease
86 Psychic Geller
87 Highway sign
88 Medium for Monet

76 ON THE UP AND UP by Martha J. Dewitt

Here's a bundle of cheers from a puzzler revered by her peers.

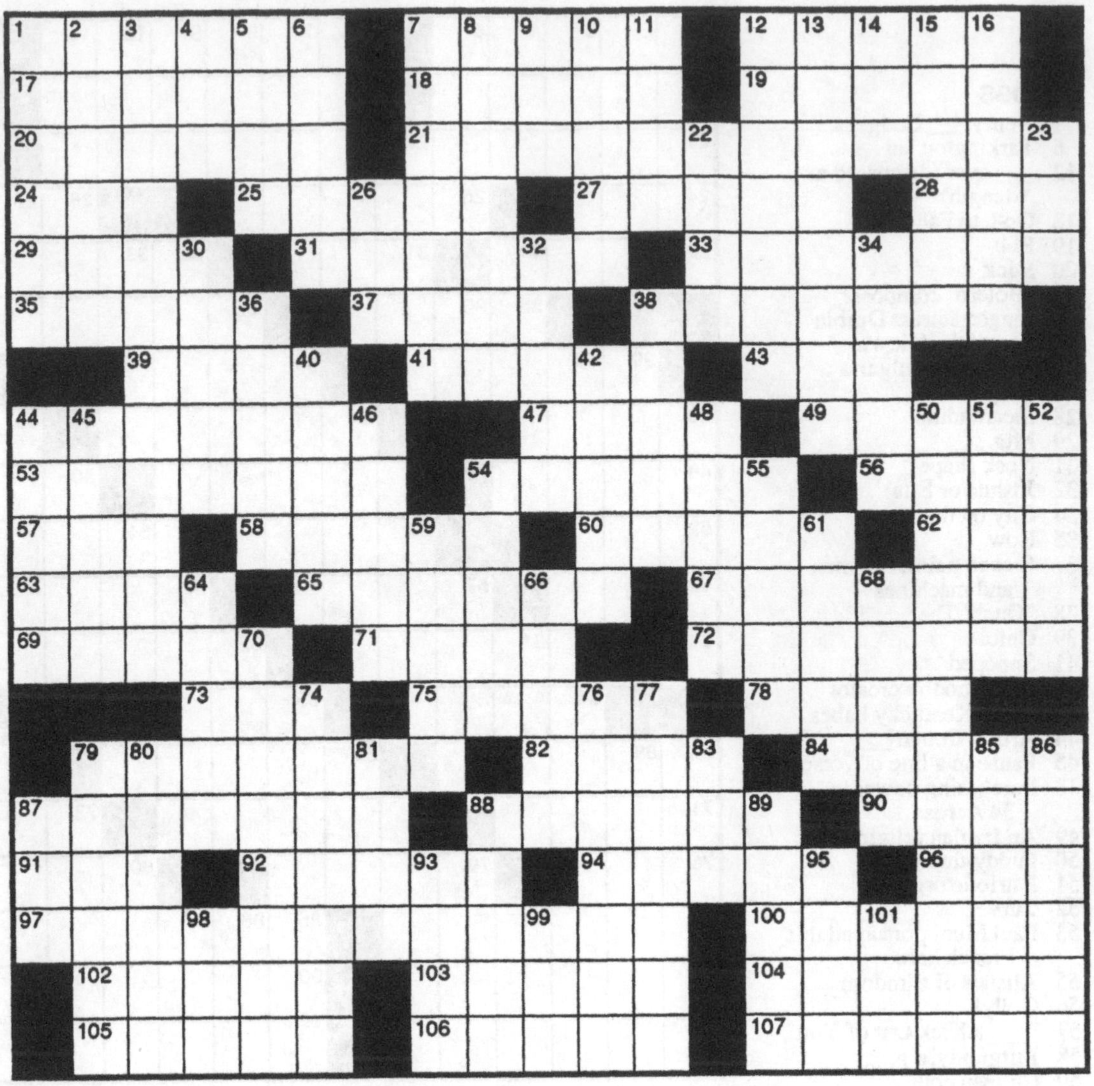

ACROSS

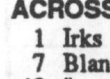

1 Irks
7 Blanch
12 "___ of Two Cities"
17 Baroque
18 Romero of movies
19 Patron saint of France
20 Feltlike
21 Definitely not down
24 Rowan
25 Drummer's ends
27 Its capital is Grenoble
28 Ferlinghetti novel
29 O.T. book
31 Nominators
33 Woo makers
35 Site of Krupp Works
37 Hebrew letter
38 Melodic fragments
39 Privy to
41 Chanticleer rules here
43 Russia, formerly
44 Disseminate
47 Doris and Dennis
49 Kind of basin
53 Quiescent
54 Keened
56 Genus of water scorpions
57 A Great Lake: Abbr.
58 Later
60 Approaches
62 Hungarian city on the Danube
63 Elevator man
65 Frame a statement
67 Grille
69 Concentrate
71 Josip Broz
72 Hollywood hopeful
73 Sniggle
75 Graph
78 Thailand, formerly
79 British soldier at Bunker Hill
82 Antitoxins
84 Apollo's Roman sister
87 Kind of delivery
88 Join a meeting
90 Russian UN vote, often
91 Baba or Pasha
92 Intent, in Ayr
94 Was loose-tongued
96 Saw
97 Definitely not down
100 Tie an artery
102 Zola
103 Aesop's point
104 Accustoms
105 Kind of butterfly
106 Growing outward
107 Abandon

DOWN

1 Ointment
2 Deles
3 Definitely not down
4 Tun
5 Summers, in Soissons
6 Family car
7 Cabal participant
8 "___ ask what the morrow will bring" (Horace)
9 Uraeus
10 Latin stone
11 Volstead's followers
12 Worshippers
13 Popular media means
14 Babylonian god
15 Reindeer moss
16 Serpentine glacial ridges
22 Polite bloke
23 Time periods: Abbr.
26 Can. peninsula
30 Camp units
32 Valerie Harper role
34 Sungari River port
36 Away
38 Milady's interest
40 Under no circumstances
42 Holy one
44 Hoax
45 Ezra Pound poem division
46 Dampen again
48 Signets
50 Definitely not down
51 Fast
52 Crochet trimming
54 Spleen
55 Mild oaths
59 Ukase
61 Decorous
64 Supple leather
66 Move easily
68 Retinue
70 In a clandestine way
74 One with a strong aversion
76 Back off
77 Trolley platform
79 Depends (on)
80 Puzzle
81 Der ___, Adenauer
83 Sothern or Rutledge
85 Asexual
86 Substantiate
87 Eight pts.
88 Science of flight: Abbr.
89 Distributed
93 Unconvincing
95 Novena number
98 Clobber
99 La-la beginner
101 Entertainer Edwards

77 FIRE WHEN READY by Patterson Pepple

A clever constructor from Columbus has discovered a new way to call the shots.

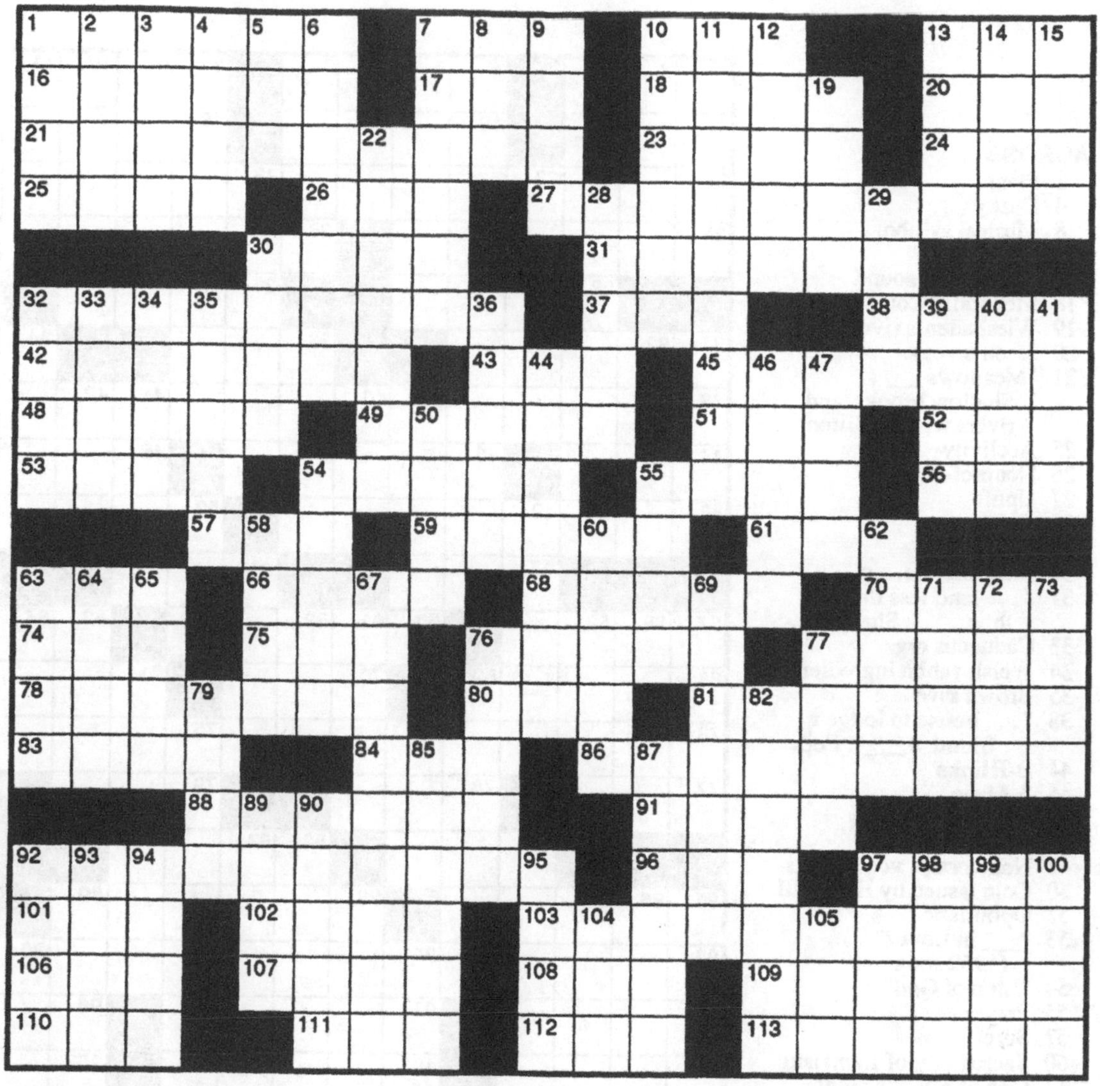

ACROSS

1 Fire a hypocrite
7 Blithe
10 W. F. Halsey, e.g.
13 Popular Boston fish
16 Macho Parisian dance
17 Past
18 Container for medicine
20 Beer's cousin
21 Fired a bill collector
23 Concerning
24 Sales agt.
25 Feline, make a beeline!
26 B-F connection
27 Uproar
30 A memorable Huntley
31 Early rustlers' come-uppances
32 Fired a lawyer
37 Ohio - Ill. neighbor
38 Grill a rare T-bone
42 Deductively
43 Summer time in NYC
45 Cuffed glove: Var. sp.
48 Rule
49 Roof parts
51 Lamb's dam
52 "Roses ___ red . . . "
53 Do followers
54 Like a leaky faucet
55 Holland cheese
56 Dreamland
57 With 103 Across, fired an anti-racist
59 Radiant
61 Hijack
63 Charisse of Hollywood
66 Baseboard
68 Holey pan
70 Highland girl
74 Latin I word
75 P.G.A. position
76 Stupid
77 Pentateuch
78 "For Whom ___ Tolls": Hemingway
80 Pindar opus
81 Trout feature
83 Poet Teasdale
84 Eastern league
86 Fired a printer
88 Form of rock'n'roll
91 He has his pride
92 Fire a sorceress
96 Dancer Miller
97 Beginner for phone or prompter
101 Author John ___ Passos
102 Biz letter wd.
103 See 57 Across
106 Powerful explosive
107 Require
108 Repent
109 Selective angler's activity
110 Swed. airline
111 N.F.L. goals
112 Omega
113 Fire a cryptanalyst

DOWN

1 Pops
2 C. B. De Mille specialty
3 Pedro's pad
4 C.P.A.
5 Sabres' org.
6 Pedagogue
7 Haploid cell
8 Vital statistic
9 Hebrew letter
10 Catalina Island town
11 Fired an innkeeper
12 Hari's namesakes
13 Reiner or Sandburg
14 Bread spread
15 With 41 Down, fired a vintner
19 Ear part
22 "___ them still": Shak.
28 Motel sections
29 Adjut.
30 Plant bud
32 Black tern
33 Fencing foil
34 Where the cup runneth over
35 Inflexible
36 Old Scratch
39 Panache
40 Gas: Comb. form
41 See 15 Down
44 Fired a model
46 On the qui vive
47 Verne's captain
50 Jason's command
54 "And cried ___!": Coleridge
55 Observes
58 Loaf
60 ___ and dined
62 Voting coalitions
63 Hit musical
64 Jewish youth org.
65 "A speaker of words and a ___ of deeds ": Iliad
67 Fired an electrician
69 Waspish
71 Clumsy craft
72 Shopper stopper
73 Lean-to
76 Senior group member
77 Harold of comics
79 Paul Bunyan's blue ox
82 Like a fork
85 Food
87 Joyful
89 ___ even keel
90 Group of eight
92 Pesticides: Abbr.
93 Inner Hebrides Island
94 JFK speedsters
95 Radial, e.g.
97 Nursery powder
98 Cause: Comb. form
99 Afford temporarily
100 Win narrowly
104 Buoy or sister
105 Female ruff

78

FLOWERY VERSE by Avery P. Bromfield

Poets from four different centuries are represented below. The editor is responsible for the clue at 65 Down.

ACROSS

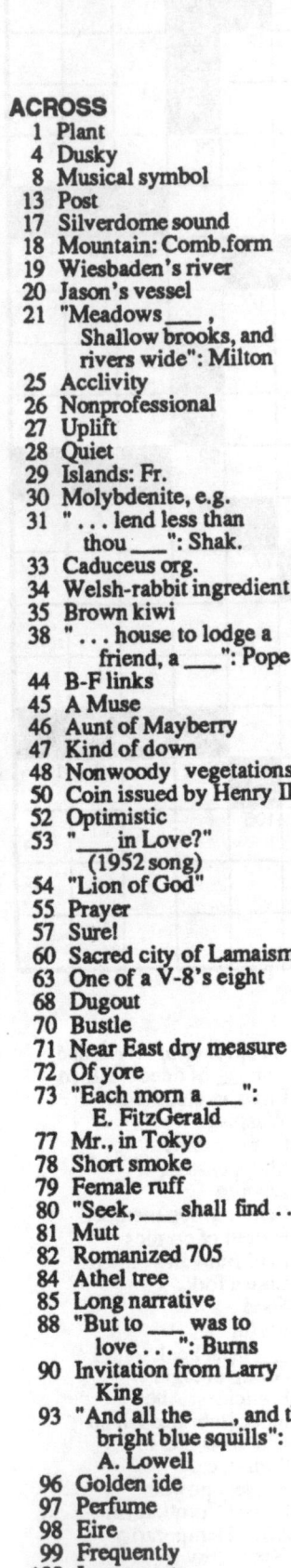

1 Plant
4 Dusky
8 Musical symbol
13 Post
17 Silverdome sound
18 Mountain: Comb.form
19 Wiesbaden's river
20 Jason's vessel
21 "Meadows ___, Shallow brooks, and rivers wide": Milton
25 Acclivity
26 Nonprofessional
27 Uplift
28 Quiet
29 Islands: Fr.
30 Molybdenite, e.g.
31 ". . . lend less than thou ___": Shak.
33 Caduceus org.
34 Welsh-rabbit ingredient
35 Brown kiwi
38 ". . . house to lodge a friend, a ___": Pope
44 B-F links
45 A Muse
46 Aunt of Mayberry
47 Kind of down
48 Nonwoody vegetations
50 Coin issued by Henry III
52 Optimistic
53 "___ in Love?" (1952 song)
54 "Lion of God"
55 Prayer
57 Sure!
60 Sacred city of Lamaism
63 One of a V-8's eight
68 Dugout
70 Bustle
71 Near East dry measure
72 Of yore
73 "Each morn a ___": E. FitzGerald
77 Mr., in Tokyo
78 Short smoke
79 Female ruff
80 "Seek, ___ shall find . . ."
81 Mutt
82 Romanized 705
84 Athel tree
85 Long narrative
88 "But to ___ was to love . . .": Burns
90 Invitation from Larry King
93 "And all the ___, and the bright blue squills": A. Lowell
96 Golden ide
97 Perfume
98 Eire
99 Frequently
100 Loom parts
101 Burnsides, e.g.
102 Moves heavily
103 We: Latin

DOWN

1 Madrid Ms.
2 Trireme sights
3 Any one that
4 With the current
5 One of the 3 R's: Abbr.
6 Soak flax
7 Chancellor Schmidt's successor
8 Wild goose
9 Announce the hour
10 Bonet and Eichhorn
11 Blue-grape pigment
12 Charge
13 "The ___ Leaf Forever"
14 Melody
15 "___ the drift"
16 Rich source
22 Verdun's river
23 Japanese feudal baron
24 Unclouded
30 Violinist Bull
31 Abbr. on some tickets
32 Far and ___
33 Measures: Abbr.
34 Gland: Comb. form
35 Refurbish
36 Bucks
37 Thirsty, once
39 Potter's clay
40 Inventor's monogram
41 Rock shelter
42 American caricaturist
43 Temptress
49 Marshy inlet
50 Neighbor of Ga.
51 Sanborn's Chase
54 Old Hebrew instrument
56 Tremors
57 Fall mos.
58 Proboscis monkey
59 Soon
61 Dangle
62 Annex
63 Manitoba tribe
64 Furlong's 220: Abbr.
65 Flower for a foppish celebrity?
66 Like Humpty
67 America's flower
69 Coin of Chile
71 A complimentary close
74 Cause of inflation
75 Grove
76 Result of marriage
81 Coffee houses
82 Actress Burke
83 Composer Franck
84 Wing it
85 Simulacrum
86 Actor Teeter
87 Doubtful
88 Position
89 Stagger
91 Lowdown
92 Owlish times: Abbr.
94 Pat
95 Frat mem.

79 ASK ME NO QUESTIONS by William Canine

For a quick start, complete the title by filling it in diagonally from the top-left corner to the one at the bottom-right.

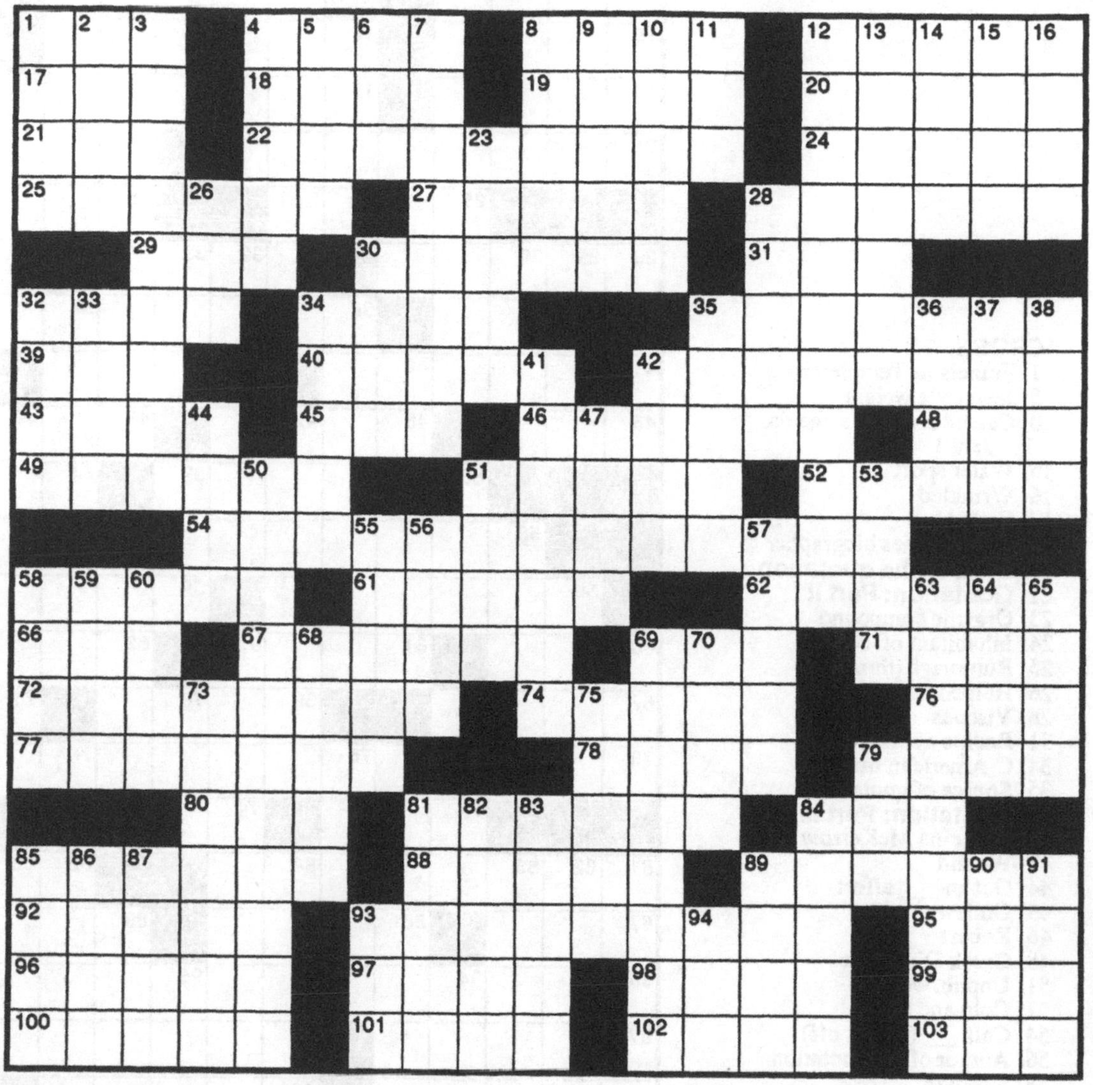

ACROSS

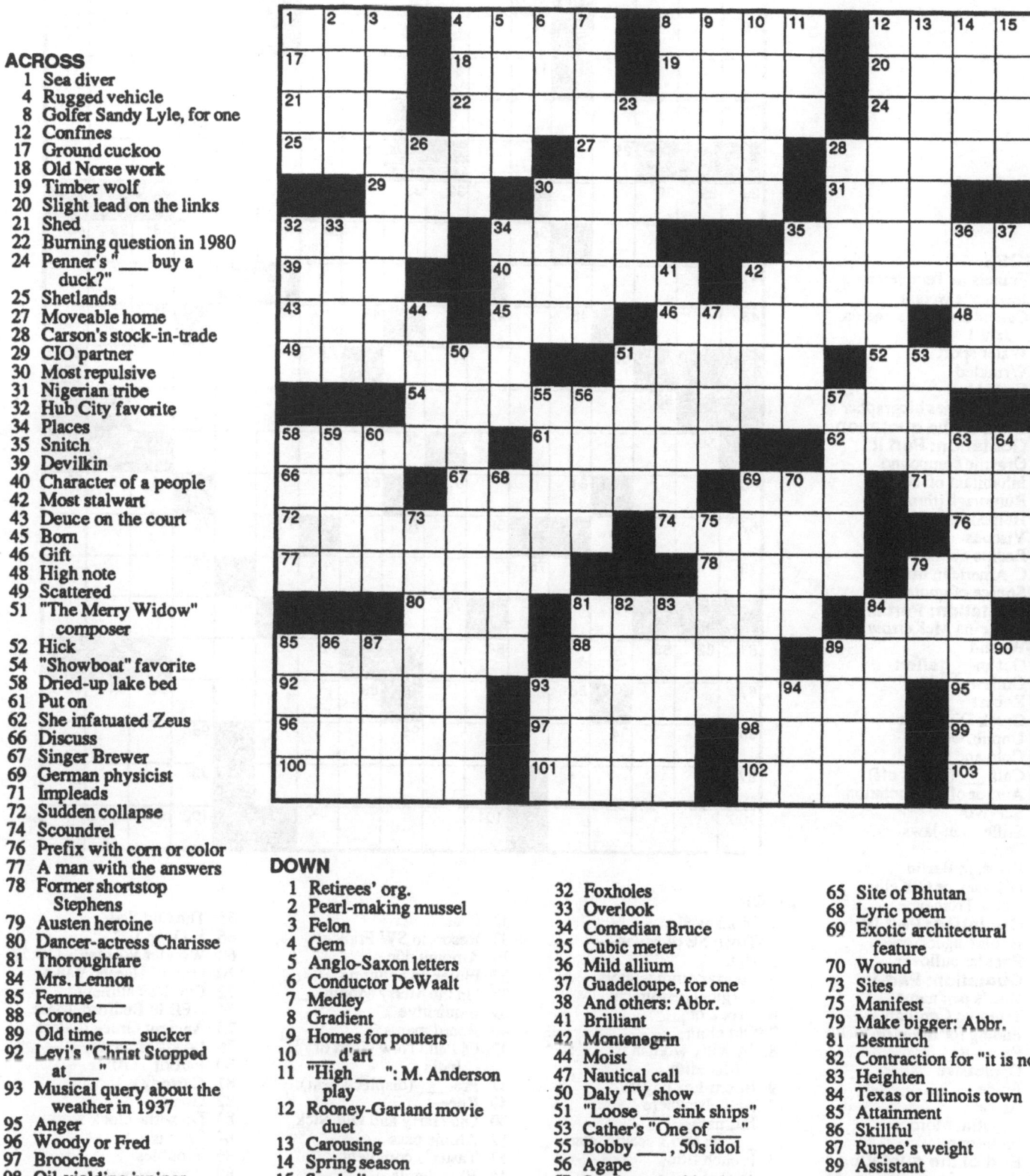

1 Sea diver
4 Rugged vehicle
8 Golfer Sandy Lyle, for one
12 Confines
17 Ground cuckoo
18 Old Norse work
19 Timber wolf
20 Slight lead on the links
21 Shed
22 Burning question in 1980
24 Penner's "___ buy a duck?"
25 Shetlands
27 Moveable home
28 Carson's stock-in-trade
29 CIO partner
30 Most repulsive
31 Nigerian tribe
32 Hub City favorite
34 Places
35 Snitch
39 Devilkin
40 Character of a people
42 Most stalwart
43 Deuce on the court
45 Born
46 Gift
48 High note
49 Scattered
51 "The Merry Widow" composer
52 Hick
54 "Showboat" favorite
58 Dried-up lake bed
61 Put on
62 She infatuated Zeus
66 Discuss
67 Singer Brewer
69 German physicist
71 Impleads
72 Sudden collapse
74 Scoundrel
76 Prefix with corn or color
77 A man with the answers
78 Former shortstop Stephens
79 Austen heroine
80 Dancer-actress Charisse
81 Thoroughfare
84 Mrs. Lennon
85 Femme ___
88 Coronet
89 Old time ___ sucker
92 Levi's "Christ Stopped at ___"
93 Musical query about the weather in 1937
95 Anger
96 Woody or Fred
97 Brooches
98 Oil-yielding juniper
99 What's ___?
100 Pester
101 Stake
102 Long-gone Long
103 Petrol

DOWN

1 Retirees' org.
2 Pearl-making mussel
3 Felon
4 Gem
5 Anglo-Saxon letters
6 Conductor DeWaalt
7 Medley
8 Gradient
9 Homes for pouters
10 ___ d'art
11 "High ___": M. Anderson play
12 Rooney-Garland movie duet
13 Carousing
14 Spring season
15 Sand pile
16 Shadowbox
23 Sun: Comb. form
26 Conditions
28 Climber's spike
30 Aye or nay
32 Foxholes
33 Overlook
34 Comedian Bruce
35 Cubic meter
36 Mild allium
37 Guadeloupe, for one
38 And others: Abbr.
41 Brilliant
42 Montenegrin
44 Moist
47 Nautical call
50 Daly TV show
51 "Loose ___ sink ships"
53 Cather's "One of ___"
55 Bobby ___, 50s idol
56 Agape
57 Southern Arabian land
58 Caresses
59 Yellow Sea feeder
60 Seed covering
63 Making obsolete
64 Urals metropolis
65 Site of Bhutan
68 Lyric poem
69 Exotic architectural feature
70 Wound
73 Sites
75 Manifest
79 Make bigger: Abbr.
81 Besmirch
82 Contraction for "it is not"
83 Heighten
84 Texas or Illinois town
85 Attainment
86 Skillful
87 Rupee's weight
89 Assistant
90 District
91 Conifers
93 Fed. agency: 1935-43
94 Sports org.

80

SPLIT QUOTATION by A. J. Santora
A. J.'s clever title does not refer to Wall Street, as the solver will soon discover.

ACROSS
1 Francis or Templeton
5 Jeweler's weight
10 Calendar moon's age on Jan. 1
15 Water sport
16 Wrinkled
17 Forbidden
18 Henry James biographer
19 **Start of the quotation**
21 **Quotation: Part II**
23 Organic compound
24 Inhabitant of: Suffix
25 Rummage (through)
26 Helped out
28 Viscous
31 Recipe abbrs.
34 C American tree
35 Source of quotation
36 **Quotation: Part III**
41 Ballerina McKerrow
43 Wound
44 Get an ___ effort
45 Outlaw
46 Robert ___
48 Greek Discordia
51 Unpub. works
52 Cold and damp
54 Call ___ (knock off)
56 Author of the quotation
58 Survivor
59 Stiller's in-laws
60 Pelt
61 Rope, in Berlin
63 O'Casey or O'Kelly
64 Actor Tremayne
67 **Quotation: Part IV**
69 Butterfingers' cry
71 Popular pullover
73 **Quotation: Part V**
77 C.L.'s pen name
78 Truth, to Confucius
79 Ending for Burns or Victor
80 Pass out
81 Oppressive
85 Brace
87 Arikara
88 ___ Ifni, Morocco
89 Fluttering
93 **End of the quotation**
96 Aware of
97 Narrow: Comb. form
98 Purloins
99 Cantor's "Palesteena" queen
100 Ryan's daughter
101 Overlords
102 Start of a letter

DOWN
1 Monkeyed
2 Town SE of Milan
3 Hgt.
4 Sports commentators
5 Surgical instrument
6 "Rock of ___"
7 Old cloth
8 "A witty woman is ___": Meredith
9 Boom-box buyers
10 And elsewhere
11 Intimate
12 ___ on one's escutcheon
13 French title
14 Trifled
16 Puerto ___
20 Voir, to a French student
22 Judge Bean
27 Pop
28 Attempt
29 Ohio city
30 Noted model
32 Plan
33 Resort in SW France
36 Amount due
37 Flutes on columns
38 "In the Merry Month ___"
39 Inquisitive
40 Board mems.
42 Old and New cities of India
47 Pre-___ (displacement)
49 Repeat
50 Old Harry and Old Nick
52 Alpine pass
53 Taster's comment
55 Blue devils
56 Cured meat
57 Class
58 Downfall
60 Gainesville loc.
62 Philosophers
64 "Darling ___": 1970 Andrews film
65 The Old Sod
66 K.O. or T.D.
68 Wonder Woman's Candy
70 Org. of Harper Valley
72 Cureless ailment
74 AFB in Bedford, Mass.
75 Ancient Greek dialect
76 Loads of money
80 Part of TGIF
81 Custody
82 Gossip
83 Do some clock work
84 That is
86 Troubles
89 At a distance
90 Kind of socks
91 An active volcano
92 Howl
94 Former P.M. of Burma
95 Carson's "The ___ Around Us"

81 ON CUE by James E. Hinish, Jr.

The title is a hint as to what lies ahead, but you'll need more than that to complete this unique toughie.

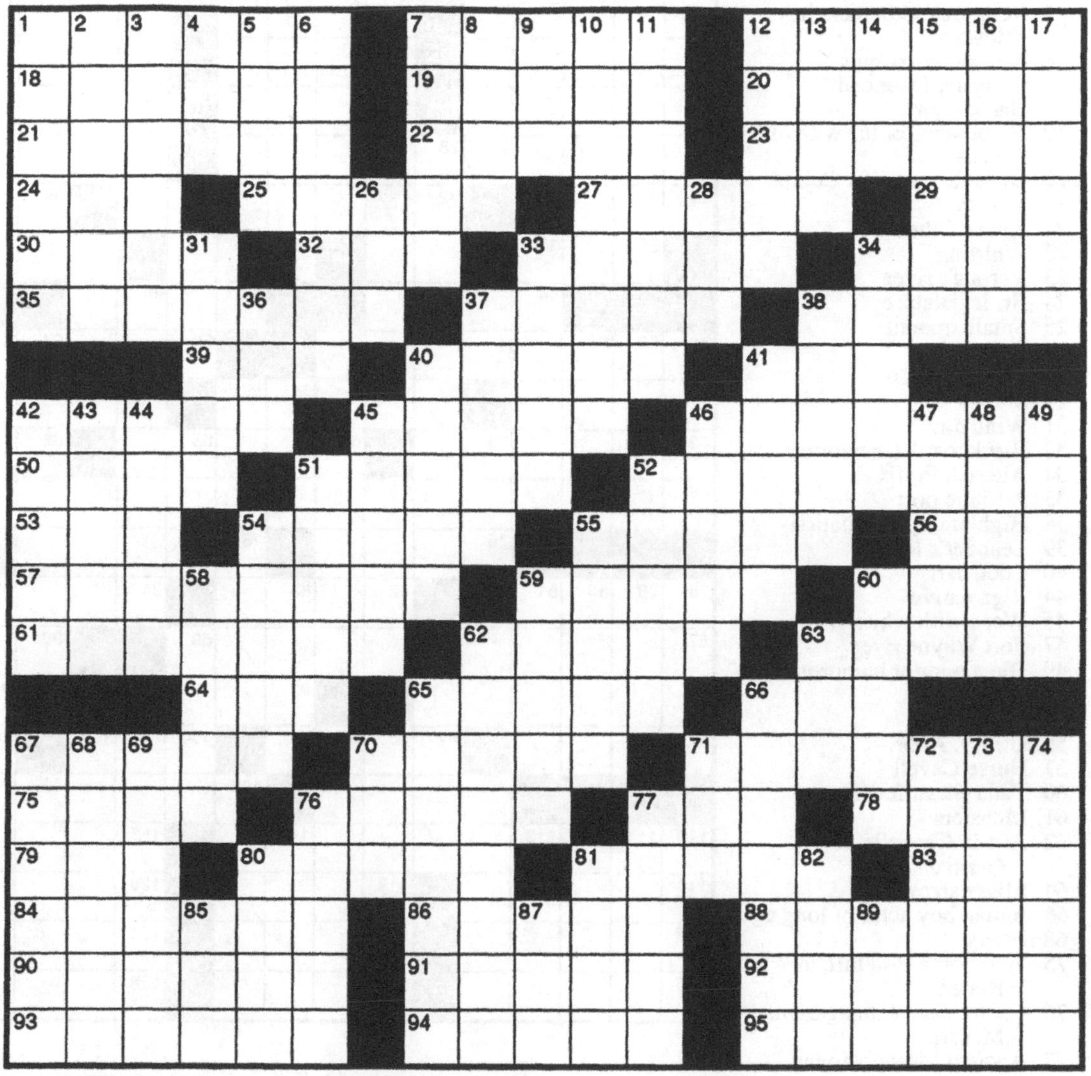

ACROSS

1 Too, to Cato
7 Baghdad native
12 Walled city of N.A.
18 Actor Ed and family
19 Deck officer
20 Land between Zaire and Zambia
21 Wall St. nos. system
22 What a genius doesn't have
23 Nineveh's river
24 Sched. abbr.
25 Enticed
27 Helicons
29 Cartoonists' org.
30 "___ Well . . . "
32 Plural endings
33 Actress Garson
34 Cunard liner: Abbr.
35 Read my lips!
37 Quixote's venture
38 Preset proportion
39 Four quarters
40 Five-card sequence
41 Sine ___ non
42 Kind of army ant?
45 Bedspread
46 Oak genus
50 Item in Bartlett's bk.
51 "The ___ Fellow": Behan
52 Tranquillity
53 Spirit of man, in Tut's time
54 Horseshoe's relative
55 "___ sabe?"
56 London's Old ___
57 Feasts
59 Punting pole in Yorkshire
60 Egyptian city on the Nile
61 WWI P.M.
62 Sand or silver starter
63 Peculiar
64 Summer in Quimper
65 Mannerism
66 "___ pasa?"
67 Kind of economics
70 Completely
71 Prefab hut
75 ___ even keel
76 Wanted pounds
77 Offstage word
78 Here, in Hermosillo
79 Hind
80 Actor Anthony
81 P-V links
83 Script or text ending
84 Off-color
86 Line
88 Old French measure
90 Even
91 Dark
92 Osceola's county
93 Compelling
94 Settle in a new habitat
95 Group of seven

DOWN

1 Australia's airline
2 Practicable
3 Sign that delights bargain hunters
4 Mathematician's abbr.
5 Eurasian river
6 Noted periodical
7 Convert and collect conclusions
8 Crucifix
9 Nav. combat against U-boats
10 Feudal payment
11 Coroner's examination
12 Persian Gulf sheikdom
13 Les États ___
14 Something to be coddled
15 Indonesian island
16 Provoke
17 Chinese cinnamon
26 Arikara
28 Quinella
31 Yell
33 Cunning
34 Dairy purchase
36 Tolkein creature
37 Riding whip
38 Lee-Dannay detective
40 Seine stopovers
41 Hush!
42 Gulf of ___, off Arabia
43 "Sorceror's Apprentice" composer
44 ___ Public
45 "___ the raven . . . "
46 ___ goose (brant)
47 Bulk wine
48 Italian province
49 To dry, in Iquique
51 Street musicians' payment
52 Panacea peddler
54 Andean capital
55 Paper quantity
58 Nut grinder
59 Call it ___ (retire)
60 Reed flute of S.A.
62 Busybody
63 Status ___ ante
65 V
66 Alsatian plum brandy
67 Finicky feline
68 Rub with oil
69 Quintillus, for one
70 On the ___ vive (alert)
71 Fourths of dols.
72 Jet
73 California's motto
74 Like a stadium
76 Caine's captain
77 Minos's realm
80 Agatha Christie's Harley ___
81 Prof's surprise
82 Ubangi feeder
85 Page size: Abbr.
87 Part of Reo
89 Spigot

82 FAMILIAR PHRASES by Joy L. Wouk

Joy wants you to be happy as a lark. And so she presents a puzzle that should make you feel wise as an owl.

ACROSS

1 Religious settlement in Iowa
6 Notorious marquis
10 Gangster Diamond
14 Game stew
19 Namesakes of the wife of Zeus
20 Of same quantity: Comb. form
21 Kind of phobia
22 Whirling
23 Verona's river
24 Br. legislature
25 Small amount
26 Rent
27 Occupied
29 Stupid
31 Wind dir.
32 Blackboard accessories
34 Altered: Prefix
35 Adriatic port
38 Highlands precipitation
39 Leander's love
40 Lock part
44 Riga native
45 Word with white or fire
47 Fort Wayne river
49 Did a poor or humorous imitation
53 Impudent
56 Utility: Abbr.
57 Nurse Cavell
60 Tatar Strait feeder
61 Monsters
62 Aix-la-Chapelle, to Germans
64 Miss narrowly
66 Indian boy actor of long ago
68 Jittery
75 Word on a paid bill, in Rouen
76 Center near Allinagaram, Madras
77 Ancient Mesopotamian city
78 Quebec city
82 Gaelic
84 Violinist Isaac
86 Charges
87 Unfettered
90 Most spacious
92 Receive
93 A continent
95 Melee
96 Totem poles
97 Ancient Persian Gulf kingdom
100 That: Sp.
102 Consumes completely
105 Ran
106 "Moby Dick" narrator
108 Serbian city
110 Suffering
115 Blushing
118 Uncaps
119 Opera by Haydn
120 Winged
121 What "Shalom" means
122 Skin holes
123 Weight allowance
124 Coin
125 Goose genus
126 Ostentatious
127 Thessaly mountain
128 Obi
129 Songstress Della

DOWN

1 Namesakes of Jezebel's husband
2 A Gorgon
3 Up
4 Hungarian leader, Imre ___
5 On the Black
6 Apart
7 Jordanian port
8 Compulsion
9 McKenny and Farrell
10 Alan and Cheryl
11 Beige
12 British unit of weight
13 Gloomy
14 Latin American dance music
15 Region
16 Slim
17 Intermediate: Comb. form
18 Holly
28 Consciousness
30 Jots
33 East Indian coarse sugar
36 Bell-shaped hat
37 Ref. work
39 Tiller
40 Hamlet
41 General Bradley
42 ___ majesté
43 Hardy heroine
46 Hates
48 Teem
49 Carillon
50 Jai ___
51 Concern, formerly
52 Annoy
54 More powdery
55 Smell ___ (be suspicious)
58 Ring letters
59 They suggest
63 Winter-hat feature
65 Stadium sound
67 Every-other-year events
69 Plural suffix in zoology
70 Que. neighbor
71 Alters again
72 Hosea, in Douay
73 Carbohydrate suffixes
74 Speedy
78 Tunisian port
79 Killer whale
80 R.C. priest's house
81 Shoe widths
83 Thailand, once
85 Cerium or erbium oxide
88 Paces
89 Withers
91 Acquired
94 Hindu places for the simple life
98 Shed
99 Vipers
101 Menotti heroine
103 Restlessness
104 Bits
105 Fresh
106 "___ Woman," Ray Charles hit
107 Moslem calls to prayer
109 Cubic meter
110 Bribes
111 City in Perak, Malaya
112 Large mackerel
113 Was aware of
114 Galena and bauxite
116 On ___ with (equal)
117 Nota ___

83

KIN SPIN by Jean Davison

The old rhyming game is applied specifically to relations. Relatively speaking, this one is Einsteinian!

ACROSS

1 Cut
5 ". . . and carry ___ stick": T.R.
9 Make a sound track
12 A descendant of jazz
17 Poet Millay
18 Silent
19 Actress Ward
20 Macbeth's first victim
21 Tom's mom?
24 Getaway
25 Madrid uncle
26 "Time ___ Hands," 1930 hit
27 Shows partiality, with "to"
28 Conditions
29 Blow up
31 Vivacious
32 Bakery items
33 ___ out (makes do)
34 Loblolly
35 Police statistics
39 Furor
42 Della's relatives?
46 Luau treat
47 Space opener
48 "Band of Renown" leader's first name
49 Cole, et al.
50 Firewood measure
51 Theater posters
55 No-nos
57 "___ Were the Days," 1968 song
58 Electric eyes
59 Actress Marta: 1926-57
60 Spanish skies
61 Joyce's sib?
65 Ameche sci-fi film
68 Medicinal plants
69 Destroyer, e.g.
73 Actor-comedian Joslyn
74 Mixture
75 Humbug; nonsense
77 "Pretty ___ pretty does"
78 Claim on property
79 "___ the land of . . ."
80 Major ending
81 Oui's opposite
82 Robert Webber's role?
87 "The heat ___"
88 "This other Eden," to Shakespeare
90 Valley
91 West Germany region
93 Memorial Day's ___ 500
94 Haunted-house sounds
95 Serial segment
99 Wheel rim
102 Causes for contributions to the IRS
103 Snakes
104 Sidekick
105 Taking more time
106 Antiseptic inventor's kin?
109 Proprietors
110 Do they have nephews?
111 To ___ (exactly)
112 "Laugh-in" comic's first name
113 Jury members
114 ___ Plaines, IL
115 Average scores for Crenshaw
116 Scoffing words

DOWN

1 Last word of a Wren title
2 Combine
3 Spy
4 What a kook talks through
5 Penitent person
6 Rangoon natives
7 Bitsy's partner
8 Peridot or tigereye
9 Actress Gloria from L.A.
10 Author of "Feeling Fine": 1978
11 Forbids
12 Light robes
13 If
14 Specialty of Ella Fitzgerald
15 Costume item for Superman
16 Snake eyes, at a dice table
19 Ale containers
20 Wants
22 Catch a cod
23 Hardy and North
30 W. C. Fields' baby's babies?
31 Church areas
32 Agreements
36 Bobbin
37 Schwarzenegger's pride
38 Factions
39 Dunderheads
40 Part of TV
41 Qum's locale
43 Building wing
44 Secret
45 "His wife could ___ lean"
50 Chastity and Elijah Blue?
52 Chemical element
53 Symbol of strength
54 Utah Beach transport
55 Gave medicine to
56 Symbols of empire
57 Cake layers
59 Jeff Bridges film
60 Biggers detective
62 Forced to go, as to court
63 Nicholas Gage bio
64 Couple
65 Actor in "Sleuth"
66 Boxer Bobo
67 Trolley sound
70 Wade Boggs's collection
71 Absorbed with
72 Hammer part
74 Hen
75 Wealth
76 Fort ___, CA
78 Dear Abby's sib
79 Danish port
82 Crèche components
83 They have "I" trouble
84 Cants
85 Backstage assistant
86 Upscale types
89 Stay
92 Show disapproval
94 "As ___ goes . . ."
96 Met work
97 Vader of "Star Wars"
98 Red ___, shrubs of southern Africa
99 Turkey
100 Rob of films
101 "Green Gables" girl
102 Delighted
103 Star with a tail
107 Gavel sound
108 Hunter of Hollywood

84 GREAT COMMUNICATORS by Martha J. DeWitt

Martha dedicates this puzzle to R.W.R.

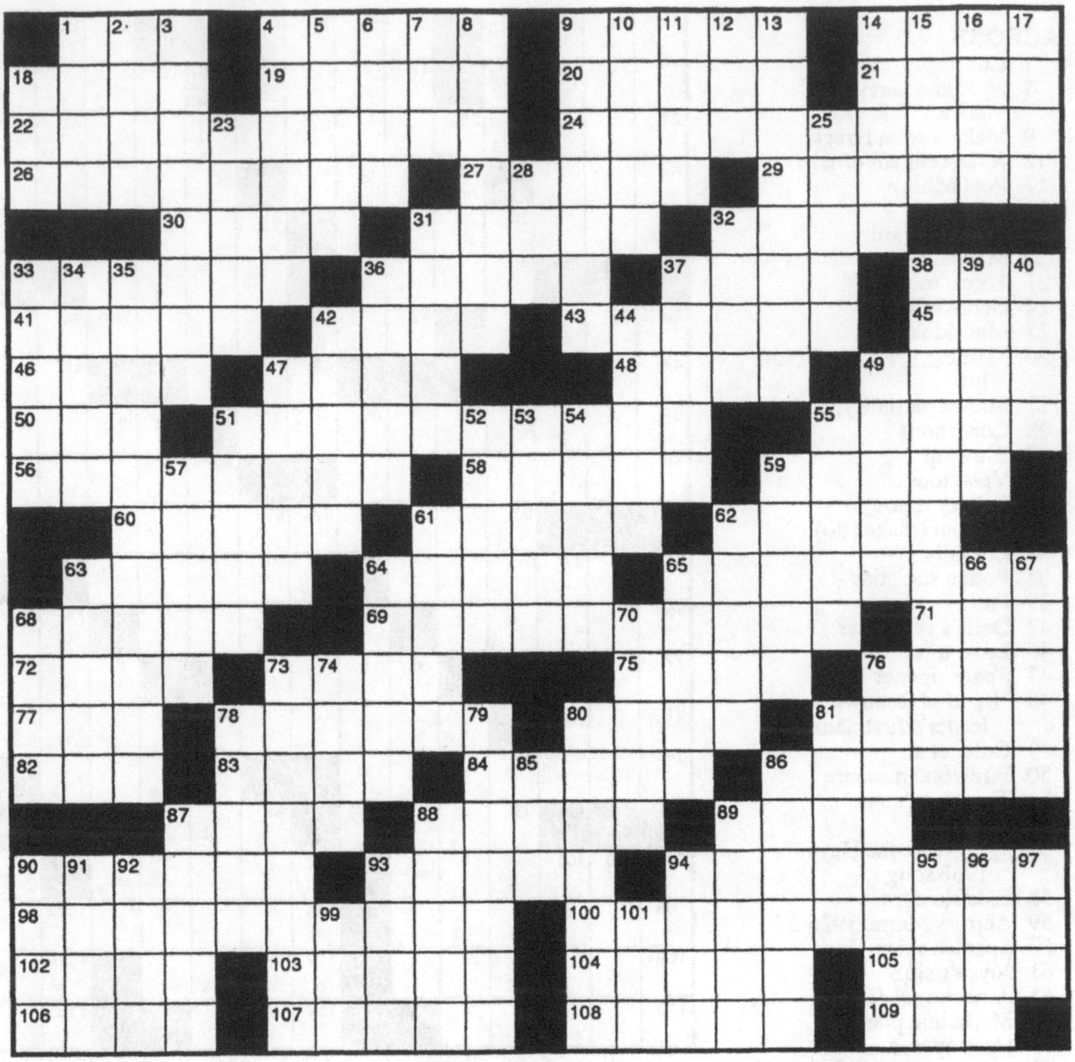

ACROSS

1 Conceit
4 Bounds' associate
9 Actress Day
14 Page
18 Tel ___
19 Muscat native
20 Zola
21 Sutherland solo
22 Teenagers' aids for reaching out
24 Overseas messages
26 Begs
27 Flans
29 On time
30 Where a downspout begins
31 Skirmish
32 Piggin
33 Whist card-combination
36 Cake
37 Syconia
38 Make "it"
41 Mountain ridge
42 Averages
43 Perry Mason's sec'y.
45 Drs'. org.
46 Barn lofts
47 Advantage
48 Scuttles
49 Hullabaloo
50 McMahon and Wynn
51 Rumor lines
55 J. Paul, the oilman
56 Embellish
58 Torpid
59 Ilex
60 Calm down
61 Boards
62 ___ Mesta, memorable hostess
63 Dramatist's ploy
64 Alan Ladd's great picture
65 Ran in
68 Dull surface
69 Emmy medium
71 The Altar
72 Olympic hawk
73 Throwaway ever since Eden
75 Cast off
76 Bet on a horse
77 Crag
78 Listless
80 Prune: Scotch
81 "Gin a body ___ a body": Burns
82 Quartet in "No, No, Nanette"
83 Warm-up activity
84 Kind of hose
86 Individual
87 Byre
88 Fold
89 Bikini tops
90 Per
93 Robbery
94 Generated
98 Envoys
100 Squealer
102 "Dies ___," Judgment Day hymn
103 Fortune-telling card
104 Expunge
105 ___ City, San Francisco suburb
106 Gossip
107 Wingspreads
108 Parking misfortunes
109 W German river

DOWN

1 Deuce, in tennis
2 Female pig
3 Is gluttonous
4 Calif. desert: Var.
5 Ham it up
6 Toasts
7 $67\frac{1}{2}$, by compass
8 The Brontës
9 Irades
10 Peruvian volcano
11 Kids
12 Indisposed
13 Transudations
14 Actress Channing
15 Biblical name of Syria
16 Flaccid
17 Wear well
18 Didn't go hungry
23 Dove's delight
25 Mill feed
28 Elev.
31 Describing a telegraphic code
32 Describing Hamelin's piper
33 Describing a busted bronco
34 Frazzle gradually
35 Peter Jennings, et al.
36 Brownish gray
37 He wrote "New Hampshire"
38 Informers
39 Friendliness
40 Ex-Sen. Hart
42 Kind of glass
44 "___ but for the grace of God . . ."
47 Yap
49 Peddles
51 Classify
52 Important
53 Silly
54 Israeli desert region
55 Big bridge man
57 R.I.P announcements
59 Judean king (Matthew 2:1)
61 Gloss
62 Got nosy
63 Nadab's father (Exodus 6:23)
64 Divest
65 Pale
66 One of Clio's siblings
67 Moshe, the Israeli politician
68 Spouse
70 "Love ___ love/Which alters . . .": Shak.
73 Sailors' concerns
74 Honest
76 Prevail upon
78 Astronauts' milieu
79 Joins the Navy, e.g.
80 Like a venetian blind
81 Nobelist in economics: 1977
85 Si or oui
86 Investigations
87 Lay siege to
88 Argentine dictator
89 French seaport
90 At the center of
91 Persian elf
92 Munich's river
93 Juno, to Plato
94 Machinate
95 Steve ___, famed miler
96 Spitchcocks, possibly
97 Desiccated
99 Hiatus
101 "For manners ___ not idle": Tennyson

85

FEAST FOR FANS by Rhoda Kraus
Noshers will devour this one with delight. We especially like 29 Across, a term unknown in our *salad* days.

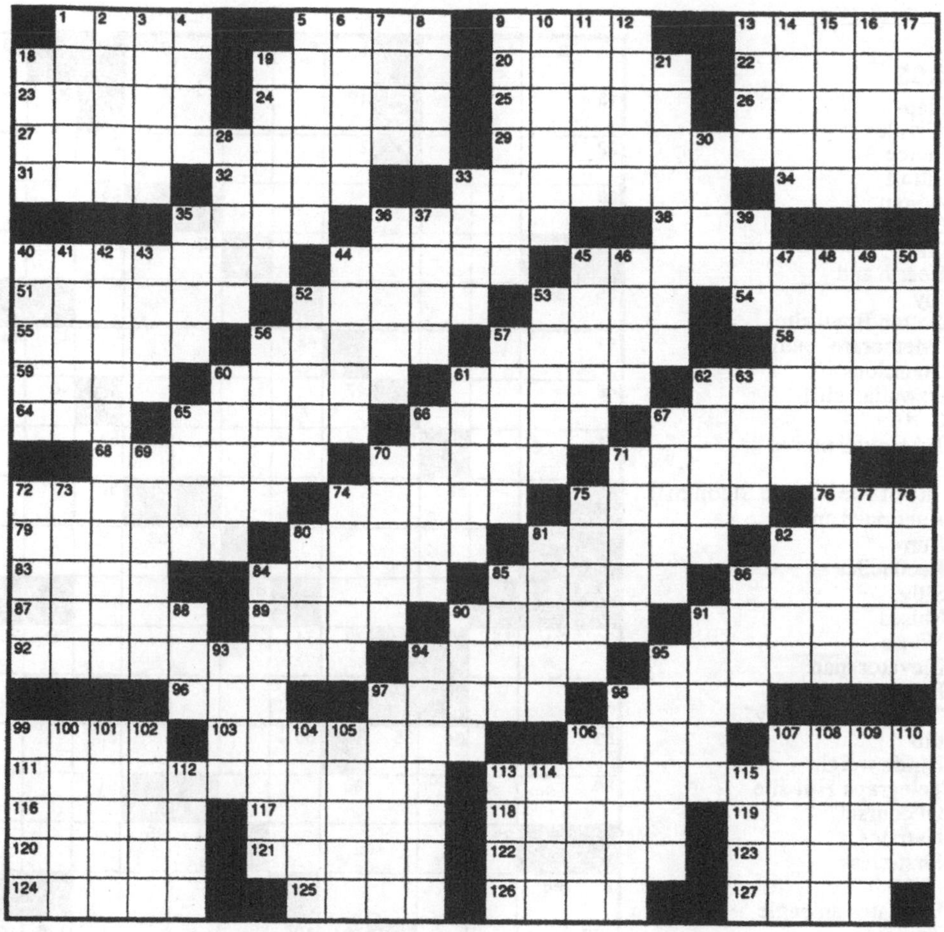

ACROSS

1 Regulations
5 "Out, damned ___!": Shak.
9 File
13 Stop
18 Danger
19 Lean
20 Enroll
22 Theatrical family
23 Dispatch boat
24 Mountain lakes
25 Shop
26 Worker in mosaics
27 Bronx cheers
29 TV addict
31 Three spot
32 Oath
33 Writer-reporter, John ___
34 Warehouse: Abbr.
35 Verdi opera
36 Tree trunks
38 All in good order
40 Shoe parts
44 "___Johnny!"
45 Takes a liking to
51 Bread units or companion to fishes
52 Speaks: Fr.
53 Have fond feelings
54 Religious
55 Still ___ (certain paintings)
56 Apologetic
57 Amor
58 Plays on words
59 Utilizer
60 Confused
61 Fathered
62 Flower child
64 Dry
65 To the matter: Lat.
66 Adored (with "on")
67 The Orient
68 TV's Dan
70 Dressed for the bedroom
71 Interest on capital
72 City bird
74 Bathed
75 Rose pest
76 M.D.s
79 Frigid region
80 Cookie
81 Tasty
82 ___ chance! (unlikely happening)
83 Polynesian image
84 ___ beaver
85 Bit
86 Arrange in a row
87 Middle East ruler
89 Ripener
90 Place of the "soggy plain"
91 Nearer
92 Pistol
94 Rub
95 Detests
96 Nothing
97 Intended
98 Brings forth lambs
99 Pouches
103 Migrating rodents
106 Opposed
107 Toddlers
111 Caspar, "The Timid Soul," ___
113 Could be a jaw breaker
116 Love affair
117 Aquatic mammal
118 Hawk's nest
119 Hat parts
120 Vladimir Ilyich Ulyanov
121 ___ Dame
122 Growl: Var.
123 News bits
124 Yorkshire city
125 Stinging fish
126 ___ a bill of goods
127 Simple

DOWN

1 Actor Burton, of "Roots"
2 "___ fair moon . . .": Shak.
3 Insubstantial
4 Messy one
5 Ancient rival of Athens
6 City of 121 Across
7 Alençon's capital
8 Hardy heroine
9 Saves
10 Chekhov and Dvorak
11 Hefty
12 Place for Polly
13 Roman statesman
14 Blue-pencils
15 ___ once (in an instant)
16 Attend
17 Mistake
18 Portion
19 Famous fiddles
21 Warmed over
28 Iroquoians
30 Christian group: Abbr.
33 Mirth
35 Pub potables
36 Baseball's Yogi
37 Airport of 6 Down
39 One of the Keystone group
40 Picture: Abbr.
41 Din
42 This one is more likely to be dangerous
43 Done
44 Stag's group of does
45 Handled difficulties
46 Roman poet
47 Pincers
48 Formal wear
49 Mediterranean capital
50 One from the Caucasus region
52 Puzzler
53 Enticed
56 Scatter
57 Quoted
60 ___ committee (organized for one purpose)
61 Sedate
62 Detested
63 "Odyssey" beggar
65 Italian town
66 Strait, city, or sole
67 Smelly
69 More of a dilettante
70 Olympian Johnson
71 Mature
72 Stuffed
73 First class
74 Beer suds
75 Dressler, Curie, or Antoinette
77 Indian princess
78 Suffix with team or young: Pl.
80 Stipend
81 Get the ___ (be victimized)
82 Thanks ___!
84 Ex-senator from Missouri
85 Bridge
86 Too bad
88 Oysters ___ season
90 Type of rug
91 Shaped like an ice-cream holder
93 Mediterranean feeder
94 Hubs: Var.
95 Suds
97 Unhappiness
98 Wrap around
99 Wee
100 Actress Anouk ___
101 Asexually produced progeny
102 Cuttlefish
104 Car engine
105 Modern, Chilean-born painter, Roberto ___
106 Pertaining to the ear
107 Spanish omelet
108 One-time migrants
109 Nickname for namesakes of early Christian saint
110 Legis. meeting
112 Vases
113 Labels
114 Wine: Prefix
115 Off-Broadway award

86 SIGHTS AND SITES by H. H. Reddall

H. H. was nice enough to take a few days off from working in his large garden to construct this puzzle for us.

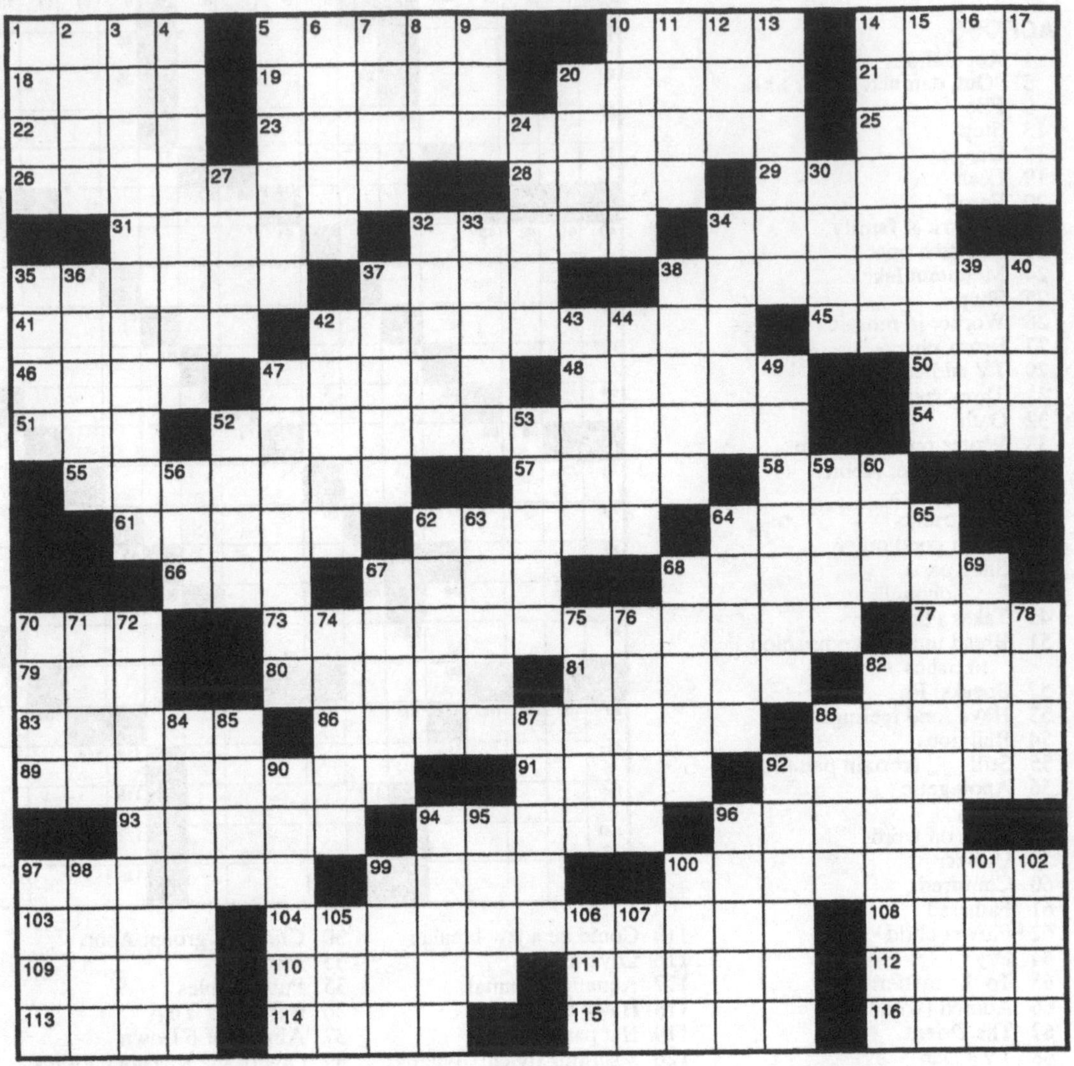

ACROSS

1 Flaps
5 Missiles
10 Pierce
14 Pitfall
18 Adjoin
19 Caroline, to Ted
20 Flat
21 Hearth and ___
22 Joy
23 Cotton Bowl site
25 "Memorare" ending
26 Conscious
28 Hawaiian cliff
29 Certify
31 Tskhinvali native
32 Strand
34 Site of Joe Robbie Stadium
35 Auctioned anew
37 Burn
38 Reconciles
41 Silly
42 Mused
45 Noose
46 Elevator man
47 Fathered
48 "The ___ of Araby"
50 Fib
51 Hindu weight
52 Telegraph Hill site
54 Of course!
55 Narrates
57 First-class
58 Hot tub
61 Emulates an eagle
62 Teases
64 Hindu nurses
66 Musical deg.
67 Roman garment
68 Under the clock ___ Central Station
70 Tun
73 Independence Hall site
77 Suffix for baron
79 Rocks
80 Sub finder
81 Suppress or repress
82 Greek peninsula
83 Goofed
86 Newspaper notices
88 Ten-speeds
89 Home wreckers
91 Repudiate
92 Challengers
93 Ventilated
94 Dodger Hall-of-Famer
96 Vexer
97 Subtracts
99 Philippine tribesman
100 U.S. sculptor: 1883–1952
103 ___ from the blue
104 Site of Hsin-kao
108 ___ meridien
109 Czech river
110 Sen. Kefauver
111 Biblical number
112 Composer Janácek
113 Encumbrance
114 Sax, for one
115 Arbor elements
116 Mature elvers

DOWN

1 Tickets
2 Talented
3 Plaza de Mayo site
4 Cowboy hats
5 Without a doubt
6 Laughing
7 Sock
8 CCXXX x V
9 Red or Black
10 Stone monument
11 Cab
12 ___ carte
13 "Much may ___ on both sides": Fielding
14 "I'm Gonna Wash ___ Right . . . "
15 Piazza del Popolo site
16 Iowa State University site
17 Shut up
20 Texan symbol
24 Recreation
27 Key
30 Mai ___ (cocktails)
32 Jewish feast
33 British Columbian tribe
34 Intern
35 Ocho ___, Jamaica
36 Stage direction
37 Slaves
38 Reagan cabineteer
39 Keystone State city
40 Observes
42 Tunnels
43 Neckwear
44 Makes tenuous
47 Ancient Persian governors
49 Russian statesman: 1904–80
52 Old Thailand
53 Aquatic nymph
56 "Old Cape ___"
59 Prefix for chute
60 Exclamation or rock group
62 Of clay
63 Culture mediums
64 Mount of 82 Across
65 Large knife
67 Prongs
68 Appropriately
69 Postal machine
70 ___ Nam
71 "Hell's Half ___," 1954 film
72 Pulverized gypsum
74 Wished
75 Anglo-Saxon laborers
76 Woody vine
78 Minus
82 Terrier type
84 Sent forth
85 Calamitous
87 Start of title of a Keats poem
88 Indonesian island
90 Bed canopy
92 Couches
94 Oared
95 Periods
96 Rajah's wife
97 First victim
98 Machete
99 Widow's ___
100 Gainer, e.g.
101 Ear doctor: Abbr.
102 Suffix for soft
105 Peer Gynt's mom
106 Okla. time
107 "___ 12 Men," Garson film

87 SUBSTITUTIONS by Guido Scarato

A standout puzzle with a stand-in theme. Don't expect to *fill in* this one quickly.

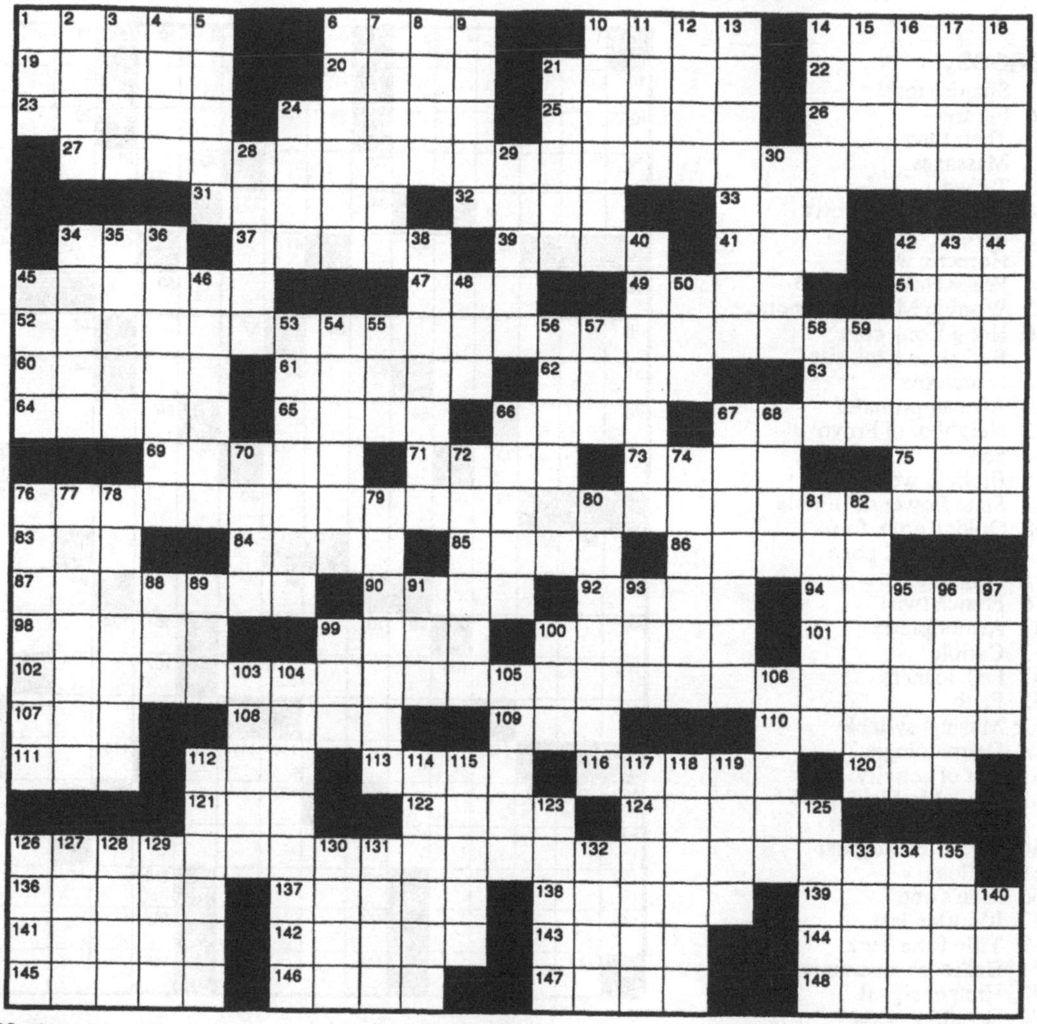

ACROSS

1 Four-star reviews
6 Not a strike
10 Denver's is one mile
14 Fool
19 Draper's fold
20 Jewish month
21 Reconcile
22 Musical study
23 Papal headdress: Brit.
24 " . . . wife could ___ lean"
25 "Green Acres" actress
26 More pleasant
27 INSTR. TO DOROTHY GALE
31 Anoint, old style
32 Kohl's three
33 Narrow shoe width
34 Vitality
37 Fear
39 Anxiously awaiting
41 The Angels hit: 1961
42 Grampus
45 It's fit for a king
47 Choose
49 Curb
51 Kanga's kid
52 SONG FOR CHEVALIER
60 Pavilions
61 French magician's word
62 Actor Salinger
63 Feeling of anxiety
64 Take ___ at (glimpse)
65 Small suffix
66 Quote
67 Disturb
69 Prefix for rocket
71 River of NW Luzon
73 Sioux City locale
75 Not pos.
76 TUNE FOR DINO
83 Forty winks
84 Apollo's mother
85 Part of S.W.A.K.
86 "___ ed Euridice"
87 Mineral pitch
90 Small songbird
92 Mail
94 Smells
98 Termagant
99 Great Indian Desert
100 Dot, in Salerno
101 River in Hades
102 WORLD'S LARGEST PLATE MAKERS
107 Wil Wright's brother
108 Feather: Comb. form
109 Writer Rand
110 Square-dance groups
111 Three before double-U
112 Ramla loc.
113 Periods
116 Looker
120 Food scrap
121 Common, in Tahiti
122 Word of division
124 Danger
126 TONY BENNETT CLASSIC
136 ___ Haute
137 Perfume
138 Dupes
139 Magna ___
141 Par ___: Fr. airmail
142 Rankle
143 Arezzo's river
144 Miffed
145 Like legal paper
146 Emperor
147 Aggravation
148 Fifer's drum

DOWN

1 Record's 45
2 Arabic letter
3 Prohibit
4 Actor Holliman
5 Commemorative pillar
6 One of the Fab Five
7 Gibson of tennis fame
8 Crescent
9 "Back To The Future" star
10 And others
11 Timber wolf
12 Enough, once
13 Word for word
14 Servile
15 Of the ear
16 Wrinkle
17 Opole's river
18 Pee-wee Herman, e.g.
21 Shoelace sheath
24 Pitcher
28 French waves
29 A sister of Urania
30 Drizzly
34 Orchid meal
35 French for 89 Down
36 Decorative design
38 Leash for Fido
40 Soybeans' asset
42 Pot marjoram
43 Circus worker
44 Retinue
45 Tampico hemp
46 Small chest for jewels
48 Bluegrass genus
50 Newt
53 Topple
54 In, à la Webster
55 Shoo!, Dogpatch style
56 Eskimo boats
57 Tit for ___
58 Airport code for Al Qahirah
59 Toronto loc.
66 Weepin'
67 "Let me give you ___ advice"
68 Lobsterman's hook
70 Like redwoods
72 Coll. in Baldwin City, Kansas
74 Tooth: Comb. form
76 Between a rock and a hard place
77 "Kilroy ___!"
78 Ratify
79 "___ Man," 1966 hit
80 Emergence
81 Ancient Greek dialect
82 City in C California
88 Drill sergeant's word
89 Shoemaker's friend
91 Séance sound
93 Ref. book
95 Further
96 Mitchell's Butler
97 Sch. term
99 R's number, to Mario
100 Single thickness
103 ___ salts
104 Homeless grimalkin
105 Stop, in Siena
106 Column style
112 Mean
114 Carwash component
115 Goose genus
117 Where planes are parked
118 Fanatic
119 Flying fishers
123 Available
125 Legitimate
126 Type of type: Abbr.
127 Harrison's Morton
128 Hibernia
129 Cleaver
130 ENCOURAGES
131 Actress Swenson
132 Shout from Strange
133 Parton known as "Fanny Fern"
134 Neptune-salad ingredient
135 Astronomer Knopf
140 Gas: Comb. form

88

APHERESIS by June Boggs

If you should find this puzzle to your liking, *drop a letter off* to the publishers and tell them about it.

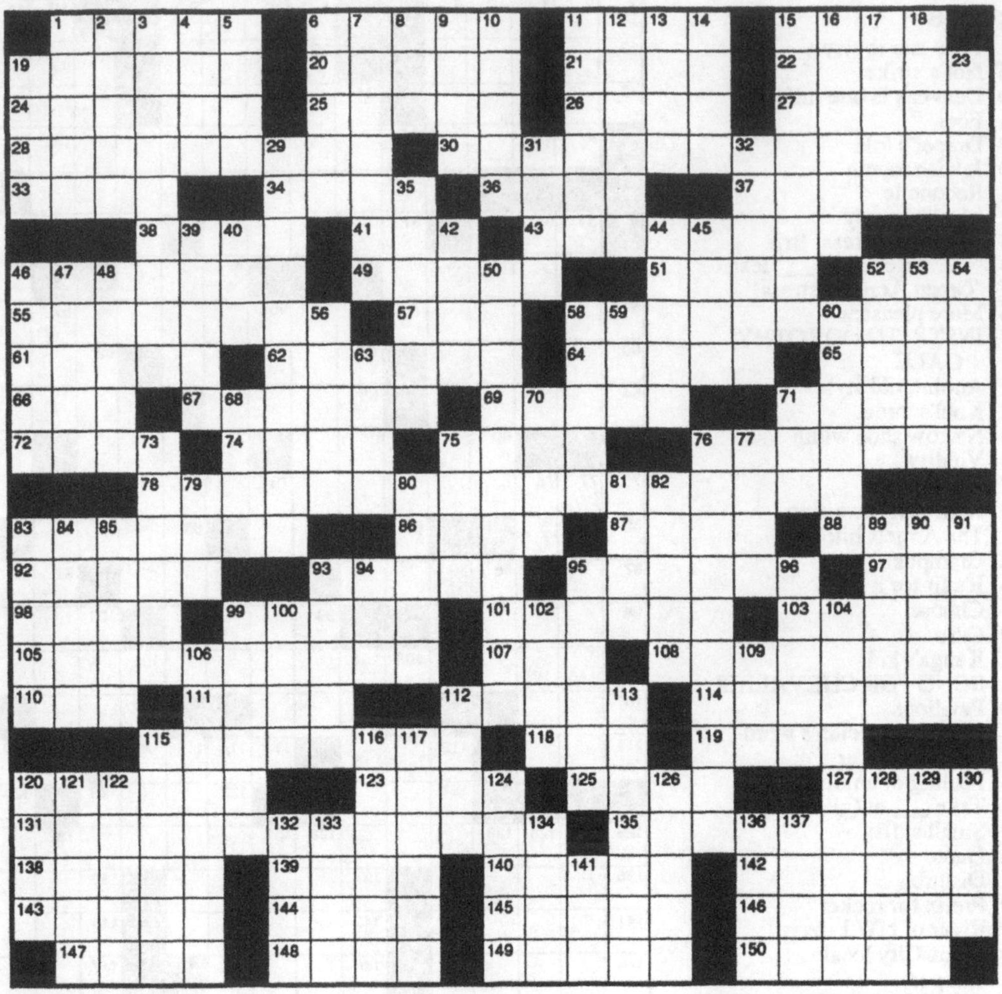

ACROSS

1 Spanish toast
6 Fig tree
11 Therefore
15 Massages
19 Tufted
20 Socialite Longworth
21 Spruce
22 Homeric works
24 Peace Nobelist: 1965
25 Word in Montana's motto
26 Hong Kong coin
27 Berkshire track site
28 Scarecrow
30 African primate?
33 Neighbor of Provo
34 Settled
36 Biblical weed
37 State flower of Illinois
38 Gold: Comb. form
41 "The Great" pope
43 Fragrant
46 French twist
49 Armor plates
51 Cariole
52 Fed. loaners
55 Faith
57 Musical syllable
58 Dermatologist?
61 Out of activity
62 "___ Marble," 1946 Carradine film
64 Prefix for surgical
65 Callous
66 Juan's one
67 It's often last
69 Title for a Turk
71 Bellicose chauvinist
72 Hunger signal
74 Reedlike grass
75 Sinecure
76 In pieces
78 Fisherman's part of speech?
83 Leanest
86 Dutch portraitist: 1618–80
87 Ballerina Nemtchinova
88 Beat it!
92 Emulate Deimos
93 Of dubious character
95 Goatmen
97 Initials for a Tudor
98 Boudreau and Brock
99 Heavenly whale
101 Governor of Mecca
103 Excuse
105 Tool sheds?
107 Suffix for cannon
108 Voice-over specialist
110 "The Catcher in the ___"
111 Speck
112 Town near Baltimore
114 Joseph ___ Kipling
115 Knight
118 Literary collection
119 L-Q links
120 French region
123 Red-dog
125 ___ meridian
127 Rainbow
131 Leaping Olajuwon, e.g.?
135 Shrewish
138 Madrid neighbor
139 The former Mrs. Reynolds
140 Dayan of Israel
142 C New York lake
143 Painter's cap
144 Actor Roberts
145 Expect
146 Undo
147 Surf sound
148 Ending for differ
149 Carnal craving
150 Wing

DOWN

1 Asdic
2 Liturgical vestment
3 Be disenchanting?
4 Mormon State team
5 Nimble
6 Pontifical
7 Enmity
8 Actress Zadora
9 Records of deeds
10 Bounded
11 Once more!
12 Shortened, as a topmast
13 Crew
14 Philanthropist Kahn
15 Infer
16 Outcome
17 Malayan Christian
18 Rifle adjunct
19 Stephen King chiller
23 Proofer's dotty directive
29 Seasonable shower?
31 Gable's were famous
32 Cook too long
35 Silver service
39 One of an "odd" pair
40 Reine's consort
42 Adventure tale of 1847
44 Present itself
45 He roared to fame
46 Laryngeal ailment
47 Reddish brown
48 Trojan's Troy
50 Brownie's psychotherapies?
52 Stomach
53 Pianist-punster
54 Passion
56 An in-law of Ruth
58 Unsuited
59 Peg for Tway
60 Spines
63 Scottish swift
68 Torte ingredients
70 Painter Cassatt
71 Summer mo.
73 Too gaudy
75 Gunned it
76 Lofty granger?
77 Boom or gaff
79 Snood
80 Obsidian
81 Nobelist Giaever
82 Soap base
83 ___ plexus
84 Substitute
85 Maltreatment
89 Actress Rivera
90 Bower
91 I Don't Know's base
93 "Family Album" author
94 "Ben ___"
95 Evening song
96 Cagliari citizen: Ital.
99 Divided
100 Place or Kett
102 "___ Rebel," 1962 hit song
104 Secular bird?
106 Waste away
109 Melt and flow
112 Formerly, formerly
113 Yellowish
115 Pill form
116 Peaceful
117 Burnett character
120 Whaler played by Peck
121 Gallant
122 Coil: Comb. form
124 Of blood
126 Piranha features
128 Remove a siege
129 ___ finger
130 English Laurel
132 Merriment
133 Midwestern Belt
134 "Tamerlane" playwright
136 Ocean sunfish
137 Ever's partner
141 Teen's test

89 TRICK OF THE WEAK by Eugene T. Maleska

Dieters who are dying to get this advice may do just that!

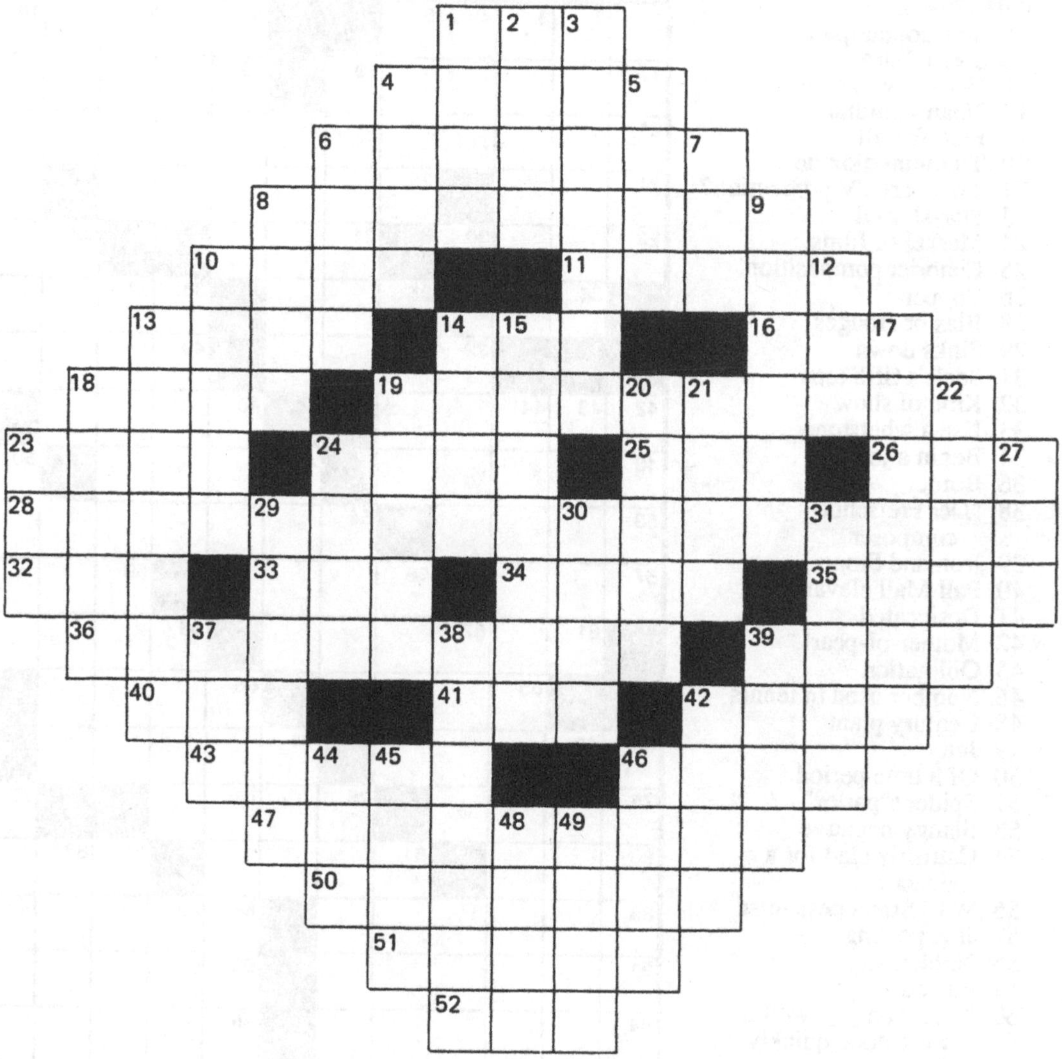

ACROSS

1 William Blake's "The Book of ___"
4 Tether for a caballo
6 Fourth-largest state
8 **Start of the quotation**
10 "Pipe to the spirit ditties of no ___": Keats
11 Prefix with lace and weave
13 First James Bond film
14 Nautical dir.
16 Hebrew months
18 Part between the femur and the thigh
19 Places replete with "cabbage," "lettuce," "bread," etc.
23 Winnie-the-Pooh, for one
24 Dance of the early Sixties
25 Prefix with cycle or corn
26 Snooker stick
28 **Middle of the quotation**
32 Treat for a Nigerian native
33 Sparks' desperate plea
34 Barrett or Jaffe
35 "___ Angel," Mae West film
36 Seizes and occupies again
39 Milt Gross's "Nize ___"
40 Act like Xanthippe
41 B. & O., etc.
42 Where many a strike occurs
43 Brightly colored fish often seen in a tropical aquarium
46 Alley Oop's beloved
47 **End of the quotation**
50 These caused DeQuincey and Coleridge to be addicts
51 Charmed
52 Govt. aid to opera, etc.

DOWN

1 Capp's ___ the Hyena
2 Meal for Spectacular Bid
3 Asset for a marathon runner
4 Mechanical repetition
5 Faulkner's "Requiem for ___"
6 Vicious Hawaiian shark
7 Vaudeville feature
8 Mind-boggling time
9 "I ___ in the deep heart's core": Yeats
10 Seaport in Nova Scotia
12 Stat for a diamond star
13 Carters of a sort
14 Actor Estrada
15 "... And ___," source of the quotation
17 Harry ___, author of the quotation
18 Composer Franck
19 End of an O. Henry story
20 Flabbergasts
21 Word with Major or Minor
22 Jerome Kern musical
23 Table ___, at Capetown
24 Physician in "Tristram Shandy"
27 Eisenhower's post in WW II
29 Lexicographers' concerns
30 Blow and College
31 Prince Charles's bride
37 Beamy boat, for short
38 Of a Russian range
39 Latvian or Lithuanian
42 Grandmother of Timothy
44 Number of moons around Mars or Neptune
45 Carried away with love, joy, etc.
46 Author Wister
48 George or Victoria
49 Great Barrier Island

90 SIGN LANGUAGE by Gloria Evans

Our terrific Texan has had fun with parts of the zodiac. You will, too!

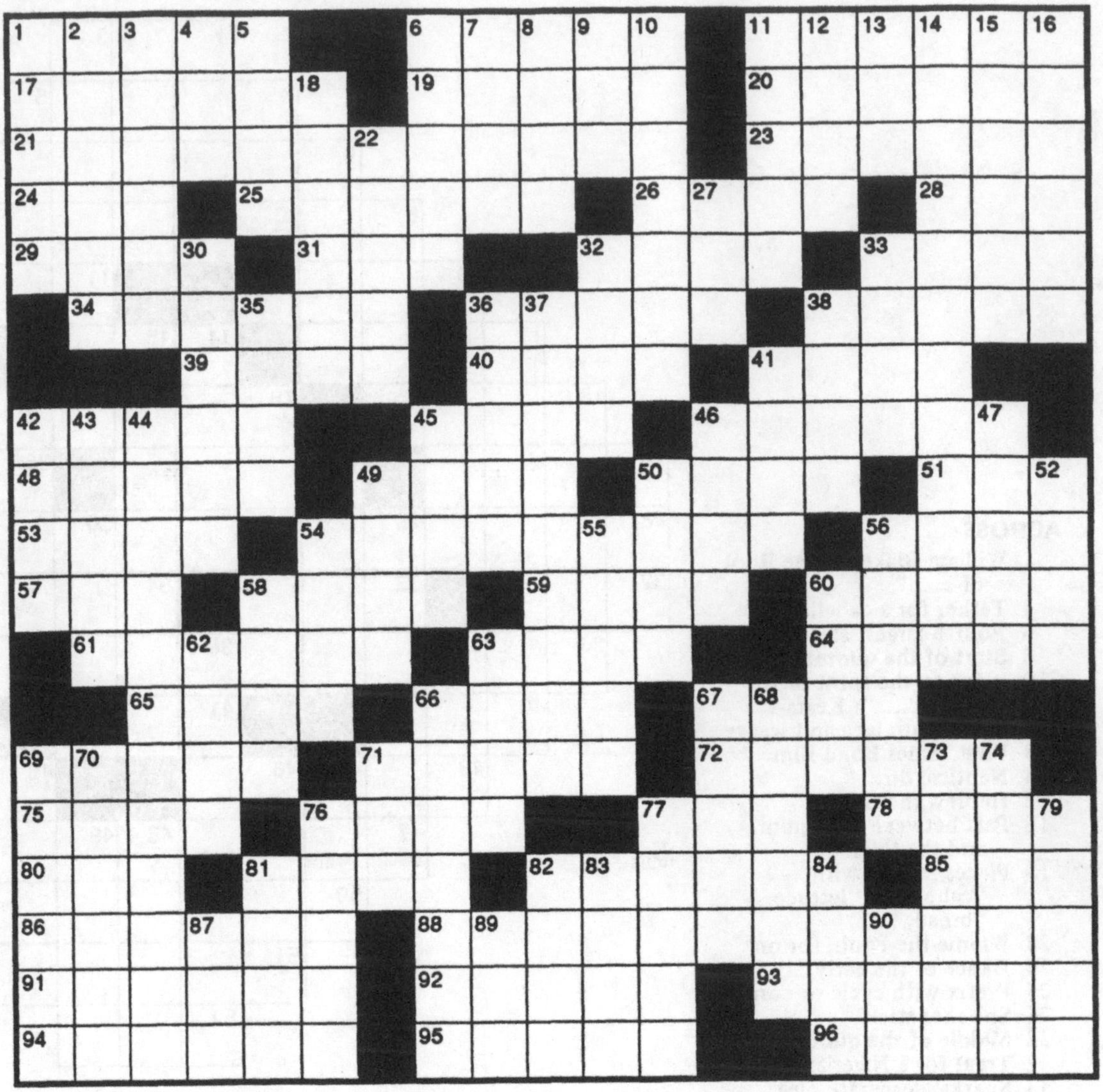

ACROSS

1 Sir's counterpart
6 Steam burn
11 Hedge evergreen
17 Noah's landfall
19 Free-for-all
20 Titanium dioxide
21 Two-part TV production?
23 Star-shaped
24 Merkel of films
25 Chabrier composition
26 Copper
28 Blas or Hodges
29 Sinks down
31 Scale's fifth tone
32 Kind of show
33 Use a whetstone
34 Begin a journey
36 Border
38 "Der Freischütz" composer
39 Iron and Stone
40 Pall Mall elevator
41 Desiccated
42 Mother-of-pearl
45 Obligation
46 Number used in tennis
48 Century plant
49 Jetty
50 Of a time period
51 Spider's"parlor"
53 Slangy negative
54 Cattishly clad for a dance?
56 Wall Street pessimist
57 JFK posting
58 Nobleman
59 Fits out
60 ". . . then ___ well it were done quickly": Shak.
61 Quinn of "Annie"
63 Pons or Tomlin
64 Mark ___, Ohio politico: 19th cen.
65 Irish port
66 Newcastle redundancy
67 Ancient Egyptian deity
69 Twenty
71 Classic oater
72 Quagmire
75 Evreux's department
76 Unheeding
77 Bandleader Calloway
78 Queens diamond
80 Marine raptor
81 Storyteller
82 "Ars ___ artis"
85 Gallic pal
86 Celtic tongue
88 Water-bearing loan shark?
91 Roving adventurously
92 Nincompoop
93 Ingenuous
94 Grayish green
95 Let up
96 Church recesses

DOWN

1 Sorcerer
2 Grounds for competition
3 Harm
4 Greek tycoon, for short
5 Amen anagram
6 First NOW president
7 Geneva research org.
8 Memorable Jordanian queen
9 Shelter
10 Counterpoint above a melody
11 Shenanigan
12 Corrosion
13 Communications inits.
14 Vestal mediator?
15 Astolat's "lily maid"
16 Fermi Award winner: 1962
18 Gauzy paper
22 Dalmatian's distinction
27 An Exalted Ruler is one
30 Famish
32 Heaviest U.S. president
33 Munich mister
35 Gula
36 Armada
37 Balanced book custodian?
38 French philosopher Simone
41 Caviar fish
42 Dog in "Peter Pan"
43 Where Greeks gathered
44 Butter's intersections?
45 Fashionable Christian
46 Very, in Versailles
47 Long
49 Hammer part
50 Tense
52 Town west of Los Angeles
54 Onion's cousin
55 Lunar trench
56 Swahili bosses
58 Dumas or Goriot
60 Odin's son
62 Body of knowledge
63 Lallygag
66 Blatant deception
67 Fine fiddle
68 German mathematician-astronomer: 19th cen.
69 Folk singer Pete
70 Arrow poison
71 Kind of chest or change
73 C# and G#, e.g.
74 A daughter of Cadmus
76 Judicial assertions
77 Gave a hoot
79 Buenos ___
81 Swedish soprano
82 Bren and sten
83 Hare vs. tortoise event
84 Big land mass
87 New Guinea port
89 Sine ___ non
90 Ref.'s kin

91 EDENIC by Dorothy Smitonick

The title gives two hints: first, that it's a pleasant puzzle and second, that a certain pleasant word appears in all the main entries.

ACROSS

1 Mus. assn.
6 Quarry
10 Gives the green light
13 Slander
18 Duplicate
19 Great destruction
21 "The Princess and the ___"
22 Acclimate
23 Question for Mary
27 Kind of alley
28 New York lake
29 "___ keepers"
30 Free from danger
33 Long time
34 Holiday times
35 Ancient god
39 Simple
41 Sail nearer the wind
44 A prefix for mural
47 ___ Royale National Park
48 Up to
50 Seine feeder
52 Tai Buddhist
54 Prairies, as described by Wm. Cullen Bryant
60 Maiden in the "Faerie Queene"
61 Wk. day
62 Cash, in Italy
63 Lover
64 Filament
66 Frosts
67 Church steeple
68 Horticultural fete
73 Bar, as in law
78 Hat ornaments
79 Cavalry swords
84 Nine-inch measures
85 Thought
86 Picnic intruder
89 Female demons
91 Request from Lord Tennyson
95 Before, poetically
96 Slave of yore
97 At no time
98 Stake
99 Verb on a penny
102 Formerly, formerly
104 Witnesses
106 British gun
107 Seaport in Okinawa
109 Age
111 Trade
113 Clouseau portrayer
116 Some are electric
118 River in West Africa
122 Advice for Peter and friends: "But don't go ___"
127 Chinese poet ___ Po
128 ___ Claire, city in Wisconsin
129 Jewish feast
130 Forty-___ (San Francisco gridder)
131 Taters
132 Desiccated
133 Pro ___ (proportionately)
134 Seaport in Japan

DOWN

1 Berliner's lament
2 Oscar Madison, e.g.
3 Monk's hood
4 "The King ___"
5 Laborers
6 City dept.
7 Beam
8 Bacchanal's cry
9 "___ the Top"
10 WW II agency
11 Cut made by a saw
12 Hawkins or Thompson
13 TV's Barney Miller
14 Consume
15 Novel by Gore Vidal
16 God of love
17 Ayres or Cody
20 Spanish American of European ancestry
24 Netherlands town
25 Kneelike part
26 Was jealous of
31 Vendetta
32 Sea birds
35 Little pieces
36 These buried Pompeii
37 Warn
38 Fernand ___, French painter
40 Sight from Taormina
42 Daughter of Mohammed
43 Hitler's title
45 An oleoresin
46 Not so common
49 Adherent
51 Lions and tigers
53 Sioux
55 Library collection
56 Pealed
57 ___ flop
58 Vocalized pauses
59 Bribe
65 Devices used for lowering small boats
66 Hosp. employees
69 Made over
70 Calorie counter
71 Valley where David fought Goliath
72 Inventor Linus ___
73 Suffix to form inchoative verbs
74 Big spender
75 More docile
76 "___ Touch of Venus"
77 Penultimate Greek letter
80 Prohibit
81 Bovary and Lazarus
82 Cheerful
83 Fry quickly
86 Ripen
87 Hub of a wheel
88 Playing cards
90 Delightful place
92 Infernal
93 Menu offerings
94 Sketched
100 Get rid of cargo
101 Ragouts stewed in wine
103 Fortuneteller
105 Emulated Caruso
108 ___ forces
110 Ragged Dick's creator
112 Instrument for Van Cliburn
113 Cut quickly
114 "___, Brute!"
115 Identification mark
117 Mixer
119 Painter, Juan ___
120 Ferber or Millay
121 Give off fumes
122 They, in Tours
123 ___ Fawkes Day
124 Soak flax
125 Sp. title
126 New Deal org.

92

CATCH ON? by Sidney L. Robbins

A veteran puzzler features offshoots of a single word. After you find it, note his droll title.

ACROSS

1 Kind of school
5 Misses a pop-up
9 Yemen port
13 "Born in the ___"
16 Sports spots
18 Diving duck
19 Honduras seaport
20 Bandleader Brown
21 Revolutionary War heroine
23 In the wrong key
25 Indian or vehicle
26 Frighten
27 Fuzzy
29 Flag
30 Marmara, e.g.
31 French spirit
32 Oakland and Mercury
33 ___ de menthe
35 Curves on roads
38 Short-legged hounds
40 Biblical mount
41 Acute incline
43 Sontag or Hayward
45 Lion in the sky
46 Far Eastern weight
49 Barker
54 Droop
57 Another barker
59 African veranda
61 Selection
62 Sharp scarp
64 Finn neighbor
67 Spelunker's spot
68 Scooped out
69 Land measure
70 Farmhand's tool
73 Dreadful
74 Pestle's companion
77 O. Henry product
78 Edom
80 Gets tanned
81 Insect areas
82 Sound from an aviary
84 Sault ___ Marie
86 Western time zone: Abbr.
87 Fixed tone
89 Glacial ridges
91 Landon
93 Parts of corsets
95 Extremely dark
101 Metal-hard
104 Math branch
107 Home-run champ
108 Lena or Marilyn
109 Less fettered
110 Mimic
112 Small combo
113 Pharoah after Rameses I
114 Palindromic title
115 "A clear conscience is ___ card": Lyly
117 Toronto is its cap.
118 Baseball ploy
121 Name for a short golf course
124 Pub drink
125 Eject
126 Cohesion
127 Amber wine
128 Sailor
129 Three-spot
130 Belittling exclamation
131 Part of a dance step

DOWN

1 Object
2 Statement sent to reporters
3 Like some G.I.s: Abbr.
4 Remits
5 ___ signum (look at the proof)
6 Short cheer
7 Sorry
8 Goblin
9 Molecule parts
10 Challenge openly
11 Brownie
12 Doze off
13 ___ Thule
14 Secluded
15 Tennis great
16 Titillates
17 Animal org.
18 Bond or Oxford
22 Poetic feet
24 Roman road
28 Profit's antithesis
32 Eastern bigwigs
33 Manger, old style
34 Mexican spread
36 Slippery one
37 Raced
39 Emote
40 "___ was saying . . ."
42 Spot for swimmers
44 Plate section
47 Certain artists
48 Take life easy
50 Grabs
51 Nodule in the skin
52 Oaks, early on
53 Latest
54 Rascals
55 Napoleon won here: 1796
56 Loft
58 Break
60 Cry at Greek orgies
63 Outfit
65 Abounding in a viscous substance
66 Egyptian deity
71 Muse of history
72 Dutch cupboard
75 Gone upward
76 Baby's toy
79 Salt Lake's state
83 Kind of tiger
85 Exile site
88 Small island
90 Josh
92 Ga. neighbor
94 Chalcedony
96 Of low quality
97 Naples neighbor
98 British passions
99 Wide open spaces
100 Troublesome
101 Mezzo-soprano Nadler
102 Wobble
103 Norse explorer
105 Jump high
106 Castor and Pollux
109 Arbuckle of early films
111 Pelagic predators
113 Quarrel
114 Erato, e.g.
115 Protein hormone
116 Old English letters
119 In great demand
120 Wilder's "___ Town"
122 "___ the season . . ."
123 Little in Nice

93

PUTTING ON PAIRS by Judith Perry
New meanings are derived from old combos in this pleasant puzzle from the Green Mountain State.

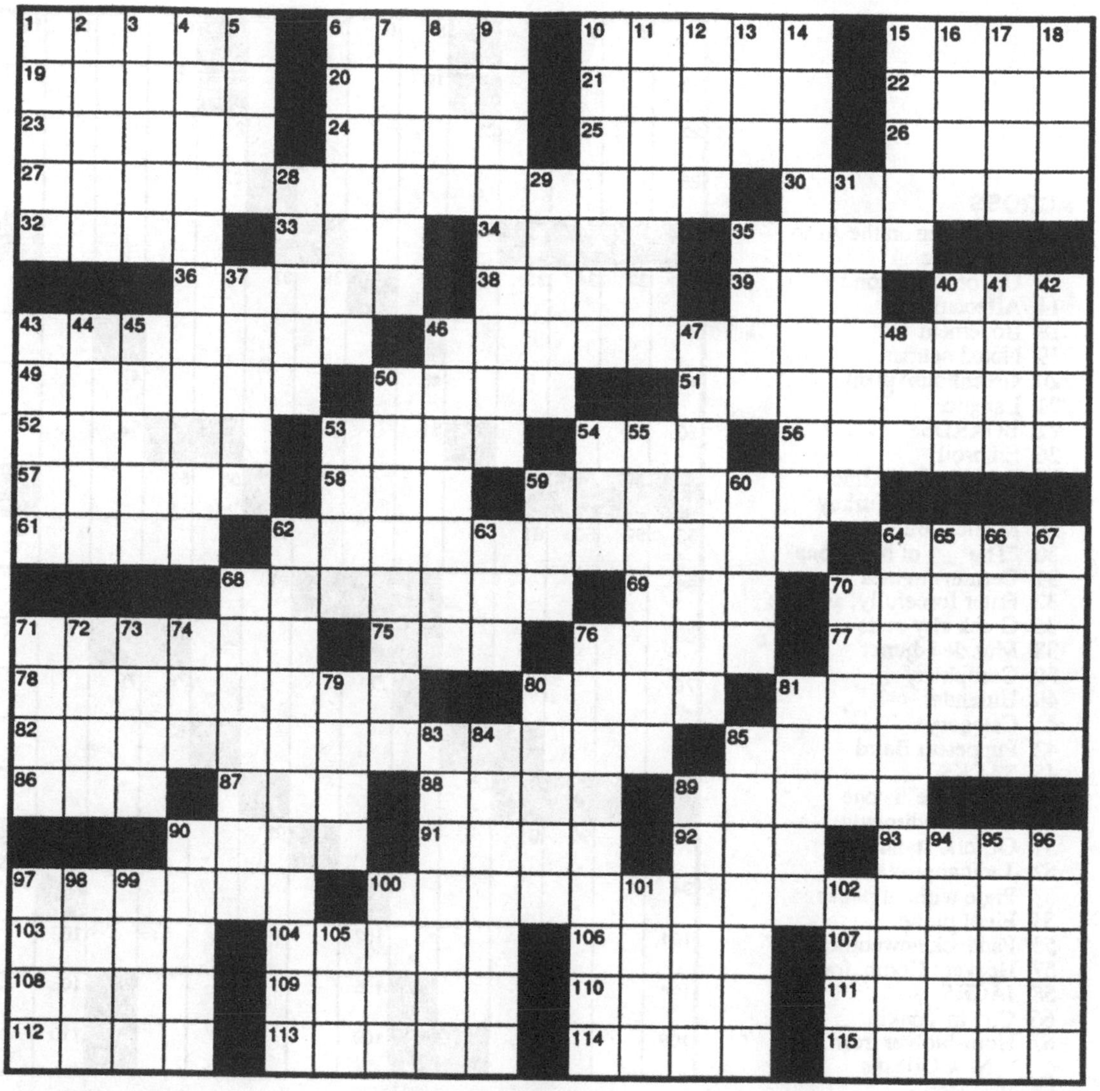

ACROSS

1 Bay on the Maine coast
6 Consequently
10 Good, in Guatemala
15 FBI agent
19 Section of the small intestine
20 Biblical pronoun
21 Reach an ultimate point
22 Like Lowell's June day
23 Yawps; blusters
24 Gothic novelist, Victoria ___
25 British parsonage property
26 ___ Royale, Michigan
27 Props for Macbeth?
30 Wise old man
32 Merit
33 Chicken or pork follower
34 Cobra genus
35 Inclination
36 Computer software
38 Rackets
39 Household pest
40 Spelling contest
43 Cuts of meat
46 Like Mike Tyson?
49 Buck and Bailey
50 ___ ex machina
51 Unguent
52 Golfer Palmer
53 Religion unit
54 Author of "Fables in Slang"
56 Greece
57 Gunpowder ingredient
58 Scotch negative
59 Burdensome
61 Propagative source
62 Like a Clemens pitch?
64 Spate
68 Lacking vitality
69 Deputy, for short
70 Small greenish bird
71 Fireplace shelf
75 Pindar creation
76 Indian of Manitoba
77 Spa at Lake Geneva
78 "___ Adano": Hersey
80 Tickets
81 Produce
82 Like a newspaper?
85 Kinsmen of 76 Across
86 Robert Burns' locale
87 Bank abbr.
88 Tennis star Mandlikova
89 ___ of Troy
90 Church calendar
91 Tied
92 Wonderment
93 Scoot
97 Arab chief
100 Supermarket staples?
103 Public survey
104 Sci-fi film: 1979
106 Flamboyantly stylish male
107 Maison compartment
108 Other
109 Slow, to Solti
110 Wide-mouthed jar
111 Outdoor sport
112 Pair
113 Bundle of twigs
114 Manxman
115 Reposes

DOWN

1 Temptress in the Odyssey
2 Greek war cry
3 Granada gentleman
4 What the inept shaver did?
5 Siberian city
6 Members of a cultural group
7 One kind of scholar
8 Symbol of goodness
9 Double play?
10 Suppliant
11 Loose
12 German river or reservoir
13 Crux
14 Test an umbrella?
15 Ground grain
16 Spar
17 Singer Guthrie
18 At no time, to Tennyson
28 Church areas
29 Caesar's first name
31 Steak and lobster
35 N.T. wedding site
37 Danube feeder
40 Security money
41 Actress Best
42 Scrutinizes
43 Bridges
44 Lofty stronghold
45 He wrote "Il Convivia"
46 Ebbed
47 Pars
48 English linear measure
50 Start of a hymn by J. G. Whittier
53 Reach the breaking point
54 Song from "A Chorus Line"
55 Revolutionist in "A Tale of Two Cities"
59 Switch positions
60 Italian host
62 Football game?
63 Peer Gynt's mother
64 Christmas?
65 The 'umble Mr. Heep
66 Military and diplomatic acronym
67 Sharpens
68 Reputed original of Robinson Crusoe
70 Zest
71 Genus of tropical trees
72 With skill
73 At hand
74 Hosp. desideratum
76 Two fish leaders?
79 Aware of
80 Ringworm
81 Joshua's Biblical companion
83 Whither
84 Victim of deprivation
85 FDR's economic policy
89 Treat
90 Lubricated
94 Salt trees
95 Lease again
96 Waste allowances
97 Cannonballed
98 Sacrosanct
99 Late actress Lanchester
100 Former opera impresario
101 German hall
102 Moscow was its capital
105 Greensward

94

FORERUNNERS by Pauline Bray
Each noun in the answers to the main entries precedes the capitalized clue.
Ms. Bray, by the way, is making her debut.

ACROSS

1 Commune on the Arno
5 Substance
9 Up, on a diamond
14 Affectation
18 Bodement
19 Noted netman
20 Greenhouse plant
21 Languor
22 BOARDS
26 Embroil
27 End of a Stein line
28 Mountain in Turkey
29 Musical Bull
30 "The ___ of Navarone"
31 Certain engines
32 Enter forcefully, as a foe
36 Greek city-state
38 Muzzle adjunct
39 Cacophony
40 Uitlander
41 Category
42 Puppeteer Baird
45 SACKS
48 "Miserere" is one
50 Caen condiments
51 Official standing
52 Tacit approval
53 Prate without pause
54 Fit of pique
55 Paddock newcomer
57 Heaven: Comb. form
58 JACKS
66 City in Tonkin
67 Horn-blower from New Orleans
68 Widgeon
69 Eniwetok is one
70 Peruke
71 Pokey, to its residents
72 "___, poor Yorick . . ."
76 Ductile material
77 HEADS
81 Anterior to: Prefix
82 "Jailhouse ___," Presley hit
83 Coalesce
84 Monsoonlike
85 Zap
86 Hebrew letter
87 Kansas Indian
88 Drops off
92 Bludgeons
93 Small follower
94 ". . . a man or ___?"
95 Contravene
96 Carte item
101 HORN(E)S
104 Thomas Gray work
105 Short stop
106 Non-professional
107 Shroud
108 Dehydrated
109 Ancient kingdom of Burgundy
110 Architectural fillet
111 Slothful

DOWN

1 Quince, e.g.
2 "___ your list": Burns
3 Spanish painter
4 Pier
5 Soothe a sore throat
6 Cordage fiber
7 Brake part
8 Vietnamese New Year
9 Increasing
10 Eagles' weapons
11 Nirvana
12 Mont Blanc, e.g.
13 Far East pagoda
14 Saturn's ring projections
15 Season
16 Arcadian
17 Screens out
21 King of England: 10th cen.
23 Cathodes' counterparts
24 Shot two under par on a hole
25 Water nymph
31 Gainsay
32 Prepares a press
33 "___ but the Lonely Heart"
34 Ampule
35 African cobras
36 Florae
37 Berkshire sound
38 Make adhere
40 James ___, pioneer Indian trader
41 Grassy hillock
42 Jejune
43 Actress Massey
44 K-Q connection
46 "Judith" composer
47 Inappropriate
48 Nice Nellie
49 Swell of the sea
54 Dexterity
55 Dissemble
56 Poet's preposition
58 Show impatience
59 Grader
60 "___ to follow sol"
61 Fountain favorite
62 Cogitate
63 First ___ (the clergy)
64 Ammonia derivative
65 Wimp
70 Candle core
71 Fish-tailed
72 "There oughtta be ___"
73 "The unlit lamp and the ungirt ___": Browning
74 Skin bane
75 Terrier type
77 Coloratura from Cannes
78 Patronage and guidance
79 "Nothing is sure ___ fight": Admiral Nelson
80 Ground fine, as mortar
82 Elmo, the former pollster
85 Late CIA director
86 He wrote "Honor thy Father"
87 Royal scion
88 Sable and Verde
89 Soap substitute
90 Airport sight
91 Elbow
92 Olympics site in 1988
93 Emaciated
95 Kolarian tribe
96 Adrenalin producer
97 Half MCXII
98 Now hear this!
99 W Indian shrub
100 One of the Maldives
102 Ems, for one
103 Arafat's gp.

95 CHROMOSOME by Peter Swift

Don't let the title fool you. The puzzle has nothing to do with genetics—and yet, in a sly way, it does!

ACROSS

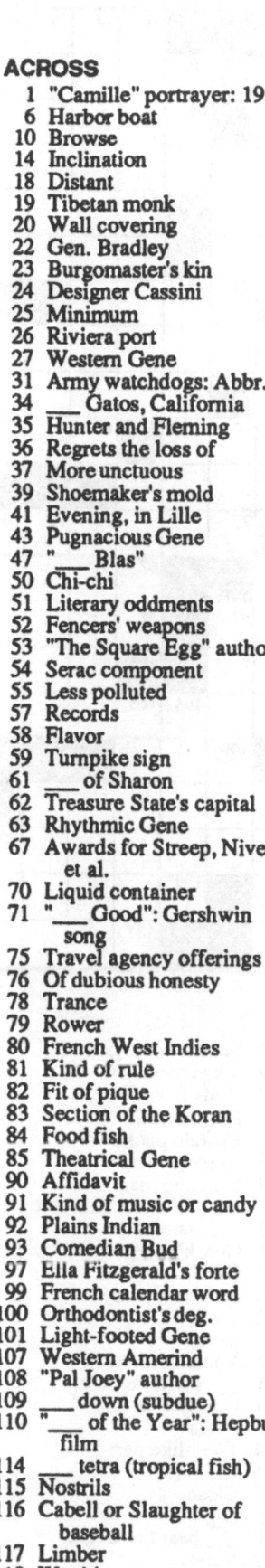

1 "Camille" portrayer: 1937
6 Harbor boat
10 Browse
14 Inclination
18 Distant
19 Tibetan monk
20 Wall covering
22 Gen. Bradley
23 Burgomaster's kin
24 Designer Cassini
25 Minimum
26 Riviera port
27 Western Gene
31 Army watchdogs: Abbr.
34 ___ Gatos, California
35 Hunter and Fleming
36 Regrets the loss of
37 More unctuous
39 Shoemaker's mold
41 Evening, in Lille
43 Pugnacious Gene
47 "___ Blas"
50 Chi-chi
51 Literary oddments
52 Fencers' weapons
53 "The Square Egg" author
54 Serac component
55 Less polluted
57 Records
58 Flavor
59 Turnpike sign
61 ___ of Sharon
62 Treasure State's capital
63 Rhythmic Gene
67 Awards for Streep, Niven, et al.
70 Liquid container
71 "___ Good": Gershwin song
75 Travel agency offerings
76 Of dubious honesty
78 Trance
79 Rower
80 French West Indies
81 Kind of rule
82 Fit of pique
83 Section of the Koran
84 Food fish
85 Theatrical Gene
90 Affidavit
91 Kind of music or candy
92 Plains Indian
93 Comedian Bud
97 Ella Fitzgerald's forte
99 French calendar word
100 Orthodontist's deg.
101 Light-footed Gene
107 Western Amerind
108 "Pal Joey" author
109 ___ down (subdue)
110 "___ of the Year": Hepburn film
114 ___ tetra (tropical fish)
115 Nostrils
116 Cabell or Slaughter of baseball
117 Limber
118 Wapitis
119 Kind of bone
120 Adore, in a way
121 Eli

DOWN

1 Shapely leg: Slang
2 Lobster ___ Newburg
3 Painter Lichtenstein
4 Audience sounds, at times
5 Life ___ (easy living)
6 Plods
7 City in Colombia
8 Black cat, to some
9 Arch
10 Drawingroom
11 Gangs
12 Saracen, e.g.
13 Ovid's surname
14 Windfall of a sort
15 Gives off
16 Mother-of-pearl
17 Playing cards
21 Thwarts
28 Scand. country
29 Suffragette Carrie
30 Ethereal
31 Upholstery fabric
32 Pres. Fillmore's successor
33 Schedules
38 ___ League
39 Hereditary
40 Food thickener
41 Snick's partner
42 Wallet stuffers
44 Like some seals
45 Thistle-like flower
46 Higher in rank
47 Stare wonderingly
48 Byzantine image
49 Cambio coin
53 Salmagundi
55 TV's Jack and family
56 Amphoras
57 Present time
58 Part of a calyx
60 Stowe transports
61 Made a sudden sally
62 Diplomat Cordell
64 Sidestep
65 Russian coin
66 Scarlett's husband
67 Auricular
68 "Star Wars" captain
69 Prompted
72 "___ I": 1941 hit song
73 Made canine noises
74 Expunges
76 Blind part
77 Dry's companion
78 Risky business: Abbr.
81 Assigned post
83 Compass pt.
85 Boozers
86 Dies ___
87 Took turns
88 Girasol
89 Transportation system
93 Make up for
94 Nut or palm
95 Put up with
96 Uncorks
97 Lesions
98 Racing driver's ___ helmet
99 One of Reagan's friends
102 Quid of tobacco, to some
103 Mata ___
104 Something forbidden
105 Granny or hitch
106 Hindu discipline
111 Part of USMA
112 Actress MacGraw
113 Bess Truman, ___ Wallace

96

COLOR SCHEME by Ernie Furtado
Personages from all walks of life run across and down within Ernie's opus.
(Solvers wondering about 68 Across can find it listed in RHD II.)

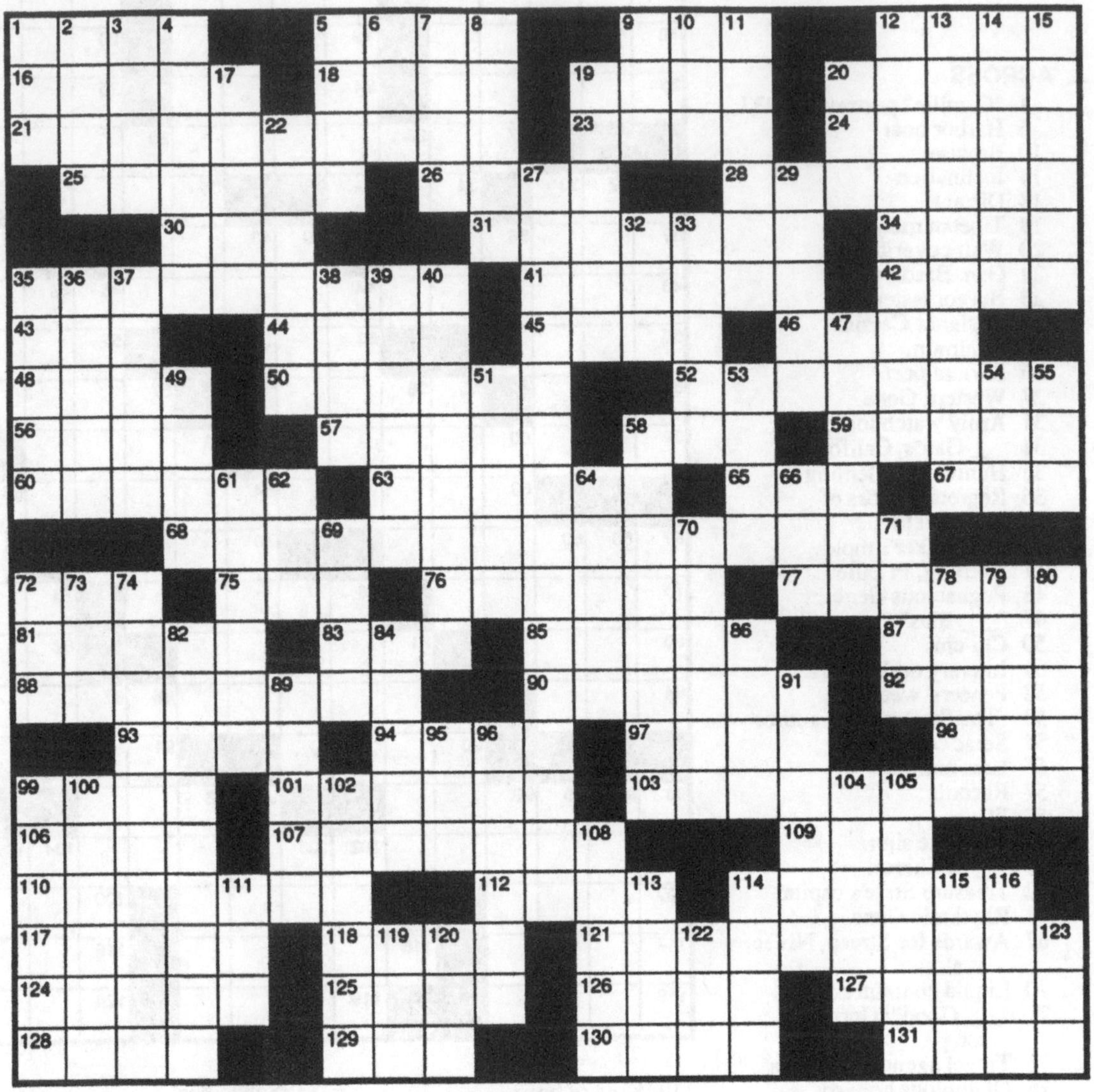

ACROSS
1 Caspar, Melchior and Balthazar
5 Profound
9 Nagpur loc.
12 Hodges or Columbo
16 "American Bandstand" host
18 Designer Jacobsen
19 Field of study
20 Paganini's birthplace
21 Baseballer Bob's candy?
23 Uriah of fiction
24 ___ Ababa
25 Birchbarks
26 "Square Dance" star
28 NFL field generals
30 SW Peru river
31 Butcher-birds
34 Ontario tribe
35 Karen's teetotum?
41 Interpolate
42 Filed Chapter 11
43 Varnish ingredient
44 Whale
45 Rend
46 "___ Window"
48 Waterford locale
50 Temperament
52 When whistles blow
56 Wife of Camelot
57 North and South
58 "Born in the ___"
59 "Maltese Falcon" star
60 Take away
63 Put in a word
65 For shame!
67 Suffix for crossword
68 John O'Connor's method?
72 Lively dance
75 Rorqual
76 "___ Fideles"
77 Letter closer
81 Sun-dried brick
83 Host follower
85 Kind of snatcher
87 Departed
88 Ancient catapult
90 Illegal jobs
92 Location
93 Sting film
94 Crimson Tide, for short
97 Actress Foch
98 ___ Cayes
99 Sinatra role
101 Carney character
103 Asa's old horse?
106 ___ volat propriis
107 In the world
109 Abbr. at LAX
110 Some are TV
112 ". . . shall bring forth ___": Matthew
114 O'Neill creations
117 Orly sight
118 Cousin of etc.
121 "Third Man" Harry's halo?
124 Wash cycle
125 Sound
126 Land west of Nod
127 Slowdown
128 "Riders of the Purple ___"
129 Unit for Cash
130 Uproars
131 JFK arrivals

DOWN
1 Twice DLXXV
2 Wilder or Baldwin
3 Vasco da ___
4 Sardonic
5 June honorees
6 Transgress
7 Chemical compound
8 Gourds and melons
9 Wrath
10 Once-named
11 Smart
12 Grange's garments?
13 Insure
14 Evening gathering
15 Sauced
17 Start of a joke
19 Brian in "I Confess"
20 Sign for motorists
22 Dry, as lumber
27 Betty's pachyderms?
29 Texas athlete
32 "Love ___ Simple Thing"
33 Composer Jerome's family
35 Extort: Slang
36 "Mule Train" singer
37 Bitter
38 Gin
39 They're all arms
40 Hermione's friend, et al.
47 Mother's relatives
49 NEA concern
51 Line anew
53 Dobbin's delight
54 Dec. and Sept.
55 Long or now preceder
58 Unnerve
61 Cheese protein
62 Quattro minus uno
64 Offspring
66 Actress Hagen
69 Regimen
70 Polite answer
71 Mundy and Ryan
72 Tyson has a good one
73 Actress Lupino
74 Forty-niner's forte
78 French interjection
79 Stage direction
80 Della from Detroit
82 Ben's beak?
84 Buffalo puckster
86 Active volcano
89 Durango man
91 Lord Wimsey's creator
95 ___ standstill
96 Coach's concern
99 Fuzzbuster foes
100 Actress Hussey
102 Starts
104 Delay
105 Van Doren, et al.
108 ___ up (hibernated)
111 Compass pt.
113 Nests
114 Toothlike part
115 IRS reps.
116 Close
119 Digit
120 ___ bear (aardvark)
122 Valets
123 BSA units

97

OFFSHOOTS by Nancy Scandrett Ross

Nancy said the idea for this puzzle came to her while she was watching "Family Ties."

ACROSS

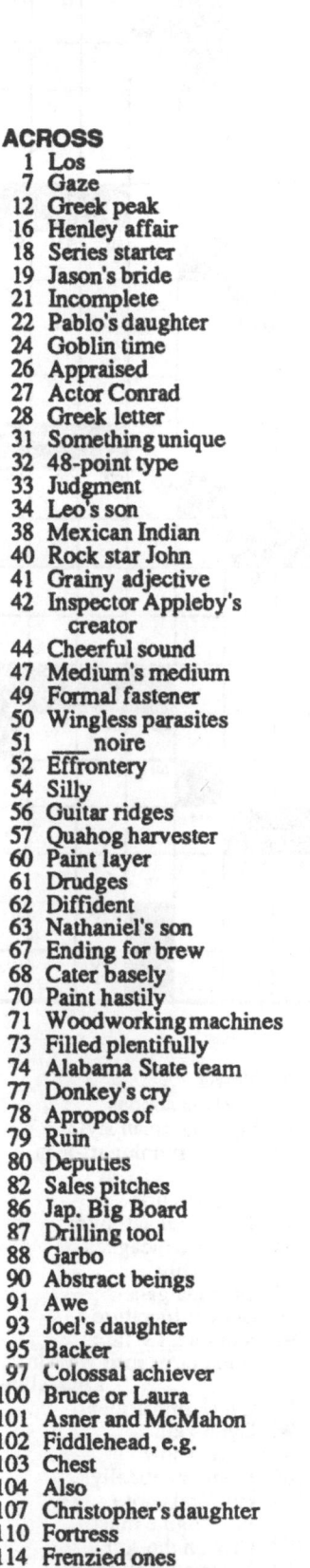

1 Los ___
7 Gaze
12 Greek peak
16 Henley affair
18 Series starter
19 Jason's bride
21 Incomplete
22 Pablo's daughter
24 Goblin time
26 Appraised
27 Actor Conrad
28 Greek letter
31 Something unique
32 48-point type
33 Judgment
34 Leo's son
38 Mexican Indian
40 Rock star John
41 Grainy adjective
42 Inspector Appleby's creator
44 Cheerful sound
47 Medium's medium
49 Formal fastener
50 Wingless parasites
51 ___ noire
52 Effrontery
54 Silly
56 Guitar ridges
57 Quahog harvester
60 Paint layer
61 Drudges
62 Diffident
63 Nathaniel's son
67 Ending for brew
68 Cater basely
70 Paint hastily
71 Woodworking machines
73 Filled plentifully
74 Alabama State team
77 Donkey's cry
78 Apropos of
79 Ruin
80 Deputies
82 Sales pitches
86 Jap. Big Board
87 Drilling tool
88 Garbo
90 Abstract beings
91 Awe
93 Joel's daughter
95 Backer
97 Colossal achiever
100 Bruce or Laura
101 Asner and McMahon
102 Fiddlehead, e.g.
103 Chest
104 Also
107 Christopher's daughter
110 Fortress
114 Frenzied ones
115 Asian palms
116 Buck's trademark
117 Monster loch
118 Eur. sea
119 Adapted

DOWN

1 Dada's Hans
2 Meadow
3 Husbandry: Abbr.
4 ___ Grosso, Brazil
5 Auricular
6 Turbine part
7 Mast
8 Wire: Abbr.
9 Parka
10 Change shifts
11 Poetry muse
12 Tolkien villain
13 "South Pacific" sailor
14 John's daughter
15 Seated, by the Seine
17 Cuban ballerina
18 "The Desert Song," e.g.
19 Scotland Yard dept.
20 Top-notch
23 Contrition
25 Bartok and Lugosi
28 Rams' dams
29 Hoffmann product
30 Edmonton's prov.
32 Edgar's daughter
33 Luke and Mark: Abbr.
35 Friendly Islands
36 Like some vacationers
37 Greek god
39 Zed
42 Pelvic artery
43 Final innings, usually
45 Pronounces
46 Like most teenagers' rooms
48 Evangelist Gantry
51 Bikini part
53 Permit
55 Negative prefix
56 Swatter alternative
57 Some necklaces
58 Michael's daughter
59 Decorated anew
61 Cooks quickly
62 Fountain favorite
64 Less usual
65 Dancer's coiffure
66 Gridiron abbr.
69 Aberdeen's river
72 Ogling
74 Kind of car
75 Gull's cousin
76 Profligate ones
79 Feathery scarf
81 Pigs' digs
83 To be, in Monaco
84 Prevaricated
85 States
87 "Un ___ Di"
89 Dark Continent
92 Brittany city
93 Played in a session
94 Finale
95 At a distance
96 Baltic feeder
98 Eastern religion
99 Guinean president: 1958-84
103 Degs.
104 Policeman's territory
105 Novel ending
106 Reception room
108 Hospital VIPs
109 Twelfth-century date
111 "___ Freischütz"
112 Before
113 Hallucinogenic letters

98 DOUBLE ENTENDRES by Maura B. Jacobson

Crosswords' recognized Queen of Pundom offers you one of her usual treats.

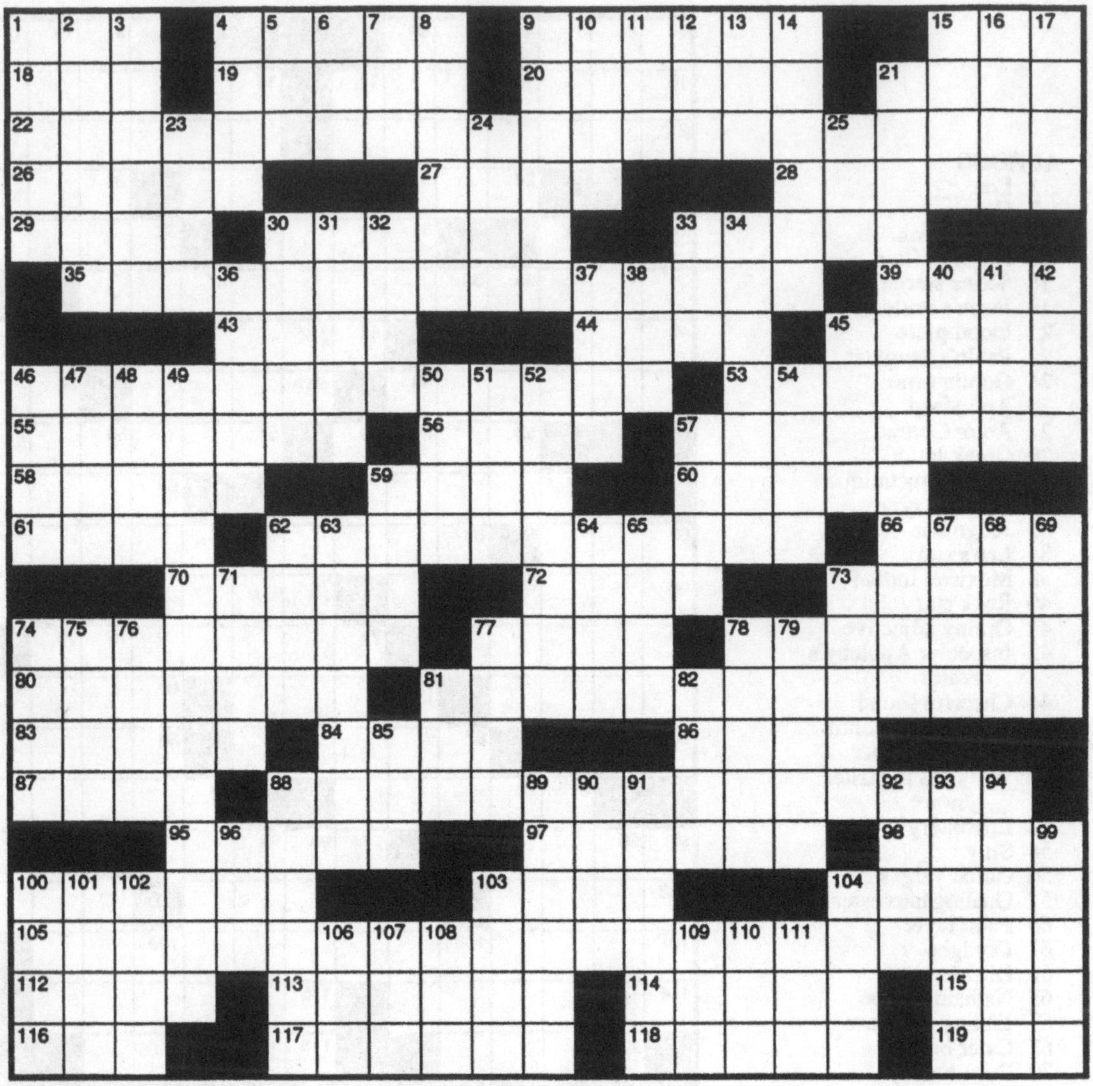

ACROSS

1 Name of 13 popes
4 Deepest-voiced opera singers
9 Minimum group for a meeting
15 Gun the motor
18 Director Grosbard
19 Alan of films
20 Illinois city
21 Fiji's capital
22 How vegetable markets arrange lettuce?
26 Takes it easy
27 Outermost Aleutian island
28 Almost
29 Shipshape
30 Like a flight of steps
33 Stem's opposite
35 How milady cared for her toes?
39 Lackluster
43 Surname in spydom
44 It's south of Minnesota
45 Flora and fauna
46 Cost of a one-way ticket?
53 Marlon's "Streetcar" role
55 Duelists' sidekicks
56 Holy Tibetan
57 Doctors' signposts
58 Small-time
59 Hurt grievously
60 Human trunk
61 Coin drop
62 Leave Bob stranded?
66 Have status
70 Macho type
72 Harvesters do it
73 Ford flop
74 Foliage
77 Without a stitch
78 Iroquois tribesmen
80 Plunderers' activity
81 Lion-tamer's fear?
83 Worked the Old Vic
84 Droughty
86 Western pact
87 Big butte
88 Jewelry for the household help?
95 Faculty bosses
97 Shining examples
98 Peter, Paul or Boris
100 Make urgent appeals
103 This might be light
104 Myanmar, formerly
105 Squeezed Smokey?
112 Drying kiln
113 Convoy
114 Part of USNA
115 One's born days
116 Carrie or Louis
117 Eye interior
118 Shelled out
119 Jackie's sister

DOWN

1 Arsene ___, fictional detective
2 Gives the slip to
3 Posse's quarry
4 Put-downs from Scrooge
5 "Right you ___!"
6 Go schussing
7 Round Table title
8 Bisected
9 French four
10 A language of India
11 Extinct: Abbr.
12 Double-crosser
13 Numero ___
14 Lodestone
15 Essen's valley
16 Knievel the daredevil
17 Diversify
21 Thou shalt not sit?
23 Place for a chapeau
24 Peary's Greenland base
25 Eterne
30 Not flighty
31 Problems brought to podiatrists
32 Not care ___
33 Ply the needle
34 British bistro
36 Impostor
37 Costa ___
38 Hostile one
40 Rock's go-with
41 Suit to ___
42 Howls at the moon
45 Embargoes
46 Recipe abbrs.
47 Achilles' weakness
48 Prefix for plasm
49 Eviscerated a pencil?
50 Blueprint
51 Speakeasy incident
52 Lacking virtue
54 Flag
57 Way station
59 More than several
62 Last word of the Bible
63 Shopper's delight
64 Wimp's kin
65 Hic, ___, hoc
67 Fungus spore sacs
68 Furniture wood
69 Ultimatum word
71 Wife of Geraint
73 Insect sci.
74 Metric weight unit
75 Paddy product
76 Newts
77 Auction actions
78 Steel, German style
79 Adlai's running mate in 1956
81 Harpo's curls
82 Theatrical acronym
85 M.D.'s colleagues
88 Preferably
89 Granada gala
90 Lyrical literature
91 Summer TV fare
92 What three men were in
93 "Life ___ . . .": Longfellow
94 Cause impairment
96 Dyne's kin
99 Street show
100 Black, poetically
101 Hospital photo
102 Fire engine must
103 City on the Aar
104 Make a break for it
106 ___-tung, now Zedong
107 In every hundred: Abbr.
108 Reine's mate
109 Seance sound
110 She never had a mother
111 Thrash

99

BIG BANDS by Betty Jorgensen

A noted constructor remembers the kings of swing and their nostalgic era. There are plenty of "thematic" entries below, starting with 22 Across.

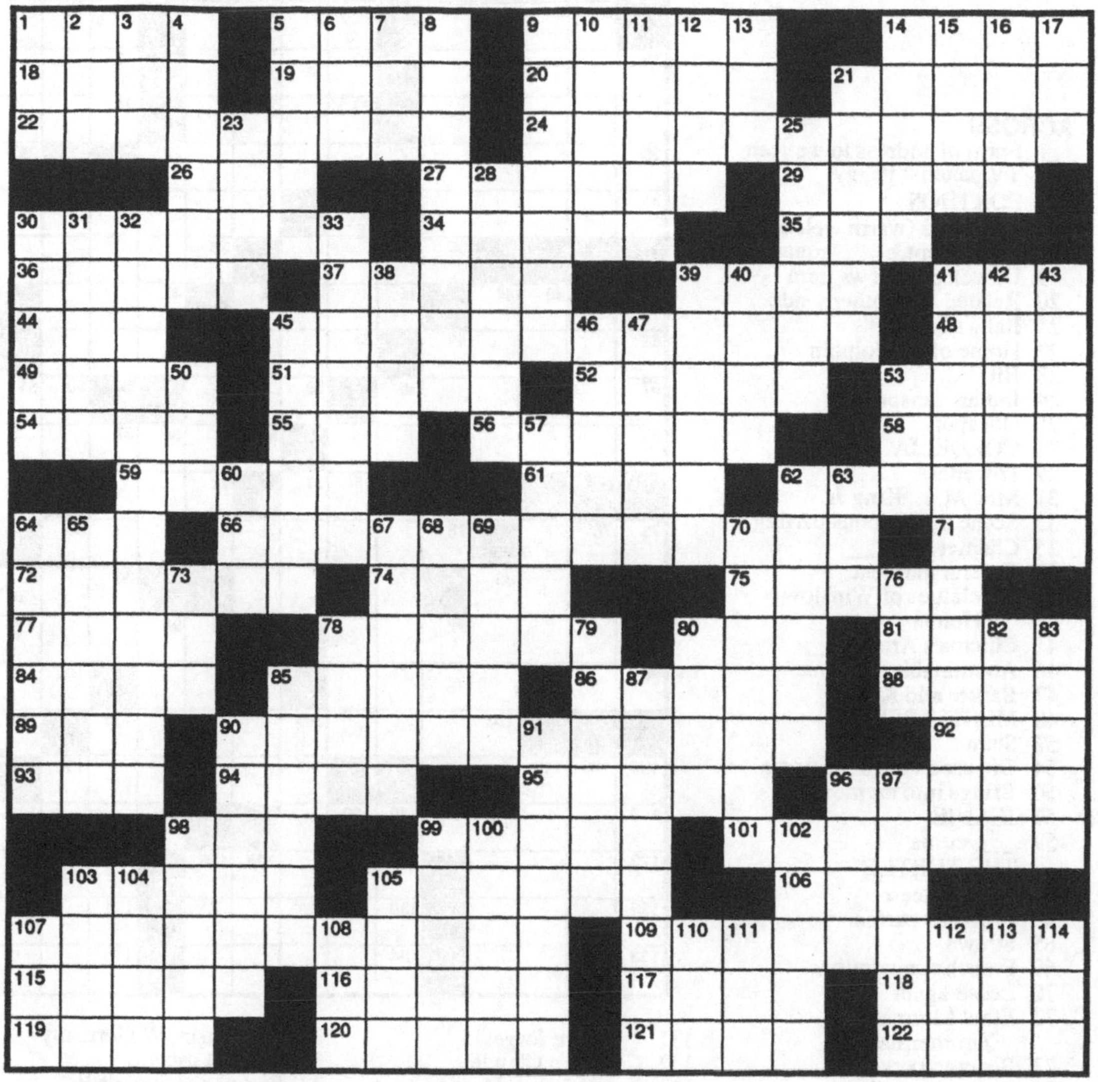

ACROSS

1 Reimbursed
5 Chard genus
9 Oscar de la ___
14 Speech flaw
18 Comparison words
19 Dramatic conflict
20 Remove from jurisdiction
21 Purvey
22 Big band's ID
24 "I'm Getting Sentimental Over You"
26 ___ longa, vita brevis
27 Storehouses
29 "When the ___ Played at Twilight"
30 Charlatan
34 Compare
35 Hgwy.
36 Designer ___
37 Selassie
39 Attica township
41 "And so to ___": Pepys
44 Old French coin
45 "Nola"
48 Bard's "before"
49 Cato's 251
51 What the virgule represents
52 Horse opera
53 Fit of pique
54 Shooting marbles
55 "Double Wedding" star
56 Sally
58 Formerly
59 Sun: Comb. form
61 Nothing, in Nîmes
62 Babe's master
64 Greek letter
66 "Take the 'A' Train"
71 GMT's astral rel.
72 Psychiatric disorder
74 Guillaume's gal pal
75 Maine college town
77 Competed
78 Feared fly
80 Driller's deg.
81 Uh-uh
84 Vapor: Comb. form
85 "___ she is, Miss . . ."
86 The last frontier?
88 A cheese
89 Common, in Maui
90 "Puttin' On the Ritz"
92 P preceders
93 Maritime eagle
94 Slaughter of baseball
95 Treaty site of 1814
96 Braid
98 California fort
99 Loss of breath
101 Hamlet's last word
103 "___ is me!": Shelley
105 Permits
106 Coq au ___
107 "Moonlight Serenade"
109 "Begin the Beguine"
115 Buenos ___
116 Tearful one
117 When banks open
118 Overhang
119 Droplet
120 Old hat
121 Small fry
122 Editor's instruction

DOWN

1 Orchestral area
2 Timber tree
3 Suffix for Gotham
4 Realm
5 "Asleep in the Deep" singers
6 Self
7 Ending for wan or won
8 Dominican painter
9 Captured anew
10 Go to Gretna Green
11 Name, to Julius
12 Conway and Holt
13 ___ which way
14 Goodly
15 ___ boy!
16 Sighted
17 Crowbar
21 Mexico's conqueror
23 Lapses
25 Window type
28 Masonic doorkeepers
30 Oust
31 Hajji's goal
32 "Rhapsody in Blue"
33 Wind of the Rockies
38 Judge Hardy's son
39 Overly fond
40 Rapier
41 "Let's Dance"
42 Heathers
43 Watch part
45 Muscle relaxant
46 Shinto temple gate
47 Make tardy
50 Honshu bay
53 See 15 Down
57 Heraldic borders
60 Mormons: Abbr.
62 Ignominious Lizzie
63 Numero ___
64 Court dance for Henry VIII
65 Wooer
67 Loom bars
68 Grinder's wheel
69 Metrical measure
70 Caterwauling creatures
73 "___ declare!"
76 Compass reading
78 Among: Archaic
79 Avoid
80 Rhett Butler's last word
82 Button not to push
83 Ham it up
85 Bicycle built for two
87 Ring-necked bird
90 Long-necked birds
91 Slighted
96 Ballet movement
97 Shutterbug's purchases
98 Had
99 Apportion
100 VMI rat
102 Campus climbers
103 "It's a sin to tell ___"
104 Greek Juno
105 Jordanian princess
107 Jabber
108 Gary loc.
110 Jem's friend
111 Trotyl
112 Castor, for one
113 Mad. or Lex.
114 Sodden

100 CHARACTERS/CREATORS by Jeanne Wilson

Here's an interesting idea. Jeanne has chosen a literary character. Your task is to identify the author.

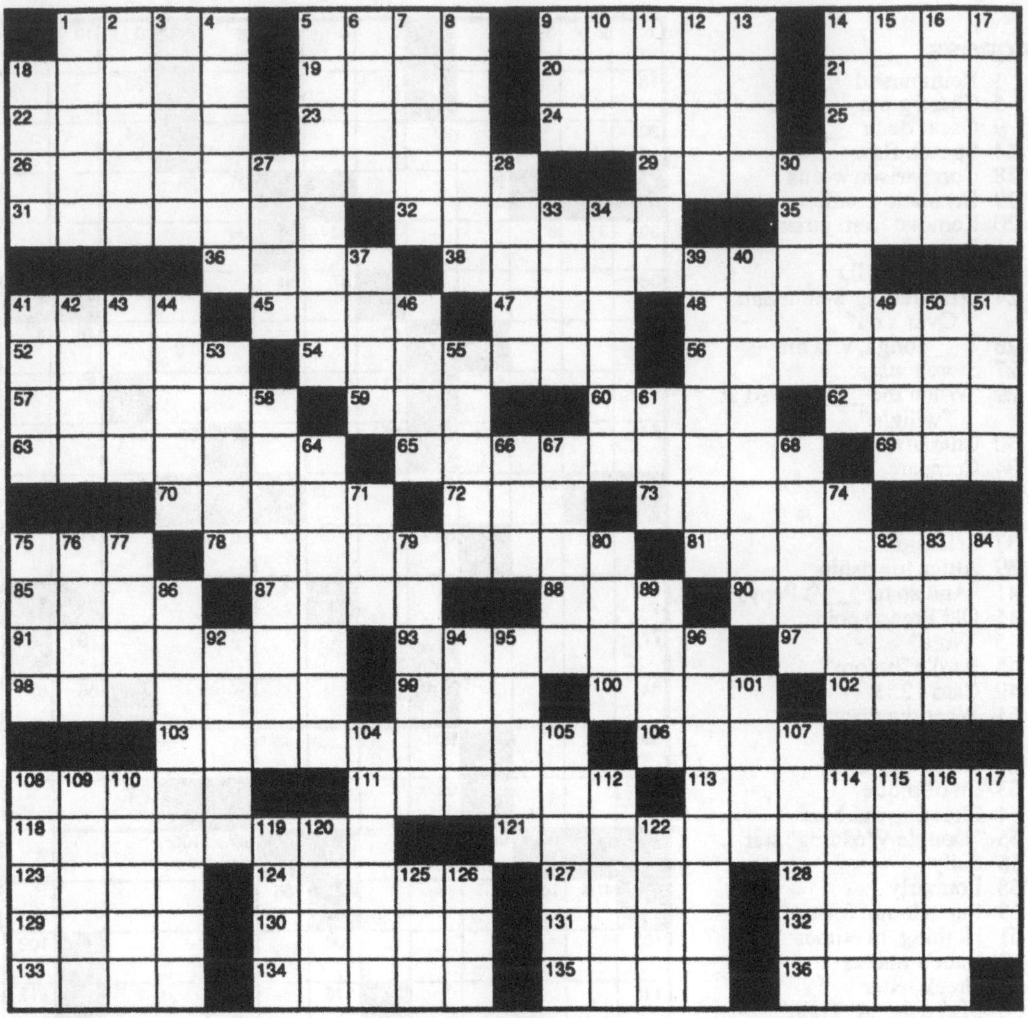

ACROSS

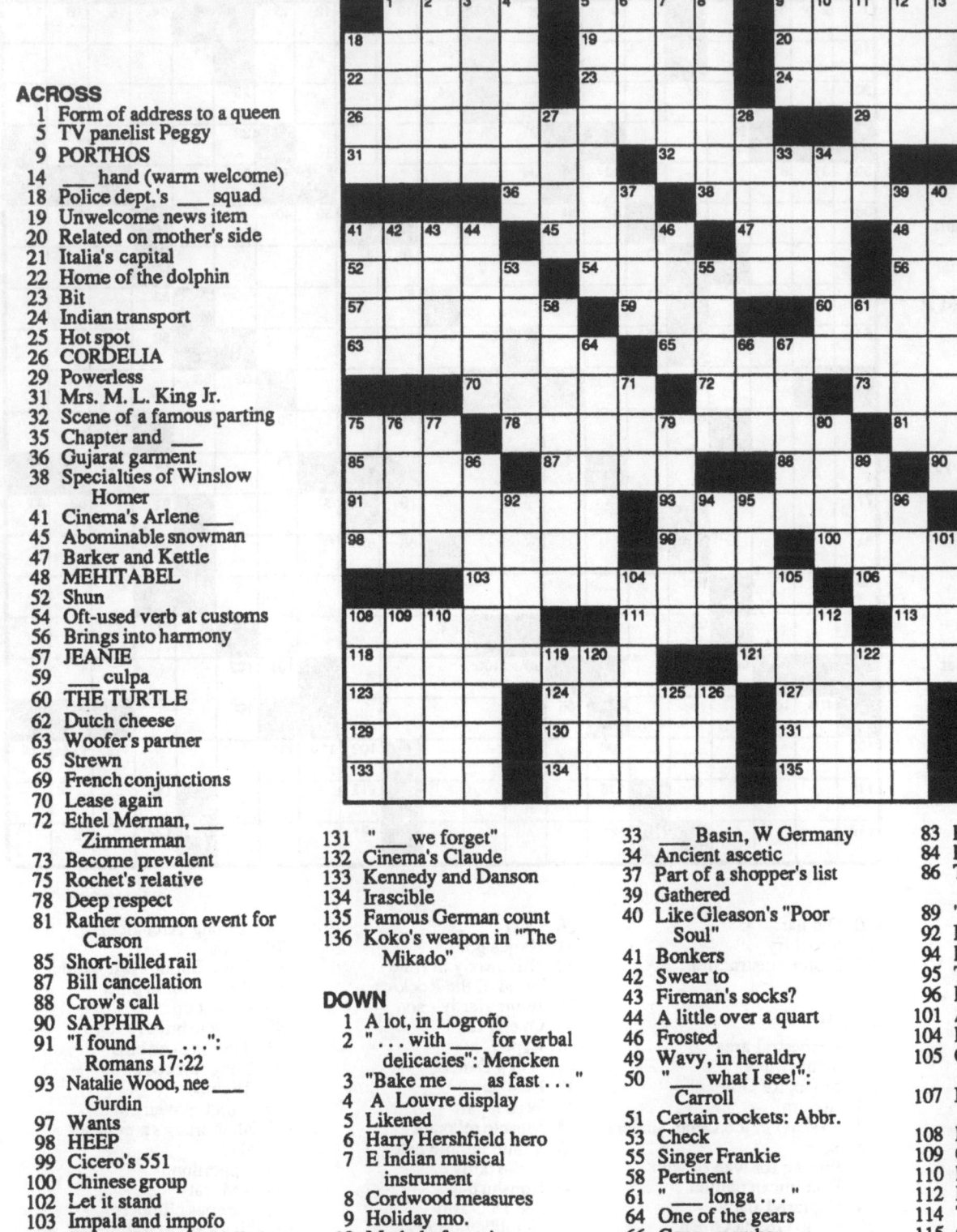

1 Form of address to a queen
5 TV panelist Peggy
9 PORTHOS
14 ___ hand (warm welcome)
18 Police dept.'s ___ squad
19 Unwelcome news item
20 Related on mother's side
21 Italia's capital
22 Home of the dolphin
23 Bit
24 Indian transport
25 Hot spot
26 CORDELIA
29 Powerless
31 Mrs. M. L. King Jr.
32 Scene of a famous parting
35 Chapter and ___
36 Gujarat garment
38 Specialties of Winslow Homer
41 Cinema's Arlene ___
45 Abominable snowman
47 Barker and Kettle
48 MEHITABEL
52 Shun
54 Oft-used verb at customs
56 Brings into harmony
57 JEANIE
59 ___ culpa
60 THE TURTLE
62 Dutch cheese
63 Woofer's partner
65 Strewn
69 French conjunctions
70 Lease again
72 Ethel Merman, ___ Zimmerman
73 Become prevalent
75 Rochet's relative
78 Deep respect
81 Rather common event for Carson
85 Short-billed rail
87 Bill cancellation
88 Crow's call
90 SAPPHIRA
91 "I found ___ . . .": Romans 17:22
93 Natalie Wood, nee ___ Gurdin
97 Wants
98 HEEP
99 Cicero's 551
100 Chinese group
102 Let it stand
103 Impala and impofo
106 Where Socrates strolled
108 Rousseau classic
111 Campaign subjects
113 As an alternative
118 Some magicians can do this
121 JEEVES
123 Rainbow
124 Deli item
127 Plane preceder
128 Shove; jostle
129 Molding
130 "Maria ___," 1933 song
131 "___ we forget"
132 Cinema's Claude
133 Kennedy and Danson
134 Irascible
135 Famous German count
136 Koko's weapon in "The Mikado"

DOWN

1 A lot, in Logroño
2 ". . . with ___ for verbal delicacies": Mencken
3 "Bake me ___ as fast . . ."
4 A Louvre display
5 Likened
6 Harry Hershfield hero
7 E Indian musical instrument
8 Cordwood measures
9 Holiday mo.
10 Merkel of movies
11 Wild one
12 Anagram for moat
13 Ooze
14 Gargoyle description
15 Romeo
16 Prayer endings
17 BEATRICE
18 Pear
27 Corset component
28 Tissue swelling
30 Aboveboard
33 ___ Basin, W Germany
34 Ancient ascetic
37 Part of a shopper's list
39 Gathered
40 Like Gleason's "Poor Soul"
41 Bonkers
42 Swear to
43 Fireman's socks?
44 A little over a quart
46 Frosted
49 Wavy, in heraldry
50 "___ what I see!": Carroll
51 Certain rockets: Abbr.
53 Check
55 Singer Frankie
58 Pertinent
61 "___ longa . . ."
64 One of the gears
66 Cong. member
67 Blemish, in Bologna
68 Parlor piece
71 Hanoi holiday
74 Do, re, mi
75 Author of "The Road to Mecca"
76 WKRP's secretary
77 Bric-a-___
79 Sonata movements, often
80 Orient
82 Bombast: Abbr.
83 Relinquish
84 Formerly, formerly
86 Takes an indigestion dose, in Britain
89 "___ on first?
92 Belief
94 Pennines or Dolomites
95 Traffic jam
96 Poison opposer
101 Auctioneer's word
104 Feudal lords
105 Cinema's George and Vivienne
107 Namesakes of a son of Jacob
108 PRUFROCK
109 Get together
110 Like Harvard's walls
112 He does chimneys
114 TV actor Michael ___
115 Composer/jazz pianist Blake
116 ". . . can live as cheaply ___"
117 ". . . fresh ___ of night": Milton
119 Aid, pejoratively
120 Fable, e.g.
122 "The ___, he knows . . .": Kipling
125 Suffix with persist
126 Minstrel's song

101 IN ALL DIRECTIONS by Dorothy Cannan

Dorothy says she had a hard time concentrating while she constructed this one. For some reason, her mind kept wanting to go every which way.

ACROSS

1 Castilian hero
6 Muslim princess: Var.
11 Clerical robe
14 Swedish name of Turku
17 Interstice
18 Deli staple
19 Shies, as a horse
21 Hades
23 Thane of Cawdor
24 IQ-test man
25 Swiss river
26 Flock member
28 Dull color
29 Bionomics: Abbr.
30 Cornice molding
31 Andiron
34 Big ___, Cal.
35 Glut
36 Edgar ___ Masters
37 Yearned
38 Pictures of health
40 Promoted
42 Orwell's alma mater
43 Arctic explorer
46 Large vat
47 "Catalina" author
51 Alegre and Novo
52 Iniquity
53 Skittle's cousin
56 Nebraska Indian
57 Hindu soul
58 Fosse
60 "I ___ Write a Book"
61 Arabic letter
62 Polo ___
63 Outward appearances
65 Shortened the rough
67 One with a clutch
68 Porter's "___ Men"
70 Abstract beings
71 City NE of Venice
72 Venetian three
73 London suburb
75 Opponent
76 O.T. book (Douay)
77 Notice
79 Soft sheepskin
81 Issei's child
82 Cracked
83 Directly adverse
86 Air anew
88 Ask
89 Help
90 Barter
94 Alexandrite, e.g.
95 Word with bank or bond
97 ___ Benedict
98 Camouflage
99 Morocco capital
101 Begley and McMahon
102 Tubercle
103 Petcock
104 Grieve
106 Ornamental cultivated area
110 Brandy cocktail
111 Cling
112 Develops
113 Vessel's curved plank
114 Urban rails
115 Unworldly
116 Watchful

DOWN

1 Beethoven's 3rd
2 "___ your heart be troubled": John 14:1
3 Small rib
4 Cay: Archaic
5 Hoover or Aswan
6 Iraqi port
7 Additional
8 Interval
9 Nice friend
10 Made picture frame corners
11 ___ forces
12 Actress Thompson
13 Movie mood maker
14 ___ as pie
15 Bear Hall-of-Famer
16 Biblical land
17 French clerics
18 Coastal bird
20 19th U.S. pres.
22 Lamina
27 Joined
30 Surfeits
31 Bona ___
32 Lethargic
33 Kind of soup
37 "Purple Rain" star
39 Neighbor of Zamb.
40 Roy Bean's concern
41 "___ and cry mew": Shak.
42 Hobgoblin, in 49 Down
43 Clary, for one
44 Stoats
45 Salieri opus
48 Keyless way to start a car
49 Greek capital, to Spiros
50 Union general and family
51 Language of W Pakistan
52 LX, to Chaucer
54 Transitional zone
55 Cormorant
58 Las Vegas employee
59 Otto I's realm: Abbr.
64 Disgrace
66 Turf accountant's concern
69 Cigar or city
74 "Lyrical Pieces" composer
76 Bagnold, et al.
78 Maize spike
80 Rowers
83 Town in Maine
84 Hindu poet
85 Eleanor of song
86 Wassermann antibody
87 Incarnate
88 Four times a day: Rx
90 "Blood Oath" author
91 He played Willy Wonka
92 Period before Christmas
93 Hammer heads
94 Kind of roots
96 Deviates
97 Finnish lake
100 Dijon donkey
102 Ukraine capital
103 Colorado ski spot
105 Rustam's father
107 Harem room
108 Greek letter
109 Sweetheart, in Sligo

102

ANIMAL ANTICS by Jean M. Hunt

Jean has packed eleven "beastly" puns into this puzzle. When you hunt them down, you'll agree that she comes in feat first.

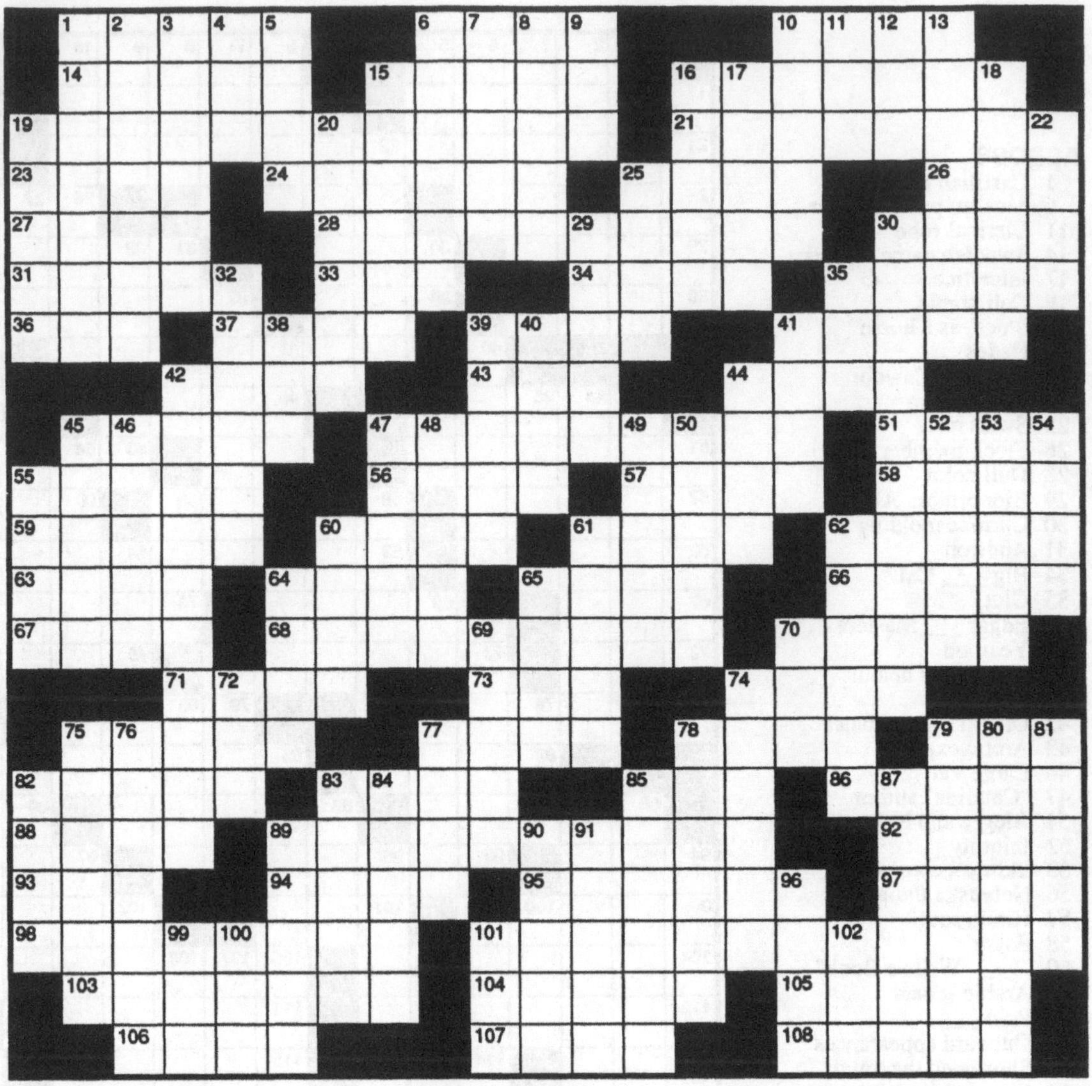

ACROSS

1 Carp
6 Swedish liquid measure
10 Synthetic rubber
14 Stage whisper
15 Book by Richard Byrd
16 Safekeeping
19 Wandering wildcat?
21 Beautiful bunny?
23 Jacob's brother
24 ". . . he was fain ___ on Cupid's name": Shak.
25 Folk wisdom
26 T. A. Daly's "___ Carlotta"
27 Part of the defunct SEATO
28 Coxcomb cats?
30 Indian princess
31 Esther ___, actress
33 Where future lts. train
34 Takes aliment
35 Necessity for John Williams
36 Town near Liège
37 British Poet Laureate: 1715–18
39 Winged
41 American artist, Winslow ___
42 Preserve in brine
43 Headland
44 "___ Timberlane," S. Lewis novel
45 Fine china
47 German deer?
51 Male cervid
55 Penitent's emotion
56 City north of Des Moines
57 Mars, to Aristotle
58 Celebes ox
59 Injures
60 Sweetsop
61 Capital of South Yemen
62 Thespian
63 One of Chekhov's "Three Sisters"
64 Opposite of the windward side
65 Mother of Horus
66 Decree
67 Hammer part
68 Steer stampedes?
70 Tip of a shoelace
71 Judge
73 "___ victis" ("woe to the vanquished")
74 Fit of shivers: Scot.
75 Tiresias, et al.
77 Conflagrate
78 Belfry denizens
79 Spring that may give some zing
82 Disconnect
83 Outer portion of earth
85 Son of Hermes
86 Ryan's daughter
88 Leather, in Lille
89 Following Fido?
92 Medicinal grape syrup of old
93 Prince Valiant's son
94 Nanny in Nanking
95 Irritate
97 Tastes a drink
98 Put money on a rodent?
101 Simian sparkles?
103 Courtyard
104 Took out knots
105 "___ her poor dog a bone"
106 Animal fat
107 Reduce a fever
108 Mates of 51 Across

DOWN

1 Ammunition wagon
2 Donkey is sick?
3 Optical
4 First name of a Ugandan exile
5 It follows Mardi Gras
6 Candidates for naturalization
7 Single-celled organism
8 Talus
9 Legal matter
10 Dull speakers
11 Suffix with depart
12 Apprehend
13 Twin, e.g.
15 ___ Lorraine
16 Sprout
17 Mountain lakes
18 Author Wylie
19 Stiller's partner
20 Musical request to Moses
22 An anagram for nail
25 Mendacious one
29 Tether
30 Straitjacket for a sheep?
32 Disintegrates slowly
35 Cattle genus
38 Pay dirt
39 April 1 baby, e.g.
40 Resins
41 Beldams
42 Ordinary caribou?
44 Neighbor of St. Lô
45 Fine-grained rock
46 Coat with plaster
47 Honey badger
48 Moslem ruler
49 Thompson or Hawkins
50 Lock
52 Square columns
53 Avian abode
54 Common vetch
55 Talk ___ (discuss one's work)
60 Astringent
61 White, as with fright
62 Distinguished
64 Burrows and Vigoda
65 Munich's river
69 Neighbor of the epiglottis
70 Buchwald or Carney
72 Stray
74 Rawboned
75 Eminent pointillist
76 Manifests
77 Aquae Sulis, to the Romans
78 Buttressed
79 Tarnished
80 Darling doggies?
81 Save or pile up
82 Incrustation
83 Plant of the cashew family
84 Teed off
85 Little finger
87 Delegate
89 Jeweler's measure
90 Subtle sarcasm
91 Catches a carp
96 Balt
99 French vineyard
100 One hundred square meters
101 Danish measure
102 ___ polloi (common people)

103 DOWN MEXICO WAY by William Canine

This puzzle's title has also been heard following 108 Across.

ACROSS

1 Rope
6 E Lansing inst.
9 Play divs.
12 Covenants
17 Makes adjustments
19 Yellowish-orange
21 Hokkaido port
22 Meryl of "Ironweed"
23 Chiron, for one
24 ___ down (subduing)
26 Quetzalcoatl or Lawrence title
29 Confusion
30 Shoe size
31 Flop
32 From: Lat.
33 Of the hipbone: Comb. form
34 Fact
37 Victim of Spanish treachery
43 Linksman Sam
44 Pester
46 Confections
47 In a gentle manner
48 Outdone
52 Former Turkish leader
53 Tumble
54 Orderly
55 Got up
57 Watergate senator
59 Melville character
63 Actress Cheryl
64 Weighty books
65 Snuffle
66 Surfeit
67 Devoured
68 Stowe character
69 Meadow
70 Little peaks
71 Cornmeal dish
73 Garrulous bird
76 Fresco painter Leonello
78 Excalibur's handle
79 To see ___ believe
80 On reserve
81 Actress-dancer Leslie
82 Out of the wind
83 Celebes gulf
85 American seer
87 Contorted
89 Flotow opera
92 Pine relative
94 Snake
95 Places
96 "The Mexican Spitfire"
98 Former labor leader
102 Muang Thai formerly
103 Dowel
104 John or Jane
106 Comparative suffix
107 To Ozawa, theme
108 1939 Autry hit
116 "___ Dallas"
118 "Fidelio" heroine
119 Curb
120 Doctor
121 Neighbor of Mali
122 Ascends
123 Burros
124 Literary monogram
125 Punkish
126 Vigilant

DOWN

1 Held out
2 Gibson of tennis
3 Lewis's "Main ___"
4 Exude
5 Soviet city
6 Alexander of ___
7 Hastened
8 Samovars
9 Capone's was famous
10 Brilliant stroke
11 Arroyos
12 Annie of "Designing Women"
13 ___ Z
14 Famed Mexican comic
15 Poem of eight lines
16 Timepiece
18 Tater
20 Suffix for Israel
25 Hot dog!
27 Silent
28 Bird's org.
35 Single
36 Hombre
38 Uproar
39 Habaneras, e.g.
40 Conceit
41 Author Grey and namesakes
42 It's rarely legal
43 Peruvian coin
45 Mexico's neighbor
47 Loser at San Jacinto
48 Thuringer's brother
49 Lacuna
50 Most peculiar
51 Condition
53 Andiron
56 Muscat man
58 Of the sole
60 Mark of "Star Wars"
61 Churchill's successor and predecessor
62 Won over
72 Tijuana fast food
74 Put 2 and 2 together
75 "Atta Troll" poet
76 Breadth
77 Jury
78 Zeppo's brother
84 Exclamations
86 The Sun King, Louis ___
88 Residue
89 Spankers and mizzens
90 Brief Verdi or Wagner air
91 Rotary tools
92 Of the throat
93 Skelton or Ball
96 One of XIII Popes
97 Writer Akins
99 Grand Ole Opry instrument
100 Antenna
101 Hold up
103 High school exams
105 Subsides
109 Recount
110 Greedy ones
111 Individual
112 1040, e.g.
113 Half a sextet
114 Grampus
115 Teheran coin
117 New Guinea port

104

REVERSE DISCRIMINATION by Lynn Lempel

Here's one of the best puzzles we've had the pleasure of editing. Feminists won't be the the only ones to enjoy it!

ACROSS

1 Stroke for Becker
4 Conforms
10 Devise
15 NASCAR member's concern
18 Word with pick or pack
19 Range
20 Employee in a paint factory
21 Act human
22 Fare for Alice
23 Deli delights?
27 Impair
29 Umpire's palms-down call
30 Speck of dust
31 Cone contents
32 Provide
34 Koppel or Turner
35 Luxurious
37 Division of Fr. Indochina
39 Air passages in one's head
41 Was a stool pigeon
43 One trillion: Comb. form
44 Crowning achievement?
49 Dwelled
51 Moved slowly
52 Doublet attachment
53 Falcon feature
54 Civil-rights leader Randolph
55 Anthropoids
58 Roman charioteer
59 Highway to Fairbanks
63 Product ID or logo
65 Bouquet ___ (herbs for soups, etc.)
66 A people of C. Sudan
67 Caesura
68 Gounod contemporary
69 Facts and figures
70 Yes siree!
71 Beat
72 Entries, as in a column
74 Shortly
75 Heroic narratives
77 Revs. around the sun
78 Arrangement
79 Demure, in England
80 Seats of power
82 Strauss's "___ Italien"
84 Calms
86 Suffix for an endurance contest
87 Lacking a key
89 Rosalind's pursuer
92 Forever?
95 Re the USN
96 Singer Nina
98 Start
99 "Tomorrow" singer
101 Odin's worshipers
102 Fire starter
103 Capital of Nigeria
107 Upbraid
109 Anne, Geneviève, et al.: Abbr.
110 Performed to perfection
112 Robin Goodfellow
113 TV talker?
117 Successful puzzler's exclamation
118 Soul, in Savoie
119 Photo color
120 Wobble
121 J. Herriot, e.g.
122 Submissions to a pub.
123 Darrow depicter
124 Presbyters
125 ". . . and they ___ ours": Perry

DOWN

1 Pliant
2 Monitor's graveyard
3 Blue follower
4 Pallor
5 Engravers' tools
6 Vents
7 State
8 Trustworthy
9 Juan or José preceder
10 Act
11 Open
12 Rambler's word
13 Ecclesiastical enclosures
14 Writer Jong
15 Sharpened anew
16 Emulate the Boy Scouts
17 Sra.'s counterpart
24 Carlotta or Josephine
25 Comfort
26 Subgroup?
28 Datebook division
33 Merchandise; stock
36 Asian range?
38 Provoked
40 Make another hole
42 Crandall of baseball
44 Actress Farrow
45 Establish
46 Enraged
47 Operagoer of note
48 Greece's ___ Islands
50 Tear-jerker
53 Trinidad's partner
56 Dinner entree?
57 Descendants of Darius
58 Pres. of Indonesia (1945-67)
60 Cassis ingredient
61 According to custom
62 Bill
64 Inhabitants?
66 Absentee
68 Fleur de ___
73 Copied Rumpelstilzchen
76 Penn and Connery
80 "___ crowd"
81 Girder material
83 Cunning
85 Joseph Smith, e.g.: Abbr.
86 Showed strain
88 Ready for use
89 Stop ___ dime
90 Forced payments
91 Business perks
92 Delineate
93 Cadged
94 One of the Mouseketeers
97 Arrangement of tesserae
100 German surrealist
102 Bialy relative
104 Fruit of the myrtle tree
105 Earthy pigment
106 Execute a camel
108 Detective, at times
111 Jody Baxter's pet
113 Predicament
114 Apr. analyst
115 Shoshonean
116 Vanderbilt emp.

105

HIDDEN HANDLES by Dorothy Smitonick
Referring to Dorothy's title, we counted sixteen different ones below. How many can you uncover?

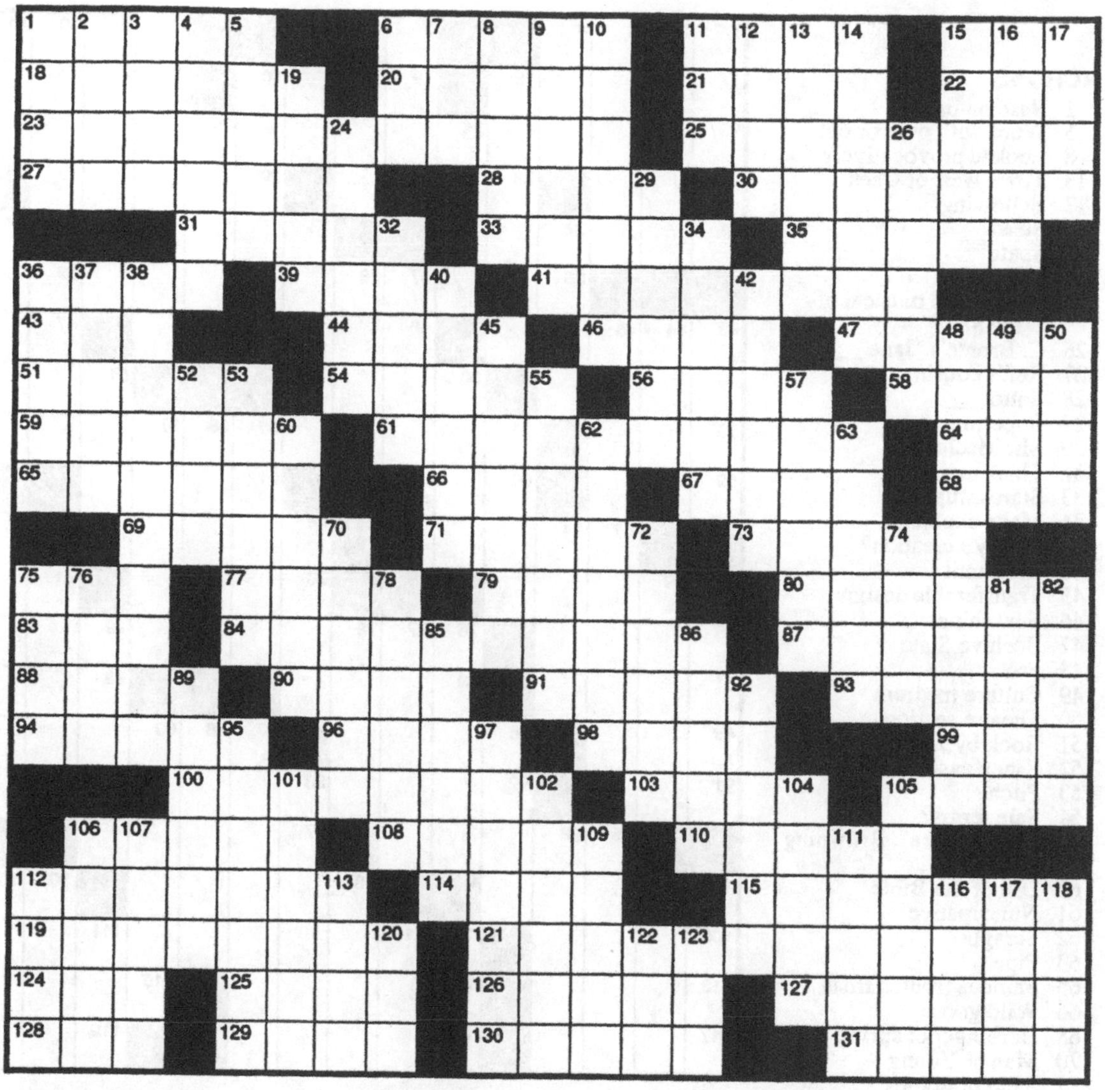

ACROSS

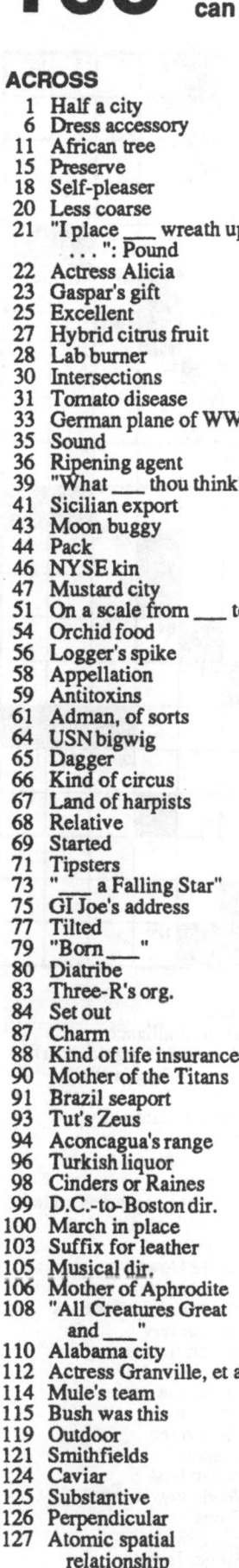

1 Half a city
6 Dress accessory
11 African tree
15 Preserve
18 Self-pleaser
20 Less coarse
21 "I place ___ wreath upon . . . ": Pound
22 Actress Alicia
23 Gaspar's gift
25 Excellent
27 Hybrid citrus fruit
28 Lab burner
30 Intersections
31 Tomato disease
33 German plane of WW II
35 Sound
36 Ripening agent
39 "What ___ thou think?"
41 Sicilian export
43 Moon buggy
44 Pack
46 NYSE kin
47 Mustard city
51 On a scale from ___ ten
54 Orchid food
56 Logger's spike
58 Appellation
59 Antitoxins
61 Adman, of sorts
64 USN bigwig
65 Dagger
66 Kind of circus
67 Land of harpists
68 Relative
69 Started
71 Tipsters
73 "___ a Falling Star"
75 GI Joe's address
77 Tilted
79 "Born ___"
80 Diatribe
83 Three-R's org.
84 Set out
87 Charm
88 Kind of life insurance
90 Mother of the Titans
91 Brazil seaport
93 Tut's Zeus
94 Aconcagua's range
96 Turkish liquor
98 Cinders or Raines
99 D.C.-to-Boston dir.
100 March in place
103 Suffix for leather
105 Musical dir.
106 Mother of Aphrodite
108 "All Creatures Great and ___"
110 Alabama city
112 Actress Granville, et al.
114 Mule's team
115 Bush was this
119 Outdoor
121 Smithfields
124 Caviar
125 Substantive
126 Perpendicular
127 Atomic spatial relationship
128 Mistake
129 Within: Comb. form
130 Endures
131 Walk-of-Fame sights

DOWN

1 Crossthreads
2 Taj Mahal site
3 Advance
4 Stay around
5 Questioned
6 Certain NCO
7 French company
8 Queen ___ lace
9 Sir Henry Wotton on angling: "A ___ his mind"
10 Tongue folds
11 Rule, in India
12 Of the ear
13 Asian robe
14 Humanlike robot
15 Bamboo stems
16 Spy of 1776
17 Some votes
19 Barred to outsiders
24 " . . . stone gathers ___"
26 Base for dyes
29 With arms ___
32 Takes ___ at
34 Reluctant
36 At ___ for words
37 "The Maids" playwright
38 Manicurist's need
40 Lever, to a French student
42 Not native
45 Comfortable
48 Rock drill
49 Atlanta arena
50 Inert gas
52 Bulrush
53 Greek letters
55 Insect's lateral plate
57 Scold
60 "___ 17," 1953 film
62 Roman plates
63 Eye part
70 "___ more blithe than he": Bickerstaff
72 Pay in full
74 Crowd
75 Theatre org.
76 Hammer head
78 Accordion and box
81 Lorna of fiction
82 Piscivorous birds
85 Washington city or river
86 Stops
89 Bio
92 Triangular sail
95 Liquid hydrocarbon found in pine-needle oils
97 "Master, ___ how the fishes . . . ": Shak.
101 Motive
102 City W of Binghamton
104 Island in New York Bay
105 Official seal
106 Grief, in poesy
107 Conclude
109 Trigon relatives
111 Supermarket section
112 Au naturel
113 Run before the wind
116 O'Hara home
117 Arabian prince
118 Medals
120 Yoko ___
122 Greenwich time: Abbr.
123 "___ a boy!"

106

SPICY GROANERS by Norman S. Wizer

Our Pennsylvania punster suggests that you approach his thematic entries *gingerly*.

ACROSS

1 Base on balls
5 Word with over or out
8 Looked provocatively
13 Town west of Caen
17 Bellowing
19 Stead
21 Spate
22 Caprice
23 Hollywood musical of 1948?
26 C. Brontë's "Jane ___"
27 Ref.'s cousin
28 Sotto ___
29 Impertinent
30 Mr. Macho
31 Thick mixtures
33 Stares stupidly
34 Make exultant
36 Ripley's creation?
40 Elec. unit
43 Transferable design
46 Fuel ships
47 Beehive State
48 Pro
49 Culture medium
50 Theatre section
51 Book by J. C. Oates
52 Fancy case
53 Pitch
54 Sale terms?
58 "___ is more": Browning
59 Trouble
60 Dill of the Bible
61 Nuncupative
62 Seraglio
63 Pipe
65 Famous frontiersman
66 Wild goose
68 Harbinger of spring
70 Man or Young
71 Kind of grapes
72 Rhode Island Red
75 Arabian gulf
76 Divorce edict?
80 Singer Sumac
81 Drop; globule
82 Words of comprehension
83 A Bobbsey twin, et al.
84 Struck, old style
85 Half of a candy
86 Book of the Bible
87 Lend
90 Care for
91 Business abbr.
92 Looney Tunes sign-off?
95 Romulus's twin
97 Raiments of Roma
98 Bridal paths
102 Disney dog
104 Claw
105 Eject
107 Time period for Gina
108 Cut of meat
109 Catty remark about an aging actor?
113 Handle for Hadrian
114 Expect
115 Does hand work
116 "If I ___ Rich Man"
117 Football holders
118 Juniper
119 Saul's grandfather or uncle
120 Mamie's predecessor

DOWN

1 Settle a debt
2 Fragrance
3 Bisque, borsch, and broth
4 Rustic musical instrument
5 One of the Waughs
6 Kind of light or house
7 Wahine's garland
8 Counterbalances
9 Tongue or language: Comb. form
10 Australian parrot
11 Business abbreviation
12 J.F.K. predecessor
13 Like Sue or Georgia Brown
14 Repeatedly?
15 Milano moola
16 Augury
18 Disclose
20 Hazardous
24 Optimistic
25 Nocturnal animal
30 "Music ___ charms . . ."
32 Stowe transportation
33 Helmet-shaped anatomical structure
34 Infiltrate
35 Consisting of topsoil
37 Not so tight
38 "The ___" (Ashcan School)
39 German steel center
41 Timid person
42 Crystal polyhedron
43 Computer input
44 Victorian oath
45 Relaxing vacation?
50 Singer Cantrell
51 Cattail or pickerel weed
52 Verve
54 Man often raised
55 Slipknot
56 Humorous
57 Beat with a stick
62 A leporid
64 Cocktail garnish
65 Twining stem
66 ___ the purple (of royal lineage)
67 Has compunctions about
68 Religious leader
69 Music hall
71 Babushka
73 Exude
74 Western alliance
76 Woman's triangular scarf
77 These in Puebla (Fem.)
78 Nidus
79 Related maternally
84 Mtg.
86 Sphere preceder
87 Seclude
88 Biblical people descended from Japheth
89 Venus, e.g.
90 See 32 Down
93 Balanced state
94 Word with eye or back
96 Lab burners
99 French river or region
100 Pelagic predators
101 Grandiose stories
102 Lot plan
103 Unescorted
104 Despot
105 Italian host
106 World power, formerly
109 Crone
110 ___ Jima
111 Singer Janis ___
112 Arachnid's trap

107 FLORA OR FAUNA? by Elizabeth Arthur

Botanists *and* zoologists should both appreciate this Chicagoan's clever theme.

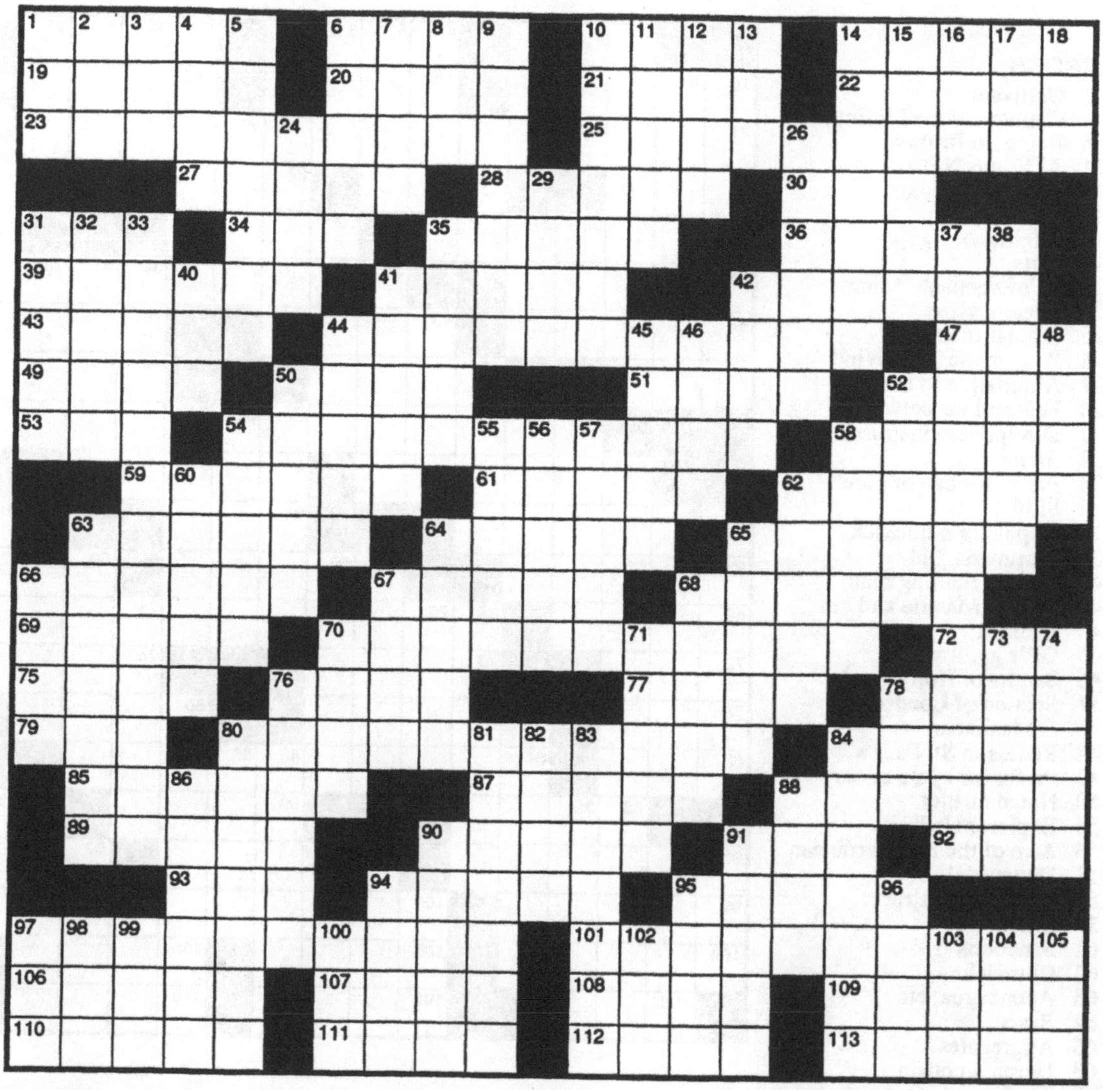

ACROSS

1 Accumulate
6 Secular
10 Knock down
14 Lifts at Vail
19 French soldier of WW I
20 Singer Guthrie
21 Met solo
22 Caravan stop
23 Geraniaceous herb
25 Leopard lily
27 Kind of bank
28 After some time
30 Zilch
31 Harem room
34 Flub
35 Jades
36 After land or sea
39 Hairy
41 Manners
42 Crown
43 "Canterbury ___"
44 Showy, vinelike plant
47 Abner's hillbilly partner
49 Author Bagnold
50 Buckeye State
51 "The Last Emperor" star
52 MX home
53 Mr. Hammarskjöld
54 Overseas
58 Summary
59 Smooth off
61 Her cat was Dinah
62 Rids of vermin
63 French star
64 Adhere
65 Red cedar
66 Ascus contents
67 Net
68 Nape
69 Whittles
70 Chief foundation
72 Amphib. vessel
75 Quart's four
76 Fizzy drink
77 Congers
78 Lavish love (on)
79 Ginger ___
80 Skunk cabbage
84 Cringe
85 Automat sight
87 Pinch together
88 Lustrous cotton
89 State-police unit
90 Praying: Lat.
91 Roost
92 Scot. author
93 Goddess of plenty
94 Kind of hunt
95 Stomata
97 Galax
101 Peruvian daffodil
106 Ms. Lauder
107 Of an age
108 Bailiwick
109 Like the otary
110 Approaches
111 Tyne of TV
112 Seal schools
113 Color changers

DOWN

1 Away from: Prefix
2 A Stooge
3 Overhead space
4 Oscar Madison, for one
5 Like ocean depths
6 ___ of love
7 Like Death Valley
8 Indisposed
9 Coal miner
10 "The ___ Gun Alive," Ford film
11 Bald-eagle relatives
12 Pinocchio at times
13 "Mighty ___ a Rose"
14 Of current interest
15 "The ___ of Reading Gaol"
16 Gray or Candler
17 ___ Tin Tin
18 Arrival at J.F.K.
24 Annoyed
26 Preserve fodder
29 Tuscany river
31 Chose
32 Anka's first hit
33 Avocado
35 Neophytes
37 Aristolochia
38 Imitate
40 Ref. book
41 State with a rocky coast
42 Eat in style
44 Transient fad
45 Sleek
46 Off-white
48 Swabs
50 Some exams
52 Letter extension
54 Attempts
55 Morning prayer
56 Actress MacMahon
57 Kitchen utensil
58 Variety show
60 Puts to sleep
62 Mends
63 Shoulder ornament
64 Ice pinnacle
65 Tongue-lash
66 Humane org.
67 Menu fish
68 Soak
70 Mountain passes
71 Appears
73 "Family Album" author
74 Sea swallows
76 "The ___ Came C.O.D.," 1947 film
78 i part
80 ___ Republic of China
81 In a bitter manner
82 Kind of door
83 Winter apple
84 Served a party
86 Horn blower
88 Beget
90 "The Main Event" star
91 Fountain treats
94 Evening, in Naples
95 Particolored
96 Do in
97 Jonson or Blue
98 Suffix for crossword
99 Zeta follower
100 United
102 PGA member
103 Wrath
104 Irish sea god
105 Furlong's 220: Abbr.

108 STATELY NAMES by Ernie Furtado

Solvers from all over the U.S.A. will find something of interest here.

ACROSS

1 Gallivant
4 Country singer McEntire
8 Being, to Brutus
12 AFC plus NFC
15 Actress Verdugo
17 Dash
18 Lifeline of Egypt
19 Parts
21 "Unforgettable" singer
24 Theatricalize
25 Glacial matter
26 "___ to the West Wind"
27 Alternative to man?
28 Few and far between
29 Disciplinary instruments
32 *Annie* ___
33 Prefix for cab or cure
34 Silly
35 Hopalong's sidekick
39 Hammarskjöld
42 Adlai's running mate
43 NBAer Manute and kin
44 Inclined
45 GP's gp.
46 Sandra of Hollywood
47 Section of London or Manhattan
48 Recess in St. Paul's
49 Prefix for cycle or carp
50 Noted hustler
55 Explorer Hedin
56 Arm of the Mediterranean
57 Dictatorial
58 Windy City airport
59 Brook
61 Sanctions
62 Church key
63 Aconcagua, etc.
64 Bract
66 Aggregates
68 Heron's cousin
69 *The Voyage Out* author
72 Edmond O'Brien movie: 1950
73 Laura Nyro's "And When ___"
74 Newcastle upon ___, England
75 Kin of aves.
78 Sea bird
79 Discharge
80 Gaucho weapon
81 Absinthe ingredient
83 Cellular initials
84 Three-time Super Bowl MVP
87 Bedding
88 Mock
90 Heraldic border
91 Grommets
93 Range buckers
95 Polite
97 Hydrocarbon suffix
98 Stars and Bars org.
99 Charge
00 Tenor sax great
04 Acts as accomplice
05 Secular
06 Shortchanged quartet
07 Imprecation
108 Nationality ending
109 Dummy's perch
110 Sojourn
111 Ovett rival

DOWN

1 Bring into being
2 Anecdotal collection
3 Morse sound
4 Peruses
5 Where preceder
6 Scrooge's expletive
7 Fauna
8 Immerse
9 Minds the baby
10 Kind of gin
11 Poetic nightfall
12 Gypsy
13 Maude's maid
14 Wimbledon do-overs
15 Enlightened
16 Driver's document
19 Battologize
20 Bishopric
22 Tribulation
23 ___ me tangere
28 Book backs
30 French one
31 Nessman of WKRP
32 Angelic headwear
35 Senator from Maine
36 Namesakes of a Norwegian king
37 Avenge
38 Tweed twitter
40 Current unit
41 Full ___ (dive)
43 ___ fide
47 Agitated state
50 Double agents
51 Feminine suffixes
52 Ancient Greek coins
53 Symbol
54 Very, in music
55 Bookcase part
56 Harrison Ford role
58 October birthstone
59 Los Angeles footballer
60 Future
62 Siouan
64 Light bender
65 "I know that ___ age succeeds . . .": Tennyson
66 Choreographer Tharp
67 A Chaplin
69 Vitalities
70 Notion, in Nantes
71 Make amends
75 Cushy position
76 African flies
77 With feeling
79 Plays bouncer
80 Things to cast
81 Nut-brown quaff
82 Zilch
85 Tyro
86 Triplet
89 Related maternally
91 Take pleasure in
92 Pro vote
93 Lingerie item
94 Hayseed
95 Highlands group
96 Netter Nastase
97 Far East container
100 Kind
101 NYC subway
102 New Deal agcy.
103 "___ Vadis"

109 SPRIGHTLY by James E. Hinish, Jr.

We think 85 Down is a fitting description of this puzzle.

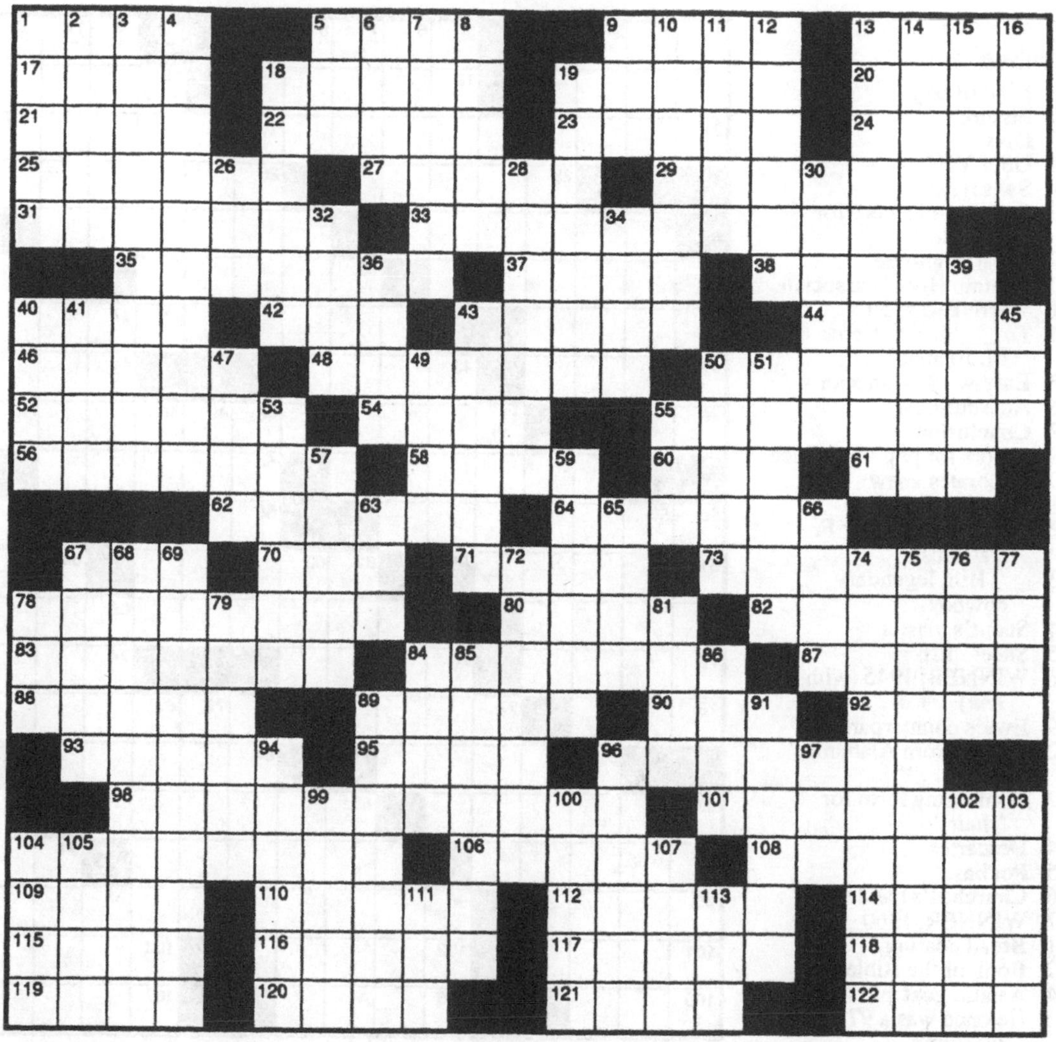

ACROSS

1 Queries
5 Cath. fraternal group
9 Dressing gown
13 Spanish spouses: Abbr.
17 Kashmiri queen
18 Moon valley
19 Item for Rosie
20 Caron role
21 Not a fac.
22 Ryan or Tatum
23 "___ man with seven . . ."
24 Sikorsky or Stravinsky
25 Mouse of fame
27 *The ___ Archipelago*
29 Kindles anew
31 Butt holder
33 Red-eye
35 Author of *The Waste Land*
37 Being, in Brest
38 Attached to a tugboat
40 Court's king Arthur?
42 Biol. categories
43 Forty days of rain
44 Gather
46 Serenaded the villain
48 Conspicuous
50 Estate entrance
52 Beloved
54 Diamond of the underworld
55 Hot event for shoppers?
56 Patty McCormack, in a 1956 film
58 Chan's comment
60 Avis output
61 One of the Chaplins
62 Predicament
64 Snow of songdom
67 Very quiet, musically
70 Spenserian heroine
71 In ___ (as originally positioned)
73 Seismology name
78 B & O charges
80 Milieu for Tai Babilonia
82 "Old ___ tyrant . . .": La Rochefoucauld
83 Admitted
84 ". . . ___ in the house?"
87 Indications
88 Topsy's creator
89 Mortgages, e.g.
90 With it
92 Indian butter
93 Lobby, in Livorno
95 Paella pot
96 ___-of-hand
98 135-pounder, in the ring
101 Maritime debris
104 ___ *Casablanca*, Marx Bros. film
106 Things to shift
108 Kirghiz grassland
109 Dry's partner
110 West Indian sorcery
112 Rent
114 Negations
115 Eight, in Eisenach
116 Assail
117 Mortise insertion
118 Miss Kett
119 Vegas transactions
120 Formerly, formerly
121 Fret
122 Brit. mil. decorations

DOWN

1 Bouquet
2 Garments for 17 Across
3 System of chivalry
4 Tourists
5 Relatives
6 Designer Cassini
7 Display conspicuously
8 Stringed players
9 Border
10 Stuffed
11 Chewy nut
12 And others, to Cato
13 Frailty
14 Passage precedence
15 Piles
16 Camelot titles
18 Kansas City nine
19 60's phrase of agreement
26 Due follower
28 Eternal
30 Reach the kindling point
32 Kennel sounds
34 Meadowlands gait
36 October gemstone
39 The ___, region of SE England
40 Rhyme scheme
41 Pop
43 Madison Square Garden events
45 Manhattan ingredient
47 Profound
49 Jacob's wife
50 Donor
51 Saudi ___
53 See 43 Across
55 Egg ___ yung
57 Ate elegantly
59 Light science
63 Kind of mask or meter
65 Go with the pack
66 Heart charts: Abbr.
67 Avocado
68 Power indicator
69 Olivier's in-laws
72 Archaeological period
74 Increased
75 Squeezes
76 Medieval menial
77 Tear down a Soho flat
78 Headland
79 Atrip's cousin
81 German Chancellor
84 French wing
85 Pleasure
86 Great Barrier, for one
89 Ignobility
91 Bohemian brewing city
94 "___ in England . . ."
96 Urban roadway
97 Acquired
99 Rome's river
100 Brings to a stop
102 Words of likelihood
103 Western scenery
104 White whale pursuer
105 Delightful
107 All there
111 At the age of: Lat. abbr.
113 Plant

110

OSCAR WINNERS by Roger M. Courtney
Movie buffs should sail through this one from our Missouri maven.

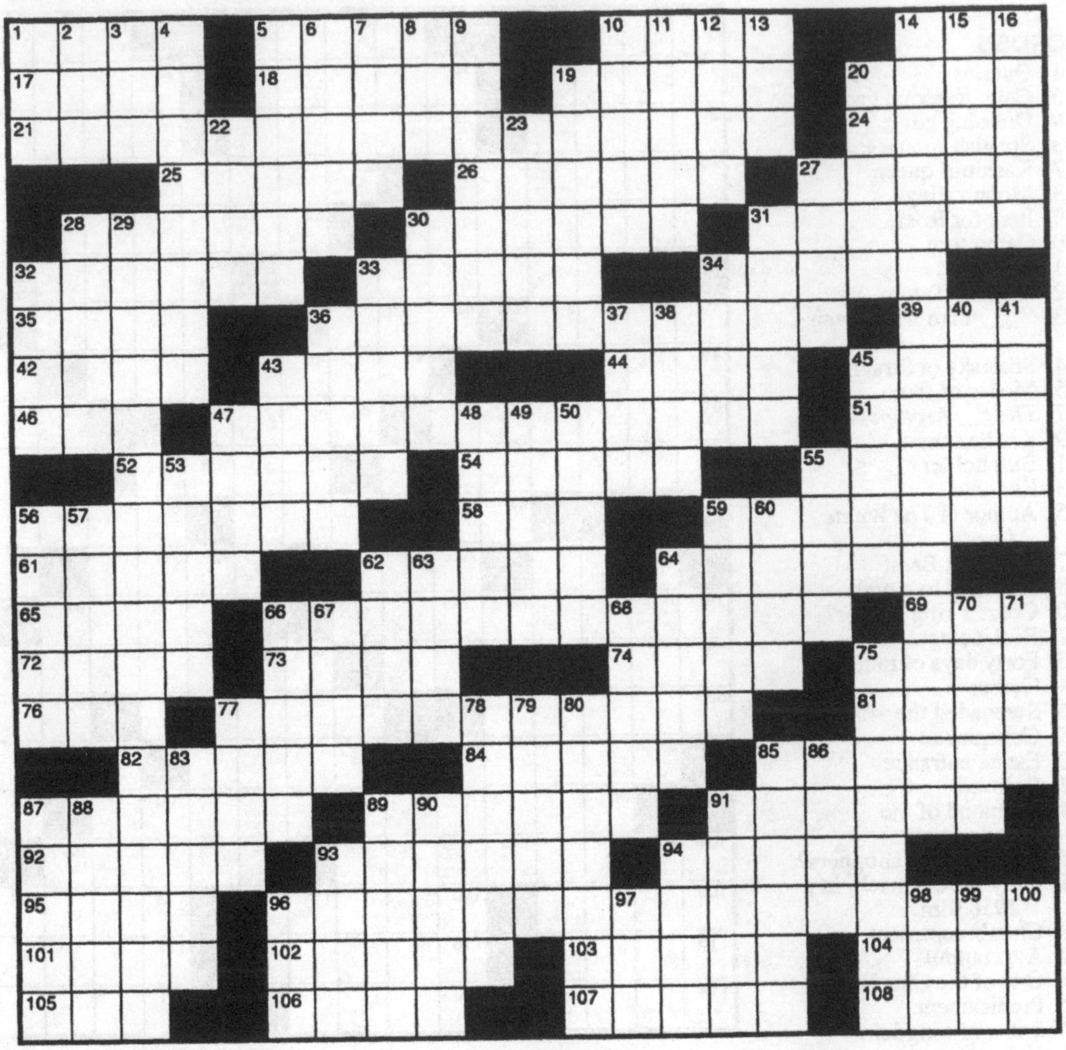

ACROSS

1 Kind of bag
5 Fissure
10 Divs.
14 USN VIP
17 Swiss river
18 Palindromic word for "allude"
19 Avian high-rise
20 Captain Hook's associate
21 WINNER: 1936
24 *To ___ And to Hold*: M. Johnston
25 Easy wins, as in sports
26 Acts curiously
27 Conclusion
28 Colors for pop star Prince
30 Decorates anew
31 Deaden sounds
32 Pierre ___-France: Fr. statesman
33 ___ Bill, legendary cowboy
34 Scout's master
35 Sheer cliff
36 WINNER: 1945 (with *The*)
39 Ewe's counterpart
42 "I ___ from Alabama, with . . ."
43 Combining form for "hair"
44 Descartes
45 Poi base
46 Churchill's hand sign
47 WINNER: 1960
51 Bread coating?
52 Book of the Bible
54 Asiatic goat antelope
55 He once was a 97-lb. weakling
56 Cromwell and Hardy
58 Indonesian island group
59 Cul-de-sac
61 Praline or pie ingredient
62 What the chair wields
64 Small pit
65 Amo, amas, ___
66 The OSCAR
69 Conf. of non-pro athletes
72 Finnish poem
73 *Little ___*, comic strip of old
74 Garden spot
75 Sales instruction
76 Kind of angle
77 WINNER: 1950
81 Cupola
82 Unusual
84 Anagram for señor
85 Comedienne Gilda
87 Clones
89 Anticipates
91 Traveler's companion
92 Russian mountain chain
93 Sap spout
94 Bribe
95 Type of breed
96 WINNER: 1934 (after *It*)
101 Hoosegow
102 City on the Rhone
103 Inflexibility
104 Obligation
105 Degs. at MIT
106 ___ Piper
107 Passes over lightly
108 Certain painting

DOWN

1 Roscoe
2 Sound at a rally
3 Have being
4 Envy
5 De cacao and de menthe
6 Bounds' partner
7 Newts
8 Tasseled, red felt hat
9 Make three equal parts of
10 English novelist (1660–1731)
11 Gets ready for the big exam
12 Sesames
13 But, to Brutus
14 WINNER: 1966
15 Daniel Webster's debate foe
16 One of Reagan's attorneys general
19 As silly as ___
20 Change gears
22 Move aimlessly
23 Enrich
27 See 23 Down
28 Ancient city on the Nile
29 WINNER: 1951
30 Soak up again
31 He painted "Impression: Sunrise"
32 Early part of the 13th c.
33 Actress Negri and namesakes
34 Home of Vanderbilt U.
36 Mortgages
37 Bombeck
38 Howard of musicals
40 Regions
41 Lodge member
43 Drugstore: Abbr.
45 All of the parts
47 Feds
48 Century plant
49 American composer Ned ___
50 For sure!
53 Egg-shaped
55 Footless
56 Abstract movement of the 1960's
57 Madagascan mammal
59 Up in arms
60 Pure and simple
62 Festive
63 "Rub-___ . . ."
64 "Oh, lift me as ___ . . .": Shelley
66 Everything in Germany
67 Choose
68 Antiquing devices
70 Evangelist McPherson
71 Utility customer
75 Annex
77 Rarae ___
78 Oranges or Indians
79 Teamsters' group
80 Threatens to fall
83 Houston athlete
85 Quality controllers, e.g.
86 Ladd or Young
87 Bane
88 Speak pompously
89 Baldwin, e.g.
90 Dried a tear
91 Malevolence
93 Hindu lady's wrap-dress
94 Grant of songdom
96 General Arnold's nickname
97 Cartoonist Browne
98 Homophone for knew
99 Newman-Neal movie
100 Half an African fly

111 AT ARM'S LENGTH by Harold B. Counts

We gotta 35 Across it to Harold for this one!

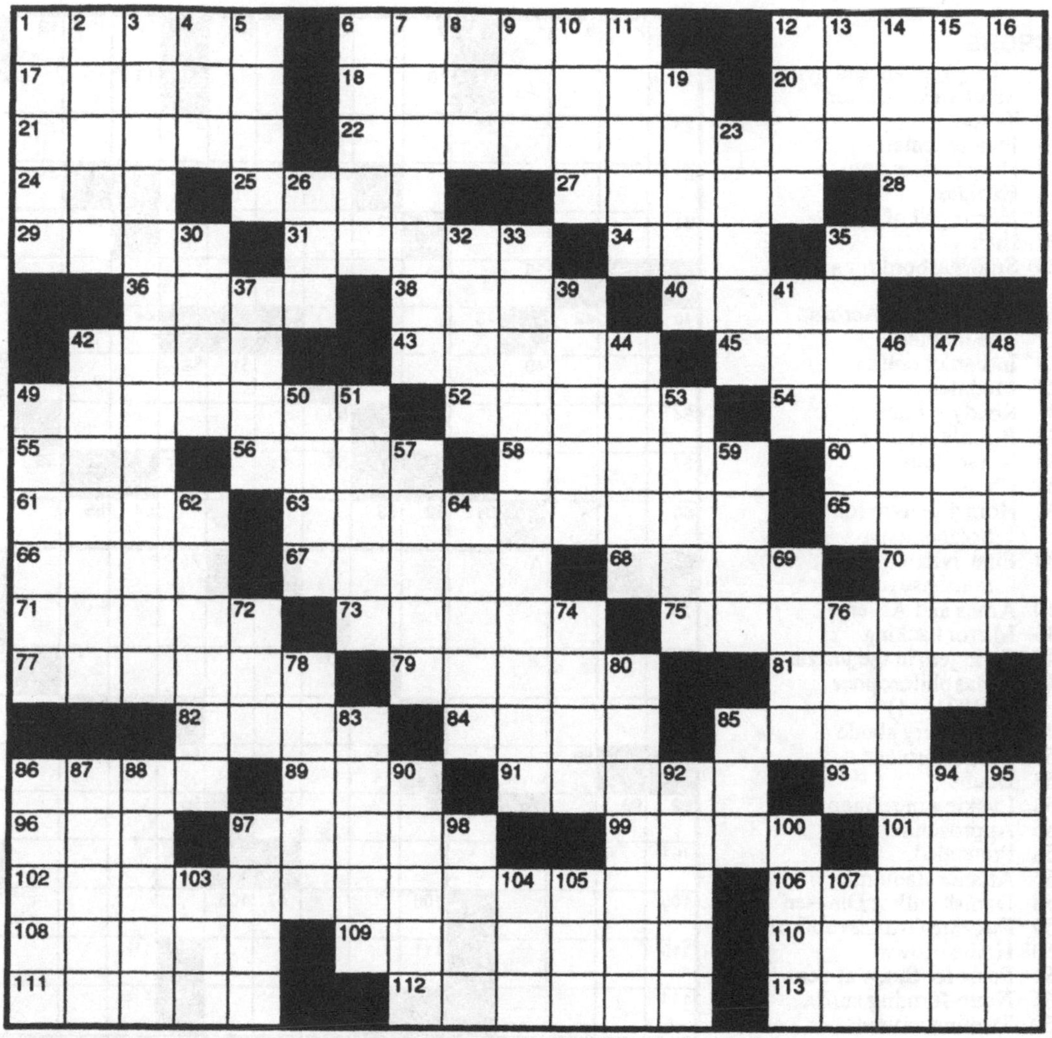

ACROSS

1 Glacial ridge
6 Royal residence
12 Map; outline
17 Alice's cat
18 Magi, e.g.
20 Boring tool
21 Harden
22 Show contempt
24 Tic-toe connection
25 Top-drawer
27 Custom
28 ___ Tin Tin
29 Scouting outing
31 Wife of Abraham
34 Mess up
35 Bridge holding
36 Coins for a fountain
38 Historic times
40 "Tonight Show" host
42 Splitsville
43 Bruce and Laura of films
45 ___ Dome scandal
49 Egyptian stone site
52 Minstrel Allan-___
54 Dauntless
55 Aussie bird
56 Scatters seed
58 Blazing
60 Gun for a Tommy
61 Beatles tune, "___ Buy Me Love"
63 Jaggery
65 French I verb
66 Within: Comb. form
67 Hunter of the skies
68 Elevator man
70 Thus far
71 Bloodhound's clue
73 Dazzling display
75 New York Indians
77 "The Perils of Pauline," for one
79 Walt Disney's middle name
81 Stampede
82 Mild oath
84 Narrow cut
85 Gaunt
86 Mimic
89 Test for a college sr.
91 Ooze
93 Cauterize
96 Brown from the sun
97 Smiles
99 "Darn!"
101 Roguish
102 Fumbler
106 Plant louse
108 "Set me as ___ upon thine heart": Bible
109 Eight-line poem
110 Expiate
111 ___ firma
112 Way up or down
113 Less refined

DOWN

1 Mrs. Bunker
2 Biblical mount
3 Gives in
4 Attention
5 Relative of 55 Across
6 City on the Ganges
7 Held fast
8 Comic Costello
9 Outfielder's asset
10 Philippine island
11 Like a moth hole
12 Job for Mason
13 Vandal
14 Athenian marketplace
15 Lac
16 General drift
19 Tangle
23 White-plumed heron
26 Carbohydrate suffix
30 "___ Kleine Nachtmusik"
32 Kind of code
33 Tough
35 Raspy-voiced
37 Blights
39 Foul-up
41 Bill
42 Love affair
44 Yeats's birthplace
46 Sitcom of 1963–6 (with *The*)
47 Gluttonize
48 Doctrines
49 Break
50 Place: Comb. form
51 Cognizant
53 Muse of poetry
57 Duffer's shot
59 Hibernia
62 More high-class
64 Gun gals
69 Immunizing fluids
72 Make "it"
74 Follow
76 Charged particles
78 Light beer
80 Swizzle stick
83 Sketch
85 Permit
86 Facing Hershiser
87 Hesitate
88 Log in
90 Moslem rulers
92 Sail supports
94 Make parallel
95 Golf's ___ cup
97 Early Hungarian king
98 Tizzy
100 Germany's coal basin
103 Old salt
104 Malabar Coast port
105 Samuel's mentor
107 Sch. affiliate

112

INTERNATIONAL MENU by Dorothy Cannan
You'll like the way that the servings are supplied to appropriate celebrities.

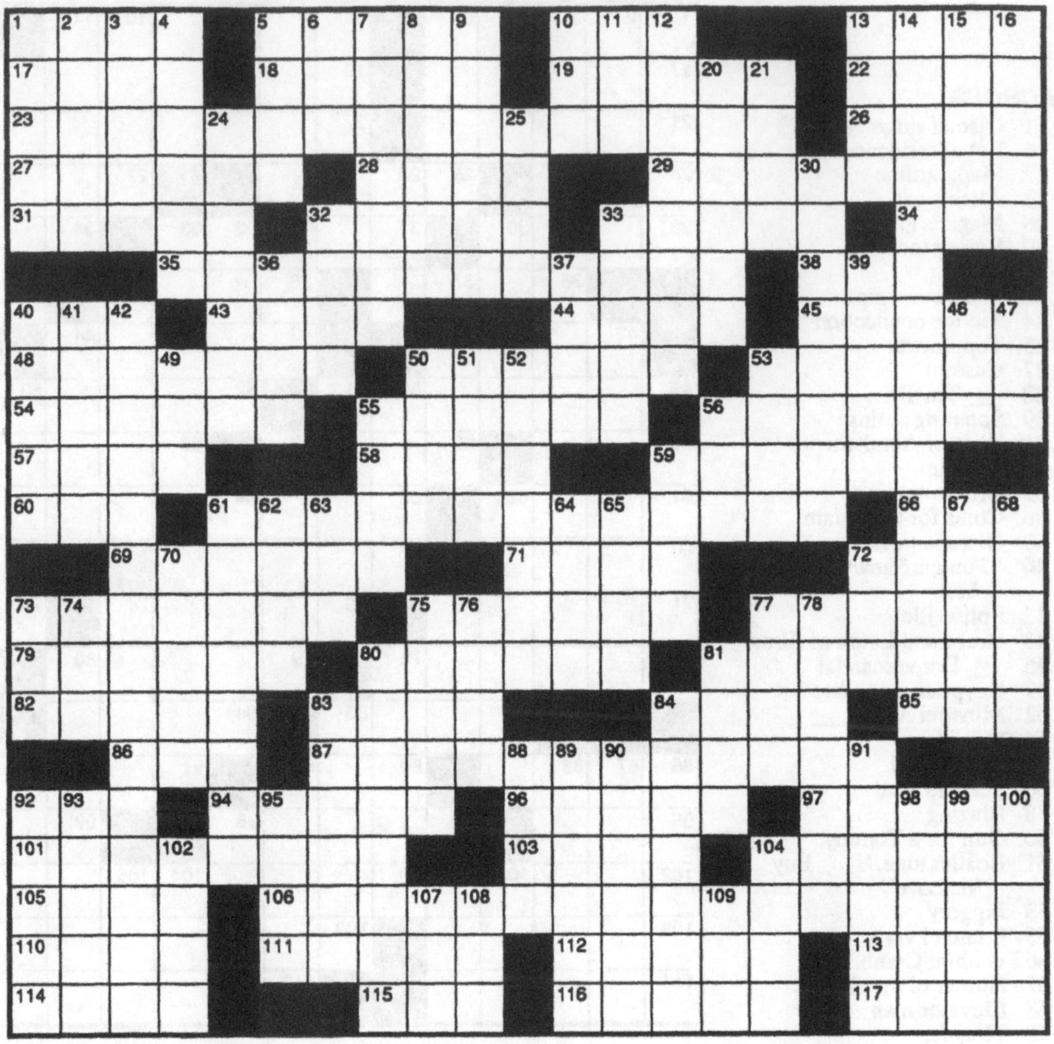

ACROSS

1 "Te ___," ancient hymn
5 Southwestern river
10 Triton
13 Fundamentals
17 How loafers live
18 Expiate
19 Norse god of poetry
22 Etch
23 Smorgasbord for actress Bibi
26 Enemy of 73 Across
27 The movies
28 Indian or cotton
29 Meddler
31 Ready for action
32 Birch's relative
33 Norse Zeus
34 Choler
35 Hors d'oeuvre for writer Solzhenitsyn
38 First syllable in a nonsense refrain
40 Ames and Asner
43 Mirror backing
44 Swingers in the jungle
45 Swiss philosopher (1821–81)
48 Temporary abode
50 Yon's partner
53 Daubs
54 Lacking in refinement
55 Approaching
56 Pretended
57 Atlanta stadium
58 Danish author Dinesen
59 *Eugénie Grandet* author
60 Honshu town
61 Pasta for Sun Yat-sen
66 Noun-forming suffix
69 Turning around
71 Bungler's interjection
72 Spanish enclave in Morocco
73 Shakespeare's Moor
75 Philomen's mate
77 Houston Oiler (1978–83)
79 Pergola
80 "___ ramparts . . ."
81 Rustic
82 Desire strongly
83 Fit of anger
84 Volume
85 City in Gelderland province
86 These, in Tours
87 Fruit for poet Khayyam
92 Invite
94 Island greeting
96 Small egg
97 Auto necessities
101 Know ___ (have the essential information)
103 Film star Garr
104 Observation
105 Entice
106 Native fare for singer Pavarotti
110 Skipper's command
111 A neighbor of Turkey
112 Crystalline stone
113 Jazz trumpeter Baker
114 Polio conqueror
115 ___ *Men*, 1987 film
116 Depside is one
117 Rocky peaks

DOWN

1 Nightclub, for short
2 Drood of fiction
3 Fraud ending
4 Letter opener
5 Spanish raisin
6 Old English letter
7 Canonical hour: Var.
8 Geographical hub of New York State
9 Mariners
10 Recede
11 ___ Mauro, lunar area
12 Discuss
13 Stulm
14 Beverage for racing driver Fittipaldi
15 Larry Bird, for one
16 Pledged
20 Volplanes
21 Russian log hut
24 Ascribes
25 South Sea staple
30 Malign; vilify
32 ___ were (so to speak)
33 Performed a dishwashing chore
36 Logical
37 Actor in *The Wizard of Oz*
39 Finale
40 Disney World Center
41 Florence's famed cathedral
42 Food fish for golfer Ballesteros
46 Soon, to a Glaswegian
47 Hallucinogen, for short
49 Beginning for angular
50 Flexible pipe
51 "As ___ going to St. Ives"
52 Type of food service
53 Retail
55 Single, ringing sound
56 Passing craze
59 TV's *Who's the* ___?
61 Blind alley
62 Seed scars
63 Wife of Athamas
64 Still, in Berlin
65 *Murder of Rizzio* painter
67 "The Lady ___," 1935 song
68 Electron tube
70 GI's vacation
72 Those holding office
73 Grampus
74 Feather's companion
75 Mozambique seaport
76 Beaux ___
77 Sloping runway
78 Mascara recipient
80 Bridge bid
81 Rhode Island's motto
83 Loud and flashy
84 Fan palm
88 Jot
89 Exact satisfaction for an injury
90 Hospital workers
91 Anticipate
92 Globe supporter
93 Miami Dolphins' coach
95 Clark Kent's friend
98 A print, for short
99 Consumer
100 Plackets
102 Be zetetic
104 Elbe tributary
107 Cato's 52
108 Fleming or Paisley
109 "Fables in Slang" author

113 JOHNNY CAN'T SPELL, EITHER by Frances Hansen

This puzzle is a good example of the unique Hansen touch—inimitable cleverness and humor.

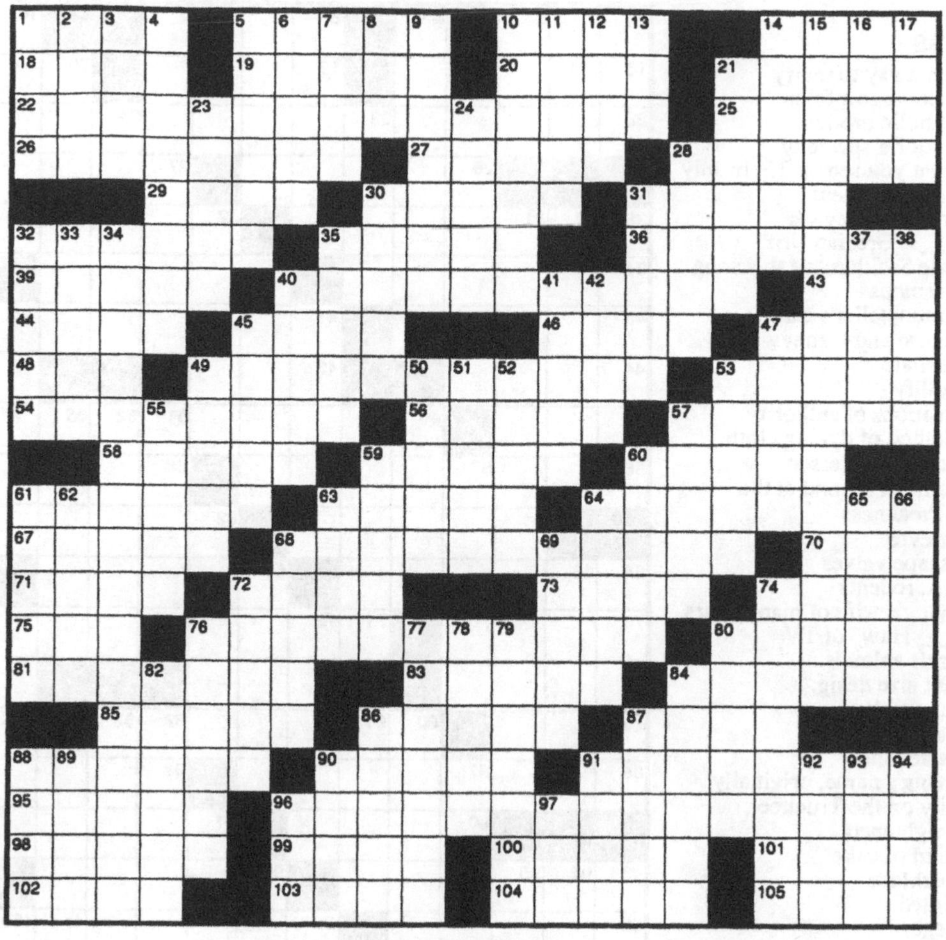

ACROSS

1 Burns's bonny hill
5 Lyric poem
10 "Drop the handkerchief" was his game
14 Club bar bill
18 Miss Schneider of *Qui*?
19 TV tube element
20 Rode down the banister
21 Letter after eta
22 Johnny describes his kid sister?
25 Communion bread
26 T. A. Daly's "Mia ___"
27 St. ___ fire, sea phenomenon
28 It may be vérité
29 Judith, of B'way's *Steaming*
30 "___, a sigh, a sob . . . ": Arnold
31 Popular roll
32 Memorable conductor Fritz
35 "Baby Snooks" comedienne
36 Certain socks
39 TV actress Georgia
40 How Johnny's rash buddies behave?
43 Author Levin
44 Get wind of
45 A bed has four legs but only one ___
46 Actress Nettleton
47 Medical student's subj.
48 Usher's offering
49 Caused devastation, à la Johnny?
53 All together, in music
54 Quail with a distinctive cry
56 Israel's P.M. (1974–77)
57 "Sleepy" pool of song
58 Univ. of Maine site
59 King with a gilty look
60 "When You ___ Tulip . . ."
61 Christmas carol opener
63 French assembly
64 Rolls-Royce, for a shining example
67 Actress Papas from Greece
68 Romeo and Juliet, to Johnny?
70 Sweet Sioux's cousin
71 Housman's "lightfoot" boys
72 Fireside talk
73 Hoarfrost
74 GI's need
75 Literary collection
76 Johnny's busiest times at the shore?
80 Butter beans
81 Heartfelt
83 Uncouth
84 Will or Ariel
85 Senior member
86 ___ du monde (man of the world)
87 Gravy vessel
88 Orchestra members
90 Columbus's birthplace
91 Manitoba's capital
95 "Like ___ from the blue"
96 Johnny's advice to a troupe assailant?
98 WW II riveter
99 Spar for a camera on a crane
100 Artoo Detoo, e. g.
101 He saves the damsel in distress
102 Part of a.m.
103 Nimble
104 Noted photographer Diane
105 Western art colony

DOWN

1 Bric-a-___
2 Church roster
3 Cupid
4 Cleopatra's was kohl
5 Devonshire cathedral town
6 Like an Irish bog
7 Wave, on the Spanish Main
8 Female rabbit
9 Peculiar to a locality
10 Survivor of the Pequod
11 ___ *Is in the Streets*, 1953 film
12 Hodges and Blas
13 Bizarre
14 Early *Phantom of the Opera* star
15 Johnny explains a grammarian's faint?
16 Newspaper squib
17 Plantation where Pork was butler
21 Tune's "My One and Only" co-star
23 Wretched abode
24 Stocking adornment
28 Sandburg and Bernstein
30 Mountain ridge
31 Fundamental
32 Restore to good shape, for short
33 January in Juarez
34 Johnny recounts his Las Vegas trip?
35 Bankrupt
37 Sappho's muse
38 Wedding gown material, often
40 "___ the vanquished": Livy
41 First name in rock-and-roll
42 By and by
45 Boxer's ploy
47 Wood-boring tool
49 Lyons's department
50 Zvornik's river
51 Attacked with vigor
52 Take ___ (lose heavily on Wall St.)
53 Pacific staples
55 Ladies of the British Royal Navy
57 Lehmann or Lenya
59 Sporting events
60 Unsavory Diet of ___?
61 Miser Marner
62 Teheran resident
63 Letters on the envelope of a billet doux
64 Down East
65 Soul, in Sanskrit
66 What the chickens come home to do
68 Luster
69 Eat away
72 Daughter of Ops
74 Like a perfect alibi
76 Mescal
77 Keynesian subject
78 This isn't throwaway mail
79 Java's neighbor
80 ___ Prabang, former Laos royal capital
82 Lassie, notably
84 "Dunkin'" treats
86 "___ God only, . . . ": Milton
87 Exquisite trinket
88 Williams of *Pete and Gladys*
89 Black, poetically
90 Close kin of glop
91 Friday's portrayer
92 This could be copped
93 Eliel's architect son
94 ___ point, embroidery stitch
96 Literary monogram
97 Opposite of vert.

114

BERI IN DIARY by Jeanette K. Brill
One of our top constructors pays fitting tribute to a great songwriter who became a centenarian in 1988.

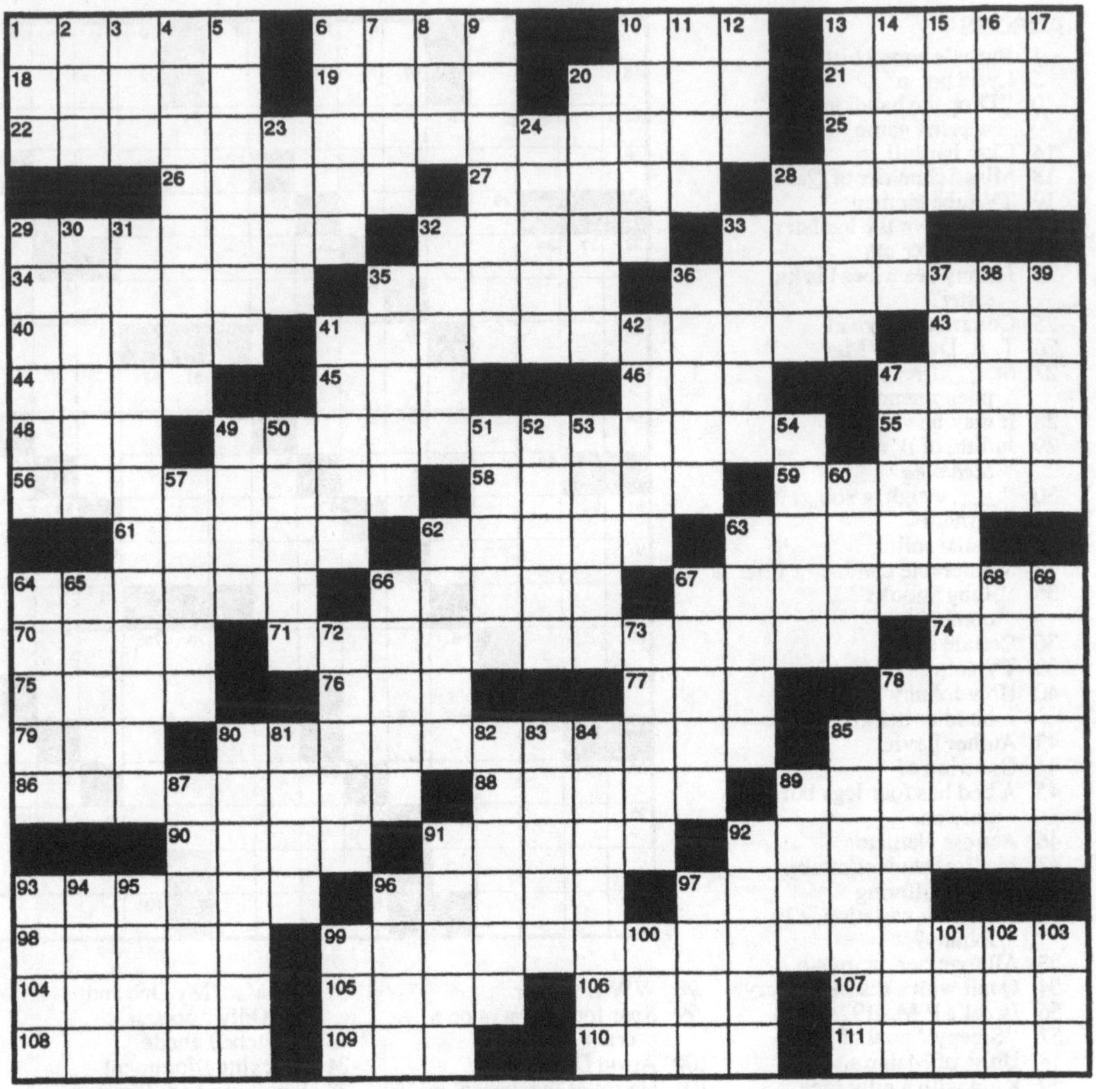

ACROSS

1 Run away to marry
6 Encourage a felon
10 Catholic brother
13 Trattoria specialty
18 What you see on TV in July
19 Indian garment
20 British trolley car
21 "___ a Grecian Urn"
22 Kate Smith made this song famous
25 Fortuneteller's card
26 Louise and Geneva
27 Hesitate
28 Nullify
29 Positions of authority
32 Method of dyeing cloth
33 Actress Anderson
34 Came in second at the Preakness
35 Grieves
36 Escape valves
40 S.A. rodents
41 Irving's wife of many years
43 "___ Haw" of TV
44 Draft animals
45 Suit size desig.
46 Atlas abbr.
47 Hammer head
48 Established
49 Irving's name, originally
55 City on the Truckee
56 Heightened
58 Kind of cake
59 Necklace
61 Sidled
62 Begets
63 European weasel
64 City near New Haven, Conn.
66 Polynesian garment
67 French songs
70 Needlecase
71 Song featured in "Alexander's Ragtime Band"
74 Bee chaser
75 What athletes sometimes suffer
76 ___ volente (God willing)
77 Greek god of the forests
78 "And ___ There Were None"
79 Cuckoo
80 Irving's birthplace
85 Casts off
86 Divided into segments
88 Stock or horn preceder
89 Addison's partner
90 "___ go bragh"
91 Mr. de Laurentis and namesakes
92 Plankings on boat hulls
93 Guard against
96 Lazy___
97 ___ ease (uncomfortable)
98 Humiliate
99 Ethel Merman starred in this musical by our hero
104 Oscar winner for "Two Women"
105 West Germany's capital
106 Old tongue
107 Italy's banking center
108 Without power to move
109 Female sheep
110 Expensive
111 Fragment

DOWN

1 Work unit
2 Sign of the Zodiac
3 California's Ft. ___
4 Innkeeper in Britain
5 Intertwines
6 Onagers
7 Kind of clef
8 Stat for Roger Clemens
9 Kettledrums
10 Search for concealed weapons
11 Speed
12 Dr.'s org.
13 Strength
14 Slow movement in music
15 Evening in Napoli
16 Bender
17 Pot sweetener
20 Platitude
23 Barely managed (with "out")
24 Corroded
28 Nick's wife in fiction
29 Set against
30 Straw-colored
31 What Irving would do at the piano?
32 Nonsense
33 Compare
35 Beg
36 A protein in muscles
37 How Irving liked to dance?
38 New Hampshire city that sounds sharp
39 Spanish gentleman's title
41 Made a mistake
42 Where Van Gogh painted
47 Malayan boats
49 Pulitzer playwright: 1953
50 Part of "Hamlet"
51 Longest river in France
52 Less clothed
53 Devoured entirely
54 Outward, to a zoologist
57 ___ Ababa, Ethiopia
60 Sharpen
62 Squelched
63 Journalist-author Alexander
64 French interjection
65 Expiate
66 False: Comb. form
67 Actress in "State Fair"
68 Goad
69 Sight and smell
72 Madison Ave. denizens
73 Church sections
78 Adjective for part of Irving's world
80 Flood
81 Lake or canal
82 "A ___ in the Sun," Hansberry play
83 Forearm bones
84 Cadged
85 Composer of "Salome"
87 Ecdysiast
89 WW II battle site
91 Creator of Mr. Dooley
92 More wily
93 Indonesian island
94 Deep black
95 Hard or soft follower
96 Flatter, colloquially
97 "___ girl!"
99 Beame or Fortas
100 Before, poetically
101 Belg. is one of its neighbors
102 Actress Merkel
103 Siesta

115 KIND OF SURE by Marjorie Pedersen

If you're wondering what Marjorie's title has to do with her theme, think of her title as a crossword clue.

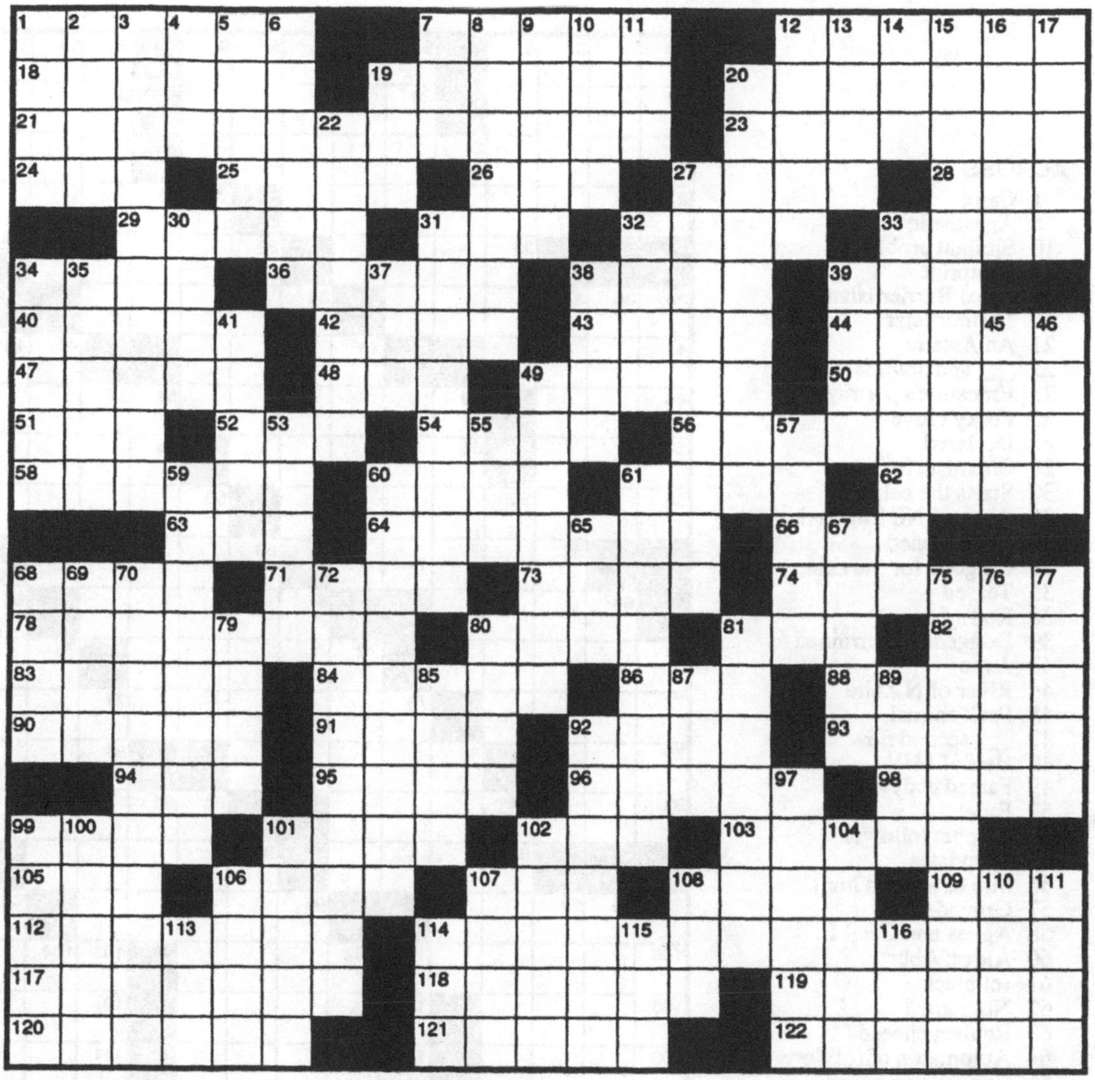

ACROSS

1 Settle
7 One-celled organism
12 Good-luck object
18 Presser
19 Muppet drummer
20 Not thorough
21 Lady is one
23 Patrolman
24 Alas. native
25 Funambulist's need
26 Kind of verb: Abbr.
27 Hundredth pts.
28 Scottish jackdaw
29 Author St. Johns
31 Morns
32 Odin's adopted brother
33 Cushions
34 Mr. C
36 Kind of diving
38 Atap palm
39 "How Great Thou ___"
40 Tropical vine
42 Jewish month
43 Hook or J. Cook
44 Bellini opera
47 Egyptian dancers
48 Hose "ladder"
49 Nut: Comb. form
50 Fir genus
51 Defendants, in law
52 Logotypes: Abbr.
54 Honey
56 Little lenses
58 Singer Franklin
60 Reiner or Rowan
61 Mislay
62 Actress Edna
63 Cookbook subj.
64 Dreamy
66 Cub. contents
68 Strong box of yore
71 Part of IRA
73 Bash
74 Chooses
78 Bible
80 Miss Gale's pet
81 Bikini half
82 ___ Ridge Boys
83 Man with a mike
84 Cup and pound followers
86 Jamie ___ Curtis
88 "The Most Happy ___"
90 Turkish liqueurs
91 Kubla or Genghis
92 Lake named after Elwood
93 Burst
94 S & L offerings: Abbr.
95 Grounds for a suit
96 Bizarre
98 Comfort
99 They're sipped in summer
101 British pokey
102 Elec. unit
103 Western
105 Snatch
106 Send
107 ___-fi
108 Land measure
109 ___ mot
112 Beetle Bailey's sergeant
114 Royal seat of Iran once
117 Linotyper's goofs
118 Narrate
119 Poet Heinrich and family
120 Essay anew
121 Praying figure
122 Passover feasts

DOWN

1 Some are loaded
2 Love god
3 Ridiculous
4 Sign
5 Plow pioneer
6 Leon and Flynn
7 Literary collection
8 Least
9 Potentates of puzzledom
10 Jethro Bodine's portrayer
11 Every bit
12 Civilian clothes
13 Barks
14 Fed. aid to the disabled
15 Legendary serpentine monster
16 Companion of Artemis
17 British radials
19 Copy
20 White parrots
22 Typewriter bars
27 Nonsense
30 Iberian lady
31 Copious
32 Fibber
33 Likely
34 Barton or Bow
35 Gretzky was one
37 Arctic knife
38 Raleigh loc.
39 Henry Gray's conc.
41 "___ World Turns"
45 N.L. team
46 Gal Fri.
49 Piebalds
53 Where St. Francis Xavier died
55 Before, in poesy
57 Not even once
59 Cars in some car deals
60 Boastfully elated
61 Floorcover
65 Decay
67 Kings of Norway
68 "Who Cares?" composer
69 City of the Seven Hills: Lat.
70 Ship-to-shore craft
72 Grasshopper and salty dog
75 Clavicle
76 Such: Lat.
77 After ice or cheap
79 Actress Armstrong
80 Scout's shelter
81 Flintstones' hometown
85 Astronomer Schwarzschild
87 Lunch or brunch
89 Sword
92 Uncas was the last one
97 "When ___ last picture is painted": Kipling
99 Goose genus
100 Poet who loved Beatrice
101 Capital of East Flanders
102 Florida city
104 Giggle
106 Snowmobile runners
107 Prophet
108 King topper
110 Lulu
111 Costner role in 1987
113 Lobster coral
114 Quid ___ quo
115 Mel of Cooperstown
116 Exterminate

116

BLOOMER GIRLS by John Greenman
Solvers will soon discover Mr. G's title does not refer to Amelia Jenks Bloomer or her dress-reform movement. (By sheer coincidence Amelia's famous newspaper is also the first name of 23 Across.)

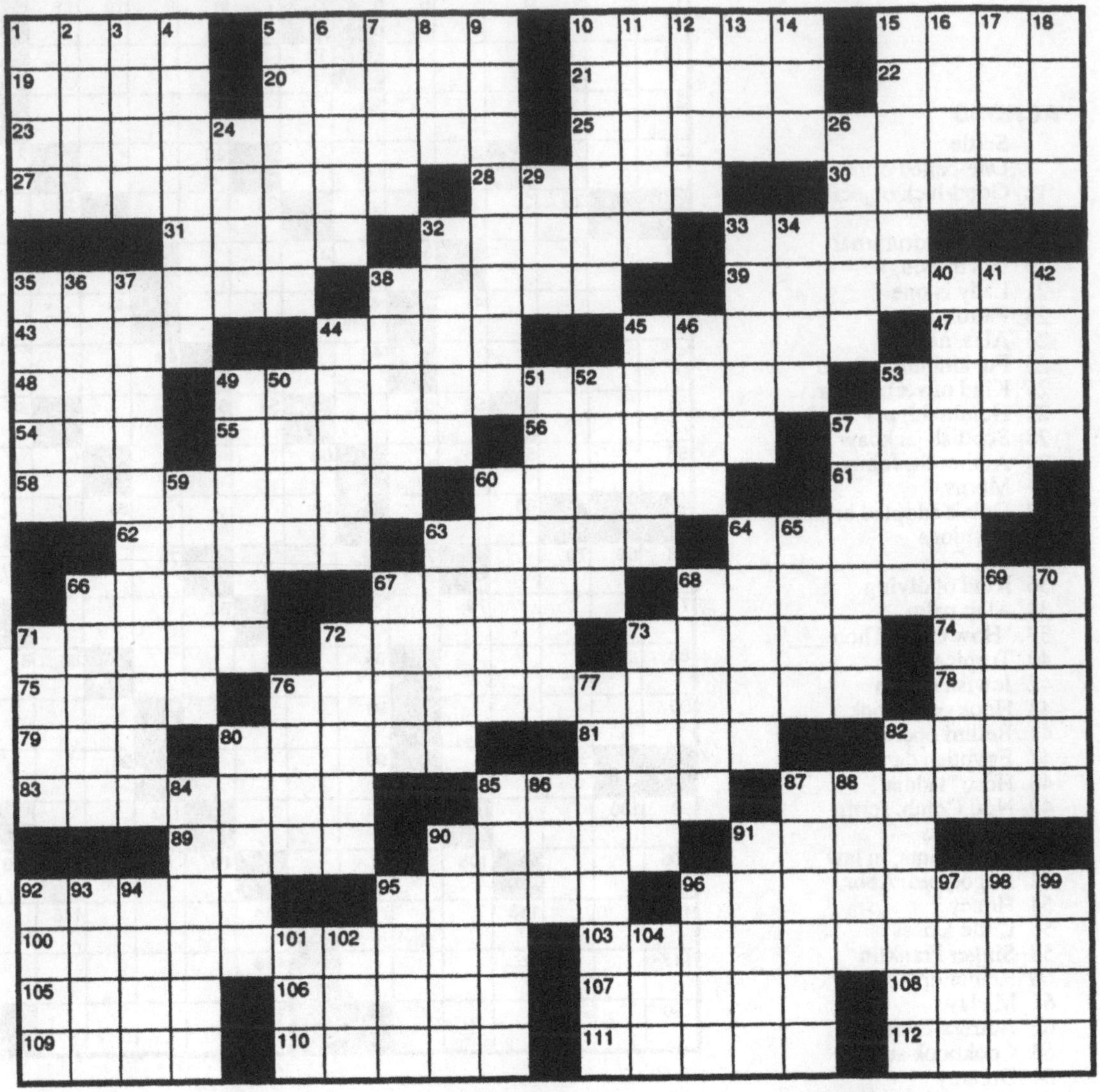

ACROSS
1 Carol
5 Anesthetic
10 Sibilant problems
15 Footprint
19 Great Barrier island
20 "Arthur" star
21 An Astaire
22 ___ and hounds
23 Ernestine's portrayer
25 Porky's love
27 Declared
28 Chemise, for one
30 Starts the betting
31 River of NE England
32 Apportioned
33 It's good for the skin
35 Teased
38 Rod's $5\frac{1}{2}$
39 Doggedly determined
43 As to
44 River of N Zaire
45 Pack animal
47 ___ second now
48 Half of MIV
49 Famed ecdysiast
53 Facet
54 Prophet follower
55 Alleviates
56 Site of a witch hunt
57 Grounded
58 Agnes and Cecil B.
60 Aides: Abbr.
61 Jet black
62 Not rented
63 Reuben cheese
64 Automaton of folklore
66 English composer
67 Piquant
68 A food service
71 Annexed
72 Factotum
73 Wan
74 Household deity
75 Othello, e.g.
76 "The Great Gatsby" character
78 ___ detector
79 Parabola
80 Pittypat and Polly
81 Friend
82 "___ Only Just Begun"
83 English Channel port
85 Kales
87 Gazed
89 Beat endings
90 Newman and Hogan
91 Spoken
92 Straighten
95 Mottled mare
96 Winslow Homer work
100 Gail Godwin novel
103 Dogpatch doyenne
105 Grafted: Heraldry
106 Town in a Hersey title
107 Buoy up
108 Skirt type
109 Scan
110 Mortise's partner
111 Stormed
112 London's ___ End

DOWN
1 Felix Arndt melody
2 Singer Redding
3 Morays
4 Newborn's wardrobe
5 Hammed it up
6 Voluminous volumes
7 After strong or toe
8 "___ tu," Verdi aria
9 Verdict giver
10 Zoot-suit features
11 That is
12 Sound stages
13 Not sing.
14 Indonesian coin
15 Sculptor, for one
16 Record
17 One of the Waltons
18 Throws
24 Chinquapin, e.g.
26 $\overline{X}$
29 Film of 1986
32 John and Tyne
33 Relevant
34 Learning
35 Awaited
36 Pernod ingredient
37 "The Black Prince" author
38 Okays
40 Henry James heroine
41 Forefinger
42 Like some old potatoes
44 Horse that beat Man O'War
45 Regions
46 Little ones: Suffix
49 Solidified
50 Brown rival
51 Small bone
52 Pert
53 More reasonable
57 Henry VIII's second wife
59 Tube type
60 Where there's ___, there's . . .
63 Tiffs
64 Flatulent
65 Preminger
66 Dote on
67 Ilk
68 Summons
69 Ingenuous
70 Cupidity
71 Merged: Abbr.
72 Units of force
73 Stacks
76 Gloom
77 Lambaster
80 Of birds: Var.
82 Glad-hand
84 Fished
85 Steve of comics
86 Excuse
87 Supplicated
88 "___ Money," Dangerfield film
90 Kind of bar or wire
91 West, in Toledo
92 Allege
93 Wrinkle
94 Jot
95 Blueprint
96 Impediment
97 Poisonous shrub
98 Quibbles
99 Exude
101 Tit for ___
102 Alphabetic sequence
104 ___ carte

117

BOZ by Elizabeth Arthur

The clue to 93 Across says it all. We have great expectations regarding the popularity of this puzzle.

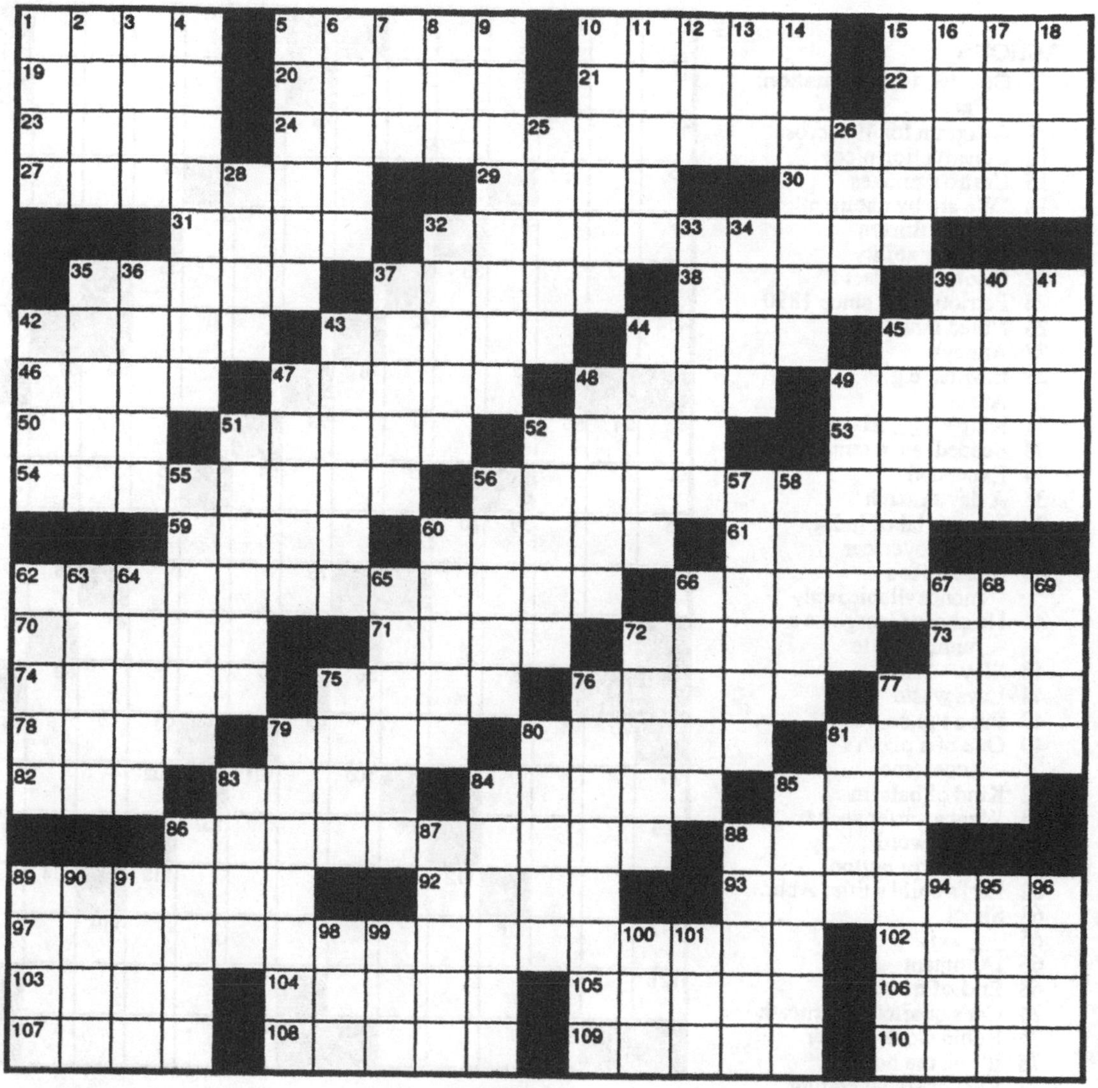

ACROSS

1 Daredeviltry name
5 "Out!"
10 Trapshooting
15 Rounds
19 Met star
20 Beethoven's "Für ___"
21 Rodeo rope
22 Sense
23 On the rocks
24 Mr. Murdstone's stepson
27 He was helped by 54 Across
29 Jason's craft
30 Leatherback, e.g.
31 Dances, to Balzac
32 Where Esther Summerson lived
35 "Mona Lisa" star
37 Famed Greek doctor
38 Little pitchers have big ones
39 Life-saving tech.
42 Young cohos
43 "Bet-you-a-million" man
44 Uncover
45 Alone: Comb. form
46 Saharan
47 Frosted
48 English horns
49 Vermont product
50 ___ Alamos
51 Kind of tax
52 Catcalls
53 Mother's relative
54 Scrooge
56 Novel about Paul and his father
59 Ancient town of Lucania
60 Tidal waves
61 Jai ___
62 She married in Marshalsea prison
66 Employee of 54 Across
70 Adjective for Humpty Dumpty
71 Inlets
72 Borscht ingredients
73 Cather's "___ of Ours"
74 Famous pollster
75 Franklin and Cross
76 Adjective for Odin
77 "Of course!"
78 Ticked
79 Storm
80 I.Q.-test name
81 Maples
82 ___ Darya
83 Prefix for space
84 Bow-shaped
85 Plait
86 He mysteriously disappeared
88 ___ du Salut
89 Circuitous route
92 "It ___ Necessarily So"
93 England's greatest novelist
97 Boz book of London-Paris settings
102 "Thanks ___"
103 Painter of limp watches
104 "It ___ two to tango"
105 Ephron and Hellmer
106 "The Oath" poet
107 Auricular
108 Jagged
109 Wipe out
110 Scotch uncles

DOWN

1 Emend
2 Veni, vidi, ___
3 Uniform
4 She beautified America
5 Church chancel seat
6 Quahogs
7 Randall's "6 Rms ___ Vu"
8 "___ Lay Dying": Faulkner
9 Emulated Janet Evans
10 Catchword
11 Pillow stuffing
12 Nostradamic gift
13 Compass dir.
14 Rack
15 Blazing
16 Assemble
17 Partner of pell
18 Ye ___ Shoppe
25 Canadian tribesmen
26 Commotion
28 Flogs
32 "The Darling Buds of May" author
33 Black vehicle
34 Sculls
35 St. John's bread
36 Get up
37 Winning hit
39 Mrs. Dithers, et al.
40 Disney dog
41 Mature
42 Pasty
43 Mountain in Jordan
44 Dunces
45 Civil magistrate
47 Low-decked warship
48 One of Santa's sledders
49 French legislatures
51 Vendor
52 "___ Godunov"
55 Cleared
56 First wife of 24 Across, et al.
57 Most agile
58 Like Hermes' hat
60 Ocean
62 Slow lemur
63 Creamy white
64 Wick
65 Mount Hood locale
66 Like a parrot's beak
67 Hebrew prophet
68 Like neon
69 North Sea feeder
72 Filleted
75 Port on the Adriatic
76 Smokers crave this
77 Emulate Hans Brinker
79 Scripted anew
80 Rodeo beast
81 Novelist Waugh
83 Together: Music
84 Songlike
85 Crinkled fabric
86 Wind-blown
87 Peace Prize Nobelist: 1925
88 Notions
89 Pedestal part
90 Coup d'___
91 Ankles
94 Jack of Westerns
95 Memo
96 Thérèse and Marie: Abbr.
98 Remote
99 Ring dec.
100 Rocky hill
101 Evangelist Sankey

118

WALL STREET BULL by I. Judah Koolyk
The speaker of the quotation below has become immortalized for committing one of the worst gaffes in history.

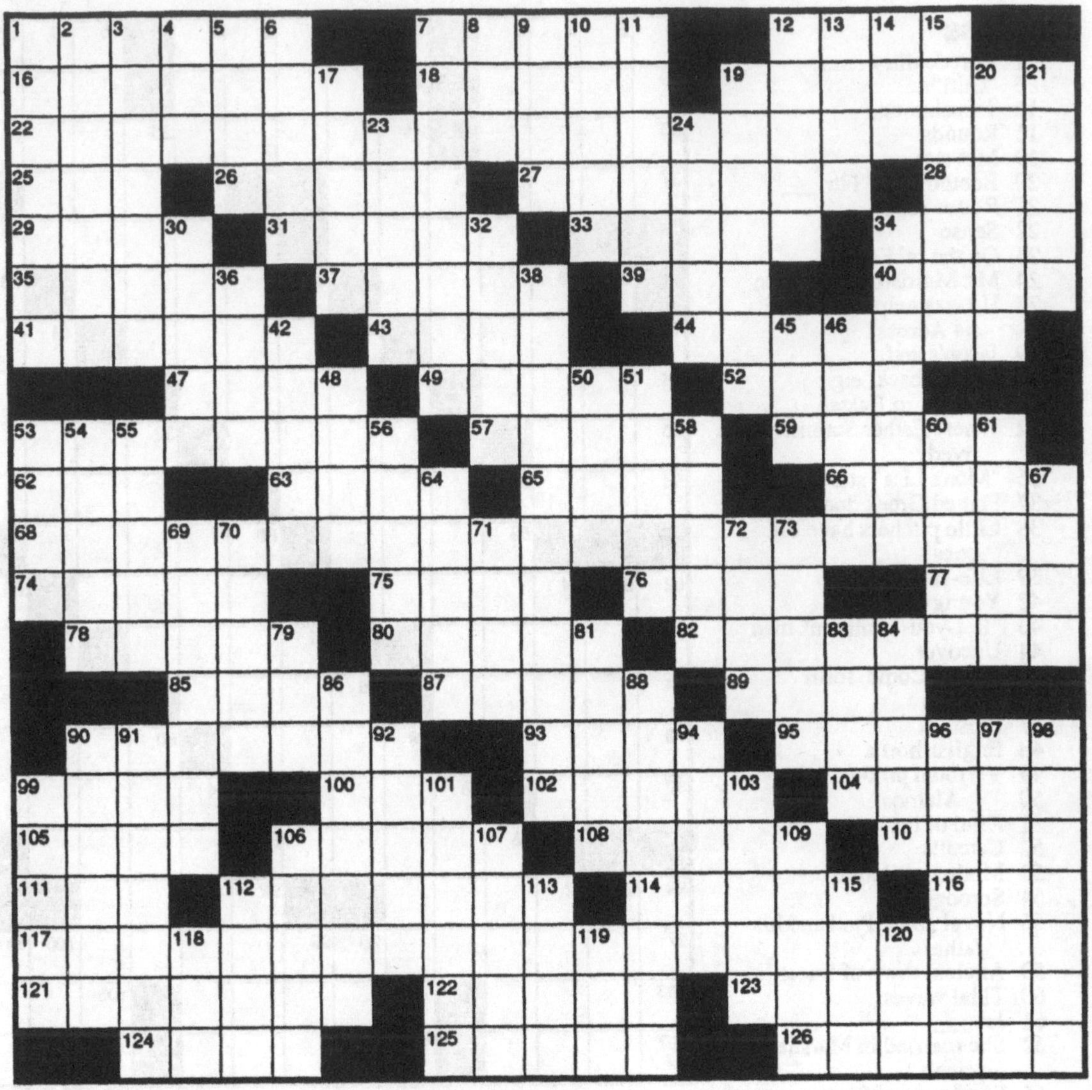

ACROSS

1 **Oct. 15, 1929 quotation: Part I**
7 Anagram for 49 Across
12 Construction piece
16 Castro's smokes
18 "We are by nature all ___": Burton
19 Superior ability
22 **Quotation: Part II**
25 Patriotic org. since 1890
26 Noted Israeli
27 Annoys
28 E.M.K., e.g.
29 Anent
31 King's "___ Macabre"
33 Seeded, as in tennis
34 Expended
35 A day's march
37 Jawaharlal of India
39 AMEX overseer
40 McAuliffe's monosyllabic reply
41 He chose George as a running mate
43 Slay
44 Lays waste
47 Put a top on
49 One of a piano's threesome
52 Kind of balsam
53 What a surfer seeks
57 Psalms word
59 Calculator button
62 Earl's child's title: Abbr.
63 Shoot
65 ___ avis
66 Dominant
68 **End of quotation**
74 Car's quartet underneath
75 Robin Cook thriller
76 It's on the house
77 Real or social ending
78 Deer sirs?
80 Work on a text
82 Part of SDS
85 Overfeed
87 Ceased
89 Old English bard
90 Cricket player
93 Susa was its capital
95 Expulsion
99 Baseball's Petrocelli
100 In one's cups
102 Check
104 Mother of verse
105 Lulu
106 Items often beaten
108 Hero stores
110 Pooch without papers
111 Grappler's must
112 Job for a justice of the peace
114 Boston's airport
116 Abecedarian trio
117 Speaker of the quotation
121 Nervous-system part
122 Iberian country
123 Conceal
124 Gaelic
125 Rigid
126 Erected

DOWN

1 More disreputable
2 Italian port city
3 Defeated decisively
4 See 8 Down
5 TV adjunct
6 Did carpentry work
7 Three gold balls site
8 Depth charge, with 4 Down
9 Kind of shark
10 Record a debit
11 Daedalus had two
12 Annoyed
13 Tweed's title
14 Shoemaker's tool
15 Circulate again
17 "Cosmos" man
19 Weasel's kin
20 Track star Nehemiah's nickname
21 Transmits
23 Forked
24 Weasel's kin
30 Difference between calendars
32 Ohio Indians
34 Salve
36 Robert ___
38 Sly
42 Maxims
45 Grammatical case: Abbr.
46 Scottish burgh
48 Suburban sward
50 Asian range
51 Extensive
53 "___ fools these mortals be": Shak.
54 Arizona Indians
55 Like argon
56 Pawn's superior
58 Sunk fences
60 Dined at home
61 Butcher's sale
64 Creature of folklore
67 Defers (with "off")
69 Atomic pile
70 Catholic prelates: Abbr.
71 Counterfeiter's nemeses
72 Noncom's troops: Abbr.
73 White: Comb. form
79 Actor Levene
81 Struck out
83 Fairbanks, for short
84 Certain salts
86 Discomfort or lethargy
88 East and west separator
90 Involving two
91 Paint ingredient
92 Peteman's liquid
94 NYSE bonanza
96 Less yielding
97 Connoisseur
98 Emeritus
99 Is frolicsome
101 What a quaff quenches
103 Bobby of tennis
106 Roulette bet
107 One of the sandpipers
109 Less precarious
112 ___ up (animates)
113 ___ Paradiso, Italian mount
115 Pleasing
118 Remote
119 Force, to Caesar
120 Madrid Mrs.

120

BOND CONNECTION by Marjorie Pedersen
The double 0's add up to far more than seven, and it's an interesting adventure.

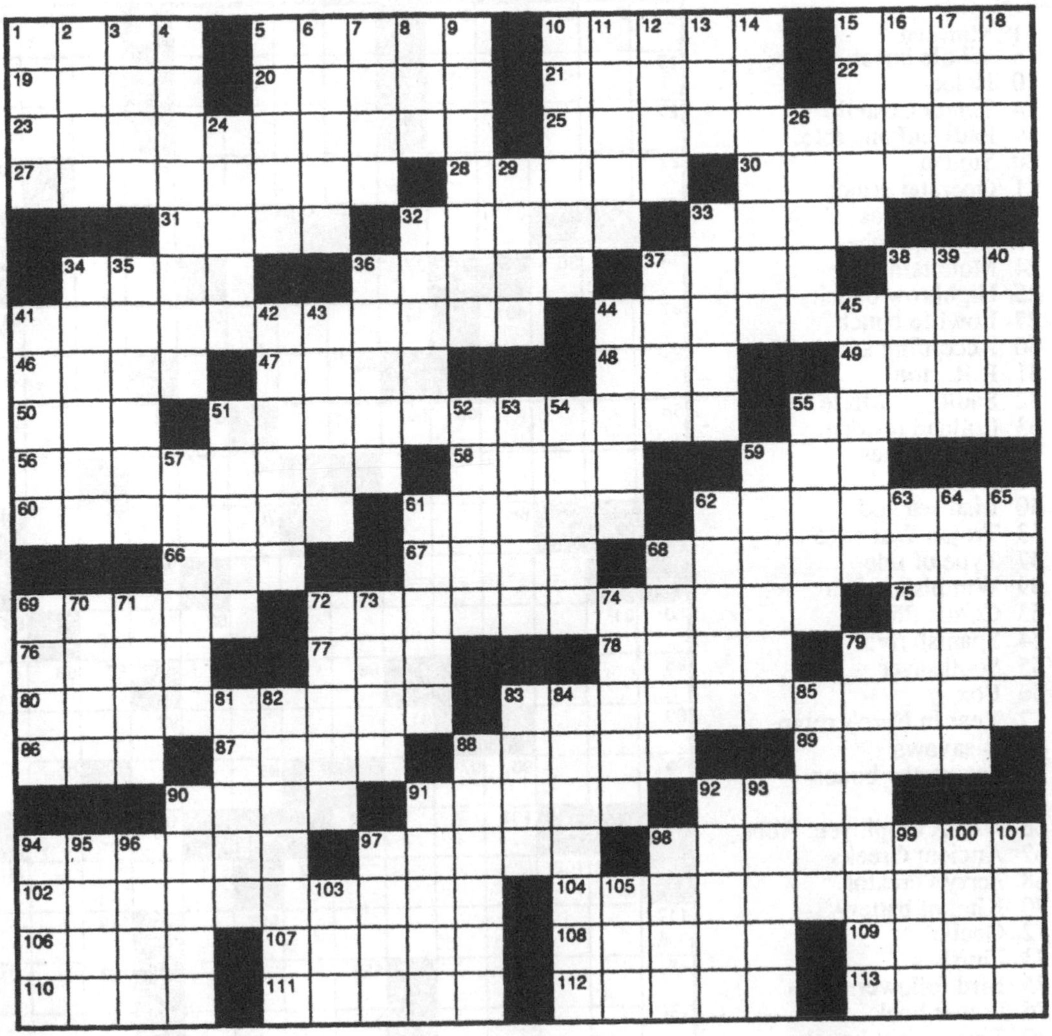

ACROSS

1 Metal door-fastening
5 Songs at sunrise
10 Bottomless gulf
15 Cheese related to Edam
19 Cold capital
20 Racket
21 Lariat
22 Breathy sound
23 Fancy dresses
25 "High Noon" hero
27 Project
28 Rhone feeder
30 Cave
31 A "Bonanza" star
32 Portents
33 Mine car
34 Holier-than-___
36 Sounds to scare chickens
37 Former UK airline
38 Try a drink
41 Springtime campus activity
44 Battle cries
46 Elec. units
47 Lachrymal drop
48 Book by Peter Evans
49 Mountain in Thessaly
50 Nancy's man
51 TV audience indicator
55 Dart
56 Feelings
58 Daredevil Knievel
59 For what reason?
60 Black Beauty's creator, et al.
61 Algonquians
62 "Oh, how ___ get up in the morning!"
66 Lobster coral
67 Stag
68 Chronic lack of appetite
69 Underworld ruler
72 Amusement park device
75 RAF aircraftsman
76 Ginger beverages
77 Debtor's letters
78 Entre ___
79 Mine, in Marseilles
80 Items twirled in a mid-century craze
83 "Our Boarding House" character
86 Naught
87 Actresses Harding and Blyth
88 Lawmaker
89 Formicary denizens
90 Minor prophet
91 Describing an alligator
92 Unadorned
94 Lew Wallace novel
97 Balance: Comb. form
98 Lassoed, in a way
102 Vessel larger than a gunboat
104 High jinks
106 More than a few
107 Bent
108 Artist's prop
109 Grad
110 Biblical patriarch
111 ___ Mae (mortgage money)
112 "Wreck of the Mary ___": Innes
113 Hodgepodge

DOWN

1 Merry sounds
2 Left without ___ (penniless)
3 Pigeonhole
4 Pawnbrokers' stores
5 Singer Paul and family
6 Cuts of meat
7 Larry of N.B.A. fame
8 An eastern time: Abbr.
9 Meeting
10 Inert gases
11 Boston and lima
12 Easily handled, as a ship
13 Unkempt abode
14 Ali, of films
15 Sweeper
16 Engrossed
17 "___ a song go out of my heart"
18 Architect Saarinen
24 Turmoil, in Glasgow
26 Goosefoot plant
29 Excited
32 District or region in Great Britain
33 Translation for équiper
34 "... for all good men ___ to the aid of their party"
35 "___, brown cow?"
36 Insults
37 Word with yard or storm
38 Passable
39 ___ facto
40 Exam for h.s. juniors
41 Swift mammals
42 Portrayer of Lawrence of Arabia
43 Spinks and Errol
44 Pitiful cries
45 Primary egg
51 City and Bay of the Big Island of Hawaii
52 Knock again
53 Prevent
54 Incisors
55 Acerb
57 Avila's saint
59 Rushing sound
61 En-lai's family
62 "___ Time": Hemingway
63 Free from obligation
64 ___ capital is Innsbruck
65 Late comedian Jack
68 Crazy as ___
69 Nobelist for Chemistry; 1944
70 His, in LeHavre
71 "Farmer in the ___"
72 Maned beasts
73 Bungler's cry
74 Relish
79 League champs, without a doubt
81 Emote
82 Switch option
83 Ditch around a castle
84 Sanctioned
85 Propelled a small boat
88 Bearing marks of wounds
90 Seafarer's calls
91 Discolor
92 One who jeers
93 Ingredient in Waldorf salad
94 College deg.
95 Zest
96 "___ Nanette"
97 The Ugly Duckling, really
98 Sub ___ (secretly)
99 Unemployed
100 Right end
101 DiMaggio and DeLuise
103 A neighbor of Ala.
105 "Some ___ meat and canna eat . . .": Burns

119 BUNCHES by Ernie Furtado

Groupies young and old should appreciate this gaggle of gags from Fun City.

ACROSS

1 Minimal
6 Whole bunch
10 Helot
14 Singer Costello
19 Patti LuPone role
20 Siouan
21 Operatic prince
22 Card classes
23 Cryptographer
24 Mountain lake
25 Highbrow bunch
27 Lowlife bunch
30 According to rule: Fr.
31 R.R. stop
32 Sault ___ Marie
33 Lolland resident
34 Tail suffixes
37 Siamese
40 Irish sea god
43 Trojan War sage
47 Type of tide
49 Wimpish bunch
53 Comic Philips
54 Spanish river
55 Soothsayer
56 Box
57 Year in Nero's reign
58 Disavows
61 Seaworthy bunch
65 Nova ___
66 NASA employee: Abbr.
67 Ancient Greeks
68 Perry's creator
70 Kind of battery
72 Gaelic
73 Finishes
75 Bird followers
76 Prayer book
80 Transparent bunch
83 Benefit: Fr.
85 Certain retired players
86 Parrot fish
87 Heraldic border
89 Opposed to aweather
90 Compass pt.
91 Vexatious bunch
94 Wrest
95 Chest: Comb. form
98 Slalom
99 Rx amount
100 Rds.
101 Hash-house sign
103 ___-fi
105 Conducted
108 Chamber
111 Afrikaner bunch
117 Poetic bunch
119 Rue ___ Paix
120 Ready to serve
121 ABA scoring leader: 1971
122 Autocrat
123 Experts
124 Regarding
125 Bergen dummy
126 Law chasers
127 Printer's term
128 Finals

DOWN

1 Walesa
2 Bacchanal cry
3 Verdi opus
4 "The 39 ___"
5 Card for 55 Across
6 School military gp.
7 Salieri opera
8 Front
9 Precept
10 Billy of the NFL
11 Feelings
12 Academic gown
13 Fern leaf
14 Ancient Jewish ascetic
15 Plunges
16 Anchor line, of old
17 "Let ___": Beatles
18 Induction gp.
26 Painter Hals
28 Nautical length: Abbr.
29 Filthy lucre
34 Unique people
35 Medieval instrument
36 Florentine painter: 1486-1531
38 Command, once
39 Brother of Eris
41 ___ far that
42 Tinkers
44 Michener title
45 Neglect
46 French face cards
48 Omens
50 "___ ed Euridice"
51 Short time: Sp.
52 Hum
57 Appellation for 44 Down
59 Cockney coiffure
60 Part of UCLA
62 The bed: Fr.
63 Terra ___
64 Street of song
66 Classifies
69 "Always the Land" novelist
71 Famed fabulist
73 Lauder of cosmetics
74 Bengali Theatre founder: Var.
77 Garage goings-on
78 Deputy
79 Yorkshire city
80 Dan Blocker role
81 Eject
82 Cow call
83 "The Sun ___ Rises"
84 Docs for Dobermans
88 Change the focus of
91 ___ this world (alien)
92 Exchequer
93 Prefix for restraint
96 Haymaker
97 Byron's Childe
102 Like some sweeps
104 Pas de deux conclusions
106 Small craft of WW II
107 "Twicknam Garden" poet
108 Naval warrant off.
109 Comfort
110 Goods.: Abbr.
111 Ukr. and Uzbek, formerly
112 Robert ___
113 Tobacco kiln
114 Hot times in Le Havre
115 Rave
116 Harbors: Abbr.
117 Lille lily
118 Anvil locale

121 WHAT'S MY LINE? by Bernice Gordon

A *personnel* computer may prove useful in overcoming some of the occupational hazards below.

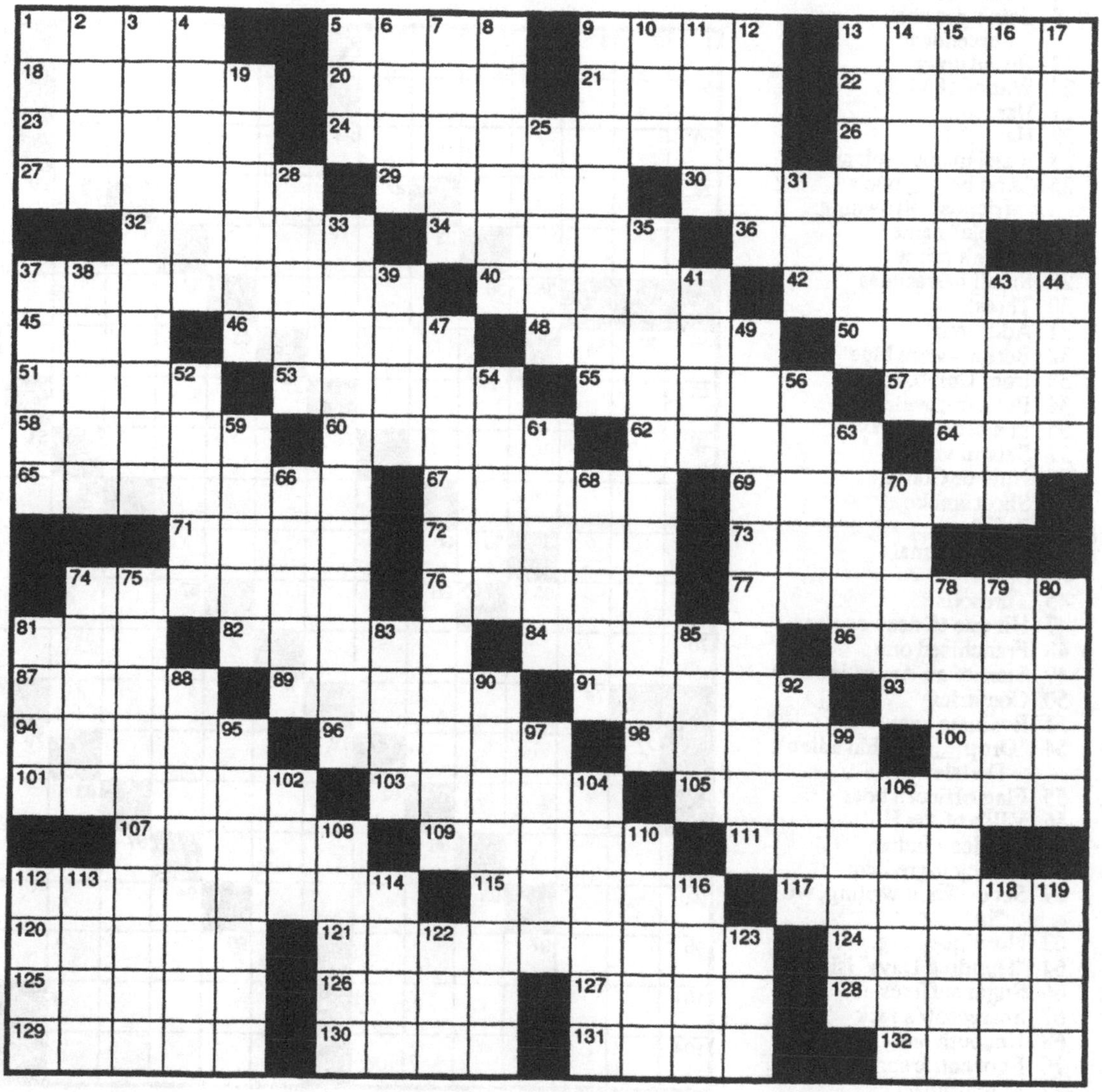

ACROSS

1 Ignoble
5 Prefix for dextrous
9 Vulnerable
13 Of a dowry
18 Pyrenees' Pico de ___
20 Weather word
21 SE Kansas city
22 Sidestep
23 Register
24 Announcer?
26 Link
27 Look back on
29 Small sandpiper
30 Napoleons, e.g.
32 Suffix for sacro
34 Near East dry measure
36 Show position
37 Elevator, in Seville
40 Thomas Hart Benton work
42 Parka
45 ___ Age
46 Case or well preceder
48 Nut pine
50 Employee under Nero
51 Thumb and Terrific
53 Ethyl acetate, e.g.
55 Adjoined
57 Fifty-fifty
58 Bass basket
60 Of a tissue layer
62 Olympian Carl
64 Corrode
65 Magical Doug
67 Ascended
69 Father of Jupiter
71 Felipe of baseball
72 Gossip
73 After a bit
74 ___ rima, verse stanza
76 Made over
77 Lady-in-waiting, to Portia
81 What Norman breaks
82 Magna ___
84 "Maria ___"
86 Papier-___
87 Where Bountiful is
89 Command
91 Sing heartily
93 Math course
94 Allude (to)
96 Cubic meter
98 Less aboveboard
100 Silkworm
101 ___ as a bird
103 Cape worn by Pius XII
105 Their hopes are high
107 Kaffir warriors
109 Hill resort of NW India
111 Montana river
112 Peoples of antiquity
115 Sorrow
117 Talks volubly
120 City on the Ocmulgee
121 Barmen?
124 Bone cavities
125 "___ Care"
126 Disparaging remark
127 Resort SE of Palermo
128 Kind of poker
129 Scruffs
130 Razorbacks
131 Oriental weight
132 Whilom

DOWN

1 Max who played Jethro
2 Actress Revere
3 Waiters?
4 Prima ballerina
5 Pen name of C. H. Smith
6 Bellona's brother
7 Regional flora and fauna
8 Lacking vitality
9 Colorful climber
10 Daybreak deity
11 Askew
12 Auric measure
13 Tooth part
14 Annulled
15 One who does hackwork?
16 Together, in music
17 Minus
19 Textile lubricants
25 Hold one's ___
28 Squander
31 ___ Na Na
33 Certain ACC cagers?
35 Robin Hood, et al.?
37 Gee follower
38 Two decades
39 Baptism, e.g.
41 Comstock ___
43 "___ and hungry look . . .": W. S.
44 Maidstone locale
47 Anchormen?
49 Shrink for anchormen?
52 French legislature
54 Street show
56 Varsi of "Compulsion"
59 The color purple
61 Type of script
63 Attack
66 Super stars
68 Long-legged bird
70 Eastern Christian: Var. sp.
74 Hall's partner
75 He sees the light?
78 Veil Vega?
79 Bake eggs
80 Sponsorship
81 Agua ___
83 Tenor Schipa
85 Lopez's theme
88 Gingold in "Gigi"
90 Quislings
92 Pariah
95 Is contrite
97 Borden bull
99 Ceremony
102 Uno, in Essen
104 Small kite
106 Actor Schell
108 Hide the loot
110 Kind of football
112 Infamous Idi
113 Nothing to Julio
114 Historic town W of Caen
116 Since, to Burns
118 Stowe's "The Pearl of ___ Island"
119 Cartoonist who tarnished a ring
122 Ex-pitcher McGraw
123 Gal of song

122 KALEIDOSCOPE by Sally Coyle

Colorful symmetry and clues that sparkle await the eye of the solver.

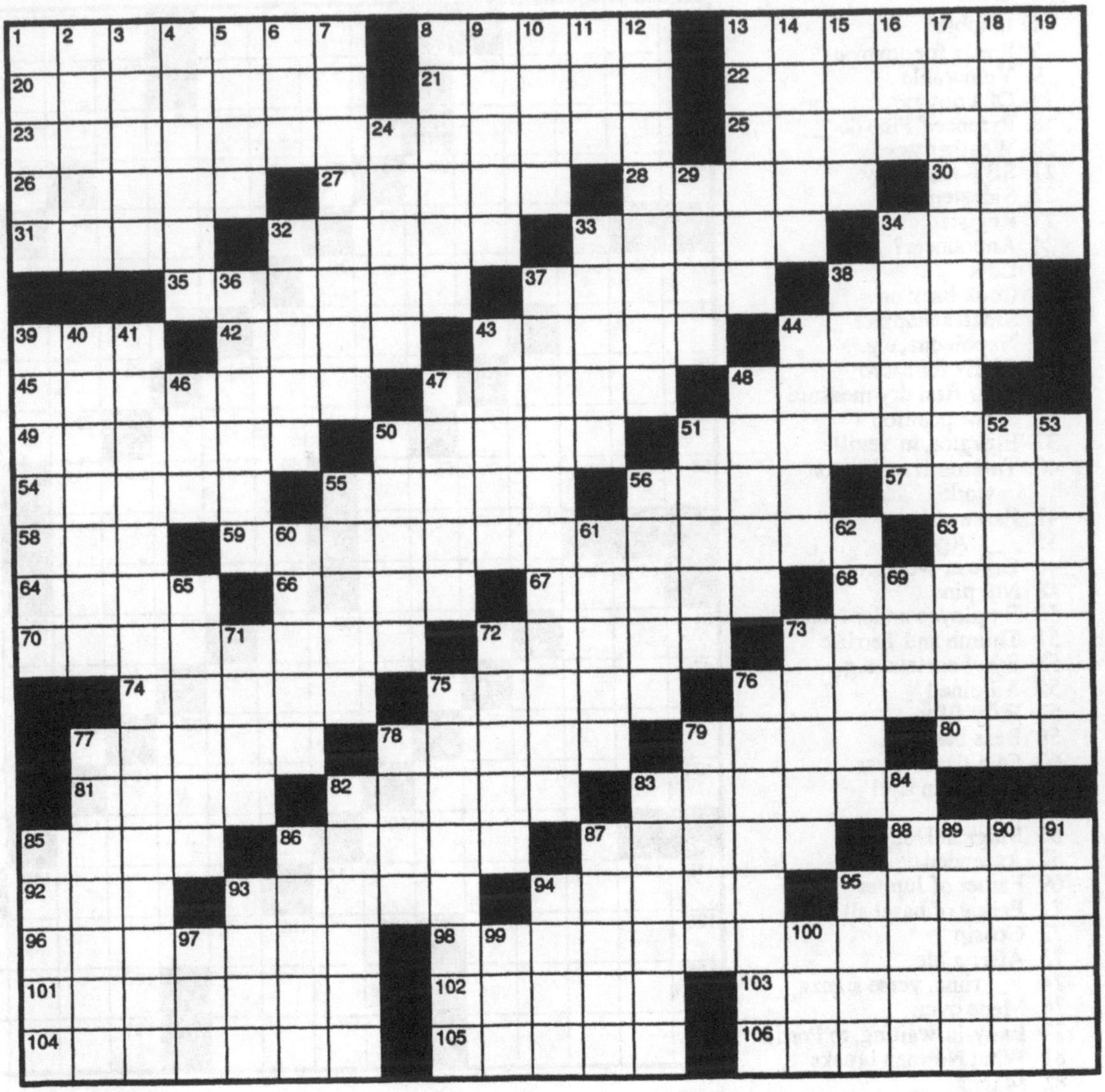

ACROSS

1 Predicaments
8 Cain's musical descendant
13 Hosed down
20 War of 1853-56
21 Harden
22 Hat
23 Russian house plans?
25 "And be ___ one's friends": Browning
26 "Noble" name
27 Torch's crime
28 Small barracudas
30 Thrash
31 Additional
32 Berlin's were blue
33 Iron: Comb. form
34 Boxcar traveler
35 In a sensible way
37 Salami variety
38 Hula or Cotton
39 Short smoke
42 Spin logs
43 Clan's animal
44 Spree
45 Turmoils
47 Hit one to deep center
48 Franchised one
49 Start of an Argentine city
50 Countries
51 Evaluate anew
54 "Drop ___ and bid adieu": Dodsley
55 Flag officer's boat
56 VIP's of the Hill
57 Mexican Indian
58 Rickey ingredient
59 Set down in writing, with "in"
63 Nordiques' org.
64 "Hundred Days" island
66 Sugar suffixes
67 Scarecrow's lack
68 Uncouth one
70 Egocentric sorrow
72 Main impact
73 Orange flower oil
74 Forsaken
75 Upswings
76 North Star
77 Sacred pictures
78 Avian crops
79 Caliber
80 Turner of history
81 Card game for three
82 Birthplace of Abel Tasman
83 French legislatures
85 Part of R. F. K.
86 His daughter became aureate
87 Soubrettes
88 "Spellbound" star
92 Ending for Gotham
93 Founded
94 1/40 inch
95 Californian oak
96 Herring relatives
98 Wintry Wisconsin city
101 Square mile's 640
102 End of an Argentine city
103 Whatnot
104 Pettifogger
105 Leaven
106 Effaced

DOWN

1 Begone!
2 Testament
3 "Easy ___," 1969 film
4 Strolls
5 Brazilian soccer great
6 Vichy water
7 NBA Hall-of-Fame sights
8 Breed of cattle
9 Mussels
10 Roll, once
11 ___ Deco
12 Abated
13 Eye part
14 Print
15 Beams
16 Paraguay River tributary
17 Cowardly dude?
18 Fit to be munched on
19 Cathedral
24 Small pellet
29 Dance with a king
32 Fits of anger
33 Galas
34 Upright
36 Assimilate
37 Russet's relative
38 Dollar's eight
39 Volumes
40 Useless
41 An unripe fruit
43 South Pacific islands
44 Crow
46 Alfonso's queen
47 Central and Hyde
48 Constituent in snake toxin
50 Cagney's partner
51 Knock again
52 Marginal comments
53 One in the limelight
55 Tack, to a seamstress
56 Cygnets
60 Cuts of meat
61 Rich played them
62 Grommet
65 At sea
69 Parrot genus
71 Bridge over the Seine
72 Big pigs
73 Charles and Hellmer
75 Great White Way
76 Ruminated
77 Line on a weather map
78 Napoleonic ___
79 "___ There," 1979 Sellers film
82 Angry goose
83 Most judicious
84 Cadge
85 Moreno and Coolidge
86 Skin disease
87 They cause 86 Down
89 Common newt
90 Ennis locale
91 Like a typewriter
93 After show or row
94 Coin for Trevi
95 Not illusory
97 Footlike part
99 Hurry
100 Opposite of hiver: Fr.

123 PHONIC FUN by Alfio Micci

Teachers of TEFL should particularly enjoy Alfio's facetious four-liner.

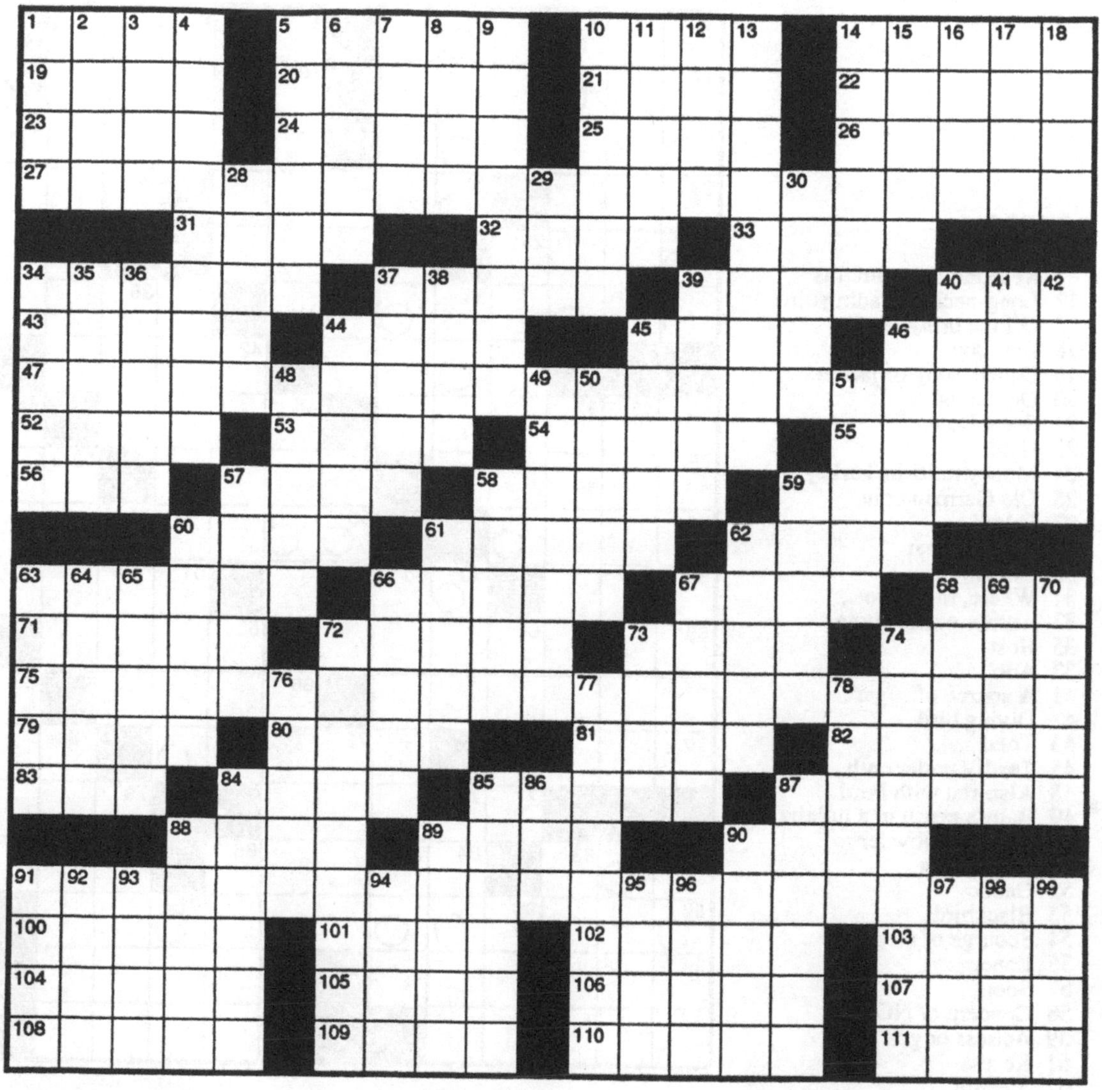

ACROSS

1 Remedy
5 Ticket: Slang
10 Sharp turns
14 Pres. Grant's original first name
19 Rockweed
20 Cape for John Paul II
21 Fairy-tale heavy
22 "A Bell for ___"
23 Glide
24 Yawning one
25 Fait accompli
26 Music for nine
27 **Start of a four-line verse**
31 Red and Dead
32 Smell ___
33 Entre ___
34 Foam
37 Down Under soldier
39 "Cool it! "
40 Abbr. on a VCR
43 Homeric classic
44 Don Juan's mother
45 Actor Mowbray
46 Dancer Montes
47 **Second line of verse**
52 Shoe size
53 Broadsword part
54 Literary device
55 E. Power Biggs's instrument
56 Curved plank
57 Sheet of stamps
58 "___ a Letter to My Love"
59 Curls the lip
60 See 1 Across
61 Springe
62 Adam's eldest
63 Reddish antelope
66 Desires
67 "Otello" baritone
68 Garfield is one
71 Unfettered
72 Unspoken
73 Pay to play
74 ___ fide
75 **Third line of verse**
79 Bellicose god
80 Pitcher Saberhagen
81 Mexican laborer
82 Log-rolling contest
83 Josephine of mystery
84 Tear
85 White bird
87 Light
88 Socials
89 Female wild buffalo
90 Like most colleges
91 **End of verse**
100 Auburn
101 Footnote abbr.
102 Indochinese capital
103 Madison Ave. award
104 Russian co-op
105 Add liquor
106 Before iota
107 Summit
108 ___ Janeiro
109 Historic times
110 15th Hebrew letter
111 Compos mentis

DOWN

1 Metal fastener
2 Sommer of films
3 Exchange premium
4 Light softener
5 Bookmark
6 Russian range
7 Ann or May
8 Epithet of Athena
9 Mosaic flooring
10 It has a dozen signs
11 Ten-percenter
12 Actor Morris
13 Like a desk job
14 Personal problem
15 Objects of worship
16 Delhi princess
17 Donkeys of Dieppe
18 Closet pest
28 City of W Yorkshire
29 Blue Eagle org.
30 Not a soul
34 London elevators
35 E. T., e.g.
36 Shoddy
37 Anoint, old style
38 Salamander
39 Bias
40 Cosmetic
41 "Dream of Gerontius" composer
42 Songwriter Sammy's folks
44 Chemical compound
45 Together
46 Golfer Roberts
48 "The Quiet Man" actress
49 Italian rice dish
50 Garb
51 "Pagliacci" character
57 Whined
58 Heavy-faced type
59 More like Solomon
60 Examples
61 Schönberg's "Verklärte ___"
62 Start of a Williams title
63 ___ ease (uncomfortable)
64 Silk with a wavy pattern
65 Hoosegow
66 Carried on a campaign
67 ___ water (troubled)
68 Was able to
69 Broadway backer
70 Western resort
72 Subway sight
73 Critic James
74 Sticks
76 Form of witchcraft
77 Goal posts
78 Pipe
84 Entertain
85 Ravages
86 Swift antelope
87 Brown bear
88 Melodious
89 Port in N Chile
90 Big bill
91 "___ she blows!"
92 Soprano Grist
93 Hep
94 Flanged I-beam
95 Sounds of merriment
96 Wind: Comb. form
97 Arm bone
98 ___-Carlo Menotti
99 It remained in Pandora's box

124

CIRCLES IN THE SQUARE by Jeanette K. Brill
Starting on the top line, the circled letters from left to right will reveal the stings of the sport of kings.

ACROSS

1 Probe
7 Respond to a stimulus
12 Long-necked wading bird
17 Off the briny
18 Boo-boo
19 Dance, song or jacket
20 On the list
21 See 4 Down
23 Haul
24 Money units in Turkey
26 Old German coin
27 Fairy
28 Fencing gear
30 Condition
31 Where, in Taxco
33 Author of the quote
35 Host
37 Ado
41 A source of sugar
42 Diving bird
43 Total
45 Testify under oath
48 Also-ran with Ford
49 Baby's perch in a lullaby
50 Abrasive powder
51 Prohibition
52 Gaelic
53 Blackbird
54 Scourge of serge
55 Loner
57 Soon
58 Concern of NOW
59 Actress or gun
61 Recess
62 Steeple
63 Rags
65 Sibelius, e.g.
66 Involuntary
67 Forever, in poesy
68 Relative of a butte
69 Copter
70 He loved Lucy
71 Not together
73 Birthplace of the author of the quote
77 Grasping person
79 Algerian port
80 Golfer Ballesteros
81 Bashful
84 Medieval court
86 Singer Ronstadt
88 Thing, in law
89 Newspaper in which the quote appeared
92 Purpose
94 Mysterious
95 Relating to a space
96 Sculptured likeness
97 These appear on graphs
98 Dustin Hoffman role
99 Rope for towing

DOWN

1 With more speed
2 On the slant
3 Melted
4 With 21 Across, article in which the quote appeared
5 City on the Oka
6 Word with man or ball
7 Present in another form
8 Irregular
9 Airport abbr.
10 Outlay
11 "Don't ___ me"
12 Hidden supply
13 Urban district in E England
14 Hazardous obstruction
15 Odd in Aberdeen
16 Inquisitive
19 Kitchen appliances
22 Farm implement
25 Deserve
29 Accompany or accompanier
32 Familiar Italian family for puzzlers
34 Quite a few
35 Profession of our author
36 Fish eggs
38 Of enormous strength
39 A natural resource
40 Fretted
42 Rounded projection
44 Bess Truman, ___ Wallace
45 Erased
46 Arabian kingdom
47 Companions of lares
48 "___ That Dream," 1939 song
49 "Star ___"
51 Golfers' gadgets
52 Collar or jacket
56 Island of the Inner Hebrides
57 These can be seen at airports
59 Colleague of a Rep.
60 Cherish
62 Tender
64 Adorn
65 Chemin de-___ (French railroad)
66 Diabolical
68 Conjugal
69 River in Suriname
72 Get animated (with "up")
73 Gruesome
74 Visorless caps
75 Fifth or Seventh
76 This precedes day or year
78 Religious representations
79 A New York city
81 Kind of bean
82 "___ in My Arms," 1925 hit song
83 Community org.
85 River in Yorkshire
87 Architectural pier
90 Long-haired ox
91 "___ in White"; Kingsley
93 Marble used as a shooter

125

BEASTLY QUOTATIONS by Dorothea E. Shipp
Some of the extracts are familiar; others are not. But an animal hides in each of the long ones.

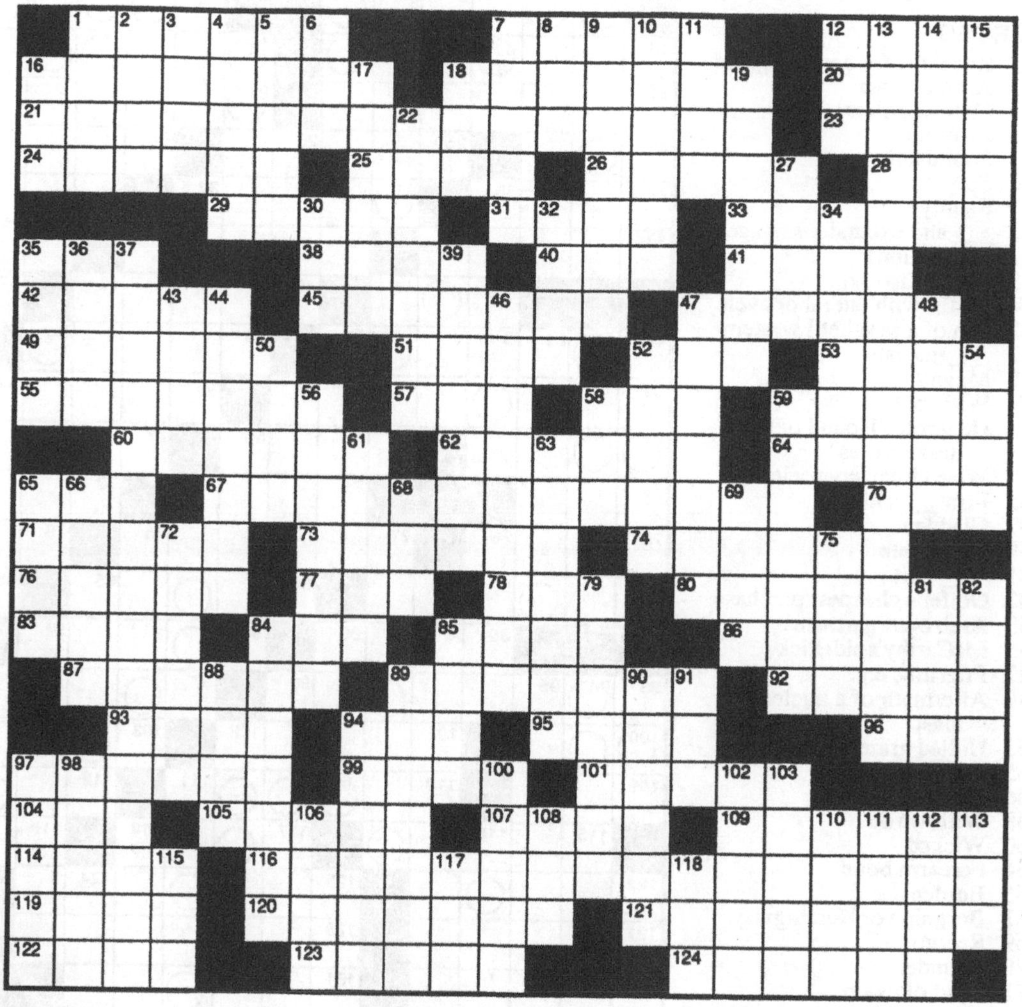

ACROSS

1 Shape of some eyebrows
7 Haydn's "Harmonie ___"
12 Common Irish vegetable
16 Tries to equal or excel
18 Most peppery
20 George Burns contemporary
21 Like Belloc's "Tall Goltman"
23 Baseball's Hall of Famer ___ Rixey
24 City of W Texas
25 First-class
26 Get new weapons
28 Come together
29 Kind of turf or dome
31 Nine inches
33 Lab vessel
35 Former financier's nickname
38 Comedian Foxx
40 ___ of consent
41 Concerning
42 Brava or Mesa
45 "Sewing at once, with ___ thread . . . ": Hood
47 Metamorphic rock
49 Barrymore and Waters
51 City north of Kursk
52 Sweet one
53 ". . . the scole of Stratford ___ Bowe": Chaucer
55 Hem decoration
57 Old Arab measure
58 New Zealand clan
59 Eastern rulers
60 Blair and Mitchell
62 Certain veil or suite
64 Marsh plants
65 Austrian born composer Hans ___
67 Shylock's accusation to Antonio
70 Tiny
71 "The Zoo Story" playwright
73 "Voila le ___ d'Austerlitz": Napoleon
74 Lenni ___ Indians
76 Disburse
77 Goddess of the dawn
78 Drugged state: Arab.
80 Let go
83 Stone
84 Town dweller
85 Genuine
86 Certain machine cycles
87 Don
89 Relative of an oboe
92 Pool person
93 Physicist's suffix
94 Year of the death of Pius I
95 "___ girl!"
96 Capt.'s underlings
97 Order
99 Female ruffs
101 ___ a fox
104 Client follower
105 Family in "A Rage to Live"
107 Of anger: Lat.
109 Emanation from a swamp
114 Nervous spasms
116 Mrs. Skewton's observation, à la Dickens
119 Pierre's loc.
120 Baby's rocking site
121 Washington group
122 The Abominable Snowman
123 Poems of Scandinavian myths
124 Kind of solution

DOWN

1 Surrounded by
2 ___ of thumb
3 Keys in Toulouse
4 Medieval merchants' guild
5 Kett and James
6 "___ gratias"
7 A Malone of basketball
8 Old English letter
9 Mink's summer home
10 Calm
11 Pronoun for the Andrea Doria
12 Haggard work
13 W. R. Mandale ditty
14 House or berth preceder
15 Started a poker game
16 Within: Comb. form.
17 Netted
18 Hebrew measure
19 Party fare
22 Bringers of bad luck
27 Handwriting-on-the wall word
30 Refrain syllable
32 Weary
34 Hospital system in times of emergencies
35 Top pitchers
36 Military org.
37 Quotation re bravery, by Archibald Douglas
39 Lasting
43 Type of printer
44 Tempered
46 "How a ___ honey": Milne
47 Netherlands money
48 Greek measure
50 Dancer Osato
52 Writer Baroness de ___-Holstein
54 Word in N Carolina's motto
56 "Comes a ___ the day's occupations": Longfellow
58 Navy man: Abbr.
59 Wild sheep of Asia
61 Dart
63 "As ___ painted ship . . . ": Coleridge
65 Sound of surprise
66 ___ Maritimes
68 Pacino and Hirt
69 Nonpareil
72 Unbroken
75 Caged
79 Atlantic debris
81 Mailed
82 Those, to Carlos
84 ___ lens
85 Angel's delight
88 Station
89 Consecrated
90 Novelist Wadell character and namesakes
91 Word of denial
94 Teamed up with other oarsmen
97 "Heavens to ___!"
98 Pass over
100 Greek island in the Cyclades
102 Religious society of Iowa
103 Strong fiber
106 Ripped
108 Relative of serge
110 ___ spumanti
111 Suffix with scan
112 Oliver Twist's request
113 Suburb of Liège
115 Perform christies
117 ___ loss for words
118 Foot, to Fabius

126 MORE CIRCLES IN THE SQUARE by Jeanette K. Brill

Starting at the top, the circled letters sequentially form a quotation from an operatic star.

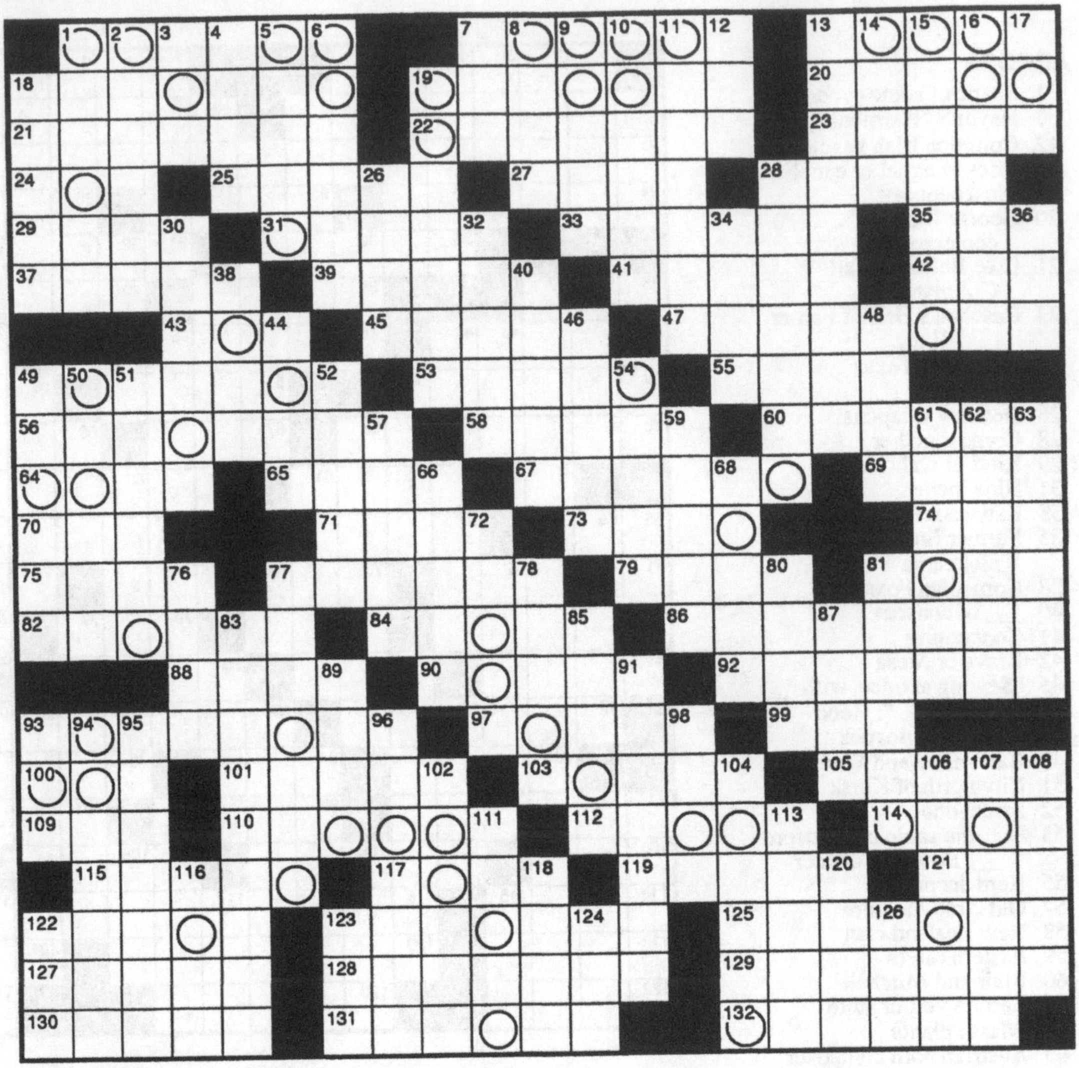

ACROSS

1 Requisite for some degrees
7 Aromatic tea
13 Critical juncture
18 Juvenile
19 Sound unit
20 Spry
21 Saintly
22 ___ and excursions (stage direction)
23 Voices, to Ovid
24 Prefix with lateral or cycle
25 Kin of a spaghetti western
27 ___ majesté
28 Magna ___
29 Withered
31 He wrote "Hound of the Baskervilles"
33 Wise Greek counselor
35 Fish ___ chips
37 Gladden
39 Roi's mate
41 "___ evil . . ."
42 Golfer's cheapest purchase
43 Arab outergarment
45 McCarthy's sidekick
47 Pilgrims, e.g.
49 Aftermath of a nuclear blast
53 Hulled grain
55 Allot
56 Consecrated
58 Willow rod
60 Wicked
64 Forearm bone
65 Burden
67 Borgnine or Hemingway
69 Record
70 Bounder
71 Kind of exam
73 Slangy affirmative
74 Half of a two-piece bathing suit
75 Relatives of ids
77 Ancient Roman magistrate
79 Allowance for waste
81 Town in SW Switzerland
82 Member of the graduating class
84 Anagram of "gears"
86 Pericarp
88 Highest point
90 Gunpowder ingredient
92 Primped
93 Specialized painter
97 Quoted
99 "Stout-hearted ___," Romberg song
100 Bog
101 Stitch quickly
103 Aweigh
105 Imbue with fresh courage
109 P.I.
110 Certain brick structures
112 Comedian Jack ___ (1903-78)
114 Tolerable
115 Song from "Seventh Heaven": 1927
117 Gouda cousin
119 Tropical fish
121 Q-U link
122 Freshman at West Point
123 SW Massachusetts city
125 Passerine bird
127 Extend a subscription
128 Acquitted
129 Whatnot
130 Kefauver
131 Enisle
132 Lecturer

DOWN

1 Lincoln is one
2 Journey
3 Before, poetically
4 Missile-storage place
5 Homeric epic
6 Portion of a military front
7 ___ Aviv
8 Suffix with method
9 Temptress
10 Maltreats
11 Formidable rivals
12 Urban transp. lines
13 Person to whom the quote is attributed
14 Conductor Buketoff
15 Wink
16 Charwoman
17 "For ___ a jolly . . ."
18 Linger for a time
19 "___ Je Vous Aime Beaucoup"
26 "The ___ of Laura Mars"
28 Challenge
30 And others: Lat.
32 Winter month in Barcelona
34 Abound
36 ___ Plaines
38 Black
40 Irregular
44 Maxwell or Marmon
46 Where cheese is made
48 Fast time
49 Oral cavity
50 Rudiment; germ; bud
51 ___ broil
52 Singer like 13 Down
54 Belief
57 He painted "Four Apostles"
59 Erects
61 Cautious; conservative
62 Came into view
63 Inclined
66 Lucifer
68 Timid one
72 Particular mode of reasoning
76 Thailand, at one time
77 Introductory performance
78 Anatomical networks
80 Duration
81 Locales
83 Where the quote appeared
85 Brief spat
87 ___ Park, N.Y.
89 Alien: Comb. form
91 Appraised a second time
93 Newt
94 Goads to action
95 "___ Evenings," 1983 Mailer book
96 Measles
98 Artificial watercourse
102 Itinerant vendor: Var.
104 Pockmarked
106 Old Dutch land measure
107 Declare positively
108 ___ Dame
111 Brazilian soprano, Bidu ___
113 Greek muse of love poetry
116 "Sting like ___": Ali
118 Italian Prime Minister: 1963-68
120 Archaic form: Abbr.
122 Grand ___ (Evangeline's home)
123 Monogram of a Hanoi VIP
124 Barbie's friend
126 Ripen

127 DOUBLE CLUES by Mary Snyder

Clues marked with asterisks are *double clues*. As a further hint, we suggest you put your pen down and use a pencil when solving this one.

ACROSS

1 High plateaus
6 Cheryl or Diane
10 O.T. book
14 In the bunk
18 Turn outward
19 Pierre's gal pal
20 Like a judge
22 Arena sound
23 They pin medals on speakers*
25 They reform the clergy*
27 Twists
28 Miler Steve
30 Wings it
31 Anger
32 Juicy fruits
33 Fateful date
34 Stands fast
38 Canine teeth
39 They babble to diners*
43 Out-of-the-money finisher
44 Kinds
45 Negative contraction
46 Place
47 Formal attire
49 Haddock relatives
50 Word in Mass. motto
51 Gas: Comb. form
52 They are demanding siblings*
56 Let him go out: Lat.
57 Section
59 Poison: Prefix
60 Riotous parties
61 Foch and Simone
62 NYC time
63 Sacred song
65 "Candid ___"
68 He played Jethro Bodine
69 Mercenary of 1776
72 Eared seal
73 They discharge landlords*
75 Sgts.
77 Bows
78 Mil. addresses
80 "___ Name" (Gabriel hymn)
82 Household deity
83 Salty "Stop!"
84 Pelvic artery
86 Get by effort
87 They look for lutrine creatures*
89 Play the role
90 Maidens
91 Sister of Zeus
92 "... went away in ___": II Kings 5.12
93 ___ Paul, S African statesman
94 Periodical publication
96 Branches
97 Pledgee
102 They dispatch fishermen*
104 They punish speeders*
106 Lily of opera
107 Uncanny
108 Self: Comb. form
109 Large quantities
110 Cummerbund
111 Girl
112 Scrawny
113 Bristles

DOWN

1 Ancient Persian
2 Level
3 Amish, for one
4 "... maids all in ___"
5 They compete on waterways*
6 Popular paint
7 Famous cookie man
8 NNE or SSW
9 Part of mountain climbing
10 "Gandhi" won several
11 Some are sonic
12 Shorten: Abbr.
13 Off the track
14 Pointillist, e.g.
15 Nitwit
16 Corn spikes
17 AMA members
21 Flushes
24 Chem. suffixes
26 Shoe adjunct
29 Teases
32 First section
34 Soprano Frances
35 Egotists, e.g.
36 River to the Rhone
37 They plot against initialers*
38 Palms off
39 Ringling ___: Abbr.
40 Laborers of yore
41 Convened again
42 Marginal words
44 Koran supplement
45 Topmost: Comb. form
48 Loudonville college
50 They study gold diggers*
53 Take
54 Voir, to a French student
55 Additional
56 Cloth measures
58 Like a swamp
60 Low voices
63 Home of Alcestis
64 Ice pinnacle
65 Rake over the ___
66 Like a rat in ___
67 Large: Comb. form
68 All for the ___
70 Pains
71 Clamor
73 Polar explorer
74 Rancor
76 Concordes
78 Mean
79 Equal
81 They float in French seas*
83 Supped at home
84 Moslem prayer leader
85 Reasonable
88 Flog
89 Obliterates
90 Kind of mock court
92 Molding edge
93 Actor Bean
94 Meeting place for Zeno
95 Shore eagles
97 ___-cake
98 Arrow poison
99 Kind of belt
100 Ms. Bombeck
101 Being
102 Gobs' jobs
103 Christian ___
105 Tint

128 HOLLYWOOD ECHOES by Arthur S. Verdesca

By their roles, ye shall know them while stargazing. A clever puzzle!

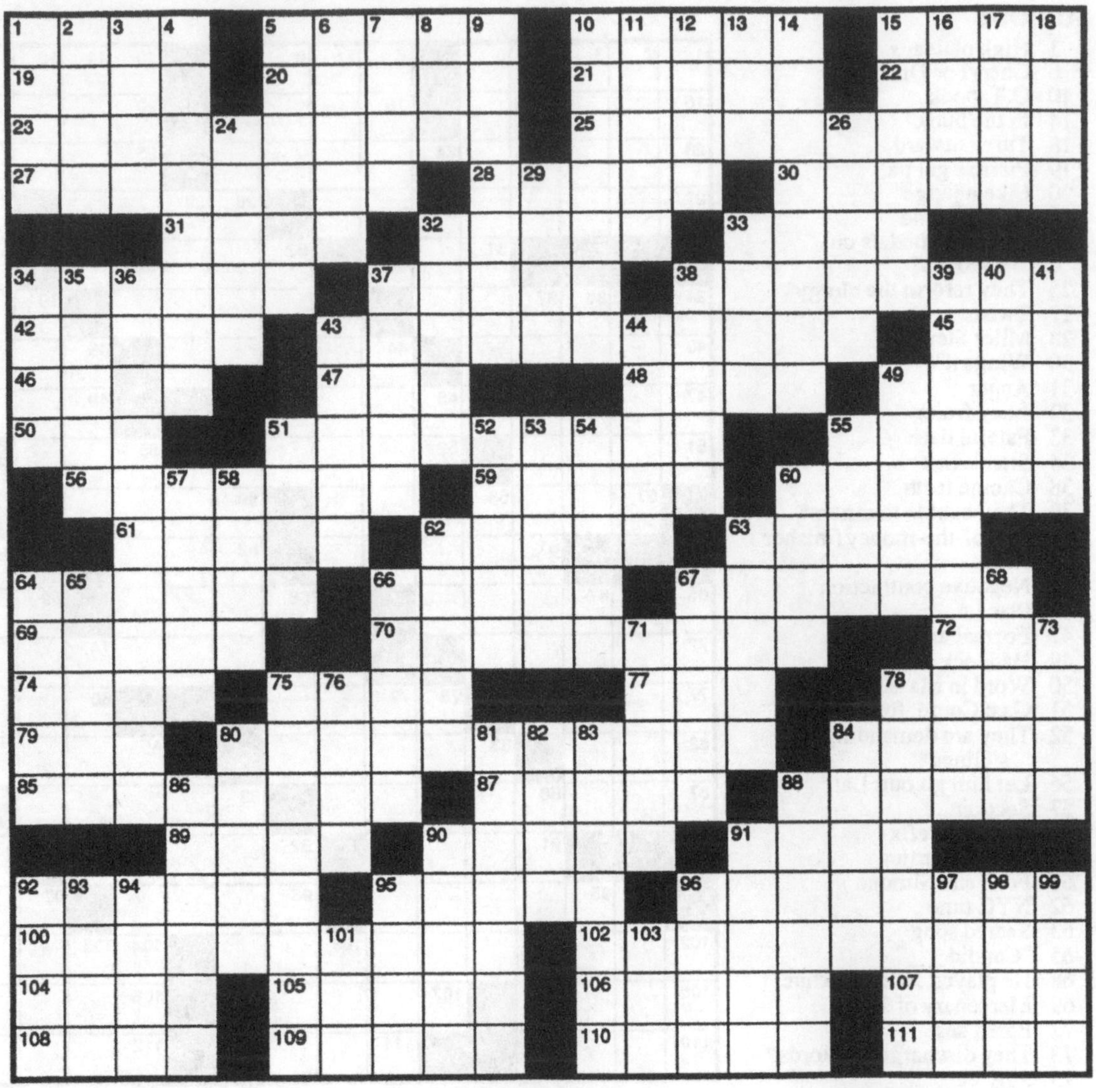

ACROSS

1 Scots uncles
5 Aftermath
10 Letter in Acre
15 H. James biographer
19 Roman statesman
20 Where Papa Doc ruled
21 Ex-NKVD head
22 Lachrymatory
23 Flash Gordon, grouch?
25 The Invisible Man's restraints?
27 Immoderate degrees
28 Lounges
30 Trumpet call
31 Angered
32 Thirties' dance
33 Paddock newcomer
34 Distributors on the farm
37 Italian bowls
38 Trisyllabic verse
42 Michelangelo masterpiece
43 Davy Crockett's anorak?
45 Nigerian native
46 Friend in a fray
47 Charles V's polit. terr.
48 Wallet stuffers
49 U.S.A.
50 Dolores ___ Rio of films
51 The Quiet Man's wagon?
55 Athos's creator
56 Quitclaim
59 Marbled
60 "All roads lead ___"
61 U.S. physicist
62 Anjous
63 Gussie of tennis
64 "Hud" star
66 Attend
67 Operatic diva from Spain
69 Tatum, for one
70 Madelon Claudet's confusion?
72 NOW goal
74 Deeply
75 Newcastle surplus
77 Fort ___, California
78 Feds
79 French salt
80 More affectionate Young Mr. Lincoln?
84 Barrel block
85 Like some winds
87 Roof borders
88 Subbase
89 Simple
90 Perfume base
91 Wild hog
92 Cheap thing
95 Ectal
96 Combed
100 M's truck?
102 Dr. Kildare's legatees?
104 Talented
105 Flynn of films
106 Depart
107 Cheese in red wax
108 Cull
109 Goad
110 Physically disabled
111 Back of neck

DOWN

1 Lo! to Pilate
2 Zeppo, e.g.
3 Elève's state
4 Sedateness
5 Short essays
6 Tore
7 Haughtiness
8 "Call ___ day"
9 No. 9 iron
10 Scraper
11 Laminate
12 Ares' sister
13 Thole
14 Church cushions
15 With fairness
16 Hammett's "The ___ Curse"
17 Helot's cousin
18 For fear that
24 Yogi of baseball
26 Lariat
29 Former
32 Sophia of films
33 Cabbie's customer
34 Hooked nail
35 Houston football player
36 Citizen Kane's oil holdings?
37 Metric pressure measure
38 The late Mr. Kaye
39 Ensign Pulver's Edsel?
40 Construction item
41 Lifeless body, to the Bard
43 New moon, e.g.
44 Prince Hal's attendant
49 Of the ear or air
51 Inform re danger
52 Partner of each
53 Emulate Penelope
54 Buenos ___
55 Dickens's Miss Spenlow
57 USAF General
58 Pierre's equal
60 Cary's "___ a Pilgrim"
62 Washington portrayer
63 Zoroastrian deity
64 Clamor
65 Nine: Comb. form
66 Disreputable
67 Wags
68 Build
71 Stropper
73 Egyptian cross
75 Trunk armor
76 "It's ___ Love," Beatles song
78 Baker's dozen
80 Unravel a ship's rope
81 Fashion anew
82 Kismet
83 Total
84 Brawl
86 Lacrimated
88 Composed
90 Wallaroos
91 Vowel mark
92 Cabbage dish
93 Ear end
94 Perry's creator
95 Odd: Scot.
96 Stuff
97 Verdi's Ethiop
98 Rodent catcher
99 Salinger heroine
101 Prill or mispickel
103 Assent

129

WESTWARD HO! by Dale Storms
From the East comes a delightful blend of historical and roundabout clues. Hours of research prove Dale's occidental theme was not accidental.

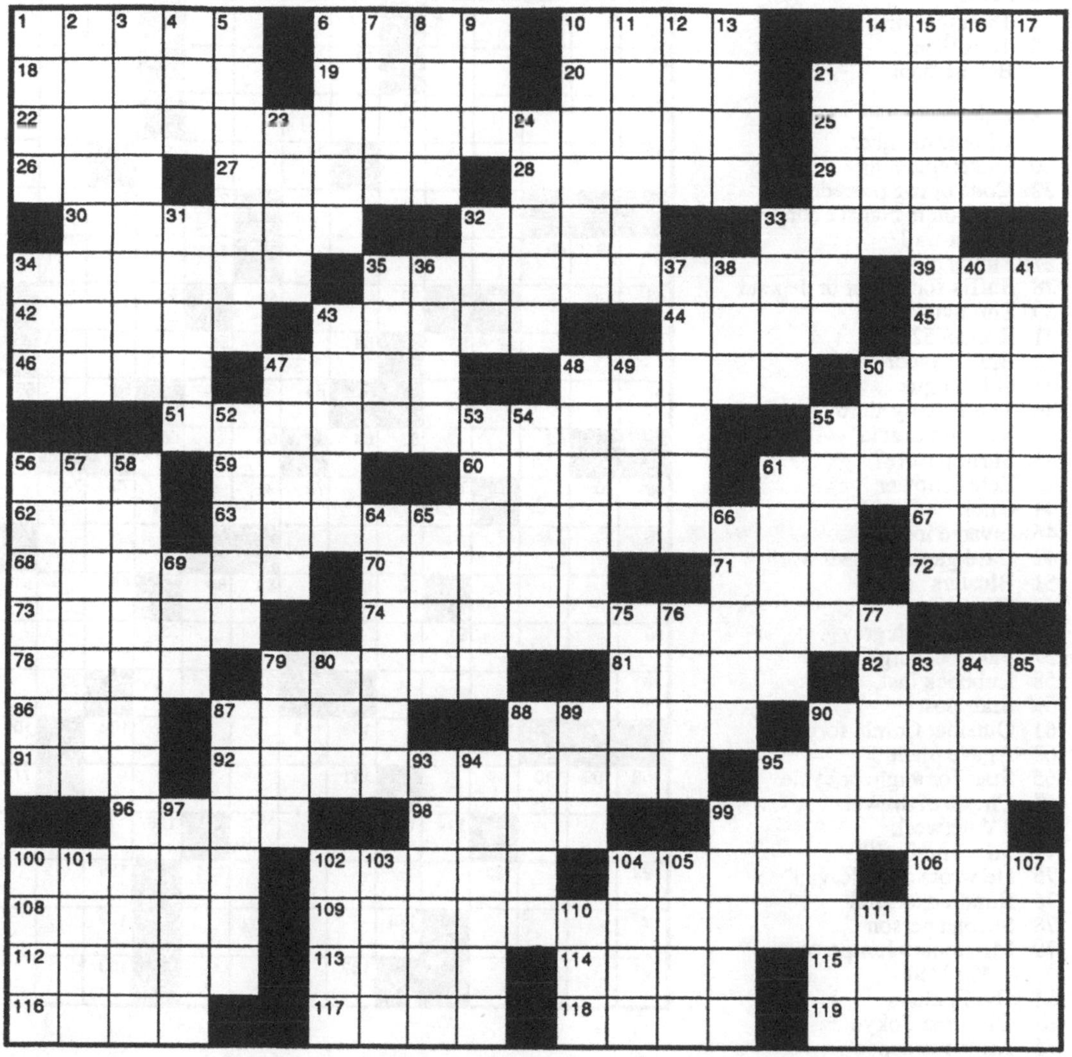

ACROSS

1 Doctor who wrote "Aequanimitas"
6 Peck
10 Jumella's twin
14 Hexagram
18 Kind of wine
19 Cuzco citizen
20 ___ Minor
21 Emulate Charon
22 Prairie-schooner relatives
25 Tropical vine
26 Veneration
27 Quail
28 Bad checks
29 Vidalia namesake
30 Bathhouse
32 Newtonian subject
33 "The Clan of the Cave Bear" author
34 Femme ___
35 Outlaw born Myra Shirley
39 Menu abbr.
42 Grenoble's river
43 City S of Milan
44 Charity
45 Actor Jacobi
46 Italian biologist: 1626–98
47 Snatch
48 Close-fitting garments
50 Follower of FDR
51 Wranglers
55 9A and 9B
56 Small harbor
59 American cartoonist
60 "Wings on My Feet" author
61 Purveys
62 Mary in "Sons and Lovers"
63 Jerry & Roy?
67 Louis XIV, to Louis XIV
68 Chamber-music group
70 Silk design
71 Middle note
72 They'll give you a no.
73 Braid
74 Buffalo Bill rode for them
78 Facilitate
79 Congregational responses
81 Reagan followers
82 Sheet of stamps
86 NBA pos.
87 Wicked
88 Spanish snacks
90 Eastern Church council
91 Elevenses beverage
92 Wantod man of 1882
95 What squirrels squirrel away
96 Refusals
98 Sunscreen ingredient: Abbr.
99 Swahili bosses
100 Penn and Teller's forte
102 Jerk
104 Kettle emission
106 French possessive
108 Suffix for fraud
109 Golden Spike Monument site
112 Songbirds
113 Seedy part
114 Hubbub
115 Adjective for some leaves
116 Fewer
117 Kind of test
118 Opera and ballet
119 Resume

DOWN

1 Killer whale
2 Display
3 Striped
4 Air-sock dlr.
5 Make smaller
6 Plains Indian
7 "Bus Stop" playwright
8 Lasting aftereffect
9 Proverb
10 Silicate mineral
11 Consommés
12 Laborer of crosswords
13 Colleen
14 River 482 miles long
15 Portland team
16 "New Yorker" cartoonist
17 Robert in "Horizons West"
21 Farina and durum
23 ___ poem
24 Hawaiian shrub
31 Of atmospheric weight
32 Roman's 1051
33 Up in ___ (outraged)
34 Coniferous tree
35 Azerbaijan capital
36 Divisible by two
37 Corn silk
38 High: Music
40 Spanish dances
41 Bitterwood
43 Tropical fruit
47 Chirp
48 Buyer
49 Actor Stoltz
50 ___ to be tied
52 Column molding
53 First-down determiners
54 Bald boy of comics
55 Asian liquors
56 Cher film of 1987
57 Bishop
58 Baseball team
61 Saskatchewan tribesmen
64 Presses on
65 Promptly
66 Lands
69 Cravat
75 Aztec god of planting
76 School orgs.
77 "___ River Anthology"
79 Rosary beads
80 Prefix for trial
83 Scraped spot
84 Balderdash
85 Ervil
87 Expels
88 Banned
89 Org. for Spock
90 Dash
93 Spartan magistrates
94 Packed
95 Absent
97 Porcine grunts
99 Parks and Lahr
100 A funny Martin
101 Wings
102 Stray's friend: Abbr.
103 Swamp reptile
104 Excite
105 Whistle
107 Oyster ___
110 Marksman's org.
111 Salem loc.

130 ELUSIVER by Judith C. Dalton

Judith claims that Lucifer did not inspire her theme. At any rate, you R in for some extRa excitement!

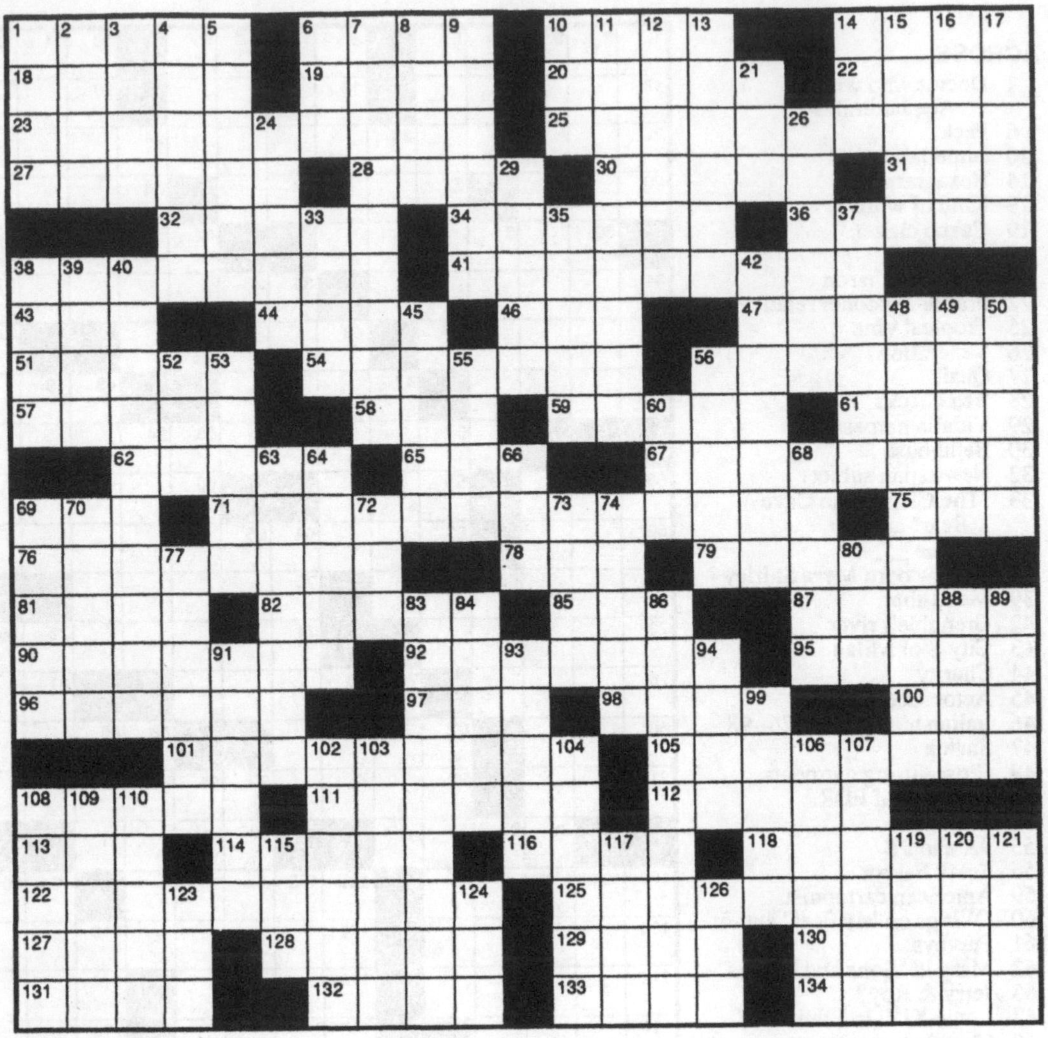

ACROSS

1 Twenty: Comb. form
6 Topgallant
10 Bd. offshoot
14 Engrave
18 Law
19 Chorus member
20 Uncomplaining
22 Code or rug preceder
23 Environmentalist's concern?
25 Finger trail?
27 Singer Nixon
28 Suffix for confer or depend
30 Slur over
31 Roman 52
32 Bradshaw or cloth
34 Gill fungus
36 The Twenty-third, e.g.
38 Vitamin C acid
41 Shrimp store?
43 Zeta follower
44 Click
46 Inverse ire
47 Card game for two
51 Blusters
54 Caves
56 More bluish gray
57 Pakistan neighbor
58 Lubbock inst.
59 Stair post
61 Outside: Comb. form
62 Agave plant
65 Start for angle or cycle
67 Chests of drawers
69 TV network
71 I do, you fool!?
75 He wrote "The Raven"
76 Bundled to send
78 Second person
79 Missionary Junipero: 1713–84
81 Ovid's altars
82 Old-time Tokyo
85 Amb. residence
87 Rand's "___ Shrugged"
90 Paid a penalty for a coach
92 Beseech
95 N. Vincent or C. Willson
96 Takes the rudder
97 Fin. advisory bd. to Pres.
98 Shortened forms of works: Abbr.
100 Crow cry
101 Overshoe ache?
105 Granters
108 Zoroastrian
111 Ancient Bavarian province
112 Shipworm
113 Gourmandized
114 Nigerian dollar
116 Pinocchio was one
118 Age, energy or mass preceder
122 Cute currency?
125 Amusing abode?
127 Assistant
128 Make allusion to
129 MC
130 Church parts
131 Endure
132 Cong. meeting
133 Hottentot
134 Endings for electro and hydro

DOWN

1 Missile letters
2 "___ Mia," 1954 song
3 ___ about (approximately)
4 ___ be released (coming)
5 Denser; darker
6 Ewe sound
7 A wagon in a bowling establishment?
8 Flabbergast
9 Shoe part
10 Ark. time area
11 Else
12 ___ Rouge, Paris attraction
13 Apes
14 Corn spike
15 Singing syllables
16 DeMille of film fame
17 Moslem potentate
21 Downtown area designation: Abbr.
24 Words of action
26 Cape ___: Mexico
29 Wading bird
33 Boxing stage
35 Moses' brother
37 Outpourings
38 Atmosphere: Comb. form
39 Laurel or Getz
40 Sugared bird?
42 Greek
45 African lemur
48 Oriental grain mansion?
49 Black, in Old Spanish
50 Irregular
52 Germanic war god
53 Holy, in LeHavre
55 Surf companion
56 Ancient Chinese
60 Hosp. units
63 Trinidad rhythm
64 "Mr Lincoln" playwright and family
66 Frost's fire mate
68 Thong
69 Armadillos
70 Campus in Lake Forest, Ill.
72 Prof. deg.
73 Finished
74 Scene of Hercules' first labor
77 Movie stars and moguls, for short
80 Ave. or st.
83 Wanes
84 ___ a time (singly)
86 Infant's sweeper?
88 Winglike
89 Stitches up
91 Begone, to Shakespeare (with "thee")
93 Ceylon or S India native
94 The Kingston group
99 Of ecological stages
102 Hauls up and secures on a ship
103 Container for liquid
104 ___ full (debt canceled)
106 Deadly
107 Wilted
108 Kind of bull
109 Entrance halls
110 Clarinets, oboes, etc.
115 Firth of Clyde seaport
117 Opera solo
119 New wine
120 "Peekaboo, ___ you!"
121 Assessment in Ireland
123 Asian holiday
124 What mins. make
126 Mauna ___

131 ALPHABET SOUP by Nancy Nicholson Joline

You'll like this one! It's ingenious and informative—an editor's delight and a solver's source of fascinating fun.

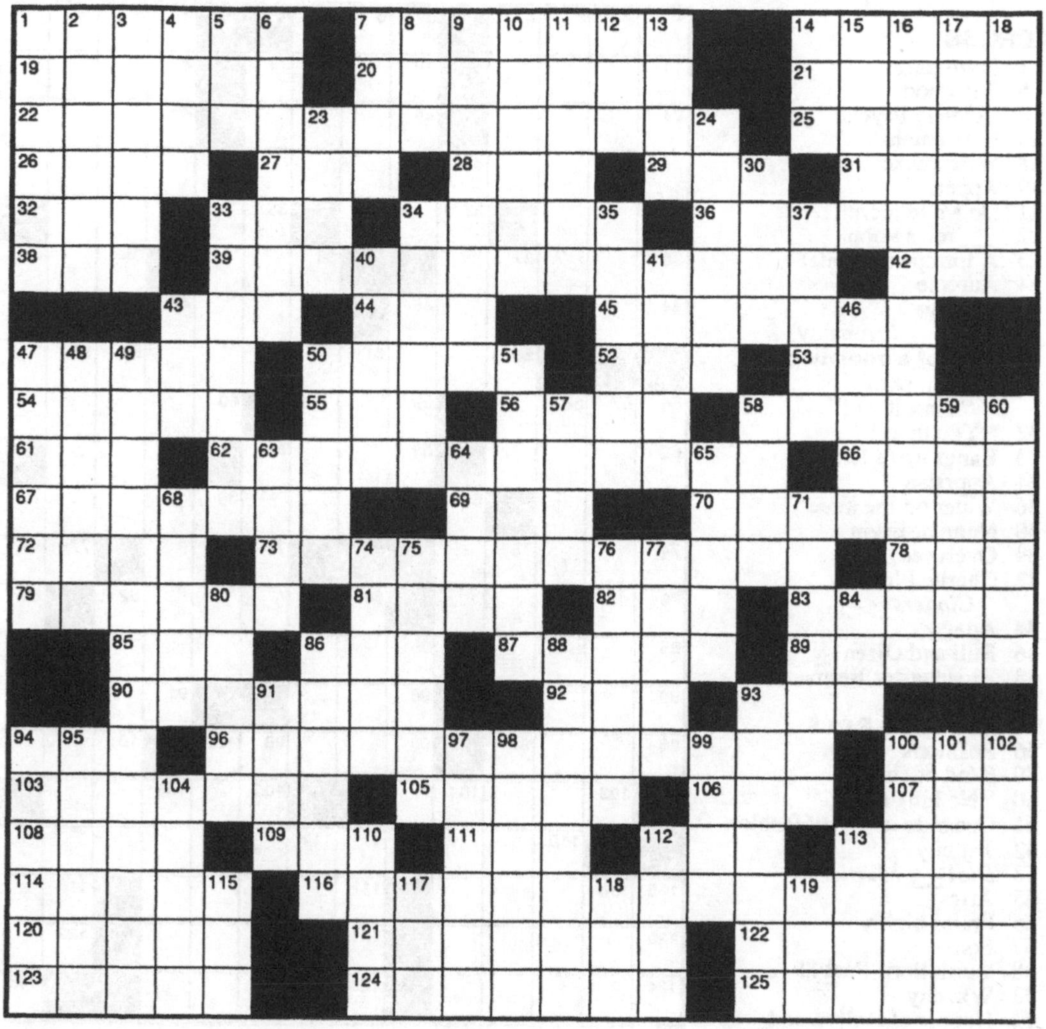

ACROSS

1 "Honor Thy Father" author
7 Rout
14 "Speed-the-Plow" playwright
19 Catalina Island port
20 Ancient Semitic language
21 "Swan Lake" black swan
22 SECNALG
25 Poisonous substance
26 Pieces' partner
27 One of the Three Stooges
28 Ending with union
29 Syn. for dep.
31 ___ Sweeney, "Anything Goes" role
32 Yalie
33 Tolstoy
34 Extraordinary folks
36 Exuberance
38 Mil. award
39 TESSAT
42 Woolf's "___ Dalloway"
43 Officeholders
44 Anatomical duct
45 Howl
47 Slang
50 Glutted
52 Joad and Kettle
53 NYC trans. line
54 Lend-___ Act: 1941
55 Tokyo, formerly
56 "Heaven's ___ vault . . .": Shelley
58 Revels or crows
61 ___ annum
62 ELOR
66 ___-daisy
67 Zog's former kingdom
69 Word with pick or wit
70 "Tougher Than ___," 1988 rap album
72 Breton's ancestor
73 ROTHS
78 Baseball great
79 Christmas-carol word
81 Boat for Wynken, Blynken, and Nod
82 "Life" in a Piaf classic
83 Left-hand page
85 Kingsley's "The Sands of ___"
86 Word with date or process
87 Clue for a hunter
89 To eat, in Erfurt
90 Physics Nobelist: 1909
92 Adam's early loss
93 Treas. Dept. branch
94 British miler
96 SGEG
100 Poe's "The ___ of the Perverse"
103 Speeds
105 T. Geisel, a.k.a. Dr. ___
106 Swedish ski resort
107 Patriotic org.
108 Old tongue
109 "The end is not ___": Matt.
111 Henri's pal
112 Novelist Levin
113 Muscovite, e.g.
114 Muscat money units
116 RUTDEN
120 Fireplace
121 Some money-makers
122 Settle snugly
123 Discharge
124 Israeli parliament
125 Puzzler's tool

DOWN

1 Identified
2 Benefits
3 Kind of acid
4 Part of B.P.O.E.
5 Disseminate
6 Champlevé and cloisonné
7 Miami's county
8 Energy unit
9 Indonesian language
10 Stunned
11 Some chair repairers
12 What a practicing M.D. must have
13 Habitats
14 Bon ___ (witticism)
15 Ornament
16 THORSEPAM
17 Novelist Glyn
18 Inserts for mortises
23 Secretary of State: 1905–9
24 Standing
30 Third man
33 What Diogenes carried
34 Bryan, e.g.
35 Numbness
37 "A Ship without ___," 1929 tune
40 Dodge
41 Arkin and Bates
43 One of the Cyclades
46 Rainbow or steelhead
47 Vicuña's cousin
48 Whirled
49 SAMEGES
50 Old word used 71 times in Psalms
51 Contrivances
57 One of the "Little Women"
58 Kind of club
59 Trypanosomiasis transmitter
60 Poet/novelist May ___
63 Seine feeder
64 Inner: Comb. form
65 Rags-to-riches author
68 Bewildered
71 Allen's "Anthony ___"
74 U.S. Open singles champ: 1963
75 French cathedral city
76 Bypasses
77 "Like ___, all tears": Hamlet
80 Concise
84 Giant follower
86 Hardy country
88 What a chairperson does
91 Baruch was a grad. of it
93 King Arthur's mother
94 Marilyn's "Bus Stop" role
95 Sculler's occupation
97 Headgear for a schoolboy
98 Arterial passageways
99 Needlefish
100 Sherwood's "___ Delight"
101 Skin blotch
102 Vienna park
104 Archer William and son
110 Diving position
112 Va. Mil. ___
113 ___ Verde National Park
115 Egyptian god of darkness
117 Darling with tantalizing curves
118 Irritate
119 "___ Alte" (Adenauer)

132 TWO GIFTS by A. J. Santora

A gifted contributor has given us a fine quote which he found in *Gift from the Sea*.

ACROSS

1 Love song
5 Bat wood
8 "Ode to Psyche" poet
13 Enticement
18 Wisecracker Jack
19 Appear
21 De Mille recruit
22 ___ fell swoop
23 A European capital
24 Aureole
25 Courage
26 Like ___ (probably)
27 **Start of a quotation**
31 Westmore of "Tinseltown"
32 "You there!"
33 Bangs up (a fender)
34 Appraise
36 Water on the knee
38 Nunn or Ervin
39 Overused
42 Charlie Plumb's ___ *Cinders*
44 Adage
46 Bull and Olsen
48 Broadcaster Berman
49 ___ Aviv
50 **Quotation: Part II**
56 Positions
59 Kind of code
60 "Nothing doing!"
61 Oscar de la ___ of fashion
62 Taj city
63 *Dial ___ Murder*
65 Aries
66 Praise highly
67 For
68 **Quotation: Part III**
73 Wk. day
74 Hopper of Hollywood
76 Chin
77 Life of Riley
78 Actor Connery
79 Lab compound
80 "Diamonds are ___ best friend"
83 Pit-a-chaser
84 Kind of vision
85 **End of the quotation**
89 Puzo's *Fools* ___
90 NYC wagering
91 Detected
92 Rusts
96 Boo-hoos
98 Catches red-handed
101 "___ your old man!"
102 "Once ___ time . . ."
103 Hubbub
105 Set ___ (ensnare)
107 Former Arab org.
109 Enl. men
110 Author of the quotation
115 T-shirt size
117 Give a grant
118 Norse poem
119 Loren's town
120 Confuse
121 Martin or Allen
122 Profound
123 Brit's exclamation
124 Model or puzzle
125 More tender
126 Tate offering
127 Sad or glad ending

DOWN

1 Climaxes
2 Winning manager in 1988 World Series
3 Hogwash!
4 ". . . rule them with ___ of iron"
5 ". . . lived in ___"
6 Sordid
7 Tiller
8 Romine or White
9 Requires
10 Finally
11 Yankee Bambino gait
12 Santha Rau's dress
13 Princess of Wales
14 Stow the mow
15 Charge of the site brigade?
16 One of Japan's top golfers
17 Still
20 Former Ariz. politician
28 Gregorian ___
29 Hercules' ___ Lion
30 Hot spots
35 Kind of college
37 Beethoven's "___ Solemnis"
38 ___ the day (menu item)
40 Seaweed
41 Vault
43 Tiger Hall of Famer
45 Gadget
47 Toys in the attic
51 Offend
52 "This ___ order"
53 ___ plume
54 A Maverick
55 Actor Barker
56 Fools
57 A going out
58 Acted
64 Thespian Toomey
68 Singer Vicki
69 Nobleman
70 Lacquers
71 Air arm of Amer.
72 Brief fight
75 Juno or Ceres
78 Denude
80 "___ boy!"
81 Asian desert
82 Playground device
86 Dough-getter?
87 Colonized
88 Princeton, to NYC
93 Pink flower
94 Riddles
95 Glides, struts
97 Unwed
99 Pantry
100 Competed
104 Scoff
106 Crewman
107 Beneath
108 Go with the flow
111 Predicament
112 Hep or hip
113 Thought
114 Actress Gray
115 Front seat?
116 Fuss

133 "JUST AS I FEARED!" by T. W. Underhill

A problem little shavers never encounter is discussed in the nonsense verse quoted below.

ACROSS

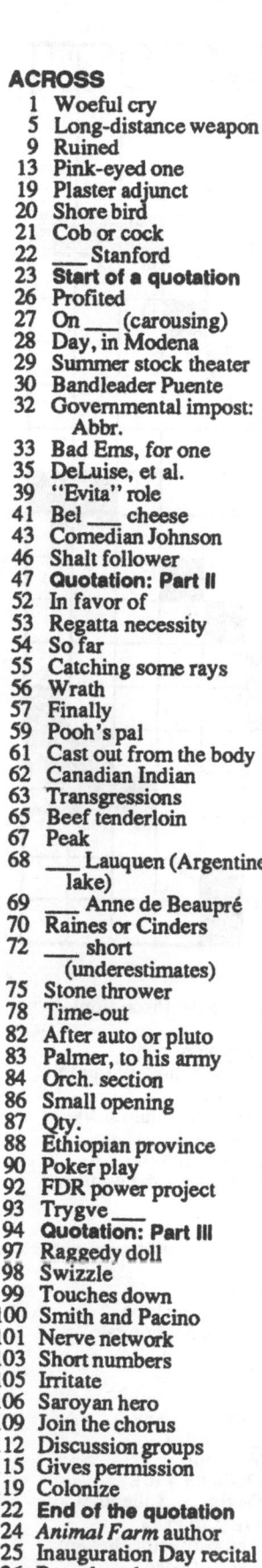

1 Woeful cry
5 Long-distance weapon
9 Ruined
13 Pink-eyed one
19 Plaster adjunct
20 Shore bird
21 Cob or cock
22 ___ Stanford
23 **Start of a quotation**
26 Profited
27 On ___ (carousing)
28 Day, in Modena
29 Summer stock theater
30 Bandleader Puente
32 Governmental impost: Abbr.
33 Bad Ems, for one
35 DeLuise, et al.
39 "Evita" role
41 Bel ___ cheese
43 Comedian Johnson
46 Shalt follower
47 **Quotation: Part II**
52 In favor of
53 Regatta necessity
54 So far
55 Catching some rays
56 Wrath
57 Finally
59 Pooh's pal
61 Cast out from the body
62 Canadian Indian
63 Transgressions
65 Beef tenderloin
67 Peak
68 ___ Lauquen (Argentine lake)
69 ___ Anne de Beaupré
70 Raines or Cinders
72 ___ short (underestimates)
75 Stone thrower
78 Time-out
82 After auto or pluto
83 Palmer, to his army
84 Orch. section
86 Small opening
87 Qty.
88 Ethiopian province
90 Poker play
92 FDR power project
93 Trygve ___
94 **Quotation: Part III**
97 Raggedy doll
98 Swizzle
99 Touches down
100 Smith and Pacino
101 Nerve network
103 Short numbers
105 Irritate
106 Saroyan hero
109 Join the chorus
112 Discussion groups
115 Gives permission
119 Colonize
122 **End of the quotation**
124 *Animal Farm* author
125 Inauguration Day recital
126 Barcelona boy
127 Ellington's *Take ___ Train*
128 *Sons of the Desert* co-star
129 Soft cheese
130 School on the Thames
131 Done for

DOWN

1 Can. province
2 Statutes
3 At the summit of
4 Marathoner Frank
5 Cay
6 Lettuce type
7 Toot one's own horn
8 Marx-Engels writing
9 Spruces up
10 Chemistry Nobelist: 1944
11 Bread spreads
12 Bo's number
13 Simple plant
14 Author of the quotation
15 Subterfuge
16 Hunter or Fleming
17 Compass letters
18 Unmatched
24 River to the Huang Ho
25 Ciardi's *How ___ Poem Mean?*
29 Queen's counsel
31 Nashville landmark
34 Foe of the Sioux
36 Burning
37 Grace, Archie and Garry
38 "On the ___ Where You Live"
39 Raccoon kin
40 Throws
42 Statuesque singer Karen
44 Wigwam
45 Chang's closest relative
47 Froth
48 Surgical devices
49 Fall flower
50 Dawn combatants
51 Of the Ch. of Eng.
58 Mature
60 Nerves ___ (cool headedness)
62 Jalopy
64 Taking away
66 Disciple's suffix
67 Bordeaux
71 Smallest
72 Graduated
73 Royal fur
74 Dormant
76 Complete, in Córdoba
77 Trevi throw-in
78 Make pigtails
79 *Heartbreak ___*
80 Singer of 79 Down
81 Bring up
83 Smell ___ (be suspicious)
85 Main telephone connection
88 Inquisitive sounds
89 ___ *Family*
91 Mrs. Victor Laszlo
95 Divulges
96 One-horse towns
102 Fragrant compound
104 Assegai
107 Silklike fabric
108 Priest's garment
110 Pronoun for Caesar
111 Dickens heroine
113 Wine city
114 Tiny tantrum
116 Pearl Harbor location
117 St. Paul's architect
118 Neighbor of Minn.
119 The sun
120 NOW goal
121 Bus driver's org.
122 ___ Hill, San Francisco
123 L-P filler

134

MED. SCHOOL DROPOUT by Bert Kruse
Bert has doctored up some answers on a test for would-be-interns. The results are hilarious.

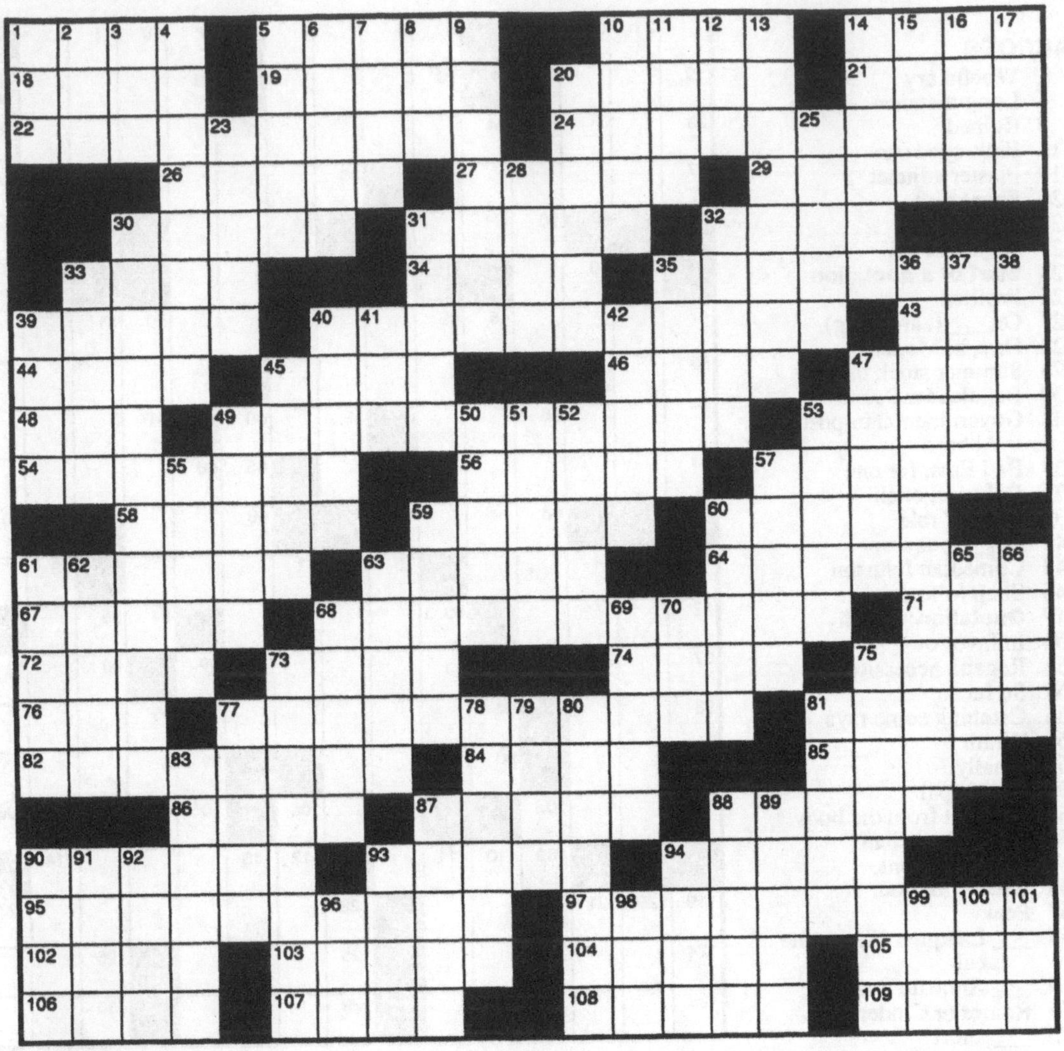

ACROSS

1 Computer fodder
5 Nerd's kin
10 Ali of Arabia
14 One of Willy Loman's sons
18 Writer Bagnold
19 Cut in two
20 Less furnished
21 Where Perry triumphed
22 Genes are vital. What are they?
24 Name a major artery.
26 Shoppers' aids
27 Kaye or Thomas
29 Quickest, as a student
30 Makes the wild mild
31 Ice masses
32 To laugh, in Paris
33 Chisel
34 Fairy tale beginning
35 Sign up
39 Campus figures
40 What is an auricle's function?
43 Charlemagne's dom.
44 ___ Islands off New Guinea
45 Early Briton
46 Dozes off
47 Unhearing
48 Chatter
49 What exactly does the palate do?
53 Kind of porridge
54 Implicate in confusion
56 Lab heaters
57 Aesop, e.g.
58 Clothing sizes
59 Attempts
60 Trojan War site
61 Transported
63 "... ___/Told by an idiot ...": Shak.
64 Mud accumulation on a river
67 Stormed
68 What are platelets?
71 TV "Squad"
72 Harem rooms
73 Venison source
74 Denials
75 Hill's partner
76 Cereal unit
77 What is the stirrup?
81 Giant
82 Deep
84 She gets what she wants!
85 Cooker
86 Poilu's weapon
87 Court proceedings
88 Kind of face or game
90 Friend of Porthos
93 Sky blues
94 Down producer
95 Name some digestive organs
97 What are syndromes?
102 Bonn salute
103 In a tizzy
104 *Adam Bede* author
105 Ending for buck
106 Whirlpool
107 Peter or Ivan, e.g.
108 Same
109 Gainsay

DOWN

1 Fox's home
2 Literary collection
3 Dickens tad
4 South Australia's capital
5 Selected
6 Lots
7 *Desire Under the* ___
8 Actress Arden
9 Hanging
10 Marriage notice
11 Bohemian
12 Busy one
13 Accuses
14 Davis and Midler
15 Dies ___
16 Suits
17 Trilbies
20 Toots
23 Goofballs
25 Bit, as of mistletoe
28 St. Louis sight
30 What follows the medulla?
31 Kicks out
32 Whitelaw and Ogden Mills
33 ___ nobis (a writ)
35 Peasants of India
36 The pia mater's atop what brain cover?
37 Obliterate
38 Ascribe to a source
39 Pen
40 Markets
41 Hoary
42 Pavlova and Held
45 Good observation post
47 Opening
49 Sharpened
50 Potpourri item
51 In any way
52 Ilka Chase's ___ *We Cry*
53 Buckets
55 Spatiates
57 Soars
59 Descriptive of naked
60 Knows what's going on: Slang
61 Sag
62 Detection device
63 Correct
65 Near-East ___ Heights
66 Where the Pison flowed
68 Net
69 Early Peruvians
70 Old coin, now of minimal worth
73 Expels ignominiously
75 Amused
77 Kind of column
78 Most under the weather
79 Carol
80 Paned
81 Remembrancer
83 Kind of tree
87 Longer
88 Decorative loop
89 "___ a Nightingale": Keats
90 Tennis great
91 Clarinet, e.g.
92 Surrounded by
93 ___ Nostra
94 Way out
96 Discs for a d.j.
98 David ___ Lilienthal
99 Prior, to Prior
100 Actor-director Howard
101 Type of bean

135 UP TO NO GOOD by Virginia L. Yates

An ingenious new theme is expertly carried out by one of Oregon's finest puzzlers.

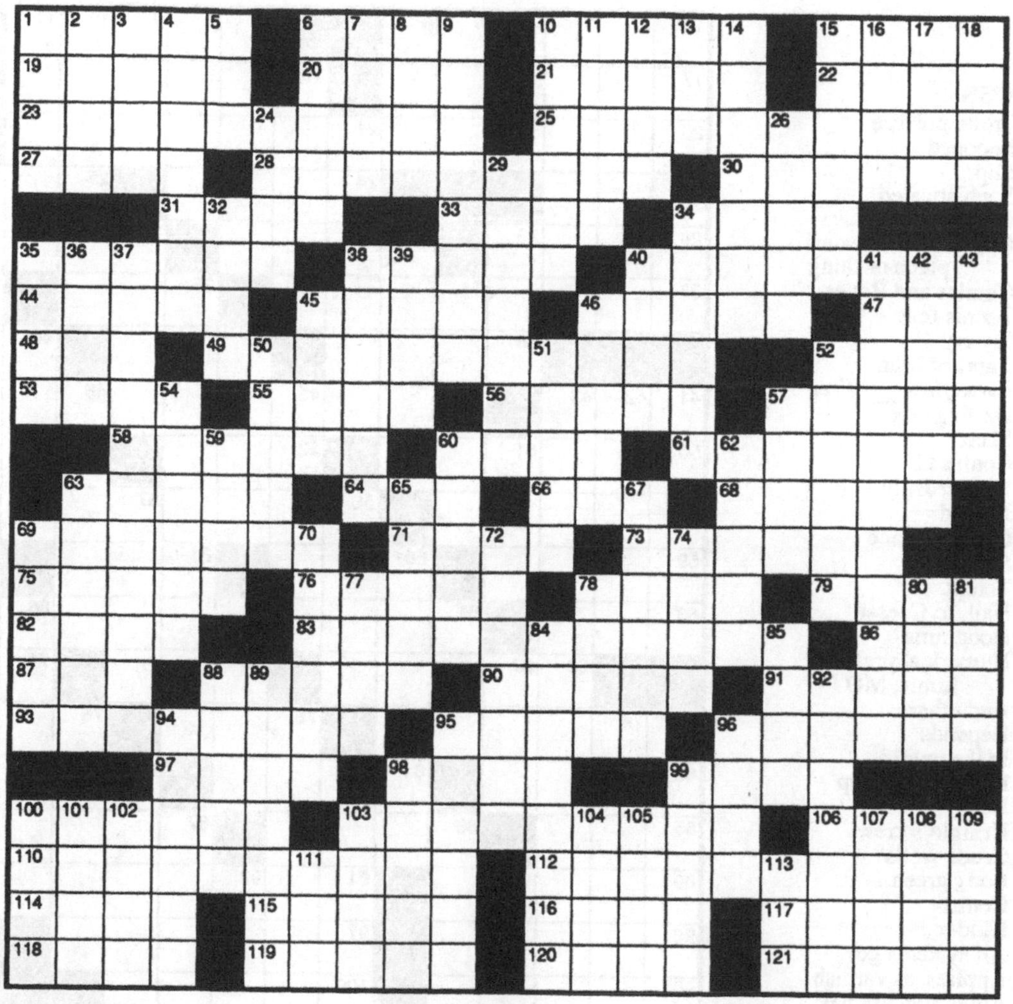

ACROSS

1 Sponge
6 N European
10 A poetic Guest
15 Bogey's *Casablanca* role
19 Acclimate
20 Testify
21 Dishcloth gourd
22 Palindrome words which end in Elba
23 Destination for Diaz: 1488
25 Donat-Garson film: 1939
27 Entry
28 Cloyingly-proper prude
30 Applies the gum elastic
31 Norse god of discord
33 Kind of hall
34 Vive's opposite
35 Useless
38 Simmers
40 Cy Young award winner: 1985
44 "Once ___ time . . ."
45 Wampum beads
46 What parties vie for
47 "___ Believer": Neil Diamond song
48 WW II command
49 Kris Kristofferson hit tune
52 Dextrous beginning
53 Plenty
55 Garb for Suzanne Farrell
56 Apply effort
57 Dolorous toll
58 Lazy; idle; pointless
60 Kiri Te Kanawa specialty
61 Makes clear
63 Porterhouse's cousin
64 Heater
66 Swing of a pendulum
68 Unit of electrical resistance
69 ___ *Picture Show*, 1971 film
71 ___ Porsena (Horatius' foe at the bridge)
73 Its main street was once Last Chance Gulch
75 "___ a jealous mistress": Emerson
76 Pepe's pal
78 American painter, FitzHugh ___
79 Camber
82 Funny one
83 Contemplate strongly
86 Law, in Lyons
87 Ames coll.
88 Filé or fennel
90 No-nos
91 Pickings
93 Pearl Buck's Pulitzer prize novel: 1932
95 Occludes
96 Stop
97 Half of MCIV
98 Word with check or light
99 Olive genus
100 Termination
103 Basis of a US diplomatic policy since 1933
106 Half a train
110 Behaves well à la Tiny Tim
112 Scalawag
114 Normandy town
115 Musical Mel
116 ___ fruit (citrus variety)
117 Laurie or Hall
118 Slot fodder
119 Sub sleuth
120 Potassium hydroxides, et al.
121 Balzac's *La Cousine* ___

DOWN

1 This: Fr.
2 Pre-med course
3 Cat's-paw
4 Glitch maker
5 Fair-hiring practices: Abbr.
6 City NNE of Helsinki
7 Acknowledge
8 Casaba, e.g.
9 Renown
10 Jostles through a crowd
11 Kingpin of a group
12 Takes off
13 Musicmaker's org.
14 Welsh ___
15 Same old stuff, in new form
16 Rainbow goddess
17 Edible mushroom
18 Smack or peck
24 Bag-shaped fish net
26 Yosemite features
29 Gunslinger's need
32 Popular name in Oslo
34 "The expense of spirit in ___ of shame": Shak.
35 Stoke
36 Thus far
37 Unbelievably fine
38 Mending
39 Part of a Pacific state
40 Whitetails
41 Bon vivant
42 Badge
43 Hardware items
45 Part of the Ger. Emp. once
46 Muckrake
50 Certain Amerinds
51 S African irises
52 Sweetsop
54 Showing no emotion
57 Heel chilblain
59 Balin and Claire of films
60 Saw
62 Gentleman's gentleman
63 Whomp
65 Oyl or oil preceder
67 Plainsongs
69 Understood
70 *The Moon and Sixpence* locale
72 Mingy motorist
74 Winds up
77 Jet speed unit
78 The scourge of serge
80 Slammer dwellers
81 Attention-getting sound
84 Pertinent remark
85 Grim Grimm character
88 Peppery Mexican sauce
89 Hierophants
92 Weaver of mythology
94 Kinetoscope creator
95 What Athena turned 92 Down into
96 Besides
98 Historic Ala. city
99 Avifauna
100 Platter
101 "___ Perpetua": Idaho's motto
102 Senegal neighbor
103 Skuld, for one
104 Bugbear
105 Architect's fillet
107 Word to the wise
108 Step ___ (hurry)
109 Cyma reversa
111 Gunk
113 Bill

136

VANISHING ACT by Jean Davison
Some of the clues below may appear a bit spacey, but Jean's theme certainly isn't! This opus was a strong contender for the Margaret Award.

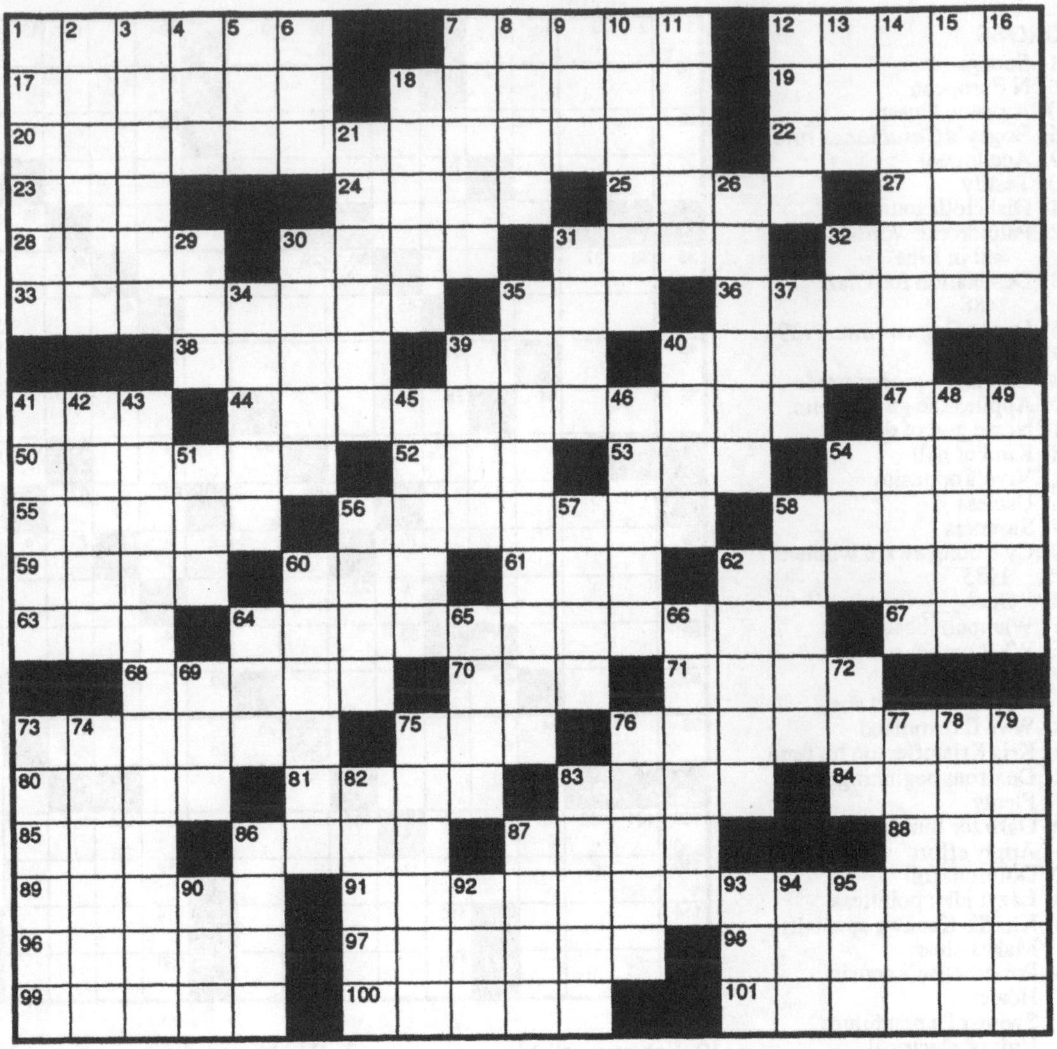

ACROSS

1 Proud posture
7 Snooped
12 Slip
17 Sophisticated
18 Freeloader
19 City on the Missouri
20 ___, place or thing
22 Charles and Bayes
23 Tennis feat
24 Sty cry
25 Capri or Man
27 *Butterflies ___ Free*
28 Darling dog
30 Slant
31 Confused
32 Rocker Billy
33 Job bid
35 Can. province
36 Smarts
38 Tempt
39 Hail, to Caesar
40 Hoodlums
41 Numerical prefix
44 ___ Louis, MO
47 And others
50 Depends
52 Make public
53 Kaline and Capp
54 Dull
55 Kringle's crew
56 Crude wells?
58 Long green
59 Control
60 Kidder
61 All systems go!
62 Applies, as varnish
63 Ames and Bradley
64 Out of ___, out of mind
67 Explosive trio
68 Lendl and Olbracht
70 They loop the Loop
71 "Atlantis" assoc.
73 *Who's on First?* straight man
75 Ballet step
76 Fill in, at work
80 Tra followers
81 Ancient Olympics site
83 Pouting grimace
84 Bog
85 Unity, in math
86 Hindrance
87 TV actress Mitzi
88 Zilch
89 Les Cayes locale
91 *The ___ of Positive Thinking*
96 Finney film
97 Most immaculate
98 Include at seven-up
99 Asian liquors
100 Fashion
101 Duration

DOWN

1 Compassionate
2 Heathers
3 Not here
4 ___*Kapital*
5 Relative of 41 Across
6 Big house
7 Exhausted
8 Word with barrel or belly
9 Public officials
10 Solipsist
11 Dumb
12 *The Last Emperor* star
13 Amas preceder
14 Stallone's ___ *Alley*
15 Gless of TV
16 Masking frames
18 Backbone
21 Chin hider
26 Works
29 Trouble
30 Carries
31 Again
32 Suffix for Orwell
34 Ponders
35 Reworks
37 Anonymous Richard
39 Sans alteration
40 Hair fixatives
41 Yonder
42 Het up
43 Pen-and-___ drawing
45 Chortle
46 Lends an ear
48 Claw
49 Repeated cry
51 O.T. book
54 Tarzan's child
56 Jokes
57 Ages and ages
58 Parsonage
60 June-August in Sydney
62 Make tracks
64 Brother of ACT
65 Socials
66 Plenty
69 USIA broadcaster
72 Branch
73 Greetings from Oahu
74 Ecuadorean fruit
75 A ___ in a poke
76 Freewheel
77 End
78 Derivation
79 Give in
82 Homophone of 12 Across
83 Former senator from Oregon
86 Gives up the ghost
87 Loaf part
90 Connection
92 Crooked
93 Verse with a strophe
94 Critic Reed
95 Make a doily

137 TUNNEL'S END by Martha DeWitt

If you're wondering about Martha's title, simply fill in the letters to 24 Across—we guarantee you won't be in the dark any more—or will you?

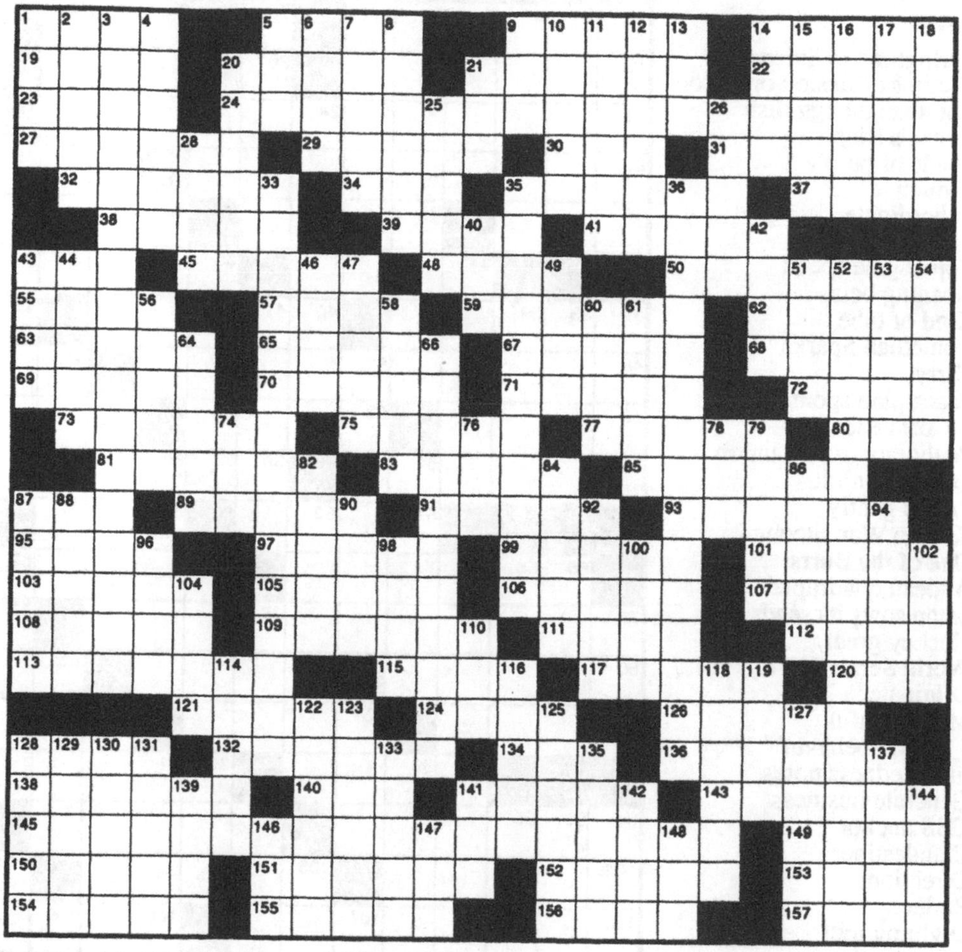

ACROSS

1 Away from the wind
5 Almost nonexistent
9 He wrote *Pal Joey*
14 Black, to Browning
19 Caplet
20 Economized
21 Daniel Webster, e.g.
22 Doxy
23 Appear
24 Kipling novel
27 Calif. live oak
29 Costs
30 Moon vehicle
31 Iroquois Indian
32 Amble
34 Still
35 Isolated
37 Cong. meeting
38 Diameter's duad
39 Painter of limp watches
41 One of Uranus's moons
43 Japanese food fish
45 *Bus Stop* playwright and family
48 Roman robe
50 Complained
55 Principal
57 Applause
59 Old English roof
62 English county
63 Tsar
65 ___-Rivières, Québec
67 Speckled fish
68 Tidal bore
69 Stay
70 Solo
71 Wasteland
72 Oates title
73 Texas A & M team
75 Plow man
77 Entries
80 CFL scores
81 Alcanas
83 Water vapor
85 Kind of toast
87 Danish county
89 Moslem month
91 Abaddon
93 Porpoise
95 Holds up
97 Run off to Gretna Green
99 Eat into
101 Gushes
103 Puts to flight
105 Profit
106 Songstress Shore
107 Henequen
108 His prophet was Mohammed
109 Where love is nothing
111 Songstress Turner
112 Nerve network
113 Day of rest
115 Teen chaser
117 Trundles
120 Opener
121 Frock
124 Congeries
126 Wake
128 Hindu garment
132 Likely Taos resident
134 Power: Lat.
136 Yelped
138 Mushroom
140 $67\frac{1}{2}°$ by compass
141 Martinique's 1902 catastrophe-maker
143 Permeate
145 Okays
149 Grant
150 Paris-lover at home
151 Adak natives
152 Its seat is Forfar
153 Do a Tuesday job
154 Exodus commemoration
155 Skin layer
156 Balance
157 Being

DOWN

1 Polygonal recess in a building
2 Security agreements
3 Could this be 24 Across?
4 City on the Chemung
5 Cheer
6 State
7 Shift
8 Revised
9 Table scrap
10 "Little Iodine" creator
11 Pallas
12 Gypsy
13 "How Great Thou ___"
14 Look over hurriedly
15 The Ram
16 Contradict
17 City on the Aire
18 Elder and Younger of Iceland
20 Trotsky's rival
21 Zeroes
25 Influence corruptly
26 Lobby
28 Difficult situations
33 Of negligible weight
35 Woozy
36 Henry Lee
40 Plat
42 Tick too slowly
43 Scarlett's home
44 Oranjestad locale
46 Writer Biggers
47 Hairnet
49 Bern's river
51 Who's friend on second
52 They don't scrub floors
53 Dropped a fly
54 Considers
56 Privet
58 Eats in style
60 Natterjack
61 "... most unkindest ___ all": Shak.
64 Maple's controls
66 Understand
74 Last queen of Spain, before Franco
76 Turmeric
78 Female ruff
79 Breaks suddenly
82 "___ Regina"
84 Earn
86 Angelic order
87 Tapestry
88 Scratch
90 Sorrel
92 Kind of boom
94 Rasp
96 Run through
98 Pineapple: Sp.
100 Actor Andrews
102 Weaver's reed
104 Anadromous fish
110 Bishopric
114 Pamphlet
116 Corvine bird
118 Skoal, prosit etc.
119 Theater extra, for short
122 He started *The Tatler*
123 Sewing machine man
125 Stele
127 Coin
128 Caspar, Melchior, et al.
129 Nimble
130 Ranted
131 Goodnight girl
133 Antitoxin
135 Net
137 Antics
139 Munich's river
141 Zoological foot
142 Ova
144 Crossword goose
146 Owned
147 Zeta follower
148 Shack

138

ORCHESTRATION by Stanley Glass
Lots of instruments are assembled here. You're invited to be the maestro.

ACROSS

1 Springtime in Salerno
7 Victims of fission or fusion
12 Lightweight egg dish
19 Bonzo's friend
20 Shade of purple
21 Seductive
23 Subordinate
25 Prepare
26 Top engine speed
27 Opening bets
29 Kind of tube
30 Comedian Sparks
31 Tarry
32 Peace plan sponsor from Costa Rica
33 Withdraw from a union
34 Leonine hairdo
35 Propel gently
36 Korean War sitcom
37 One of the Burrs
40 Andean quadruped
42 Satan sows its seeds
44 Hockey great
48 World Series MVP: 1987
50 Originate
51 More painful
52 "___ Misbehavin'"
53 Indebtedness notes
54 Generate business
56 CBS anchor
58 Clandestine
60 Directions
61 Reduce
63 Divining tool
64 Pay attention to
65 Subject for litigation
68 Chicago hoodlum of yore
70 Buries
75 Chess opening
77 Expression of regret
79 Part of QED
80 News item
81 "God's Little ___": Caldwell
82 Cliff Edwards
84 Group of vendors
85 Easily laminated mineral
86 "I'm a Dreamer, ___ We All?"
87 Arrival
88 Footnote expression
90 Legitimate
92 Solitary
94 Woman St. Peter restored to life
97 Turner, et al.
98 Kind of food
99 Military award
102 ___ fixes
103 Cobra's weapon
104 Watchmen
106 Assembled systematically
108 Drop the subject!
110 Critic-author Lionel
111 Cato was one
112 Ingredient of hydriotic acid
113 Kind of terrier
114 Ernest ___, naturalist-author
115 Early anthropoids

DOWN

1 Hot felony
2 Irk
3 Tore
4 Operatic prince
5 Farmers' loan agency
6 An insecticide
7 Surviving
8 Neap or ebb
9 Like Father William
10 Equatorial ailment
11 Travel folder adjective
12 Wise people
13 Cheers for a torero
14 Extreme: Abbr.
15 Alecto, Tisiphone and Magaera
16 Corne
17 Unsocial climber
18 Wound up
22 Spiral motion
24 Beethoven opera
28 Fast-food option
32 ___ Mater
33 Maglie or Mineo
34 Lunar unit
35 Quiz option
36 Tiny
37 At a distance
38 Domingo offering
39 Carry on
41 Rotter
43 Pep
45 Mouthward
46 Hitches up
47 Poetic "prior to"
49 Shrew
50 "I believe," to Brutus
51 Great violinist
54 Former Red Sox first baseman
55 Eulogize
57 Means of lunar chronology
59 Aquatic bird
62 Avenged
64 Ship launcher
65 Sutherland or Price
66 Leopold or Mischa
67 Jefferson's home
68 Traveling group
69 Stripped
71 Lilliputian
72 Troublesome goddess
73 Roué
74 Printer's instruction
75 Exceptional specimen
76 RR regulator
78 Stop west of Johnstown
82 "Exodus" author
83 Juvenile treat
85 Prefix with lay or play
86 Fashionable
89 Wedgwood's favorite rock
91 Battery terminals
93 Brown fur
94 Webster bk.
95 Scents
96 Archaeologist's prize
97 Architectural shelf
98 To see, in Stuttgart
99 Overalls fabric
100 Move on ice
101 East, to Hans
103 Start of Caesar's boast
104 Normandy town
105 Lump or bump
107 Small bird
109 Basketball tourney: Abbr.

139

AU PAIRS by Nancy Atkinson
If you're wondering what the *AU* stands for in Nancy's title, we can tell you this: in this instance it does not stand for the element gold.

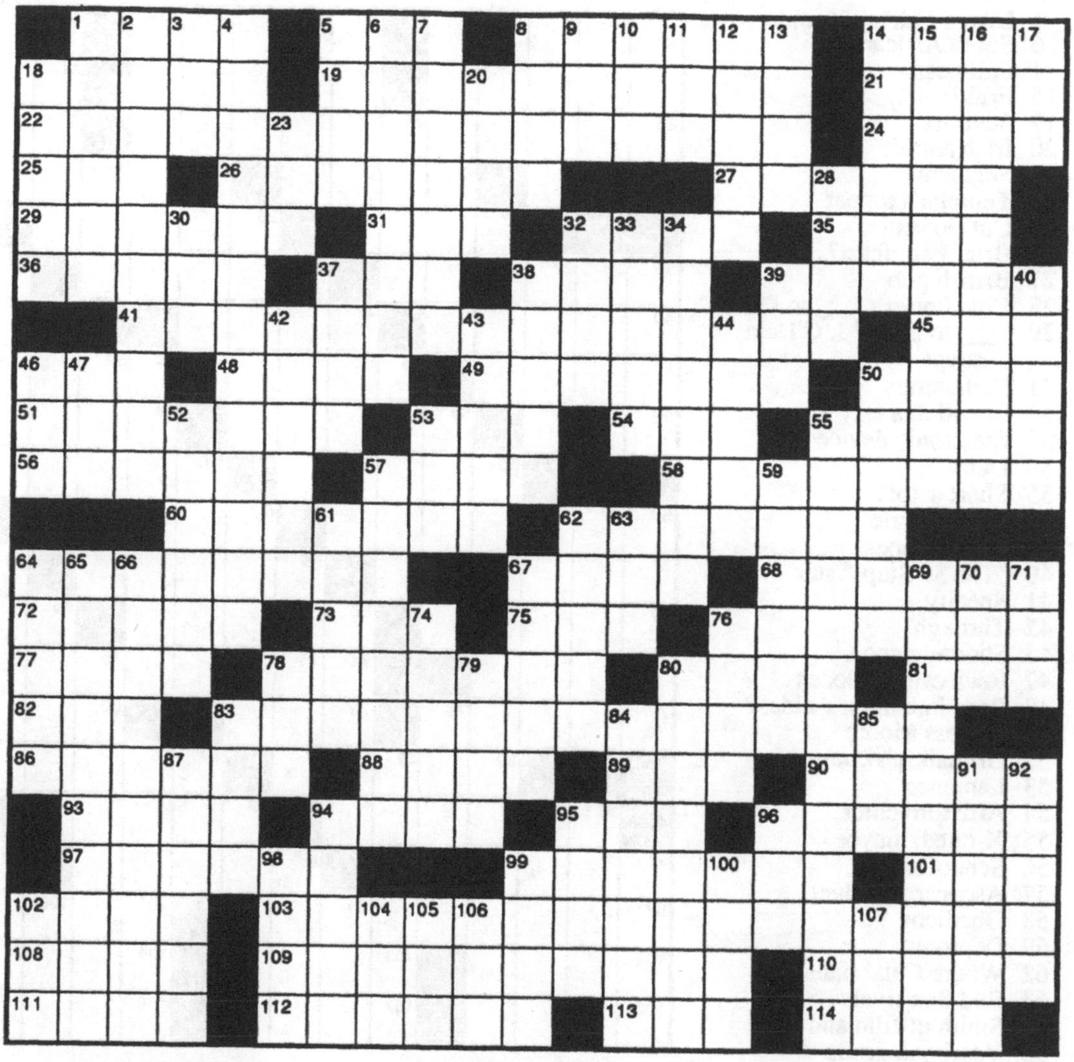

ACROSS

1 DEA agent
5 Actress Arthur
8 Deadly
14 Arabic name prefix
18 Judicial seat
19 Free
21 O.T. book
22 Courage within Martin?
24 Mr. Ed's dinner
25 Plains Indian
26 "The Tortoise and ___"
27 "___ as I live": Middleton
29 Meets after long parting
31 Numero ___
32 Attack time
35 Mister, in Münden
36 Nine: Comb. form
37 Part of i.e.
38 Puppeteer Tony
39 Simplest
41 Oceanographer on location?
45 Coll. in Blacksburg
46 Swiss canton
48 Celtic poet
49 Winter apples
50 Hairy hog
51 Leaf division
53 Fairbanks footwear
54 Behold
55 Electricity: Slang
56 Eat
57 Place for a Devil
58 Voiced scruples
60 "___ the limit": T. Roosevelt
62 Excelled
64 Transvaal capital
67 City W of Caen
68 Ancient love feasts
72 Ruhr iron
73 Ring legend
75 Prosciutto
76 Opens
77 Kelp
78 Worker on a crane
80 Brother, to Harris
81 Triton
82 Texas coll.
83 Signature of a French painter?
86 Aquiline adolescent
88 Sward
89 Pt. of the itinerary
90 Moslem scholars
93 Regretted
94 To dare, in Dijon
95 Fleshy
96 Like a look-alike
97 Trying time
99 Be honest, at customs
101 "Green for Danger" star
102 Musical medley
103 Walter becomes involved with gourmet cooking?
108 Sharp-witted
109 "End of message"
110 McKinley's birthplace
111 Cape fox
112 Figure of speech
113 Coll. in Troy
114 Ending for road

DOWN

1 Trig up
2 Curt Gowdy's forte
3 Accepted: Abbr.
4 Estate in a French tapestry town?
5 Kind of china
6 Raring to go
7 CNN's home
8 ___ majesty
9 Sounds of surprise
10 Weight for bricks
11 Color
12 Test
13 Minus
14 Idolater
15 Bridges bids adieu?
16 "Enterprise" milieu
17 Syllables replaced by do
18 Eric in "Fancy Pants"
20 Sub
23 Word-searching sounds
28 Evergreen genus
30 Prefix for classic
32 Paters
33 Kind of rehearsal
34 Acceded
37 French-1 verb
38 Went like a thief
39 ___ amis
40 Bushed
42 NaCl maker
43 Heavens: Comb. form
44 Incitatus, for one
46 Reuters' rel.
47 ___ Tin Tin
50 FBI center
52 Asexual
53 Abyss
55 Swiss mountain attracts German maidens?
57 Down-to-earth ones
59 Bewailer
61 Feline sound: Var.
62 Hokkaido city
63 Einstein's birthplace
64 "___-porridge hot . . . "
65 Time-wasting procedures
66 Omens from Jacob's twin?
67 Quiver
69 Like a monkey's tail
70 North Pole worker
71 Heathrow arrival
74 Offspring
76 Press to action
78 Sizzling
79 Piazza: Abbr.
80 Suppress
83 Advise, once
84 Farmer's friend
85 Org. founded in 1964
87 ___ a merry chase (lured)
91 Down-Easter
92 Alexandrian dancers
94 King of Norway: 995-1000
95 Vendetta
96 Vineyard
98 Freeman Gosden role
99 Alborg resident
100 Theatrical start
102 Volga tributary
104 President pro ___
105 Part of TNT
106 Lyricist David
107 Canine command

140

KICK THE CAN by Louis Sabin
You may have played the game when you were a child, but it was never like this!

ACROSS

1 Like a Shirley Temple
6 South Africans
11 Fall pear
15 Fruitless
19 Severity
20 Irish patriot
21 Segment
22 Templar's topper
23 Cut flower?
25 Brief Feb. feast?
27 British gob
28 Cole Porter's "___ to Dance"
29 "___ to Live," J. O'Hara novel
31 Red entries
32 Friend in a fray
33 Electronic device
34 Deny
35 Short actor?
38 Poetic cleric
39 Picker-upper
40 "The 39 Steps" star
41 Specify
42 Through
43 Shooting sport
47 Iowa campus locus
48 Part-time nurses' aides?
51 Actress Moore
52 Grimalkin's comment
53 Lenience
54 Artist-inventor
55 X-rated, maybe
56 School sign?
57 Ascocarp product
58 Obedient
59 Deplores
62 Where Calabrians live
63 Red Sox rivals
64 Smith of film and stage
65 Yearbook group
66 Conventions
67 Louis XVII's mother
68 Spoil
69 Dervish or yogi
70 Humdinger
73 Snail's journey
74 Half-hearted dancer?
76 Stoic school founder
77 Mao or Ito
79 Shawn or Lewis
80 Cheese choice
81 Crush
82 Smidgens
84 Folklore image
86 Short-order meal?
87 Box
89 Packaged hay
90 Completed
91 Slate
92 Woody Allen film
93 Gangster Diamond
94 Hollywood's Erwin
97 Partly-filled flask?
99 Curtailed meeting in Rome: 1869-70?
102 Nettles
103 Zebra's parent
104 Upper layer
105 Seine city
106 Climbers' challenges
107 Handicap
108 Slender
109 Movie mob member

DOWN

1 Unwelcome tyke
2 Soy's kin
3 Antiquing device
4 Kind of easter?
5 Ort
6 "Min and Bill" star
7 Sultanate since 1970
8 Ostrich's cousin
9 Legal fee
10 "Sophie's Choice" author
11 Scout's goal
12 Voided escutcheon
13 Bishop's concern
14 Delaware River city
15 Partly-fallen birds?
16 Attend a lecture
17 Hot under the collar
18 Senate rejections
24 Trunk of a tree
26 Patronage
30 Punch's cousin
32 Lamentation
33 Loco
34 Viking
35 He got a ribbing
36 Stadium topper in Houston
37 Yet again
38 Oerter's supply
39 Pointedly
41 Persian king
42 Della's boss
44 Like "Psycho"
45 Rousseau novel
46 Surges
48 Hollows
49 Art style
50 Office groups
53 ___ ball (conical bullet)
55 Stag
56 Doubly deprived dog?
57 Kiosk
58 Singer Bobby
59 Sorceress
60 Trammell and Mowbray
61 Toulon "thanks"
62 B.C. classic
63 See 88 Down
65 Matters for Mason
66 Title of respect
68 Mogul
69 Dicer's "covered"
70 Rose of baseball
71 Balin and Claire
72 John Paul II, e.g.
75 Banish, long ago
76 Court defense
78 Famous
81 Monk's haircut
83 Objects of worship
84 Western lass
85 Oscar-winning musical
86 Beanery cry
87 Mubarak's capital
88 With 63 Down, a Dogpatcher
89 Artist's headgear
90 Minimize
91 Tease; taunt
92 Mostel of B'way fame
93 Twisted the truth
94 Rabbit tail
95 Level at a stadium
96 Arm bone
98 Emulate Honi Coles
100 Title opener
101 Roman goddess of night

141 THE OPPOSITE SIDE by Richard Platt

Lexicologists will enjoy this light-minded look at the English language. We wonder why 22 Across never went over with the populace.

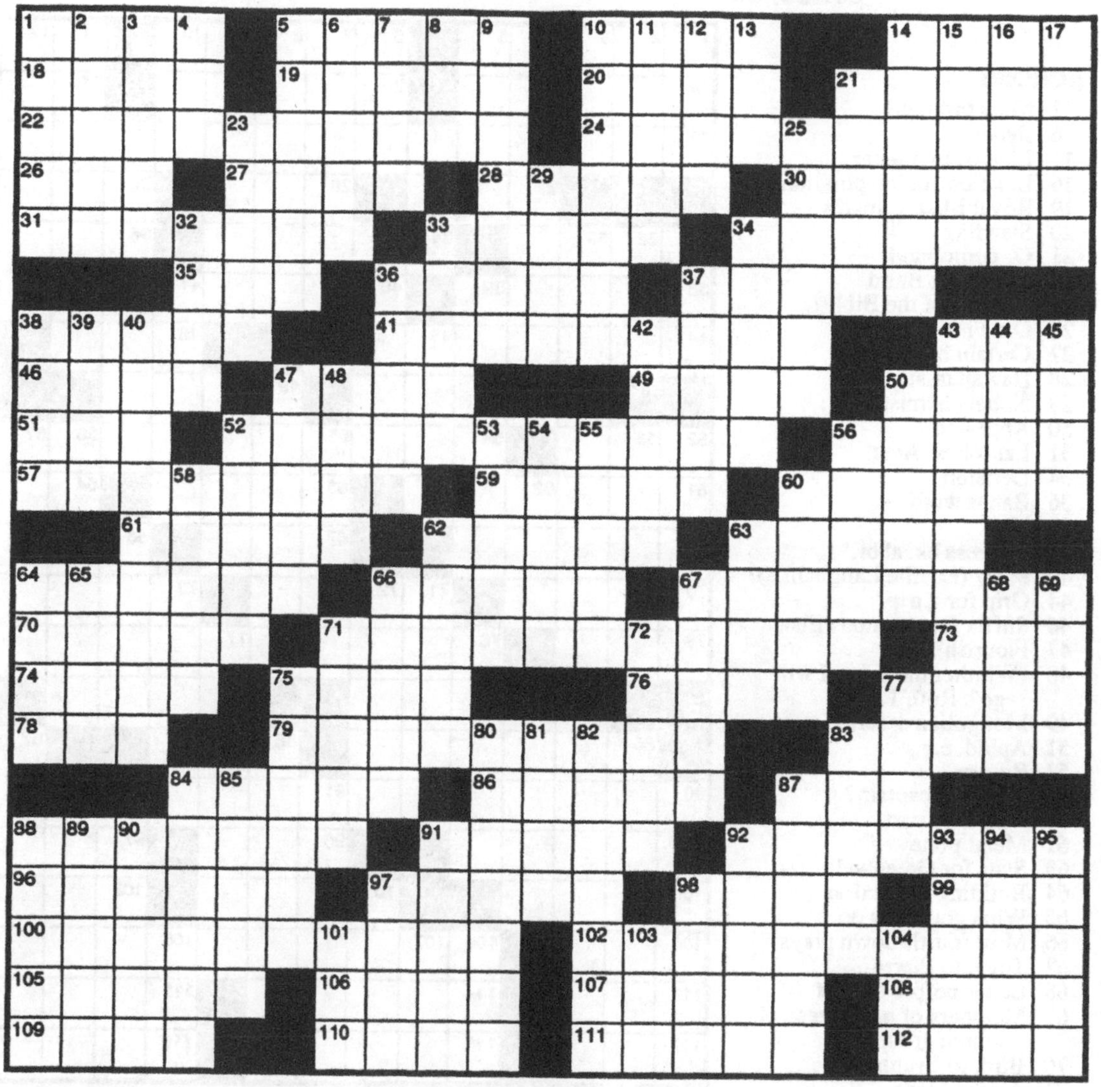

ACROSS

1 Paid attendance
5 Kind of code
10 Tuesday of fame
14 There's no place like it
18 Famous cookie man
19 Uneven
20 Response from the pews
21 Paddock papas
22 The masses?
24 Crewel and needlepoint?
26 Siderite, for example
27 "___ o'clock scholar . . . "
28 Four: Comb. form
30 Dapper Dan's concern
31 A Giza attraction
33 Lachrymose
34 Stirs
35 Actor Heflin
36 Kind of mackerel
37 Janet of swimming
38 Bittern's kin
41 A snap?
43 "The Way" in Chinese thought
46 "___ and a Woman," 1966 film
47 Oho relatives
49 Voice of America org.
50 Craw
51 Dram
52 Brainy garçon?
56 Mock
57 Computer product
59 Insurer's concern
60 Makes baby food
61 Posterns
62 Occupies
63 Nonunion worker
64 French physicist: 1775-1863
66 Japanese-American
67 Kind of window
70 City in Dorset, England
71 Whisperer?
73 Dawn deity
74 B.P.O.E. members
75 Suffix for luncheon
76 City in Oklahoma
77 Black: Prefix
78 Ike
79 Jilted lover?
83 ". . . House of ___"
84 Fact
86 Sound
87 Three in Treviso
88 Ebb-Kander musical
91 Slider's cousin
92 Luzon native
96 Syracuse U's color
97 SE Asian capital
98 Wash
99 "___ to the West Wind"
100 Sauna?
102 Sunburn?
105 Pallid
106 Hautboy
107 Anxious
108 Lover of Aphrodite
109 Exigency
110 Fearless
111 Fantail locale
112 Balzac's "Le ___ Goriot"

DOWN

1 Lively dance
2 "The Proper Bostonians" author
3 Loom
4 Suffix for Sudan
5 Jelly ingredient
6 Slipped
7 Substantive
8 Jack or jenny
9 Alpha and omega
10 Good-for-nothing
11 Board for nails
12 Wife of Tyndareus
13 Genetic essential
14 Gap
15 Fragrant iris
16 Canadian unit of length
17 Sidewinder's trail
21 She was canonized in 1975
23 Indian Nobelist in physics
25 "___-Boom-Der-E" (1890s hit)
29 Effortless
32 Severn feeder
33 Prosit, for one
34 French-1 verb
36 Core
37 "Barnaby Jones" star
38 Metal fastener
39 Mideast millionaire
40 Speedster?
42 Franklin and Nash
43 Real chompers?
44 Welk's opening
45 Chooses
47 Love, in Livorno
48 Abode in Aachen
50 Billiards shot
52 Hoard
53 Some watch this
54 City on the Rhone
55 Resort on Long Island
56 Yam, for one
58 Seasonal songs
60 Attitudinized
62 Drummer's companion
63 Turkish liquor
64 Did a Little thing
65 Part of blue cheese
66 Bug's back
67 Italian song
68 River of SE Eire
69 Mikhail Romanov, e.g.
71 Archie Goodwin's creator
72 Spectral
75 Prize
77 Not landward
80 Emulated Slimer
81 Wallaroo
82 Diplomatic report
83 Pressed
84 Clogged
85 Inert gas
87 Alewife's concern
88 "Over There" composer
89 Got up
90 Immerse
91 Comedienne Kane
92 Donee
93 Nantes' river
94 More singular
95 Gaggle members
97 Bindlestiff
98 Box at the Met
101 Watch chain
103 Avena sativa
104 General Arnold

142 APPELLATION EXPANSIONS by Robert H. Wolfe

Just when we think there's nothing new under a solver's sun, along comes another innovation! Note how the first few letters of each theme answer are enlarged to perfection.

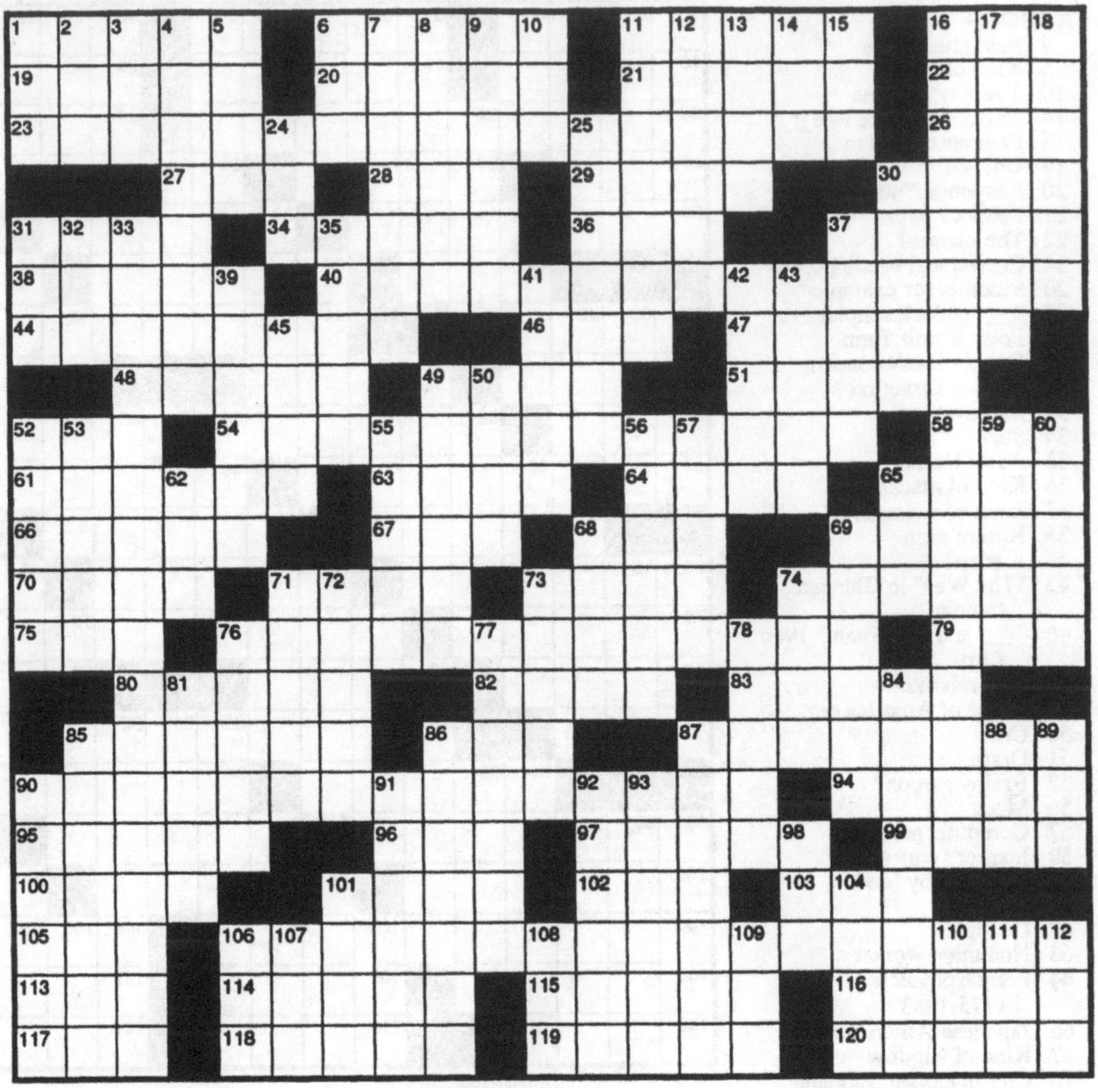

ACROSS

1 Mink product
6 Bender
11 Line from a letter
16 Libation station potation
19 Royal Madras mates
20 Standing
21 O_2 compound
22 Puppeteer Baird
23 Hebrew of the Bible?
26 Old French coin
27 Certain ball booster
28 Hawaiian staple
29 Nobel chemist
30 Appealed
31 Ear lobes: Anat.
34 Derision
36 Banns word
37 Net
38 Address bk. abbr.
40 Mary (Lucille Langhanke)?
44 Grip for a trip
46 Suffix for a famous Elsa
47 Flourish
48 "Whither thou___, I will go": Ruth 1
49 Mongolian desert
51 Aphid, e.g.
52 Rowan
54 Pequod's captain?
58 Umbrella part
61 Metal plate
63 Stats for Greenwell
64 Building projection
65 What gourmets do
66 Most fourth-down plays
67 They, to Pierre
68 Letter before omega
69 Members of a Japanese ethnic group
70 Bird, to Brutus
71 A gray blade
73 Serum measurement
74 Chemical sugar
75 Actor Cariou
76 Author George from Indiana?
79 One of a N.J. five
80 Range
82 Rom. and Holy Rom.
83 "The Wreck of the Mary ___"
85 Where the veldt is
86 Priest's robe
87 What Grant did at Vicksburg
90 Edie or Julie?
94 Teacake
95 Jitneys
96 Old car
97 Maternally related
99 Track word
100 Hts.
101 Paint or draw
102 Printing quads
103 Lunar lander
105 ___ Mahal
106 Greek god of war?
113 Zeta follower
114 Ringworm
115 Network of nerves
116 Laughing
117 Mister, in a synagogue
118 Hoard
119 "Do, ___, a female . . ."
120 Needlecase

DOWN

1 Mrs., in Madrid
2 Cap for Burns
3 Yoko ___
4 ___ reason (consider sound advice)
5 Italian nobleman of yore
6 Indian weight
7 Pop the question
8 Explosive noise
9 Prickly: Comb. form
10 Season for Mitterrand
11 Evening parties
12 Pass
13 Frosty
14 Mount ___, in Crete
15 Bog
16 Second son in Genesis, probably?
17 Liberty
18 Dodges
24 Foot, to Fabius
25 Country on the Mediterranean
30 Lovely lasses
31 Laotian money
32 Rumanian coin
33 Forte of a former ring king?
35 Social class, to Pedro
37 Swagger
39 Indian and Arctic
41 Picture puzzle
42 World's biggest hold-up man
43 Bile: Comb. form
45 Wimbledon champ: 1975
49 Turkey part
50 Revolutionary statesman
52 Dismay
53 ___ qui peut (every man for himself): Fr.
55 Terse
56 Riatas
57 Espionage expert
59 Working, as machinery
60 Harry
62 "___ a Wonderful Life"
65 Completed
68 Companion of circumstance
69 Chinese mountains
71 Evoke
72 Plant part
73 Disney creation
74 Enzyme endings
76 Faulty
77 Actress Katherine ___
78 That is to say: Lat.
81 Weapons for poilus
84 Refer back to a committee
85 Praise too highly
86 Blood deficiencies
87 Scot's little animal
88 Finis
89 ___ Plaines, Ill.
90 Easer
91 Rainbow and crocus
92 Swerved
93 One who dwells in cells
98 English measure
101 Horne with a great sound
104 Rochester's Jane
106 ___ loss for words
107 Edge
108 NOW objective
109 Scull adjunct
110 Manhandle
111 Relative of ein
112 Sault ___ Marie

143

SOUND REASONING by Michele Hyams

Homophonic humor abounds in this marvel from Michele. If you decide to look up the clue for 36 Down, you may wish to consult a foreign language dictionary.

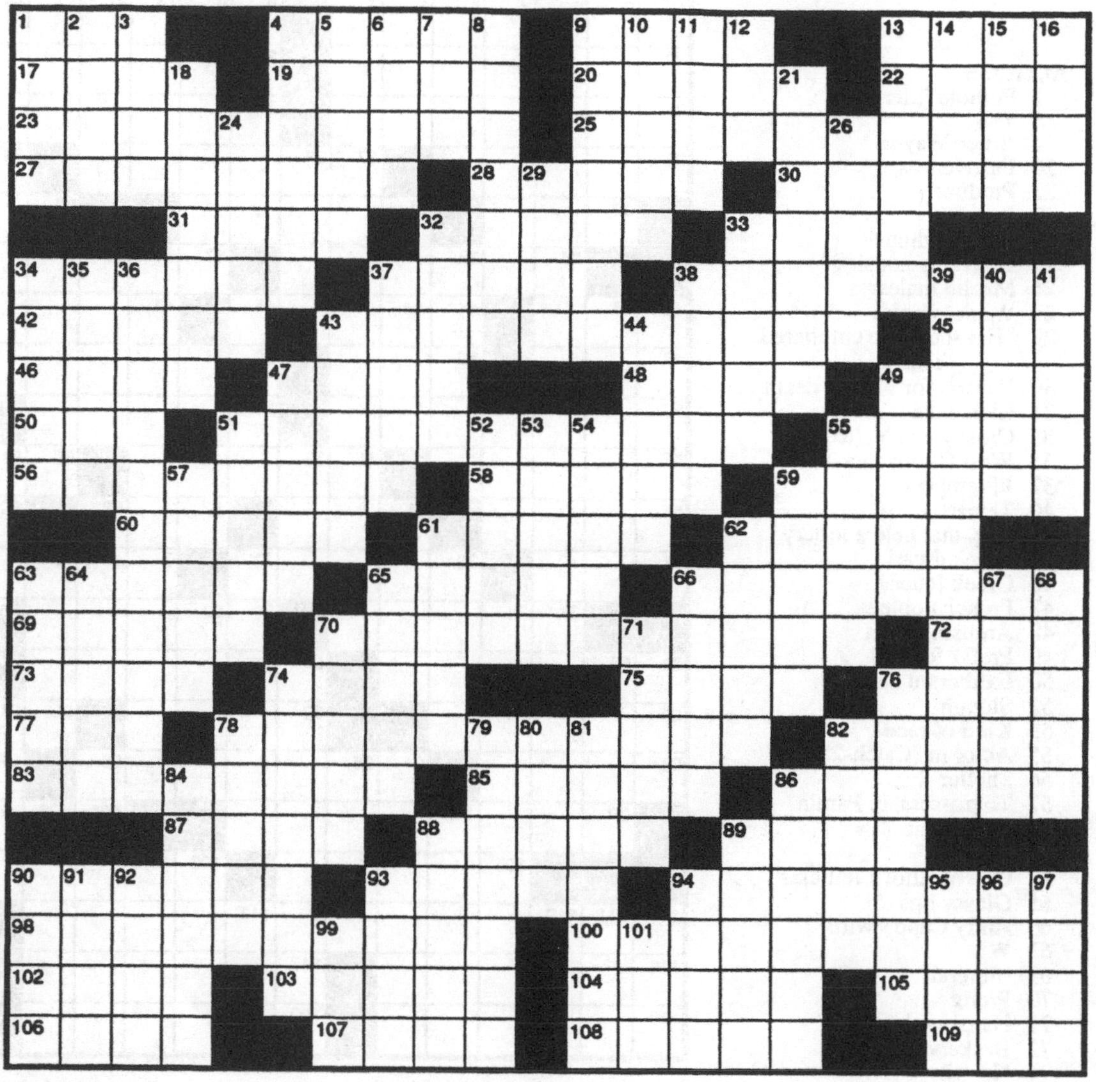

ACROSS

1 Mother Goose's Margery
4 Bel ___, Gigli specialty
9 Susiana
13 Till
17 Cenozoic and Mesozoic
19 "___ a Grecian Urn"
20 Metalliferous veins
22 Chesty rattle
23 Upper and lower fares?
25 Preppy's wrath?
27 Bars
28 Pocus' pal
30 Havoc
31 Eternities
32 Egyptian natives
33 Gorge
34 Fleet of 1588
37 Way follower
38 Subjoined
42 Scars
43 Y chromosone?
45 Soho residence
46 "___ Above All"
47 Ground
48 Frankfurt's river
49 Eighth century opener
50 Shire film of 1986
51 Bookbinder?
55 Embankments
56 Final notice
58 John of rock
59 Official seal
60 Ingenuous
61 Fat: Comb. form
62 ___ Domingo
63 "In the leafy month ___": Coleridge
65 Cut of beef
66 Glassworks worker
69 President from Ohio
70 Christmas Eve gathering?
72 ___ du Diable
73 Totally absorbed
74 Loop
75 Bone: Comb. form
76 B followers
77 Spanish queen
78 August cheeses?
82 Slice thinly
83 Pebble Beach obstacle
85 Then, in Toulouse
86 Postponed
87 Kind of dance
88 Astray
89 Douglas namesakes
90 Juarez's sister city
93 Arrange in folds
94 Oblong cut of gem
98 Pessimistic pony?
100 Miami palms?
102 Cantina treat
103 Taken ___ (surprised)
104 Capsize
105 River in SC Arizona
106 Nine inches
107 Huxtable and Rehan
108 Beverly Hills and Scarsdale
109 Redford's sign

DOWN

1 Obligation
2 Part of WATS
3 Distort
4 Crown
5 F.P.A.
6 Snoods
7 Sock part
8 Landward
9 Orestes' sister
10 Lotophagi's fruit
11 Excitements
12 "The Hollow ___": T. S. Eliot
13 Tried and true
14 Tra-___
15 Designer Cassini
16 "___ in the Money"
18 Freshets
21 Tool for icy windshields
24 Mobsters
26 With 70 Down, misogynist
29 Org. founded in Baghdad
32 Spanish street
33 Peeper
34 Houston athlete
35 Restore, for short
36 Jochū?
37 Mistress Flora, e.g.
38 "As You Like It" forest
39 Labor Day at the waterfront?
40 Host
41 Believer in God
43 Wavy fabric design
44 Dynamo part
47 Urbane
49 Pronouncements
51 One of five
52 Joined with
53 Scottish names
54 Vampire's bane
55 Odense natives: Ger.
57 Gibe
59 Hiawatha's conveyance
61 Oil source
62 Piques
63 Monsters
64 Landslide: Ital.
65 Use a curling iron
66 Ninnies
67 Sorbonne student
68 Stoked anew
70 See 26 Down
71 Evenings in Paris
74 Erotica
76 Follow-up drinks
78 Cache
79 Radar beacons
80 Oscilloscope spot
81 Kane's obsession
82 Show off
84 "Year of the ___," 1985 film
86 What tourists take in
88 Betel palm
89 Phase
90 Tolkien trees
91 Kind of year
92 12-point type
93 Couple
94 First or second
95 Greenish blue
96 From a distance: Comb form
97 Pedro's 46 Across
99 Garment for Abdul
101 Prefix for dermis

144 FILM FLAM by Calista Luminati

Movies with unusual names are punfully clued by one who also has an unusual name.

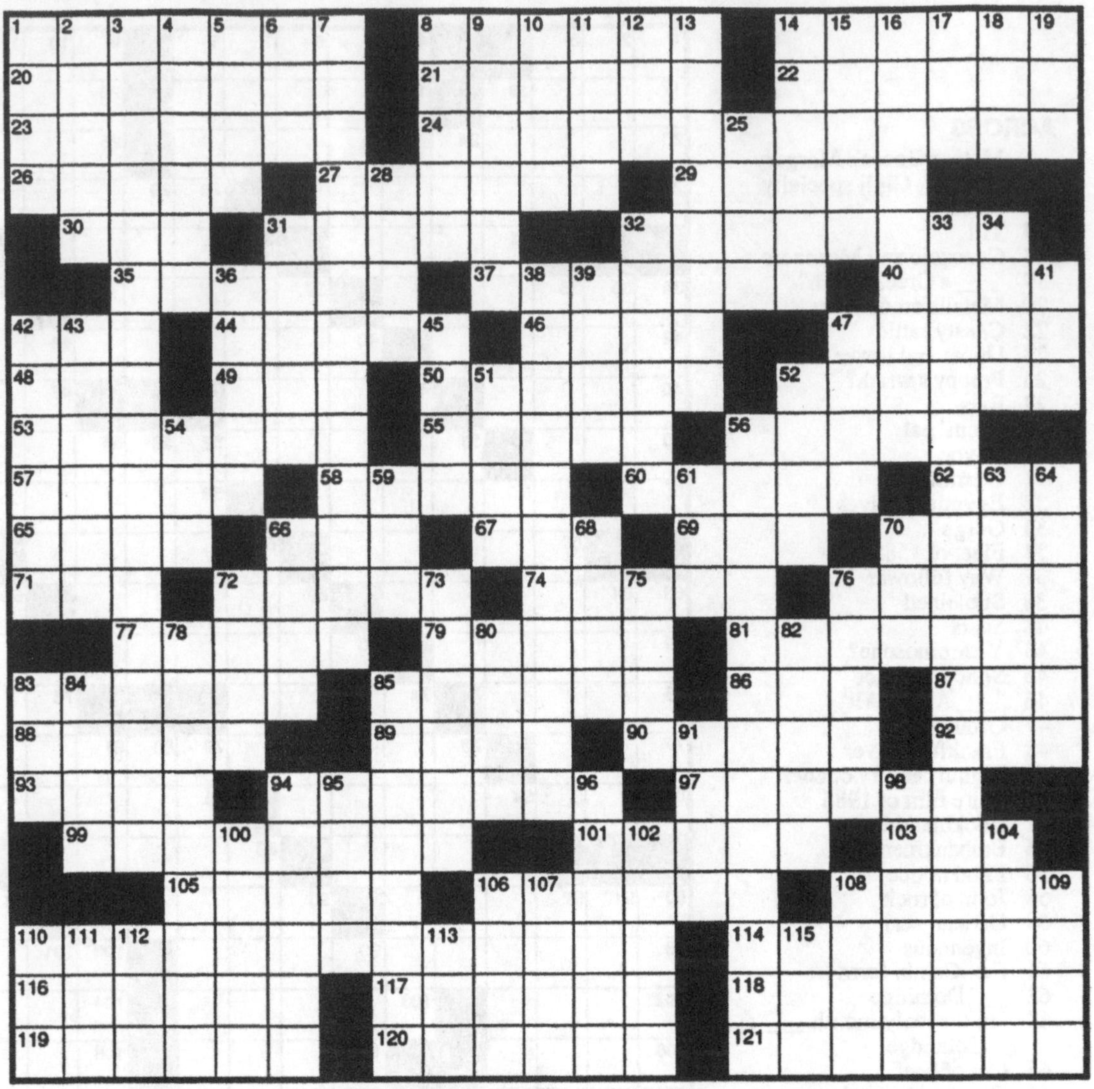

ACROSS

1 Pothole filler
8 Tell
14 Bruce Wayne
20 Furtiveness
21 Producer
22 Beached
23 Compendious
24 Heavenly housing?
26 Macho males
27 Winless horse
29 "His soul is so enfettered ___": Shak.
30 Reason for sudden death
31 Rich cake
32 Crosby and Vallee
35 West Orange genius
37 Ill tempers
40 Thwart
42 Org. that held a lottery
44 Greek dwarf
46 Greek letter
47 French noble
48 Amusing alien
49 Prefix for pod
50 Exuberant dance
52 Slough
53 Kind of race
55 Actor in "Catch-22"
56 Shelter
57 To possess, in Pantin
58 Jazz of the '40s
60 Eat into
62 One of Eliot's Jellicles
65 Glassy lips
66 Andy Capp's wife
67 Wit
69 Mineral
70 Prong
71 Hans' exclamation
72 Baskervilles' beast
74 Nostrils
76 Line at a party
77 Université
79 One-to-one, for one
81 Emanates
83 Nurtured
85 Skill: Comb. form
86 Craze
87 ___, quatro, cinque
88 Vaishnava holy man
89 Almost extinct
90 Kind of stealer
92 Pres. from Lamar
93 Commoner
94 Streep-Hoffman roles: 1970
97 Annoy
99 Maternal relationships
101 The 400
103 Important govt. org.
105 Histories
106 Affix
108 Overloves
110 Concords not in concord?
114 Example
116 Straw, to Satie
117 Compound sugar
118 Profits
119 Save
120 Home wreckers
121 Girl-watchers

DOWN

1 "Salvation" author
2 Porter relative
3 Godsends for some loafers?
4 Cut
5 Baba and MacGraw
6 NCO's superiors
7 What astronomers rarely say?
8 Mus. style
9 Ducks
10 Ear part
11 Analogous
12 Taps' time
13 Asmaran
14 Anticlimax
15 Blanched
16 Consequently
17 Annual doz.
18 Joan Van ___
19 "Prometheus Bound" sculptor
25 Koestler's "Darkness at ___"
28 Tuscany river
31 Michael and Peter
32 Oil in petroleum
33 Daily happening at Blarney Castle?
34 Poses
36 Prefix for faith
38 Coral cat?
39 Places
41 Paul of music
42 Bogart film: 1943
43 Czech or Slovak
45 Strikebreaker
47 Inlet
51 ". . . maids all in ___"
52 ___-to-order
54 Serbian city
56 Filly's fluff?
59 Unfathomable time
61 Small deer
63 Riles
64 China service
66 Origami feature
68 Win
70 Home for an aerie
72 Weeder
73 Fond hopes
75 Aussie hoppers
76 Gives up
78 Jelly fruit
80 Realty unit
82 Pastor's place
83 Chew the fat
84 Fashion magazine
85 What Mr. Roberts wanted
91 Cartoonist Young
94 Love's partner
95 Newspaper section
96 Long-haired dog
98 Ransacker
100 Liangs
102 Wry-faced Bert and family
104 Have scruples
106 Mesa loc.
107 Dull
108 Sutherland or Sills
109 Bishoprics
110 USSR police
111 Japanese epic film: 1985
112 Ache
113 Depression agcy.
115 Dear

145

ANIMAL CRACKERS by June A. Boggs

June preferred puns to guns when she caged this merry menagerie. You're invited to set them free.

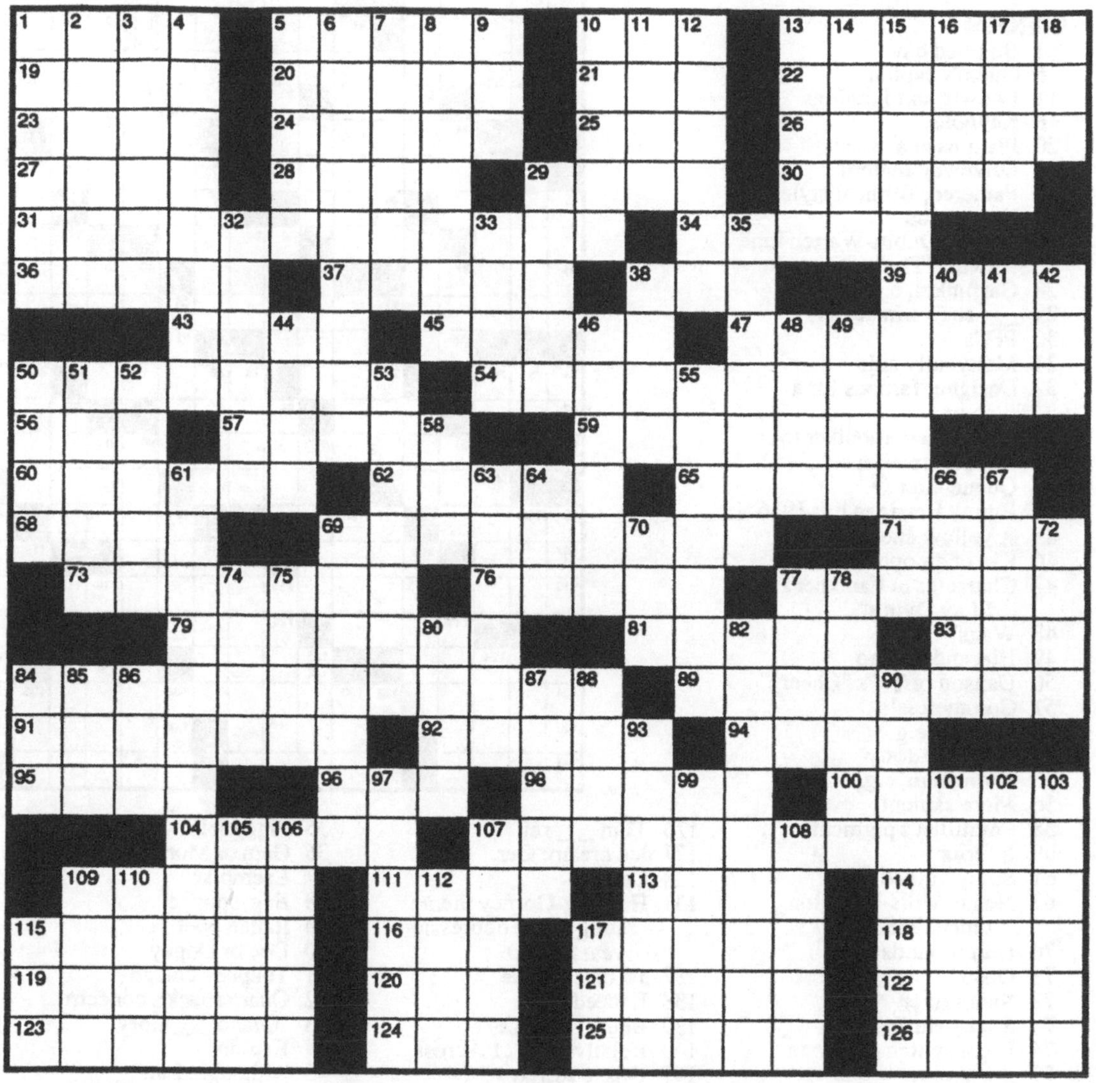

ACROSS

1 Part of S.A.S.E.
5 Couples
10 Rattle
13 Cotton of the cloth
19 U.S.
20 Hall-of-Famer Flick
21 Ripen
22 Revolted
23 Creeper
24 Morning songs
25 Type of turtle
26 Slovenly
27 Balanchine ballet
28 U.S. publisher: 1882-1947
29 Colombia's neighbor
30 Pith helmet
31 Gray-haired Chicago team?
34 Singer Lopez
36 Weird
37 ___ Gordo, Veracruz sight
38 Aitch preceder
39 Native Egyptian
43 Herb, in Verbania
45 Lyricist Cahn
47 Subject to court action
50 Freebies
54 Sir Edmund Hillary, e.g.?
56 Adj. ending
57 Endeavor
59 Abrupt drop
60 As long as: Dial.
62 South African grassland
65 "Bathers" and "The Box"
68 Jurist Woodbury
69 Sweet spelling contests?
71 Hood's knife
73 Worse than a harpy
76 Computer inspections
77 Arrangement
79 Piquancy
81 Miss Hungary of 1936
83 ___ es Salaam
84 Scotch liqueur glass?
89 Healthful
91 Roll along
92 Soul
94 Reluctant
95 Convoy member
96 He ran with DDE
98 Recoiled
100 Stadler of the links
104 "For it is ___ that speak": Matt. 10:20
107 Two-bit piece of gymnastic equipment?
109 Like Rose's twelve men
111 Wildebeests
113 Rayong resident
114 Nobel physicist: 1911
115 Moorish drum
116 Reine's mate
117 Canines
118 Turned
119 Ascribe
120 "___ Never Smile Again"
121 Napoleon in 1814
122 ___ Royale
123 Inadequate
124 Witty remark
125 More amiable
126 NBA team

DOWN

1 Wild
2 Deportee
3 City near Granite Falls
4 In a dither
5 Form of mica
6 Jazzmen of Tin Pan?
7 Drink
8 Proofers
9 BMOCs
10 "Daisy Miller" author
11 Chinese gelatin
12 Good name
13 Civvies
14 Raggedy Ann wears one
15 Sultry schoolmates?
16 Gordie of hockey
17 Being
18 Curious George's creator
29 Advance man's concern, for short
32 Binary digits
33 "My Name Is ___": Saroyan
35 Records anew
38 "Peer ___"
40 West Indies charm: Var.
41 Arafat's org.
42 Decalogue number
44 Shatter
46 "It ___ Him," 1967 Carr hit
48 Gulf of Corinth strait
49 Data
50 Bay
51 Pasty
52 Colombian city
53 Smacked one's lips
55 Brewer and Wright
58 Hankering
61 Bolts buff?
63 Moral
64 Tint
66 Roman cart
67 Priestly cassock
69 Fowl house
70 Hosp. test
72 Part of V.S.O.P.
74 Olympian's goal
75 Catania loc.
77 River of Java
78 Prop
80 Nine inches
82 Plain U.S. gold coin?
84 Address abbrs.
85 Charlemagne's dom.
86 Suffix for petrol
87 Effort
88 Youth org.
90 Gives a bonus
93 Short-flight vehicle
97 Whim, of yore
99 Cultural
101 Melodious
102 Tristram's love
103 Types
105 Speechify
106 Harrison's successor
107 Counterpane
108 After early or late
109 "Do not muse ___": Shak.
110 California valley
112 ___ contendere
115 Intention
117 Bog

146

THIRTIES SONGFEST by John Greenman
Among the ruins of the Depression there were immortal tunes, some of which reflected the times.

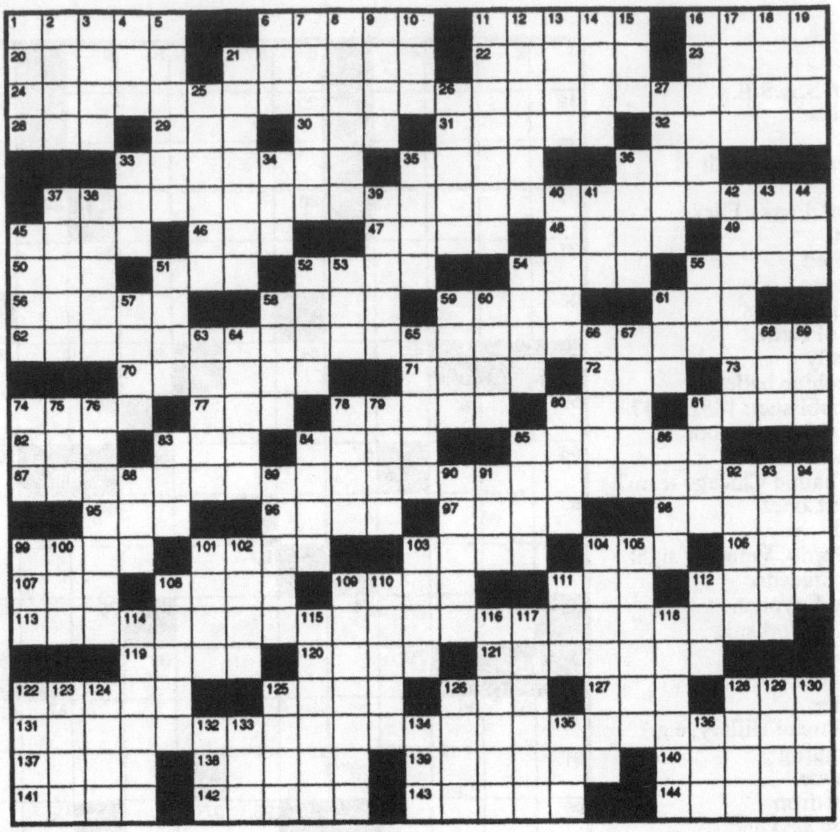

ACROSS
1 Bundled hay
6 Guam's capital
11 Ludwig and Jannings
16 Keyhole
20 Plant used as soap
21 Driveway material
22 Fathered, Biblical style
23 Use a strop
24 A 1933 Dubin-Warren tune (with "The")
28 Garfunkel, e.g.
29 ___ se (intrinsically)
30 PFCs
31 Maternally akin
32 Designer famous for a chair
33 Gave a new moniker to
35 Guppies, perhaps
36 Queue after Q
37 Bunny Berrigan hit: 1936
45 A yellow cheese
46 Kin of an ophidiid
47 Character in Faulkner's "As I Lay Dying"
48 Wags
49 Hirt and Pacino
50 Danson of TV's "Cheers"
51 Commercials
52 Rolltop, e.g.
54 Dippy or dotty
55 Hornbeam, e.g.
56 More sapient
58 Pointillist's pigments
59 Inferior
61 Spiny-finned fish
62 Nemo-Mills-Ellington tune: 1938
70 Dumbfounds
71 Goad
72 Swiss river
73 Sticky stuff
74 Light switch positions
77 Speakeasy
78 Toot; bender
80 Equestrian's seat: Abbr.
81 Previously stitched
82 Actress Arthur
83 Mountain crest
84 Athletes' org.
85 Pascal
87 Rodgers & Hart song: 1939
95 Allow
96 Reinking and Jillian
97 "Te ___" (hymn)
98 Rebuke
99 Accurate
101 Nothing more than
103 ___ down (prescribes)
104 Disciple's emotion
106 Actress Grant
107 Wherry implement
108 Artist Chagall
109 Read quickly
111 Noshed
112 Entreated
113 Romberg-Hammerstein waltz: 1935
119 Author Murdoch
120 Stowe's "The Pearl of ___ Island"
121 Tangelos' kin
122 007, e.g.
125 "___ for All Seasons"
126 Thin ___ rail
127 Ice cream: Ger.
128 Delay
131 Harburg-Gorney theme song of the depression years: 1930
137 Jacob's spouse
138 Exceedingly
139 Belief systems
140 Relative of 121 Across
141 Fabric suffixes
142 Hoard
143 Cup, in Cologne
144 Rub with rubber

DOWN
1 Rum dessert
2 Cupid
3 Oaf
4 Architectural wing
5 Excavate further
6 Timetable abbr.
7 Doodad; gismo
8 Sidesteps
9 Ship-shaped clocks
10 Priestly robe
11 Hard, black rubber
12 "Kiss ___": Porter musical
13 "___ Ideas," 1951 tune
14 Bucolic byway
15 Norm: Abbr.
16 Blade case
17 Clayey soil
18 The laugh's ___
19 Trueheart of comics
21 Shelters a car
25 Aired
26 Nurtures
27 Takes a coffee break
33 Aries symbol
34 Brooks or Blanc
35 Piggy follower
36 Gam or Moreno
37 Exemplar
38 Beg; sponge
39 Italian poet
40 Doc or Dopey
41 Toupee's cousin
42 Quarterback's concern
43 "Grand ___ Opry"
44 Exploit
45 Although: Lat.
51 Saroyan boy
52 Burrows
53 Actress Taina
54 Almost excellent
55 Tic-tac-___
57 Zeta-theta bridges
58 Ripsnorter
59 Unadulterated
60 Nebraska tribe now in Oklahoma
61 Follower of Jesus: Abbr.
63 Wooden shoe
64 Arkansas's ___ mountains
65 Winfrey of TV
66 "Call Me ___," Broadway musical
67 New Haven student
68 Set-to
69 Heavy weight
74 ___-wan Kenobi of "Star Wars"
75 Grazed
76 Misfire
78 (Had) done a lumberjack's job
79 Fido's feet
80 Svelte
81 Adam's youngest
83 Explosive
84 Top-notch
85 Heat measures: Abbr.
86 Six in dice, old style
88 Billy ___ Williams of films
89 Drug agent: Slang
90 Hersey's hamlet
91 "The Daughter of Time" author
92 Novelist Cather
93 Revoke, in law
94 Peach pit, e.g.
99 Drag
100 Super Bowl sound
101 Three Wise Men
102 Miscalculates
103 SE Asian republic
104 Expiators
105 Woman's shoe
108 Merriment
109 Leaves high and dry
110 Hackneyed
111 One ___ time
112 Footlike part
114 Certain fractions
115 "A ___ Face": Joan Crawford film
116 Wins' opposites
117 Hangs in swags
118 Used car transaction
122 Competent
123 Goodwill of yore
124 Of the dawn
125 Zoological suffix
126 Ambience
128 Peruvian capital
129 One of a radio pair
130 Heredity unit
132 A Spanish queen
133 Lang. type
134 Eight: Comb. form
135 Iced tea alternative
136 Dresden article

147 FROM SEA TO SHINING SEA by Sherwood Lane

This veteran constructor from Roslyn Heights, New York, shows his true colors at 61 Down and suggests solvers may wish to save this one for 49 Across.

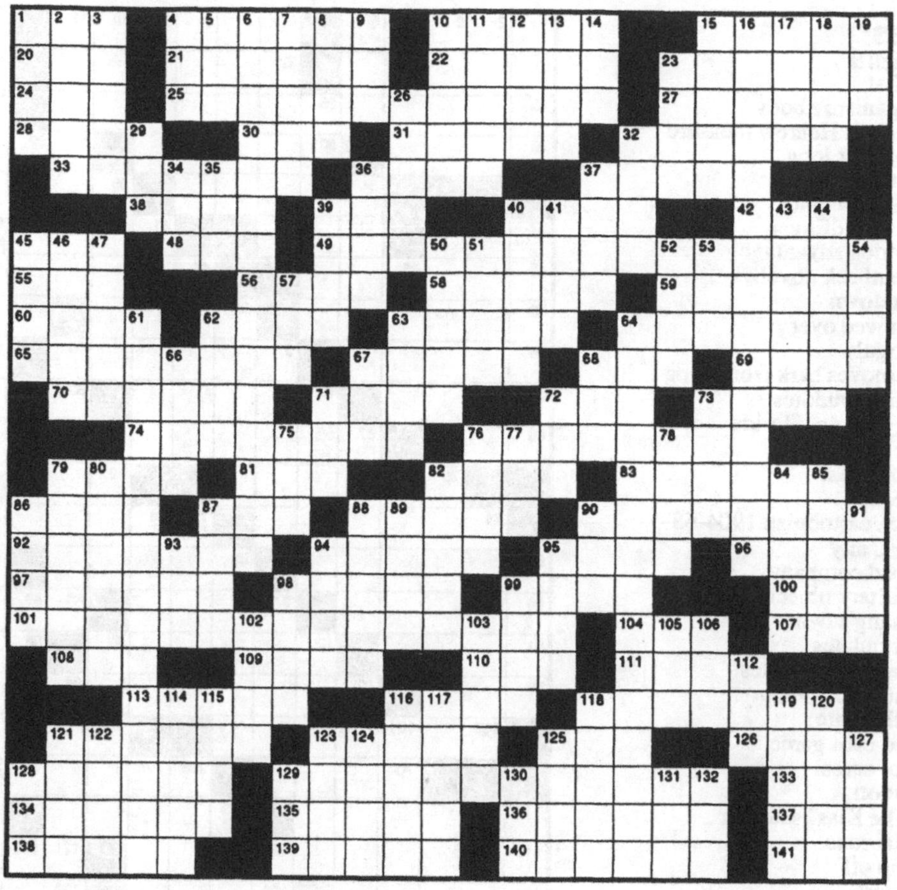

ACROSS

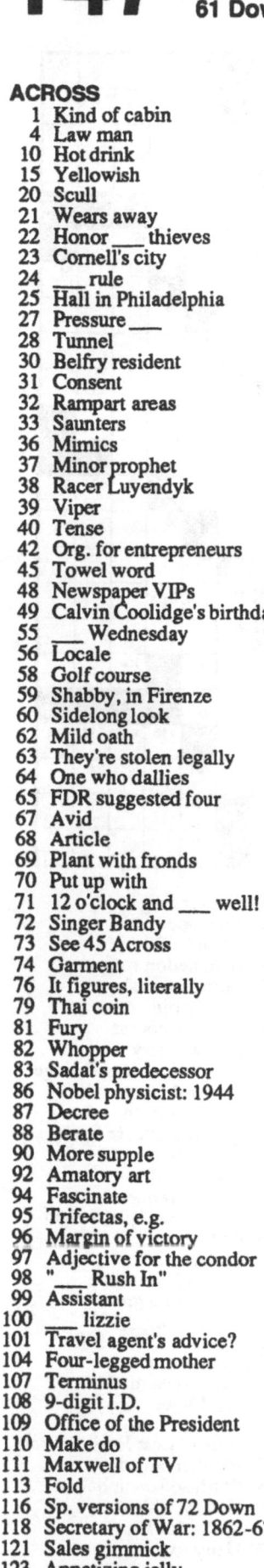

1 Kind of cabin
4 Law man
10 Hot drink
15 Yellowish
20 Scull
21 Wears away
22 Honor ___ thieves
23 Cornell's city
24 ___ rule
25 Hall in Philadelphia
27 Pressure ___
28 Tunnel
30 Belfry resident
31 Consent
32 Rampart areas
33 Saunters
36 Mimics
37 Minor prophet
38 Racer Luyendyk
39 Viper
40 Tense
42 Org. for entrepreneurs
45 Towel word
48 Newspaper VIPs
49 Calvin Coolidge's birthday
55 ___ Wednesday
56 Locale
58 Golf course
59 Shabby, in Firenze
60 Sidelong look
62 Mild oath
63 They're stolen legally
64 One who dallies
65 FDR suggested four
67 Avid
68 Article
69 Plant with fronds
70 Put up with
71 12 o'clock and ___ well!
72 Singer Bandy
73 See 45 Across
74 Garment
76 It figures, literally
79 Thai coin
81 Fury
82 Whopper
83 Sadat's predecessor
86 Nobel physicist: 1944
87 Decree
88 Berate
90 More supple
92 Amatory art
94 Fascinate
95 Trifectas, e.g.
96 Margin of victory
97 Adjective for the condor
98 "___ Rush In"
99 Assistant
100 ___ lizzie
101 Travel agent's advice?
104 Four-legged mother
107 Terminus
108 9-digit I.D.
109 Office of the President
110 Make do
111 Maxwell of TV
113 Fold
116 Sp. versions of 72 Down
118 Secretary of War: 1862-67
121 Sales gimmick
123 Appetizing jelly
125 Triptik org.
126 Porter's "Miss ___ Regrets"
128 Theater district
129 New Hampshire peak
133 Gunpowder, e.g.
134 Note maker
135 Uplift
136 "The Tatler" publisher
137 French coin
138 Captain Kirk's father
139 NBA official
140 Botched (with "up")
141 Electrical unit

DOWN

1 Good earth
2 Caravan stop
3 President from Ohio
4 Garland
5 Suffix for south
6 Kate sang it memorably
7 Notions
8 Labor's mo.
9 Half a fly
10 Sponge
11 Dry measures for Solomon
12 Volcano peak
13 Third of thrice
14 Ripen
15 Mall member
16 Monticello resident
17 Autumn tool
18 Unreturnables from Graf
19 Card game
23 Frosts
26 Tablecloth: Fr.
29 Historic period
32 The two
34 Galena, e.g.
35 Cover
36 Tennis name
37 Hovels
39 Mil. command
40 Piano doc
41 Asylums
43 Whodunit villain?
44 Changes
45 Partial
46 River to the Rhone
47 "Wall Street" star
50 Banners
51 River to the Seine
52 Monster
53 Part of T.G.I.F.
54 It's spun by a gob
57 Mid-April letters
61 Old Glory's glory
62 Poet Goodale
63 Great evil
64 Great Melting Pot
66 Song for the Judds
67 Addition
68 Tot's toy
71 Jurist Fortas
72 Mrs. in Montpellier
73 German violin virtuoso: 1859-1939
75 Humorist Buchwald
76 Serene
77 Like King Cole
78 Soviet "AP"
79 Critic Clive
80 Domiciles
82 Trunks
84 Play the ham
85 Lac, for one
86 Yellow dyes
87 Dermatologist's concern
88 Sand bar
89 Veal
90 Conducted
91 Pull apart
93 "How Dry ___"
94 Caesar's costar
95 ___ the bullet
98 After 4:59
99 Answers in "Jeopardy"
102 Kind of ladder
103 Boxer's asset
105 ___ mode
106 Neanderthal ___
112 MS. notation
114 Assessor
115 Noun-forming suffix
116 Flash flood
117 Stairway piece
118 Wise guys
119 Long-tailed animal
120 Nephew's sister
121 Soprano Stevens
122 Bridge position
123 Hun king
124 Acted fishy?
125 ___ meridiem
127 Israel's first king
128 Tear
129 Encountered
130 Doctrine
131 Inventor Evinrude
132 Governor McWherter

148

ALL HANDS ON DECK by Louis Sabin
In this clever puzzle, nothing is in duplicate—but all the main entries really are!

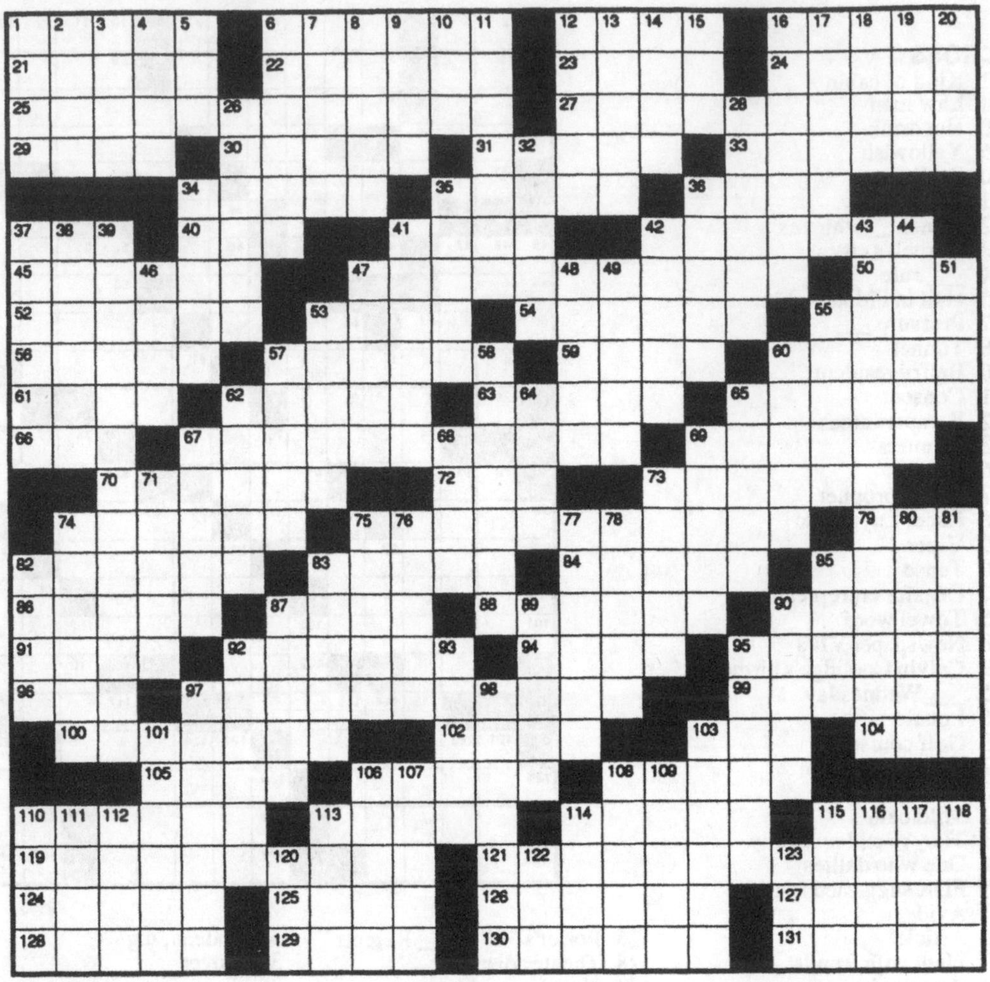

ACROSS
1 Grinder
6 D flat
12 Organism's body
16 Ancient Hebrew measure
21 Novelist Jong
22 Catapult
23 Underweight
24 Mr. Goldfinger
25 Hidden advantage
27 Steinbeck novel
29 Set down
30 Showed over
31 Moguls
33 Removes bark from a log
34 Range buddies
35 ___ Glade, Florida
36 Roll call reply
37 Downcast
40 Rocks
41 U.S. cartoonist: 1904-68
42 NFL city
45 Road company
47 Military objectives
50 Chang's twin
52 Stimulates
53 Prefix for physics
54 Shows contempt
55 Fulminate
56 Old card game
57 Hot cereal
59 Shoot!
60 "The Kiss" sculptor
61 Glabrous
62 Lop off
63 Taters
65 Cottages
66 Suffix for Sudan
67 Franchises
69 E Texas river
70 Dick, Tess and Junior
72 Mortarboard
73 Guitarist's purchase
74 Stadia
75 Boneset or joe-pye
79 Drop back
82 Kyushu volcano
83 Two-door car
84 Chimes
85 Game of chance
86 Swings around
87 Tubs
88 Actress Durbin
90 Calgary Stampede, e.g.
91 Spring goddess
92 Cherry
94 Takes steps
95 Time frame
96 Conger
97 Actress in "Charley Varrick"
99 Narrate anew
100 Pungent
102 Birds' class
103 Hardin or Unseld
104 "___ It Isn't So"
105 Lincups
106 With ___ breath
108 Chemical compound
110 Rating at the pumps
113 Shane, for one
114 Europe-Asia boundary
115 North Sea feeder
119 Park place
121 Annual mail item
124 Agra coin
125 Baxter or Bancroft
126 Underwrite
127 Turkish sultan: 1703-30
128 "Through the ___," Rogers hit
129 Skates
130 More precious
131 Eucalyptus lover

DOWN
1 Kind of ticket
2 Bo Derek film
3 Mortgage
4 Etcher's need
5 Made tracks
6 Hold fast
7 Bergen dummy
8 Laugh track sounds
9 Dramatic conflict
10 Cath. or Prot.
11 Feign
12 Bargain
13 Midwest airport
14 It's as good as a mile
15 Worker or queen
16 Attempts
17 Button on some coffeemakers
18 Mortar trays
19 ___ in one's bonnet
20 They peck at their food
26 Indications
28 Hill nymphs
32 Moves through mire
34 One to pay
35 Actor Aherne
36 "Sweeney Todd" star
37 Shutterbug's light
38 Pervasive qualities
39 Presley film of 1967
41 More bohemian
42 Tarot readers
43 Streep and Hepburn
44 Fire follower
46 Duped
47 Swiss canton
48 Terminate
49 Gambler's call
51 Caesar's clan
53 Heavy hammers
55 Dick Grayson
57 Ravels
58 Abashed
60 Hydrophobic
62 Pie type
64 Gehrig replaced him
65 Solicitudes
67 Wynter and Andrews
68 Porgy
69 Stone pillar
71 View anew
73 Cob and pen
74 Retired
75 Comedienne Fields
76 Charlotte ___ (dessert)
77 Calendar differentials
78 Extra inning
80 Interstice
81 Considerable
82 Wimbledon winner
83 Partner of cash
85 Stronghold
87 Changes course
89 Like an otary
90 "Don't You Know" singer
92 One with a cud
93 Growing from
95 Fourth estate, in Spain
97 Lives off
98 Whist goof
101 Solemn request
103 "Our Town" playwright
106 Pretty
107 Chilean chain
108 Pianist Schnabel
109 U.S. skiing great
110 "Grand Ole ___"
111 Whodunit film, 1985
112 Cloth from bark
113 Pale-green moth
114 ___ Major
115 Repeat
116 Jaffe's "Lost Horizon" role
117 Belgian balladeer
118 Sturluson compilation
120 Henley athlete
122 Suffix for hero
123 Hairy ox

149 FOR AILUROPHILES by James E. Hinish, Jr.

Barrels of feline fun await you from 1 Across to 128 Across.

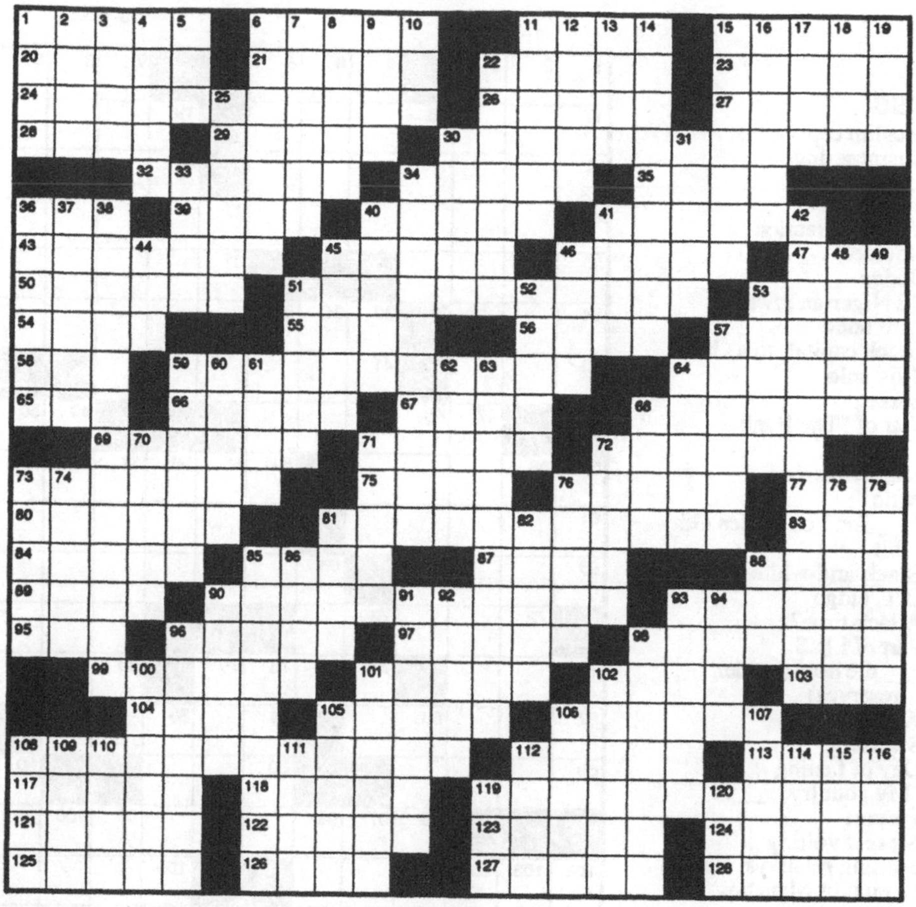

ACROSS

1 Common house cat
6 One of the Marxes
11 Small containers: Abbr.
15 West Coast shrub
20 Eyes, to Cato
21 Love affair
22 Decree, in Dijon
23 Win by ___
24 Children's game
26 ___ move (open an adjourned chess match)
27 Name meaning "lioness"
28 Auricular
29 Cat, Tigre, St. Kitts et al.
30 Kids of the comics
32 "___ on the Keys"
34 Contest coupon
35 Actress Moore
36 Terps' conference: Abbr.
39 "The liner, ___ a lady": Kipling
40 Ville VIP, in Verdun
41 Hamlet's playfellow
43 Talk
45 Succinct
46 Les ___, theirs in Tours
47 Kitten ending
50 Author of "One of Ours"
51 Sweetened the pot
53 "___ Brute!"
54 Plains tribesman
55 Double exclamation
56 Bourbon rulers
57 Canon's cap
58 Sloth, for example
59 Pulitzer Prize historian: 1954
64 Coupe roof tops
65 Chinese village
66 Litigate again
67 Singapore sarong
68 Skunk
69 Sailor, to a Greek of old
71 Pivot; swing
72 Start of a T. Williams title
73 Royal mace
75 Kitchen ending
76 Grasshopper's sound
77 Realm of John Paul II: Abbr.
80 French yellow
81 Made a harsh cry
83 Mauna ___
84 "He had ___": Proudfit
85 Cat or curtain follower
87 Catcher's ___
88 Clan symbol
89 "___ is the cat that ate the rat . . ."
90 Disaster that produced a stuffed leopard (aurally)?
93 Tapeworm larva
95 Part of a word: Abbr.
96 Stealthy; spiteful
97 Despises
98 Barcelona native
99 Roman robes
101 Essential parts
102 ___ mia (my dear)
103 Byzantine, for one
104 Girasol
105 Cosecants' cousins
106 "To ___ Thief": 1955 film
108 Equivocation is their forte
112 Emulate Catfish Hunter
113 Anatomical tissue
117 A church member, for short
118 Mrs. Coolidge
119 Richard I's sobriquet
121 Skin fungus
122 Sidled
123 Sandy's companion
124 Tropical vine
125 Horse laugh
126 Felines' foe
127 Yellow jackets
128 Felice's felines

DOWN

1 Large toucan
2 "No room to swing ___"
3 "___ cain't say no"
4 Poe's "The ___ Cat"
5 Yang's opposite
6 Youngster's pet
7 Soap plants
8 French cathedral city
9 "___ in Boots"
10 Galena, e.g.
11 Relative of a curé
12 ___ Kat of comics
13 Kind of type or vision
14 Lalapaloozas
15 Site of naval battle: 480 B.C.
16 Lacking vitality
17 Weaver's instrument
18 Editors' org.
19 "The Owl and the Pussycat" author
22 ". . . a poem lovely ___": Kilmer
25 In a ___ (agitated)
30 Delicatessen specialty
31 Tom's companion
33 That man, to Catullus
34 Star of "Timbuktu"
36 Confront
37 Small S.A. tigers
38 Type of whip
40 Bordeaux wine
41 Himalayan creature
42 Mrs. Moss Hart
44 "___ Cat," old TV crime series
45 Titter
46 Detroit player
48 Ancient gravestone
49 She wrote "Lummox": 1923
51 Concentrate (upon)
52 Danish dollar
53 Unite: Ger.
57 Piaf song
59 Cruel
60 Attempt again
61 Beneficiary, at law
62 "La Plume de ma ___"
63 Woolly bear caterpillars, someday
64 "A ___ santé!"
68 Beach bucket
70 Plant-pest genus
71 Restores
72 Flume
73 Chases away
74 Heathcliff's love
76 Members of 77 Across: Abbr.
78 Cat's ID
79 Connected series
81 Cat and ___ (building material)
82 Uses a hanky
85 Classified, in a way
86 Bar membs.
88 Kipling's python
90 Prince in Puccini's "Turandot"
91 "The ___ Line": James Jones novel
92 Deserves
93 Bon ___ (cheap)
94 North Atlantic air base
96 Mimic
98 Snares
100 Restless one
101 Fragments
102 Favorite of 1 Across
105 Amos Alonzo ___ of football fame
106 Grafting shoots
107 Sitting rooms
108 Kittens, e.g.
109 ___ arms (angrily aroused)
110 Chinese: Comb. form
111 Church publication
112 ___ colada
114 "L' ___, c'est moi"
115 Marquisette
116 Summer coolers
119 Order's partner
120 School subj.

150

WHEN IN ROME . . . by Robert H. Wolfe

Perhaps a more accurate title for Dr. Wolfe's challenger would be "When In Crosswordland . . ."

ACROSS

1 Muslim cap
4 Business deg.
7 ___ la la
10 Spigot
13 Vanity attraction
17 Novices
19 Budge
20 SE Nigerian town
21 Arm bone
22 Greek capital, to a Greek
23 Sills' solo
24 Biking
26 Star of "The Bank Dick"?
29 Maiden-named
30 Attic
31 "___ for You," Glen Gray hit
32 Black-and-white ducks
34 O.T. judge
35 Attack time?
40 Part of I.R.S.
41 ___ the hole (hidden reserves)
42 Actress Balin
43 Swelling
47 Day of fasting
49 "My country, ___ . . ."
51 Purport
52 More revolting
54 Starling relatives: Var.
58 Capital of Manche
60 Long time
61 Wed
62 Their pupils don't learn
63 Fab Five name
65 Novelist O'Brien
66 Bond's boss?
70 HST and AES
72 Drone
74 Ring of color
75 Opposed to intaglio
76 More, to Duran
77 And elsewhere: Abbr.
80 "Laura" lyricist
81 Mortgages
82 Growl
84 Tribal emblem
86 Fortify anew
88 Indian of Honduras
89 Scull
90 Flavors
93 Druggist's deg.
96 U.S. labor leader?
101 Blake's "before"
102 Bottle with a lip
105 Awn
106 Not kosher
107 ___ mode
108 "Ben Hur" star of long ago?
114 Adjective for George Gobel
116 A son of Jacob: Douay
117 Pacify
118 Ogle
119 Printing quads
120 Jamaican exports
121 Stutter
122 Perplexed
123 Tosspot
124 Affirmative rock group?
125 Rocky pinnacle
126 Circular contents

DOWN

1 Fishing boat
2 She played L. Lang in "Superman III"
3 Former NYC mayor?
4 Ho Chi ___
5 A Bridges
6 B ___ boy
7 Precede
8 Egg-white protein
9 Foliaceous
10 Magnetic ___
11 Inventor of cordite
12 Like some expense accounts
13 Suffix for soul
14 Dress design
15 ___ Mongolia
16 Storms
18 Young guinea fowl
19 Belafonte's birthday
25 An Olympic ring
27 Expires
28 King of Libya: 1951-69
33 Unit of force
35 "Rabevel" novelist
36 "Fire and ___," 1983 film
37 Rats
38 Slaughter of baseball
39 Loony
44 John Van Druten play?
45 Concierges
46 Eagle-eyed avian
48 Gold, e.g.
49 Proven proposition
50 One passing out
51 Toddler
52 Sight, in Sèvres
53 Jones of films
55 Choler
56 Kind of picker
57 "Ain't It ___ ?": Domino hit
59 Hallucinogen
64 Iowa or Kentucky county
66 Post-meal particle
67 Assn.
68 Libation-station potation
69 Like AA or AAA
71 Abba hit of 1975
73 Grig
75 Caste
76 Leo the Lion's co.
78 Like ___ of bricks
79 Loll
83 Indian chief: Var.
85 Dimmer switch
87 Silkworm
90 Methods
91 Modifies
92 Song of praise: Var. sp.
94 Wrinkled
95 Hugh and daughter Chris
97 Cricket sides
98 Subs
99 Mendicant monastery
100 Kleenex
102 Marsh plant
103 Succulent plants
104 Wife of 83 Down
106 Sci-fi film of 1954
109 Rounds
110 Aery
111 Phloem
112 ___ no good
113 Box
115 Epoch

151 NAME GAME by Mary S. Snyder

If you've played the name game before, you may be in for a pleasant surprise—Mary has taken it a step further.

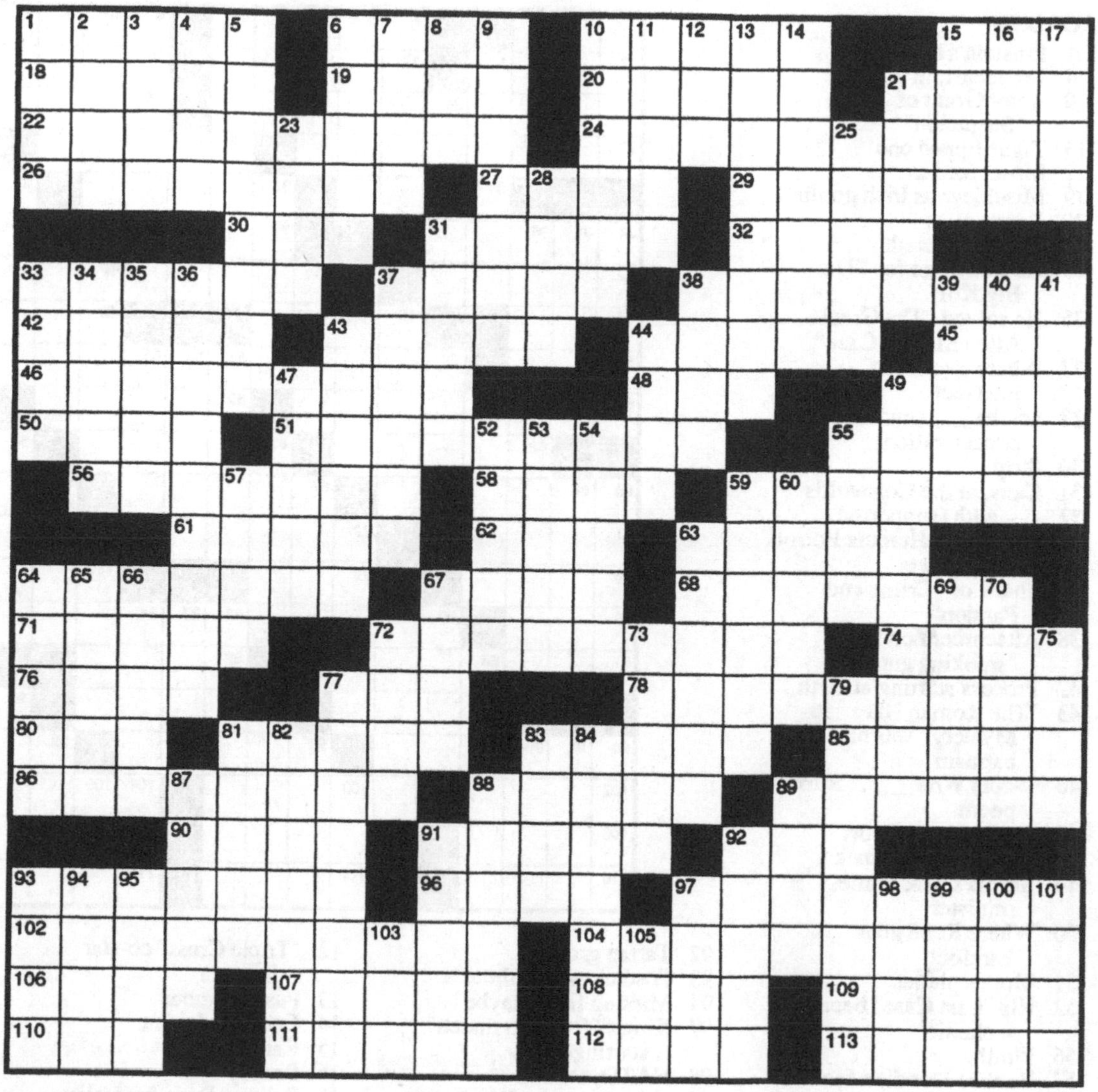

ACROSS

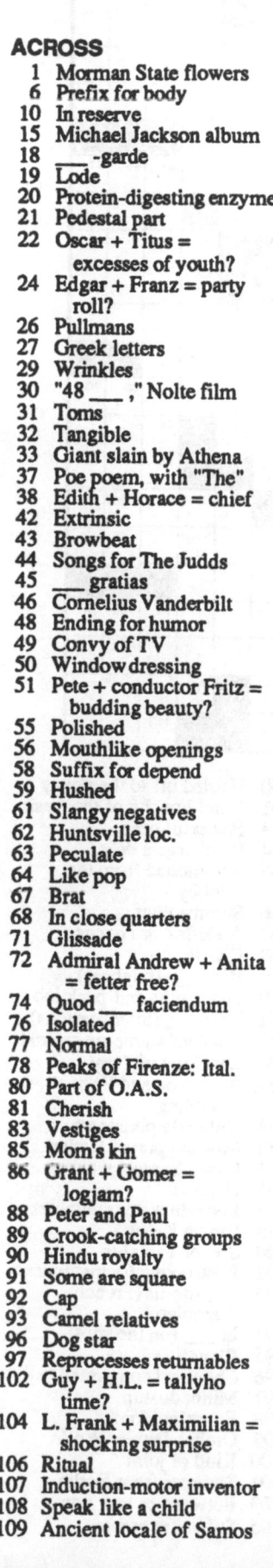

1 Morman State flowers
6 Prefix for body
10 In reserve
15 Michael Jackson album
18 ___-garde
19 Lode
20 Protein-digesting enzyme
21 Pedestal part
22 Oscar + Titus = excesses of youth?
24 Edgar + Franz = party roll?
26 Pullmans
27 Greek letters
29 Wrinkles
30 "48 ___," Nolte film
31 Toms
32 Tangible
33 Giant slain by Athena
37 Poe poem, with "The"
38 Edith + Horace = chief
42 Extrinsic
43 Browbeat
44 Songs for The Judds
45 ___ gratias
46 Cornelius Vanderbilt
48 Ending for humor
49 Convy of TV
50 Window dressing
51 Pete + conductor Fritz = budding beauty?
55 Polished
56 Mouthlike openings
58 Suffix for depend
59 Hushed
61 Slangy negatives
62 Huntsville loc.
63 Peculate
64 Like pop
67 Brat
68 In close quarters
71 Glissade
72 Admiral Andrew + Anita = fetter free?
74 Quod ___ faciendum
76 Isolated
77 Normal
78 Peaks of Firenze: Ital.
80 Part of O.A.S.
81 Cherish
83 Vestiges
85 Mom's kin
86 Grant + Gomer = logjam?
88 Peter and Paul
89 Crook-catching groups
90 Hindu royalty
91 Some are square
92 Cap
93 Camel relatives
96 Dog star
97 Reprocesses returnables
102 Guy + H.L. = tallyho time?
104 L. Frank + Maximilian = shocking surprise
106 Ritual
107 Induction-motor inventor
108 Speak like a child
109 Ancient locale of Samos
110 Lt.'s alma mater
111 Belgian violinist: 1858-1931
112 This makes a room small
113 Uncomfortable neckwear

DOWN

1 Proverbs
2 Kind of eye
3 Dorothy of Kansas
4 Wave, in Normandy
5 Shakespearean butler
6 Russian nomads of yore
7 NBA team
8 Fasten
9 Put in
10 Refutes
11 "Green Eggs and Ham" author
12 Carol ending
13 Prudent
14 Beseech
15 Salvatore Baccaloni, e.g.
16 Lumberman's tool
17 Dowries
21 Knot's "___ for Murder"
23 Poetic contractions
25 Certain roles
28 Actress Sheedy
31 Confusion
33 Covenant
34 Then, in Troyes
35 Put a ceiling on
36 Jack + George = popular potable?
37 Anatomical sacs
38 Kind of puppy
39 "Let's Make ___"
40 Audacity
41 Eminent
43 Kicked
44 Bones
47 Fall in folds
49 Ole + Sean & William = pitching places?
52 Keno's cousin
53 Dark
54 Shaft of a column
55 Chon Buri's gulf
57 Speck
59 Tonsorial sharpeners
60 Rag
63 Darrow's client
64 Radiant
65 The gold, to Cortez
66 Rock Starr
67 Angered
69 Silkworms
70 Italian poet
72 Get along
73 "Oz" actor, and family
75 Digits
77 Refines
79 An antibiotic
81 Quickly
82 TV's Forsyte saga?
83 Hindu realm of nonexistence
84 Suitable for purchase
87 "Golden Hind" captain
88 Seed coverings
89 Larrigans
91 Virile
92 Neighbor of Phoenix
93 ___-American studies
94 Secular
95 There are 20 in a troy oz.
97 Paint remover
98 Loco sound
99 Jester Jay
100 Old Olympic site
101 Blackthorn: Scot.
103 CATV network
105 Eyot

152 A SLEW OF SLEUTHS by Frances Hansen

This clever, well-researched puzzle has won the Margaret Award for its creator. Enough said!

ACROSS

1 Einstein's birthplace
4 Broadcast, in a way
9 Actor Grant of "Suspicion"
13 Tight-lipped one
17 Mosel feeder
19 Mischievous Irish goblin
20 Poppy juice
22 Like hens' teeth
23 He was there for "The Big Kill"
25 He solved "The Gracie Allen Murder Case"
27 Where two roads intersect
28 On the ___ (under consideration)
30 Strip
31 Cans, in the Cotswolds
32 ___ with (supported)
33 Luxury, to Hercule Poirot
34 Church tenets
37 Sharif of "Crime and Passion"
38 Attachment on the "smoking gun"
42 Process starting at birth
43 "The Roman Hat Mystery" was his baptism
46 "Scots Wha ___," Burns poem
47 Sindbad's transport
48 Kimberley entrance
49 Burma's first prime minister
50 Where René goes barefoot
51 Mork's planet
52 His "Last Case" became a classic
56 Plinth
57 Yankee Doodle's feather?
59 A mite wary
60 W. C. Bryant's Long Island address
62 "Do I ___ Waltz?": 1937 song
63 Dustin Hoffman role
64 Spokes
65 Blood-bank supply
67 Actor Bruce of "Homicide Bureau"
68 Contrite
71 Danish island in the Little Belt
72 He pitted himself "contre Herlock Sholmes"
74 Arch
75 Big swig
76 Bee chaser
77 Neighbor of Iraq
78 "With it"
79 Gelderland town
80 "The Nine Tailors" took their toll of him
85 Spook, in a way
87 Had it coming
89 Last of a Latin trio
90 Smoothed a piece of wood
91 Architect ___ Van der Rohe
92 Tartan groups
93 Fosdick was without it
94 Missing link, maybe
97 King's "freedom march" starting-point
98 NATO, for one
102 "Murder at the Vicarage" occupied her
104 "The Dead Man's Knock" didn't faze him
106 "Thanks ___!"
107 Full of fissile rock
108 "This ___" (warning on crate)
109 Satie or Estrada
110 Soften the steely eye
111 Sweet Sioux's cousin
112 Gets up on one's hind legs
113 Unclose, to Shakespeare

DOWN

1 Leatherneck's org.
2 Animal's snuggery
3 Mackerel shark
4 Gives rise to
5 ___ Masaryk, first Czech president
6 Actress Schneider of "Triple Cross"
7 Monogram of a musical Duke
8 Period to be deplored
9 Of a bronze hue
10 Plant pest
11 Social reformer Jacob
12 "Triple Cross" co-star Brynner
13 Pusillanimous
14 Druy or Maiden
15 Rainbows
16 Seemly
18 Pulitzer Prize journalist
21 Spacecraft's detachable unit
24 Double this for Ling-Ling's mate
26 Foxy lady?
29 Month after Shebat
32 Symphonic conductor Sir Georg ___
33 Sarge's superior
34 Bounce back
35 Where Xanthippe bought her veggies?
36 He was a contrast to Sam Slade
38 Cheerful
39 He understood "The Chinese Parrot"
40 Betimes
41 Mil. scouting expedition
43 Minneapolis suburb
44 Leslie Caron role: 1953
45 Interrogate
48 Now, in the barrio
50 Postulate
52 Hyde Park baby buggy
53 Lowly West Point cadet
54 Mortise insertion
55 French income
58 Fabulous Greek
60 Hauled off to the pokey
61 Chief honcho of the Aesir
63 Powerful beam
64 Discharge a debt
65 Summoned from the lobby
66 Summa cum ___
67 Apostles' or Nicene ___
68 Chaste
69 Bête ___ (bugbear)
70 Did a hunt-and-peck job
72 Entr' ___ (intermissions)
73 Jousters' stamping ground
80 Last king of Troy
81 "(___ you and I!)": Kipling
82 Unlovely pikeperch
83 Moslem prayer leader
84 Casey Stengel was one
85 Done in
86 Bedside water container
88 Clown Kelly
90 Son of Tantalus
92 Rostropovich's instrument
93 ___-de-lis (French emblem)
94 In ___ (on the spot)
95 Blanch
96 Chemical compound
97 Minor dustup
98 Egyptian skink
99 Orchid-fancier Wolfe
100 Kind of joint
101 Sommer from Berlin
103 Between pi and sigma
105 Suffix for serpent

153 MARVELOUS MIXTURE by Jim Page

An oleo of familiar and unusual words and clues has been concocted by our N.Y.C. veteran

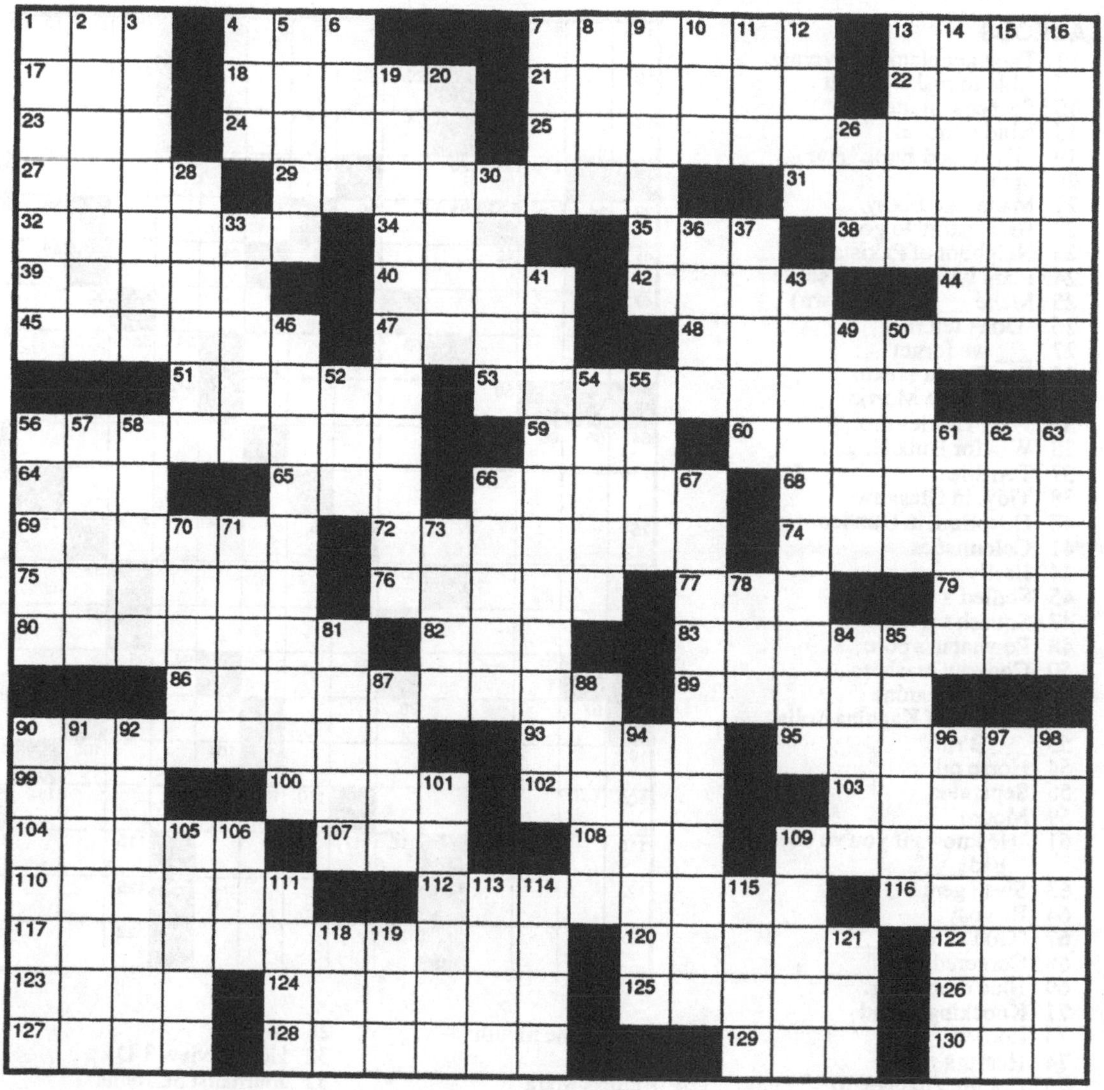

ACROSS

1 German article
4 "___ on parle français"
7 "___ aux Folles"
13 Hebrew month
17 Brit. honor
18 List for imps
21 Meltdown's his bane
22 Canada's Lévesque
23 Nitwit
24 Zero
25 Like the George Washington Monument
27 High: Comb. form
29 Milton subject
31 Big-wedding skipper
32 Acts; events
34 Brooklyn's Wallach
35 Russian coins: Abbr.
38 Mountain spur
39 She shone in "Paper Moon"
40 British servicewoman
42 City on the Mures
44 R.R. depot
45 Hoisted
47 Blockhouse?
48 Collared
51 Artery maneuver
53 Fanned
56 Dish for Elia?
59 Faroe winds
60 Ponderosa, et al.
64 Pull-over part
65 Amin
66 "The Adventures of ___ March": Bellow
68 British leading man, Edmund ___
69 Chaplin's "___ Times"
72 Recurring at 48-hour intervals
74 Sect member of yore
75 Composer de'Cavalieri
76 Minds
77 Playwright Mosel
79 ___ Dee, Carolina river
80 Scolders
82 AEF's York, e.g.
83 Esau's descendants
86 Spiced the dish
89 Post-diet need
90 Tobacco graders
93 Pack the hold
95 Crêpes suzette, often
99 Rumanian coin
100 Flanges
102 Toolhouse
103 Xenophobe's concern
104 "I will make thee think thy swan ___": Shak.
107 Bone: Comb. form
108 Buckeyes' inst.
109 Duke among "Dem Bums"
110 Rubberneck's object
112 Colonize anew
116 Kind of sax
117 Separated forcefully
120 Socket holding
122 Mountain-valley shelf
123 Whodunit first name
124 May or Stritch
125 Juan de ___ (conquistador)
126 Born
127 Ottoman rulers
128 ___-day (modern)
129 One of the Three Stooges
130 Drillmaster's deg.?

DOWN

1 Quadrille move
2 Sea otter's favorite prey
3 Placekicker Rafael
4 Actress Lupino
5 Masterstrokes
6 Actress Swenson
7 Attrice Virna
8 Four ___ (singing group)
9 Et follower
10 Simenon's "Mon ___ Maigret"
11 Maldives island
12 Ending for exist
13 Chain mail, e.g.
14 Superlative for Baikal
15 Actress Funicello
16 One returning to military service
19 Joined the mob
20 "___ 17": Oscar movie
26 Guido's note
28 Trio's spot
30 Channel changers
33 Satiates
36 Bric-a-___
37 Shirts in the Shetlands
41 Playthings for little girls
43 Fell asleep
46 Arranged alphabetically, e.g.
49 The southeast wind
50 Medieval Eng. pennies
52 Comedian Buttons
54 Actor Toomey
55 Murrow was its dir.
56 Weaker, as an excuse
57 Bouquet
58 2502, to Cato
61 Having natural aptitude
62 Heir, for one
63 Pintails
66 Betel palm
67 Started, as a project
70 Greece, to Greeks
71 Family of a 16th century architect
73 Poetic nights
78 "Artie" author
81 Kind of comic
84 Lombardy city
85 Francia neighbor
87 Mil. decorations
88 It's drained by the Truckee
90 Shook another's hand
91 Prof's address
92 How to listen
94 Defunct car
96 West Texas city
97 Jutted out
98 Coats with chocolate
101 Bering, e.g.
105 Heraldic borders
106 Like Willie Winkie
109 Arena match
111 Henry James biographer
113 Lake in Ireland
114 Wing: Comb. form
115 Brick-making ingredient
118 ___ carte
119 Boone or O'Brien
121 "___ Haw," TV show

154

UPTOWN, U.S.A. by Joel Lafargue
Although 1 A is an A-1 clue, this "Uptown" theme is strictly in the DOWNS. (See 30 D.)

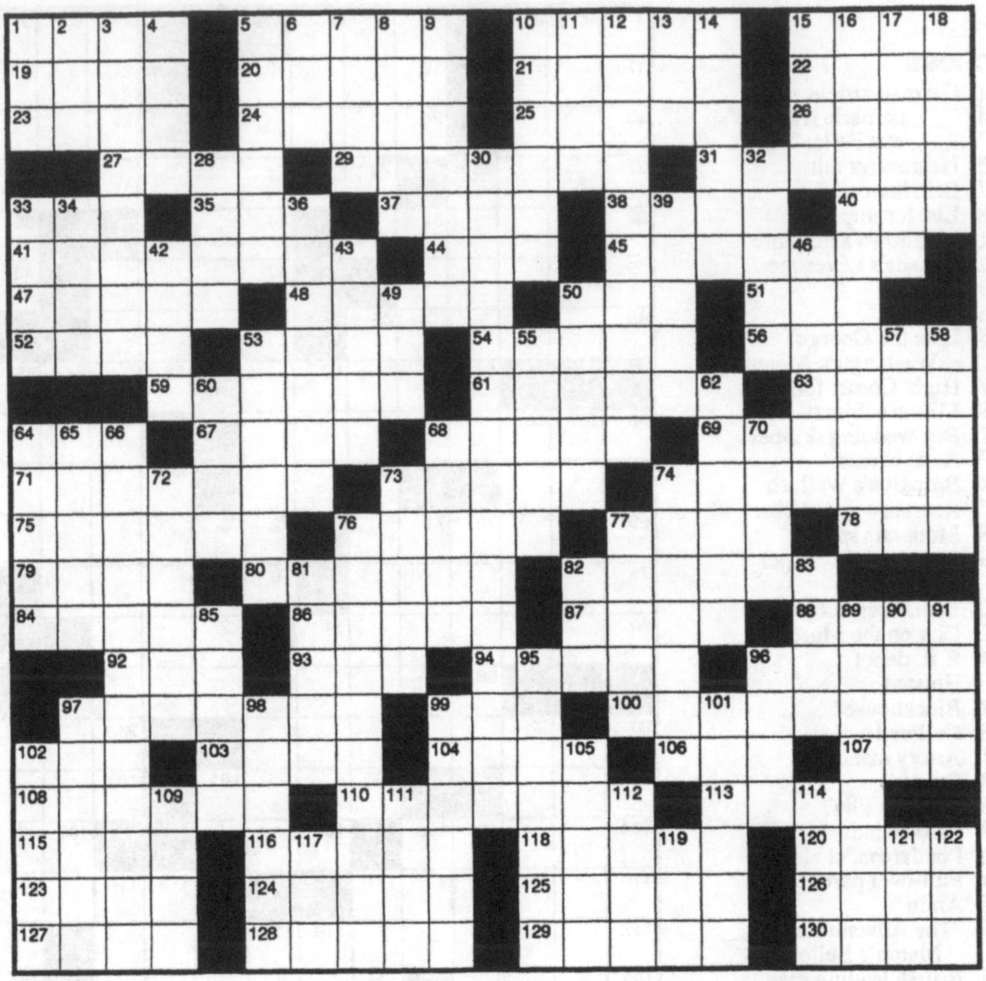

ACROSS

1 They get blanket coverage
5 Able to make the cut
10 Seabees' motto
15 Kind of novel
19 "The Good Earth" star
20 Spud
21 Made like Bossy
22 He's roarin' to go
23 Neighbor of Pakistan
24 Plant with aromatic seeds
25 Make ___ of (jot down)
26 "Don't tell me!"
27 ___ we forget
29 Pacific sea bream
31 Drank like Morris
33 World Series mo.
35 Win for Hulk Hogan
37 Terrible
38 Tidy, in Glasgow
40 Devotion, in Dundee
41 Colonnades
44 Barfly
45 Settled a score
47 Squash variety
48 Powhatan's pole
50 Cookout crasher
51 Terhune canine
52 Makers of Kachina dolls
53 ___ B'rith
54 Horse pill
56 Separated
59 Mourn
61 "He knows if you've been bad ___"
63 Swan genus
64 Be nosy
67 "God's Little ___"
68 Cornered
69 Blue moon, e.g.
71 Knocking sound
73 Loosen
74 Hearing range
75 Couldn't happen to ___ guy
76 High-hat
77 Pelt
78 He's paid to play
79 They get rolled
80 Hag
82 Diamond's 1971 hit
84 "And ___ grow on!"
86 Tilting
87 Souvenirs of summer
88 Minot loc.
92 Hebrew dry measure
93 Little extremist
94 Musical works
96 Carried
97 "___ Hoffmann": Offenbach
99 ___ snail's pace
100 Gershwin's "___ Loves Me"
102 Kingklip, e.g.
103 Cape Town loc.
104 What Scrooge was to Scott
106 L. ___ Hubbard
107 For shame!
108 Tube-nosed seabird
110 Fatty
113 Warped
115 Brynhild's brother
116 Metalliferous veins
118 Giraffe's relative
120 Toward the mouth
123 Fellow
124 Actress Mara
125 John Paul II's original first name
126 Chesty rattle
127 Kinski role
128 Carp's cousins
129 Aardvark on Boner's Ark
130 Attention-getter

DOWN

1 Org. of Tin Pan Alley
2 Where Eng. is
3 OREGON'S CITY OF ROSES
4 Function in 42 Down
5 Showing little change
6 Solo in "Star Wars"
7 Eagerly expectant
8 Put in new turf
9 Postulate
10 Purplish red
11 Super
12 STATE UNIVERSITY IN OHIO
13 L. Archer or M. Helm
14 GREAT LAKES PORT
15 Swill
16 WHERE BETSY ROSS LIVED
17 Infatuated with
18 Electrode
28 Joy ride
30 How to view 3-D
32 Journalist St. Johns
33 Colorful fish
34 Gabrielle Chanel
36 CITY ON THE DELAWARE
39 Untrue
42 H.S. math, sometimes
43 Softly, in music
46 Mists
49 Reason for overtime
50 Pond scum
53 Indigestion remedy, for short
55 Pluto's path
57 Chopper blade
58 "___ Remember"
60 Have status
62 Enervates
64 Where Goyas hang
65 Arrested
66 MORMON TEMPLE SITE
68 Dwarf buffaloes
70 Designer Jacobsen
72 Chemical solvent
73 Annulled
74 GATEWAY TO THE SHENANDOAH VALLEY
76 U. OF NORTHERN IOWA STATE
77 Binary and red giant
81 Learn like a Cockney?
82 ___ Anne de Beaupré
83 See 76 A
85 What beanpoles aren't
89 WHERE WHALERS SKATE -- NOT SAIL
90 "___ in my cap . . .": Moore
91 Actor Luke
95 Fisher's fighter
96 Part of n.b.
97 Grow canines
98 COWBOYS' HOME
99 Gets up
101 Crib adjunct
102 Solar-lunar year differential
105 Ridge of gravel: Var.
109 Tears
111 Take-out order
112 Deserve
114 Asta's mistress
117 Seraglio chamber
119 Luau chow
121 Milwaukee product
122 RFK was one

155 AFFAIRS OF STATE by Bert Rosenfield

Unusual theme; clever rhymes and clues; all in all, a peerless puzzle.

ACROSS

1 Midlothian miss
5 Watery
13 Another name for a papaya
19 Speedily
21 Produce mal-de-mer
22 Popular uprising
23 Food-processor attachment
24 Marooned in Georgia
26 Lanai
28 Old Roman wicker carriers
29 "___ You Glad You're You?": 1945 hit
30 Perceptive in Montana
34 Count-out commencement
36 Lunar vehicle's module
37 Memo inditers
38 Neighbor of Twelve Oaks
40 Muslim scholar
44 Augment
46 Headland
47 They're traversed by 1 Across
48 White or Blue stream
49 Clinkers in Illinois
54 "Blood hath been shed ___": Macbeth
56 Dark pigment
57 Monster: Comb. form
58 Down-under parrots
59 Diamonds to Legs Diamond
60 Bus. letter addendum
62 Late English actor Reginald
64 ___ même: oneself, in Orne
65 Former World Series star Luis
67 Squiffed in New York
71 Pinnacle of glacial ice
75 Capri ending
77 Finishing nail
78 Emulate Maxwell Perkins
80 Long follower
81 Mangle
84 ___ a time: serially
87 Vigorous
89 Sensitive plant
90 Gives thumbs-down in California
92 Moroccan coastal region
93 Journalist-author Alexander
95 Morsel for Fido
96 One of the psi phenomena
97 Ja's opposite
98 Fish dish
99 Roof technician
101 Federal bldgs.
104 Greek peak
106 Clamorous in Idaho
109 Port on the Shatt-al-Arab
112 Spoor
115 Cyclist's device
116 Graceless in Minnesota
121 Reflex motion
122 Posture for Payne Stewart
123 Theater section
124 "Cold Pieces" composer
125 The Minutemen, e.g.
126 More expeditious
127 "___ we forget"

DOWN

1 Immature, in a way
2 Get ___ of the action
3 Vertebral column part
4 Anglo-Saxon coin
5 Neonate
6 ___ dai: Indo-Chinese religion
7 Charioteer Ben ___
8 Bill Donovan's org.
9 Executes a knee-jerk
10 Chaplin's cinematic co-dictator
11 Salt Lake City team
12 Stamped and posted
13 Con's milieu
14 Where King Hussein holds forth
15 Worn-out in Pennsylvania
16 Eureka red
17 Like ___ of bricks
18 ___ with: dated
20 Turn-of-century lightweight champ
25 Rhone River feeder
27 Haughty indifference
31 Swiss city with a bear pit
32 Not likely
33 ". . . ___ the queen"
35 Atelier accessories
38 More old-hat
39 Road-service org.
41 Kind of van or bus
42 ___ hemp: agave
43 Stable area
44 Screw pine
45 Kitchen adjuncts
47 Brains' companion
49 Struck hard, old style
50 This, in Thiers
51 Olive-tree genus
52 Progress gingerly
53 Imitation gold alloys
55 Bucolic arousers
61 Women's ___
63 American humorist Bill
66 Forbidden in Maine
68 Post-prandial sounds
69 Dancer-choreographer Holm
70 Former UK prime minister
72 Riches' antithesis
73 Opposed to, in Dogpatch
74 Hepburn role on Broadway
76 Expunges
79 Conflagration
81 "___ the Mood for Love": 1935 ballad
82 Current
83 Where the Hawks hold forth
85 Chameleon's cousin
86 Hartebeests
88 One of 13 from NJ
90 Frivolous lady of song
91 Bitty preceder
94 Erica
99 Solvent's victim
100 One or the other
101 Procurator of Judea
102 Egyptian fertility god
103 Rhyme royal, for one
105 Bigarade or bechamel
106 Kol ___
107 1948 White House name
108 Eighth
109 Kind of jacket
110 Preliminary donation in poker
111 Heidelberg memento
113 Libertines
114 Take ___: doze
117 Symbols for Element 52
118 Emulated Mehta
119 Altdorf's canton
120 Due follower

156

SYNONYMIC GEOGRAPHY by Jim Page
This highly unique creation is the result of long hours of research spent at the New York Public Library. The streets found in the answers below actually do exist. Excellent job, Jim!

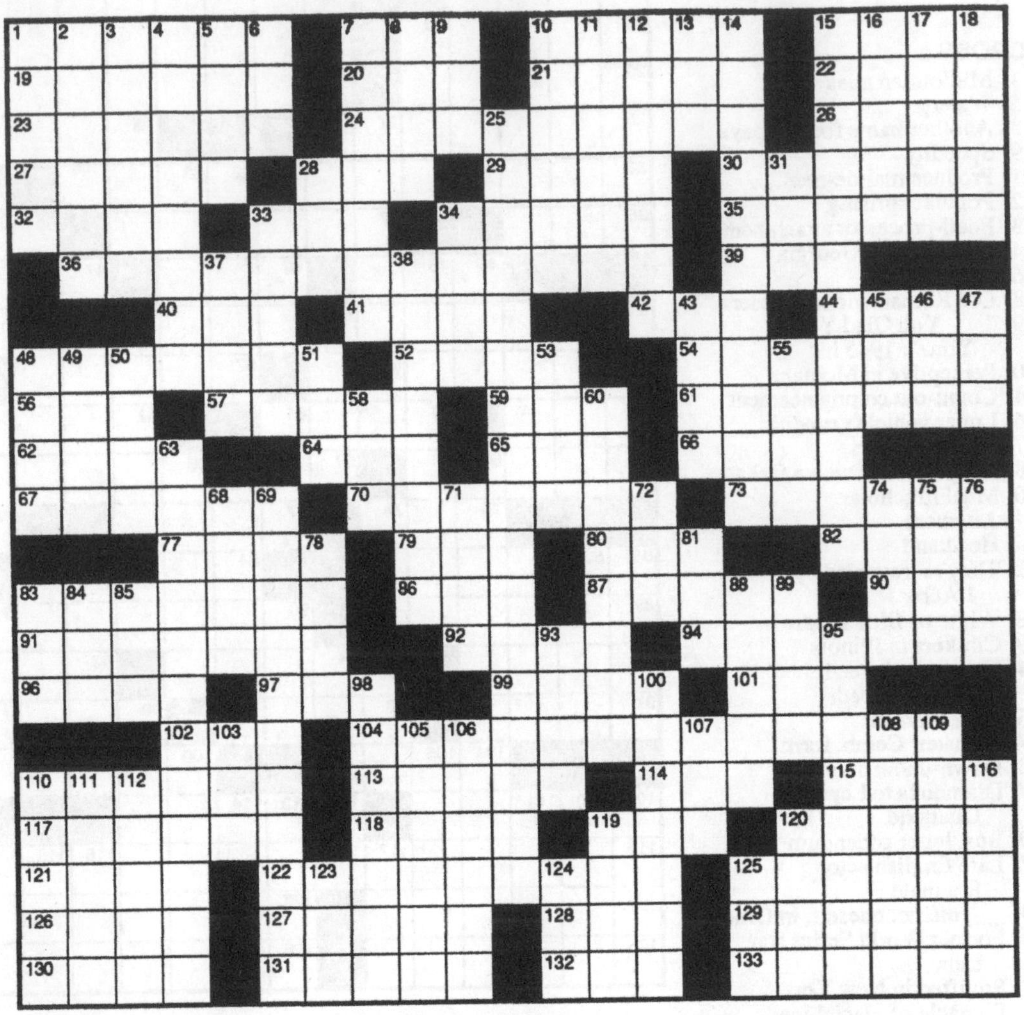

ACROSS

1 Messenger of the gods
7 ___ vous plaît
10 Conductor Caldwell
15 "Shucks" kin
19 Mountain nymphs
20 "___ my heart beats . . ."
21 ___ de Chine
22 Russian mountains
23 Gridiron list of players
24 Unheeded prophetess
26 He dispatched Octavia
27 Fragrant oil
28 Dined
29 ___ bien
30 Thomas Moore poem
32 Told a whopper
33 Spanish year
34 Former Reagan counselor
35 Wolf-pack members
36 Pass over a drive in Costa Mesa
39 Sock sound
40 Tire's groove
41 "The big house"
42 Part of D.O.D.
44 Actress Patricia
48 Officers on the QE2
52 Facial contractions
54 Moon pits
56 Sched. info
57 "The Velvet Fog"
59 Roman deity
61 Blue-pencil
62 Attire
64 Director Peckinpah
65 "The Name of the Rose" author
66 C Sicilian city
67 Close-fitting dress
70 Talk louder
73 Field hand
77 ___ Huang-ti (Chinese emperor)
79 Prescription's "three times"
80 Saturate
82 Knowledge
83 Breeding ground for cheaters?
86 Angel's delight
87 It takes a licking
90 ___ of worms
91 Publishing houses, e.g.
92 "All ___": 1931 song
94 Grappler's grip
96 Tide type
97 ___ Chiang, Chinese writer
99 "___ I say, not as I do"
101 Social gathering
102 Actor Erwin
104 Rocket along a drive in Tallahassee
110 Slumbering
113 The sniffles, et al.
114 Slippery fish
115 Greek letters
117 Typewriter part
118 Few: Comb. form
119 "And fades awa' like morning ___"
120 ___ -pat
121 ___ sapiens
122 Detached, in a way
125 Traction devices
126 Tree of Life locale
127 ___ limit (draws the line)
128 Tiny
129 Sonnet's last six lines
130 Jerk
131 Waste maker
132 Ex-Bruin great
133 Spuds

DOWN

1 Timely adjective
2 Amatory
3 One abed
4 They work the capes
5 West German river
6 Latvia, formerly
7 Circle portions
8 Dies
9 ___ Cayes
10 Hobgoblin, for one
11 Dillon portrayer
12 Marine crustaceans
13 Spring mo.
14 Move along a street in New Orleans
15 Motor on an avenue in Dallas
16 Omni or Joe Louis
17 Fortuneteller's card
18 Vegas "bandits"
25 Avoid a street in Wichita
28 Picnic pest
31 Nigerian
33 One of a Houston nine
34 1,007 to Cato
37 Tallow source
38 Endeavors
43 ___ homo
45 Shoe size
46 Longbow shape
47 Landing vessel
48 Thole pins
49 Wasatch Range state
50 "O ___ Ben Jonson!"
51 H.S. gp.
53 First or second
55 Tuscany river
58 Suffix for Christ
60 "The Social Contract" author
63 Go in reverse on a NYC avenue
68 "Of ___ I Sing"
69 Floor it on a street in Chicago
71 Saarinen
72 With roast or luck
74 Crazed
75 Epochal
76 Tear apart
78 Wall Street org.
81 Tap gently
83 ___ Tin Tin
84 Carbohydrate suffix
85 Explorer/author Johnson
88 Tourist's stopover
89 Chick's sound
93 Witticisms
95 Most lighthearted
98 Ball figures
100 Trooper's target
103 Peg for Strange
105 Jan C. Smuts follower
106 Certain Roman wreaths
107 Bench
108 Real ___
109 Star of "Three's Company"
110 Pallid
111 Chinaware
112 More unsatisfactory
116 Methods: Abbr.
119 Roebuck
120 ___ bargaining
123 Teachers' org.
124 ___-by-four
125 Minn. time

157 DOLLARS AND SENSE by Bert H. Kruse

With glasnost part of our language now, the epigram below assumes a timely perspective.

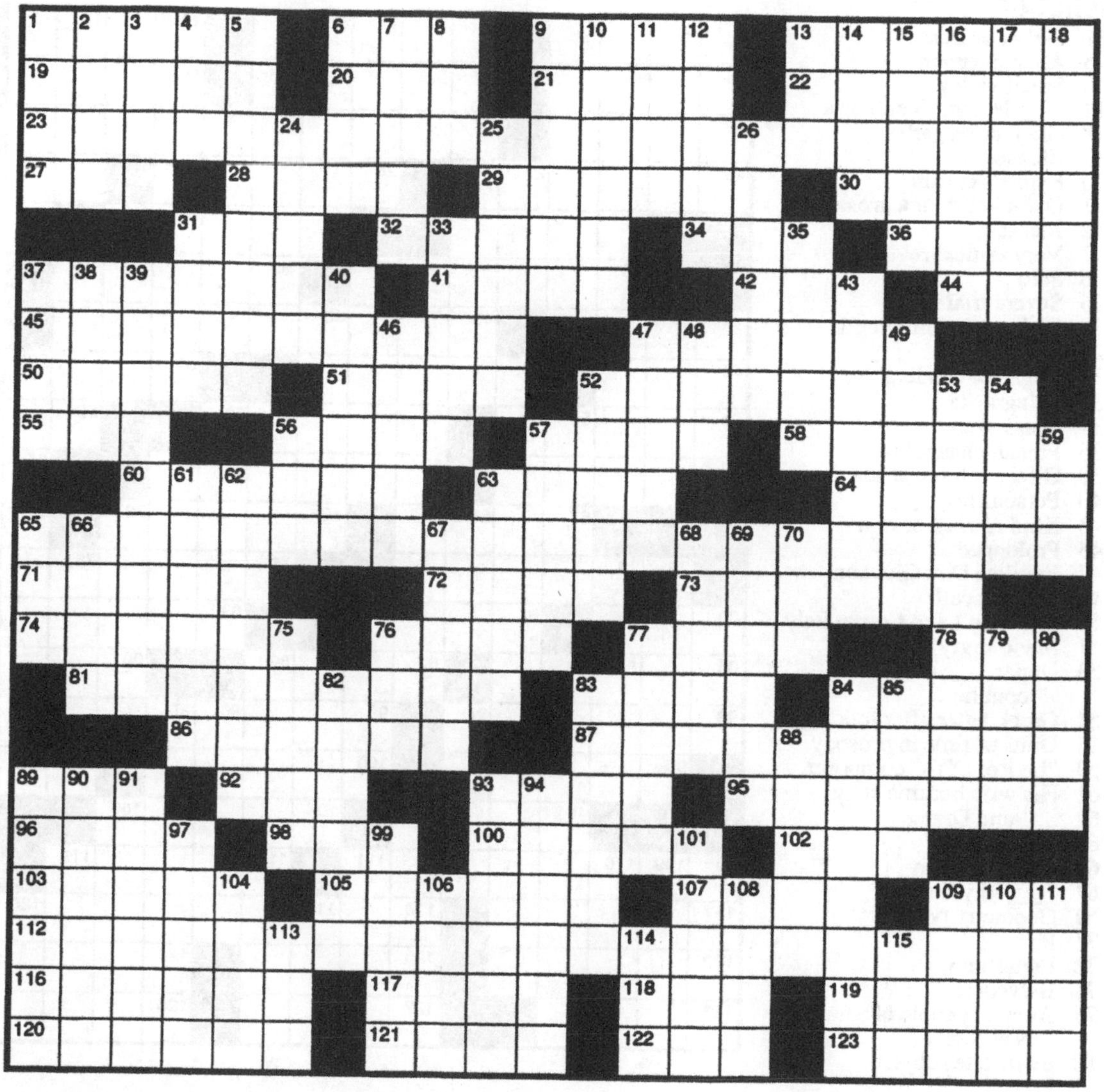

ACROSS

1 Tam-tams
6 Do in
9 Film Fido
13 Like Nike or Pegasus
19 Make up for
20 Literary collection
21 Nervousness
22 One who worships
23 **Start of an epigram**
27 Forever
28 Snick's pal
29 Flutist Jean-Paul
30 Brown shade
31 "Shoo!" in the Ozarks
32 Kind of infinitive
34 Please Satan
36 Feat
37 Tonsil
41 Saarinen
42 ___ es Salaam
44 Grads-to-be: Abbr.
45 Capitalists
47 Soft leathers
50 Samples
51 Make the grade
52 Deepened a well
55 Letters on a Cardinal cap
56 Italian arts patron
57 Saintly symbol
58 Poured
60 Fifth, e.g.
63 Napoleonic victory site
64 Alexander's birthplace
65 **Epigram continued**
71 Sinking, as a ship
72 Awful, with "the"
73 Basque beanies
74 Certain leagues
76 Contradict
77 Kind of house
78 Fielding's Jones
81 Accord
83 Colorful ware
84 Lobster claw
86 Bank customers
87 Parts of beds
89 New Deal org.
92 Thy, in Tours
93 Dock
95 Bone cavities
96 Dr. Zhivago's love
98 Drop off
100 Call off
102 Explosive
103 Dye-producing shrubs
105 Hat
107 Abhor
109 Flab
112 **Epigram concluded**
116 It may have eyes
117 Indian garb
118 Rehan
119 Not good for you
120 Indicates displeasure
121 Lanchester
122 Attorney's place
123 Tennis ratings

DOWN

1 Water or Golden follower
2 Roman emperor
3 Brown-bag time
4 Antelope
5 "Montezuma" composer
6 Grey of westerns
7 High range
8 Dance step
9 Romance
10 Appear so
11 Pipe tool
12 Opera highlights
13 Event in 1812
14 Roman date
15 Pried
16 Delaware and Catawba
17 More weird
18 Fears
24 Dido
25 More ___ (approximately)
26 Quiet plane
31 Little pest
33 Intrinsically
35 Acme's opposite
37 Ship areas
38 Take it off
39 Enthralling to excess
40 Serves the soup
43 Backslide
46 Nibbler
47 Pause in the Psalms
48 Japanese herb
49 Most foxy
52 Carries on
53 Recruiters
54 Poet Walter ___ Mare
56 King's lang.
57 Like a pro lineman, e.g.
59 ___ Cupid
61 Sun protectors
62 Beg
63 Dive
65 Flee
66 Pelvic bones
67 Begins
68 Congo tributary
69 Goes to the altar again
70 Vase
75 "___ come eleven!"
76 German article
77 "___ is human . . . "
79 Ye ___ taverne
80 Celebration of the Eucharist
82 Minnesota ore range
83 "Relativity" is one
84 Gets a hit
85 ___ monde (high society)
88 Please, in Potsdam
89 Embraces
90 Grand or Bryce
91 "The Count of Monte ___"
93 Dads of Etonians
94 Spanish peninsula, once
97 Where "I do's" are heard
99 Western law bunch
101 Bara of films
104 Cobblestone's cousin
106 Grandparental
108 Distant, poet.
109 Idée ___
110 Straining at the bit
111 Gumshoes
113 Yr. units
114 Flounder
115 Golf club part

158 VERTICAL DISORDER by Kenneth Haxton

You'll have your downs and ups when solving this tricky creation.

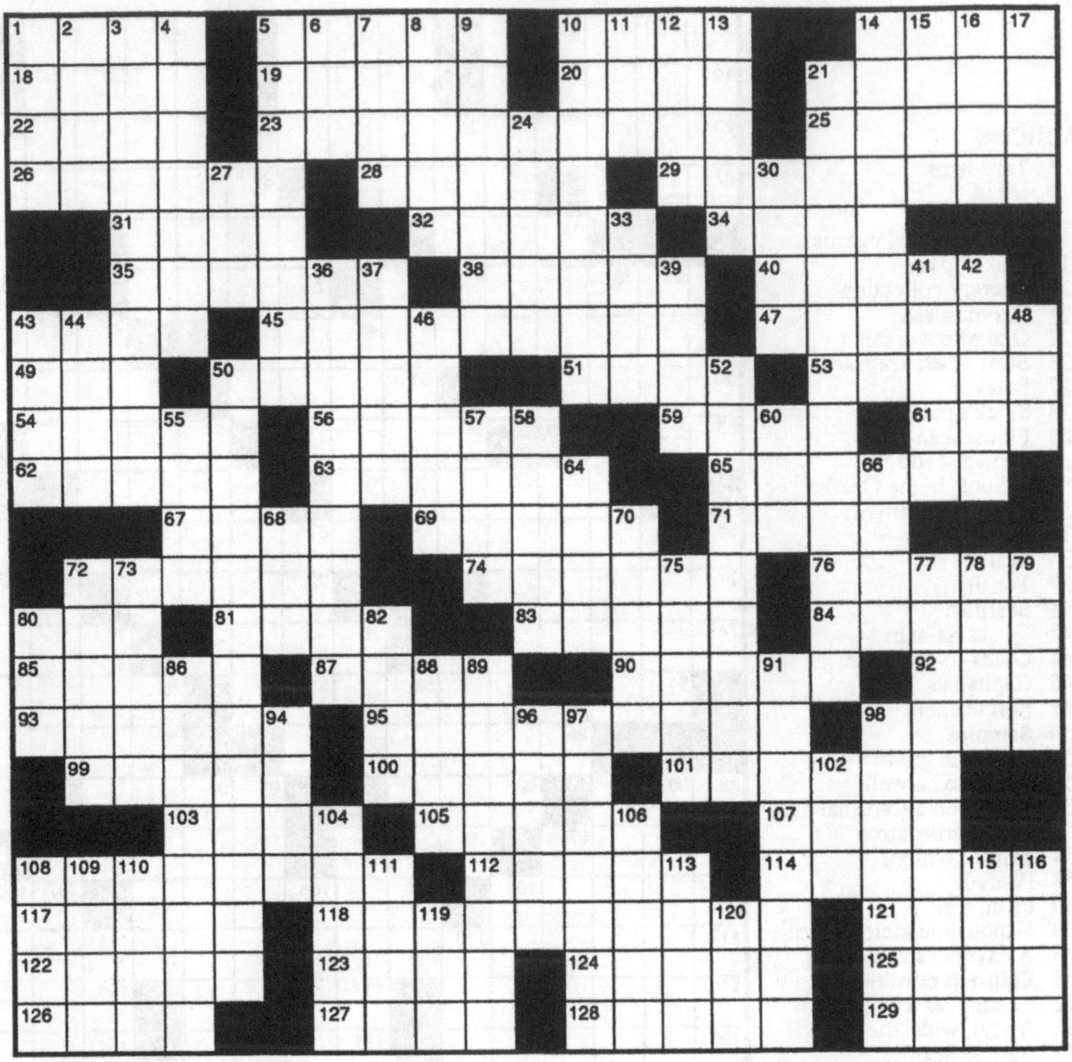

ACROSS

1 Ferber or Best
5 A younger son
10 Small valley
14 "___ Nome," Verdi aria
18 Graduation garb
19 Ellipses
20 Rapier's cousin
21 One-twelfth of a gross
22 Blessing
23 Very critical review
25 Solo
26 Severe trial
28 He burns midnight oil
29 Coup
31 Logan or Cinders
32 Telegraphs
34 Glass oven
35 French channel city
38 Gilbert's force at sea
40 Persona non ___
43 Kind of rock or rain
45 Prolonged
47 Emulate Don Giovanni
49 Distress call
50 Town on Lake Como, Italy
51 Made angry
53 Upper ___, ex-African republic
54 Greek letter after iota
56 Units of time in prosody
59 "Le Roi D'Ys" composer
61 His wife became salty
62 ___ und Drang
63 Papal capes
65 Spring holiday
67 "___ Rhythm"
69 Geometry type
71 Pit
72 Lodestone
74 Belvedere
76 Ancient people of NW Sicily
80 Swift-tale subject
81 Press
83 Spartan serf
84 First name in rock
85 "Sweeney ___ the Nightingales"
87 Sonar sound
90 Sassy
92 One ampere turn per maxwell
93 Stage parts
95 Learning
98 Choreographer Tommy
99 Subway appurtenance
100 Extinct ratites
101 Washington portraitist
103 Ruffian
105 Western lilies
107 Lady Jane
108 Cuban cutlasses
112 Shining
114 Gamal Abdel
117 Tennyson's Arden
118 Conventionalized representation
121 Agile
122 Mr. Chips of screen
123 Verboten
124 Lap dogs, for short
125 Town in Texas or Louisiana
126 Fictional midshipman
127 Small island
128 Antony and Clarissa
129 Small automatic gun

DOWN

1 Nigerian secret society for males
2 Aperture
3 Vertical disorder
4 Red-blooded worm
5 Prostration
6 Actress Gardner
7 Humid
8 Jostle
9 Russian ruler's spouse
10 Vertical disorder
11 Finial ornament
12 Forerunner of 65 Across
13 Within the law
14 Paul Whiteman's home state
15 Black Sea arm
16 Lacoste of tennis
17 Singular person
21 Vertical disorder of two kinds
24 Eastern inn
27 Stout
30 Containers for 27 Down
33 Foreteller
36 Vertical disorder
37 Flight, in France
39 Henry James biographer
41 Thin silk
42 Thespian
43 Interrogates
44 Chesterfield
46 African antelopes (anagram for roast)
48 Have brunch
50 Vertical disorder, re a tarot card
52 Vertical disorder
55 A precisionist
57 Like a bump on ___
58 Biblical pause
60 Indo-Chinese language
64 Dimensions
66 Swiss archer
68 Above, to Swinburne
70 Home of Vermeer
72 "Swell" disease
73 Cancel a shuttle flight
75 Netman Becker
77 Vertical disorder
78 Aspect
79 Dot on a map
80 Chinese pagoda
82 Necessity
86 New Providence Island, Bahamas
88 Psyche's beloved
89 Vertical disorder
91 Condition of feeling close or warm
94 Boiler plate
96 Stray calf
97 Almost identical species of an atom
98 Long locks
102 Palm cockatoo
104 "Beau ___,": Wren
106 Located
108 Ancient Asiatic
109 Celebes ox
110 Bilks
111 Corset part
113 Mound to prevent inundation
115 Dashiell contemporary
116 Tatum's dad
119 Central American tree
120 Female swan

159

NAME GAME by Louis Baron

You may have played this game before, but never quite like the way you are about to play it now. Mr. B. has added a few variations of his own just for the pun of it.

ACROSS

1 Sprays with gunfire
8 Kaiser's kin
12 Have, in Fife
15 Jalopy
19 Free time
20 Large kangaroo
21 Maritime bird
22 Killer whale
23 Mainstream writer of Turin?
25 ___ said than done!
27 Pristine retreats
28 Ballistic missile
29 "Wild Dog" of rock?
31 Nabors role
32 "The Breeze ___," 1940 song
33 Suborder of reptiles
34 Tibetan gazelle
37 Irish
39 Suffix for journal
40 Died down
44 He went to town in Chungking?
49 Leblanc's Lupin
50 "I ___ Camera"
51 "___ Gang"
52 Malayan boat
53 T, in Tel Aviv
55 Black
56 Potala priest
58 Snitch
60 Not attended to
62 Nidus
63 Canines
65 Uncommunicative
67 Composer de la Halle
68 Stuff oneself
70 Newsy bit
74 May's stones
77 In bondage
81 Seem
85 Menotti's "The ___"
86 Tear
87 Henri's head
88 Sand's "___ et Lui"
89 ___ and outs
90 Shocked reaction
93 Dracula's alter ego
95 Dir.
96 Jehovah
98 Cutting-room emperor?
101 Oppenheimer colleague
102 Singer's syllable
104 Hindu fire god
105 Prefix for center
106 "Strangers on ___," 1951 film
108 Hodgepodge: Abbr.
110 Wind
114 Sheriff in a western?
118 Concerning
119 Pulpits
120 London's "The ___"
121 One of five Zorbas?
124 Little Caesar
125 Wish one hadn't
126 Dies ___
127 Poet Cullen
128 Part of LIFO
129 Agent
130 Extol
131 Stevedores

DOWN

1 Realm of Hypnos
2 Kind of bear
3 Orion star
4 Fragile ___
5 Miniver and ermiline
6 Epoch
7 Author Lagerlof
8 Start of a cry
9 Windshield shade
10 French sculptor: 1887-1966
11 Cross
12 Hair tints
13 "O, what ___ . . . am I!": Shak.
14 Pre-surrealist: 1860-1949
15 Cowboy playwright?
16 Soprano Sack
17 Maple genus
18 Young trout or salmon
24 Like some coats
26 Willow
30 "___ Your Face Before Me"
35 Ear: Comb. form
36 Sky-blue
38 Hummer of "Symphonie Espagnole"?
41 Actress Daniels
42 Seth's son
43 Impression
44 College since 1701
45 Dancer Carmen
46 Put the finger on
47 Part of Q.E.D.
48 Uhlans' weapons
49 State
53 Audrey of films
54 Babylonian sky god
57 ___ standstill
59 Spines
61 Through: Prefix
64 Ayr uncle
65 Dravidian language
66 Zilch
69 Anatomical duct
71 Make Alençon
72 Levels off
73 Bandwagon jumper's words
75 Ovidian 1102
76 Ages and ages
78 Avian bills
79 NASA milieu
80 Earl ___ Biggers
81 Caterpillar's dinner
82 Ye ___ inne
83 Cygnet's genus
84 Repressed cowboy?
91 Rho followers
92 Disciplined
94 Waiter's expectation
97 Gee follower
98 Goodall or Pauley
99 To place, to Virgil
100 Romberg or Freud
102 Bind with adhesive
103 Man to believe—or not!
107 Afrikaners' rifles
109 End: Abbr.
111 Have ___ to eat
112 Party shunner
113 ___ Park, CO
114 Lass
115 Sortita
116 Legendary avians
117 Part of RR
119 Greenish-blue
122 New Deal agcy.
123 ___-hoo

160

MISSING VOWL by Robert H. Anderson
Solvers should study Robert's title carefully. It relates to a theme which directly affects 50% of the answers below.

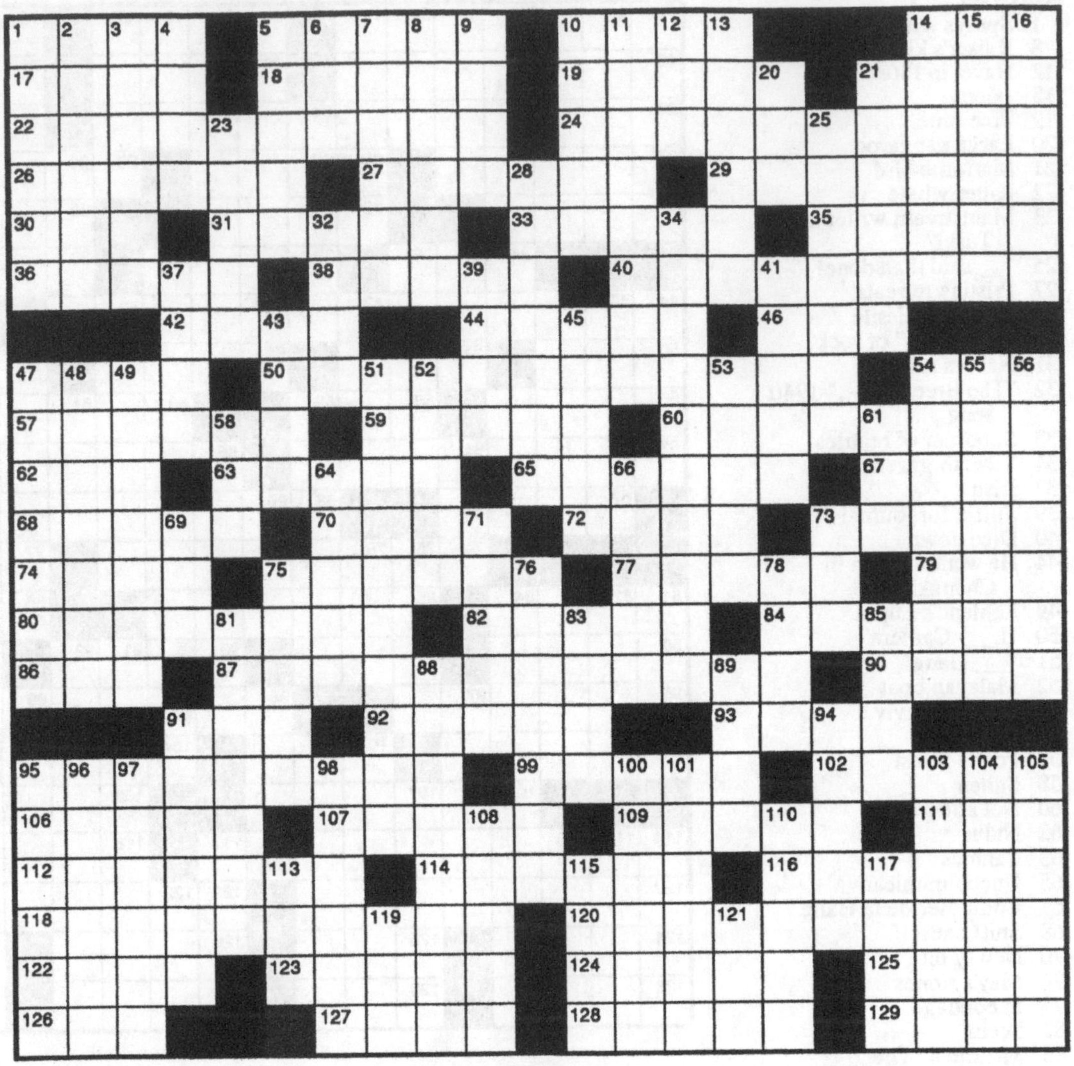

ACROSS

1 Khan, et al.
5 Spanish coins
10 ___ de force
14 Sour compound: Comb. form
17 Palm tree
18 Cleaner
19 Tapestry
21 Tropical American tree
22 Westwall
24 Planetary measure
26 Go aboard
27 Kind of hornblende
29 Unpolished
30 Very, in Vichy
31 Scamper
33 Hilo hello
35 ___-marie (steam tables)
36 Floating island, e.g.
38 Laudatory piece
40 Flighty ones
42 Whitish
44 Diversified
46 Hemisphere gp.
47 Tolerably
50 Author of column "My Day"
54 Actor Waterston
57 Affixes
59 Topics
60 She hosted "Beat the Band"
62 Thespian's delight: Abbr.
63 Omit
65 Colorful fabric
67 Nothing, in Seville
68 Weight unit
70 Constitution, e.g.
72 Triplet
73 It's at one's fingertips
74 Carry ___ (sing on key)
75 Essential oils
77 Birthplace of Jainism
79 Fr. pronoun
80 Nylon, e.g.
82 Quite ___ (difficult)
84 Tense
86 BMOCs
87 1823 declaration
90 Beginning
91 Skirt insert
92 St. Peter's nun
93 Someone else's child?
95 Warhol, e.g.
99 Brick buildings
102 Ounce's sixteen
106 Rumor
107 IRA, for one
109 Three (horses) in line
111 Meadow sound
112 Flowering cactus
114 Scamp
116 Helpful
118 Dense celestial object
120 Hawthorne's "A"
122 Tallied
123 Essay
124 Sacrificial place
125 Pentateuch: Var.
126 Rigid
127 ___ up (learns)
128 Used-car deals
129 Curtain

DOWN

1 Went along
2 Spats
3 Make an attack
4 Furniture piece
5 Rupert, for one
6 Was apparently true
7 Aromatic hydrocarbon
8 Patience is ___
9 Evening love song
10 Dravidian language
11 Choral work
12 Homophone of earn
13 Give forth
14 Qatar locale
15 Harvard president: 1933-53
16 Fills with wrath
20 Geometric ratio
21 Fastenings
23 Give ___ (cause)
25 Denied
28 Roman royal standard
32 Stem-borer beetle
34 Analyst: Slang
37 Avignon's river
39 Venerates
41 Exactions
43 Moreover
45 Optimistic
47 Some Homer works
48 Ma Bell employee
49 Seeds
51 Slumberland attire
52 Port of ancient Rome
53 Delicious dish
54 Tentacled marine animal
55 Difficult
56 Happy Olympian
58 Dexterous
61 Wildebeest
64 ___ peace
66 Most jejune
69 ___ which way
71 Madrid museum
73 Father of Regan
75 Lifeless, once
76 Warehouses
78 ___ tube
81 Little cupid
83 Sch.
85 Registered one
88 Swaps superiorly
89 "Peer Gynt" author
91 Collected
94 Acknowledge
95 Turn the palm downward
96 Controvert
97 Certain pigeons
98 Agitated
100 Divine revelations
101 Sapodilla
103 Nuisance ridder: Law
104 Mystic formula
105 Petty tyrant
108 Cooper and Hart
110 Casino workers
113 The elected
115 Romero
117 Expunged
119 Ornamental case
121 Abnormal rattle

161 HEAR IT NOW! by Bert Rosenfield

Famous inventors of the past have been brought to the present through the magic of crosswords and Bert's witty mind.

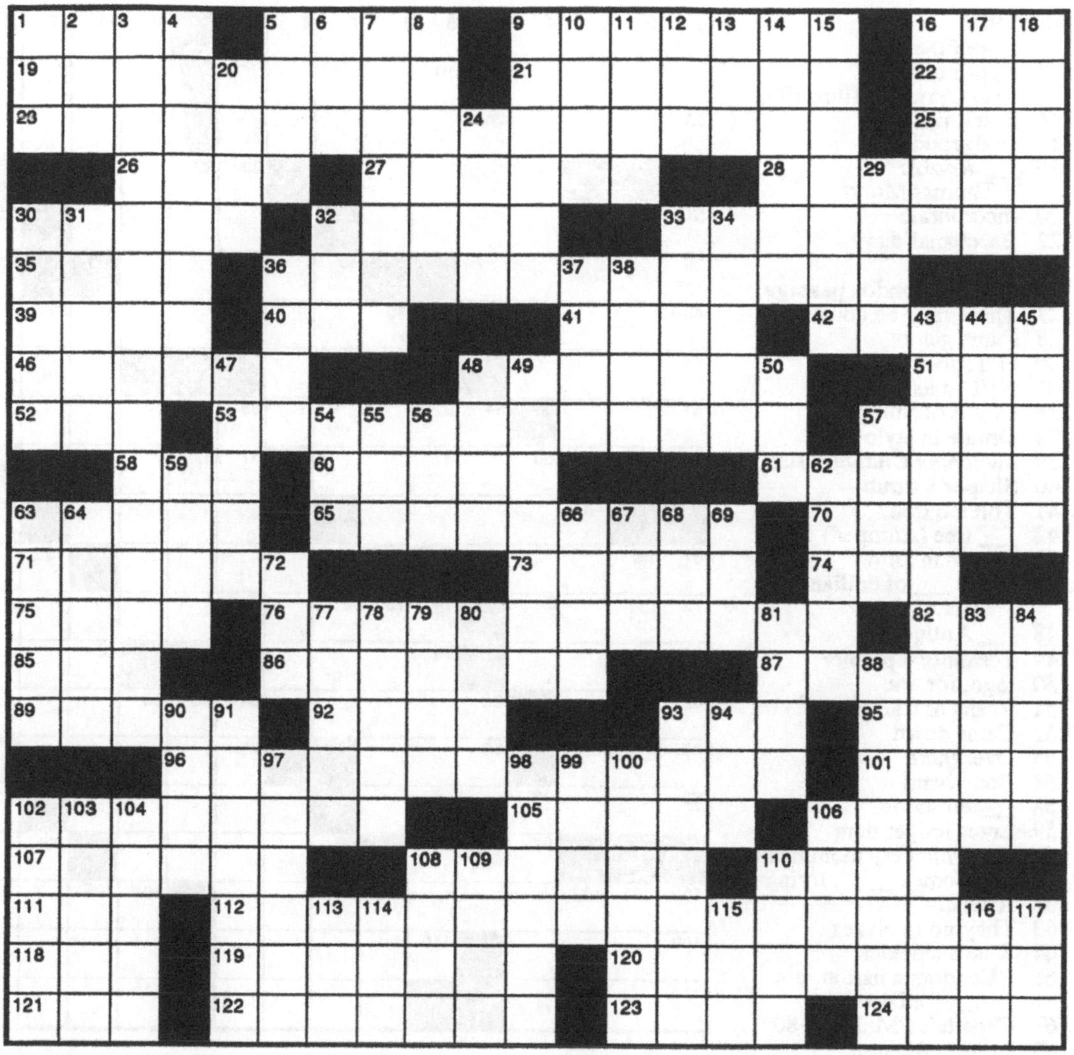

ACROSS

1 Singer Cantrell
5 Kind of distinction
9 Least craven
16 Spring berry
19 Fervent
21 Trattoria offering
22 ___ carte
23 Whine from Henry Ford?
25 Beiderbecke
26 Too
27 Galeazzo and Edda
28 Summer flounder
30 ___ Kaigi: Japanese labor union
32 Elegant billiard shot
33 Divinely designated
35 Litter member
36 Beef from Johann Gutenberg?
39 Thine, in Thiers
40 ___ vous plaît
41 Carryall
42 De Valera of Eire
46 ". . . ___ pail of water"
48 Presumptive living cell sources
51 Peruvian soprano Sumac
52 Singer's syllable
53 Grumble from Samuel F. B. Morse?
57 Ottoman Empire standard
58 Through
60 Rides a hang-glider
61 Asylum
63 Bergen's bumpkin
65 Yelp from Guglielmo Marconi?
70 Former TV show set in Nevada
71 Embroidery decoration
73 Bribe
74 Part of a joule
75 Where the collar rubs
76 Snarl from Thomas Edison?
82 Ripen
85 Corrida cry
86 He hit over .300 eighteen times
87 Old ___: veteran performer
89 Request to the waiter
92 King known to Steed
93 Major TV ntwk.
95 "Concert of Angels" painter
96 Scream from Alexander Graham Bell?
101 End of a billion
102 Emulsifying agents
105 Greenspan and Cranston
106 Orbits
107 Spoonbill relatives
108 Modugno's 1958 song hit
110 Etc. relative
111 Friday, for one
112 Groan from Robert Fulton?
118 Ear: Comb. form
119 Bent like a bow
120 Medical assays
121 Ball or total
122 1961 U.S. Open golf champ
123 In the know
124 Pennsylvanie, e.g.

DOWN

1 ___ Zeppelin of rock
2 Boss, in Bilbao
3 Squawk from Galileo Galilei?
4 Strapping
5 De ___: afresh
6 Saturn or serpent ending
7 Unkind form of criticism
8 Kay Thompson's Plaza kid
9 Sarawak's neighbor
10 Puerto ___
11 Opens the dicker
12 Tenn. footballer
13 Hiver's opposite
14 Blackout
15 Predominant
16 Wont
17 Faye or Brady
18 Like some mustaches
20 Former Romanian capital
24 Sparafucile, for one
29 Buffalo's kin
30 Kind of beer
31 ___ Mongolia
32 D + D + XXX + XXI
33 Less irrelevant
34 Exceedingly
36 ___ example
37 Take on cargo
38 W African republic
43 Wail from Wilbur Wright?
44 Last of a sequence
45 Appoints to a post
47 Insect or cannibal group
48 City on the Aare
49 "Screaming Eagle" or "Big Red One"
50 Armenia or Est., once
54 Omaha Beach transp.
55 "___ Do Something to Me": Porter
56 Gob
57 The southwest wind
59 Della's creator
62 6-time U.S. tennis champ
63 Ballesteros, formally
64 African antelope
66 Hotfoot it
67 Mel of Cooperstown
68 Copier product: Abbr.
69 6-ft. naut. depth
72 Turner ntwk.
77 Author Sinclair
78 Toronto team, for short
79 Upchuck
80 Card game for three
81 Evan or coal ending
83 Kind
84 Cat Nation
88 Plains Indian
90 Concerns of Fichte and Hume
91 Renovation
93 One member in an alley game
94 Units led by lt. cols.
97 First Jewish month
98 Restrain, in a way
99 King in I Kings
100 Texas city of song
102 Paul or Carly
103 Wane
104 ___ Blanc (wine)
106 Abbr. on an envelope
108 Schnitzel component
109 Bony prefix
110 Such being the case
113 External: Comb. form
114 Same old 9-to-5
115 Feedbag morsel
116 Grassland
117 Mass. time

162

VERY VIATIC by Mary Murdoch

If you're wondering about that word in Mary's title, it is found in a few unabridged dictionaries. Anyway, after solving the puzzle below, you won't be wondering what *viatic* means.

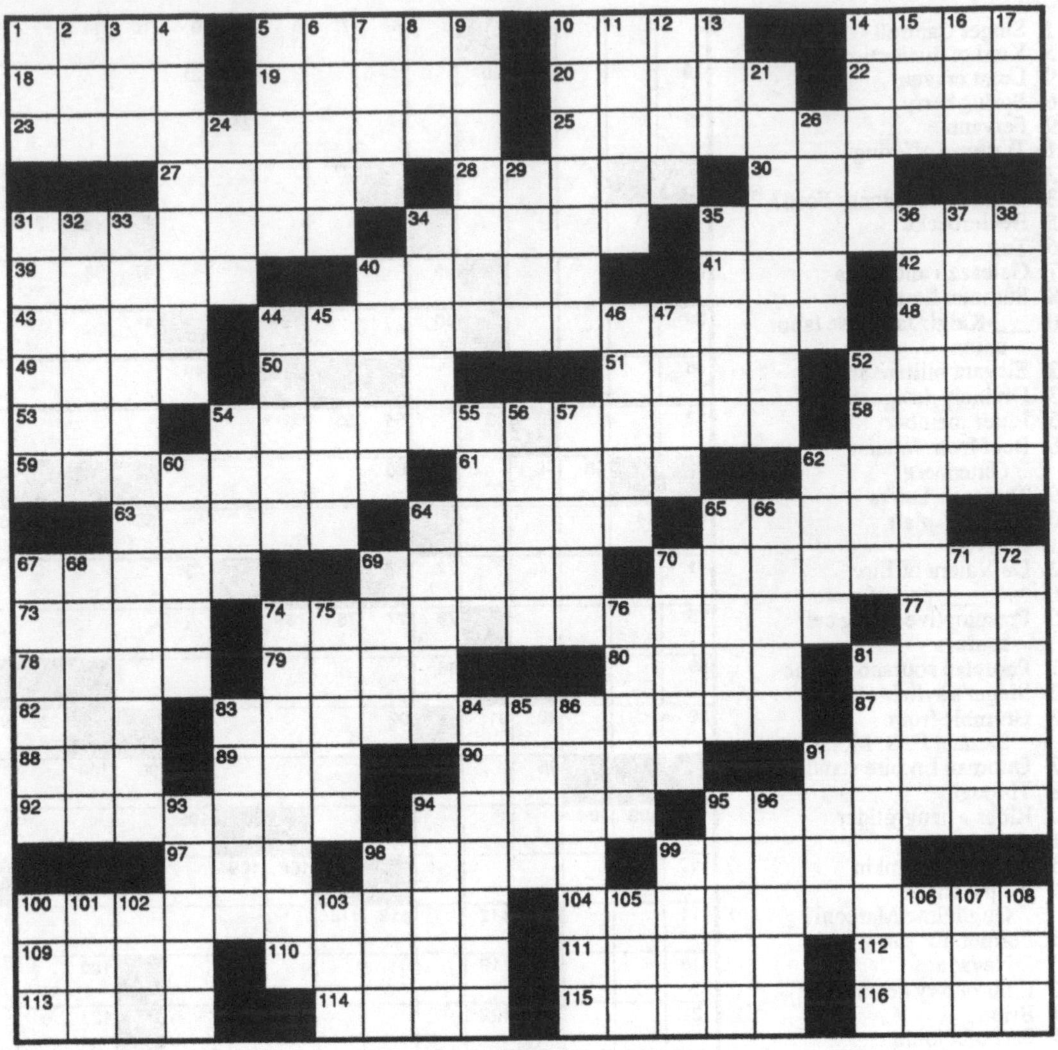

ACROSS

1 Not of the cloth
5 Cyprinoid fish
10 Joan Crawford film: 1932
14 Entertain
18 Hodgepodge
19 ___ *Rookh*: Thomas Moore
20 Incorporate
22 Bacchanal's cry
23 Cul-de-sac
25 Famous London passage
27 These may be counted
28 Puma genus
30 N. T. book
31 NHL stats
34 City E of Stuttgart
35 Ornate in style
39 *Switching Channels* star
40 Shapes a shrub
41 Tolkien tree
42 ___ tree (stumped)
43 Dream in Dijon
44 "The ___ of dalliance": Shak.
48 ___ Antiqua
49 Terminer's partner
50 Iago, for one
51 Evans or Carnegie
52 Came down
53 Over there
54 Bon vivant
58 ___ en scène
59 Lives longer than
61 ". . . his very monument becomes ___": Irving
62 After
63 They go to blazes
64 Kate's sidekick
65 "London: a nation, not ___": Disraeli
67 Canada's PM: 1979–80
69 Actress Burstyn
70 Nonbelievers
73 Great review
74 Joan Crawford film: 1949
77 Turf org.
78 Birds' class
79 Leinster locale
80 Pervade
81 Hindu titles
82 Sportscaster Scully
83 Liz Taylor film: 1954
87 Luck of the Irish
88 Col. in Tempe
89 Mailing to the IRS
90 Ada from Limerick
91 Ready, in Rouen
92 Till ___ come home
94 ___ of roses
95 Flew
97 Stir
98 Forerunner of bridge
99 Edge along
100 Sierra Nevada col
104 *Tales of a* ___: Longfellow
109 In ___ (routinely bored)
110 Implied from actions
111 Egyptian Zeus
112 Author Jaffe
113 Words for Nanette
114 Scads
115 O'Casey and Penn
116 Snick's partner

DOWN

1 Shot for Steffi
2 Alternative to nothing
3 Timely numerals
4 Schemer
5 Slangy good time
6 Chesty rattles
7 Old measures of length
8 Bock's brother
9 Fashionable district of London
10 Like some eyeglasses
11 Forcefully
12 Nile bird
13 Buntline
14 "___, Goodbye": Beatles
15 Eggs
16 Robbie, to Evel
17 Football holder
21 Wine holder
24 Medicinal measure
26 Bridge position
29 Pollster Roper
31 Southwestern gulch
32 "I'll ___ in my Dreams"
33 Norman Bogner novel
34 French fighters
35 "___ Street Blues"
36 J. M. Barrie play
37 Ascend
38 When bonnets are bought
40 Works the soil
44 Matter-of-fact
45 Rummages about
46 Foy or Murphy
47 Ache
52 Fine fiddle
54 Soak up the rays
55 Actress Alida
56 *The Green Hat* author
57 Contrite
60 Erudition of varied cultures
62 What Pinocchio did
64 Dancer of Cairo
65 Coral reef
66 Score
67 Tie
68 Posh
69 Famed gunfighter
70 Suffix for sect
71 Sad, in Sèvres
72 Talked back
74 Woolly-leafed plant
75 Property claims
76 *The Winds* ___: Wouk
81 Tools for icy windshields
83 Ravage
84 Daubigny and David
85 Lacrosse goals
86 Part of *TW3*
91 Varicolored
93 Poetic division
94 Harte's Heathen Chinee
95 A felony
96 Lodes
98 Baylor U site
99 Classical arch. molding
100 Quayle or Coats
101 Start of Montana's motto
102 Sister
103 Mr. Paulsen
105 French soul
106 A son of Apollo
107 Vane reading
108 Negative in Paisley

163

A LITTLE HUMOUR by Dale Storms

Brit wit is featured by our bright wit from Norwich, New York. The subtlety of Dale's title may elude some Canadian solvers

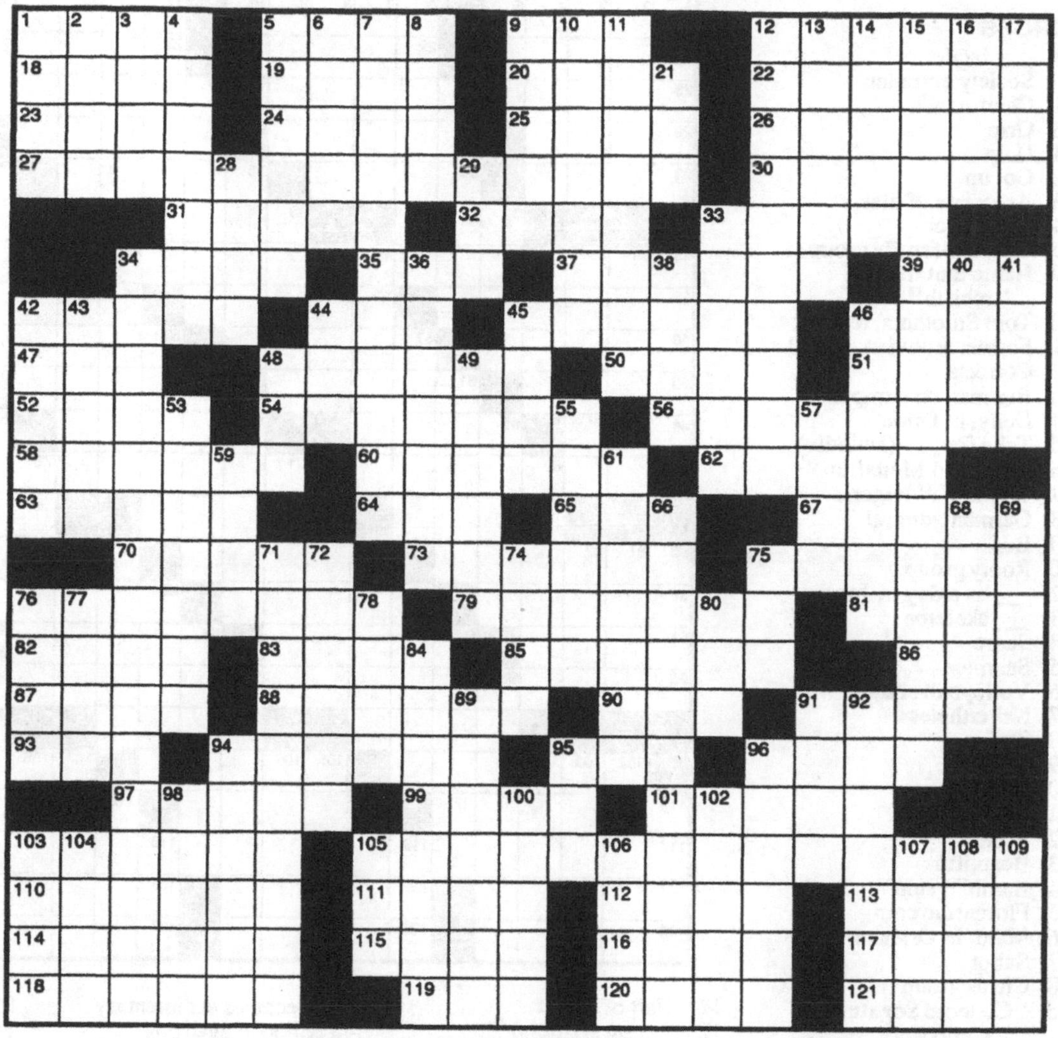

ACROSS

1 A Bridges
5 Christian rel. gp.
9 Globe
12 Muncher
18 Jai ___
19 Nomadic Muslim
20 Ziegfeld's Anna
22 *From ___ Eternity*
23 With hard or soft
24 Teased
25 Enthusiastic
26 Best: Comb. form
27 Robin's retreat
30 Straight muscle
31 "I Can Dream, ___?"
32 Tired
33 College in Ohio
34 Longings
35 Heat or Jazz org.
37 Smooth and even, to 40 Down
39 Miss Hogg
42 Nautical adverb
44 Big Ottoman
45 In Hinduism, the four life phases
46 Danish king of England: 1017–35
47 For each
48 Half a rack
50 Thick slice
51 Bone: Comb. form
52 Exasperates
54 Stone Age tool
56 Shuttle of NASA
58 Size up
60 "His wife could eat ___"
62 Hatchet handle
63 Kind of jacket
64 ___ Anne de Bellevue
65 Target for boo birds
67 Sumatran goat antelope
70 Metrical feet
73 Silk fabric of yore
75 European principality
76 Sedan shelters
79 They have dendrites
81 Lift for schussboomers
82 S-curve
83 Vexes
85 Ejected
86 Sandwich
87 Agents
88 Earl Grey holder
90 Stop the bidder
91 Voodoo fetish
93 East Lansing col.
94 Detroit hoopster
95 Mid.
96 Attack time
97 Kind of code
99 Harvest
101 Longhorn
103 Chic
105 Conflicts among climbers?
110 Narcotic
111 Bustles
112 Over-50 gp.
113 Disney dog
114 Lessee
115 New Zealand island
116 Genu
117 Arabian sultanate
118 Mysterious awards
119 Minn. time
120 Churchill's foreign secretary
121 Dotted, in heraldry

DOWN

1 Spielberg film
2 Where David killed Goliath
3 Diet
4 More hostile
5 Feudal vassals
6 Walking
7 London station and lovable bears
8 Not kosher
9 Airport with the ORD code
10 Displays
11 Signs of a bad paint job
12 Benevolent
13 Namibia native
14 Susan Lucci role
15 London lovelorn columnist?
16 Words for Brutus
17 Outback leapers
21 Banned insecticide
28 Crave
29 African tribal ruler
33 Biblical city in W Syria
34 Dessert for a terrier?
36 Votes
38 Festive
40 Maestro Riccardo
41 Sweetsop
42 Adjective for a drone
43 Deep blue
44 Chem. suffix
45 Johnson of TV
46 Nunnery
48 Abbreviated reply
49 Actress Brennan
53 Juárez wraps
55 In dire straits
57 Too
59 Mat sport of Matsue
61 Most intimate
66 Where Eliza Doolittle worked
68 Floridian city
69 Value
71 What Anglophobes hate and Anglophiles love
72 Suffix for seam
74 Hatchling's home
75 Medical deg.
76 Crocus bulb
77 Mellows
78 ___-of-the-pants
80 Catch, as a monarch
84 Occasional
89 Burdensome
91 River of SW Poland
92 Dry red Italian wines
94 Bug
95 Naval noncom
96 Dredge
98 Lariat
100 Poise, for one
102 ___ *Men and a Baby*
103 Knighted saint
104 Newspaper page
105 Pallid
106 Humbug
107 Corresponding in essentials
108 Town or cheese
109 Since, in the Highlands

164 GROUPTHINK by Joy Wouk

Joy says it's okay to get together with others while solving this one.

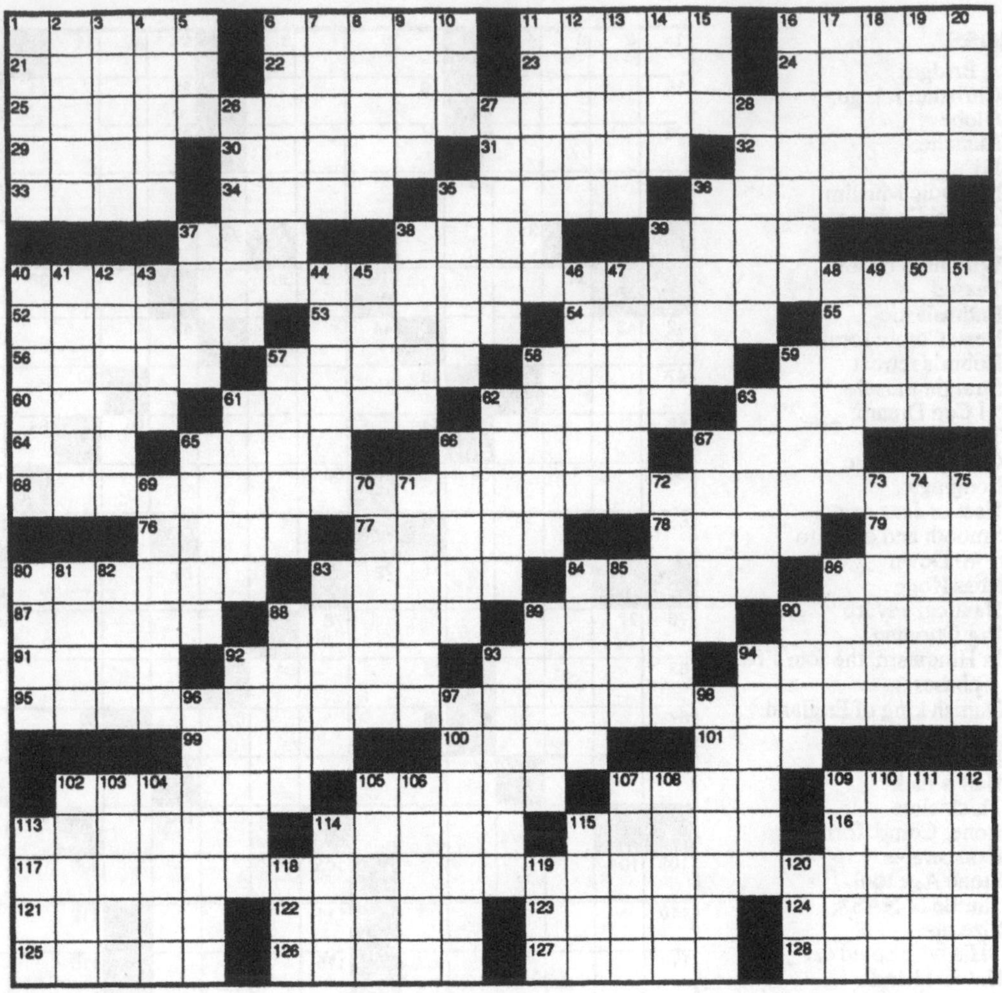

ACROSS

1 ___ fatale
6 Society entrance
11 Chair man?
16 Grip
21 Help
22 Got up
23 Associate of alas
24 Beekeeper
25 Mustard-family group
29 Name that means "rebirth"
30 Tom Smothers, to Dick
31 Former Bolivian capital
32 Corrects
33 Big man on campus
34 Deny, in Dijon
35 Take for ___ (swindle)
36 Lazar and Meredith
37 City in SW Nigeria
38 German admiral
39 Box
40 Rooty group
52 ___ as a day in June
53 ___ skeleton
54 Score
55 Saarinen
56 Volleyball slam
57 Nevertheless
58 Stale
59 Vacillate
60 Reserve
61 Taj ___
62 Winds
63 Beautiful
64 Bambi's aunt
65 Florentine coin
66 Maid, in Orléans
67 Sabot
68 Citrus group
76 "Concord Sonata" composer
77 Saltpeter
78 Contends
79 CEO's deg.
80 Did some sleight-of-hand
83 Aphids and borers
84 Corvine group
86 Barbecue item
87 Lithe
88 Billiards stroke
89 Value
90 Gem State city
91 ___ majesty
92 Dry, in Siena
93 Fragrance
94 More beautiful
95 Salad-bar group
99 Forget-me followers
100 Substantive
101 US biomedical agcy.
102 Political pamphlets
105 Ibsen play
107 Der ___ (the boss, in Bonn)
109 Box of beer
113 Site of some tempests
114 Raccoon's relative
115 Bedeck
116 Vipers
117 See 95 Across
121 Smart ___
122 Category of legal rights
123 Cicero's books
124 Part of an act
125 ___-nest (mess)
126 How a rhymester rhymes
127 Dutch genre painter
128 Throngs

DOWN

1 Confronted
2 Skirt
3 ___ Loa
4 Site of La Scala
5 Whitney
6 Idler
7 Eat away
8 Shady place
9 Consumer
10 Thrice: Comb. form
11 Kind of pigeon
12 With speaking voice
13 Mother-of-pearl
14 Here, in Napoli
15 Marquee monogram
16 Lion-headed monster
17 Compare
18 ___ garde
19 Unites
20 LBJ or HST
26 Swiss dish
27 Northern
28 Bequest
35 Dismay
36 Jonathan, for one
37 Being
38 Utter freely
39 Becomes sedimentary
40 Short-legged dog
41 Sevilla's location
42 Capital of Armenia
43 Seize
44 Hale
45 Corn lily
46 Kind of quartet
47 Brad's driver?
48 Orange squeezer
49 Dream of Nancy
50 Russian oblast
51 Disraeli or Thatcher
57 Rani's raiment
58 Color modifier
59 Weavers' concerns
61 Bogged
62 Arrives
63 Place for a peck
65 Quay
66 Reply to "danke"
67 Cardamom, e.g.
69 Borer
70 Rumanian composer
71 Supple
72 Lawyer, in Avignon
73 Arbiter
74 Stork-family members
75 Spuds
80 Lose strength
81 Former Amazin' Met
82 Roll
83 Agreements
84 Exhibit displeasure
85 Succotash bean
86 Evening in Eure
88 Pays (the bill) in full
89 Elated
90 *Brandenburg Concertos* composer
92 Soprano from Savona
93 Unaccented
94 Intimate
96 Opens a port
97 Detailed analysis
98 Board the Twentieth Century
102 Inventor who competed with Edison
103 Sullivan or Rahal
104 Quickly
105 Council
106 Untwist
107 Brick of Durango
108 *M* star
109 Portland's bay
110 Signs of smoking
111 Exhausted
112 "Satisfactory" letters
113 Tag or A follower
114 Supper, in Cadiz
115 UMW member's approach
118 Women's ___
119 Caiola and Hirt
120 Suffix for boy

165

A MANY-SPLENDORED THING by Joan Leemhorst
Our puzzler from West Hollywood says she's dedicating this one to Karen and Scott Valentine.

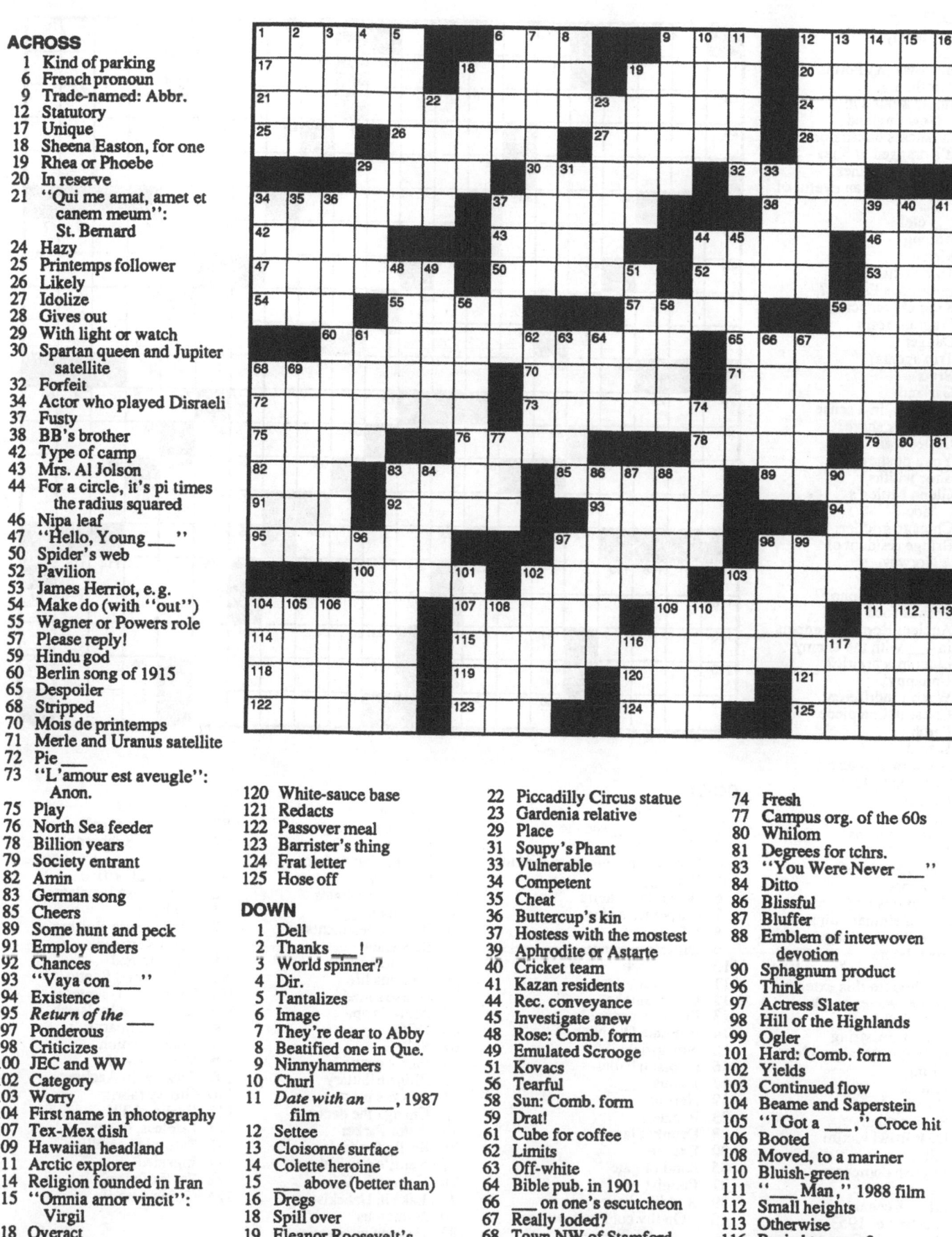

ACROSS
1 Kind of parking
6 French pronoun
9 Trade-named: Abbr.
12 Statutory
17 Unique
18 Sheena Easton, for one
19 Rhea or Phoebe
20 In reserve
21 "Qui me amat, amet et canem meum": St. Bernard
24 Hazy
25 Printemps follower
26 Likely
27 Idolize
28 Gives out
29 With light or watch
30 Spartan queen and Jupiter satellite
32 Forfeit
34 Actor who played Disraeli
37 Fusty
38 BB's brother
42 Type of camp
43 Mrs. Al Jolson
44 For a circle, it's pi times the radius squared
46 Nipa leaf
47 "Hello, Young ___"
50 Spider's web
52 Pavilion
53 James Herriot, e.g.
54 Make do (with "out")
55 Wagner or Powers role
57 Please reply!
59 Hindu god
60 Berlin song of 1915
65 Despoiler
68 Stripped
70 Mois de printemps
71 Merle and Uranus satellite
72 Pie ___
73 "L'amour est aveugle": Anon.
75 Play
76 North Sea feeder
78 Billion years
79 Society entrant
82 Amin
83 German song
85 Cheers
89 Some hunt and peck
91 Employ enders
92 Chances
93 "Vaya con ___"
94 Existence
95 *Return of the* ___
97 Ponderous
98 Criticizes
100 JEC and WW
102 Category
103 Worry
104 First name in photography
107 Tex-Mex dish
109 Hawaiian headland
111 Arctic explorer
114 Religion founded in Iran
115 "Omnia amor vincit": Virgil
118 Overact
119 Like sixteen
120 White-sauce base
121 Redacts
122 Passover meal
123 Barrister's thing
124 Frat letter
125 Hose off

DOWN
1 Dell
2 Thanks ___!
3 World spinner?
4 Dir.
5 Tantalizes
6 Image
7 They're dear to Abby
8 Beatified one in Que.
9 Ninnyhammers
10 Churl
11 *Date with an* ___, 1987 film
12 Settee
13 Cloisonné surface
14 Colette heroine
15 ___ above (better than)
16 Dregs
18 Spill over
19 Eleanor Roosevelt's column
22 Piccadilly Circus statue
23 Gardenia relative
29 Place
31 Soupy's Phant
33 Vulnerable
34 Competent
35 Cheat
36 Buttercup's kin
37 Hostess with the mostest
39 Aphrodite or Astarte
40 Cricket team
41 Kazan residents
44 Rec. conveyance
45 Investigate anew
48 Rose: Comb. form
49 Emulated Scrooge
51 Kovacs
56 Tearful
58 Sun: Comb. form
59 Drat!
61 Cube for coffee
62 Limits
63 Off-white
64 Bible pub. in 1901
66 ___ on one's escutcheon
67 Really loded?
68 Town NW of Stamford
69 Ditchmoss or waterweed
74 Fresh
77 Campus org. of the 60s
80 Whilom
81 Degrees for tchrs.
83 "You Were Never ___"
84 Ditto
86 Blissful
87 Bluffer
88 Emblem of interwoven devotion
90 Sphagnum product
96 Think
97 Actress Slater
98 Hill of the Highlands
99 Ogler
101 Hard: Comb. form
102 Yields
103 Continued flow
104 Beame and Saperstein
105 "I Got a ___," Croce hit
106 Booted
108 Moved, to a mariner
110 Bluish-green
111 "___ Man," 1988 film
112 Small heights
113 Otherwise
116 Buried treasure?
117 Star Wars: Abbr.

166 TRAVEL TRAVESTY by Mary Snyder

Below is proof that traveling violations aren't restricted solely to the basketball court!

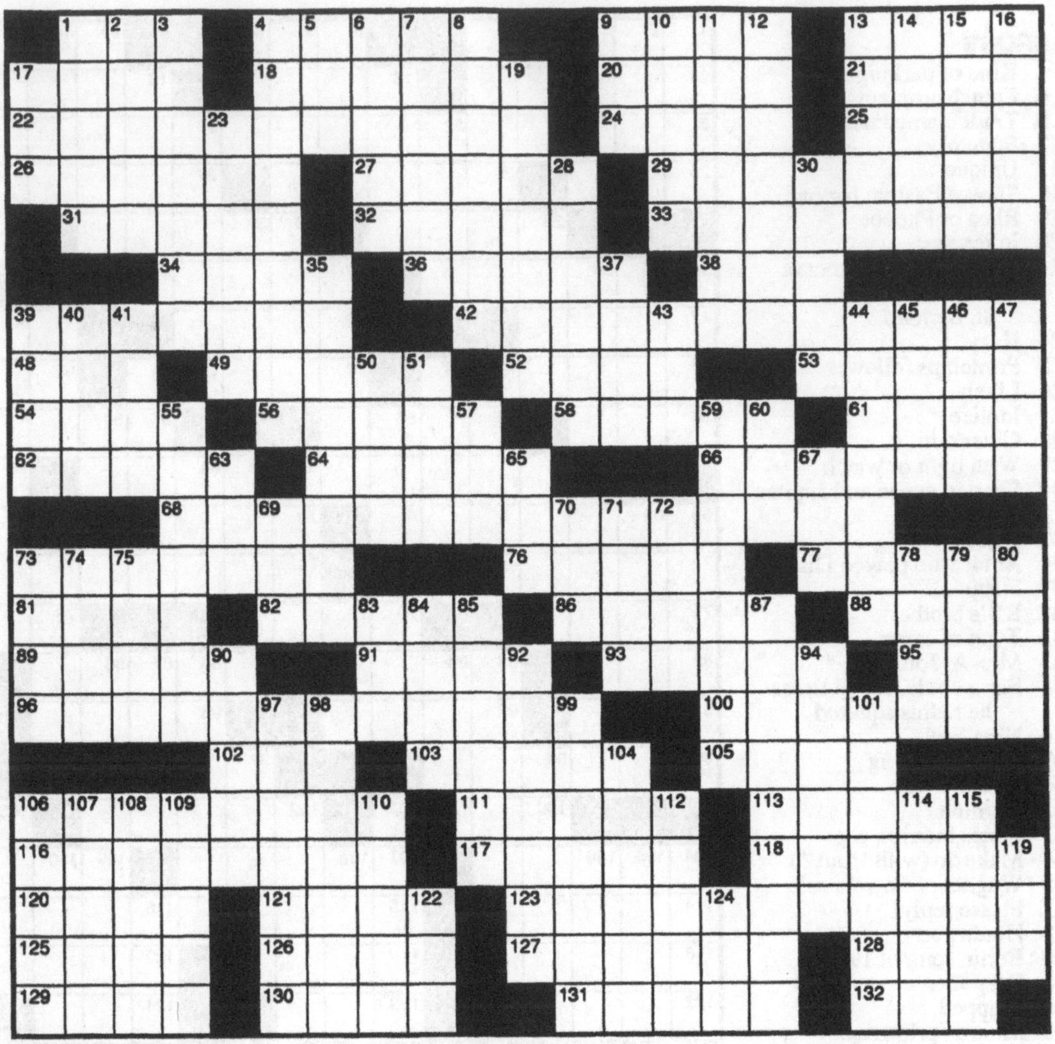

ACROSS

1 Extremely
4 En ___
9 Burrows and Fortas
13 Alioth, e.g.
17 Horse around in New England
18 Jamaica's banana bird
20 It's dragged at Shea
21 Gorgons' mother
22 Where to get an eyeful of Paris?
24 ___ clef
25 Among
26 Mean
27 To no extent
29 Enormous Empire?
31 Kind of contact lens
32 Fragrant resin
33 Dagger
34 Trip agents?
36 Brats
38 Garland
39 Walk-on, in a sense
42 Heavenly shore?
48 Geller's gift
49 Yoga posture
52 Shoe widths
53 Glenn Miller's "___ Mood"
54 Chicago gridder
56 Bridge resident of Norway
58 Fear
61 Streetcar of Soho
62 Orchid-food
64 Ancient Roman trumpets
66 In ___ with the enemy
68 Lincoln's prairie?
73 Unhappy
76 Wasn't indifferent
77 Construction piece
81 Lamb
82 Lizard
86 Additional clause
88 Asmodeus' love
89 Omens
91 Jitneys
93 Pyle, of reruns
95 Hied
96 Othello in kilts?
100 In theory
102 Columbus Day's mo.
103 Site of Roman ruins
105 Metallurgists' org.
106 Postulators
111 ___ down (moderated)
113 ___ hoc (to this extent)
116 Where waves break easily?
117 Side-drum string
118 Kidney-related problem
120 Biting
121 Rancor
123 Gucci galosh?
125 Rapier relative
126 Dust Bowl victim
127 Jailer
128 English composer
129 Pudu, for one
130 Ed or Keenan
131 Western of 1953
132 Hot time in Cannes

DOWN

1 Contaminate
2 "We're ___ see the . . ."
3 Volunteer
4 Where forty-niners rushed to?
5 Pop ___
6 Ward, in Venetia
7 Carpenter's pins
8 NFL teams
9 Omar's garment
10 Some flash
11 Give a right to
12 Cheap smokes
13 Leafless peduncle
14 Emulate Old Nick
15 Not upright
16 Copland ballet
17 Agnus ___
19 Hermit
23 Puzzle
28 Drunk: Slang
30 Excuse
35 Kind of gate
37 Palmist
39 Budding belles
40 "On thy cold gray stones, ___!": Tennyson
41 A birthstone
43 A poet's monogram
44 Buries
45 Black: Comb. form
46 Colloquy
47 Haws' associates
50 Common ___
51 Priestly vestments
55 Sow anew
57 Northern Thai
59 Campus life
60 Morse sound
63 Arafat's gp.
65 NCO
67 So!
69 Parrot genus
70 Rhine tributary
71 Pirate's place
72 Change the decor
73 Actor Parker
74 Suffix for acids
75 Verdi's musical staff
78 Columnist Wilson
79 Lake in Uzbekistan
80 Numerous
83 German interjection
84 Doll's word
85 Calls off a liftoff
87 Home of Kasparov's king?
90 Botanical orifice
92 Like a wise legislator
94 Runback
97 Where to see Boitano and Kerrigan
98 Tear-stained
99 Tebaldi and Scotto
101 Causes of dysentery
104 Angel seen by Isaiah
106 Trod the boards
107 Configuration
108 Yes follower
109 Among, in Aachen
110 Glossy fabric
112 Burke of TV
114 Lifeless, once
115 Saturnian satellite
119 Ingested
122 Suffix for velvet
124 Going particle

167 NO BRIDGE DUMMY by Bernice Gordon

We liked Bernice's title so much we used it again at 37 Across.

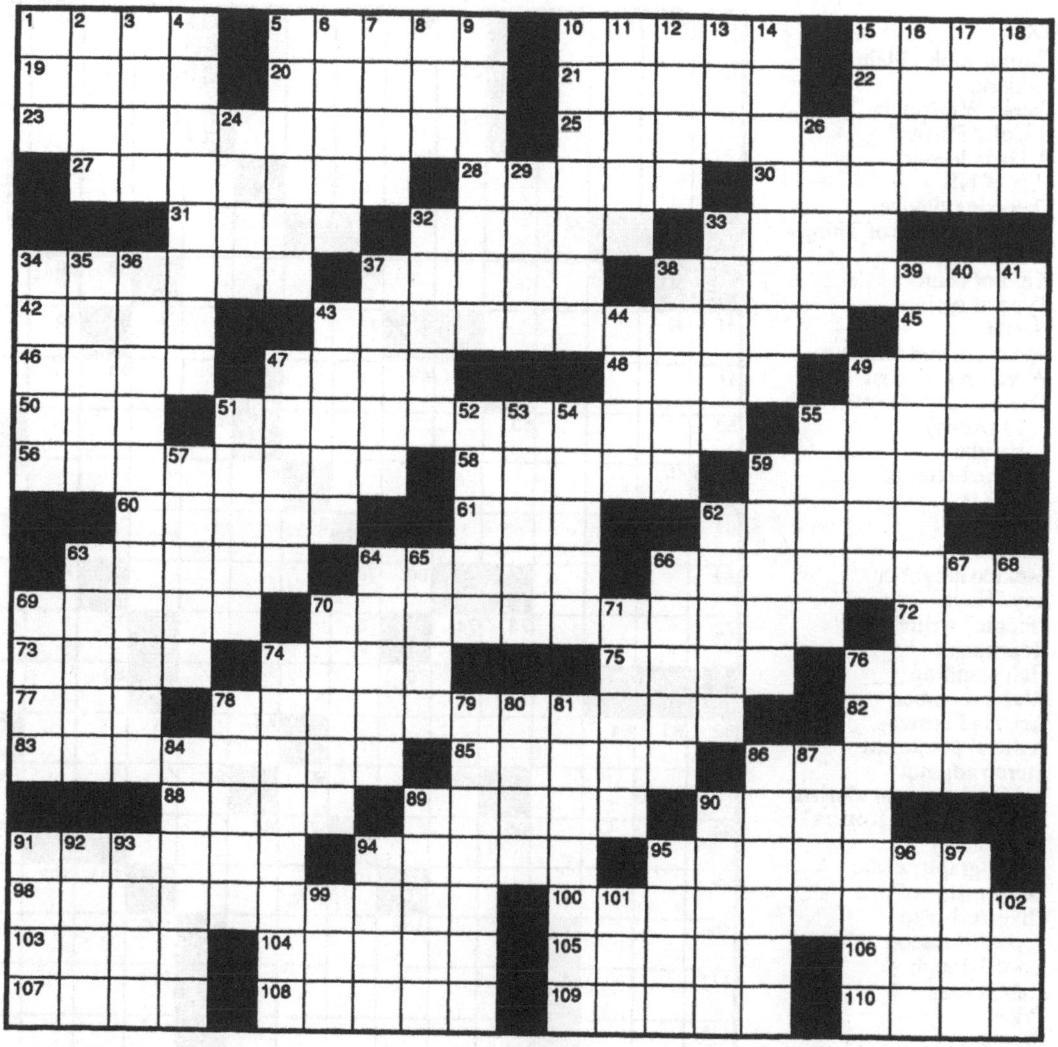

ACROSS

1 Trudge
5 Nosh with cream cheese
10 Brazil rodents
15 Hill's partner
19 Venetian magistrate
20 Luciano's love
21 S.A. serpent
22 Common abbr.
23 Span across the East River
25 Suspension to Long Island Sound
27 Testified under oath
28 Mountain-climbing tool
30 Suggests
31 German river or dam
32 Kind of surgery
33 Sacred bull of Memphis
34 Lodestone
37 No bridge dummy
38 Tabletop sight
42 Toward the mouth
43 Concrete arch at Sydney
45 Tanguay of musicals
46 Panelist Peggy
47 Sanction
48 Old Gaelic alphabet
49 ___-friendly
50 Rose fruit
51 Span over the Sabi River
55 Make up for
56 Seaport in SE Spain
58 Slightly soused
59 Overcharges
60 Clown
61 Opera division
62 Francesca's love
63 Billet on the QE2
64 Actress Saint-Cyr
66 Post-parade sight
69 *Wizard of Oz* actor
70 Continuous truss in Philadelphia
72 Beard
73 Kind of test
74 Teflon things
75 Actress Kirk
76 "___ the Mood for Love"
77 Pitcher Guidry
78 Memorial bridge in Sandy Point, Md.
82 ___ days' wonder
83 Space under a desk
85 Coal strata
86 Eskimo boats
88 Ullmann and namesakes
89 Face an embankment
90 Cervine trail
91 Mutational gene
94 Emanations
95 Crack or coke
98 Concrete arch in Catanzaro
100 Suspension of W Denmark
103 Actor Santoni
104 Moisten naturally
105 Basketry willow
106 Mahayana monk
107 Singles
108 Sound in the night
109 Spoon and baffy
110 Underworld river

DOWN

1 ASAP relative
2 Stentorian
3 Pointed arch
4 Diving-board locales
5 Hound from France
6 *Forever* ___
7 ___ Friday
8 Overthrow first
9 Spotted carnivore
10 Wooden shoes, e.g.
11 Abominate
12 Sweet ___
13 Latin I verb
14 Japanese cycad
15 Austin or Darcel
16 Solar disk
17 Tatting
18 BPOE members
24 Knob
26 Kind of cake
29 Words of understanding
32 Reluctant
33 Khomeini's Creator
34 Pliable leather for gloves
35 Thin as ___
36 Suspension over the Atchafalaya River
37 Candied
38 Kermit's Miss
39 Cable-stayed bridge in Corrientes
40 Herb of the rose family
41 Vetch seed
43 Encircle
44 You, to Yves
47 Oscar winner in *Network*
49 Practical
51 Nuts
52 Babylonian hero of myth
53 More refined
54 Chose
55 In the air
57 Was concerned
59 Colorful tropical plant
62 Composure
63 Actor Kevin
64 Laundry cycle
65 Formerly, formerly
66 Pyas and bani
67 Sparkle
68 Inspector Appleby's creator
69 Listen
70 Highlanders
71 Industrial building
74 Book of the Bible
76 Signs quickly
78 Franco follower
79 Intimidate
80 Actress Patterson
81 Remains in hiding
84 Oleoresins used in varnish
86 Worrier's ailment
87 Country of the Amorites
89 Oligarch
90 Did a cobbler's job
91 ___-American studies
92 Mortgage
93 Crescent
94 Ray of the screen
95 Erato's sister
96 Trig
97 Abounding with wahoos
99 Poetical time
101 Before bar or gram
102 Duty

168

COMIC RELIEF by A. J. Santora
Here's a cute one from the funnies. When it comes to packing a puzzle with thematic entries, A. J. has no peer.

ACROSS

1 Comic book villain
5 Athletic
10 Oprah Winfrey in "The Color Purple"
16 A Dada leader
19 Part of NB
20 Detecting device
21 "Remembrance of Things Past" writer
22 Kind of canto
23 Type of spring
24 Needs
25 Spectrum and Centrum
26 Word on a st. sign
27 The "A" in 1 Across (with 13 Down)
29 Particular
30 Got the better of
32 Out of it
33 Finished
34 Usher's job
35 Mexico neighbor
38 Say "Hey!"
40 "Picnic" writer
41 Reprimand
43 Hair standing ___
45 Was a member
47 Actress Petrova
48 Judicial document
50 Stereo adjunct
52 Ad for American tourism
54 Dr. ___ ("Buck Rogers" scientist)
55 Phonograph needle
59 Deep inside of one
60 Give-and-take confrontation
62 Lo-cal dough
63 Rabbit ears
64 Prices
65 Educated
68 "You've shown me!"
69 Doxologized
71 Shake up the troops
72 Layer of skin
75 Designer gown
76 Cheery atmosphere
78 See 91 Across
80 Juarez aunts
81 Pointer Sisters, e.g.
82 Yesman?
85 Messmate's words
87 "Where there's ___ . . ."
88 "To ___ not . . ."
89 Bone along the radius
91 The "B" in 1 Across (with 78 Across)
94 Ouster
96 "Nana" writer
98 Three, in Essen
99 Mount of Biblical lore
100 Big wind
101 Lopez's "Nola," e.g.
106 All ___ up (excited)
107 Slanderous ads
109 Authority
110 Sapling
111 "___ live and breathe"
112 Night gathering
113 Zeal
114 Suburban sight
115 Sci. degree
116 Minstreler
117 Like "The Refrigerator"
118 Diffferent

DOWN

1 Peruvian Indian
2 Kick
3 Doing a job
4 The "C" in 1 Across
5 Obliquely
6 Mitch Miller feature
7 Thumb measurement
8 Resort area
9 Forage plant
10 Outburst
11 Planetarium apparatus
12 Richard Wilbur creation
13 See 27 Across
14 Huppert of "The Bedroom Window," et al.
15 Wandering and wondering
16 Lessening
17 Tit for tat
18 In a fraternity
28 Fill trucks
29 The "I" in 1 Across
31 "Real" name of 1 Across
33 Spanish cheer
34 Double runner
35 Enterprising one
36 Damp
37 Theatrical org.
39 Film critic Roger
41 Call for help
42 Purge
44 Slapped paint on
46 Reggie Jackson's mo.
48 Disaccustom
49 Countrified
51 Some veggies
53 Brooder
56 Nighties and undies
57 Dicer or ricer
58 Down
60 Lined with grooves
61 "Maria ___," (1933 song)
63 Assistance
64 Spoil
66 Has a little lamb
67 Louisville slugger
70 Put on the glitz
71 Having regrets
73 Quest or suggest follower
74 Kind of comedy
76 Move about
77 Mr. Sunshine
79 Convince
82 First great Biblical patriarch
83 Jeane Dixon or Cassandra
84 Corporeal
86 Former Portuguese colony
87 To ___ (precisely)
90 Spring flower
92 ___ March
93 Guard headquarters
95 A concert waltz
97 Merlin of NBC Sports
100 Bug of a kind
101 Darnel
102 R.L.S. character
103 Spoken
104 TV feature
105 Mauch of baseball
108 Offer
109 Day for rel. class

169 VIP TREATMENT by Wilson McBeath

Although Wilson is from Akron, we suspect his favorite hockey team is L.A. and his favorite baseball team is Kansas City.

ACROSS

1 Indigo
5 Disencumbers
9 N.T. book
13 Heehaw
17 Servile
20 Concept
21 Peel
22 Spread unchecked
23 Double sirloin
25 Tigers' school
27 Lettering aid
28 Betel palm
30 Entrance
31 Upstairs dining room
33 Inland sea in Asia
35 Japanned metalware
38 ___ en scène
41 Kind of range
42 River in Hesse
43 High-rise occupant
45 Toady
48 Straight
50 Morse sound
51 Solomon Grundy on Thursday
52 Emporium's rural relative
55 Flower cluster
56 Seine
57 Kind of lily
58 "___ things devise": Spenser
60 Mends socks
62 Bristle
64 Scand. airline
65 Cotton thread
66 Stripped
67 French legislature
69 "Who's That ___," Madonna hit
70 Actress Massey
72 Holiday time
74 Place for a coin
76 Clare Abbey site
78 Like some mannequins
80 Bauble
82 ___ bull terrier
84 Eucharistic celebration
85 Frock coat
89 "The Princess and the ___"
90 Vane letters
91 Low bow
92 Brazen
94 Draw ___ (approach)
97 HREs
98 Kauai memento
99 Anglo-Saxon coins
100 Deneb, for one
101 Shoe insert
102 Secondhand dealings
105 Festive
107 Thirstier
109 Person in a hurry?
113 Politically powerful person
117 Whopping sum
119 Words of comprehension
120 Presidential power
121 Chemical suffixes
122 English naturalist: 1660-1753
123 Trampled
124 Take ___ (snooze)
125 Antitoxins
126 Very, in Vichy

DOWN

1 Dipl. officials
2 Nifty
3 Anent
4 Leo, in Heraldry
5 Josh
6 Epitomes
7 Plow pioneer
8 Call at Fenway
9 Manifest
10 Subcompact
11 Partner of error
12 Dispatch
13 Brest native
14 ___ cheese (cheddar)
15 Gone
16 Kyoto coin
18 Suffix for utter
19 Cut of meat
24 Wine bottles
26 Summon to court
29 Muslim judges
32 Insertion marks
34 Interstice
36 Variety of orchid
37 Cloisonné coating
38 Principal
39 Loafed
40 Babe Ruth's epithet
42 Elbow
43 Waste allowance
44 With fore or after
46 Dockets
47 Pester
49 Bellicose god
53 Dodger Hall-of-Famer
54 Commedia dell '___
55 Heap of stones
59 "___ Galileo on his turret": Browning
61 Mystical characters
63 Short response
64 Kind of pigeon
68 Alan in "A New Life"
69 First and second
70 Lake near Leningrad
71 Climbing vines
72 Pound or Stone
73 Cover-up man?
75 Mugs with mugs
77 Tuscany city
79 ___ facto
81 Disavowals
83 Makes lace
86 Impress, in a snobbish way
87 Gambol
88 West German river
93 "___ the things eternal": "The Book of Common Prayer
95 Shabby
96 London streetcar
98 Loewe's partner
101 Captured
102 Roi's mate
103 ___ Porsena
104 And others
106 Volcanic glass
108 Turner and Pappas
110 Eskers
111 "___ of your business"
112 Glasgow uncles
113 First-aid ___
114 Elath loc.
115 Recent: Comb. form
116 Hellenic letter
118 U.S. records agcy.

170

BASEBALL FILMS by Albert J. Klaus
Nicknames of teams are featured in this challenger by a newcomer from New Jersey.

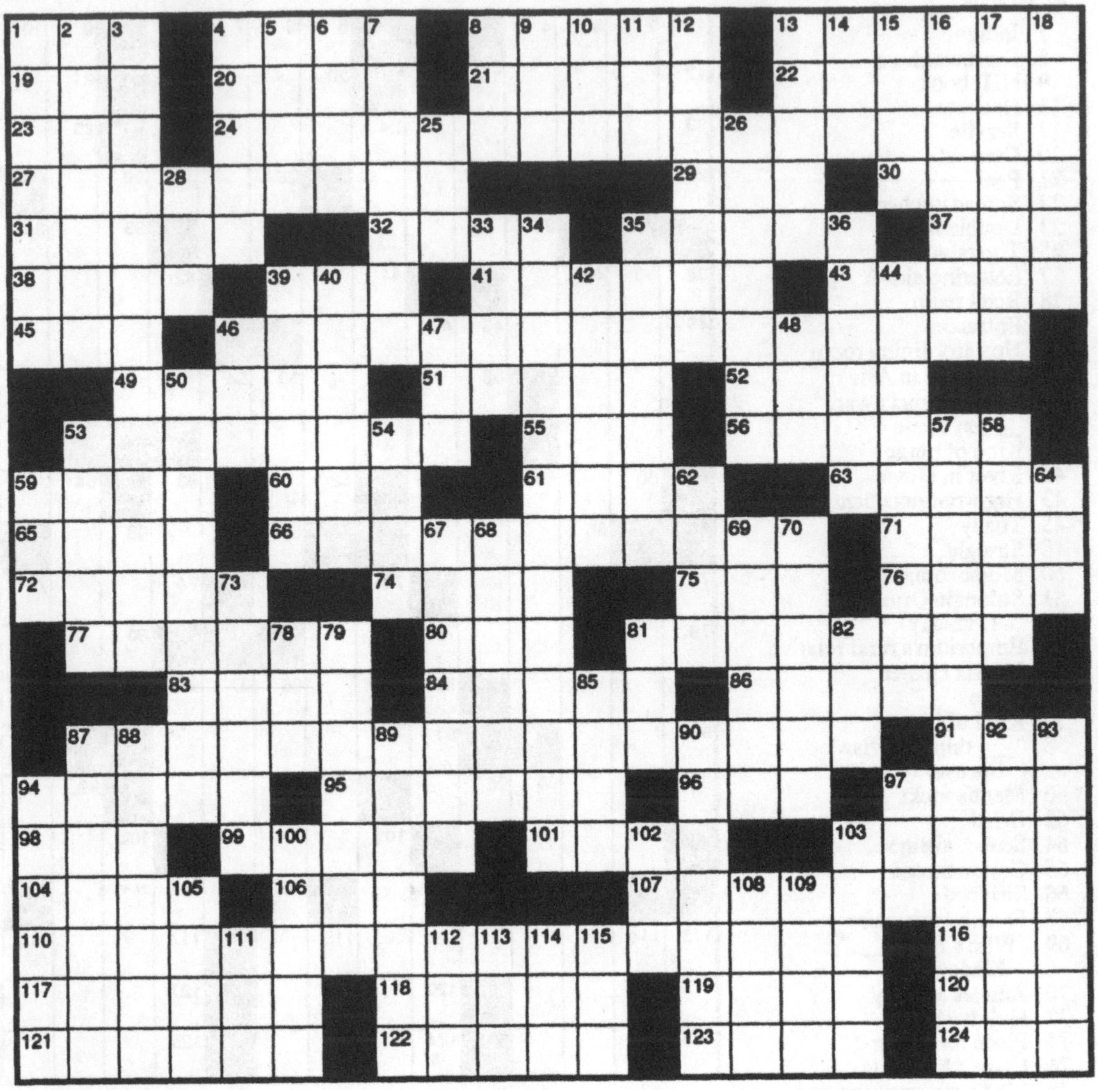

ACROSS

1 M.D.'s group
4 Linen fabric
8 Localities
13 Fumes
19 N, S, E, or W
20 Olive genus
21 Tenet
22 Shagbark
23 Up: Prefix
24 Fine N.Y. athlete dawdles in Cagney film?
27 Wage-distribution official
29 Balmoral Castle river
30 Obliterate
31 Draggle
32 Information
35 Vaulted
37 NE Thailand native
38 Lampreys
39 "The Lenin of Spain": Init.
41 Certify
43 Bradley and Khayyám
45 Some coll. linemen
46 J. Mason film with N.Y. night-game athlete?
49 Caraway plant
51 Swedish island
52 And others: Latin abbr.
53 Mangle
55 Here, in Paris
56 Revolve
59 Gasp
60 When Marcus Aurelius was thirty
61 Nancy and Hannah, to friends
63 A Barrymore
65 Caucasic language
66 Harlow's daredevil film includes California team?
71 Present
72 College officials
74 Great Pyramid feature
75 Picture border
76 In the same place: Abbr.
77 Pullover
80 Very early in 2nd cen.
81 Apronlike garment
83 Irish nobleman
84 Tree-lined passage
86 Roman goddess of hunting
87 Cleveland team is subject of H. O'Brian film?
91 Vigor
94 Perceive
95 Peaks
96 Swine genus
97 Philippine native
98 Feline
99 Porticoes
101 Gypsum
103 "Forever ___" (Winsor novel)
104 Parcel of land
106 Reply: Abbr.
107 Reversal of direction
110 G. Scott and J. Woodward film may include San Francisco team?
116 New Guinea town
117 "I ___ in the deep heart's core": Yeats
118 Expunge
119 Plumlike fruit
120 Kind of aircraft: Abbr.
121 Organic compounds
122 Repeat
123 S American wild cat
124 Cambodian coin

DOWN

1 Connecting device
2 Prayer crier's tower
3 Bankhead film in which Kansas City athlete falls into disrepute?
4 Faithful
5 Expression of regret
6 Departed
7 Barely
8 Fruit drink
9 Staff
10 Self
11 I love: Latin
12 Most sorrowful
13 Brush off
14 Small boy
15 Verve
16 Ringlike
17 Bird or gamin
18 Graphic pens, for short
25 Historic period
26 Tanned material
28 Prefix with place or take
33 Asiatic weight
34 Achievableness
35 Kind of library
36 Up to now
39 House of worship
40 Woman or girl
42 Destroyer: Navy slang
44 Insecticide
46 Three in Tivoli
47 A Stooge
48 World War II area
50 Sea anemones
53 Passageways
54 Slant
57 Ferrer-Quinn film features Atlanta athlete with official documents?
58 Weird
59 Cushion
62 Half: Prefix
64 Guided
67 Sites
68 Grins
69 Covered carriage
70 Spots
73 Spigots
78 Mouth: Comb. form
79 Borough in Morris Co. N.J.
81 Foot: Comb. form
82 Diatonic scale notes
85 Start of the Bay State motto
87 Instructs
88 Beseech
89 Condemned as worthless
90 Equal elevation line on a map
92 Repeat
93 Of a department in France
94 Denounce fiercely
97 Tot.
100 Honey possums
102 Capuchin monkey
103 Bewildered
105 Bronte heroine
108 Exclusively
109 To use, to Caesar
111 "Bei ___ Bist Du Schön," 1937 song
112 Prefix with corn or cycle
113 Nocturnal mammal
114 Superlative ending
115 Earth: Comb. form

171 GENERAL CONFUSION by Warren Reich

If you're a bit confused by all those strange upper-case clues, remember the title.

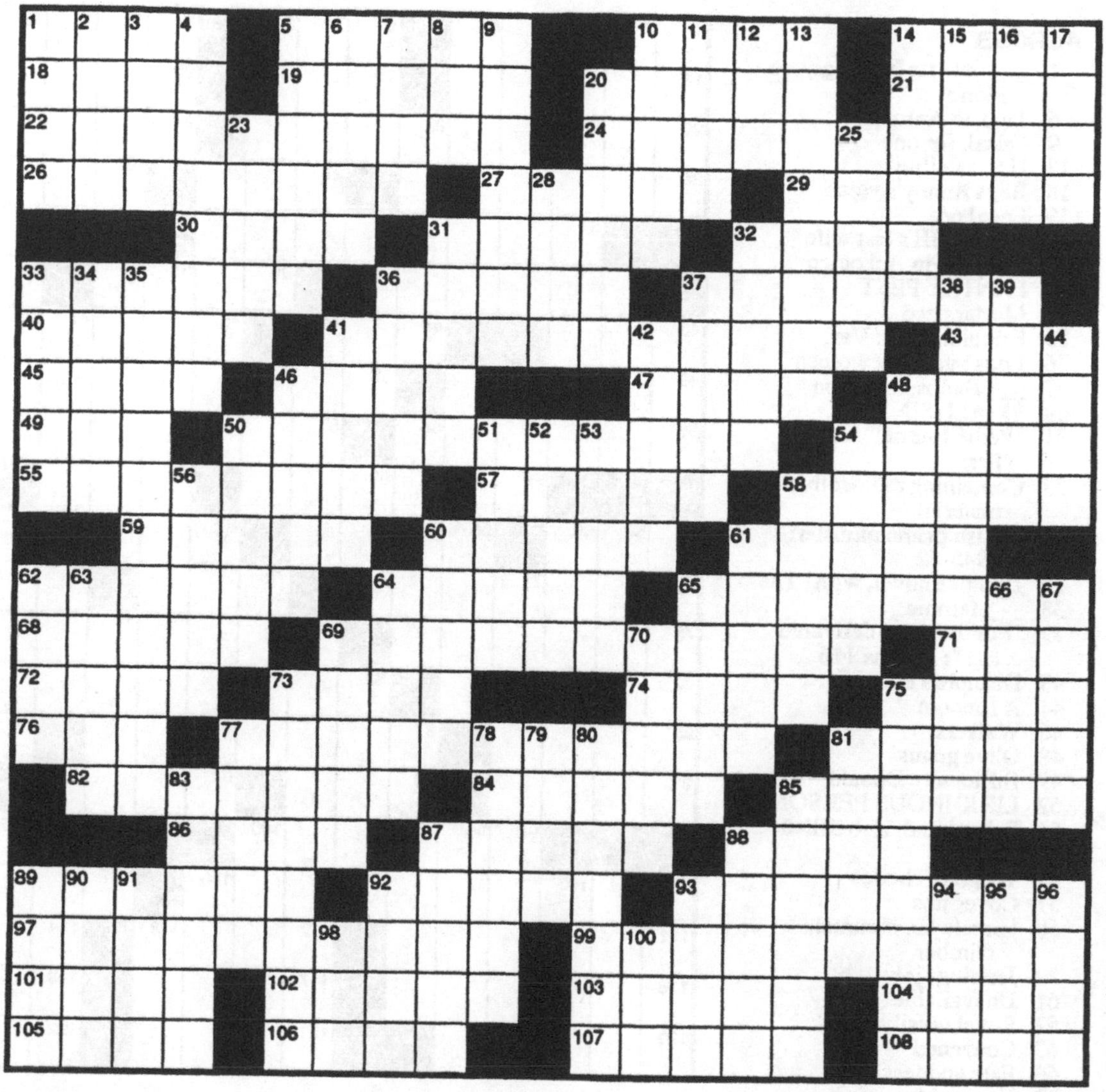

ACROSS

1 Raiment
5 Lazybones
10 Siberian city
14 Unit of matter
18 Peek follower
19 Gallows sight
20 Tati's ta-ta
21 H. H. Munro
22 GENT NOW ILL
24 CROWN IS ALL
26 Receivers of promises
27 Papal crown
29 Poplars
30 Adversaries
31 Barks
32 He homered 51 times in 1947
33 Recompense
36 Film producer Carlo
37 Assaulted
40 "Song of Roland" et al.
41 DOG IS A LAUGH
43 Make a green faster
45 Wight, e.g.
46 Prescribed amount
47 Sniggler's quarry
48 "The ___ of Genji"
49 Costa del ___
50 WIN MORE, MERL!
54 Pub pastime
55 Exodist
57 Be in store for
58 Dado
59 Molding edge
60 Shirts' opponents
61 Scout's ___
62 Famed pillar hermit
64 British carbines
65 Where trawlers trawl
68 Wedding worker
69 GO, AGED EMEER!
71 Mrs. rabbit
72 City NE of Paris
73 Letter opener
74 Galley sights
75 Yeasty film on sherry
76 Kansas Indian
77 HARDER NYLON
81 Takes a powder
82 Home of the anoa
84 Legal claims
85 "After this manner therefore ___": Matt. 6:9
86 "I smell ___"
87 Biological hook
88 High-strung
89 Writer Wylie
92 Basque headgear
93 Quotidian
97 HE-MAN MINER
99 BEET OR REEL
101 House pests
102 Deserves
103 Skirt type
104 Spline
105 Jewish month
106 Unit of force
107 Balts
108 Ranee's garment

DOWN

1 Stare (colloquially)
2 Seth's brother
3 Something to play
4 Type of type
5 A friend ___ . . .
6 Venetian bigwigs
7 Realtor's offerings
8 Inner: Prefix
9 Landlord's activity
10 Scents
11 Star in Cetus
12 Part of a yen
13 Saudis' neighbors
14 Slumbering
15 "___ in the Saddle," 1944 film
16 Dust Bowl victim
17 Overlook
20 Nova Scotia, formerly
23 Sikorsky and Stravinsky
25 Feminist Bella
28 Part of I.L.A.
31 Flaubert's birthplace
32 "And nothing brings ___ things": Shak.
33 Journey, in Bremen
34 With 41 Down, a famed racetrack
35 HOW WELL I AIM
36 Postulate
37 White sale item
38 BOER ARMY LAD
39 "The Deep" star
41 See 34 Down
42 Highway giants
44 Nod-to-Eden direction
46 Exhaust
48 Verboten
50 Diamond boot
51 Autumn worker
52 In debt
53 Rectory
54 Shag or frug
56 Like a rookie
58 They lead to Rome
60 Floor
61 "I ___ It Through the Grapevine"
62 Mope
63 Author Asimov
64 Browns a chop
65 Sigils
66 Hog call
67 Aphoristic
69 "The Maids" playwright
70 Satellites
73 Estopped
75 Condition calling for spice
77 El Cid, to Juan
78 Tocsins
79 Frost
80 On the fence
81 Cobbler ingredient
83 African falcon
85 San Diego team
87 Author of "Die Lorelei"
88 Little Nell's last name
89 Madame Bovary
90 Put down
91 Atahualpa was one
92 Swiss canton
93 Newspaper notice
94 ___ breve
95 Raise
96 Himalayan hulk
98 Secretary of State: 1898-1905
100 Comedian Olsen

172 OUR ROMANTIC HERITAGE by Calista Luminati

The answers to the capitalized clues are words derived from French, Italian or Spanish. The single exception is 76 Down, which comes directly from Latin.

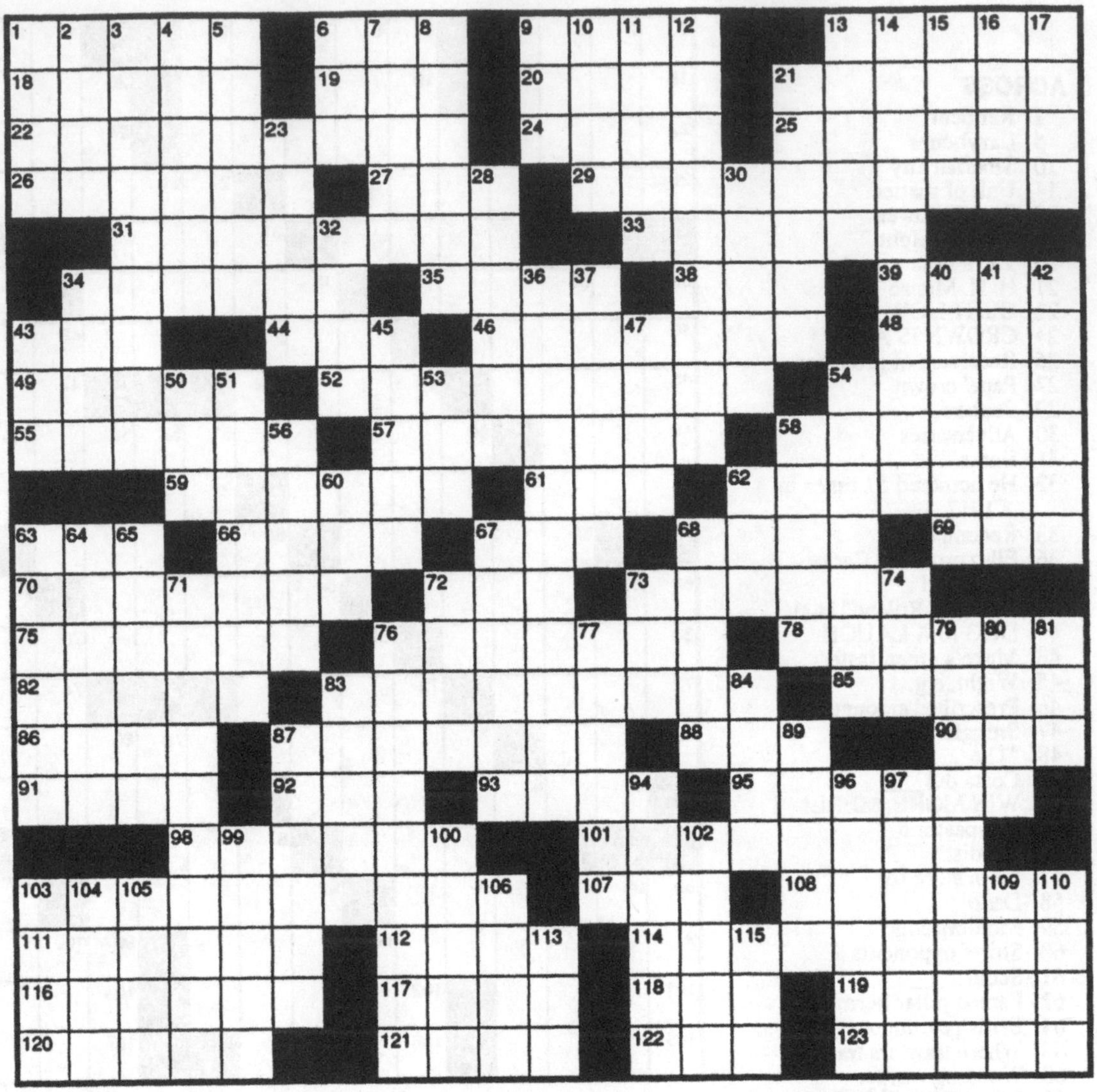

ACROSS

1 ___ ouverts (willingly, to Pierre)
6 Two, to Antonio
9 Faisal, for one
13 U.S. satellite
18 Bugs Bunny's voice
19 Legal org.
20 Henry VIII's last wife
21 Wrapper in Acapulco
22 PANTRY PEST
24 Mortar need
25 Falchion's kin: Var.
26 Loose garb for women
27 ___ Baños, in Luzon
29 SMALL SIN
31 "Pathé Journal" was the first
33 Containing radioactive material
34 British prime minister: 1945-52
35 Douglas novel, with "The"
38 ___ femme
39 "For thou ___ delivered . . . ": Psalms 116
43 Disciple's emotion
44 A Lincoln
46 Walkers
48 Olive genus
49 Billionaire Donald
52 LIBIDINOUS PERSON
54 Poker hand, also called pelter
55 Trogons' abodes
57 Cover-ups
58 Himalayan mountain climber
59 Jennings job
61 Unavailable
62 Revel noisily
63 Convened
66 Fate goddess
67 Hosp. aides
68 Energy
69 Hayden's org.
70 Swindles
72 Thieves' haunt
73 Marksmen
75 Card game
76 Frankfurter and Burger
78 Wideman novel: 1987
82 Textile fiber
83 TOSCA AND TRAVIATA TEXTS
85 Athenian lawmaker
86 Reference word
87 Tremulous
88 Bible land
90 Toupee, colloquially
91 Wax for Nero
92 King topper
93 Play or type preceder
95 Euripides tragedy
98 The Nelsons' TV neighbor
101 Extraction from rye
103 SMOKE SCREEN
107 Gob
108 Dislodges
111 In ___ (so to speak)
112 Abecedarian
114 NICKNAME
116 Armor-plated ungulates
117 Artemis attendant
118 Motherless one
119 Kind of kid
120 A code
121 Hwys.
122 Incarnadine
123 Muddled

DOWN

1 Rudiments
2 Disgrace
3 TALE TELLER
4 Sportswear
5 Hen tracks on a page
6 Day, in Durango
7 Tom or Sam
8 Imitator
9 Tropical tree
10 Inclination
11 Crusader's helmet
12 PAMPHLETS
13 ___ Arabia
14 FLOWER FOODSTUFF
15 Teens' popular gathering place
16 Silica gem
17 Brain, in Baza
21 Cows
23 Caucasia resident
28 "I Like Ike" was one
30 A French tale
32 Interpret
34 Crooked
36 GROOM'S GARNISH
37 Apocrypha bk.
40 Sirens
41 Transuded
42 Genghis Khan tribesmen
43 Rusted
45 Belial, e.g.
47 Egyptian month
50 "Cara ___," 1954 song
51 Feathered
53 Tavern
54 Gathered, in dressmaking
56 Teacake
58 More sensitive
60 Night and day pts.
62 Edge
63 Relating to atoms in a molecule
64 Where pennies count
65 Carter
67 Feel contrite
68 Wisent
71 TEMPERAMENTAL VOCALIST
72 National problem
73 A d.a. is one
74 South, in Sonora
76 WISE WRITER
77 Dagger
79 PATIO PARTIES
80 Salinas loc.
81 Wooden block
83 Halter, to Henri
84 Section of London
87 Actor Sam, et al.
89 Check
94 Pupil's aid
96 Ideal citizenship
97 Describing the Taj Mahal
99 Boric acid and lime mix
100 Peace pact partner
102 Boscage
103 Cavil
104 A county in N.C.
105 "___ Kampf"
106 City in Pa.
109 Koppel and Kennedy
110 Steep, to a Scot
113 Agency before the C.I.A.
115 Fourposter

173 FOR THE MET SET by Daniel Girardi

Put on your opera glasses and gibus (opera hat) and enter into the world of Verdi, Ravel, Saint-Saens, Scarlatti and others.

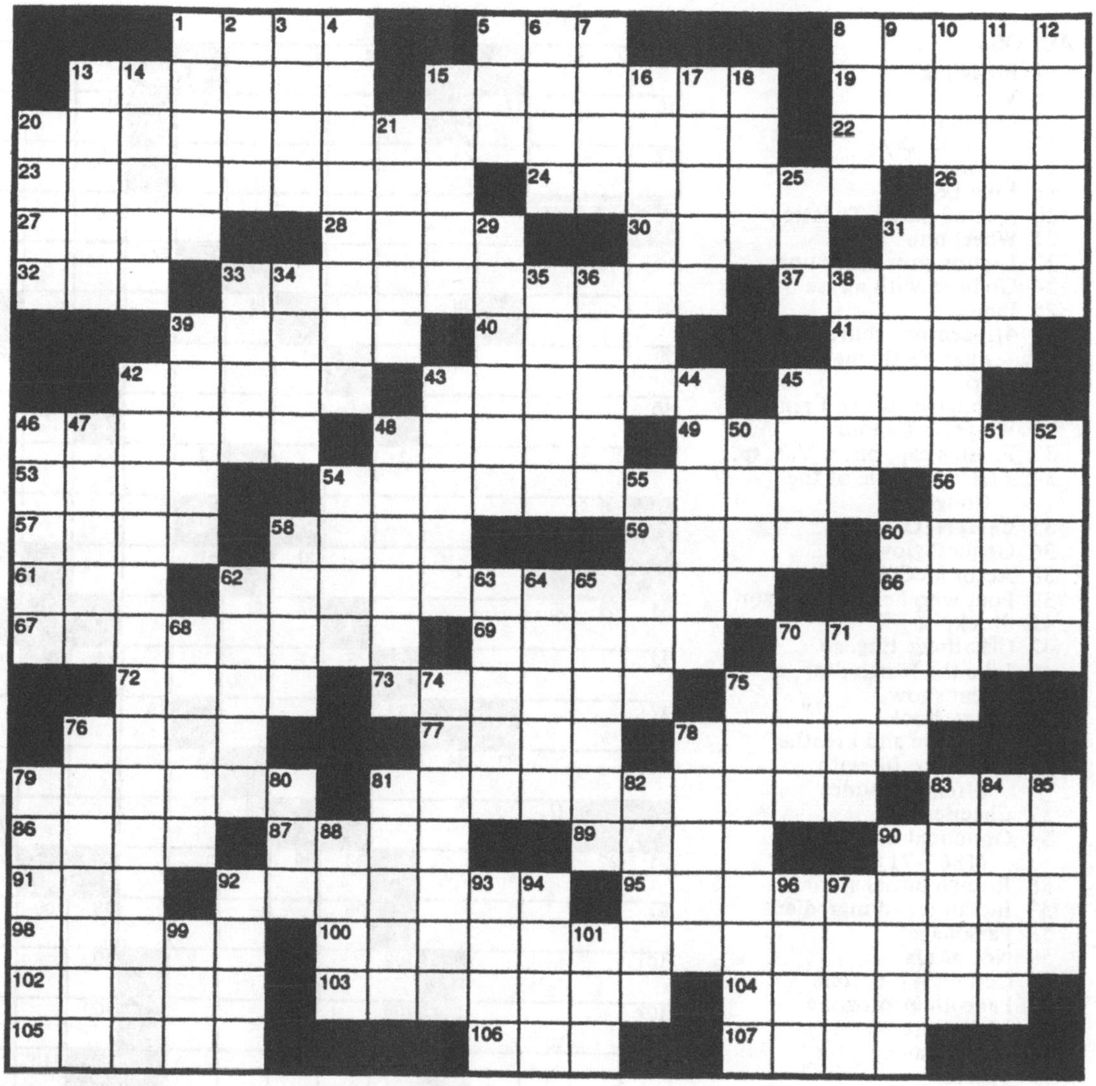

ACROSS

1 Neth. coins
5 Land measure
8 King of France: 987-996
13 "___ is a revolt against man's fate": Malraux
15 Reduced drastically
19 Protein acid
20 Ravel opera
22 Cuban revolutionary: 1853-95
23 Chicle tree
24 Folly of 1867
26 Akin: Abbr.
27 Triplet
28 Cologne loam
30 Where loughs are lakes
31 Pitch
32 Defunct campus org.
33 Auber opera
37 Plants of the madder family
39 Garden areas
40 Ancient Hebrew months
41 Peruvian tribe
42 No-goodnik
43 BB's big brother
45 Curved molding
46 Hometown of 34 Down
48 WW I battle site
49 Municipal council members
53 "Tosca" setting
54 Verdi opera
56 Soprano Marton
57 Cupid
58 Borders
59 Buzzard bills
60 Slammer
61 Debussy's "La ___"
62 Saint-Saëns opera
66 City of W Romania
67 Mother-to-be care
69 Asylum
70 Placido Domingo, e.g.
72 Slugger Winfield
73 Suppressed
75 "Pagliacci" clown
76 Half a disease
77 Muezzin's call
78 Hag
79 Pearl of high quality
81 Luening opera
83 Luck
86 Gobs
87 Hawks' home
89 Dash
90 After nose or pine
91 "Le Coq ___": Rimsky-Korsakov
92 Acts silly
95 Pen holders
98 Swelling
100 Steffani opera
102 Ice pinnacle
103 Warm salutation
104 Matador
105 North Carolina river
106 Court divider
107 Influence

DOWN

1 Particle associated with quarks
2 Fat
3 Zwei follower
4 Starry
5 Wing
6 Tatters
7 Slave of yore
8 They move tappets
9 Japanese pearl diver
10 Scarlatti opera
11 International accord
12 Sheer fabrics
13 "___ Day's Night": Beatles
14 Flake: Comb. form
15 Algerian cavalryman
16 Otherwise
17 Oil: Comb. form
18 Earl ___ Biggers
20 Mil. landing crafts
21 Coasters
25 Society flower
29 Large metal cups
31 Doc for a grand
33 Chimney duct
34 See 46 Across
35 Heifetz's birthplace
36 Language of Flanders, once
38 Beer
39 Central
42 Montemezzi opera
43 Hundredth of a rupee
44 City in Kwantung
45 Lengthy poems
46 Disney dog
47 Certain Italian, to Brünhilde
48 Murmur
50 Leg. degrees
51 Lake Geneva resort
52 Henner's "Taxi" role
54 Actress Hartman
55 "The Woman ___," Wilder film
58 Network of nerves
60 "Socrate" composer
62 She played Alice Hyatt
63 Root: Comb. form
64 Siberian plant
65 Requite
68 Nostrils
70 Mad one
71 Actress Archer
74 Town in S Texas
75 Doodads
76 Gloomy hen
78 Metallic sound
79 Least current
80 Also
81 ___ nous (between ourselves)
82 "The Cocktail Party" poet
83 Renown
84 "___ to bed"
85 Campeche coin
88 Disposition
90 Gov. Cuomo's predecessor
92 Reality
93 Merit
94 Blade of yore
96 Weather word
97 Trillion: Comb. form
99 ___ about town
101 Sept. time

174

NICK-NAMES by Jim Page

Our constructor from New York says he's dedicating this puzzle to Virginia.

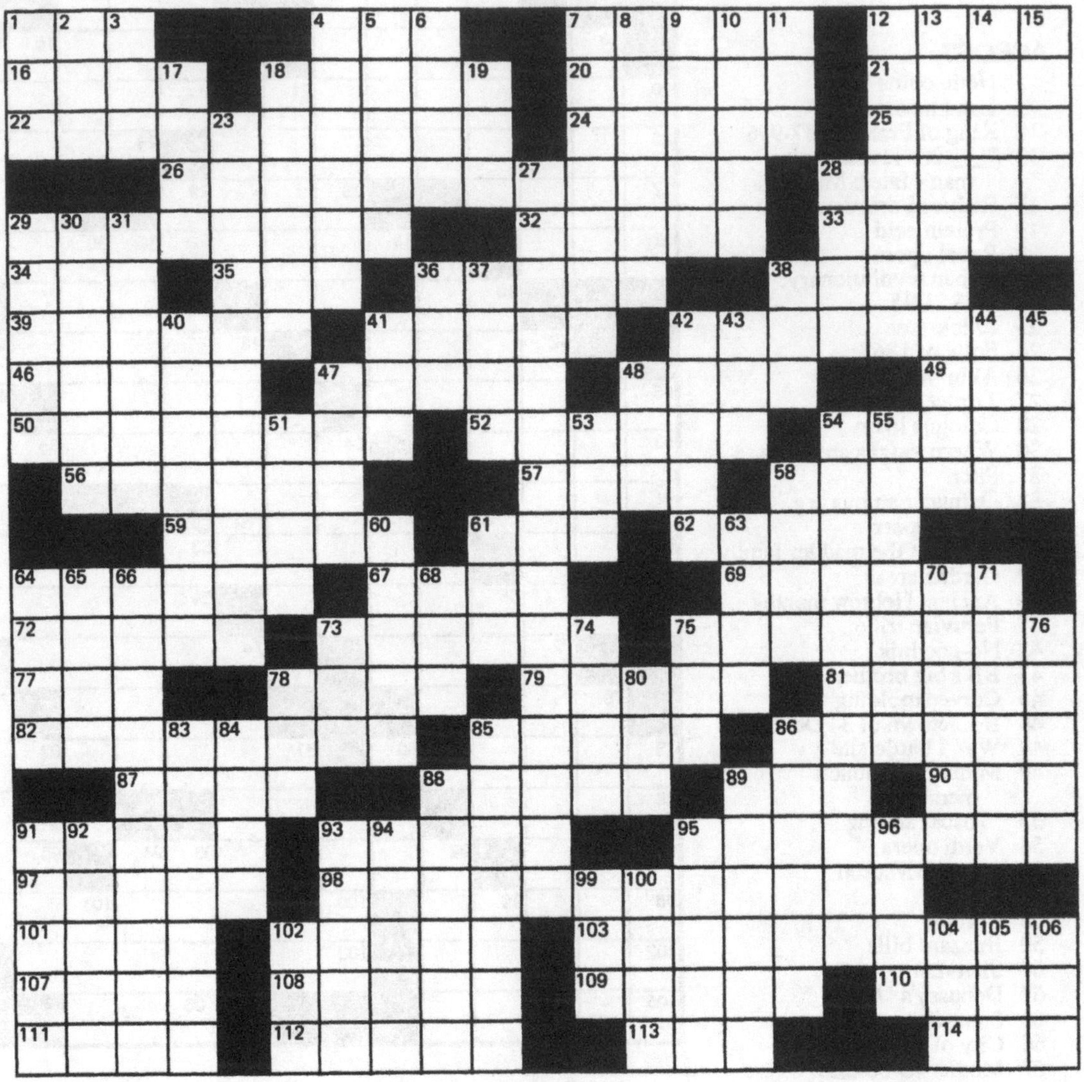

ACROSS

1 Fledgling
4 Vim
7 Overact
12 ___-friendly
16 Cupid
18 Like Leo
20 Ada of Daly's Theatre
21 Wheel hub
22 Leguminous arbor unit
24 Goddess with a lyre
25 Pique
26 4th-century source of this puzzle's theme
28 Otto
29 Annual visitor to France
32 Wings, in Cannes
33 Frosh's cap, once: Var. sp.
34 African people of the Congo
35 $C_7H_5N_3O_6$
36 Goalies' gloves
38 Actor McCowen
39 Poet who helped Emerson
41 Stockpile
42 Classified: Eng. sp.
46 Like the North Star
47 Street show
48 Heavy book
49 "___ live and breathe"
50 Caused to fill with offensive fumes
52 Cheerless
54 Opponent of Bismarck (1863-71)
56 Roman burial stones
57 Indian-bread ingredient
58 Parsonages
59 Not heads
61 Certain AL batters
62 Parasitic protozoan
64 Irish overcoat
67 Wrench away
69 Teased
72 Lugs
73 "Peter the Great" author
75 Casual promenader
77 Astronomer's billion years
78 Rx amount
79 Blackthorns
81 English ecclesiastic: 1562-1640
82 Fickle
85 Rand's "___ Shrugged"
86 Let go by
87 Chipmunk Dale's pal
88 Visored helmet
89 Incisive remark
90 Suffix for Benedict
91 N Sumatran region
93 Narrow channel
95 Annual visitor to Spain
97 Perch
98 Annual visitor to Germany
101 Prehistoric axlike tool
102 Chanukah, for one
103 Southern sole
107 Twofold
108 Wife of Jason
109 "Merry Company" author
110 Jeff MacNelly's strip
111 Irish
112 Carbines of WW II
113 Goof
114 Gist

DOWN

1 Cap
2 "___ Blue?"
3 Monk's title in Portugal
4 ___ Lao of Laos
5 Sign up
6 Cheep
7 Religious recluse
8 Streep and namesakes
9 Alternative to Midway
10 Toodle-oos
11 Wine: Comb. form
12 Soften
13 Annual visitor to the U.S.
14 Lake of Geneva spa
15 Take to court anew
17 Bishop's chimere
18 F.A.M. members
19 "Gloria in excelsis ___"
23 Annual visitor to Holland
27 Annual visitor to England
28 Qualified
29 Flashy displays
30 T.S. and George
31 Tiny brook
36 Spoil
37 Frosted
38 Saperstein or Beame
40 Actress Fabray
41 Rotter
42 Actress Patterson
43 Singer Grant
44 Latin being
45 Morse sounds
47 Scottish dance
48 Seafarer
51 Kind of implant or transplant
53 Daybreak goddess
54 Annual visitor to Italy
55 Authorizes
58 "My Life" author
60 Squirrel away
61 Russian affirmatives
63 Lawrence Tero's
64 Western Athletic team
65 Seem
66 Patron saint of children
68 Suffix for crossword
70 Blissful, in Bari
71 "Clair ___"
73 Yearly doz.
74 Fashion magazine
75 French possessive
76 Spurn
78 Dye, as an egg
80 Avena sativa
83 Prickly plant
84 Tinge
85 Bristlelike parts
86 Cork shooter
88 Out of the hay
89 Crib in a crèche
91 ___ Triomphe
92 ___ d'Alene Lake
93 Trapshooting
94 Craft
95 Echo, e.g.
96 Ship-shaped clocks
99 Auric measures: Abbr.
100 Learning process
102 Naut. lengths
104 Christian monogram
105 Old French coin
106 Throaty utterance

175 CROSS REFERENCES by Ernst Theimer

E.T. was thinking q.v. when he created this challenger. (Alternative title: "See, See, Senor!")

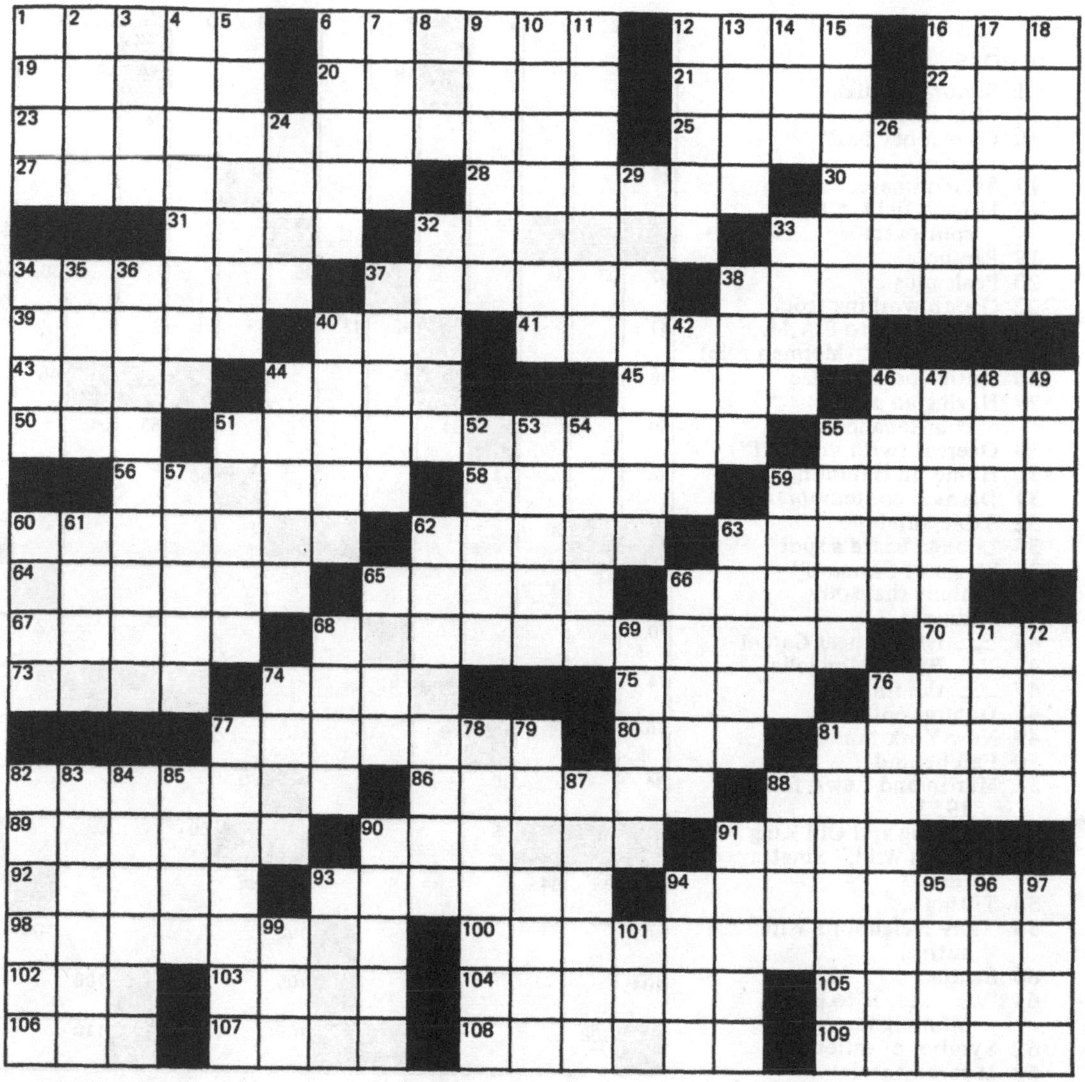

ACROSS

1 Biggs played one
6 Smiled
12 Fourth word from the moon
16 Bals.
19 Red, to 59 Down
20 At a bargain
21 Della's creator
22 Lendl or Laver
23 Work by 82 Across
25 94 Across, for one
27 Is hardly articulate
28 Tree ornament
30 Town N of Zermatt
31 Word of regret
32 Wakens
33 Thaw anew
34 Whirlybird
37 Title for 51 or 55 Across
38 Creation of 47 Down
39 Tribe of Israel
40 Edge
41 Some pens have these
43 Utters
44 See 32 Down
45 "Elmer's ___"
46 Tore
50 ___ est celare artem
51 Scottish explorer or what 38 Across became?
55 Watson's creator
56 Turkish hospice
58 Uses a combine
59 Lanky
60 Gave in
62 Bellows
63 Early
64 Coupled
65 German: Comb. form
66 A Finger Lake
67 Walking ___ (elated)
68 "Father of Medicine"
70 Resinous substance
73 Strain of Indian corn
74 Achilles had a famous one
75 Encourage
76 Corn Belt structure
77 Notched
80 Solidify
81 Fountain measure
82 Poet born in Moscow
86 Breaker
88 Sparse
89 More wan
90 Compensated
91 Four-tusked animal
92 Source of baleen
93 Pitching in
94 Ally of Mussolini or to-do over 100 Across?
98 Favorer, relatively speaking
100 Roberts' kind of kid
102 Before, to Keats
103 Language of Hibernia
104 Sergeant's welcome call
105 Outer
106 Double curve
107 Arikaras
108 Mildness
109 Inclines

DOWN

1 Spheres
2 Cheer
3 Revered teacher
4 Stirs
5 Aerie youngling
6 Louts
7 Finishes
8 Coll. in Tempe
9 Cassava
10 Declaim
11 Testator
12 Streamlined mammals
13 Hoffer's "___ Believer"
14 Urban rails
15 Mother Carey's chickens
16 Kind of 1 Across
17 Rocking bed
18 "Pathétique," e.g.
24 Low or drive
26 Thai king
29 Dinosaur genus
32 ___-fleuve
33 Like a day in June
34 Place for a sala
35 Eskers
36 One who swore by 68 Across
37 Finger or toe
38 Rayburn
40 Carried on
42 Phoenix team
44 Begot
46 Boom type
47 Shaw play or Greek sculptor
48 Haggard heroine, to Henri
49 Algerian governors
51 Longshoreman, for one
52 Set
53 Pact that ceased in 1977
54 Card game of yore
55 Appointments
57 Kind of badge
59 "The Balcony" playwright
60 Leech, e.g.
61 Type of sugar
62 Superseded
63 Climbing pepper
65 Row
66 Uhlan's weapon
68 Pal of his'n
69 See 40 Down
71 "Thanks ___!"
72 Duplicate
74 Legatee
76 Pacino or Muni film
77 Small ice-boat
78 Local
79 Come forth
81 Surgical knife
82 Caddoan Indian
83 Wedding workers
84 Forms
85 Hawaiian harbor
87 Striking London landmark
88 Menu fish
90 Marriage ___
91 Birdie + 2
93 Caama
94 Venture, in the backwoods
95 Town W of Astrakhan
96 Read like HAL
97 Ammo: Abbr.
99 Wrath
101 Chestnut horse: Fr.

176 HALLOWEEN SPECIAL by Louis Baron

Save this one for some midnight when the winds are rattling the windows.

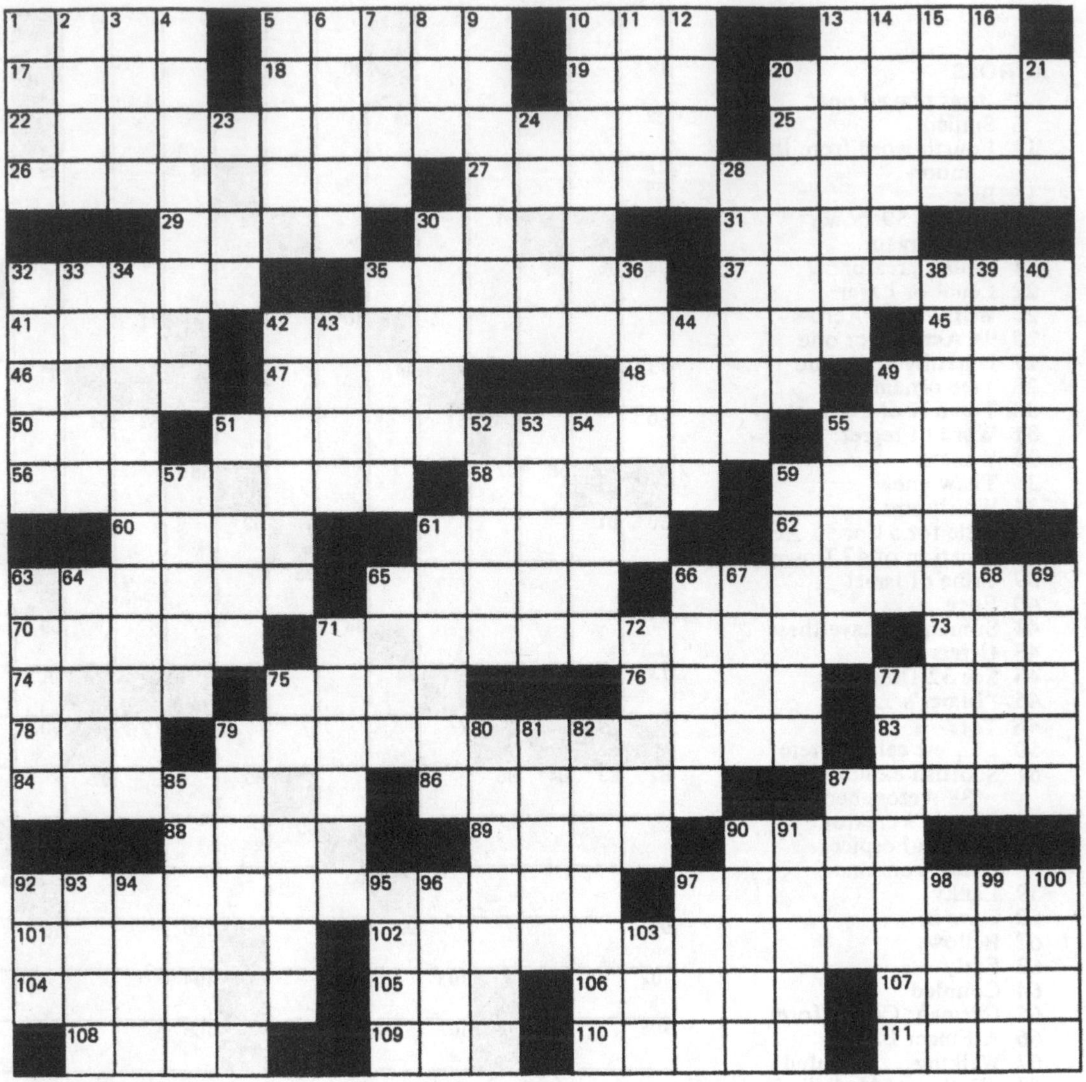

ACROSS

1 Sonoran Indian
5 "Get lost!"
10 Cousin of "baa"
13 Take off
17 Sacred image
18 Plowed field in the southwest
19 Parabola
20 Peals plus
22 Group working from midnight to 8 A.M.
25 Panama ___ (Merman role)
26 Anthropomorphize
27 Having an ashen countenance
29 Overeat (with "oneself")
30 Home, in Hamburg
31 Dashiell contemporary
32 Sable antelope
35 Lounge lizard's spot
37 "Sage of Concord"
41 Brahms rhapsody
42 Midnight
45 ___ Islands near Ceram
46 ___ Bator, Mongolia
47 ___ the finish
48 Dummköpfe
49 New York nine
50 Fall behind
51 Martin and Lewis film: 1953
55 Nat King and Old King
56 "___ Is Wild," Sinatra film
58 Tilting
59 "Thy Neighbor's Wife" author
60 Seethe
61 ". . . ___ is to live": Montaigne
62 Symbol of satiety
63 Moored Lizzie
65 "Seventh Heaven" theme song
66 Get a job done
70 Hears a case
71 Was as quiet as a mouse
73 SSW's diag.
74 Sahara areas
75 Earthy deposit
76 Cagney film, 1935
77 Pellicle
78 Kin of "ole"
79 Saint-Saens' Op. 40
83 Hamsters, guppies, etc.
84 Be a better canary
86 Caesar's name for France
87 Check casher
88 Yearn (for)
89 "Birth of a Nation" subject
90 A Waugh
92 October 31st deal
97 Show rainbow effects
101 Author Carson
102 Sweet or sad nostalgia
104 Pallas ___
105 Uraeus feature
106 Come after
107 Axillary
108 Arithmetic exercises
109 "That ___ no lady . . ."
110 Price list
111 Gold Rush center

DOWN

1 Suspiration
2 Beige
3 Digress
4 Unwelcome visit
5 "___ Isn't So," 1932 song
6 Mania
7 Like a day in June
8 Say further
9 Section of W Queens, N.Y.
10 People with many letters
11 Golden ide
12 Shortchanged ennea-
13 Noted Florida developer
14 Shaver's choice
15 Inner: Comb. form
16 Sponsorship
20 "___, orator . . .": Tennyson
21 Jet or chess chaser
23 Member of Naphtali's tribe
24 Cuba's neighbor
28 Accompany to the bus
30 Ancient Greek coin
32 ___ St. Marie
33 "The Garden of ___," Dietrich film
34 Would-be thespian's problem
35 Ringo or Bart
36 Meredith subject
38 It opens many doors
39 Writer Joyce Carol
40 Kobold
42 Bad; evil
43 Zoological suffix
44 Knife handle
49 Picon or Pitcher
51 Hungarian-Rumanian river
52 Israel's Moshe
53 Show bias
54 A car has five
55 Lorre, in "Maltese Falcon"
57 Kallikaks' contrasts
59 It goes with the crown
61 Twixt knee and toe
63 Wing: Comb. form
64 Pianist Claudio
65 E & W
66 Part of the ear's concha
67 But, in Berlin
68 Weld
69 In need of a relaxant
71 No-skating sign
72 Another time
75 Lidded street opening
77 Astronaut
79 Boz
80 Compositions
81 Part of E.A.P.
82 Kitchen cacophony
85 Indian chief
87 Having feet: Comb. form
90 Contend
91 Citrus fruits
92 Refrain segment
93 Kid's cuss
94 Andean forage grass
95 Detente
96 Tabula ___
97 Part of M.I.T.
98 Like Lindy's flight
99 Overstuff
100 Fictional Jane
103 ___ hurry

177 DUFFER'S DEFINITION by William Lutwiniak

Any neophyte on the links will agree with this description of golf.

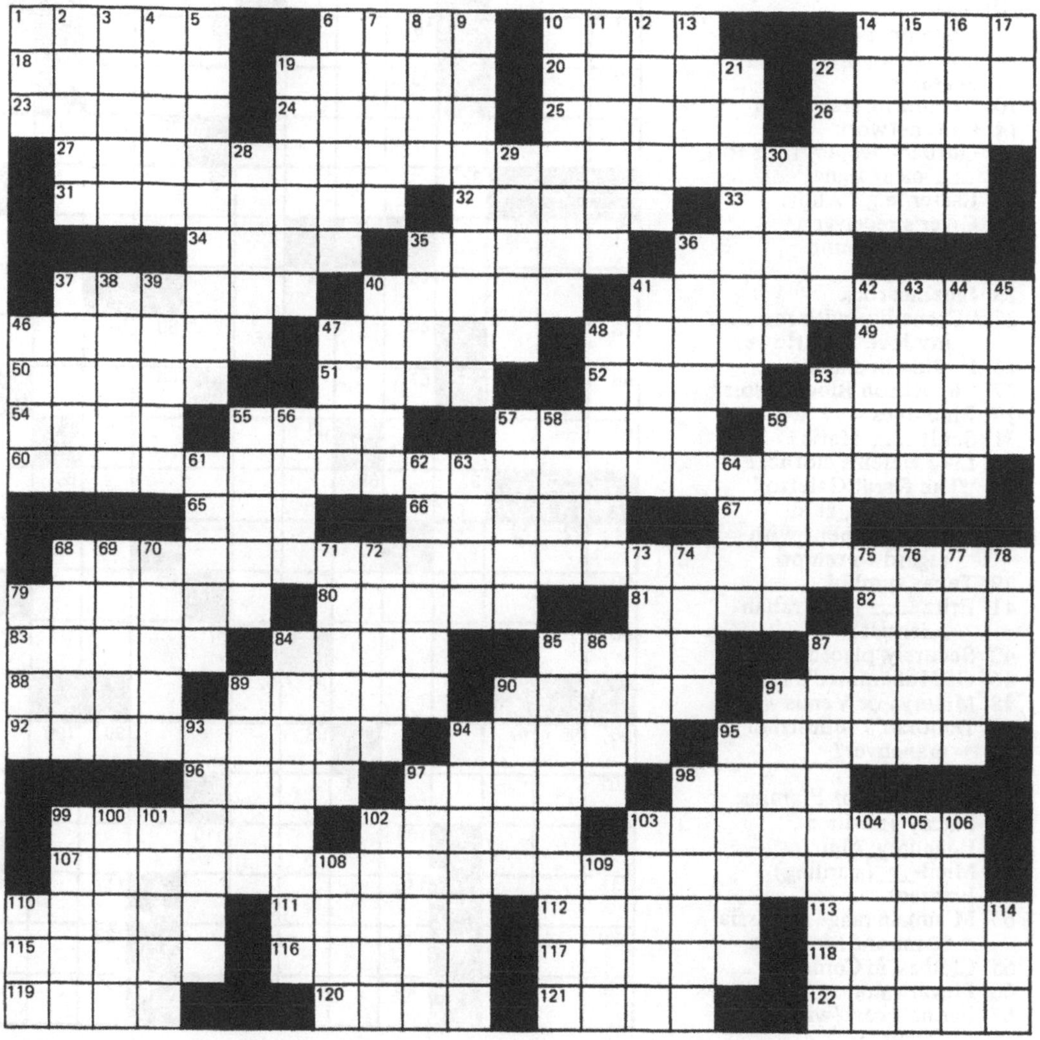

ACROSS

1 Muzhik housing
6 Roe source
10 Monks
14 PTA stalwart
18 Ceased, of yore
19 ___ citato
20 Earring sites
22 ". . . ___ her poor dog a bone"
23 Monteverdi opera
24 Vikki Carr is one
25 Smart ___ (wise guy)
26 Idealess
27 **Start of a duffer's definition of golf**
31 It's often scenic
32 Plug-uglies
33 Linen vestment
34 Pentagon department
35 Fern leaf
36 Malay craft
37 **Definition: Part II**
40 Bates and King
41 Dilly-dallied (with "away")
46 Young salmon
47 Emulates Ella
48 Absquatulates
49 Comedian Jay ___
50 Cantrell and Turner
51 Room finisher
52 Without
53 "Annie Hall" star
54 Have ___ with (rate)
55 Sparkling vino
57 Honeyed
59 Abu Dhabi moneybags
60 **Definition: Part III**
65 Popular nest egg, for short
66 Old Persian coin
67 Versailles vogue
68 **Definition: Part IV**
79 Churchman
80 Rapid: Prefix
81 Believe or trust
82 Mrs. Kovacs
83 Swimming-pool nuisance
84 Silent
85 Sch. subject
87 Gets jaded
88 Obstacles
89 Prepared, as pears
90 Actress Gray
91 Lowly abodes
92 Squeezes in
94 Eau ___ (brandy)
95 Manufacturers
96 Part of a wad
97 Loblollies
98 A Dumas
99 Shoes for Hans Brinker
102 "Alice" star
103 Laterally
107 **End of the definition**
110 Exclusively
111 Subordinate
112 Another name
113 Exhilarate
115 Turned over
116 Bowers of bliss
117 Valletta's isle
118 Expunges
119 Former spouses
120 Bologna boniface
121 Inventor of a sign language, Abbé de l' ___
122 Overpriced

DOWN

1 Kin of equi
2 Thong
3 Big at the box office
4 Rich Little, et al.
5 Corpulency
6 Gyroscope pioneer
7 Sixsome
8 Smell ___ (suspect)
9 Defame
10 Wine vessels
11 He wielded Durendal
12 Acts as spotter
13 Faction
14 Calendar unit
15 Shooting marble
16 Forget-___
17 Feasted
19 ___ rima
21 Sea rocks
22 Boy's game
28 ___ down (decrease)
29 Middays
30 Brings up for debate
35 Insipid
36 Straightaway
37 Mashhad man
38 One drop
39 Level: Prefix
40 Play part
41 Mock
42 Actress Burstyn
43 Sublease
44 Inverno month
45 Puts on
46 Tickled
47 Egyptian king
48 Defraud
53 Chemical compound
55 Of gold
56 Forest creature
57 Atomize
58 Use a whisk
59 Put on a pedestal
61 Female water spirit
62 Brought forth
63 Cummerbund
64 Whoop ___ (revel)
68 Moslem God
69 Mato Grosso river
70 Bleep out
71 Taxi maneuvers
72 "Angel of Light" author
73 ___ Island (Ocean State)
74 Robe of office
75 Change lanes frequently
76 Layabout or couch potato
77 Works the land
78 Dame Myra
79 Airport queue
84 Intricate tracery design
85 Tom, Dick or Harry
86 Original Olympic Games site
87 Garden nuisances
89 Italian nobleman
90 Tutelary deities
91 Seraglio
93 Like a cobra
94 Mixed
95 A Gorgon
97 Plain to see
98 Willie Stargell was one
99 Quartz
100 Battery terminal
101 Bad things
102 Takes on cargo
103 Fence crossover
104 Fjord
105 Much-heard
106 A Lauder
108 Dissassemble
109 Insult
110 Serve perfectly
114 Clairvoyancy, for short

178 GAMES WITH NOTED NAMES by Jim Page

If you like puns and a tough challenge, this is your cup of tea.

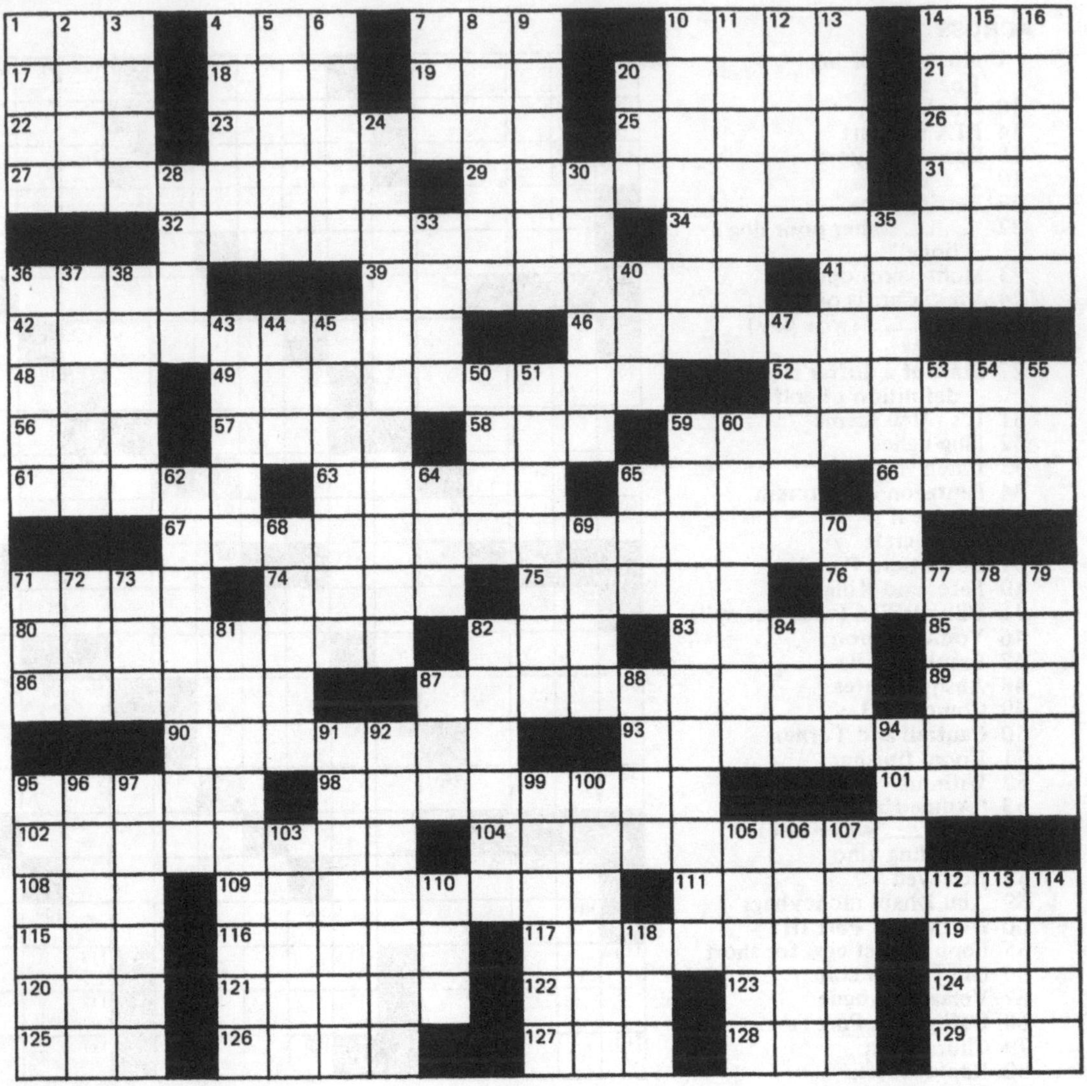

ACROSS

1 Dope on a horse
4 Son, to a pop
7 Seafarer
10 Recording star Vikki
14 Can. network
17 Outback leaper, for short
18 ___-clear signal
19 Easter, e.g.: Abbr.
20 Giver's receiver
21 Laughing sound
22 Labor gp.
23 Igneous rock
25 "Come live with me ___ my love": Marlowe
26 Ending in chemistry
27 "Brockton Blockbuster"
29 Blue dyes
31 Sault ___ Marie
32 Like Helen's clothes?
34 "The Great Galetto" character, et al.
36 Mus. movement with regard to tempo
39 Texas symbol
41 Fritz ___ (Australian scientist)
42 Securely placed
46 Of Mohammed's religion
48 Minerva or Venus
49 Deborah's equestrian maneuver?
52 Garland
56 007's creator Fleming
57 Pincay's position
58 Boundary: Abbr.
59 Mind-___(startling)
61 Embrace
63 Mountain range in Russia, China and Mongolia
65 Clothes, in Cordoba
66 Prevaricator
67 Eartha's cast (with "whole")?
71 High: Comb. form
74 Pillboxes
75 Archaeologist's sites
76 Shiftless car?
80 Calcaneus
82 Gram weight
83 Naval officer Hopkins: 1718–1802
85 Anne Jackson's Wallach
86 Author Turin, et al.
87 Earle's sea bank?
89 Downing Street number
90 Vexed one
93 One-celled fruits
95 Livy's birthplace
98 Lamb's "Dissertation" subject
101 Ronny Howard TV role
102 Animal pelt
104 Like Celeste's garden?
108 Eternity
109 Sea squirt
111 Former French coin
115 Final; conclusive: Abbr.
116 Lift spirits
117 Concerns of certain scouts
119 Homophone for air
120 Device for coining money
121 Less well-done
122 Brooklyn extension
123 ___ Brown, "Creek Mary's Blood" author
124 Railways in Chi.
125 Sch. for brass
126 "The ___ the limit"
127 Dakota Indian
128 "To ___ is human . . .": Pope
129 Soak flax

DOWN

1 Adjust, as sails
2 Locale in Kans., Tex. or Wis.
3 "___ Richard's Almanack"
4 Thompson or Hawkins
5 Trojan War epic
6 Mild; dull
7 Actress Scala
8 Gaelic hero
9 Shiny mineral
10 Jell
11 Pyrenees republic
12 Vine: Ger.
13 Della's wine?
14 Modest
15 Confer, as a title
16 Smile-inducing word
20 Bao ___ (former Vietnamese emperor)
24 Skiing conditions for Peter?
28 Gator's cousin
30 Rid a stream of sediment
33 Fashion, in Roma
35 Designated thus
36 "M*A*S*H" cast member
37 Patrick from Ocala
38 Ethiopian lake
40 Famed poet's monogram
43 Hoofed African mammal
44 Monarch catcher
45 North Carolina Indian tribe
47 Concert master Samuel
50 Attired
51 Greek letter before pi
53 Caesar's 502
54 Alfonso's queen
55 Job C. Stengel had
59 Waste of time, to Pat?
60 Marsupial of eastern U.S.
62 Like an artisan
64 Grown-up villages: Abbr.
65 Stat for Strawberry
68 "___ Were the Days" (Mary Hopkin hit)
69 "___ Lang Syne"
70 Compare
71 Word of triumph
72 Started a bridge game
73 Peg for Nancy Lopez
77 Slacken, as a storm
78 Tropical resin
79 A wash cycle
81 Theodosia's solicitors?
82 Actress Mason
84 Bath-to-London dir.
87 "Mother and lover of men, the ___": Swinburne
88 Knock out of the NFL playoffs
91 Having three parts
92 Blasting explosives
94 "Sixteen ___," Ernie Ford hit
95 Fake
96 Greek dialect
97 Count of Monte Cristo
99 Wobble
100 "___ Don't Eat the Daisies": J. Kerr
103 Exploiter, in Czarist Russia
105 "La ___," Jean Anouilh film
106 External
107 More sagacious
110 Wax: Comb. form
112 Buck, doe or stag
113 Heraldic border
114 Take five
118 Actress Grant

179

DOUBLE JEOPARDY by Bert Rosenfield

There are two "themes" in this ingenious puzzle. One deals with odd couples; the other is for you to discover.

ACROSS

1 ___ et nunc: here and now, to Nero
4 Delusion's mate
9 Make a selection
12 Half of MMD
16 Love feast
19 Hourly
20 Capital of Aisne
22 "___ la": boulevardier's comment
23 McCarthy's co-star
24 City and old car
27 Scotch partner
29 Dropsy
30 Atlantic City diversion
31 Thorny thicket
34 Alien transports
36 In the UK, they're silly
37 Tri follower in NYC
38 Pop singer and jazz singer
41 ___ out: inconsistent
42 Plays it as dealt
44 Already occupied, as a seat
45 He wrote "Seize the Time"
48 In the beginning, in a way
49 Author of "The Thief's Journal"
52 Special Academy Award winner: 1949
54 Wallaba tree
56 Flower and poet-novelist
61 Sierra Leone & Sierra Madre: Abbr.
62 ___ out: plan in detail
63 Otter genus
64 Voyaging
65 Raton and Chica
66 Lycees' cousins
68 Garfunkel
70 Source of many a bad trip
71 Signify
72 Acquire a new tenant
73 All-purpose trucks
74 Kind of space
76 Perfect game pitcher ___ Barker: 1981
77 Ball of yarn in Britain
78 Implement and marksman
81 Three-fourths of a weathervane
82 Namesakes of a Plaza moppet
84 Petrol unit
85 Lend ___: assist
87 Double boiler component
88 Old Turkish coin
91 Entered quietly
95 Where Tupungato is
96 Pitcher and musical star
99 Comstock, for one
100 Places for amants
103 Papuan gulf or peninsula
104 Light reddish-brown
106 Rivals
108 Alexander ingredient
111 Heil preceder
112 Indian and old car
115 Chou ___
118 Cottbus conjunction
119 Microscopic organism
120 Kind of coil or current
121 Rises up, Silver style
122 "The ___": 1953 Anouilh drama
123 Cleveland-to-Akron dir.
124 "I will not undergo this ___": Falstaff
125 Where to find jrs. and srs.

DOWN

1 Owns
2 Pt. of an engine
3 Salad and dessert
4 "___ sells seashells . . ."
5 Mrs. Spratt's dietary stricture
6 In jejune fashion
7 Level
8 Its capital was Susa
9 Chic's comedic partner
10 Pre-Revolution New York VIP
11 Fox-hunt calls
12 Hurdler and slugger
13 Outlays
14 Former Yankee infielder Boyer
15 Loosens, of old
17 Make a suggestion
18 Skaldic offering
21 A rhea
25 Rough-cut length of timber
26 Kite
28 Greek city, once called Ambracia
31 Paley's network
32 Time or toddy preceder
33 Cheap booze
35 Turnpike toll, for one
39 American Tel ___
40 ___ mouse game
41 Paris suburb on the Seine
43 Air-gun missile
46 Tunnel and fir
47 Worker ants
50 Printers' mistakes
51 Closed in on
52 Alaskan peak
53 Ancient ascetic
54 Invoke a penalty
55 Pius XII's family name
57 Von mir ___: (OK with me, to Hans)
58 Basketball Hall-of-Famer Greer
59 Systematize
60 Abridge
65 Dale and Yogi
67 Comedian and general
69 Taoism founder, Lao ___
71 Chester's river
73 Cheerful times
75 Crowded groups
78 Becomes rigid
79 Washington ___: Lexington campus
80 ___ water: old gas station freebies
83 "Two for the ___": Wm. Gibson play
86 Greek
88 Legree and his ilk
89 School area traffic sign
90 Bowl or line preceder
92 Vocal affirmatives
93 Musts for teeners
94 Book of the O.T.
97 French perfume city
98 George Eliot heroine
100 Treadle
101 Subject on a slide
102 Oligarch or satrap
103 "___ looking at you, kid": Bogart line
105 Catafalque
107 "___, you're it!"
109 Spring testers
110 The Earl of Avon
113 "Just Molly ___" (from "My Blue Heaven")
114 Pile
116 Part of a chevron, sometimes
117 Fool or ghoul ending

180 ECONOMY MINDED by Joan P. Leemhorst

We recommend Joan for a seat in Congress. She knows a lot about D.C. doings.

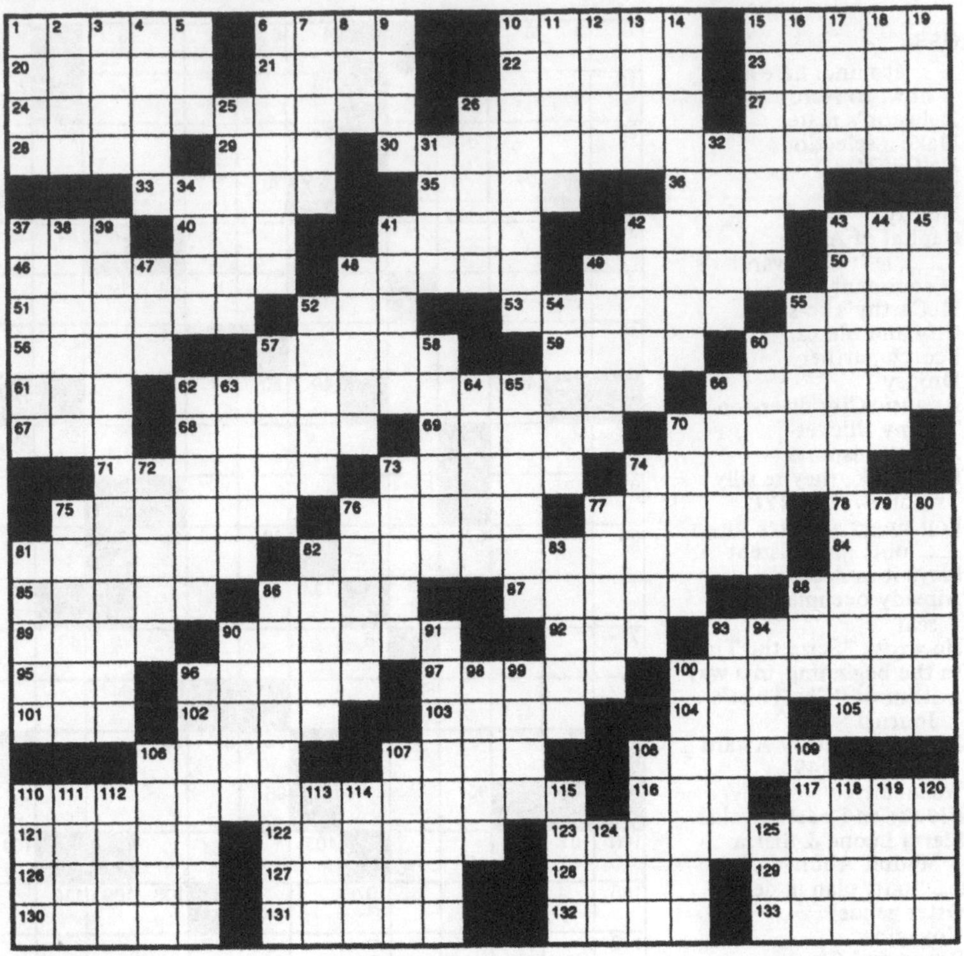

ACROSS

1 Frailty's name, per Shakespeare
6 Horner's prize
10 "___ his old age . . . ": Gen. 37:3
15 "Cradle of Texas Liberty"
20 Positive terminal
21 Trick
22 Cut back
23 Japanese-American
24 Uncle Sam's indications of future policy
26 Tainted
27 Of birth
28 Existence, to a philosopher
29 Einstein's relativity letters
30 Pay now, collect later
33 Shore from Tennessee
35 Overspreading element
36 Jacob ___ Park, N.Y.
37 Economists discuss it: Abbr.
40 Fabled bird
41 Take out
42 Bygone
43 Bus. regulator
46 Kind of rhyme or school
48 Casino patron
49 Piquant
50 U.S. painter-sculptor: 1869-1953
51 Idle; futile
52 Song syllable
53 Escargots
55 Dismal, in Scotland
56 Abbreviated raincoats
57 "Rintrah ___ and shakes his fires . . . ": Blake
59 Solely
60 Comic strip by Mell Lazarus
61 Tourist time in France
62 Fueling paroxysms?
66 Strip in L.A.
67 Dry govt. agcy.?
68 Froths
69 Addition to document
70 Didn't participate
71 Part of OPA
73 Antonym for lax
74 Grosse Pointe is one
75 Turmoil
76 Prohibition
77 La ___, Milan opera house
78 Depot: Abbr.
81 Being
82 Line of demarcation re the needy
84 April's harvester: Abbr.
85 Cole Porter hit
86 Advocate
87 Fish with a net
88 Slayer of Castor
89 Psyches have them
90 Filches
92 Deed
93 Dwell
95 Teleost fish
96 Chard or bank predecessor
97 Sample
100 Preadolescent
101 Radical youth org.
102 Party boys?
103 Stowe character et al.
104 A vestment
105 Concorde: Abbr.
106 Persian fairy
107 1,000,000,000 years
108 Hallowed
110 Marxists' bête noire
116 Mixture of gases
117 Donkey talk
121 Partitioned (with "off")
122 Accustomed
123 Slight depressions
126 Swarming
127 Witch of ___
128 Press
129 Chap
130 Result of a sudden Wall St. drop?
131 Saint-___, French composer
132 Jargon
133 "I do" site

DOWN

1 Minimum ___ law
2 Burden
3 Mai et Juin
4 Value ___ tax
5 Originally called
6 Preeminence
7 Type of counter
8 Manipulate
9 Sailor's meal
10 Racing car parts
11 Connected with: Suffix
12 Invalid
13 Singles
14 ___ funded
15 Amount payable yearly
16 Mythomaniacs
17 Italian wine region
18 Headcheese
19 Unctuous
25 Poe lass
26 Union ___
31 Oil cartel
32 Prehistoric tombs
34 Irritates
37 Small underground guardians
38 Nod one's head
39 Government anti-inflation regulations
41 Mad housewife's book
42 Buckets
43 Growing grants?
44 Where Bing was once king
45 Rope fitting
47 Mayday's kin
48 Encumbrances
49 More sensible
52 The Velvet Fog
54 Pried
55 Role Carnegie often played
57 Respond to a stimulus
58 Journalist
60 Kind of fund
62 Weak; decadent
63 Loud
64 Inflexibility
65 Sherwood's "___ Delight"
66 Pine marten's cousin
70 Smooth
72 Sautés
73 Fray
74 Perfume
75 New, raw
76 Romans' garb
77 Part of a loaf
79 Occupations
80 Concur
81 Fencing blades
82 Do some ironing
83 Irish Nobel Prize poet
86 Light and power
88 Adherent: Suffix
90 Kind of affidavit
91 Helmsmen
93 Kings and queens
94 Recedes
96 Highway menace
98 Eschew
99 Without, in France
100 Prominent
106 Annoy
107 Paved airport area
108 Roger or Francis
109 U.S. govt. obligation
110 Wife, in Stuttgart
111 What bowlers do
112 Homeric work
113 City in Sicily
114 Uncouth
115 Author Ambler
118 Cheer one's team
119 "Lonely Boy" Paul
120 North Sea feeder
124 NOW goal
125 Govt. agcy. for entrepreneurs

181

CINÉMA VÉRITÉ by Robert H. Wolfe
Familiar film titles are subjected to a game of associations and the results are fascinating.

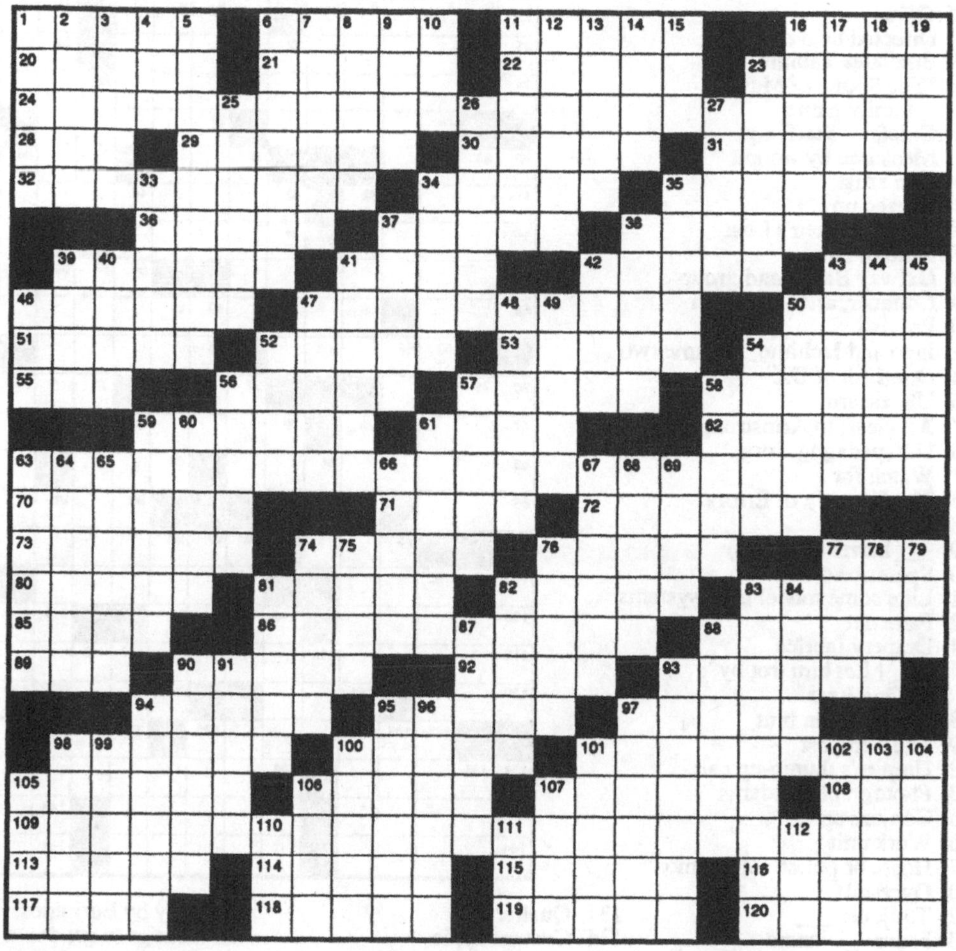

ACROSS

1 Hindu destiny
6 Comedienne Taylor
11 Write, musically
16 Chaucer's ___ of Bath
20 ". . . ___ unto my feet": 119th psalm
21 Actresses Gray and Moran
22 Former German coin
23 Frame for Raphael
24 Romeo, Juliet, Camus' antihero et al.?
28 Ethyl ending
29 Hamsun character and actress Stevens
30 City on the Rhône
31 Forevermore, in poesy
32 WW II policy
34 Writer Gertrude
35 Anagram for 98 Across
36 Odorous
37 Grand ___ National Park
38 The end
39 Frenzies
41 Ramble
42 Of vapors or ears
43 Sal of songdom
46 Etymol. terms
47 Cut-out of a Blake subject?
50 "___ 'n' Tillie": 1972 film
51 Dated
52 Connoisseur
53 ___ Gay, A-bomb plane
54 Dialects
55 ___-la
56 Architectural style
57 Impediments
58 GIs up for medals
59 Ancestry
61 Song of joy: Alt. sp.
62 Against
63 Diana with Captain Hook?
70 Greece to a Greek
71 Bivouac item
72 Makes merry
73 Salad root
74 Kringle
76 Less spicy
77 Dais denizen
80 Smart ___ (wise guy)
81 Potsherd
82 Film monster resembling an SST
83 Fish scales: Comb. form
85 Base of a bird's beak
86 Whence the sun rises on Barbara?
88 The Kaaba, e.g.
89 Bitter vetch
90 To Yaz, these were grand
92 Plays the paraclete
93 Characters like E.T.
94 ___ out (crush)
95 Sedates
97 Full assemblies
98 Daisylike flowers
100 Robert and Alan of films
101 Appraisers
105 Streep's forte
106 Ending with alter
107 Middle points
108 Brook
109 God plus Satan plus TV's Beast?
113 What negotiators hope to come to
114 Expiate
115 Author St. Johns
116 "___ of Two Cities"
117 On the briny
118 Necessities
119 Passover rite
120 More sound

DOWN

1 Superman's Krypton name
2 Solo
3 Prowl after prey
4 Mlle., when married
5 A certain fool and Eros?
6 Ron and Nancy
7 Mariel's granddad
8 Kol ___, Yom Kippur prayer
9 Baseball's Slaughter
10 N.Y. wintertime
11 Sound system
12 Comic George ___
13 Comic Ole ___
14 Soaks flax
15 To do this is human
16 Parimutuel activities
17 French river
18 Brakes
19 Besides
23 Necessitate
25 Scoffs
26 Carroll's was mad
27 Sicilian spouter
33 A beautiful Day
34 Word with seas or keys
35 Contemptuous old term of address
37 Theme
38 Liquid and natural gas
39 Dread
40 Major or Minor preceder
41 Gulley
42 Excited
43 Biological classifications
44 Certify
45 Renter
46 Govt. section
47 ___ button
48 Kind of farmer
49 ___ out (erratic)
50 Harrow boys' fathers
52 Cry; lament
54 Polite
56 Kind of stew or setter
57 Connery and Penn
58 Frolic
59 Piece together
60 Adam ___, Steinbeck character
61 False: Comb. form
63 Balkan region
64 The good doctor
65 Church officials
66 Set in motion
67 Barters
68 Type of role for Stallone
69 Tied
74 Ali, four times
75 Colleen
76 Lincoln's in-laws
77 Lode
78 Serais
79 "Israfel" poet
81 Certain junctures
82 Where Germany surrendered in '45
83 Yellow and others?
84 Foot the bill
87 Entertainer Lola ___
88 Olivier-Caine film
90 Pool people
91 Key ___, Fla.
93 Midsummer game
94 Mark of disgrace
95 Patron
96 Some brick buildings
97 Canoe necessity
98 Throbs
99 An anagram for reset
100 Greek mount
101 Ivied
102 Bach's instrument
103 Moon trench
104 Follower of sooth
105 Philippine native
106 Aleutian island
107 Created
110 Beavers' creation
111 "___ Boot," 1981 German film
112 Actress Hagen

182

TITULAR TITTERS by Bert Rosenfield
Names of plays by the Bard suggest pithy plots to our wizard from Troy, New York. Chuckles lie ahead!

ACROSS

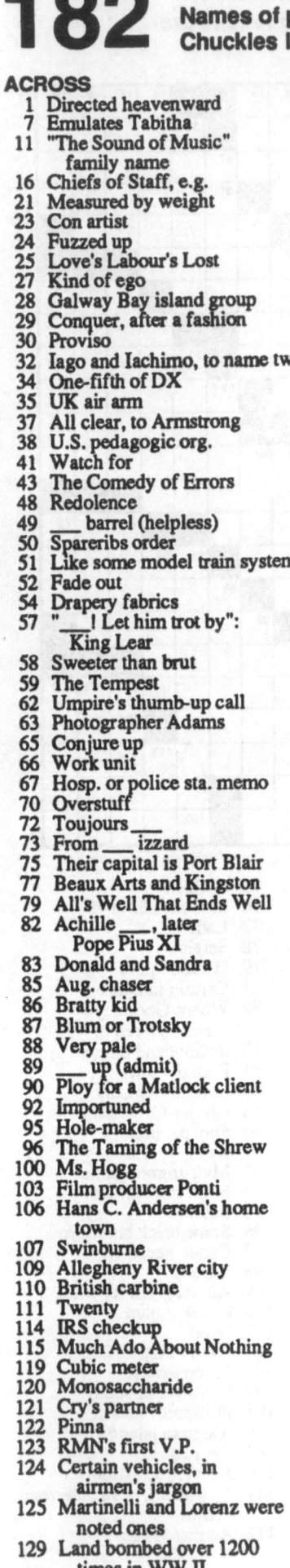

1 Directed heavenward
7 Emulates Tabitha
11 "The Sound of Music" family name
16 Chiefs of Staff, e.g.
21 Measured by weight
23 Con artist
24 Fuzzed up
25 Love's Labour's Lost
27 Kind of ego
28 Galway Bay island group
29 Conquer, after a fashion
30 Proviso
32 Iago and Iachimo, to name two
34 One-fifth of DX
35 UK air arm
37 All clear, to Armstrong
38 U.S. pedagogic org.
41 Watch for
43 The Comedy of Errors
48 Redolence
49 ___ barrel (helpless)
50 Spareribs order
51 Like some model train systems
52 Fade out
54 Drapery fabrics
57 "___! Let him trot by": King Lear
58 Sweeter than brut
59 The Tempest
62 Umpire's thumb-up call
63 Photographer Adams
65 Conjure up
66 Work unit
67 Hosp. or police sta. memo
70 Overstuff
72 Toujours ___
73 From ___ izzard
75 Their capital is Port Blair
77 Beaux Arts and Kingston
79 All's Well That Ends Well
82 Achille ___, later Pope Pius XI
83 Donald and Sandra
85 Aug. chaser
86 Bratty kid
87 Blum or Trotsky
88 Very pale
89 ___ up (admit)
90 Ploy for a Matlock client
92 Importuned
95 Hole-maker
96 The Taming of the Shrew
100 Ms. Hogg
103 Film producer Ponti
106 Hans C. Andersen's home town
107 Swinburne
109 Allegheny River city
110 British carbine
111 Twenty
114 IRS checkup
115 Much Ado About Nothing
119 Cubic meter
120 Monosaccharide
121 Cry's partner
122 Pinna
123 RMN's first V.P.
124 Certain vehicles, in airmen's jargon
125 Martinelli and Lorenz were noted ones
129 Land bombed over 1200 times in WW II
131 Quaker gray
134 Custard apple
136 The Merchant of Venice
141 "The Most Happy ___," Loesser musical
142 Marner's creator
143 Bodies of sacred knowledge
144 Where Edward III beat the French
145 Upholstery fabric
146 Police capt.'s boss
147 Alpine crests

DOWN

1 Sound to go with a shudder
2 Starter for dispose
3 A Midsummer Night's Dream
4 Odium
5 Hindu deity
6 D.C. group
7 Stampmark on some flatware
8 Progressively impairing
9 Less fatuous
10 I know, to Cato
11 Surgical bone-cutter
12 Reel's companion
13 Ottoman officer
14 What Cato was at six
15 Bear on
16 As You Like It
17 Streamlet
18 Pre-cable sights
19 Sault ___ Marie
20 A neighbor of Leb.
22 Hesitations, vocalized
26 Silk or snake preceder
31 Play by Euripides
32 Things to get down to
33 Fluttering
34 Bush cat
36 "La ___ du Régiment": Donizetti
39 Soufflé components
40 On the Black
42 Tartan trousers
43 Kind of point
44 Healer: Comb. form
45 ___-do-well
46 Shrine Bowl team
47 With 94 Down, 1951 hit song
53 Bishopric
55 Hardwood galls
56 Ellington's "___ Song Go ..."
60 Listen to
61 Disease, poverty, etc.
62 ___ Peak, Arizona
64 ___ tetra, aquarium favorite
66 Buffalo-to-Rochester dir.
67 Merry Wives of Windsor
68 Aware of
69 C ___ Charlie
70 Arrange cargo
71 Old strongbox
72 Nitrous oxide, e.g.
74 African antelope
75 Castor or Pollux
76 Cob or ram
78 The Winter's Tale
79 East or west end
80 Long
81 Skip
84 Athena's mascot
91 I.e.
92 Pickets
93 Stamp on a sweatshirt
94 See 47 Down
95 Jai ___
96 Chit
97 Ghazels
98 Perfume, ritually
99 Magna ___
101 Ballerina Shearer
102 Poker payments
103 Silver salmon
104 Pub quaffs
105 Populate anew
108 Lincoln's Ann
110 Nut-processing machine
112 "The Last Plantagenets" author
113 Utility company woes
116 ___-de-sac
117 Berber
118 Magnitogorsk's river
126 After-shave application
127 Girlfriend of Alley Oop
128 Sink's alternative
130 City on Utah Lake
131 Long follower
132 Fountain order
133 "___ out?" (poker query)
134 Potential cpl.
135 Chalice veil
137 "C'est ___": "Camelot" song
138 Marshall Plan: Abbr.
139 Actress Grant
140 Kiang

183

HOMOPHONE HUMOR by John Dreyer

This puzzling newcomer seems to be an old hand at wordplay. Every pun below is well above average.

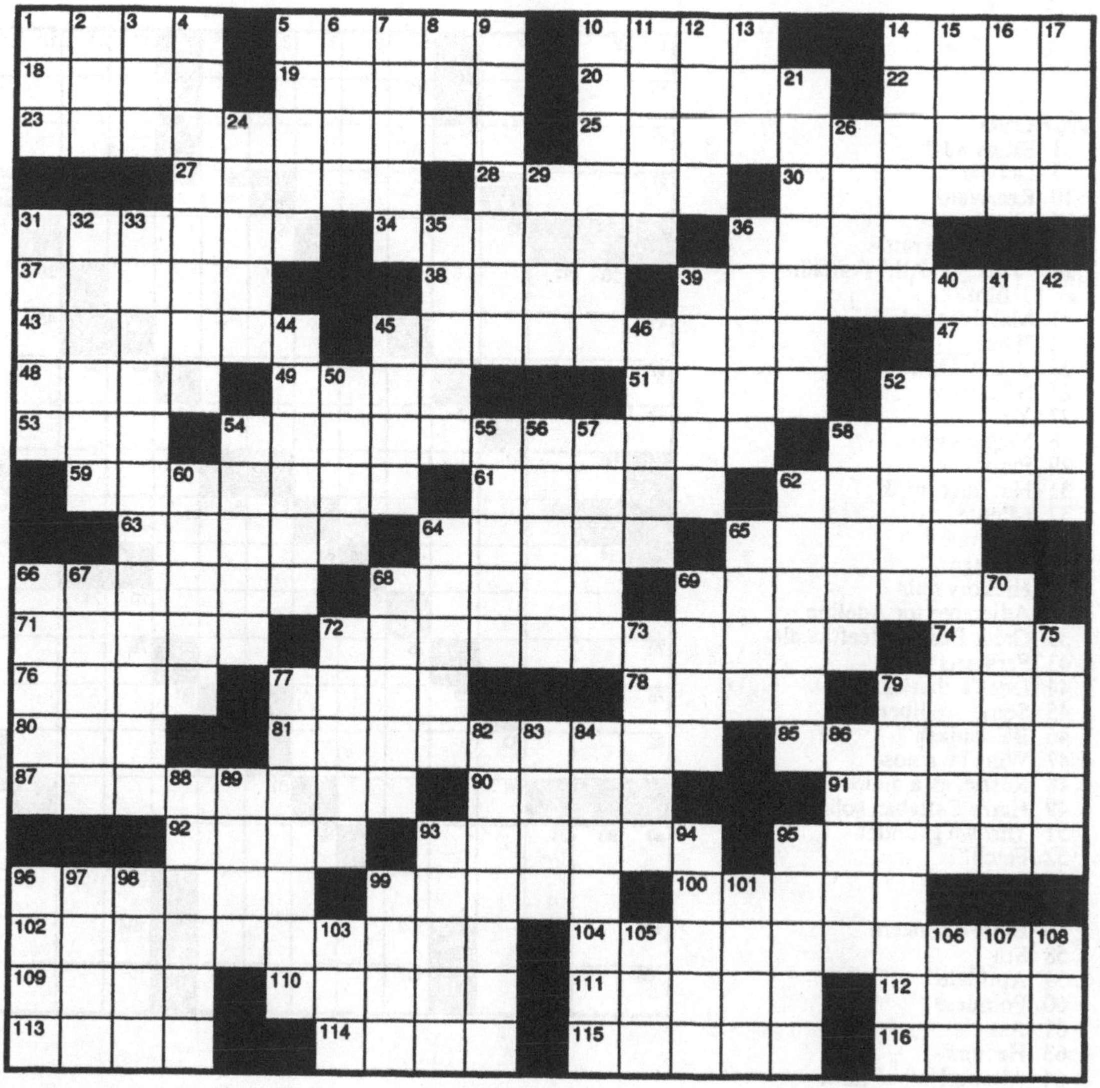

ACROSS

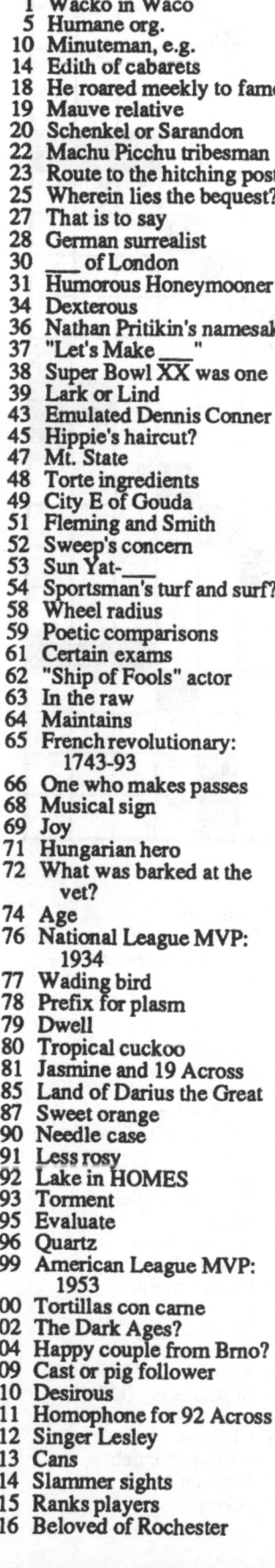

1 Wacko in Waco
5 Humane org.
10 Minuteman, e.g.
14 Edith of cabarets
18 He roared meekly to fame
19 Mauve relative
20 Schenkel or Sarandon
22 Machu Picchu tribesman
23 Route to the hitching post?
25 Wherein lies the bequest?
27 That is to say
28 German surrealist
30 ___ of London
31 Humorous Honeymooner
34 Dexterous
36 Nathan Pritikin's namesake
37 "Let's Make ___"
38 Super Bowl XX was one
39 Lark or Lind
43 Emulated Dennis Conner
45 Hippie's haircut?
47 Mt. State
48 Torte ingredients
49 City E of Gouda
51 Fleming and Smith
52 Sweep's concern
53 Sun Yat-___
54 Sportsman's turf and surf?
58 Wheel radius
59 Poetic comparisons
61 Certain exams
62 "Ship of Fools" actor
63 In the raw
64 Maintains
65 French revolutionary: 1743-93
66 One who makes passes
68 Musical sign
69 Joy
71 Hungarian hero
72 What was barked at the vet?
74 Age
76 National League MVP: 1934
77 Wading bird
78 Prefix for plasm
79 Dwell
80 Tropical cuckoo
81 Jasmine and 19 Across
85 Land of Darius the Great
87 Sweet orange
90 Needle case
91 Less rosy
92 Lake in HOMES
93 Torment
95 Evaluate
96 Quartz
99 American League MVP: 1953
100 Tortillas con carne
102 The Dark Ages?
104 Happy couple from Brno?
109 Cast or pig follower
110 Desirous
111 Homophone for 92 Across
112 Singer Lesley
113 Cans
114 Slammer sights
115 Ranks players
116 Beloved of Rochester

DOWN

1 Deg. for Belli
2 Scull
3 T'ai ___ (martial art)
4 First, second and third
5 "Paradise ___," Stallone film
6 Nurses a drink
7 Buenos Aires' river
8 Start of a Williams title
9 River in Hades
10 Fossil footprint
11 Thorax
12 Young herring
13 Russian commune
14 Ornamental loops
15 Black
16 Eagled a par-3 hole
17 Waller of jazz
21 Fracture immobilizers
24 Dancer Mara
26 Actor Vidov
29 Rake
31 Plights
32 Old truths
33 Dominio?
35 Albee's art
36 He wrote "for whom the bell tolls"
39 Uses a signet
40 Crusoe and Friday?
41 Elicit
42 Critic
44 Casino employee
45 Wilander of tennis
46 Early strings
50 Stowe novel
52 Wheel block
54 Tramped
55 Wouk's genre
56 Clad, of yore
57 Conductor Caldwell
58 Sans ___ (monotonal type)
60 U.S. naval historian: 1840-1914
62 Haymaker
64 Belts
65 Confront
66 Palindromic title
67 Type of theater
68 Evita
69 Bronze medals: Abbr.
70 Kingfisher's cousins
72 Mandel from Toronto
73 Bhutanese Bigfoots
75 Approaches
77 Striped
79 Charge for coining
82 Those who desist
83 French 1 verb
84 Slight variations
86 Derby town
88 Condescends
89 Prefix for enemy
93 "The Northeaster" artist
94 Cubic meter
95 Needs an analgesic
96 Monty Python piece
97 Letters at Golgotha
98 Columbia's animal
99 Latvian capital
101 Tannin, for one
103 Bill
105 Zuider ___
106 AKC division
107 Overthrow first
108 Diocese

184

YO-HO-HO! by Dale C. Storms

A swashbuckling surprise from a first-timer whose puzzle is strictly first-rate. Welcome aboard, Dale! (As an interesting sidenote, the city of Tampa holds an annual carnival honoring 99 Across.)

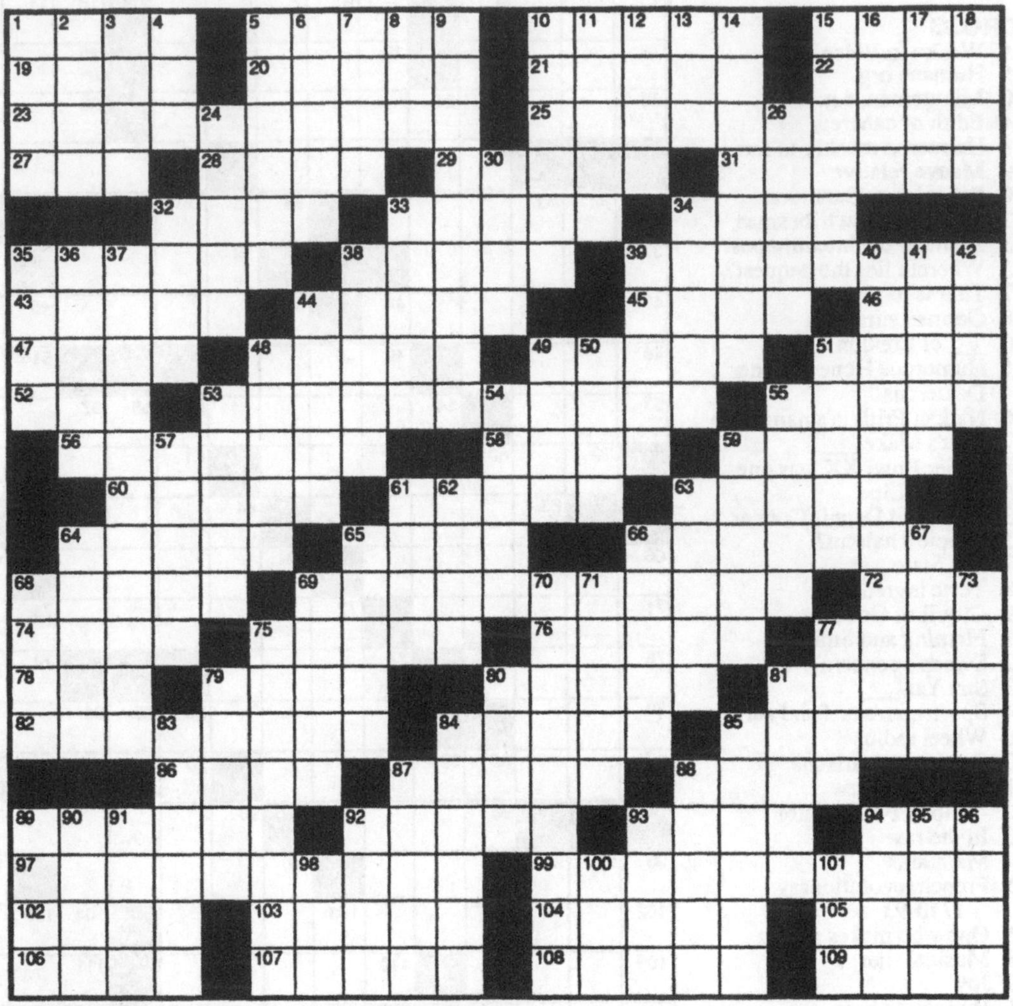

ACROSS

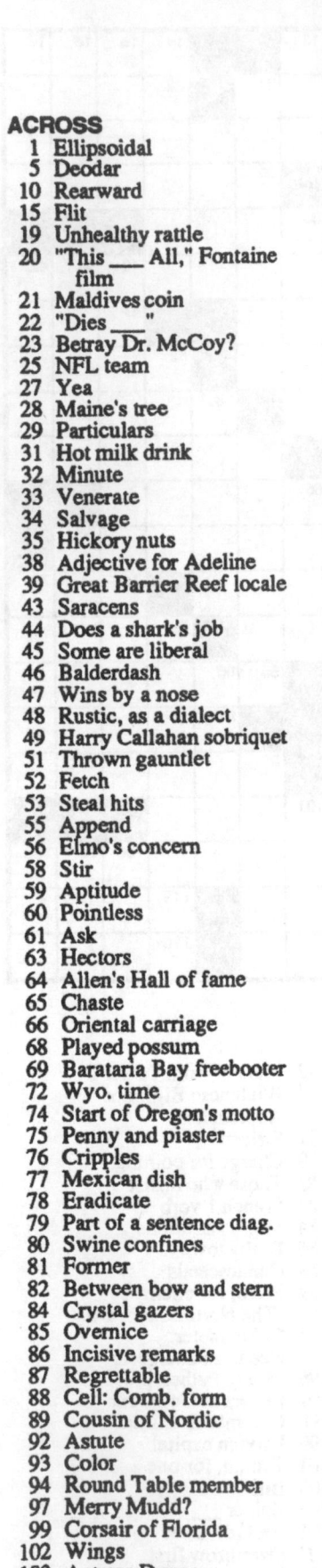

1 Ellipsoidal
5 Deodar
10 Rearward
15 Flit
19 Unhealthy rattle
20 "This ___ All," Fontaine film
21 Maldives coin
22 "Dies ___"
23 Betray Dr. McCoy?
25 NFL team
27 Yea
28 Maine's tree
29 Particulars
31 Hot milk drink
32 Minute
33 Venerate
34 Salvage
35 Hickory nuts
38 Adjective for Adeline
39 Great Barrier Reef locale
43 Saracens
44 Does a shark's job
45 Some are liberal
46 Balderdash
47 Wins by a nose
48 Rustic, as a dialect
49 Harry Callahan sobriquet
51 Thrown gauntlet
52 Fetch
53 Steal hits
55 Append
56 Elmo's concern
58 Stir
59 Aptitude
60 Pointless
61 Ask
63 Hectors
64 Allen's Hall of fame
65 Chaste
66 Oriental carriage
68 Played possum
69 Barataria Bay freebooter
72 Wyo. time
74 Start of Oregon's motto
75 Penny and piaster
76 Cripples
77 Mexican dish
78 Eradicate
79 Part of a sentence diag.
80 Swine confines
81 Former
82 Between bow and stern
84 Crystal gazers
85 Overnice
86 Incisive remarks
87 Regrettable
88 Cell: Comb. form
89 Cousin of Nordic
92 Astute
93 Color
94 Round Table member
97 Merry Mudd?
99 Corsair of Florida
102 Wings
103 Actress Dunne
104 Two caliphs
105 Tub's trouble
106 Beams
107 Aided: Abbr.
108 Species of herring
109 Subtracting

DOWN

1 Boat in "Jaws"
2 Modify
3 Lily relative
4 Bandleader Brown
5 Staterooms
6 Black
7 Cooked
8 Rosary bead
9 Domicile
10 A funny Brooks
11 French chemist: 1728-1804
12 Rainbows
13 He made it: Abbr.
14 Boston's was famous
15 Engine type
16 Enyo's companion
17 Like a day in June?
18 ACT is one
24 Whirls
26 Variable stars
30 Sloth features
32 Checks
33 Expect
34 Grades eggs
35 Twinge
36 Cat Nation tribesmen
37 "Quedagh Merchant" captor
38 Small rails
39 Hold contents
40 Madrid water pipe?
41 Raring
42 Vertex
44 "The Mask of Dimitrios" star
48 Aphrodite's mother
49 Access
50 Hoosier race
51 No-see-ums
53 "Dead Men Don't Wear ___," 1982 film
54 "Secrets" author
55 Identical
57 "The Survivors" author
59 Truths
61 Four: Rx
62 Vases
63 Nibbles
64 Hawaiian shrub
65 Remains undecided
66 Hoarfrosts
67 Place for a stickpin
68 Cultivate
69 Four-wheel-drive vehicles
70 Inseparable friends
71 Tooth taker
73 Loyalist of '76
75 Touchstones
77 Kingston ___
79 Mountebank
80 José the muralist
81 ___ Noster
83 Regards with favor (with "on")
84 Embittered
85 Hereditary ruler
87 Whiff
88 Coconut meat
89 Nearly closed
90 Dancer Montez
91 Frolic
92 "Rock of ___"
93 Autocrat
94 Swiss artist: 1879-1940
95 Sustineo ___ (USAF motto)
96 Chatters
98 Endings for debt
100 Elec. unit
101 Adverse

185

ACTING THE PART by Dorothy Smitonick
Names of fame in a name game—and more: a double-featured delight with lots of spicy clues from the Nutmeg State.

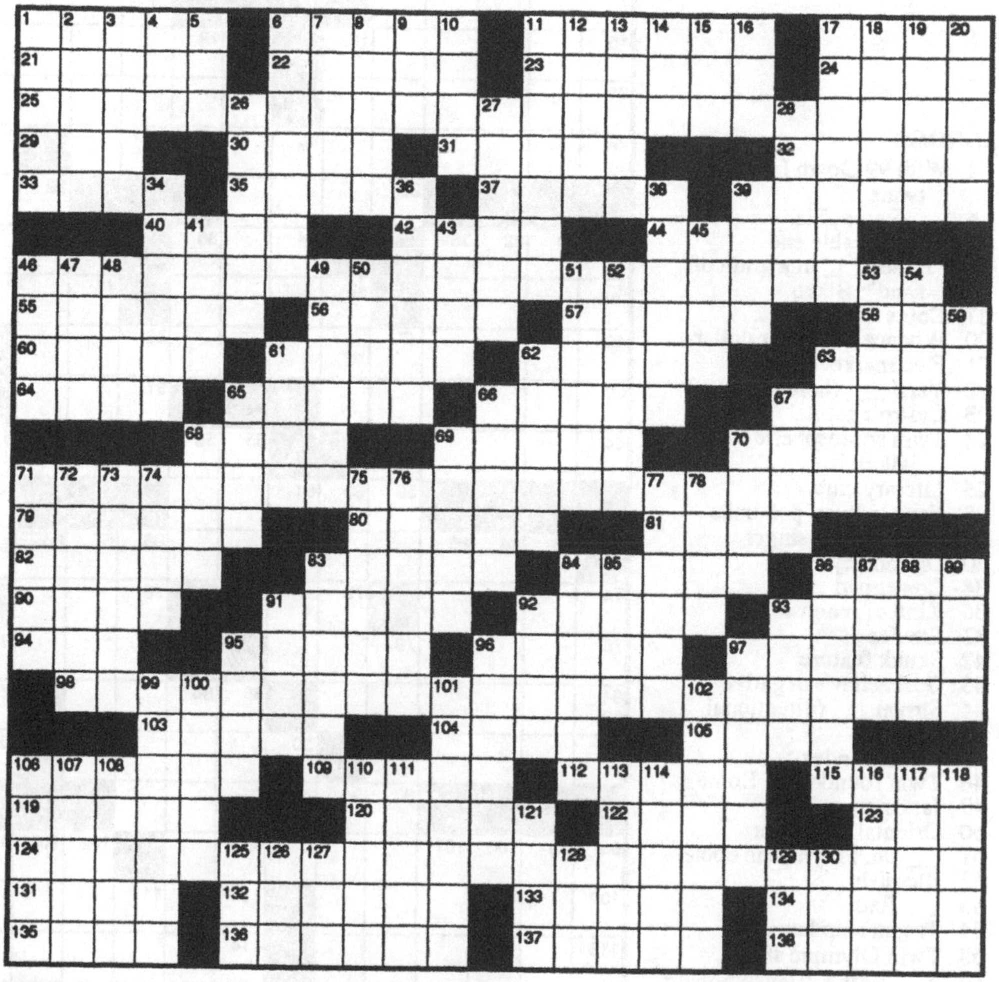

ACROSS
1 Mauna Loa outflows
6 Pair-___ shell
11 Urchins
17 "___ and Lovers"
21 Bring to bear
22 Alley score
23 Talisman
24 Resign
25 Actor requests hotel rates?
29 Vichy water
30 Escutcheon border
31 Basketry fiber: Var.
32 "Call Me ___," Merman movie
33 Part of E.E.
35 Rows
37 Plait of hair
39 Hound
40 Of the ear
42 ___ passu (side by side)
44 Gunwale pin
46 Actor pursues the Rockettes?
55 Midnight rider
56 Some Prado paintings
57 Think
58 Prefix for diazole
60 Actress MacMahon
61 English auto pioneer
62 Concerning
63 Diavolo and Angelico
64 Wire-diameter measures
65 Pub game
66 Surrounded by
67 Bath powders
68 Tops
69 Springe
70 Bully-tree gum
71 Actor crosses a SE Asian stream?
79 Bordoni and Papas
80 Goads
81 Heels
82 Gold braid
83 Disturbances
84 School heads
86 Midge
90 Australian marsupial
91 Southwestern groves
92 Wharton character
93 Hag
94 ___ loss for words
95 Biblical mount
96 "Crisis" publisher
97 Sci-fi film of 1986
98 TV host stews in Texas?
103 Halter
104 Petitions
105 SI units of resistance
106 Indian porter
109 Oodles
112 Child's kind of test
115 At all times
119 Heeling
120 Struck
122 War of 1899-1902
123 Indignation
124 Actor expecting the Thayers?
131 Capital of Manche
132 Woodland deities
133 De Niro's "Angel Heart" role
134 Greased
135 Miami team
136 Pulls away
137 Shabby
138 Rumpled

DOWN
1 White House reception
2 Of a pivotal nature
3 Scene of the crime
4 Curve
5 ___-Foy, Quebec
6 Rhea's relative
7 Empire or Grimes
8 Harder to find
9 Silkworm
10 Tenth: Comb. form
11 Of the stomach
12 Abundant
13 Slippers
14 Org. of the docks
15 ___ Percé Indian
16 Dep.
17 Back to ___
18 De la Ramée's pseudonym
19 Actress Naldi, et al.
20 Stalks
26 See
27 Bit players
28 Petite
34 Assemblies at Eastwick
36 Amounts to
38 G, D, A or E
39 Garden tool
41 Site of modern Sur
43 Sale provision
45 Seek
46 Miler Steve
47 Sun: Comb. form
48 Depraved
49 Cherished
50 River in SC Arizona
51 Balzac
52 Half of a twin bill
53 "___, nor duty bade me fight": Yeats
54 Track bet
59 Brazilian palm
61 Rajah's wife
62 Nanking nannies
63 "The Cheap Detective" star
65 Actress Diana
66 Chips in
67 Gobs
68 Honest names
69 Some NCOs
70 Fourposters
71 Regional life
72 Corrigenda
73 Antenna
74 Organized body
75 B.B. King's instrument
76 Amorous
77 Beginning of veni, vidi
78 Windmill blade
83 Palmyra
84 Most thirsty
85 Ages and ages
86 Young salmon
87 Seasonal song
88 Comedienne Held
89 Mrs. Tracy
91 Sara and Farrow
92 Sham
93 Littleneck
95 Convertiplane
96 Vantage point
97 Stick
99 Up a tree
100 "Games People Play" singer
101 Gradual absorption
102 In a remarkable way
106 Severe
107 Winged
108 Frost-flower genus
110 Simon of opera
111 Catkin
113 Upstairs
114 " . . . this too too ___ flesh": Shak.
116 Bowed instruments
117 Coastal birds
118 "Pete's Dragon" star
121 Wraps up
125 NYC-to-El Paso dir.
126 Before brake or brush
127 ___ de la Cité
128 Grand
129 ___ de guerre
130 Kind of chart

186 GEMINI by Patterson Pepple

We considered calling this puzzle "Gemini Crickets"—but that wouldn't be cricket!

ACROSS

1 With 99 Down Indy 500 twins
6 ___ Raton, Fla.
10 Jumper cable end
15 "To see ___ in a grain of sand": Blake
17 Coins for Sherlock
20 Whence came our dollar
21 Flea market activity
22 Versi ___ (heroic poetry)
23 Castro's capital
24 Twin stratospheric balloonists
26 Literary club
28 Former Russ. pol. units
29 Famed blues singer
30 Diplomacy
34 Consumed
36 Kind of renewal
37 Exudes
42 Skunk feature
43 Gorbachev's negative
44 Simon ___ (directional game)
45 Sundial index
46 Twin founders of Rome
49 Jazzmatazz
50 Oriental computer
51 ___ tai, Polynesian cooler
52 Blemish
53 ___ fixe
54 Trojan ship launcher
55 Twin Olympic skiers
59 "___ with a View": Forster
62 Kidneylike structure: Comb. form
63 Twins of the Peacock Throne
69 Moslems, collectively
74 Friendly Parisienne
75 "Follow Me___": Kipling
76 Popeye's Olive
77 Outline
78 Scapegoat
80 Mark Twain's twins
84 Kind of kingdom
85 Cassette feature
87 Bacchanalia
88 British gun
89 Sped
90 Sea eagles
91 "A ___ Named Sue"
92 Tortoise's competitor
93 Care for
95 Numbered musical composition
98 Biblical twins
102 "GWTW" Tarleton twins
109 ___ and bothered
110 Female monologuist
112 Lewis Carroll's Tweedle twins
113 Abhorrent
114 More obdurate
115 Circumlocution
116 Promote
117 Ginza need
118 Moresby and Said

DOWN

1 Actresses Main or Rambeau, for short
2 "Just ___ doch-an-dorris": Lauder
3 Soprano Ponselle
4 Persia, now
5 Spicy stews
6 Parris Island recruit
7 Caen's river
8 LI x II
9 Twin advice columnists
10 P. T. Barnum's twins
11 Etna product
12 Wings for Amor
13 Computer display options
14 Little Hilary's "wheels"
16 ___ ex machina
17 Induce confusion
18 "___ Misérables"
19 Alaskan Indians
20 Now's tagalong
25 CSA troops
27 Hebrew liquid measure
29 Neighbor to Paraguay (Sp. spelling)
30 Pentateuch
31 Taos architecture
32 Southwestern griddle
33 White flag result
35 Printemps follower
36 Customary
38 Leit theme
39 Ammonia compound
40 "Peace on the earth, good will ___": Sears
41 Cut, old style
43 Greek letters
45 Fisher's weir
47 Moonlike
48 Tacitus's 2,001
49 Rough file
52 Architect Ieoh
55 Pontiff
56 Desig. for a British aircraft
57 U.S. Patent Off. suitor
58 Author Jong
60 French king: 923-936
61 "Heart ___ Heart," Ben Ryan hit
63 Iowa commune
64 Containing an abundant element: Comb. form
65 "St. Margaret's Cave" author
66 Emulated a toad
67 Dishonest harps?
68 "The Greatest"
70 Silence!
71 Parts of a drachma
72 Middle East VIP
73 WW I battle site
74 Not near
77 Double agent
79 Social butterfly
81 San Francisco hill
82 Vallee or Crosby
83 Cleo's realm
85 Stair parts
86 Lifetime lifeline
90 Latin conjunctions
94 Vietnamese New Years
96 Cabinet post: Abbr.
97 Pol's post
98 Linear measure of India
99 See 1 Across
100 Muse of history
101 Exclamations of triumph
102 Swiss capital
103 Hose ladders
104 Suffix with Siam
105 Knob on a shield
106 Jewish month
107 Part of a brig.
108 Prepares to drive
111 Bishop's office

187

E FOR FFORT by Donald V Lee II

For this challenger Donald deserves an E for Excellence. Take a good look at the title; it points to a theme that affects *every* word in the diagram.

ACROSS

1 List
6 Weasel relative
10 Shelters for sheep
14 Short-___ the bed
18 Put into motion
20 Brought up
21 Rep
22 Senator from Maine
23 Nursery-rhyme trio
25 Less experienced
26 Hebrew dry measures
27 Minerals
28 Pantries
30 ___ later (eventually)
32 NFL team
33 Take on freight
34 Was offended
35 Wild adventures
38 Allowing
40 Wish for a traveler
44 Vicar's assistant
45 Belonging to Jason's wife
47 Hard worker
49 Good will
50 Whole
51 Fry
52 It borders Eritrea
53 Number 1 wood
54 Seaport in N Honduras
55 Less plain
57 Emphasize anew
59 Region
60 Stevens and Dallas
62 City on the Kansas River
64 Anyway
66 Else
68 ___ volens (willy-nilly)
70 Weight allowances
71 Injurious
75 Spadix enclosure
77 Trickle
81 Caution
82 Grumblers: Sl.
84 Column's slight convexity
86 Olive genus
87 Not transparent
89 Cover completely
90 Cobble or gem
91 Perspire
92 Liberate
93 Escaroles
94 Acoustic coupler
95 Purveys
96 Young arbor
98 Disney's "___ Wonderland"
100 Lewis or Biondi, e.g.
102 Practical
104 Ace
105 Akin
106 Alienated
109 Piercing
111 For fear that
114 Spicy kind of cooking
115 Liquefied
117 Amusement park thrill
119 Dahl or Francis
120 Approached
121 Russian co-op
122 Bureaus
123 Minimal
124 Shul
125 Forefathers
126 Pines for

DOWN

1 Muse of poetry
2 Earthy pigment
3 Pilots
4 Toothpaste container
5 Land
6 Commands
7 Circus performer
8 Poems of eight lines
9 Soldier of 1776
10 Imprisons
11 Bête noire of folklore
12 Volunteer State
13 More powerful
14 Type of murder or burn
15 Four-bagger
16 Pang of pain
17 Thicker
19 Like the nobility
24 Ancient Scandinavian
29 Mare nostrum
31 Amerind
32 Javelin
34 Chronicle
35 Aromas
36 Croquette
37 Antenna
38 Joy
39 Protuberances
41 Kind of ID number
42 Macadamizers
43 Abate
46 Separated substance
48 Piece of iron
51 Coast
53 Renegades
55 Weariness
56 Recovery
58 Pilchard
61 Knowledge
63 Pacific seaweed
65 He loved Lucy
67 Demolished
69 Hat with a high crown
71 Stage settings
72 Expired
73 Molasses
74 Distinctive
76 Like some arguments
78 Clown's cravat
79 Strident sounds
80 Most recent
83 "Bolero" composer
85 Wine steward
88 Tantamount
91 Part of S.W.A.K.
93 Betrothal
94 Reflected
95 Class
97 Ennead
99 Pivotal
101 Did the Watusi
103 Scene of confusion
105 Narrates anew
106 Climb
107 ___ cotta
108 Functions
109 Hawk
110 Modify
111 ___ of two evils
112 Like some taskmasters
113 Braid of hair
116 U. of Maryland athlete
118 Bewildered

188

CAPITAL GAINS by Arthur Verdesca
You don't have to be a world traveler to appreciate this puzzle's geographic gimmick.

ACROSS

1 Scop
5 10/19/87 on Wall Street
10 Chilly in Glasgow
15 After human or horse
19 Lawyer Gardner
20 Kind of cassette
21 Very, to Verdi
22 Islamic chieftain
23 Portuguese candies?
25 Japanese health food?
27 Fence
28 Lucy's friend
30 Exact
31 Pestiferous pests
34 Danish island
35 Silkworm center of Japan
36 Salvation Army founder
37 Bore
39 Disturb
43 Pigeon coop
44 Descend an Australian mountain?
47 Margin
48 Amin
49 Theatrical award
50 Discern
51 Small in size
52 Cabbage salad
54 SOS from Finland?
58 Slow driver
59 Florida State's mascot
61 Aquatic nymph
62 Rothschild's domain
63 Idolize
64 Breadnut
65 Bay window
66 Progenitor
68 Freshen
69 Like Nemesis
72 Actress Pappas
73 Iran's demand for 9 Down?
75 Chiwere dialect
76 McAuliffe's surrender reply
77 Creek
78 Insular mass
79 One billion years
80 Suffix for soon
81 Austrian pastry?
86 He, to Giuseppe
87 Three-dimensional displays
89 Bolt
90 Befuddled
91 "When I was ___"
92 Cigar ending
93 Hid
96 Higher-up
99 Tocsin
101 Like some pickings
102 Italian curative?
105 Peruvian tree?
110 Foamy potations
111 Purposes
112 Ghana capital
113 Na^+ and Cl^-
114 Thomas Wolfe hero
115 Lock of hair
116 Outmoded
117 Frank Herbert novel

DOWN

1 ___ canto
2 "Exodus" hero
3 Literary monogram
4 Compiler of British "Peerage"
5 ___ Major (Great Dog)
6 Coin in Perm
7 Annie of "Oklahoma"
8 Without: Lat.
9 Behan play, with "The"
10 Party worker
11 Italian commune
12 England-Wales river
13 Short poem
14 Bishopric
15 Warm over
16 Manchurian river
17 About: Abbr.
18 French fashion illustrator
24 Curse
26 U.S. mathematician: 1906-1978
29 Monsieur, in Mainz
31 ___-oo (ta-ta)
32 Bulgarian liqueur?
33 Geriatric
35 Unfasten
36 Heaven
38 Beame and Burrows
39 Overturn
40 Libyan courtesy?
41 Flaxen
42 Corundum
44 Companion
45 White poplar
46 Continental's neighbor
51 Precede
53 Expands
55 Empty
56 Handler?
57 Plains Indian
58 Principal pipe
60 Zip
62 City of NW Germany
64 Ada from Limerick
65 Convex molding
66 Yearned
67 Ethiopian province
68 Bit lines
69 Entries in black
70 Hung
71 Racing jib
73 Trample
74 Abydos' river
81 Sound
82 Pound or Williams, e.g.
83 Crude
84 Agave
85 Shingle a roof
86 Nasal bone
88 Least cooked
90 B ___ boy
92 Gil ___, Port. navigator
94 Nicholas and Alexander
95 Chlorination victims
96 Crow
97 SE Kansas city
98 Feds
100 Isinglass
103 Tucker, for one
104 Four after Silent Cal
106 Hosts
107 Coach Holtz
108 Imaret
109 AMEX

189 DETECTIVE STORY by Barbara Springer

Barbara has cleverly taken characters, settings, and titles from the world of mystery and woven them into her own whodunit work. The only thing lacking below is the standard chase scene, and oh, yes, a solution. We assume 38 Down is found guilty.

ACROSS

1 Curling-team captain
5 After horse or soap
10 Barely
14 Occident
18 "L'Etranger" author
20 Snake or Moose
21 High: Comb. form
22 Redolence
23 Piecemeal
24 Concerning
25 SCENE OF THE CRIME (Poe)
27 THE VICTIM (Christie)
30 Gymnasium sights
31 Supplement
32 Young ruru
33 Be contrite
36 Necessity
37 Cape for John Paul II
39 Neckwear
44 Sound of cymbals
48 THE POLICE INSPECTOR (P. D. James)
51 Let bills accumulate
52 Caravan stop
54 Footnote abbr.
55 Sunfish
56 Part of WASP
57 Turn signal
59 Badger State capital
61 Orfe
62 Madonna and Cher, e.g.
64 Mountain in Thessaly
66 Commune E of Antwerp
67 Fire opal
69 Jungfrau, for one
70 Dick Francis thriller
75 Soft shoe
76 Fish story
78 Glazed pottery
79 ___ polloi
80 "San ___ Rose"
84 War of 1853-56
86 Source of oil
88 Char
89 Alban Berg opus
91 Area of sinkholes and caverns
92 Carouse
93 LAWYER FOR THE DEFENSE (J. Mortimer)
96 Manipulate
97 Mother of Col. Paul Tibbets, Jr.
98 Super actor
99 Greenish-blue
102 Hugin and Munin
105 Squirt
106 Crony
109 Scholastic world
113 THE MOTIVE (W. Collins)
117 THE PRIVATE EYE (Stout)
120 One past puerility
121 Outstanding
122 Parts of a switchback
123 Toe, in a sense
124 Hosiery thread
125 Senator Inouye, e.g.
126 Succulent plant
127 "Desert Gold" author
128 Cultural customs
129 Adjacent

DOWN

1 Spook
2 Pillow stuffing
3 Spitting ___
4 24-karat
5 Dodona or Delphi
6 Cut with certain shears
7 Turn inside out
8 Univ. of Nevada site
9 Partner of crafty
10 John Mason's namesake
11 Eskimo knife
12 Roman burial stone
13 Greek philosopher
14 Drudge
15 Move gradually
16 Off-key
17 Uno y dos
19 CAUSE OF DEATH (Sayers)
26 Stanza of eight lines
28 Wonder
29 Sixty grains
34 Presbyters
35 Organic fertilizer
37 Master of 102 Across
38 CHIEF SUSPECT (Dostoyevsky)
40 Figure of speech
41 Corp. VIP's
42 European capital
43 Word of comparison
44 Golfer Stadler
45 Monday in Quebec
46 Madden
47 Not any, to Belli
48 Sale caveat
49 Cuban painter: 1902-82
50 Thane of ___ (Macbeth)
52 Coin of ancient Greece
53 Allen's was famous
58 Kreskin specialty
60 THE NARRATOR (Doyle)
63 Tractable
65 Globe support
68 Ethically neutral
69 Part of E.T.A.
71 Usage
72 Splinter
73 Hut
74 Succumb
77 Shrewdness
78 "No Mercy" star
80 Wimbledon winner in 1975
81 Rare gas
82 Poi ingredient
83 "___ Town"
85 Tom or drake
87 Romanian coins
90 Angler's spoon
94 American League MVP: 1977
95 Nudnik
99 Rocky's Creed
100 Cites
101 Coffee server
103 Honor ___ thieves
104 Of the soft palate
105 Compress
106 Balance
107 Append
108 For real
109 San Francisco founder
110 Do some plastering
111 Meleager's vessel
112 Medicate
114 Spy of 1776
115 Emulate Mencken
116 Mattress size
118 For shame!
119 Culbertson of bridge

190

WISE WORDS by William Lutwiniak
Here's a sagacious statement by a famous essayist. Also, note the sapience of our noted puzzler.

ACROSS

1 Green gemstone
6 Vale of Tempe landmark
10 Windsock
14 Part of OAS
18 Of the kidneys
19 Factor in lunar reckoning
20 "There ___ old woman . . ."
21 Literary form
23 **Start of a quotation**
27 In-box item
28 Actress Merrill, et al.
29 NY Bay island
30 Offended olfactorily
31 Like a pillar
33 Van Gogh milieu
34 Paraphrase
35 Forte of 55 Across
39 Zipper, e.g.
43 "___ a far, far better . . ."
44 "We ___ the World"
45 Pay to play
49 Escalates
50 Co-star on "Quincy"
51 N.J. summer resort
54 Intones
55 Author of the quotation
58 Lady of song: 1932
59 ___ clock scholar
60 The best
61 Patty Duke's ex-spouse
62 West Indies people
63 Stuttgart street
66 Semester
67 "La Nausée" author
68 An adjective for 55 Across
73 Solar phenomena
76 But, to Jose
77 Sailor's rope
81 Front-end part of a car
82 Chamfer
83 Fedora material
85 Be quite audible
87 Famed violinist
88 Autobiography by 55 Across
90 Sum of money
92 Chophouse offerings
94 Courtroom vow
95 An 18th cen. public ball
96 Towel ID
97 Sch. subject
98 Window unit
100 Certitude
101 Work by 55 Across: 1865
105 Saguaros
108 Local birds
109 In paired fashion
113 Pago Pago person
114 Parade vehicle
115 Discipline
116 Library offer
118 **End of the quotation**
122 Nile feature
123 Heart parts
124 "Waiting for Lefty" author
125 Fathers
126 Dry run
127 Grammar abbr.
128 Mrs. Truman
129 One of Reagan's Attorney Generals

DOWN

1 Demure
2 Violin's precursor
3 Wind: Comb. form
4 Phenyl salicylate
5 Whitney or Wallach
6 Alfresco
7 City on the Krishna
8 Educational insts.
9 Noshed
10 Scoundrel
11 Birthplace of St. Francis
12 Ex-D.C. nine
13 Depend ending
14 Saint whose day is April 21
15 Contrapuntal composition
16 Bring out
17 Apply to
19 Shows
20 NBA's Reed
22 In Ireland, he's a spalpeen
24 "Drums Along the Mohawk" author
25 Iron: Comb. form
26 Desk item
32 Didn't usually
33 Suburb of London
36 Willowy
37 Humble abode
38 City on the Bidassoa
39 Datum
40 Remains
41 Meager
42 Pavarotti, for one
45 Notwithstanding
46 The pits
47 Subfamily subdivision
48 ___ out (gets by)
50 Act finish
51 Pet dog of the Jetsons
52 Allow too little
53 Certain periodical
55 McCrea or Grey
56 Cramped, untidy place
57 Consumer
60 Sale condition
62 "Brian's Song" star
64 Kitchen wear
65 Unload
67 Style for Ella
69 ". . . upon ___ in Darien": Keats
70 Glacial snowfields
71 Weight allowance
72 Ille, ___, illud
73 Daudet's daughter
74 Potto, for one
75 Saudis, e.g.
78 Light-bulb gas
79 Way there
80 Scoots
81 Georgia ___
82 Portuguese poet-president
83 Señor Castrp
84 SHAEF concern
86 Autos of old
88 Writes
89 Peelings
90 Gun
91 That is, to Cato
93 ___ off (vexing)
95 Dilapidated
98 Summer topper
99 Actress Ekberg
100 Snubs
101 ___-home, kin of a shut-in
102 Certain teeth
103 X-rated, likely
104 Herons' kins
105 Sign of omission
106 Stubborn as ___
107 AFC team
110 "Dallas" matriarch
111 France's longest river
112 Penn Yan's county
113 Part of MST
114 Greek cheese
115 Ferris wheel, for one
117 Brokers' domain on Wall St.
119 NFL-er
120 ___ Hill, San Francisco
121 Doctrine

191 COLLABORATIONS by Joy Wouk

Joy has arranged for famous literary figures and others to work jointly together on her puzzling project. The results are most interesting.

ACROSS

1 Ms. Abzug
6 Lively dance
11 Bulgarian capital
16 Extinct Hawaiian bird
20 Celebes oxen
21 Leave by ladder
22 Out on ___ (vulnerable)
23 Abba and family
25 Wolfe-Hamilton work?
29 O. T. book
30 Mills of opera
31 Guido's note
32 Skulls
33 Cather-Hart work?
38 Anjou and Bosc
43 Extreme: Abbr.
44 Maseru is its capital
45 An Adams
46 Actress Duse
48 Soak flax
49 "The Name of the Rose" author
51 Science deg.
52 Green-Comden-Nash work?
59 Oozed
60 Oar
61 Peculiar: Comb. form
62 Prized prize
66 Symbol of Eire
67 Japanese Buddhist church
68 "The Sign of the Cross" actress
70 Last of a series
71 Plus
73 Miser, in Avignon
75 Doctrine
77 Excited
78 Ibsen-Marx Brothers work?
84 "___ Rhythm"
88 Longing
89 Word heard on 10/31
90 Isaac's mother
94 Eureka loc.
96 Less green
100 "Bus Stop" playwright
101 Como coins
102 Senior
103 Soothe
104 King in I Kings
105 Jack-in-the-pulpit feature
107 Hardy-Wright work? (with "The")
113 NFL division
116 Flub
117 Coll. branches
118 Most beaverlike
119 Dawdle
121 "The ___ in the Garden": Thurber
125 Curve
126 Lacoste and Coty
127 Willson-Wasserman work? (with "The")
132 ___ Madre
133 Commercials
134 Transport
135 Oak worshipers
141 Hemingway-Carson work?
146 Solos
147 Turmoil
148 "Mack the ___"
149 ___ mignon
150 Terminates
151 Makes ready
152 Tars
153 Senses

DOWN

1 Anguish
2 Adam's grandson
3 Booty
4 100,000 rupees
5 Court figure
6 Valued one
7 Pub order
8 Part of l.c.d.
9 Geometric genre
10 Danger
11 Articulate org.
12 Cities in Illinois and Texas
13 Filippo's son
14 "___ not so": Shak.
15 Lat. case
16 Canadian length measure
17 Rub off
18 Raging women
19 Of dreams
24 Bet
26 ___ pro nobis
27 Pone's neighbor
28 Impact, in Saxony
34 Gruesome
35 Buck heroine
36 Item
37 Tea genus
38 Zoological foot
39 Elijah's successor
40 Virgil hero
41 Will or Buck
42 Scrap
47 "A Chorus Line" number
48 Profit
50 Wine: Comb. form
53 Fountain of 58 Down
54 Hourly
55 Crete peak
56 Paris-born diarist
57 Fashionable dressmaker
58 Italia capital
63 Implore
64 Self
65 Straggle
67 More gingery
69 Alike: Comb. form
72 "___ will be done . . ."
74 NYC summer time
76 Greek letters
79 Suffix for auction
80 Heep, and others
81 Use a thurible
82 Uzbek city
83 Idle chatter
84 Rocks
85 Girl
86 Antique
87 Stadium feature
91 Laugh, in Rimini
92 Ascended
93 A simple sugar
95 Unfettered
97 Peter of fiction
98 That, in Ecuador
99 Roll up again
105 Hide
106 Orwell's Napoleon
108 Two-term president
109 Jug, to Jupiter
110 Bridge sequence
111 Old English ligature
112 U. in Denton, Texas
113 ". . . beg the ___ palsied . . .": Shak.
114 Excavation, in Évry
115 Enclosed within
120 Steadied
122 More foolish
123 Baby
124 Out ___ (not in conformity
125 Necessitate
128 Tasteless
129 Dominoes
130 Kind of theater
131 Fuss
136 Reeve's mate
137 Fish named after 121 Across
138 Unemployed
139 Affaire d'honneur
140 Concordes
142 Elec. unit
143 "For ___ a jolly . . ."
144 At the stern
145 Legal matter

192 WHIMSICAL MEMOS by Ernie Furtado

An up-and-coming puzzler unleashes some pretty powerful puns! If this NYC wordsmith had his way, Fun City would be called Pun City.

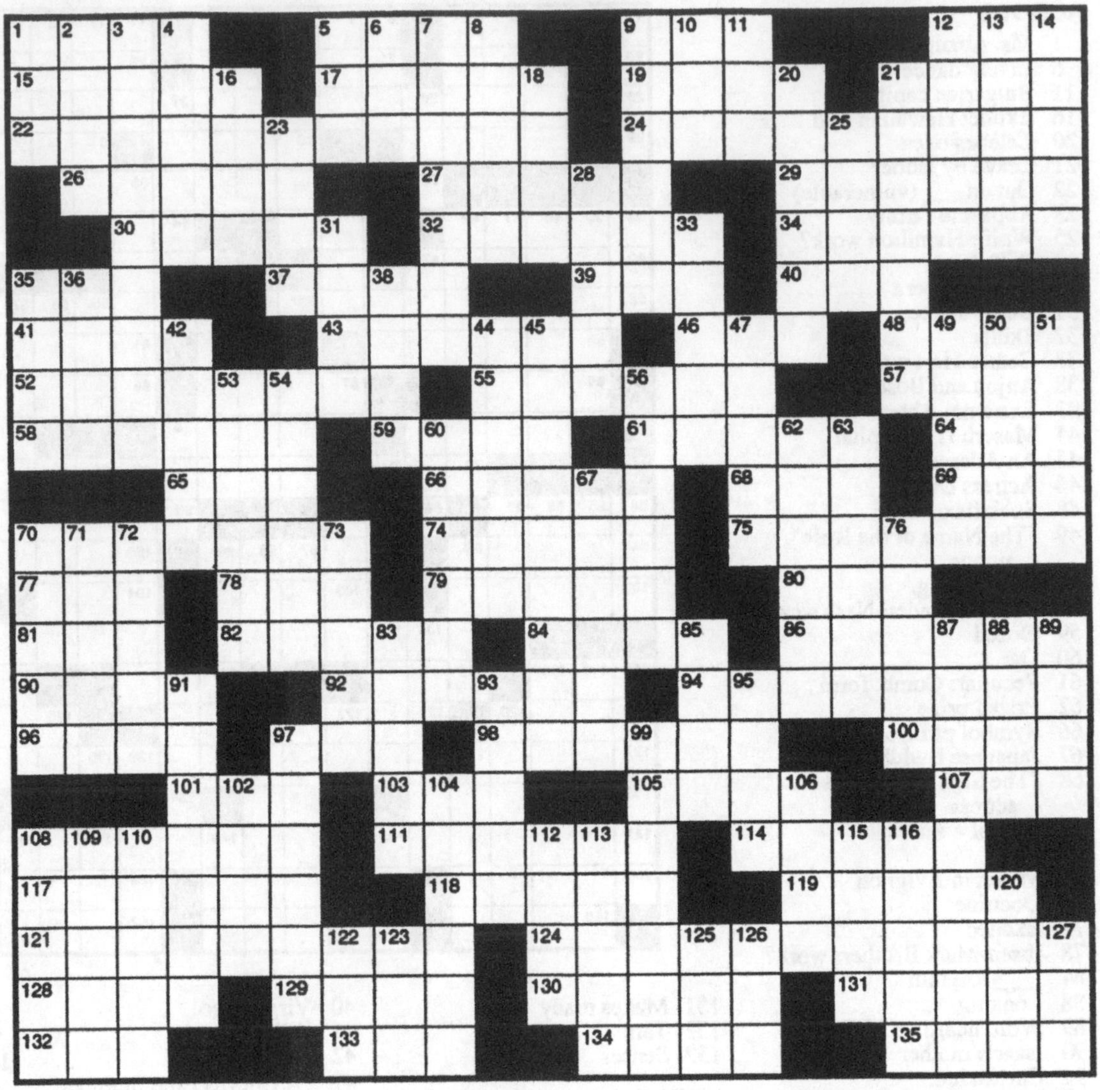

ACROSS

1 Hawkeye city
5 First name in espionage
9 NYSE's little brother
12 Pub
15 New ___, India
17 Rope fiber
19 Shortened way to the Hamptons
21 Rum cake
22 Rile Spillane's sleuth?
24 Unshackle Perry?
26 Rocky debris
27 Rose oil
29 W Louisiana river
30 Places for chapeaux
32 Honchoed
34 Mitterrand's residence
35 Ginseng relative
37 Tarn
39 Nero's 401
40 Trouble
41 Wend
43 ___ claim (plead with insistence)
46 SMU rival
48 Inventor Lilienthal
52 Watch over Fleming?
55 Silky wool
57 Brad
58 Radiant
59 European capital
61 Pulsate
64 Bucks' org.
65 Upward: Prefix
66 Popular type of book
68 Suffix for hero
69 Biblical bk.
70 Ask Lisa to settle up?
74 A funny Williams
75 City near Cleveland
77 Yoko
78 Peete's peg
79 Toughen
80 Ankle-high shoe
81 Steal, once
82 Also, to Marcellus
84 Demolish: Brit.
86 Weather-map line
90 Netman Yannick
92 ___ tuck
94 Spike's abode
96 Opposed to ecto
97 That girl
98 False
100 Caesar's 602
101 Fed. printers
103 Stat. of the mound
105 Zola novel
107 Maynard of oaters
108 Modular
111 Blunted
114 Permit
117 Thin layer
118 Graylags
119 Imprecations
121 "All-American Boy" of radio days
124 "The Boss" of rock
128 Yep
129 Prong
130 Kind of bear
131 Weepy
132 Former jrs.
133 Conducted
134 Cajole
135 Hwys.

DOWN

1 Some are classified
2 National League team
3 Vote in Roberts?
4 Apportion
5 Ovine sound
6 Missile letters
7 Like some wild ones
8 Vinegar Comb. form
9 Lunt or Newman
10 Title for Guinness
11 Before, before
12 Foundation
13 Have ___ to pick
14 Hindu queen
16 "___ a man who wasn't there . . . "
18 Liberal ___
20 Network
21 Mollycoddle Chaney?
23 Mr. Wickfield's clerk
25 Algeria neighbor
28 BMI rival
31 Spanish soup
33 Abandon
35 Links org.
36 Actor McClure
38 Yes ___?
42 Shatter
44 Gin mill
45 Delay George?
47 Lesser Antilles Indian
49 "Last ___ in Paris"
50 Italian river
51 Chan portrayer
53 Israeli tribesman
54 Turkish inn
56 Expiates
60 Kind of cocktail
62 Just ___ happy family
63 Spatter all over
67 Harangue
70 "Death Be Not Proud" poet
71 What Lincoln preserved
72 Gypsy
73 Not any, in Nuremberg
76 Deluge
83 Televised
85 Icelandic poetry manual
87 "Our Gang" member
88 French continent
89 Hold back
91 Large wrasse
93 "Behold ___ horse . . . ": Rev.
95 Mrs. Chaplin
97 College in Geneva
99 Cook poorly
102 Gasp
104 Hardy
106 Like a bump on ___
108 Gambols
109 More unusual
110 Southworth and Bovary
112 For fear that
113 Particularly: Abbr.
115 Final
116 Animal with webbed feet
120 Dry
122 Peanut ___
123 Compass pt.
125 Gilbert's princess
126 Night goddess
127 M. Cuomo's concern

193

CINEMA VITAE by Robert H. Wolfe
Film titles are cleverly converted into bios. Our favorites are 31 and 69 Across.

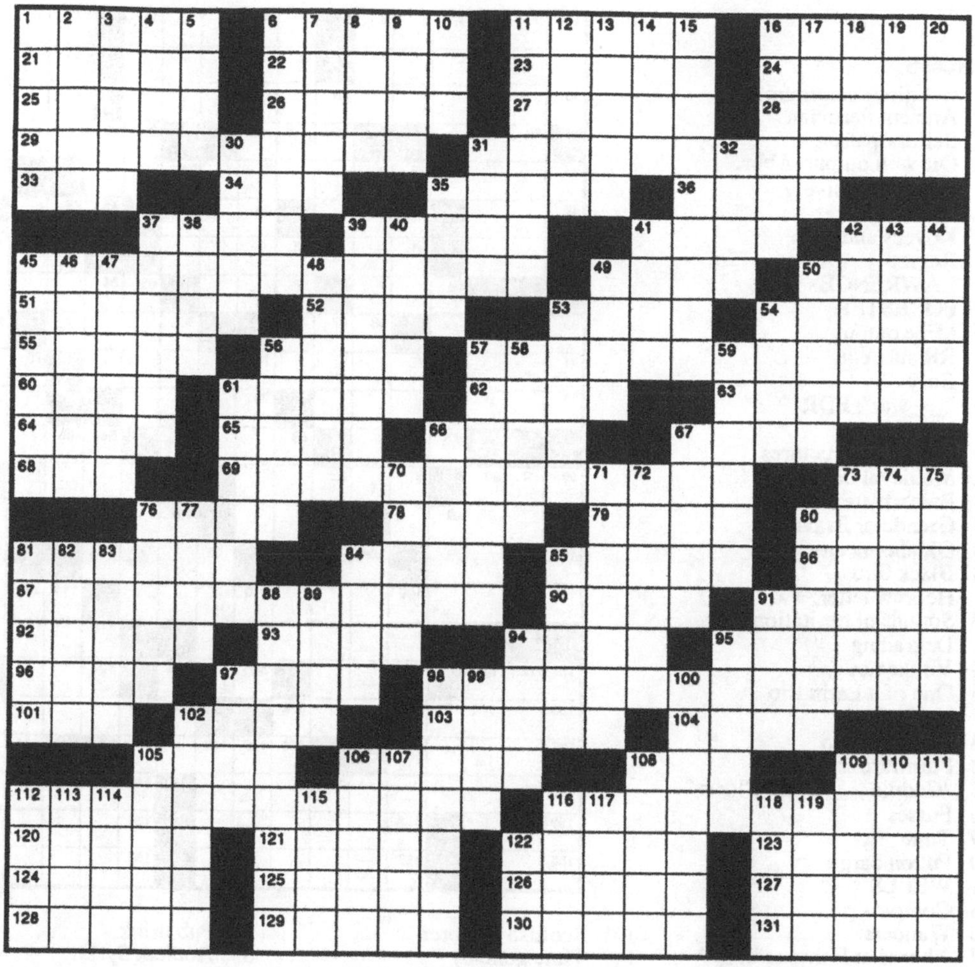

ACROSS

1 Satiated and bored
6 Brazilian dance
11 Memorable socialite, Perle ___
16 Gave out
21 Filled the hold
22 Spreads
23 Troy
24 Many ___ (often)
25 Lessen
26 Cries
27 Play part
28 Ellington's "___ Doll"
29 El toro's bio?
31 North's bio?
33 Compass pt.
34 Legal thing
35 Test rating
36 Chills
37 Portico
39 Kind of can or gun
41 A large amount
42 Pliny's 601
45 Bio of Elsa and siblings?
49 Charlie ___ of literature and films
50 Mr. T's "A" group
51 Topee
52 One, in Berlin
53 Official with a list
54 Certain stage
55 Syrians, e.g.
56 Defeat
57 Benji's bio?
60 Taboo
61 Trim before a mirror
62 Emulates Jesse James
63 Tenant
64 Boat support
65 Gas: Comb. form
66 Aroma
67 Endure
68 JFK sight
69 Tatum's bio?
73 Hot tub
76 Garden tools
78 McShane and Fleming
79 Gable feature
80 Synagogue
81 Film bio necessity
84 Mine entrance
85 Leporids
86 Milano money
87 Bio of Merrick and Levine?
90 One of the Johnsons
91 Indian follower
92 Harsh
93 Dec. 24 and 31
94 Dog star
95 Strip
96 Bohemian
97 Risked being caught by radar
98 Tony's bio? Or maybe Pernell's?
101 Kind of man
102 Antitoxins
103 Cyclotron item
104 Wide-mouthed container
105 Graf ___
106 They come in pairs
108 Coll. militants in the 60's
109 Mr. Cole
112 Mother Teresa's bio?
116 Bio of Frankie and Annette?
120 Hardness
121 Former treaty org.
122 On to
123 Type of type
124 Beautify
125 Utah's Senator Hatch
126 Networks of nerves
127 Quality of taste
128 Nuisances
129 Donna and Robert
130 Golfer Sam ___
131 Metric measure

DOWN

1 Brassy sound
2 Father of Rachel
3 Maxim
4 A king of Egypt
5 "East of ___"
6 Proteinaceous legume
7 Matty and Jesus of baseball
8 Whine
9 ___ weevil
10 Pack animal
11 Loses
12 Heston biographical role
13 Sifter
14 Air
15 Charles Kuralt's forte
16 Gathered
17 Les ___-Unis
18 Broz
19 Title for Fatima's lineage
20 Gainsay
30 Mortar for tiling
31 Algerian port
32 Survey
35 Cross-ribbed silk
37 Ideogram
38 Piggies in the nursery
39 Slip deftly to a specific place
40 Small pine
41 Ayatollah's predecessor
42 Mister who went to town
43 Buckeye, e.g.
44 Reflection
45 Merci, to you and me
46 Hogan's men on TV
47 Kite
48 Biological classifications
49 Tax
50 Lovers' meeting
53 Remove the trousers, in England
54 Eons
56 Nobel chemist and family
57 Hooky players
58 Sun god
59 Stares fiercely
61 Vilfredo ___, Italian sociologist in Switzerland
66 Iowa county
67 Dike
70 Flanks
71 Inspirit
72 Dental problem
73 Tremble
74 Most virtuous
75 Warns
76 Broad in the middle of the torso
77 Grand Ole ___
80 Splinter
81 Err
82 Odd job
83 Reposes
84 Served perfectly, in tennis
85 Must
88 M.D.'s tongue ___
89 Eye part
91 Scoff
94 Sale sign
95 Search for water
97 Spotted
98 Vowel marks
99 Black
100 Lucy, e.g.
102 Rejects
105 Nasal sound
106 Ogle
107 Cell that becomes an ovum
108 Groove
109 Artless
110 Thespian
111 "Over ___," Cohan song
112 Pitfall
113 Screen
114 Freudian terms
115 Withered
116 ___ Stanley Range, New Guinea
117 Archibald or Thurmond of the NBA
118 Mamie's predecessor
119 Israeli port: Var.
122 "___ Poetica": Horace

194

INITIALS UNCOVERED by Betty Jorgensen
We add to Betty's detective work by revealing that W. H. Auden is Wystan Hugh. Ah, those men of letters!

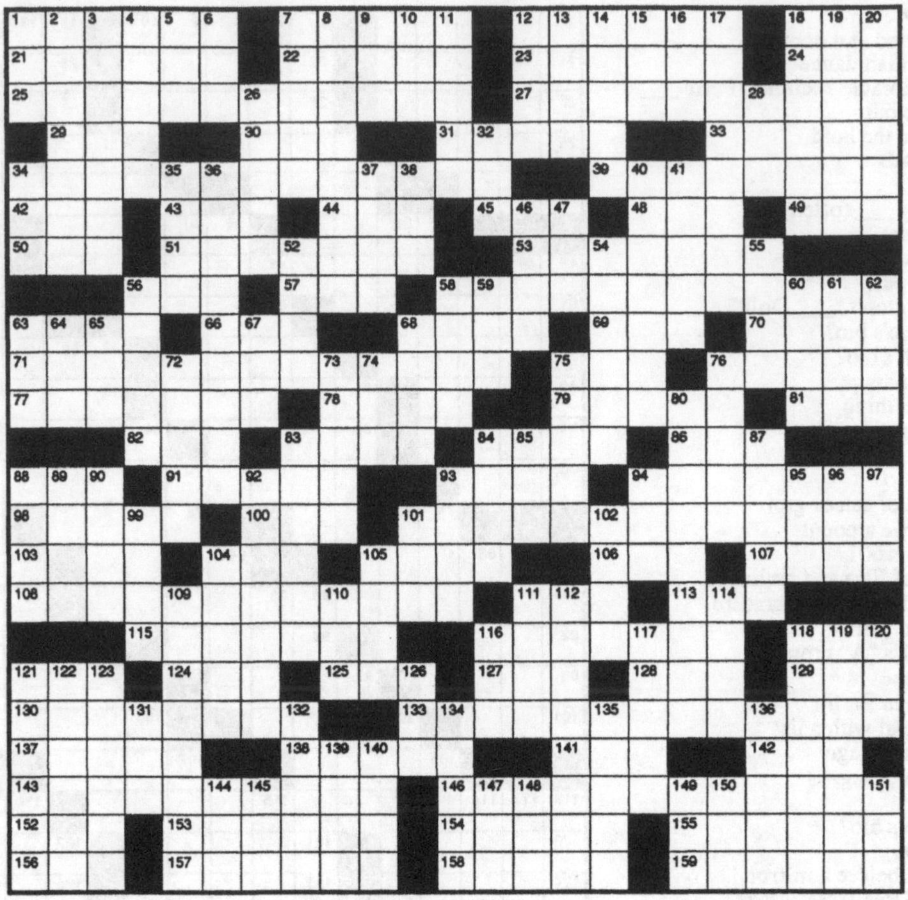

ACROSS

1 Religious community
7 Ancient Peruvian
12 Sailors' patron
18 Oil-well output: Abbr.
21 Scrubs abrasively
22 Kind of jacket
23 Kovacs and Pyle
24 Regret
25 LAWRENCE
27 FORESTER
29 Mine output
30 RR sta., e.g.
31 Bury
33 "___war": FDR
34 MILNE
39 Imposing structures
42 Medieval ballad
43 Ewe's mate
44 Grande or Bravo
45 Oklahoma city
48 Black bird
49 Hebrew letter: Var.
50 Sounds of hesitation
51 Degrading
53 Vindicates
56 One of a Latin trio
57 Half a fly
58 CUMMINGS
63 Furniture style
66 "Cuddle ___ Little Closer"
68 Fusses
69 Tune
70 Put on cargo
71 WELLS
75 Compass pt.
76 Wanders
77 Abbess at Ephesus in "Comedy of Errors"
78 Veritable
79 ___ Haute
81 ___ Consume
82 Asian holiday
83 False
84 ___-do-well
86 Notable years
88 Headgear
91 Brave deed
93 Dole out
94 Grist for a tabloid's mill
98 Suspicious
100 Make a boo-boo
101 WYETH
103 Mountain: Comb. form
104 Chinese philosophy
105 Spar
106 Saud preceder
107 Angered
108 CHESTERTON
111 Acronym for defense weapon
113 Tennessean, for short
115 Strikers
116 Slandered
118 Large
121 Russian plane
124 Buddy
125 Greek letter
127 Lubricate
128 Single
129 Important acid
130 Spread out the carpet
133 SHAW
137 Cigar type
138 French port
141 Scottish explorer
142 Time gone by
143 MENCKEN
146 FORSTER
152 Lawyer: Abbr.
153 Kind of tax
154 Well-named English novelist
155 Consent
156 Draft letters
157 Dodger
158 Possessed
159 Richard III thought it worth a kingdom

DOWN

1 Regular hrs. in Puerto Rico
2 Student
3 Cheers
4 Bambi's first stomach
5 Altar on high
6 Auth.'s submissions
7 Part of many a reference book
8 Indiana city
9 Half or third of a dance
10 JFK posting
11 Kind of beach or movie: Slang
12 Religious group
13 Word with family or shoe
14 Writing fluid, to Jacques
15 Cato's 52
16 Brooks or Torme
17 Turns to bone
18 Bring up a subject
19 Gaiter
20 Abhor
26 Swelling
28 Greek letter
32 Blue eagle org.
34 Pub drink
35 Ancient Syria
36 British party member
37 Baseball team
38 Follow faithfully
40 More excellent
41 Late star Stevens
46 Crows
47 A Gardner
52 Kind of line
54 Utensil on a pencil
55 French battle town
56 Bounds
58 Rim
59 Female deer
60 Wash
61 Thought
62 Raven's haven
63 Exclamation of discovery
64 Scotch river
65 Limb
67 Schl. group
68 Wake-robin
72 Shelley's "Adonais" for one
73 Anesthetic
74 "A feast ___ famine"
75 Pittsburgh product
76 Played again
80 Meet again
83 Caress
84 Salamander
85 Nice summer
87 Forge necessity
88 Stop up
89 Atmosphere: Comb. form
90 Rind
92 Space Needle city
93 Join smoothly
94 College deg.
95 ___ Alte (Adenauer)
96 Exist
97 Hallucinatory drug: Abbr.
99 Hijacks
101 A Turner
102 Bean or city
104 Ordeal
105 Fine vapor
109 Hired hand
110 Before, to the Bard
111 Moslem ruler
112 Capital of Yugoslavia
114 River to the Baltic
116 U.S.-Canada canal
117 Attired
118 He gasconades
119 Sudden invasions
120 Wander about
121 Even though
122 Small bays
123 Gives
126 Vital statistic
131 Hockey great
132 Ancient Celtic priest
134 January, to Juan
135 Like an otary
136 Dope dick
139 River into the Seine
140 Gas co. customer, e.g.
144 Half of CXXX
145 S American wood sorrel
147 Morning moisture
148 Pallid
149 Lamb's cry
150 Scottish exclamation of regret
151 Bess Truman, ___ Wallace

195

HAPPINESS IS . . . by Sidney Robbins
Solve the puzzle below to uncover a truth that applies to all and to all situations—at work or at home.

ACROSS

1 Israeli seaport
6 Knightly wear
11 ___-gin fizz
15 Arrive
19 Eastern religion
20 Shalom
21 Labels
22 Weather-map line
24 **Start of the quotation**
25 "Awake and Sing" playwright
26 Singer Redding
27 Muscular
28 Eggy drink
30 "___ of a Wayside Inn"
32 "The Old ___ Bucket"
33 Unhearing
37 Virginia ___
40 "___ Misérables"
41 They made a star trek
43 **Quotation: Part II**
52 Mother: Comb. form
53 Jacob's father
54 Merit
55 Mrs. Chaplin
56 Retinue
57 Fit for employment
58 Like porridge
59 Shoot
60 Brander's tool
62 Sun
63 Auto pioneer
64 Recovers
65 Woodland deities
67 "The ___ Stick," 1967 film
69 Operative
71 Lima's land
72 Do a plaster job
75 Dropping a last syllable off
77 Complain
81 True grit?
82 Author of the quotation
85 Assistant
86 Skin-cream ingredient
87 Repeat
88 Greek letters
89 Fountain drink
90 Dental deg.
91 Be innate
94 Friars' bashes
96 One to one, for one
100 King beaters
101 Palm leaf
103 Internal: Comb. form
104 Lord's residence
105 Spanish housewives
106 Lash holder
108 Part of LEM
112 Preminger
113 Kind of fall
114 Street urchin
115 Massey in "Rosalie"
116 **Quotation: Part III**
122 Observes
123 B.I.R. now
124 Facilitate
125 Hatrack
126 Japanese verse form
129 "___ Landing"
131 Kind of soup
133 **End of the quotation**
134 Bassoon, e.g.
135 Rhino's cousin
139 What 82 Across is
144 City on the Rio Grande
145 In the matter of
146 Join
147 Emulate Crosby
148 Teutonic goddess
149 "The ___ of Summer"
150 Ross or Palmer
151 Avian wader

DOWN

1 Single, e.g.
2 Silvery gray
3 ___ de France
4 Distant
5 So be it!
6 Opposite of perigee
7 Embarrassed
8 Ginnie ___
9 Fall mo.
10 Remainder
11 Taken
12 Just out
13 Eastern sashes
14 Snake-shaped letter
15 Stopper
16 Woodwind
17 Literature Nobelist: 1929
18 Unit of work
22 Polygon of equal angles
23 Homophone of stare
29 Bauxite, e.g.
31 Albee's "Tiny ___"
33 Car's low beams
34 Ancestor of the Edomites
35 Against
36 Courage
38 New Haven team
39 Mordente and Kirk
41 Food group
42 Askew
44 Hot and furious
45 Eastern VIP
46 Vintner brothers
47 Migraine
48 Easy gait
49 Mrs. Copperfield
50 Indigo
51 Droops
57 Dethrones
58 Stews
59 Diffident
61 Expensive flower
63 Soviet secret org.
65 Circus performer
66 Italian river
68 Near East liquor
69 Pierced
70 Individual
71 O.T. book
73 Fury
74 Encased
76 Toronto loc.
77 Bean stew of Paris
78 Fracas
79 Puts 2 and 2 together
80 Comedienne Arthur
83 Paths
84 Rel. degrees
90 ___ Alte
92 Kind of flush
93 Fragrant resin
95 Off-the cuff
96 Unhealthy brume
97 Marcus Porcius
98 Upon
99 Cross
100 Chinese nursemaids
102 Straighten
105 Comic Johnson
106 Excrete
107 Actress Swenson
109 Roulette bet
110 Actress Ramsey
111 Wrath
113 False
117 Inquired
118 Showy attire
119 Wears away
120 Rara avis of Maine
121 Charge
126 Listen
127 Gas: Comb. form
128 Thought
129 Numbers game
130 Stump
132 Prefix for enemy
133 Vietcong org. of 1960
134 Josh
136 Chem. suffix
137 Abyss
138 "___ Always You"
140 "You ___ My Destiny"
141 Town near Gorki
142 Pal of hiss
143 Bavarian river

196 FOLLOW-UPS by Guido Scarato

An old gimmick with a new twist is the theme of this challenger from Gotham City.

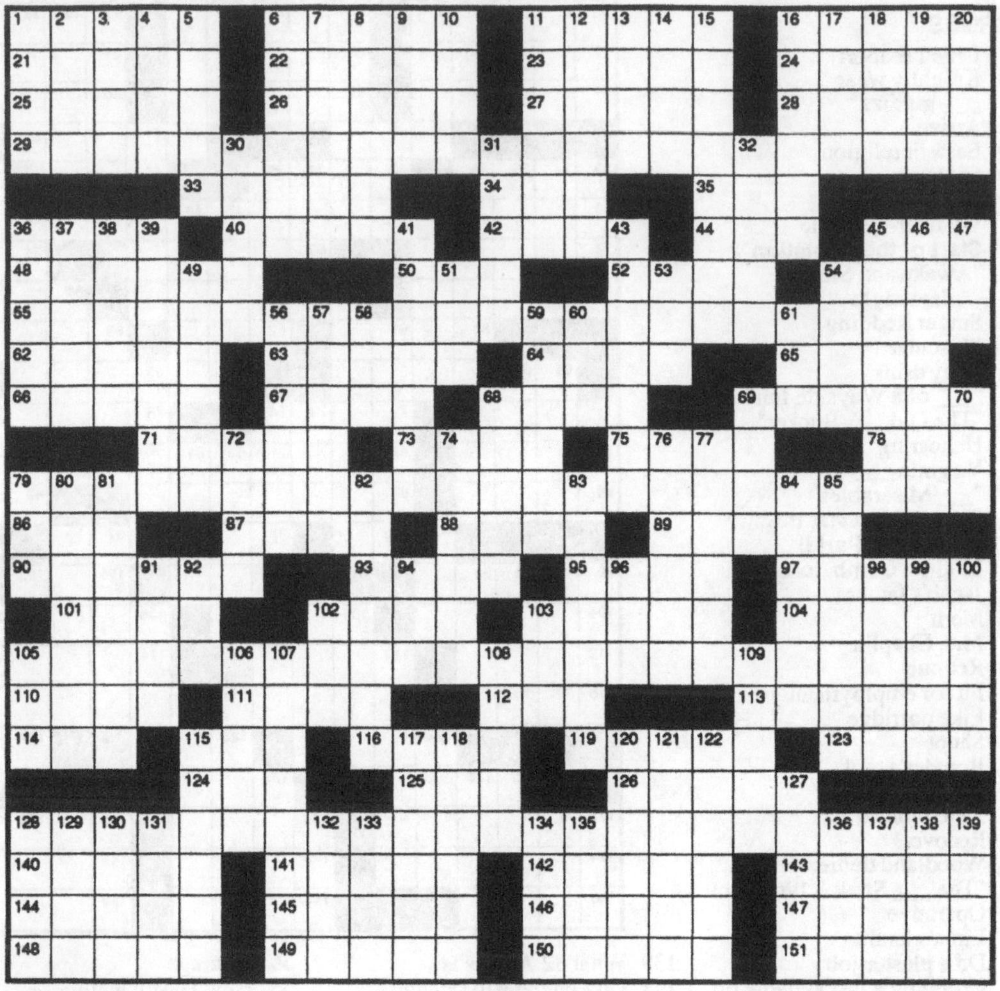

ACROSS

1 Calyx part
6 Swift snake
11 Scent
16 Castle defenses
21 Webber-Rice musical
22 Floor, in Arles
23 Put a match to again
24 Own up
25 Problem car
26 ___ down (softened)
27 Former Mrs. Trump
28 Nary a soul
29 Former President/ Ex-footballer
33 Sing from Mont Blanc
34 One ___ time
35 Leather tool
36 Slant
40 Having radials, in London
42 Ankle bones
44 Wedding-notice word
45 Small sandwich
48 Broadway backers
50 ". . . ___ I saw Elba"
52 Tiny Archibald
54 Word for poor Yorick
55 1959 movie/animal trainer
62 Chinese province
63 Ghostly
64 Noted tentmaker
65 Desire
66 Big Brother
67 Profit
68 Yemen port
69 Star in Gemini
71 Dine at home
73 Spanish river
75 Twaddle
78 Baton Rouge col.
79 French statesman/"South Pacific" actress
86 Limb
87 Infamous fiddler
88 Long sentence
89 Pretend
90 Humorously lewd
93 Mineo and Maglie
95 Gab
97 Takes ten
101 Murphy or Evans
102 Yesterday, in Leghorn
103 Threesome
104 "___ Lescaut"
105 American songwriter/Stein line
110 Light and dark liquors
111 Baseball brothers
112 Legal thing
113 Menu listing
114 Mornings
115 State further
116 A spice
119 ___, so good!
123 Take notice of
124 At once
125 ___ sequitur
126 Ship for Sextus
128 Singer/former V.P.
140 Protein acid
141 Lawful
142 Glyceride in olive oil
143 ". . . the duty which ___ to our Creator: P. Henry
144 Wyoming range
145 Rock, in Scotland
146 Getting on in years
147 Like a cornfield
148 Tête-___
149 Gary, Lorenz and Moss
150 Canine disease
151 Costume

DOWN

1 Ego
2 Continually
3 Fine cotton
4 Like ___ of bricks
5 Lean
6 Clean up anew
7 Penitent one
8 Menorah element
9 Elbe feeder
10 Make over
11 Grain beard
12 Show
13 Norse king
14 Coal deposit
15 Wife of Hippomenes
16 Disfigure
17 Smell
18 De vous ___ (between you and me)
19 Fork feature
20 Old or young follower
30 "___ luck!"
31 Of a cereal
32 'Twixt
36 Spa
37 ___ water (troubled)
38 Rocket stage
39 Anesthesiologist at times
41 Emulated Webster
43 Spanish princess
45 In an abrupt way
46 Milk sugar
47 For shame!
49 Straight
51 "Norma ___"
53 Listing at JFK
54 Down, in Dijon
56 Period of rule
57 Ewe at times
58 Mouth: Comb. form
59 Sleep
60 Highlander's uncle
61 Nigerian language
68 Musical upbeat
69 Mr. Huntley
70 Leg it
72 Manage
74 Lawyer Melvin and family
76 In production
77 Act beginning
79 Score for Strange
80 Atomic number 77
81 Preserves from oblivion
82 Biting midge
83 Ford anew
84 Bates of "Psycho"
85 Dig up
91 "___ well that ends . . ."
92 Pewter
94 Jackie's second
96 Towel word
98 Night sound
99 "The Owl and the Pussycat went ___"
100 Scoff
102 Prefix for bar
103 Uno + due
105 Bikini part
106 Hazardous gas
107 Cambrian language
108 Sphere of activity
109 Letter stroke
115 "Tennis, ___?"
117 Apply an unguent to
118 Graphite-clay crayons
120 ___ a blue moon
121 Feigning
122 Vindicate
127 Stitched
128 Pro ___
129 "___ a man . . ."
130 Summon officially
131 Clove hitch, e.g.
132 Actress Baron
133 Battle memento
134 Meander
135 Author Novikov
136 Jet name
137 Learning
138 Flock members
139 Beatty film

197

VERY VERBAL by Louis Sabin
"Words are also actions, and actions are a kind of words."—Ralph Waldo Emerson

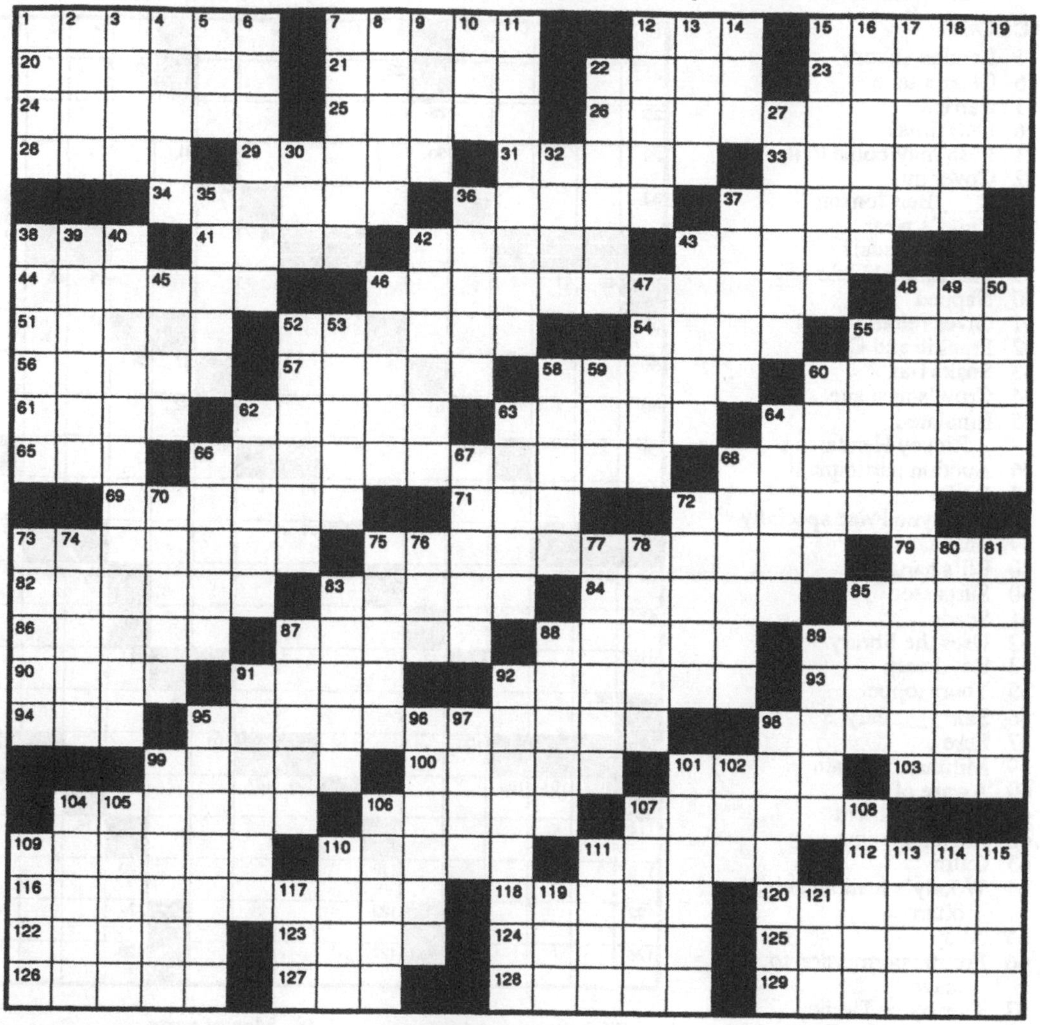

ACROSS

1 Genoa or hard
7 Overcharge
12 ___ Red apple
15 Rift
20 Arthurian isle
21 Forefather
22 Trash carrier
23 Truly
24 Sounds
25 Civil War general
26 Performed on skis
28 Within: Comb. form
29 Oneness
31 Prevents
33 NFL team
34 Courteous
36 Full of vitality
37 Loreleis
38 Kind of verb: Abbr.
41 Blue ox
42 Saguaros
43 Managed
44 Latin gender
46 Progress
48 Manner
51 ___ Dei
52 Gazed
54 Impulse
55 Cob or gander
56 Velvetlike fabric
57 Prunes
58 Coventry coins
60 Barriers
61 Nobelist Metchnikoff
62 Left Bank lapper
63 Castle or Papas
64 Wilson of baseball
65 Neon's number
66 Moves right along
68 Trucks on rails
69 Lots and lots
71 Tide type
72 Enclose
73 Frolics
75 Holds fast
79 Tomcat
82 Rhymeless fruit
83 Footsteps
84 Waters down
85 Tivoli's Villa d'___
86 Celebrations
87 Risked
88 Vapid
89 Pansy part
90 Lulu
91 Cohorts
92 Closer
93 Deftness
94 Arabic cape
95 Exercise or toy
98 Headband
99 Party poopers
100 Happy as ___
101 Valid
103 Elec. units
104 Flight of ___
106 Safaris
107 Kingdoms
109 Expert on card games
110 Where won are spent
111 June's birthstone
112 Noted archer
116 Became
118 "The Invisible Man" star
120 Spain locale
122 Vary
123 Opinion
124 Connect
125 Fleets
126 Consecrate
127 Aliens
128 Forest in N Warwickshire
129 What golfers read

DOWN

1 All there
2 English Channel feeder
3 Placed
4 U.S.political columnist
5 Singer Bandy
6 Isolated
7 Israeli or Arab
8 Boyer of baseball fame
9 An apple ___ . . .
10 Conducted
11 Introduced
12 In an unfriendly way
13 Medicos
14 Belligerent Cockney?
15 Male escorts
16 Eddied
17 Helmet insert
18 Anat. canals
19 Knight and Turner
22 Never mind!
27 Willard Scott wears one
30 Pen point
32 Chooses
35 Fleshy
36 Land ___!
37 Beaver's home
38 Vexed
39 Entertain
40 What Ike and Nixon were
42 Biblical mount
43 "Odyssey" sorceress
45 Tommy of Broadway
46 Popular streets
47 Tending to drip
48 Cane or insect
49 Ex-Yankee Reynolds
50 Agreements
52 Guides
53 Nonsense
55 New Zealand minority
58 Attends Andover
59 Sniggle
60 "As the ___ Turns"
62 Peculated
63 Wall climbers
64 Lamentations
66 Walks through mud
67 Bothered
68 Horseshoe in horseshoes
70 Doubleday
72 Subway gate
73 Try
74 Cow Palace, for one
75 Ankles
76 Top pitcher
77 Charge
78 Hustler
80 Type of type
81 Abzug and Spewack
83 Lobster feelers
85 Cries of alarm
87 Ladies at court
88 Burns
89 Song for the Sabbath
91 Copied a cat
92 Capital of Indonesia
95 Members
96 Restricted
97 Delight
98 Returning to Earth
99 Binnie of films
101 Purpose
102 Musical gift
104 Short oar
105 Pie of Paris
106 Lugs
107 Annuity of Avignon
108 Garvey or Allen
109 Attempt
110 Make mittens
111 Multi-hued
113 Buffalo canal
114 Bank holding
115 Miss
117 "___ Gotta Be Me"
119 Song
121 Place for a rail

198 INVENTION EXTENSIONS by Dorothy Smitonick

We think you'll find this puzzle patently enjoyable.

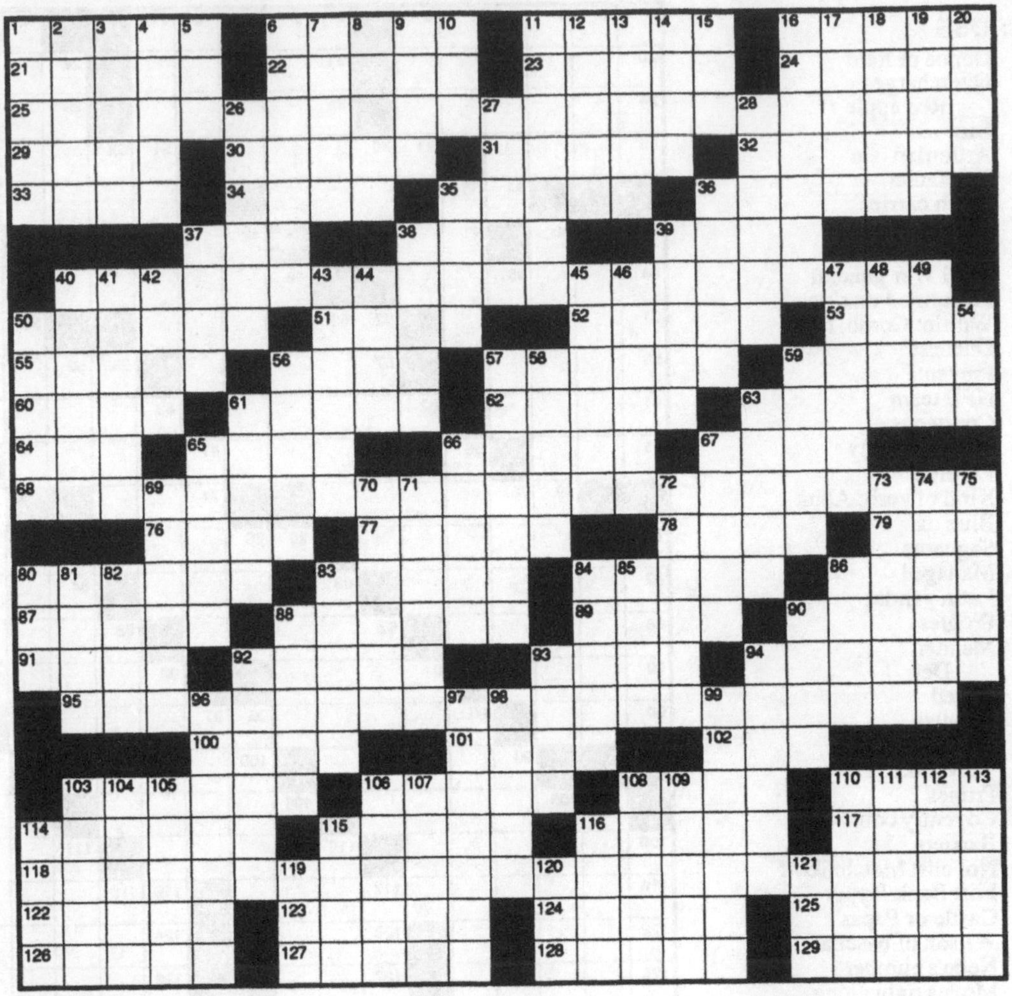

ACROSS

1 London suburb
6 Clear a tape
11 Carried
16 Dull finish
21 Push may come to it
22 Cover girl
23 "___ Ben Jonson"
24 Child's wear
25 Elias' manual?
29 The Emerald Isle
30 Napped
31 Gives felonious aid
32 Frankie and Cleo
33 Soaks flax
34 Crow's nest site
35 Emulated Rickey Henderson
36 Auction participant
37 Barfly
38 Leontyne Price specialty
39 Space
40 Eli's hangout?
50 Surpassed
51 Scads
52 Uses the library
53 Daydream
55 Tours topper
56 San ___, Italy
57 Pure
59 Military chaplain
60 Aware of
61 Paté ingredient
62 French income
63 Calm
64 Woody's leading lady, often
65 Allay
66 Formal permission to leave
67 Tunney or Tierney
68 Alexander's paperback?
76 "___ o'clock scholar"
77 Miss Massey
78 Indicate
79 Frances, Ruby or Sandra
80 Tonic
83 Satisfy
84 ___ profundo
86 ___ Verde National Park
87 Fictional uncle
88 High school student
89 "Peanuts" expletive
90 *Stagecoach*, e.g.
91 Eternity
92 Hebrew letter
93 Supervision
94 Chekhov's namesakes
95 Benjamin's topper?
100 Peepers
101 Johnson of "Laugh-In"
102 Uno y uno
103 Vaccines
106 Defies
108 Asian weight
110 Marsh bird
114 Arduous
115 Portable chair
116 Last
117 Bedazzles
118 Thomas' current release?
122 Allow to enter
123 Country crossing
124 Memorable shrine
125 Strainer
126 Tarkenton and Allison
127 Site of the Krupp works
128 Not as ruddy
129 Stage direction

DOWN

1 Son of Jacob
2 Odd job
3 Namely
4 Pizza places
5 Seine
6 Rival
7 Kentucky Derby prize, symbolically
8 Expert
9 NYSE membership
10 Urban railways
11 Harbor sight
12 Bay window
13 Plume possessor
14 Work units
15 EMK, e.g.
16 Blacktop
17 Garden pest
18 Musketeers or Stooges
19 Copy machine additive
20 Chemical endings
26 Donny or Marie
27 ". . . and ye shall ___ in haste": Exodus 12:12
28 UFO crew
35 Hit signs
36 Honeymooner
37 Let it stand
38 Man of parts
39 Small type
40 Hot dog
41 Work stoppage in India
42 Thought: Comb. form
43 Surveyor's tool
44 "___ are born great . . .": Shak.
45 Grove product
46 Built a tree home
47 Turkish inn
48 Ore deposit
49 Forsaken
50 Awesome weapon
54 Maiden-named
56 Gotten up
57 Singer like Bing
58 Auburn dye
59 Pound parts
61 Not now
63 Take care of
65 Borgia in-laws
66 Carburetor valve
67 GNP part
69 Gap
70 Actress Heckart
71 Boards
72 On the beat
73 "___ Nightingale"
74 Take umbrage
75 Century components
80 Bikini top
81 Navigation hazard
82 Love, to Livy
83 Highway haulers
84 Intrepid
85 Rhine tributary
86 SAT section
88 Scheherazade's specialty
90 Change for a five
92 Paratroopers
93 Barracks beds
94 Son of Zeus and Leto
96 Nerve cells
97 Crusader's enemy
98 Midlands river
99 "A life is beautiful and ___ the reverse": Ellis
103 Exodus commemoration
104 Patti Lu Pone role
105 Pine exudation
106 Sub shops
107 One of Fred's dancing partners
108 Thai monetary unit
109 "What's in ___?"
110 Like Ellington's doll
111 Young hooter
112 Actor Christopher
113 Fall flower
114 Ego
115 Goes like the sun
116 Threadlike structures
119 Opposite NNW
120 Seance sound
121 Exploit

199

HOW ABOUT THAT, GORBIE? by Alfio Micci
Here's a quip that Art Buchwald could well have written.

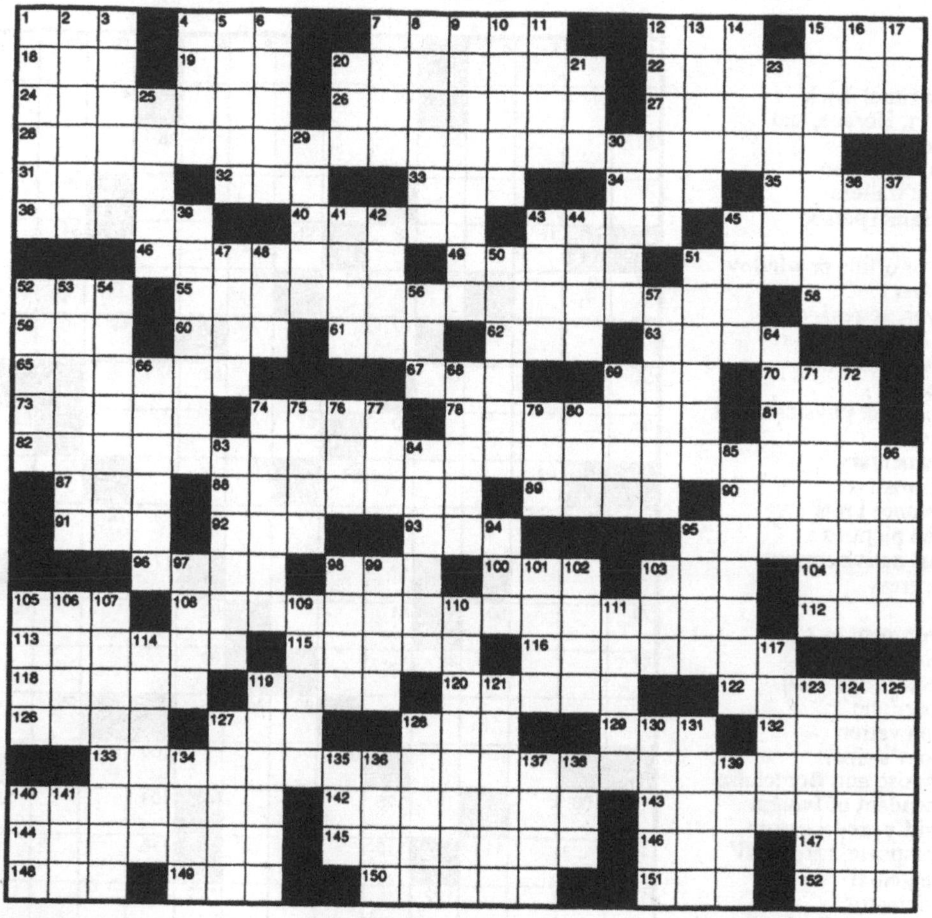

ACROSS

1 Classifieds
4 Heavenly Altar
7 ___ of the ball
12 Conservation agcy.
15 Jones's partner
18 Cumberland or Generation ___
19 "Today ___ a man"
20 Roof sights
22 Non grata lead-in
24 West African group
26 Jack Webb series
27 Mandarin and temple
28 **Start of a quip**
31 Stone pillar
32 Spanish bear
33 French connections
34 Passes, in bridge
35 Star in Lyra
38 "___ of dreadful note": Macbeth
40 "___ say more?"
43 Oates book
45 Marsh bird
46 Pepys output
49 Stout's Wolfe and others
51 Henry VIII's second
52 Hardwood
55 **Quip: Part II**
58 Cambodian's neighbor
59 Greek "h"
60 Scale notes
61 ___ *My Darling Daughter*
62 Lixivium
63 Over
65 Game fish
67 Keystone ___
69 Far from cordial
70 "There ___ tavern in . . ."
73 Woodland trembler
74 Obi
78 Former Czech province
81 ___ Aviv
82 **Quip: Part III**
87 Leandro's love
88 Sun rooms
89 Brace
90 User of 50 Down
91 NYC clock setting, at times
92 Bot. or geol.
93 Key letter
95 Madden
96 Celebrated pen name
98 Opposite of post
100 Tar
103 Joanne of Hollywood
104 Modern, in Mannheim
105 Elec. unit
108 **Quip: Part IV**
112 Roush of baseball fame
113 Appal
115 Stood
116 Principal's principal concern?
118 Actor Delon
119 Director Martin
120 Tire feature
122 Spar
126 Pilot's place
127 Trampoline
128 Mine yield
129 Become extinct
132 Collection suffix
133 **End of the quip**
140 TV offering
142 Nuke item
143 Amasses
144 On the market
145 Eban, for one
146 Guidonian note
147 Indignation
148 Artfully bashful
149 Kind of appeal
150 City on the Arkansas
151 Actor Cariou
152 Beatty or Sparks

DOWN

1 Hercule's creator
2 Participated in a track event
3 Orb
4 Japanese aboriginal
5 *Midnight Cowboy* role
6 Incorrect
7 City on the Aar
8 Expunged
9 Illumination
10 Turner and Cantrell
11 Alt.
12 One for whom a group is named
13 French fathers
14 Bedouin
15 Comic verse
16 Quarter of four
17 Part of "TWTWTW"
20 Rehan or Huxtable
21 Sault ___ Marie
23 Whine
25 Provided weaponry
29 Part of ancient Greece
30 Plump
36 "Los Caprichos" painter
37 Part of A.D.
39 Legs or Neil
41 Counting-out word
42 Notable Italian family
43 Helen's new home
44 Lifted, nautically
45 Garden item
47 Tennis term
48 Amended materials: Abbr.
50 Sniggler's trap
51 *Pilgrim's Progress* author
52 At the age of: Lat. Abbr.
53 Put by
54 ___ Ferry, W. Va.
56 Invite
57 More suggestive
64 Desiccate
66 Mescal
68 Voodoo
69 South African warriors
71 Nautical way
72 Supposed
74 Winter vehicle
75 King of the Huns
76 ___-Na-Na, entertainment group
77 ___ Govind, Sikh guru
79 School dance
80 Conductor ___ Pekka Salonen
83 Harden
84 Asps
85 Exposes
86 Montgomery Clift role
94 "But ___ on forever": Tennyson
95 Marine flyers
97 Bank transaction
98 Procacious
99 Kind of act
101 Head of a tale
102 Composer Bartok
103 ___ *Rheingold*
105 A wife of Lamech
106 About a third of a league
107 Dulcimer's cousin
109 Santo Domingo's neighbor
110 Rhythmic
111 Writers' colony in Saratoga Springs
114 Little, et al.
117 Book back
119 Involuntary movement
121 French incomes
123 "Marcher" in Bush's inaugural parade
124 Emulate Lloyd's
125 Packed down
127 Fraser of tennis
128 Japanese port
130 Force forward
131 Rousseau classic
134 Farrow and Slavenska
135 Gypsy horse
136 Command, old style
137 Indian storeroom
138 Dernier ___
139 ___ Bator, Mongolia
140 An NCO
141 Nanki-___, son in *The Mikado*

200 RHYMING TRIPLETS by Jim Bernhard

Consider the research necessary to find five 23-letter entries to fit this unusual theme. Wonderful work, Jim!

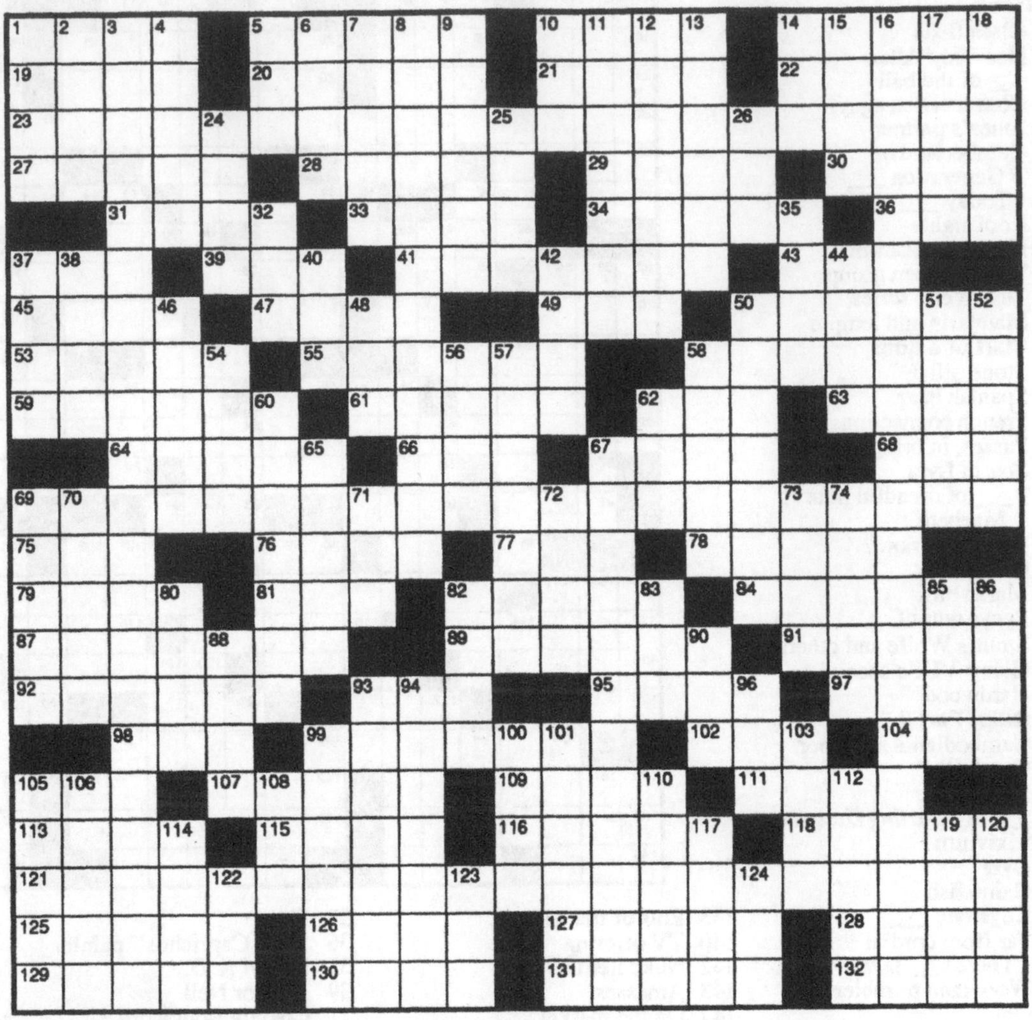

ACROSS

1 Vedic ritual drink
5 Delbert, Horace, and Thomas
10 Guitar accessory
14 Freight trailers
19 Unoriginal person
20 Cant
21 Kind of office or window
22 Discovery
23 Lawyer, actress, and folksinger
27 Violinist Mischa
28 Places
29 Nobelist for physics: 1944
30 Withered
31 Parliamentary affirmatives
33 Resistance units
34 Sacred pictures
36 Burns' native county
37 Transgress
39 State
41 Government by two people
43 Horned Frogs' schl.
45 Bert or John
47 Flat elevation
49 Bigfoot's size?
50 Béarnaise and Bordelaise
53 Descendant of Fatima
55 Leonid's predecessor
58 Shakespeare's *Henry IV*
59 More genial
61 Sub detector
62 Improvise, to Brubeck
63 Litigated
64 Legendary Phrygian king
66 Persistent behavioral trait
67 Lightweight garment
68 Mme.'s Madrid counterpart
69 Designer, silent film star, and film director
75 Played on stage
76 "Jake" from Utah
77 Thai river
78 Import
79 Western lizards
81 Campbell or Jacob follower
82 Obscures
84 Legal minority
87 Shared annuity
89 Equity members
91 All ___ Day (November 2)
92 Suffix
93 Mil. unit
95 Sap
97 Tense
98 Deg. from a church schl.
99 Like some ball teams
102 Math subj.
104 Maiden-name indicator
105 Legal benefit
107 Plant disease
109 Equivocates
111 Alum.
113 Saucy
115 Alan, Orson, or Roy
116 Hockey term
118 Imam's religion
121 Jazz singer and two movie stars
125 Maternally related
126 Recorded proceedings
127 Variegated chalcedony
128 Let
129 Principle
130 Exclamation of amazement or relief
131 Present time
132 Is in debt

DOWN

1 Marquis de ___
2 October birthstone
3 Musical comedy star, Broadway composer, and comedian
4 Impressive display
5 Cow's fourth stomach
6 Sandy's remarks
7 Marsh of mystery
8 Bismarck native
9 Fr. commune
10 Moon jumper
11 Cupidity
12 Dash
13 Eton graduate, for one
14 Dep.
15 Is wrong
16 Film star, oceanographer, and movie mogul
17 Kind of tower
18 Conduit
24 Five make a fin
25 Greek mountain
26 Feminine principle
32 Playwright Shepard
35 Aldebaran or Betelgeuse
37 Large number
38 ___ *Fugitive from a Chain Gang*
40 Propensity
42 Admiral or guard preceder
44 Meat segments
46 Absolve
48 Bro.'s sibling
50 Japanese banjo
51 First month in Mexico
52 Portable chair
54 Make over
56 "What's ___ for me?"
57 New York-Massachusetts range
58 Chums, cowboy style
60 Roaming about
62 Garber or Murray
65 Ray
67 Hispaniolan capital
69 Beast
70 First head of Harvard College
71 Before
72 Cartoonist Thomas
73 Slaughter of baseball
74 As like ___ (probably)
80 Prison
82 Ancient Persian priests
83 Marquee letters
85 Viscous adhesive
86 Line of Italian aristocrats
88 Dart poison
90 Belgian watering place
93 Second bout
94 Come forth
96 Actress Taina
99 Broadway musical of 1973
100 Foster or Silvers
101 Paint again
103 Grating
105 Discompose
106 French river
108 Fem. knighthood
110 Sam of the links
112 Pet dog of the Jetsons
114 Kind of board
117 Nurse shark
119 Sister-in-law of Fergy
120 Shea nine
122 Court divider
123 Avogadro's ___, in chemistry
124 Napoleonic marshal

201 JAPANESE ZOO by Stanley Whitten

Plenty of cagey clues were used to cage these curious creatures below.

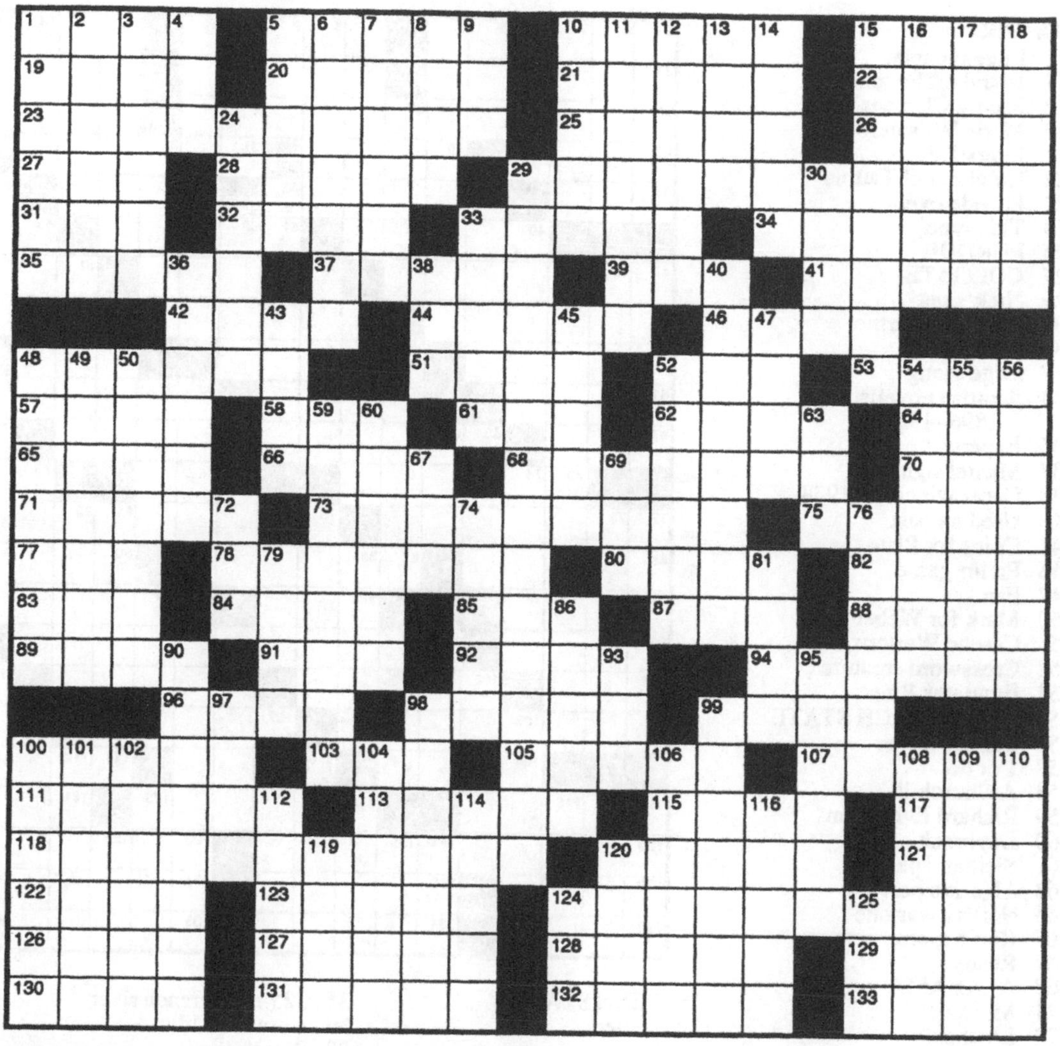

ACROSS

1 Hemingway's sobriquet
5 Grand and small, in bridge
10 Brilliant success
15 Comedian Foxx
19 Verbal
20 Clocks
21 Thither
22 Robt. ___
23 Japanese bird?
25 Hebrew prophet
26 Fires
27 Period of note
28 ___ *and Adonis*: Shak.
29 Japanese reptile?
31 Beam
32 Ovine moms
33 Incorrect
34 Black eye
35 Ringo or Bart
37 Gesture of indifference
39 Unit of work
41 Wide awake
42 Tarbell and McKinley
44 Numbered clubs
46 Wife of Louis XIII
48 Skewbald ponies
51 In addition
52 Corrida shout
53 Kewpie ___
57 Jacob's twin
58 *I ___ Camera*
61 Corp. issue
62 Tattle
64 Calendar abbr.
65 Fraternity party garb, sometimes
66 Splendor
68 Beseech
70 ___ *Lay Dying*
71 Threaded fastener
73 Japanese bird?
75 Pub game
77 Negative vote
78 Museum display
80 Despot
82 Hindu teacher
83 "Watchful" name
84 Marsh bird
85 Response: Abbr.
87 Nautical chain
88 At a distance
89 Inquires
91 ___ *Abner*
92 Title
94 Ornamental border
96 Serves perfectly
98 ___ *Attraction*
99 One-man performances
100 Happen again
103 Before corn or pod
105 *Romola* novelist
107 Brief note
111 Strikingly different
113 Adams from San Francisco
115 Weight allowance
117 Latin I word
118 Japanese felines?
120 Make amends
121 Naval NCO
122 Arabian big-wig
123 Pine Tree State
124 Japanese sheep?
126 Neighbor of Ala.
127 Asian palm
128 Envy
129 Certain
130 Old dirk
131 Fathered
132 Exchange
133 Hurried

DOWN

1 Baffling problems
2 Noah's landing place
3 Melonlike fruit
4 High mountain
5 Sprinkle
6 Pride member
7 Surprise attack
8 ". . . the best of ___ diligence": Shak.
9 FICA identifier
10 An alcohol
11 Selects
12 Jazz saxophonist Young
13 Mars: Comb. form
14 Lachrymose shedding
15 Drew back
16 Sir Galahad's mom
17 Thicker
18 Abandon
24 Exhaust
29 Japanese water mammals?
30 *More ___ a Miracle*
33 Rolls up tightly
36 Ceremony
38 Narrow inlet
40 Scottish breed of horse
43 Quick letters
45 ___ *Rae*
47 Close
48 Porky Pig's love
49 Weather-map sights
50 Japanese beast of burden?
52 Russian "province"
54 Japanese sandpiper?
55 Quinquennial
56 Suit for the seventies
59 Pedal pusher?
60 Without principles
63 Flower plot
67 Burmese money unit
69 Agt.'s ten
72 QB stats.
74 Iowa church commune
76 Common mushroom
79 Eurytus' daughter
81 Repurchase agreement
86 Tiny
90 White table wine
93 Porter's "Bingo ___ Yale"
95 Irish province
97 Neonate's place
98 Supply credit
99 Caressed
100 Places in position again
101 Study of conscience: Eccles.
102 Trig function
104 More risqué
106 ___ rima
108 Tally
109 Unclean
110 Combined
112 Unconscious states
114 Stand in good ___
116 Maternal relative
119 Seaport in SE Italy
120 Hebrew instrument
124 Witchy mo.
125 Donkey

202 TEAMWORK by Louis Sabin

Uniformed groups are uniformly hidden within the puzzle below. Another winner from Coach Sabin!

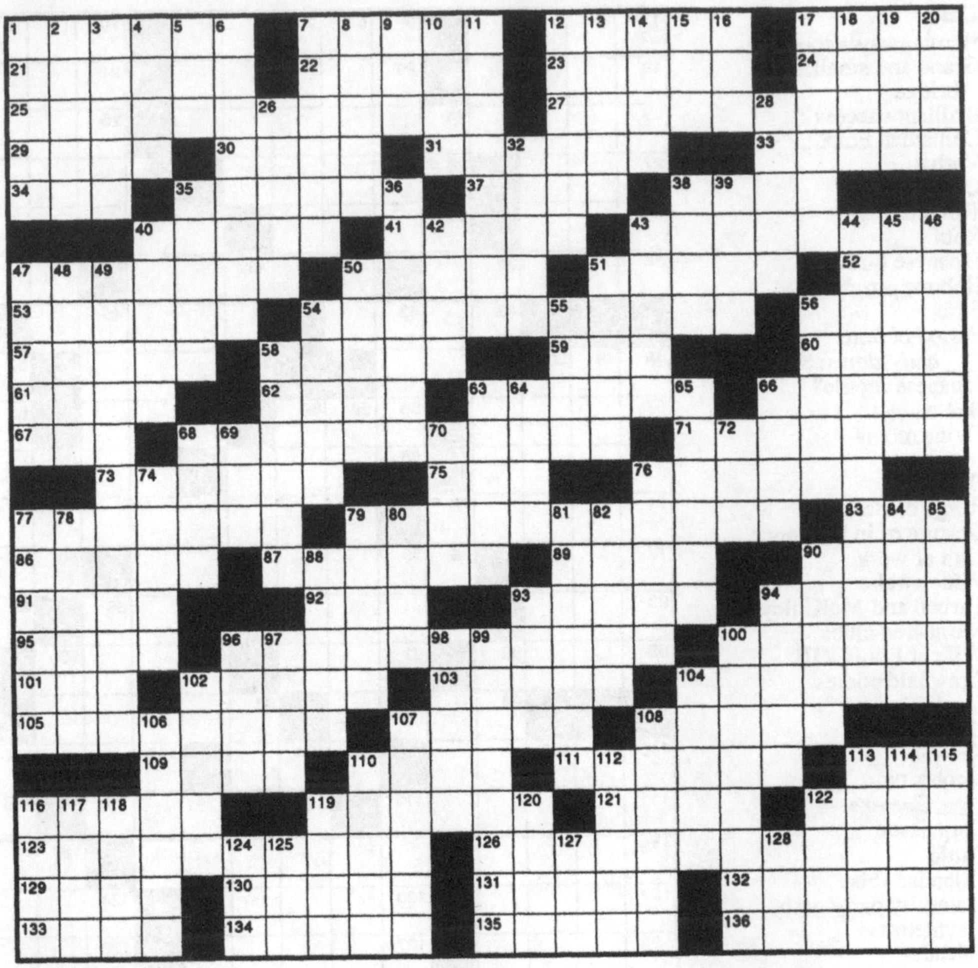

ACROSS

1 Luggage toter
7 Island off Foochow
12 Facing Clemens
17 Marie Wilson role
21 Interstice
22 Neighbor of Taurus
23 Preside over
24 Tide type
25 PURDUE
27 COLGATE
29 Nick's pet
30 Captain's partner
31 Indian poet
33 Edge along
34 Scottish novelist: 1896–1952
35 Experts
37 Mantel sight
38 Oscar winner of 1988
40 Used an oast
41 Coins for Plato
43 Parlor game
47 Fan
50 Mark for Weber
51 Classic Western
52 Crossword creature
53 Emulates Bing
54 LONG BEACH STATE
56 Sunday closer
57 1 or 66
58 A Churchill
59 Richard Everyman
60 Daybreak
61 Sicilian spa
62 Algerian port
63 Norkay was one
66 Roo's mom
67 Ready
68 ALABAMA
71 Mocks
73 Loathes
75 Summer mo.
76 Medjugorje, e.g.
77 Oared warship
79 NEBRASKA
83 "Gotcha!"
86 Keep the issues coming
87 Govt. securities
89 Black, in Blois
90 Bakery specialist
91 Tied
92 Bow
93 Wood tool
94 "The Harbor" novelist
95 Encounter
96 CALIFORNIA
100 Flag
101 NHL great
102 Short blades
103 Waugh and Wilder
104 Castro's predecessor
105 Inspect anew
107 Balance
108 Toren of *Casbah*
109 Haiku or tanka
110 Split hairs?
111 In a waggish way
113 Get-up-and-go
116 Italian poet
119 Put back in office
121 "Nessun dorma," e.g.
122 Prong
123 DUKE
126 PENN STATE
129 Settled
130 Poona princess
131 Angler's basket
132 BOSTON COLLEGE
133 Drat!
134 Signed
135 Millennium members
136 Cheerless

DOWN

1 Hassan's capital
2 Irregularly notched
3 Isis or Osiris
4 Fountain order
5 Flagon filler
6 Shares
7 Reacted to puns
8 *Catch-22* star
9 Paisley
10 Class
11 Tasteless
12 Over
13 "Over ___": Cohan
14 Invited
15 Mien
16 Chorale syllable
17 A Gandhi
18 *Reds* journalist
19 Lime substitute
20 Building "bulge"
26 Man with a van
28 Rhone feeder
32 "Father of Medicine"
35 325-mile French river
36 Horne or Mills
38 Scorch
39 Katzenjammer kid
40 Flora and fauna
42 With robe or house
43 Aerie call
44 WAKE FOREST
45 Pop out
46 Islamic customs
47 Real estate
48 Tiring sound
49 WEST VIRGINIA
50 Rails
51 REM accompaniment
54 Minor-league teams
55 Het up
56 Forcefully
58 Evening event
63 Takes off-guard
64 Partner of dry
65 Stick to
66 Malayan dagger
68 Masticate
69 Gypsy boy
70 Ancient balm
72 Drop a stitch
74 *Forty-Second Street* star
76 Shirts' contacts
77 Shaking
78 Patriotic silversmith
79 Waled trousers
80 Story opener
81 Open
82 Skyrockets
84 Slave
85 Rose Bowl, e.g.
88 Unwilling
90 Ancient district of Asia Minor
93 Strip
94 Minor
96 Yield
97 City in N Utah
98 Mother-of-pearl
99 Brazen obtrusiveness
100 Doubled up, at the track
102 Mysterious Edwin
104 Round Table knight
106 Gridiron surprises
107 Expressed disrespect
108 Ethical behavior principles
110 Martinique volcano
112 Critic
113 Pitcher Frank
114 Kind of circle
115 Disorganized
116 Aspen lift
117 Ms. Nazimova
118 Diamonds, e.g.
119 NHL site
120 Flag
122 Buster Brown's dog
124 Silkworm
125 Lee ___ Cleef
127 Taiwan export
128 Burmese gibbon

203 TRANSPARENCY by Kenneth Haxton

Kenneth says a recent trip to Corning, NY inspired the challenger below.

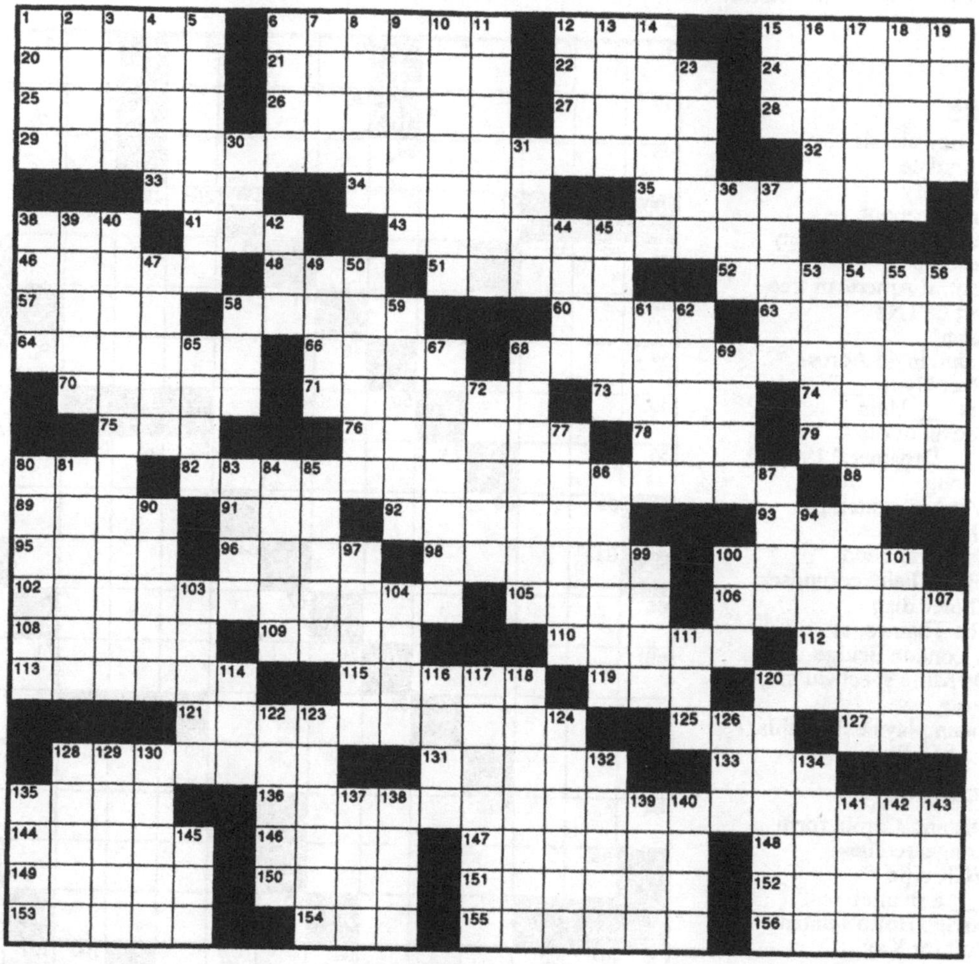

ACROSS

1 Emulates Ella
6 Paving material
12 Thoth or Thor
15 Dapper
20 Singer Branigan
21 Harrington's ideal republic
22 Attention getter
24 Beaverlike
25 Pianist Claudio
26 Yellowish astringent
27 *Educating* ___, Caine film
28 Greek Pax
29 Bahamian tourist vessel: Var.
32 Arrow poison
33 Owns
34 Trap
35 Repeat
38 ___-relief
41 Phosgene, e.g.
43 Legless lizard
46 Coeur d'___
48 Barn bird
51 Costly
52 Riddle
57 Stubby or Danny
58 *Hours of Idleness* poet
60 East Asian weight
63 British ___
64 Like some beds
66 Hungarian violinist
68 *Einstein on the Beach* composer
70 Miserable
71 Prayer, to Jeanne D'Arc
73 *Old Curiosity Shop* heroine
74 Caama
75 Employ
76 Moths
78 West or Murray
79 Belgian river
80 Team VIP
82 Instruments composed of bowls
88 RR union
89 Hence
91 Samovar
92 Floodgate
93 Off one's feed
95 Troubles
96 Kind of gin
98 Allure
100 "___ Such As I," Presley hit
102 No abodes for stoners
105 Gratify
106 Stevedore
108 Finley's Dinsmore
109 Canine command
110 Behemothic
112 Without: Lat.
113 Mignonette
115 Part of HUD
119 Reuben bread
120 Tepees
121 One with a cast-iron stomach
125 Debussy inspiration
127 Obtained
128 Seraphic
131 Confused
133 Chinese pagoda
135 Cupid
136 Williams success
144 Like an English judge
146 Merry old soul
147 Unite or separate
148 Thomas Mann's daughter
149 *Gasoline* ___
150 Fireman's friend
151 Gat
152 March of ___
153 Fashion name
154 Part of UNLV
155 Stoat
156 Leaven

DOWN

1 Smelting by-product
2 Rowan or Rochelle
3 Invisible emanation
4 It gets compacted
5 Kielbasa, e.g.
6 Miss Gale's pooch
7 Aloof as ___
8 Charters
9 Malay Peninsula town
10 Desman and saiga, e.g.
11 African ground pig
12 Apparel
13 Steubenville locale
14 Hold back
15 Half-dozen, to Luciano
16 *West Side Story* lead
17 Ten-percenter
18 Jeanmaire of ballet
19 It grew in Brooklyn
23 Modern Chilean painter
30 One of Baden-Powell's orgs.
31 N central Ethiopian town
36 Supplement
37 Fail to follow suit: Var.
38 Caucasus rug
39 Hale and Arkin
40 J.D. Salinger protagonist
42 Chinese sauce
44 Inventor Boyden
45 Valladolid locale
47 Approaches
49 Envelop
50 Portuguese city
53 Wild plum of California
54 Venetian art
55 ___ *Marco Polo*
56 Allege
58 Turkish governor
59 Whinnies
61 Resin in varnish
62 Spring bloomer
65 Residue
67 Entertains royally
68 Licenses
69 Appeal
72 TV oldie
77 Ice-cream ___
80 Scant
81 Grating
83 Sot
84 Guthrie and Hults
85 Tapir feature
86 Drink of the gods
87 Winnow
90 Actor Davis
94 Companion of fast
97 Namesakes of Jacob's twin
99 Like a Poe tale
100 Peer Gynt's mother
101 Slow, musically
103 Papyrus's family
104 Brontë heroine
107 Take five
111 Columbia, to the ocean
114 Alternative to nothing
116 Biblical idol
117 Embassy VIP
118 *Fleurette* composer
120 Calamity
122 Hydrogen's symbol
123 Barbizon ___
124 Stitch anew
126 Depot abbr.
128 Soap plant
129 High-born
130 Wet behind the ears
132 Valuable violin
134 Eaglet's home
135 Bedouin
137 Novelist Morante
138 Commands for oxen
139 Level
140 Town in Mauritania
141 *Green Mansions* heroine
142 Summer desserts
143 Hula Bowl team
145 Indigo, for one

204

SPEAK OF THE . . . by Louis Baron
Ironically, this careful creation from Mr. B. was constructed with a devil-may-care attitude.

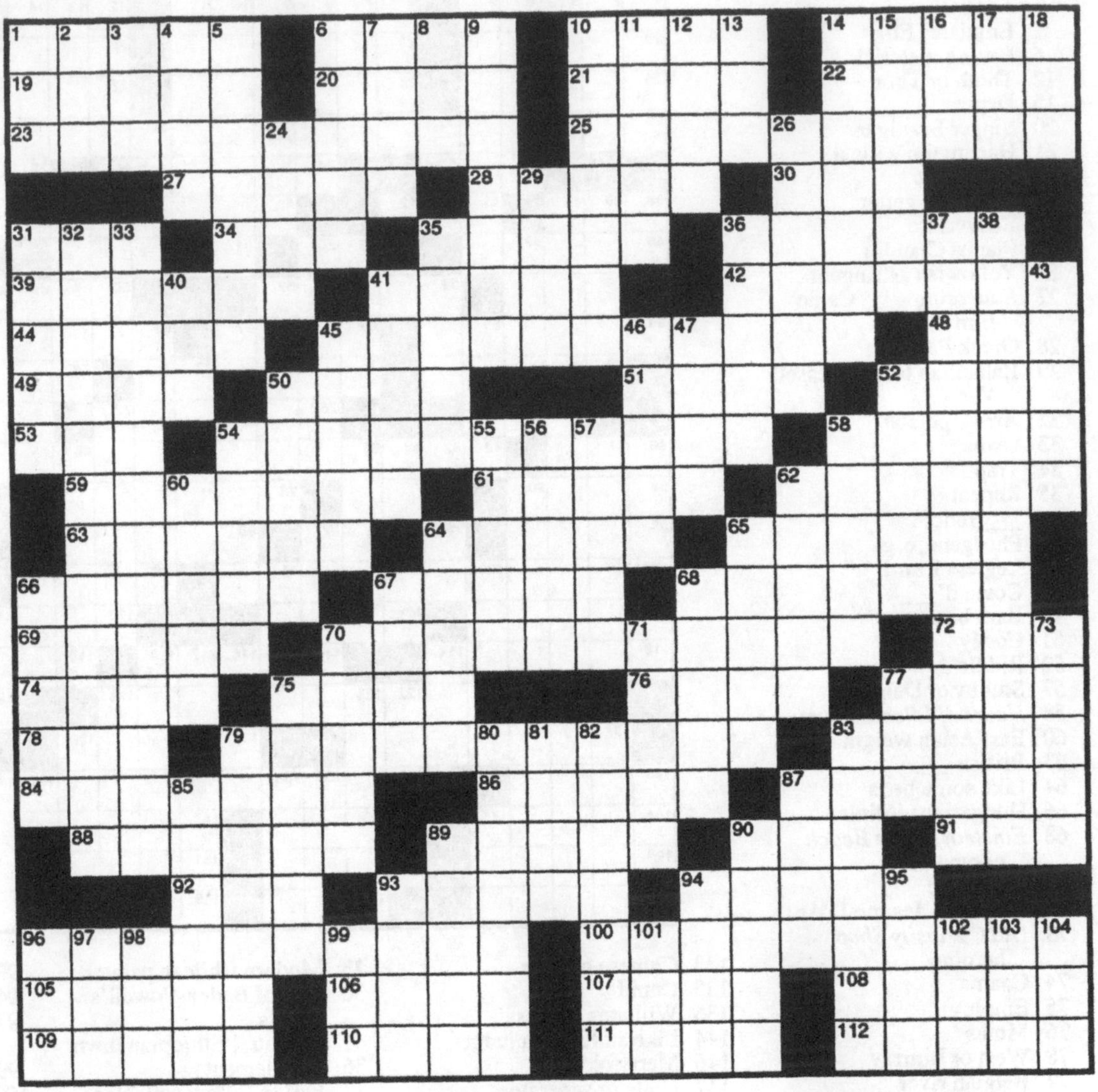

ACROSS
1 Disney classic
6 Stimulate
10 Diversify
14 Unterseeboot
19 City on the Allegheny
20 Deserve
21 Central American tree
22 Part of TNT
23 Satan
25 Satan, in 45 Across
27 "Peer Gynt ___"
28 Les ___ Unis
30 Cousin of olé
31 "___ Dreamer," 1929 song
34 Word of contempt
35 Threesome
36 Cold war's end
39 "Brigg Fair" composer
41 Choice dish
42 The Thames, at London Bridge
44 De Mille spectaculars, e.g.
45 Satan plays ball in this 1958 film
48 ___-fi
49 Chaise: Dial.
50 Distant: Comb. form
51 Long stretches
52 VCR type
53 ___ a shame!
54 Arrigo Boito's Satan
58 Suit for Kay
59 Played the yenta
61 Silent actor
62 On base, at Fenway
63 Waiter's friend
64 Japanese monasteries
65 Sharp, in Halle
66 In ___ (never)
67 Near namesake of Boru
68 Vladimir, to Mitya
69 Clumsily, old style
70 Satan, in "Heaven Can Wait"
72 Porky Pig's genus
74 Collars
75 Popular pop
76 "I don't care ___"
77 Recipe meas.
78 Scot's nappy
79 Satan, in "Angel On My Shoulder"
83 Nasua
84 Aussie's ranch
86 "Enough!"
87 Persian nightingale
88 Cash for Casimir
89 Bad bantlings
90 La Rocque of silents
91 Baby of the family: Abbr.
92 Till
93 Nincompoops
94 "The Morning After" star
96 ". . . gave his name to ___": Butler
100 Devilish, in Dijon
105 Hang loosely
106 Columnist Chase
107 Destroy
108 Utopias
109 Osborne's "Look Back in ___"
110 Forks over
111 Over
112 Mubarak's predecessor

DOWN
1 Half a blunder
2 Omitting nothing
3 Part of A.M.A.
4 Satan's voice in "Faust"
5 Nightmare
6 Fury
7 Satan spreads this around
8 Und so weiter, in Eng.
9 Mideast capital
10 Piazza
11 Slow down
12 Rogers and Clark
13 Berried evergreen
14 Loosens
15 Chess piece
16 Giant who wore "4"
17 Orinoco feeder
18 Pachydermal weight
24 Creeks
26 Ogive and ogee
29 Minuscule
31 That is
32 Satanic Liszt title
33 Satanic Milland film
35 X
36 Greek capital, to Luigi
37 Levin's devilish novel
38 Marlowe's devilish play
40 Unfriendly
41 Sound
43 N British Columbia river
45 Put off
46 Dundee turnips
47 Slavic folk dance
50 Wickiup
52 Wide
54 One of Potter's rabbits
55 Howells' "___ Wedding Journey"
56 Pair-___ shell
57 Hundred centimes
58 Loathe
60 Fiery stones
62 Like ___ of thunder
64 Took a stab at
65 Lake Victoria people
66 Pram pushers
67 Caspian oil port
68 "Michel Strogoff" author
70 Bank department
71 Complains loudly
73 Overflowed
75 Surfeited
77 Largest Truk Island
79 Medieval lutanist
80 Cries of discovery
81 Ribosomal and messenger
82 Misbehaved
83 Snuggles
85 "Like Lucifer, never ___ again": Shak.
87 Singer Sonny
89 Tom Sawyer's friend
90 Golem
93 Venomous lizard
94 Rages
95 Amneris's slave
96 Turkish room
97 Necropolis vessel
98 "Twelfth Street ___"
99 Tuck's pal
101 ___ nutshell
102 Abbr. in math proofs
103 Actress O'Connor
104 NYC time

205

WITHOUT EYES by Kenneth Haxton
If you enjoyed Puzzle 160, we know you'll enjoy Kenneth's challenger below.

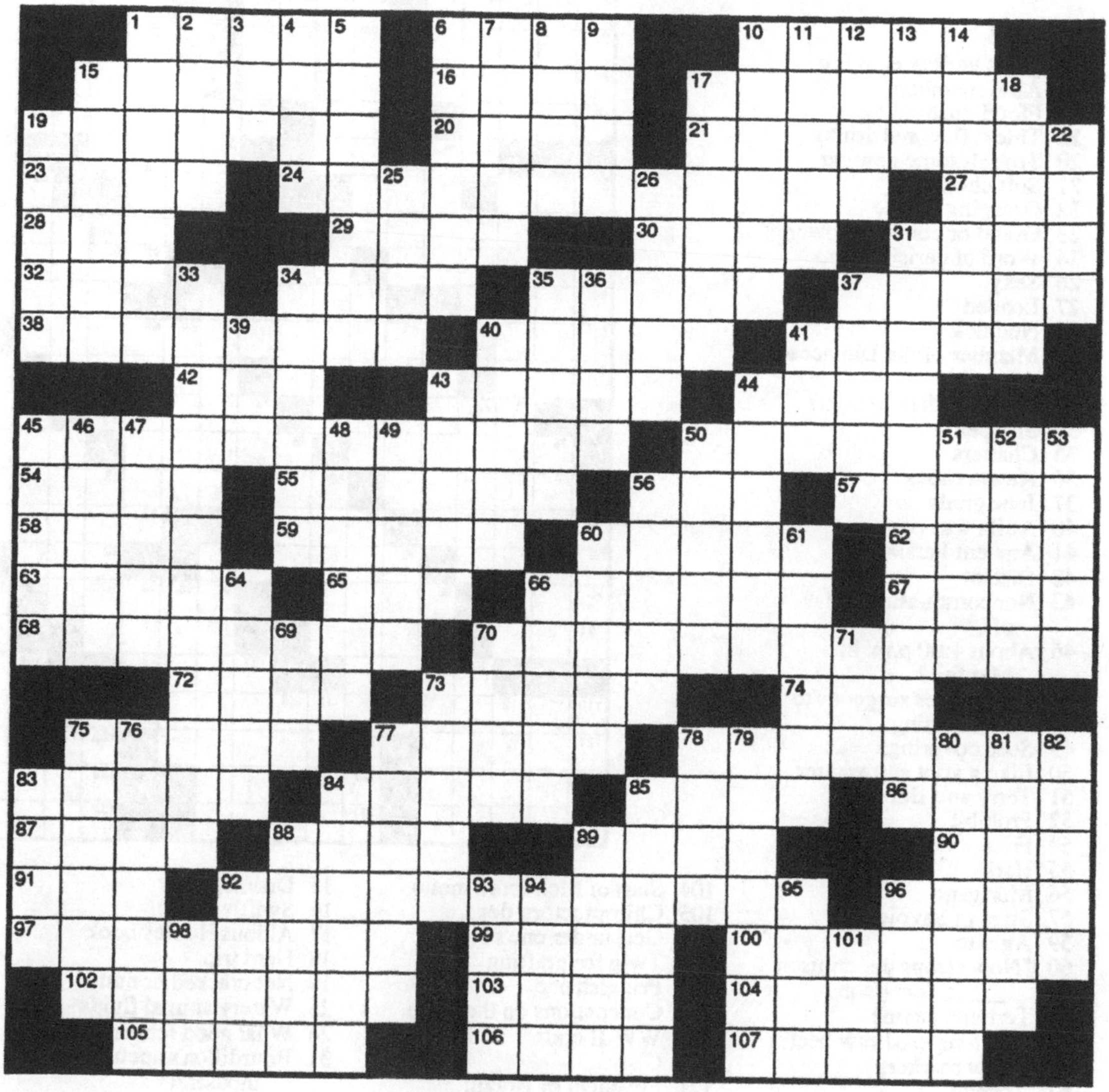

ACROSS

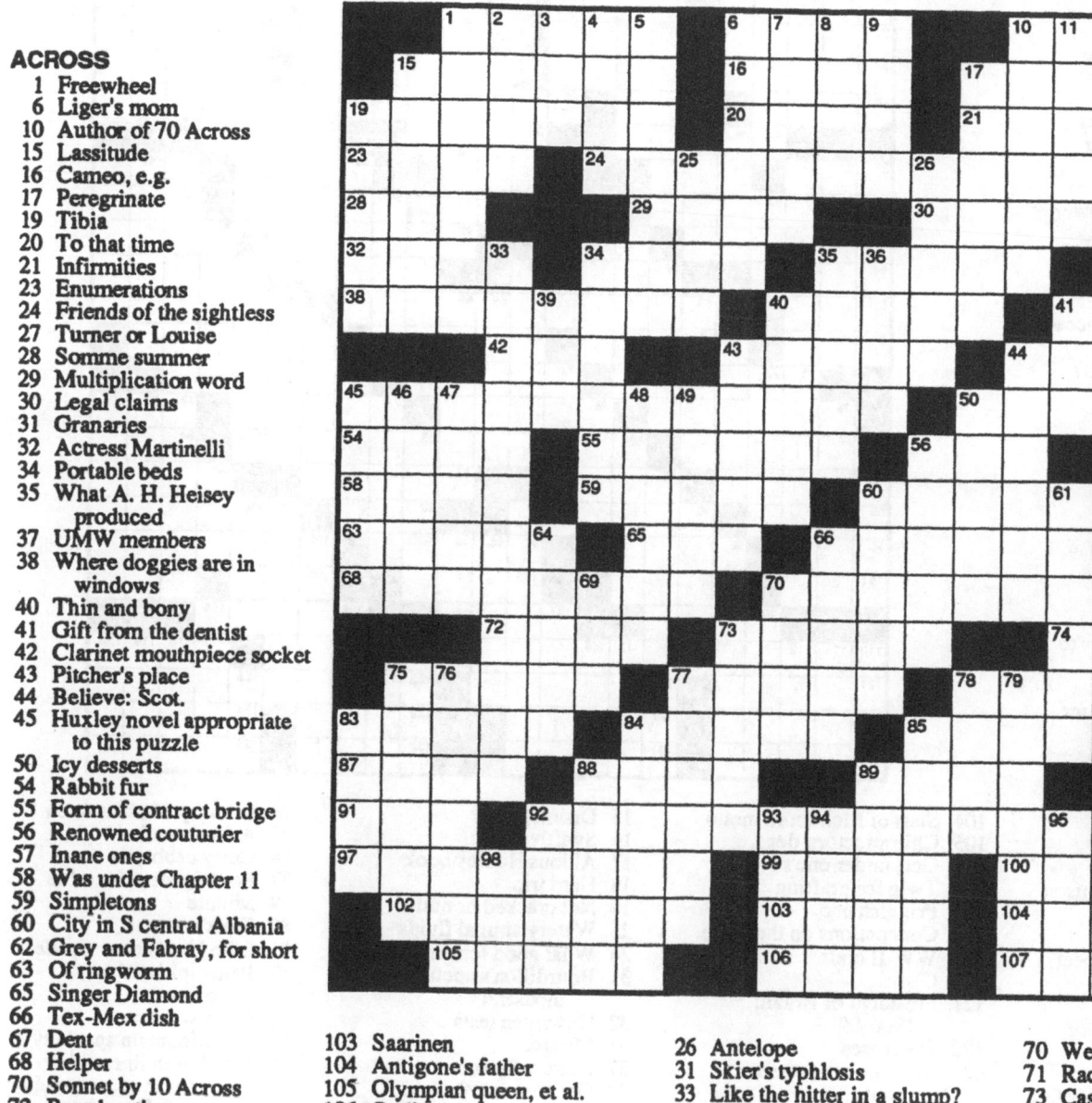

1 Freewheel
6 Liger's mom
10 Author of 70 Across
15 Lassitude
16 Cameo, e.g.
17 Peregrinate
19 Tibia
20 To that time
21 Infirmities
23 Enumerations
24 Friends of the sightless
27 Turner or Louise
28 Somme summer
29 Multiplication word
30 Legal claims
31 Granaries
32 Actress Martinelli
34 Portable beds
35 What A. H. Heisey produced
37 UMW members
38 Where doggies are in windows
40 Thin and bony
41 Gift from the dentist
42 Clarinet mouthpiece socket
43 Pitcher's place
44 Believe: Scot.
45 Huxley novel appropriate to this puzzle
50 Icy desserts
54 Rabbit fur
55 Form of contract bridge
56 Renowned couturier
57 Inane ones
58 Was under Chapter 11
59 Simpletons
60 City in S central Albania
62 Grey and Fabray, for short
63 Of ringworm
65 Singer Diamond
66 Tex-Mex dish
67 Dent
68 Helper
70 Sonnet by 10 Across
72 Broadcasting
73 Montana city
74 Without
75 Gallows
77 O and Wong
78 What Fosbury flopped over
83 Nimbi
84 Made a butt joint: Brit.
85 ___ Congwen, Chinese author
86 Maugham's Thompson
87 Suffix for rheo
88 Average marks
89 Jaeger's kin
90 North Caucasian language
91 With tic and toe
92 Nursery song
96 Worn out
97 Marine bivalve mollusk
99 Lift at Aspen
100 Progressive jazzman Lennie
102 Ballet jump
103 Saarinen
104 Antigone's father
105 Olympian queen, et al.
106 Oodles
107 Scandinavian goblins

DOWN

1 Dispute a will
2 Spheres
3 Mil. address
4 "My Three ___" (TV oldie)
5 ". . . baby on the ___ "
6 Trinities
7 Opposed to comings
8 Uppercrust
9 Depend on
10 Crenshaws
11 Taels
12 Fork features
13 ___ bodkins
14 Snuggles
15 Prickly plant
17 Least harsh
18 "Lise" and "Baigneuses"
19 "Balm of hurt minds"
22 Impudence
25 Radiates
26 Antelope
31 Skier's typhlosis
33 Like the hitter in a slump?
34 Entrust
35 Surgical dressing
36 Pale-green moth
37 Scott and Coe
39 Rent
40 Objectives
41 Give the ax to
43 San ___, El Salvador
44 Bondman
45 Mexican town in Durango
46 Shows boredom
47 Sportive swords
48 Pole climbing
49 Chamber-music music
50 Town in Karnataka, India
51 Maid of Astolat
52 Burmese measures
53 Timid ones
56 Death
60 Thai coins
61 Strain
64 Cubic decimeters
66 Stained
69 Against
70 West Sussex river
71 Rackets
73 Case for the corporal
75 They get picked and plunked
76 Somewhat salty
77 He started "The Tatler"
78 Pal
79 Countertendency
80 German art movement of the twenties
81 Extras
82 Right-hand page
83 Canine sleuth
84 Pigeon hawks
85 Urban eyesore
88 Indian millet
89 Trap
92 God with a hammer
93 "Man ___ dog!"
94 Slander
95 Eastern Amerinds
96 Short stalk
98 Wind dir.
101 Luft and Caesar

206

CUISINE FOR COGITATION by Joan P. Leemhorst
A time-honored theme gets rejuvenated by a California constructor. Have a word-feast!

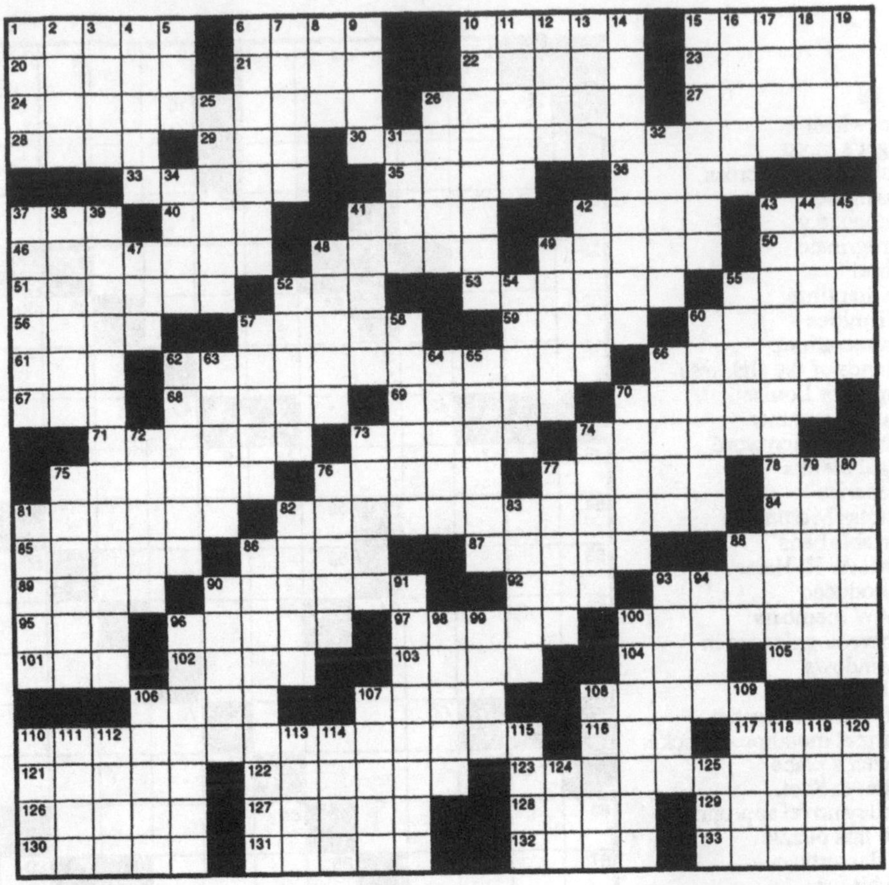

ACROSS

1 What variety is to life
6 ABA members
10 Flood; rush
15 Thick, flavored drinks
20 Troublesome new car
21 Soft cheese
22 Grasping device
23 Grand or comic follower
24 Word of derision
26 Sexy
27 Loaded
28 Nudnick
29 Member of the Ulmaceae family
30 Lucifer's dark delight?
33 Sharpen
35 Chatters
36 Autonomous
37 June grads
40 Attila was one
41 Ancient Persian
42 Distant
43 Noncommissioned nav. off.
46 About 4:00 p.m. in Mayfair?
48 This causes surgeons to be beaming
49 Seed coverings
50 Like a zoot suit wearer
51 Terry and Burstyn
52 Prohibit
53 Fries
55 Hari
56 Mortgage
57 Sires in Savoie
59 Agitate
60 "Now sleeps the crimson ___": Tennyson
61 Terhune canine
62 Bad-tempered raw beef?
66 Ballot markers
67 Append
68 Culinarians
69 Singer Mel
70 Germany's Adenauer
71 A lot of TV's summer fare
73 Leg bone
74 Setting
75 Discourages
76 Actress Black or Valentine
77 French short story
78 A source of Ger. cream
81 Beer ingredients
82 Hot and cold states?
84 Map abbr.
85 Syrian president
86 Length of 320 rods
87 Old stringed, fretted-necked instruments
88 Christian of fashion
89 Talk idly
90 Saying nil
92 Scale notes
93 Psychiatrists' fodder
95 Rooster's fancy
96 "Bubbles"
97 More underdone
100 Elf or dieter's ruin?
101 Corp.
102 Order originated by actors
103 Second caliph
104 Start of Montana's motto
105 Chiropractors' degs.
106 Gets under one's skin
107 Twig for grafting
108 Priggish one
110 Concoctions on the Main
116 WW II craft
117 Gist
121 President of Brazil: 1906-09
122 Decreases
123 Soprano who was a beauty?
126 Backer who takes the cake
127 Pool
128 Swearword
129 Yemenis and Omanis
130 Suffix for team and tap
131 Distinguishing beliefs
132 Pony with no legs
133 Units of force

DOWN

1 Stick or happy preceder
2 Le Moko
3 Small demons
4 Indianapolis eleven
5 Bath-to-London dir.
6 Rock-clinging mollusk
7 It often wins for Goren
8 Spasmodic motion
9 Pippin, e.g.: Bot.
10 Painters' manhelpers
11 Business combos
12 You can't find them in Antarctica
13 End-of-the-week cry
14 Famed French chef
15 Disintegrates
16 Swiftly
17 Aldous Huxley book
18 Hard trip
19 Not cracked or nutty
25 Watery animal fluids
26 What good fencers do
31 Bourdillon's nocturnal "thousand"
32 Unwritten tests
34 Meager
37 Actress Stevens
38 Get new ammo
39 Caesar putting on robes?
41 He painted "Boy With a Sword"
42 Lana's first spouse
43 Tenderloin Frenchman?
44 Loud firework
45 Iridescent gemstones
47 X
48 Members of an exaltation
49 Other, on the Rue de la Paix
52 British judges: Slang
54 Japanese volcano
55 A measure, in Europe
57 They toil hard for little
58 Witty exposé
60 One-ounce glasses
62 Tirade
63 French city for travelers?
64 Dressed for ceremony
65 Threefold
66 Upper ___, former African republic
70 Quirks
72 Frome of fiction
73 Charmed
74 Book by Sholem Asch
75 A Santa puller
76 Curly cabbages
77 Feed feasters for a fee
79 Minute
80 Frost's output
81 Like Hammer or Spade?
82 Items initiated in Congress
83 Circe was one
86 Soda-fountain specialty
88 Word with line or drop
90 "Whenas in ___ my Julia goes": Herrick
91 British trams
93 Media "sexpert"
94 Cross
96 Parceled yarns
98 Girlfriends, in Grenoble
99 Engrossed
100 It's hot or cold, but usually red
106 Word with man or circle
107 Fight
108 Founder of a school in the Academos garden
109 Mineral used for polishing
110 Watering holes
111 Shut up
112 Spirit of Saint-Louis
113 One life's recap
114 Sci. of nos.
115 Difficult position
118 Enthusiasm
119 French clergyman
120 Russian news agency
124 Loan to Antony
125 Senseless

207

AVIARY by Dorothy Cannan

Our feathered friends crop up ten times. The puzzle is a real "tweet!"

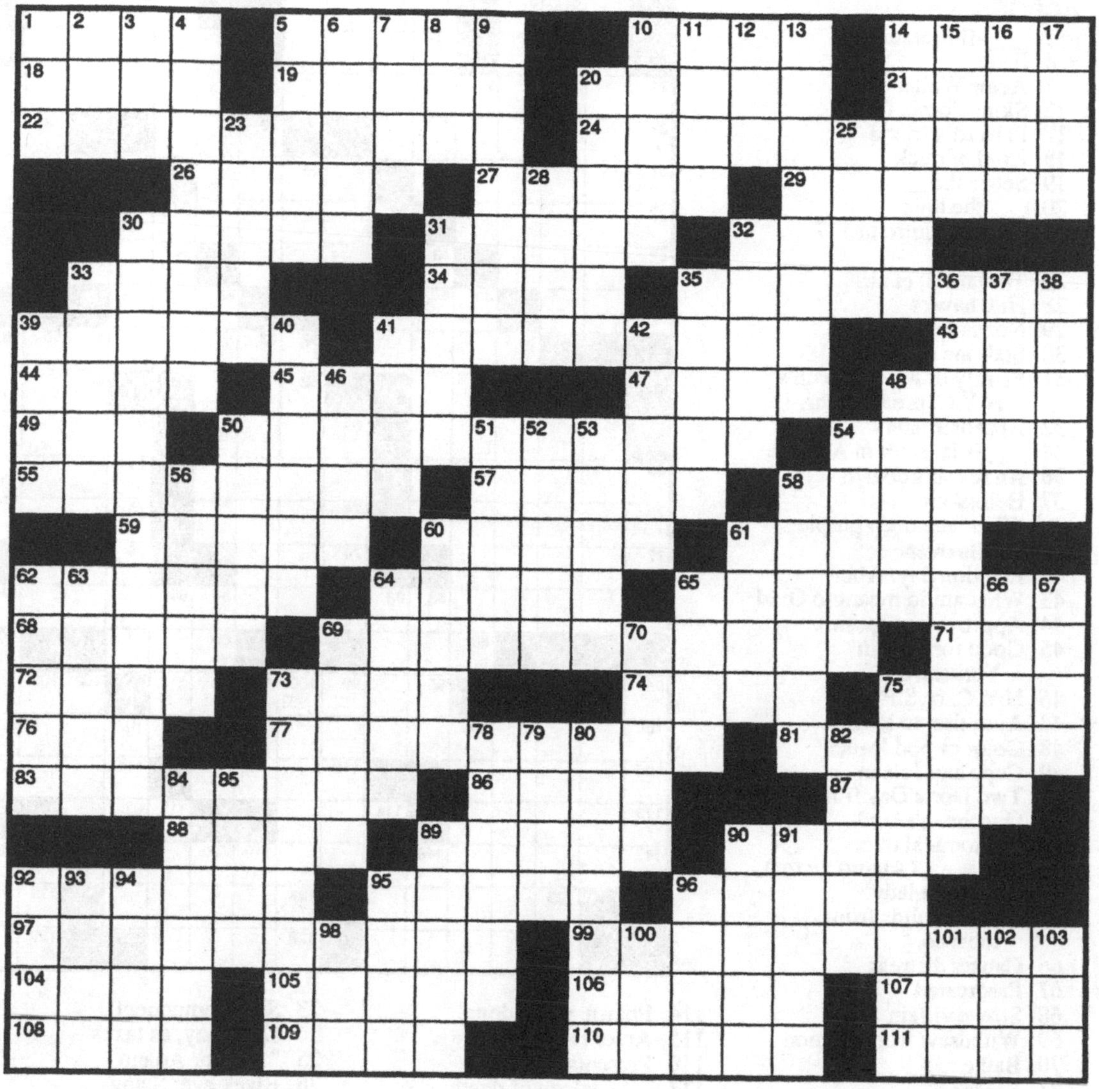

ACROSS

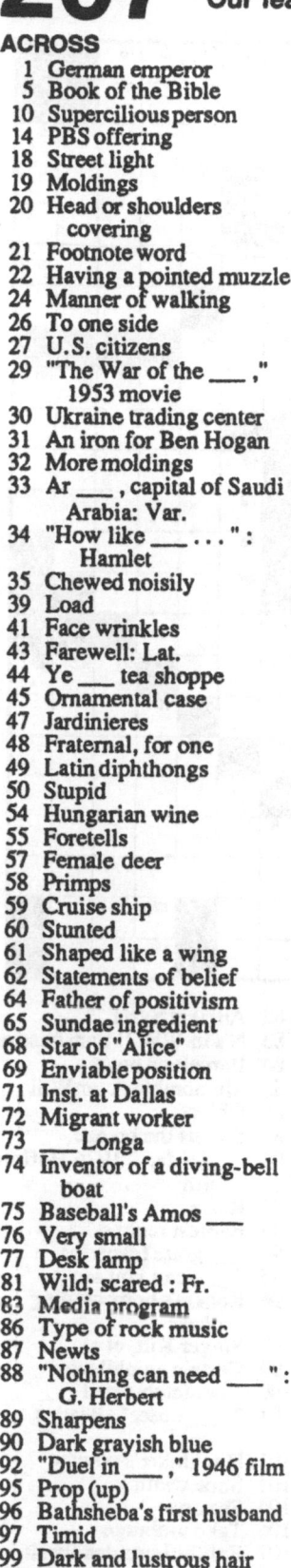

1 German emperor
5 Book of the Bible
10 Supercilious person
14 PBS offering
18 Street light
19 Moldings
20 Head or shoulders covering
21 Footnote word
22 Having a pointed muzzle
24 Manner of walking
26 To one side
27 U.S. citizens
29 "The War of the ___," 1953 movie
30 Ukraine trading center
31 An iron for Ben Hogan
32 More moldings
33 Ar ___, capital of Saudi Arabia: Var.
34 "How like ___ . . ." : Hamlet
35 Chewed noisily
39 Load
41 Face wrinkles
43 Farewell: Lat.
44 Ye ___ tea shoppe
45 Ornamental case
47 Jardinieres
48 Fraternal, for one
49 Latin diphthongs
50 Stupid
54 Hungarian wine
55 Foretells
57 Female deer
58 Primps
59 Cruise ship
60 Stunted
61 Shaped like a wing
62 Statements of belief
64 Father of positivism
65 Sundae ingredient
68 Star of "Alice"
69 Enviable position
71 Inst. at Dallas
72 Migrant worker
73 ___ Longa
74 Inventor of a diving-bell boat
75 Baseball's Amos ___
76 Very small
77 Desk lamp
81 Wild; scared : Fr.
83 Media program
86 Type of rock music
87 Newts
88 "Nothing can need ___" : G. Herbert
89 Sharpens
90 Dark grayish blue
92 "Duel in ___," 1946 film
95 Prop (up)
96 Bathsheba's first husband
97 Timid
99 Dark and lustrous hair
104 Verdi opera
105 Approaches
106 Size of type
107 Agitate
108 City Agamemnon conquered
109 French book-illustator
110 Kitchen utensil
111 Montreal athlete

DOWN

1 Cricket positions
2 Cardinal number
3 ___ polloi
4 Like a formal procession of West Pointers
5 Single-celled organism
6 Kind of coast or tower
7 ___ of living
8 House or wife preceder
9 Spanish nobleman
10 Malinger
11 Scolds
12 Be indebted
13 Tire problems
14 Bacteria or oxide
15 Old Greek coin
16 Competed
17 Annexes
20 Races
23 Horatian verse form
25 Norse goddess of fate
28 Tabby's plaint
30 Panoramic sight
31 Indian of South America
32 Drift
33 Sovereign
35 Largest asteroid
36 Iowa
37 ___ les-Bains, Lake Geneva spa
38 Patron saint of France
39 Betty ___, cartoon flapper
40 Whinnies
41 Rumina
42 Bay of ___, Canada
46 Weight allowance
48 "___ is human" : A. Pope
50 Breakfast food
51 Mariner's compass point
52 "___ something?"
53 Bury
54 Religious pamphlet
56 Maugham character
58 Satisfy
60 Medieval stringed instruments
61 Served perfectly at Wimbledon
62 Circus performer
63 S European drink
64 Henry ___ Lodge
65 Writer Dinesen
66 Moslem princes
67 Ponder
69 Stingy
70 Knocks a boxing opponent down
73 ___ again (often)
75 Kind of oil drilling
78 High priests' vestments
79 Nilotic people
80 Inserted
82 Savage
84 Square-dance call
85 Mystery-story item
89 "___ Go the Boats?" : R.L.S.
90 Actor Duilio del ___
91 One, to Helmut
92 Kipling's "The Light ___ Failed"
93 Legatee
94 Within: Comb. form
95 Asterisk
96 ___ acid, from grapes
98 Vintage car
100 Mohammed's son-in-law
101 Son-in-law of Nixon
102 Untanned hide
103 Highway sign

208

Z-Z-Z by Alvin B. Chase

Try this one before you retire. Then finish it at breakfast.

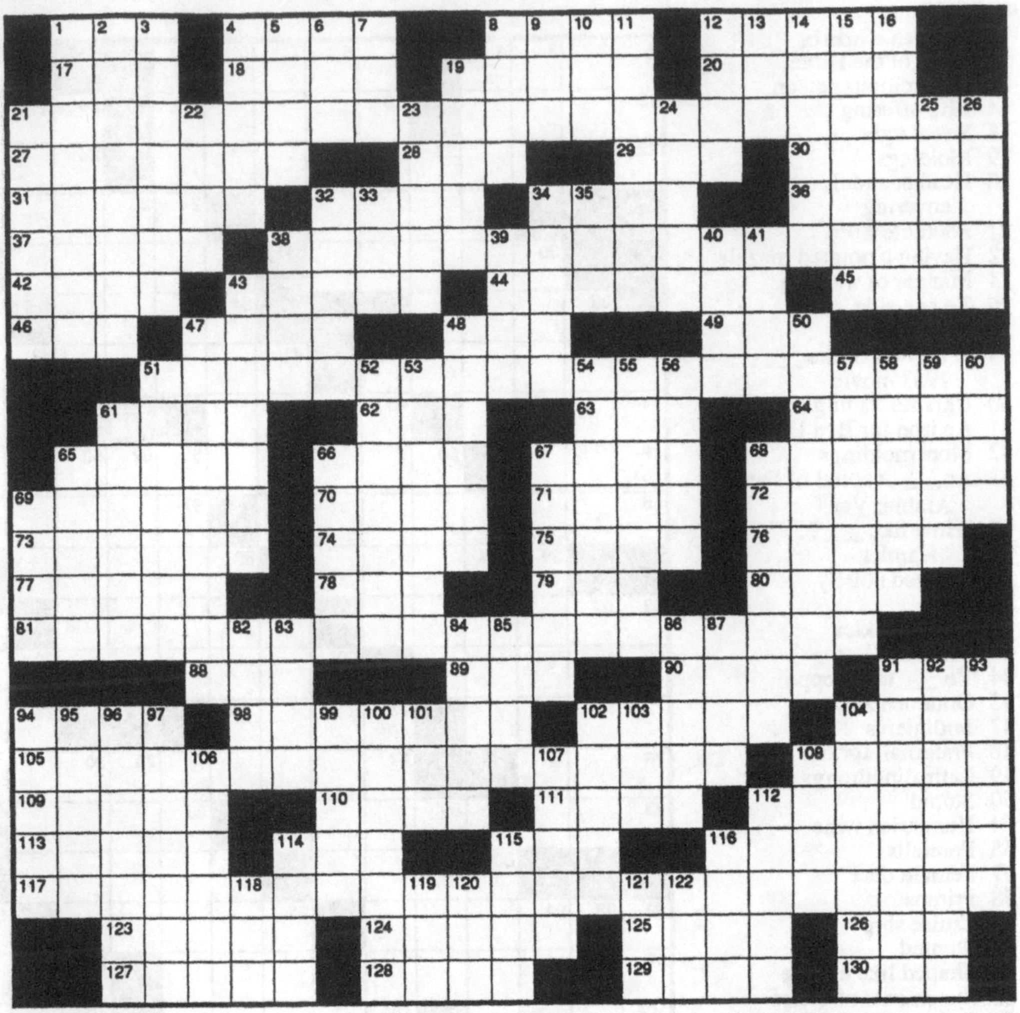

ACROSS

1 ___-fi literature
4 Fetid
7 Actor Walter
12 Skin: Comb. form
17 Falstaff's friend
18 Kind of duck
19 Settle the ___
20 ___ the hole
21 Hamlet's intro to 117 Across
27 Toscanini, et al.
28 Hilo hawks
29 Norris Dam agcy.
30 Stallone role
31 Family of Mayor Koch's N.Y.C. predecessor
32 Approximately
34 ___ Fria, river in Arizona
36 Au revoir's cousin
37 Helots' kin
38 What "the deep purple falls over"
42 Election day: Abbr.
43 What audio meant to Ovid
44 Approve a proposal
45 Good fortune, in Yorkshire
46 N.Y.C. or S.F., e.g.
47 Auto tire, to René
48 Color or pod leader
49 Capp and Jolson
51 Two Doris Day films
61 Quechuan's land
62 Anatomical duct
63 Santa ___ (Alamo victor)
64 She was a lady
65 Reduce solids from tobacco
66 Causes distress
67 Procreated
68 Stowe villain
69 Withdraw from a union
70 Bathe
71 Raison d' ___
72 Heedful: Poet.
73 Aquila's brightest star
74 Type style: Abbr.
75 Dahs' partners
76 Small barracudas
77 "The ___" (Redford/ Newman film)
78 "___ Dieu!" (Caen expletive)
79 "Is ___?": Matt. 26:22
80 Socials
81 "Mister ___" (Start of old Les Paul hit)
88 Mazatlan Mrs.
89 Night and pant followers
90 Dumbo's large features
91 Child's marble
94 Tender
98 Famed New Orleans restaurateur
102 Kelly girls, for short
104 Leo's pride?
105 Nocturnal embracers
108 Shrivel
109 French river or department
110 Maui milkfishes
111 He's sorry now
112 "... all ___ created equal"
113 Huffs and puffs
114 Pharm. watchdogs
115 Actor Hanks
116 Presents
117 "___ sleep of death..."
123 Arrested
124 Alleviated
125 Ages
126 Dawn goddess
127 City near Malmo
128 Syngman ___ of S Korea
129 National concern
130 Chemical suffix

DOWN

1 Supports; makes stable
2 Flamenco adjunct
3 Brightens, to Byron
4 Spreads on breads
5 Track circuits
6 Devilkin
7 Actress Sandra
8 Essen expletives
9 Neckwear
10 Sea scavenger
11 Lengthy rebuke
12 Computer fodder
13 Environmental prefix
14 Correct a cartoon
15 Looks; glances: Sp.
16 Denver's altitude
19 Ladle
21 Bodily feelings, in Ayr
22 "___ Tu" (old Spanish song)
23 Stair component
24 Don't pay, as taxes
25 "___ for Adano"
26 Black eye: Slang
32 Oil, to a druggist
33 Cartoonist Gardner ___
34 Texas A&M student
35 Needlefish
38 East Coast stadium
39 Animal's wail: Brit. dial.
40 Handy abbr.
41 ___ contendere
43 Tort committer
47 Outstanding models
48 Mortarboard adjunct
50 Ornamental garden plants
51 "___ Tilly," Matthau film
52 The Lone Eagle, e.g.
53 Father of zinc plating
54 Having divisions
55 Sluggishness
56 Stows cargo
57 Wrestling match duo
58 Mountainsides receiving direct sunlight
59 Mortgages
60 Young guinea fowl
61 Basis of fruit jellies
65 River mouth area
66 Out on ___ (vulnerable)
67 Darkens, obscures
68 Tools for stretching leather
69 Lip
82 Ancient Syria
83 N's in WW II transmissions
84 Barcelona boys
85 Memorable actor Will ___
86 Object
87 Shoots the breeze
91 "___ Man," 1976 Hoffman film
92 Raise
93 Earnest request
94 ___ grass (esparto)
95 "___ can you see..."
96 Rocket's homecoming phase
97 Singer Kitt, et al.
99 Certain amphibians
100 "... fetch a pail ___"
101 "___ Loser" (Beatles song)
102 Hitchhiker's pointer
103 Shoe width
104 Sea cow
106 Take umbrage
107 Exhibiting a deadly sin
108 ___ Station
112 Soggy; damp
114 ___ off (parry)
115 Ule or baobab
116 Unexciting
118 Inlet
119 Villain's cry
120 Japan or Canton follower
121 T-Man, e.g.
122 Lode load

209 COURT PLASTERED by Tap Osborn

An N.B.A. leader tells how it feels when his team takes its bumps in a protracted slump.

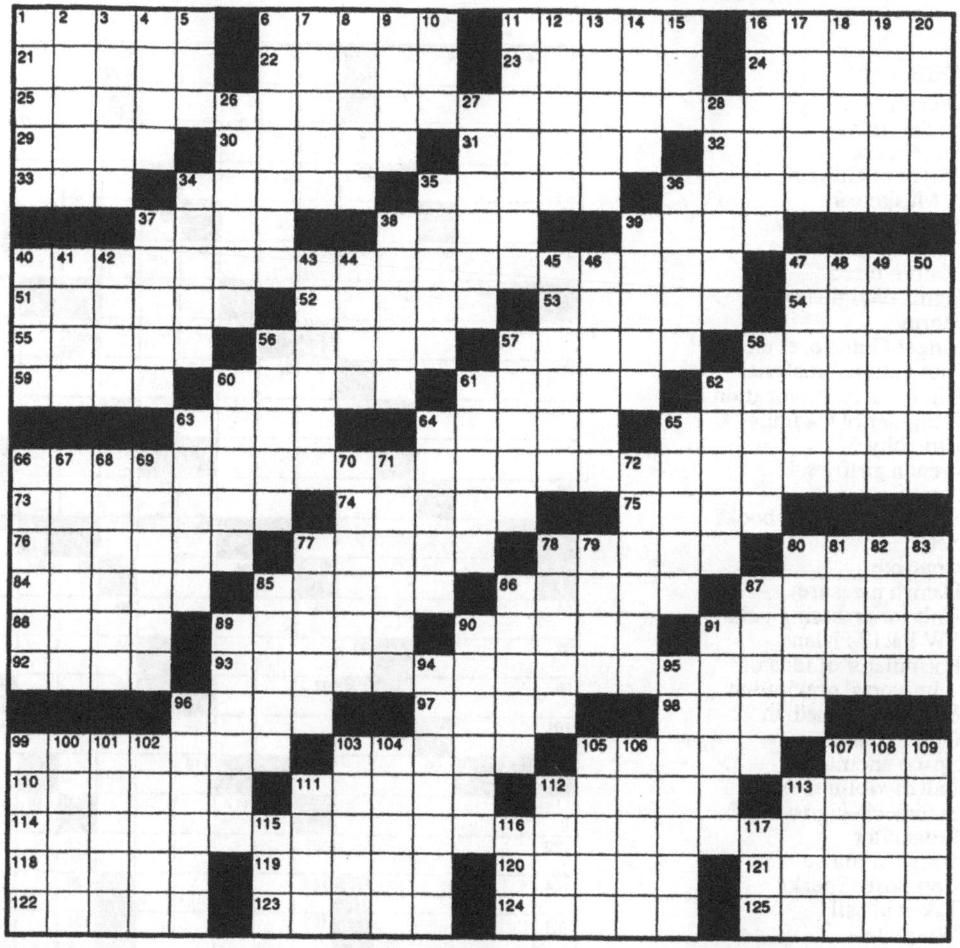

ACROSS

1 Author of the quotation
6 Aspect
11 Barrymores' milieu
16 Germ cell
21 ". . . lived in ___ . . . "
22 Attacked
23 Runner Rudolph
24 Buddhist monk
25 Occupation of 1 Across at time of quotation
29 Flag
30 ___ Gay, historic plane
31 Priscilla wooer
32 Dance: Comb. form
33 Unclose, in poesy
34 Composer Erik
35 Fred of stage, screen and TV
36 Chooses
37 His name means "I am faithful"
38 Small band
39 Egyptian goddess of law or truth
40 **Start of a quotation**
47 Hide away
51 Rams or Jets
52 Asp's weapon
53 Fraser of tennis
54 Slim-bodied lemur
55 Spent
56 Ten: Prefix
57 Italian banking center
58 Sweater-mill sights
59 Truck garden employee
60 Camping gear
61 Actress Field
62 Trumpet valve
63 Houston university
64 Cole Porter's "___ Went to Haiti"
65 Axle wrecker
66 **Middle of the quotation**
73 Deckhand or bosun
74 Vast quantity
75 Start of Massachusetts motto
76 Laborers in London
77 Painter Jan of Holland
78 Diminish
80 Exchange
84 As ___ (generally)
85 Levels, in carpentry
86 Jetés
87 Entrap
88 Gait
89 Kind of ship or trip
90 Medicine: Comb. form
91 Station-house ringers
92 Small vat
93 **End of the quotation**
96 Crocus or gladiolus
97 Conflicts
98 Caroler's word
99 Desert dweller
103 Plucks suddenly
105 Onion pest
107 Zucchetto or calotte
110 Spanish province
111 Pickler's need
112 Out front
113 Words of woe
114 When the quotation was uttered
118 White poplar
119 Wood thicket
120 Jewel-thief's need
121 Site for a kite
122 Petruchio's role, at times
123 Harris ___
124 Sham
125 Puts on weight

DOWN

1 De ___ (in reality)
2 Long Island city
3 Then's partner
4 Protected inlet
5 Haw's forerunner
6 Specter or delusion
7 Far East capital
8 Put in a dither
9 Bag, in Barcelona
10 Greek letter
11 Ingest
12 Diacritical mark
13 Foreign
14 Hoover or Webster associates
15 Head part
16 Scented bag
17 Prosecutor's need
18 Busy terminal
19 Foyt or Coe, e.g.
20 Moral code
26 Kind of electrical wire
27 Tranquilizer
28 Jam or difficulty
34 Located
35 "___ of One's Own" (Woolf)
36 Actress Prentiss
37 Yellow or scarlet ailment
38 Soprano Margaret ___
39 Memorable labor leader
40 Abel's little brother
41 ___ strut, plane part
42 Like a widow's mite
43 Smoothing device
44 Methodist, e.g.
45 Nitrobenzene derivative
46 ___ over (swooned)
47 Awash
48 " O! that this ___ solid flesh would melt": Hamlet
49 "Mosaic gold"
50 Mennonite leader Jacob (1808-89)
56 Setting or scenery
57 Personification of iniquity
58 Double-jointed
60 ___ Square, N.Y.C.
61 Cosmos expert
62 Vigilante's group
63 Dr. Richards of tennis
64 Cypress roots
65 Pub offerings
66 Join, in heraldry
67 Shoe size element
68 Theatrical company
69 Actress Wendy ___
70 Formal announcement
71 Almost extinct workers
72 Bola or blow-gun, e.g.
77 Sliver of pottery
78 Bataan group
79 Scop
80 K-9 corps warning
81 Weather forecast
82 Weapon: Fr.
83 Nuisance
85 El Greco's land
86 Comedian Bert and his biographer
87 Nocturnal blessing
89 Released from the slammer
90 Juan Peron's successor: 1974
91 Sidesteps
94 Played the guitar
95 Furious
96 Laundry worker
99 African leader of the 70s
100 One of the Antilles
101 Where a khanum presides
102 Spry
103 Feel one's way
104 Hair coloring
105 Ponder
106 Therefore
107 Colette novel
108 With full force
109 Some small dogs, for short
111 Bad setback
112 On a windjammer cruise
113 Vicinity
115 Piece of legislation
116 Askew
117 The "it" game

210 LITERARY COLLABORATIONS by Judith Perry

The fun here comes from tying titles together. We hope it won't cause knotty problems.

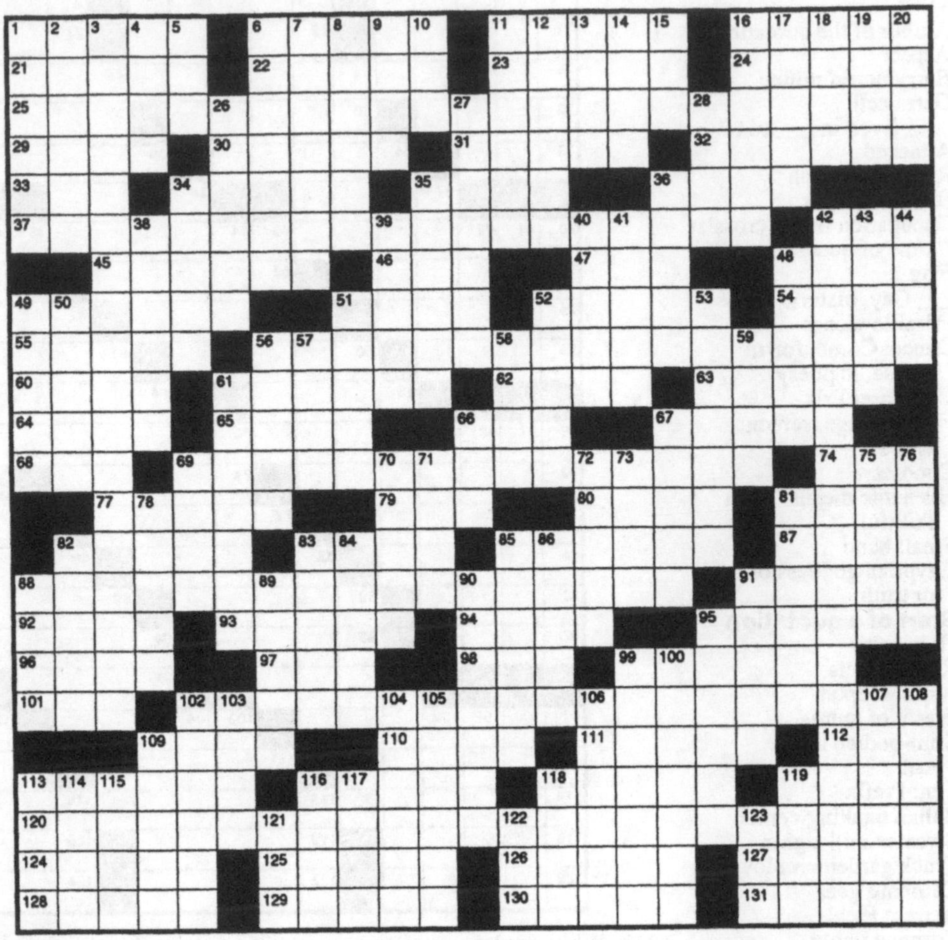

ACROSS

1 Green plays
6 Under oath
11 Storehouse
16 Slayer of Goliath
21 A Musketeer
22 Weedy plants
23 Lindens
24 Mature insect
25 Hardy-Wright book?
29 Storm
30 Singer Guthrie, et al.
31 Motivational material
32 Hindu sacred invocation
33 Daughter of Cadmus
34 Ohio city
35 French girlfriend
36 Axes
37 Shute-Tarkington book?
42 Set
45 Contrive
46 Danish measure
47 Unit for assessing pain
48 SW Pacific island
49 Formulator of idea of universal gravitation
51 Montreal comedian
52 Disseminated
54 Space anomalies
55 Italian violin maker
56 Steinbeck-Inge work?
60 Progenitor
61 Songs of praise
62 Composer Speaks
63 Takes in sail
64 Winglike
65 Spicy stew
66 Supplement (with "out")
67 Pater's better half
68 Author Deighton
69 Le Carré-Daniels book?
74 Unclose, to Shakespeare
77 Falls in globules
79 Arctic explorer
80 Near or Far follower
81 Egyptian sun god
82 Skyline landmark
83 Cupid
85 Solar system asteroid
87 City in NW France
88 Auchincloss-Hunter book?
91 Nothing, to Nero
92 Dies ___
93 Unravel
94 Allows
95 Amorous males
96 Gumshoes
97 Hasten
98 Mouths
99 New Zealand's vegetable caterpillars
101 Pindaric creation
102 Rachel Carson-Gladys Taber work
109 Virgo predecessors
110 Confident anticipation
111 Proceed from
112 Subj. of Tennyson's "In Memoriam"
113 Cotton cloth
116 English actress: 19th c.
118 Good, in Granada
119 Off kilter
120 Murdoch-Alcott creation?
124 Symbol
125 Entomb
126 Mountain ridge
127 Dig
128 Bergen character
129 Raise the glass to
130 Jacksonville sports bowl
131 Metal repositories

DOWN

1 Native land: Latin
2 Former UN secretary-general
3 Terkel-Tolstoy book?
4 Rent
5 Dir. from Reno to Carson City
6 American architect-author
7 Bellicose
8 "All ___!" (plunger's motto)
9 Old cars
10 Inits. on a rubber check
11 Racial group member
12 Cone-shaped residence
13 Japanese aborigine
14 Municipal map
15 Superlative suffix
16 Couches
17 Ratifications
18 Enormous
19 Stravinsky
20 Spanish gentlewoman
26 Estonian city in the Gulf of Finland
27 With fearfulness
28 Moslem priest
34 Closing poetic stanza
35 Greetings or farewells in Oahu
36 Biblical Israelite spy
38 Soppier
39 ". . . restless as ___": Heine
40 Worship
41 Frumpy
42 Anne Lindbergh-Jack London opus?
43 Malayan palm fibers
44 Speech impediment
48 Colored flare
49 Twangy
50 Rousseau character
51 Hamlet's "___ troubles"
52 Dried orchid tuber
53 Historians Will and Ariel
56 Chaucer specialty
57 Inheritor
58 Cooking utensils, Chinese style
59 Scottish tartan pattern
61 Corn cookers
66 Hot time on the Fr. Riviera
67 Ancient ballad singer of Provence
69 Grass genus
70 Wear away
71 Grant of Hollywood
72 Outcries
73 Amer. Revolutionary patriot
75 Salk's field of research
76 Organic compounds
78 Takes a bus
81 "Foundation and Earth" author
82 Fragment
83 Kate's TV friend
84 Expert
85 S Dakota capital
86 Asian range
88 Memorable Slav
89 Eye cosmetics
90 Clapper, in Cottbus
91 ___ Dame
95 Common sense
99 Be in compliance with
100 More complaining
102 Indicate support
103 Cousin of B.P.O.E.
104 Possessive pronoun
105 Voiced
106 Cape Cod Indian
107 Gave absolution to
108 Pungent aromatic herbs
109 The Titanic, e.g.
113 T. S. Eliot subject
114 Later
115 Patron saint of physicians
116 Reddish tropical resin
117 S.A. republic
118 Adriatic wind
119 Athena
121 Appropriate
122 Scrap of cloth
123 Theol. degs.

211 THE BARD ON BASEBALL by Edward Marchese

Since Shakespeare loved wordplay, we're sure he would root for this puzzle.

ACROSS

1 WW II military area
4 Cuts out a design
10 Get along
14 Lots of land
19 Rorem or Sparks
20 Hot Mexican dish
21 Apportion
22 Fraternity letters, e.g.
23 FIELDER'S CHOICE, ENGLISH STYLE?
27 Stan the Man
28 Estuary
29 Needle-shaped
30 Libido
31 Girdles
32 Movie part
33 Chile's northern seaport
37 Actor Cariou
38 Most populous continent
41 Male descendant
43 Rooter
45 Map deg. line
46 MANAGER'S NIGHTMARE?
52 Tristan's love
54 Adopt a cause
57 Reagan or Santo
58 Fix
60 Where Met meets Met
61 Former capital of Japan
62 Shatter
64 Spiced, curdled milk drink
65 Wrongs
66 Explode
68 Ecological community
70 Alone onstage, as a diva
71 Movie star Davis
72 Type of glove
74 Intertwine
76 Reluctant
78 Thou
79 MACBETH WITHOUT A SCORECARD?
84 Decorate cake
87 Delaying tactic
89 "You ___!" ("You bet!")
90 Of the skin
92 Farewell in Madrid
94 Spanish duke, conqueror of Portugal
98 Concise
99 Moslem law
100 Nosegay
101 River between Poland and E Germany
103 Ruhr city
106 Starting gate
107 Matador's cape movement
108 Joined to an unlike part
109 Native of Vientiane
110 ". . . a story of ___": Shak.
112 Large Nigerian city
114 STATEMENT IN A COMEDY OF ERRORS?
117 Landon
118 ___ Paulo, Brazil
120 Doze
121 Talk back to
122 Frequently, à la Keats
125 Lacks
127 "Dr. Zhivago" theme song
131 Italy's largest lake
134 Moonfish
135 Comfortable
137 Tasteless porridge
138 Perfume ingredient
140 R.B.I. FOR HENRY VI?
144 Foot-to-leg joint
145 Astaire's sister
146 Lon Chaney role: Var.
147 "The Path" in Chinese philosophy
148 Jackson or James
149 Period in office
150 Addison's co-editor
151 Person

DOWN

1 Glossy paint
2 Job permanence
3 Heavy kind of favorite
4 Ancient colonnade
5 Fuselage part
6 Morning hrs.
7 New York Indian tribe: Var.
8 Wood leveler
9 Betrays
10 Ga. neighbor
11 Place of sacrifice
12 "___ and His Brothers": Italian movie
13 Merman or Waters
14 Turkish official
15 Greek island inhabitants
16 Pass along
17 Snaky fish
18 The limit, sometimes
21 Movement
24 Sonny's sibling
25 Allows it to be thought
26 Kosher's opposite
34 LAERTES AS CONFIDENT BATTER?
35 Rhythmic
36 Army command
38 Expression of surprise
39 Pouches
40 Short newspaper piece
42 Murderous Roman
44 Ventilate
46 Bundled
47 Italian papal family
48 "To Have and ___," M. Johnston book
49 Dame Myra ___, pianist
50 ___ facto
51 Asian unit of weight
53 Caucasian
54 Opponent
55 Lanza or Cuomo
56 CLOSE CALL AT PHILIPPI FIELD?
59 Aviator Balbo
63 Tucked in
64 Salt derived from an acid
67 New Mexico Indians
69 Huge crowd
71 Moderates
73 Org. for Bruins and Sabres
75 Lake boundary of New York
77 Lutelike instrument
80 Baltic Sea island
81 "___ of Jeanie . . . "
82 "___ Death": Widmark film, 1947
83 Summers in Savoie
85 Strait near Nova Scotia
86 Happify
88 Trifled
91 India's money unit
92 Rome's famous Way
93 That can be accomplished
95 ___ Riefenstahl, German movie director
96 Prejudice
97 Dog in "The Thin Man"
102 Stitched up
104 Austen novel
105 British swells
108 Collection of sayings
109 Islands north of Sicily
111 Monogram of "Kidnapped" author
113 Attacks
115 Dicker
116 "Let ___. Time driveth . . . ": Tennyson
119 Cassini
122 Portuguese seaport
123 Card game featuring sevens
124 "The Man with ___": E. Markham
126 Writing tables
128 Major key
129 ___ la Paix
130 Reddish-wood tree
132 Trumps
133 Skim, as milk
134 Yoko
136 Dirk of yore
138 Adored one
139 "All ___," 1931 song
140 Mecca pilgrimage
141 Chemical ending
142 Mil. formation
143 Letter-carrier's terr.

212

THERE'S NO FOOL . . . by Tap Osborn
Remember the rest of that age-old saying and you'll be in the right frame of mind for the hidden quotation below.

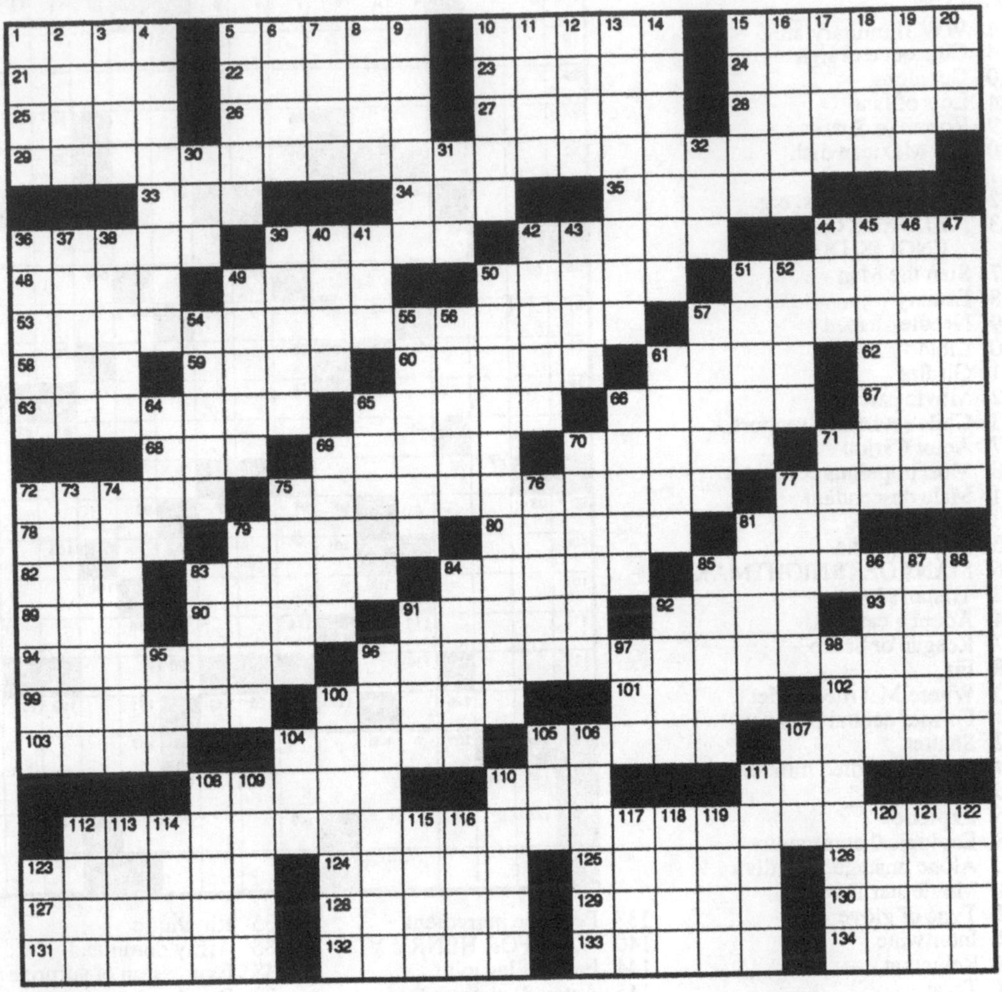

ACROSS

1 Splendor
5 Stalk
10 Tennis shot
15 Reach for
21 Notion
22 Tantalize
23 Ringworm
24 ___ de fer
25 Cans
26 Mrs. who went to Paris
27 Quechuan
28 City NW of Asti
29 **Start of a John Foster quotation**
33 Lummox
34 Bosh!
35 White with age
36 Leery
39 Eta's follower
42 Teapot part
44 Commotion: Slang
48 Roster
49 Mondrian
50 Utter unthinkingly
51 Contest
53 **Quotation: Part II**
57 Crown
58 Gained
59 Abashed
60 City on the Seyhan
61 Water hazard
62 Fingers' stat.
63 Impractical one
65 At an impasse
66 Edge
67 Gal of song
68 June bug
69 Twig
70 Sturm und ___
71 Bern coaster
72 Courtly dance
75 **Quotation: Part III**
77 Did a rodeo stint
78 Indian Ocean gulf
79 Hirsute
80 Architectural order
81 Outlaw
82 Soak hemp
83 Carried aloft
84 Tactless
85 Touching
89 Stout
90 Part of D.A.
91 City near Stockholm
92 Hawk's cousin
93 Use a scythe
94 Clemente played for them
96 **Quotation: Part IV**
99 Quick-drying paint
100 Scattered
101 Walesa, e.g.
102 Frost
103 Bedouin's "castle"
104 Reserved
105 Midler
107 Potato ___
108 Iloilo's island
110 Hurt
111 Bee: Prefix
112 **Conclusion of the Quotation**
123 Rat or mouse, e.g.
124 Sixth-century date
125 Uncertainty
126 Heap
127 Argentine sculptor
128 Caught congers
129 Banks of baseball
130 Caama
131 Pepper or Billy
132 Obliterate
133 Stop by threatening
134 ___ tetra

DOWN

1 Commiserate
2 Hatred, to Luigi
3 Bill of fare
4 Rustic
5 Kind of sergeant
6 Tin source
7 Warren
8 Conditional phrase
9 Vacation spot
10 Long-legged wader
11 Short or small
12 Suffix for avoid
13 Vacation lure
14 Rendezvous
15 Burton or Brent
16 Ostentatious
17 Fairylike creature
18 "___ the Mood for Love"
19 Hagler's milieu
20 Wine: Prefix
30 Use a pitchfork
31 Mauna ___
32 Fink
36 "Our ___" (Birmingham)
37 Distinction
38 In harmony
39 Princetonian mascot
40 Mind
41 Sched. abbr.
42 Move stealthily
43 New Zealand tree
44 To's partner
45 Arranges
46 So-so
47 Like a rose or daisy
49 Dog at the door, e.g.
50 Osier relative
51 Sun Yat-sen's widow
52 Hegira
54 Runyon
55 Sanction
56 Elicit
57 Hold tightly
61 Metz currency
64 Moslem call to prayer: Var.
65 Metric measure
66 Spread a rumor
69 Like a new car
70 Reed and Fargo
71 Yearn
72 Defensive wall
73 Sweet one of song
74 Old hand
75 Jack of Hearts' love
76 Baseball's Robin
77 Delhi princess
79 Plaza Athénée, e.g.
81 Lave
83 Moderate
84 Showed contempt for
85 Ownership
86 Fax, for one
87 Bellini opera
88 Harris ___
91 Hindu title of address
92 Sheepshank, e.g.
95 Quant.
96 Spend the night
97 Select
98 Cranium
100 Straphanger
104 Burns's white stuff
105 Whit
106 Got away
107 Town near Liège
108 Charles the swindler
109 Town SW of Des Moines
110 Stage whisper
111 Later than
112 180 ser
113 Fragrance
114 Confined
115 Lee of films
116 Stamping tools
117 "Dialogue" author
118 Fourth-down option
119 Off-Broadway award
120 Seine feeder
121 In addition
122 Quick-witted
123 L.A. athlete

213

+1 by Shirley Soloway
You'll find more than one pungent pun in this non-numerical challenger. (Shirley, you jest!)

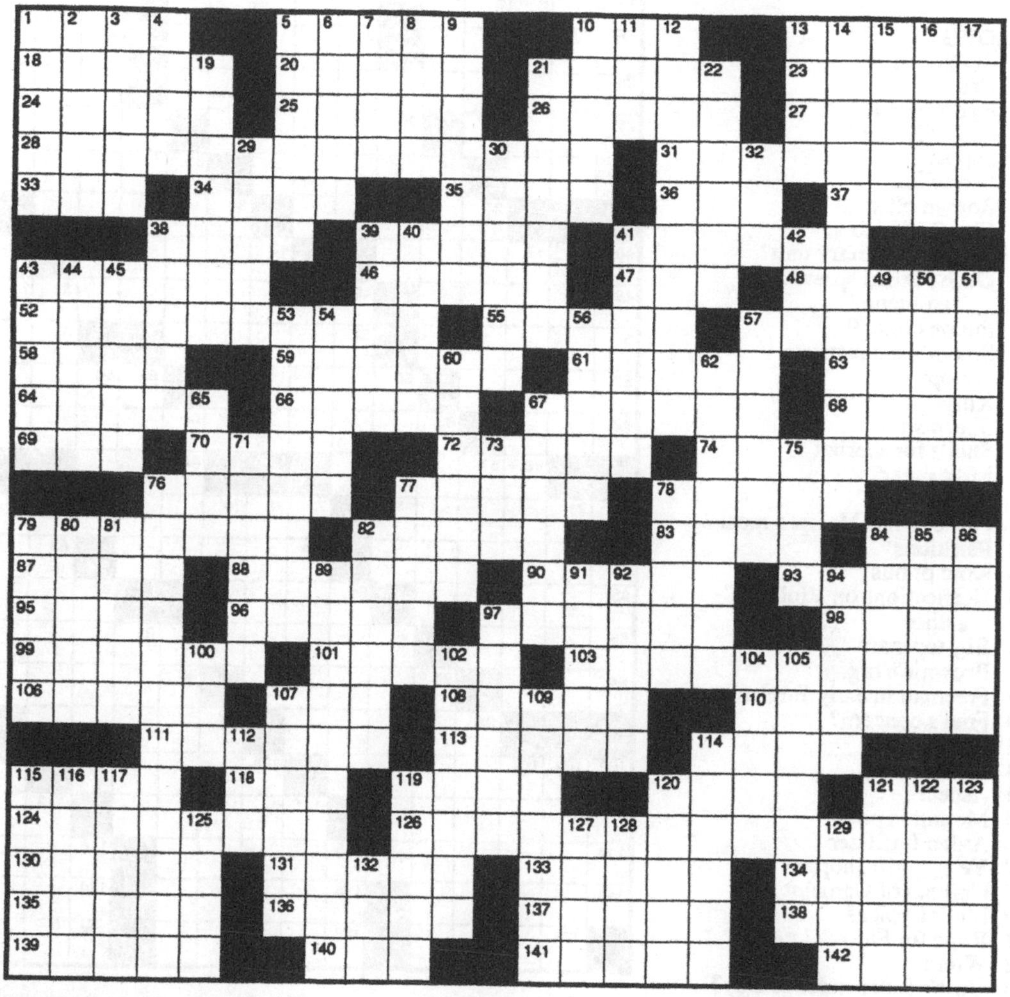

ACROSS

1 Used a bubble pipe
5 Weasel
10 WW II heroes
13 Fancy neckwear
18 Weaker
20 Georgian fruit
21 End or coffee follower
23 Make a point
24 ___ a minute
25 "A Day ___ Life"
26 Close by
27 Producer Spelling
28 Cooperstown, perhaps?
31 Things to be ironed out
33 A way to go: Abbr.
34 March date
35 Picnic crashers
36 Pasture sound
37 Simplicity
38 Cabell of baseball
39 Ankles
41 Tenor of note
43 Shred
46 Relative of Della
47 Rubber-stamps
48 Bizarre
52 Uninteresting painting?
55 Kelly or Jones
57 Loose
58 Diva Gluck
59 Actress Keyes
61 Throw out
63 Banner
64 Della of notes
66 Street performance
67 Shelters
68 "Ye ___ Gift Shoppe"
69 Madrid Mr.
70 Astonish
72 Laurel and Musial
74 Rested
76 San Andreas, e.g.
77 Overcharge
78 Cast a ballot
79 Doug of films
82 Winning
83 As well
84 Total
87 Russian mountain
88 Shrew
90 ". . . ___ man put asunder"
93 Before glycerin
95 Yin's partner
96 Join up
97 Fit in
98 Seep
99 Dudley Moore role
101 Friend ___?
103 Everyday changes?
106 Vaudeville turns
107 One ___ customer
108 Fasten again
110 Agreement
111 Zenanas
113 Critic James and family
114 Elevator man
115 Hat holder
118 "___ the Walrus"
119 Cake topper
120 Shake ___!
121 Humpty Dumpty, e.g.
124 Moorish palace
126 Someone emulating Clayton Moore?
130 Playground favorite
131 "___ Grows in Brooklyn"
133 ___ mañana
134 Rich dessert
135 Copier ink
136 Pours
137 Go in
138 Swelling
139 Stockholm resident
140 Call for help
141 Run-down
142 Printer's notation

DOWN

1 Doldrums
2 Fernando or Lorenzo
3 Zola
4 After wishing or stair
5 Steeple tops
6 Wigwams
7 Vow
8 Pain
9 Shakespeare
10 Carries on
11 Honest name
12 Poor senators?
13 Wise ___ owl
14 Late-night snack for some police?
15 "Cheers" character
16 Midwest tribesmen
17 Uptight
19 Like sugar
21 More flavorful
22 Goofs
29 Bouquets
30 Pulver, e.g.
32 Debtor's paper
38 Lab burners
39 Candle
40 Jergens or Astaire
41 Bacterium
42 Offspring
43 Ski lifts
44 Steve or Fred
45 More domesticated
49 Money boxes
50 English dramatist
51 Bordered
53 Sky blue
54 ___-garde
56 "With ___ in My Heart"
57 Aggravates
60 Before day or year
62 Atmosphere science
65 Rebekah's child
67 Manage
71 Lana or Tina
73 Pablo's aunt
75 Slave worker
76 Nervous in the air?
77 Whatnot holder
78 Miss White of letters
79 Guatemala tribe
80 Lewis's co-explorer
81 "I Can Dream, ___?"
82 Greek marketplaces
84 Entrance courts
85 Wander
86 One of seven
89 Brides, perhaps?
91 Dinsmore of fiction
92 Villages
94 Stays in neutral
97 Barry Gibb, for one
100 "Born in the ___"
102 Herbs of the goosefoot family: Var.
104 Playful creature
105 Warship
107 Lacerate
109 Sits on a fence
112 Barbecue item
114 Infamous cow owner
115 Former years
116 Permit
117 "To ___ own self . . ."
119 Units
120 Staked
121 Heron's kin
122 "___ to the Church . . ."
123 Fantastic!
125 Bare
127 Country road
128 Bone: Comb. form
129 Dozes off
132 Collector's car

214 POSSESSIVE PEOPLE by Bernice Gordon

From the City of Brotherly Love comes a rhyme scheme we know you'll love.

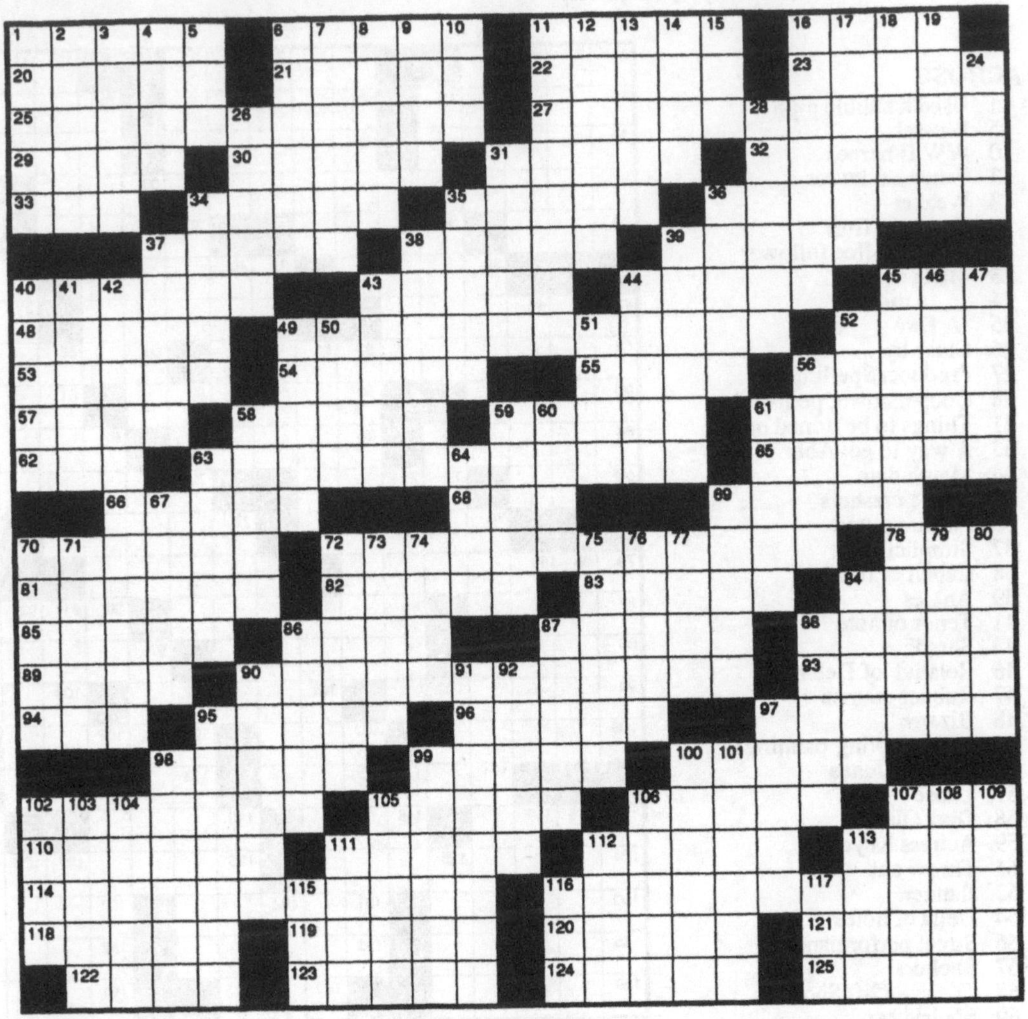

ACROSS

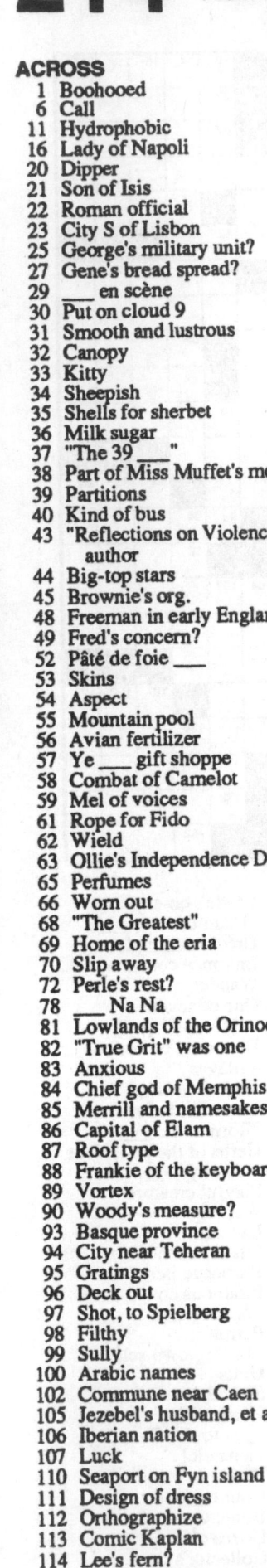

1 Boohooed
6 Call
11 Hydrophobic
16 Lady of Napoli
20 Dipper
21 Son of Isis
22 Roman official
23 City S of Lisbon
25 George's military unit?
27 Gene's bread spread?
29 ___ en scène
30 Put on cloud 9
31 Smooth and lustrous
32 Canopy
33 Kitty
34 Sheepish
35 Shells for sherbet
36 Milk sugar
37 "The 39 ___"
38 Part of Miss Muffet's meal
39 Partitions
40 Kind of bus
43 "Reflections on Violence" author
44 Big-top stars
45 Brownie's org.
48 Freeman in early England
49 Fred's concern?
52 Pâté de foie ___
53 Skins
54 Aspect
55 Mountain pool
56 Avian fertilizer
57 Ye ___ gift shoppe
58 Combat of Camelot
59 Mel of voices
61 Rope for Fido
62 Wield
63 Ollie's Independence Day?
65 Perfumes
66 Worn out
68 "The Greatest"
69 Home of the eria
70 Slip away
72 Perle's rest?
78 ___ Na Na
81 Lowlands of the Orinoco
82 "True Grit" was one
83 Anxious
84 Chief god of Memphis
85 Merrill and namesakes
86 Capital of Elam
87 Roof type
88 Frankie of the keyboard
89 Vortex
90 Woody's measure?
93 Basque province
94 City near Teheran
95 Gratings
96 Deck out
97 Shot, to Spielberg
98 Filthy
99 Sully
100 Arabic names
102 Commune near Caen
105 Jezebel's husband, et al.
106 Iberian nation
107 Luck
110 Seaport on Fyn island
111 Design of dress
112 Orthographize
113 Comic Kaplan
114 Lee's fern?
116 Ezra's dog?
118 Mallet
119 Glee
120 Napoleon's troops
121 "___ Sanctum"
122 Network of nerves
123 Navigator Islands now
124 Forbidding
125 Subway

DOWN

1 Gripping device
2 "___ Days," 1987 film
3 That is
4 Otherwise
5 Society bud
6 Fergie's father-in-law
7 "___ Heroes"
8 Hold the floor
9 Au naturel
10 Japan follower
11 Burn anew
12 Mara and Simpson
13 Fleeces
14 In a bad way
15 Actress Susan
16 Disheartens
17 Parsee Bible
18 Maestro's "much"
19 City on the Rhone
24 Point of ___, Isle of Man
26 Whoop it up
28 Kind of gun
31 More tender
34 Amerinds
35 Polonium discoverer
36 Hear about
37 Weather balloon
38 Freewheels
39 Rummage
40 Barber's belt
41 "The Big ___," 1983 film
42 W.C.'s jawbreakers?
43 Hide away
44 Skimpy
45 Greene's cable car?
46 More reasonable
47 Ancient Hebrew strings
49 On the left side, to some
50 Sealed
51 Asterisk
52 Drop, to a doctor
56 ___ kick out of (enjoys)
58 Links legend
59 Clayey
60 Firpo of boxing
61 Yummy
63 Roman historian
64 Kismet
67 Where Iloilo is
69 Blanched
70 Lee of golf
71 Playground sight
72 Musty, to a Londoner
73 Relieves
74 Getz or Kenton
75 Adobe material
76 Common Market member
77 Outside: Comb. form
79 Reduce by 50%
80 Leading
84 Loses interest
86 Glutinous mud
87 Central Africans
88 Tombstone of a sort
90 Springs up
91 Fox or Eggar
92 Diving bird
95 Cartilage
97 Falls short
98 Gooselike bird
99 Religion of Honshu
100 Church key
101 Lt. Stone's portrayer
102 Niven's worldly role
103 Saharan mountainous region
104 Permission
105 Tocsin
106 Foam
107 Frequent
108 Honest Abe's dad
109 First emperor of Brazil
111 Inter ___
112 Ilk
113 Left
115 Parl. VIPs
116 ___ de chat
117 Male objective

215 MISSING LINKS by Harold B. Counts

Hazards and other theme-related words have been carefully hidden below. Harold hopes all solvers can bring them to the fore!

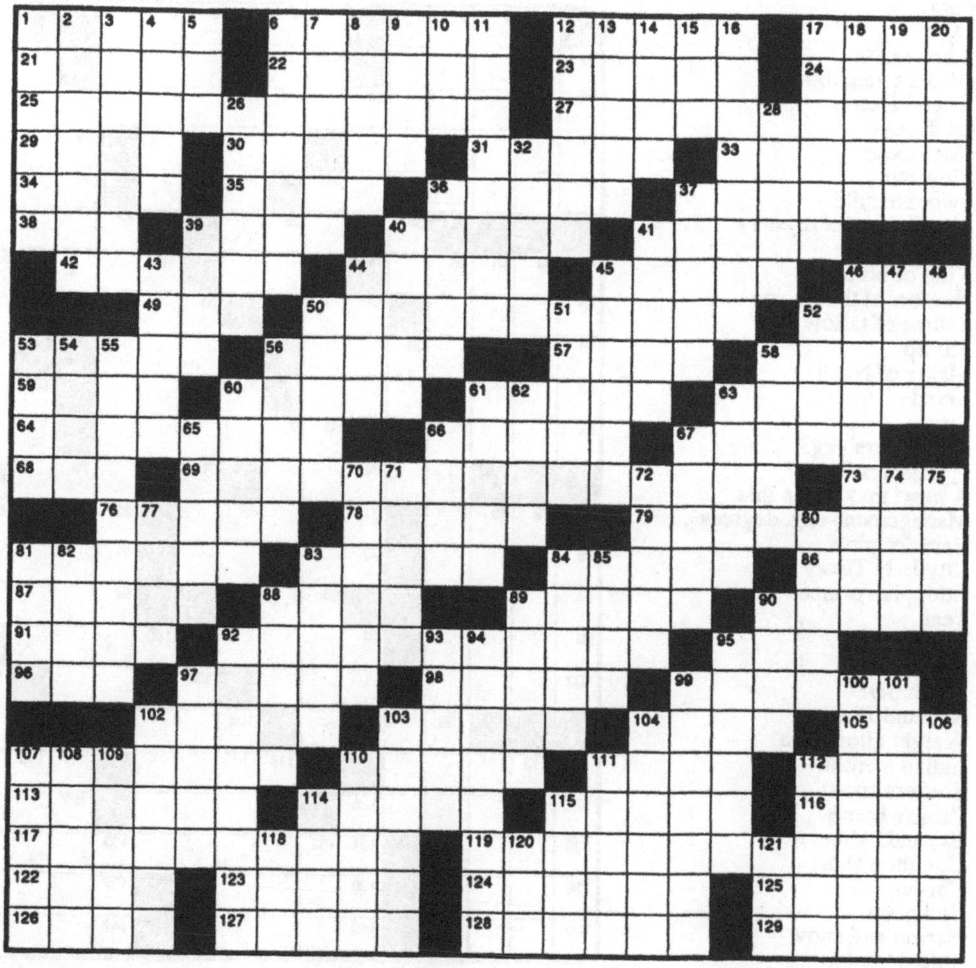

ACROSS

1 Love, Italian style
6 Zibelines
12 Amendment of 1901
17 Grandeur
21 Delivered
22 Bring about
23 Aquiline abode
24 Nichols' hero
25 Stinkweed
27 Mustard relative
29 Goofs
30 Make amends
31 High-strung
33 Winter apple
34 Hummock
35 Sesame plants
36 Danube feeder
37 Callings
38 Born
39 Behold!
40 Dugout
41 Gem State capital
42 Losing ___
44 Rafted
45 Plum
46 S Lebanon town
49 Noted model
50 Rickety old heaps
52 A Turner
53 Best Picture of 1955
56 Pieces of plate armor
57 Lothario
58 ___ dancer (railroad worker)
59 Century plant
60 Dixie dish
61 Two whole notes
63 Bouquet throwers
64 Wholehearted
66 "Personae" poet
67 Clingstone
68 Road animal
69 Sources of Vitamin A
73 GI's friend
76 Czech coin
78 Rowed
79 JFK and Charles de Gaulle
81 ___ it!
83 Deviate
84 Captures
86 Greek letters
87 Sound
88 Household cleaner
89 Renowned
90 Characin fish
91 Cuckoos
92 Londoner on the wagon
95 Spider
96 Fink
97 Armor for a horse
98 Great Lakes tribesmen
99 Assets
102 Vetches
103 Jujubes
104 Bookish deg.
105 School org.
107 Classifies
110 Foundation
111 Actor Stockwell
112 Stratum
113 Bantu language
114 Cancels
115 Quality
116 Hun king
117 Historic height in Charlestown, Mass.
119 Hidden advantage
122 Jai ___
123 Chios' ancient locale
124 Nervous ___
125 Like some stadiums
126 It comes in a skein
127 Quotes
128 Retailer
129 Oracles

DOWN

1 Nautical term
2 Unites
3 Topple
4 Hall-of-Fame shortstop
5 Tokyo
6 Comic's routine
7 Ring of color
8 Conks
9 Bathe
10 Cannes season
11 Guard
12 Plains Indian
13 Minimum
14 A Johnson
15 Four-in-hand
16 Grounds
17 Zoroastrian
18 Corpulent
19 Tight one
20 Nuisances
26 Well-heeled one
28 Anathema
32 Abrade
36 Bath ___
37 Icy dessert
39 Slippery
40 Avian shelters
41 Thicket
43 Gave an "X" to
44 Alliance
45 What Muscovites read
46 Montgomery's alma mater
47 Wavy, in heraldry
48 Irradiates
50 Poker ploy
51 City on the Adige
52 Not clerical
53 TV classic
54 Vocal range
55 Camped out
56 More devoted
58 Understand
60 Sharif's bridge partner
61 Par plus one
62 Was penitent
63 Cold ones
65 Northern hemisphere?
66 Former name of Beyoglu
67 Used
70 Write music
71 "Argonautica" poet
72 Sherlock's street
74 Pokey
75 Greek peak
77 Tut's sacred bull
80 Blossoms
81 Moselle tributary
82 Sushi fish
83 Molts
84 Lies
85 Iowan college town
88 Goddess or asteroid
89 After house and horse
90 Flexed
92 Acid found in soft drinks
93 Card wool
94 Craftsmen
95 Base of a vase
97 Intrude (with "in")
99 Braider
100 Abstract
101 Outstanding
102 Hainan's gulf
103 NFL team
104 Skullcap
106 African gazelles
107 Cornered
108 NFL coach
109 Sub finder
110 Misrepresent
111 Exercise
112 Western resort
114 Force
115 Inform
118 Hawaiian yam
120 Caesar's hundred
121 Bradley and Bullins

216

MATCHMAKING by Shirley Soloway
"It was easy arranging these unions," writes Shirley. "In each case, the celebrities have something in common."

ACROSS
1 Lip
5 Some skirts
11 Ghana's neighbor
15 Attend Exeter
19 Of the eye
20 Contribute
21 Slow bus
22 Sword handle
23 Singer marries mystery writer
26 Kind of blue
27 Number at the pumps
28 Source of tallow
29 Stir up
30 Maker of NaCl
32 Lived
34 Sts.
35 Composers' org.
37 ___ Estacado
38 A heart may mean this
40 Management-eng. degrees
41 Case for pins
43 City in N Texas
47 Ethiopian prince
48 Tear
49 Subcontracts
53 Eye part
54 Peach part
55 Red and Black
56 Weight allowance
57 Indian mentor
58 Scatters about
60 Pablo's home
61 Expand: Abbr.
62 Common abbr.
63 Chosen
64 Red giant
65 Hermit and snow
67 Shield border
68 Nobelist president
69 Slope skyward
71 Pianist Rubinstein
72 ___ gestae
73 Smelling of smoke
75 Recondition
77 It makes the cake
79 Gin mill
81 "___ Entertain You"
83 Open
85 Sponsorship
89 Symbol of virtue
90 ". . . ___ we all fall down!"
91 Nothing, in Nantes
92 Backtrack
94 Walter in "Mirage"
95 ___ to worry!
96 Commune of C Italy
97 Having an advantage
98 Transport
99 Low number, in Bonn
100 Beauty ___ beauty does
101 Rep.
102 Sawbucks
103 Overwhelms
105 Sounds of disgust
106 Title for Bovary: Abbr.
107 Pang
108 Withdraw
109 "___ of the Thousand Days"
110 Broadcaster
112 Oral
115 Wolfman Jack's milieu
117 Part of e.r.a.
119 Mountaineers
124 Equalized
126 Way out
127 The Flintstones' pet
129 Stickpin's relative
130 Spotted
131 Actress marries producer
135 Approximate phrase
136 Nostril
137 Spreads sunshine
138 Escargot
139 Suffix for mob
140 Holiday times
141 Most unusual
142 It, in Italy

DOWN
1 Variety, to life
2 Rat-___ (rappings)
3 Mideast mount
4 Malmo's ancient locale
5 Commotion
6 Deficit
7 Underwrites
8 Titled
9 Les ___-Unis
10 Amex overseer
11 Bracers
12 Sunshine State city
13 Sal of song
14 Auto pioneer
15 TV beauty marries Yankee legend
16 Gaucho's rope
17 Novelist Glasgow
18 Feather: Comb. form
19 Scent
21 Unfastened
24 Country dance
25 Plumber's concerns
31 Grad
33 Heiress marries Dodger great
36 Author marries spaceman
39 Tub
40 Actress marries tennis star
42 Three, in Capri
43 Whines
44 Province of Spain
45 Distributed
46 Comedienne marries actor
48 Secondhand venue
49 Zealot
50 Bizarre
51 Narodnaya's mountains
52 Lage bulrush
54 Before: Prefix
55 Parodies
56 Dist.
59 Luncheon follower
60 Minn. time
65 Telegraphers
66 ___ Lanka
70 Snake and dragon
74 High note
76 Loos and Louise
78 Hall-of-Famer Thurmond
79 Rum cakes
80 Attu resident
82 "Amazing" team
84 Naval CIA
86 Horse clam
87 Image: Comb. form
88 It's good when common
89 Sunk fence
93 Tolkien tree
99 Finale
100 Snub
101 "What Kind of Fool ___?"
104 River of Zaire
105 Marriages
106 Empire builder
107 Walk about
109 Aphrodite's love
111 Prefix for plasm
112 Chihuahua coins
113 Turn away
114 Baseball's "Little Colonel"
116 Idolize
117 Journalist St. Johns
118 Deputy
120 Uris and Trotsky
121 Lab burners
122 Proportion
123 To wit: Abbr.
125 Unit of force
128 Smeltery sights
132 Hebrew letter
133 German article
134 Mil. ship

217 GAMES by Kenneth Haxton

Lots of ways to spend leisure time and have fun crop up below. Some are familiar to Americans; others are British imports.

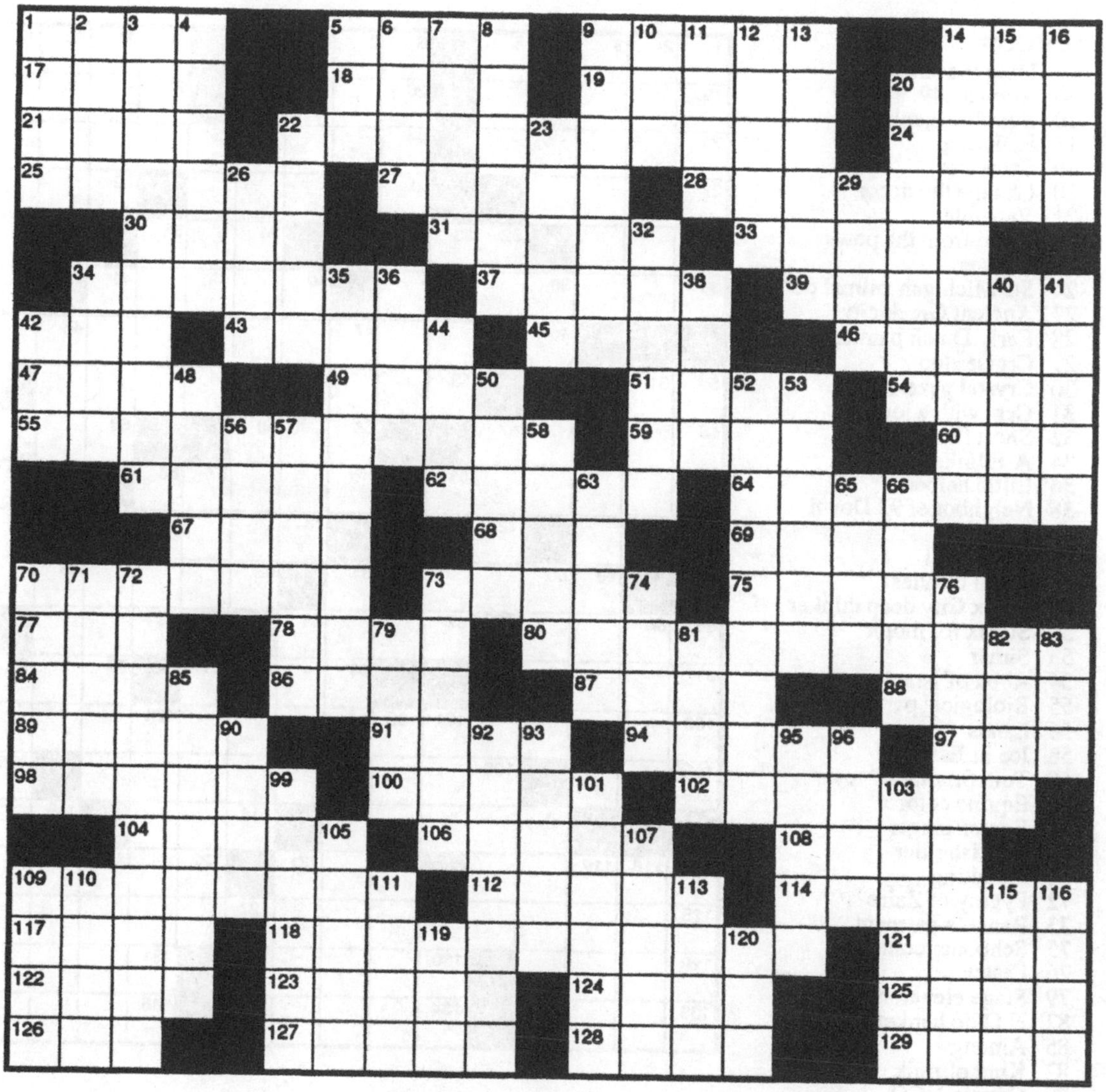

ACROSS

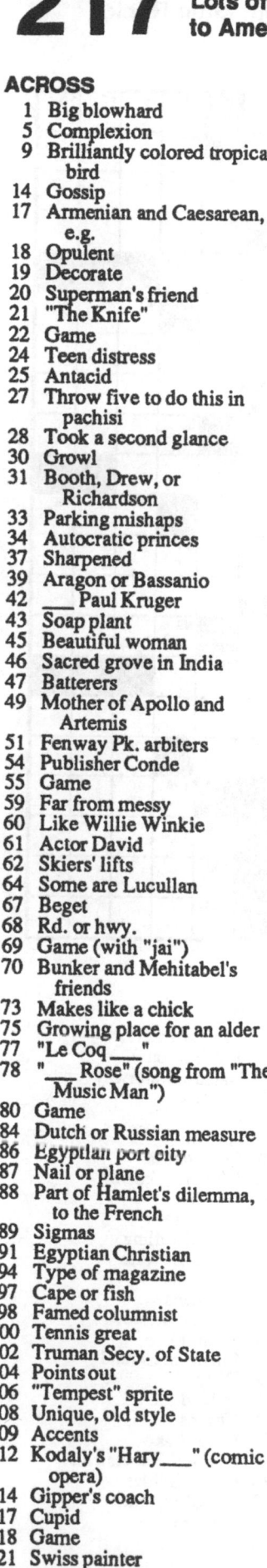

1 Big blowhard
5 Complexion
9 Brilliantly colored tropical bird
14 Gossip
17 Armenian and Caesarean, e.g.
18 Opulent
19 Decorate
20 Superman's friend
21 "The Knife"
22 Game
24 Teen distress
25 Antacid
27 Throw five to do this in pachisi
28 Took a second glance
30 Growl
31 Booth, Drew, or Richardson
33 Parking mishaps
34 Autocratic princes
37 Sharpened
39 Aragon or Bassanio
42 ___ Paul Kruger
43 Soap plant
45 Beautiful woman
46 Sacred grove in India
47 Batterers
49 Mother of Apollo and Artemis
51 Fenway Pk. arbiters
54 Publisher Conde
55 Game
59 Far from messy
60 Like Willie Winkie
61 Actor David
62 Skiers' lifts
64 Some are Lucullan
67 Beget
68 Rd. or hwy.
69 Game (with "jai")
70 Bunker and Mehitabel's friends
73 Makes like a chick
75 Growing place for an alder
77 "Le Coq ___"
78 "___ Rose" (song from "The Music Man")
80 Game
84 Dutch or Russian measure
86 Egyptian port city
87 Nail or plane
88 Part of Hamlet's dilemma, to the French
89 Sigmas
91 Egyptian Christian
94 Type of magazine
97 Cape or fish
98 Famed columnist
100 Tennis great
102 Truman Secy. of State
104 Points out
106 "Tempest" sprite
108 Unique, old style
109 Accents
112 Kodaly's "Hary ___" (comic opera)
114 Gipper's coach
117 Cupid
118 Game
121 Swiss painter
122 Requiem, e.g.
123 Say
124 Hankering
125 Composer Janacek
126 Pulver's rank: Abbr.
127 Impudent
128 Rich soil
129 U.S. satellite

DOWN

1 Subject of a sonata
2 Eurasian boundary
3 Game
4 Crookedly
5 Dernier ___ (latest fashion)
6 Assistant
7 Opera part
8 Thick hair on the head
9 Boss, Italian style
10 Cards shown to bartenders: Abbr.
11 Mark toucher
12 Cornered
13 Tarsi
14 Game
15 Boleyn or Baxter
16 Vetch
20 South Asian
22 King of Tyre
23 Colonist's greeting to Indians
26 Zhivago's love
29 Burden
32 Summer TV fare
34 Fly
35 South Sea region
36 "Rosebud," e.g.
38 Something to stop on
40 Beginning
41 Amounts to something
42 Treat for Fido
44 Hawaii, to Mitterrand
48 Cut: Shak.
50 Game
52 Hospital outrider
53 Roman pillars
56 Number of Heinz varieties, to Caesar
57 Game
58 Peter with a pumpkin
63 Autos taken in for lack of payment
65 Type of song
66 French river
70 Serpent
71 Wake
72 Game
73 Town or province of Italy
74 Partakes of a night meal
76 Game
79 Game
81 Big shindig
82 Remove wrinkles
83 Cerise or vermilion
85 Professions
90 Topers
92 Mendacity under oath
93 Event where 92 Down occurs
95 Make butter
96 Game
99 Centaur slain by Hercules
101 Outwork in the main ditch of a fort
103 Implement for Father Time
105 Nose divisions
107 Game
109 Idem
110 Federal agt.
111 Tennis divisions
113 "Bicycle Thief" director, de ___
115 Modernists
116 "W'at good ___ wife . . . ": T. A. Daly
119 These, to Deneuve
120 Measurement of resistance

218 SCHOOL TIES by Judith Dalton

Freshmen solvers may have trouble with this clever creation from Little Rock, but try, try again!

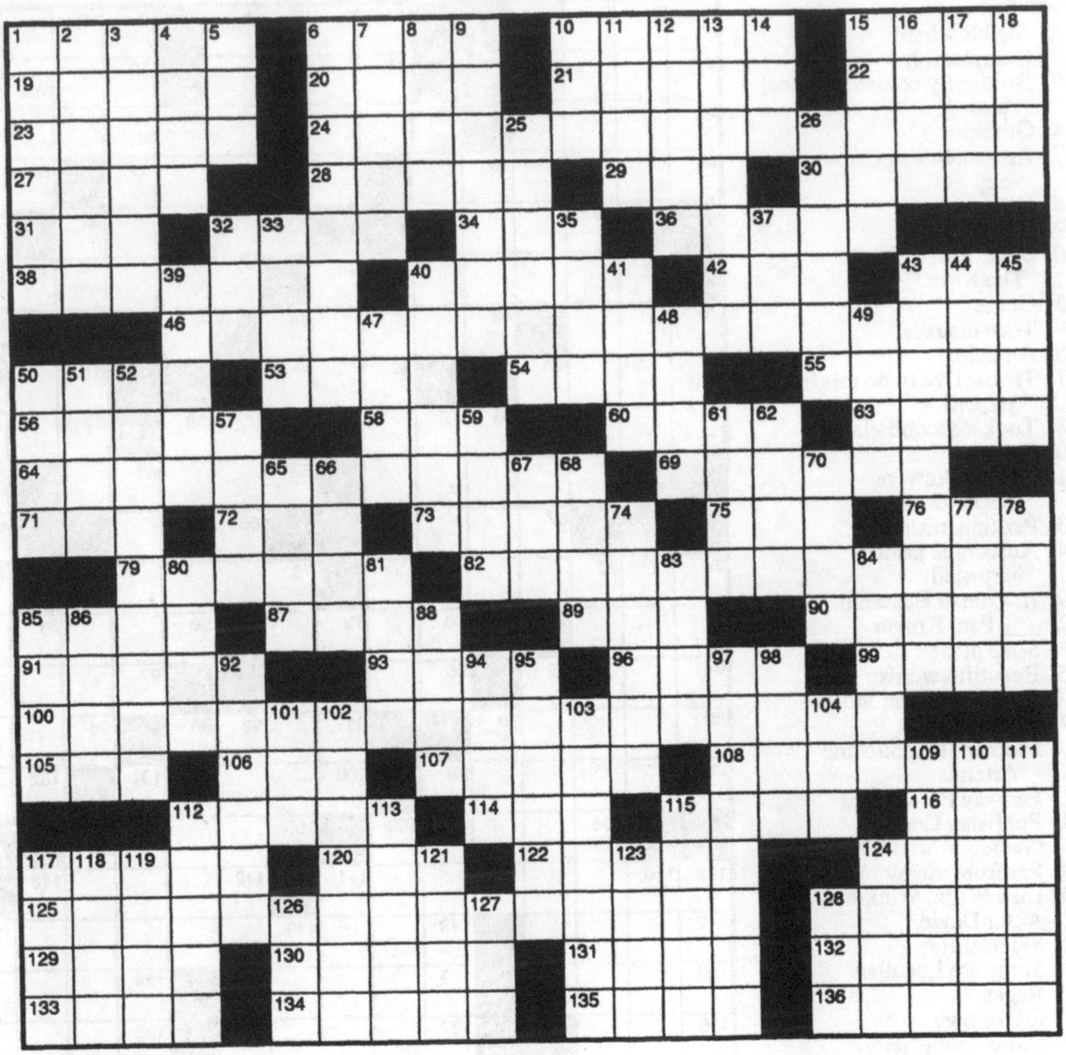

ACROSS

1 Ding the strings
6 Roman 249
10 Simple organism
15 FDR dog
19 Spore sac
20 Change the decor
21 Venerate
22 Word from the pews
23 Answer
24 SC Michigan animal doc
27 Ancient Greek city
28 Early Dutch painter
29 Cruise stop
30 Crystal gazers
31 Org. with a journal
32 Short flats
34 A-E links
36 Little helpers
38 Neighbor of 92 Down
40 Shield
42 Rocky hill
43 Legal business
46 Sioux City deep thinker
50 Suffix for motor
53 Simar
54 Abba of Israel
55 Biological partitions
56 Lands
58 Ice in Essen
60 Tom Smothers' toy
63 Equine color
64 Boston singer
69 Turkish ruler
71 Spanking ___
72 Pygmy of Zaire
73 Ranee's garment
75 Schooner contents
76 Fasten
79 Stage elevators
82 N Ohio banker
85 Among
87 Kind of milk
89 Certain NCO
90 Bulgarian capital
91 Malayan chiefs
93 Composer Janáček
96 Hops kiln
99 Skyey saucers
100 Garden City benefactor
105 Debussy subject
106 Own, in Ayr
107 Picture card
108 Ornament with engraving, etc.
112 Junk: Sl.
114 Track plug
115 Broadway opening
116 Arikara
117 Double fold
120 Circuit
122 Like argon
124 Russian river
125 Greenville producer
128 Dowitcher
129 Coin toss
130 Roman official
131 A Sinatra
132 Young moray
133 Wine casks
134 Succinct
135 Eared or earless mammal
136 Planes

DOWN

1 Bolt of lightning
2 Actress Ritter
3 Abrogation
4 Bruins col.
5 Merry month
6 Canapé, in Cremona
7 Bretons
8 "When ___," 1969 hit
9 1969 Disney comedy (after *The*)
10 Picture frame
11 Baltic feeder
12 Water wheel
13 *Orlando Furioso* author
14 Lair
15 Tokens
16 Gal-pal of René
17 Nonsense poet
18 Landers and Sheridan
25 Cover over
26 NL team
32 I love: Lat.
33 Young salmon
35 Bit
37 Shining god
39 Moslem potentate
40 Metamorphic rock
41 June 6, 1944
43 C Wisconsin pope
44 This, en Español
45 Musial of Cooperstown
47 "___ to differ with you"
48 Son of Seth
49 City in SE Germany
50 City in NW France
51 Summit
52 Madison scribe
57 Arrivals at JFK
59 Suffix for rheo
61 Hunan river
62 Stew
65 Sees red
66 One in on a bust
67 Assamese worm
68 NHL officials
70 Sawbucks
74 Attempt
77 Final four in "Old MacDonald"
78 Ages
80 Cher, for one
81 Window part
83 UN agency
84 Refinement, jocularly
85 Grandfather of 48 Down
86 Created
88 Pith
92 Lacedaemon
94 Judah's son
95 Narrow waterway
97 Ghostly
98 Hue
101 Hasten
102 Encompass
103 Brown hickories
104 ___-fi
109 Get there
110 Mud-dwelling coelenterate
111 Snigglers
112 Moistens
113 Islamic infidel
115 Stadium
117 Fizzle-out sound
118 Dilly
119 Ireland
121 Chums
123 Great Lake
124 Runnin' Rebels col.
126 Court divider
127 Middling mark
128 Discern

219 DOG PAGEANT by June A. Boggs

A parade of canines awaits you. What an excellent show June has put on!

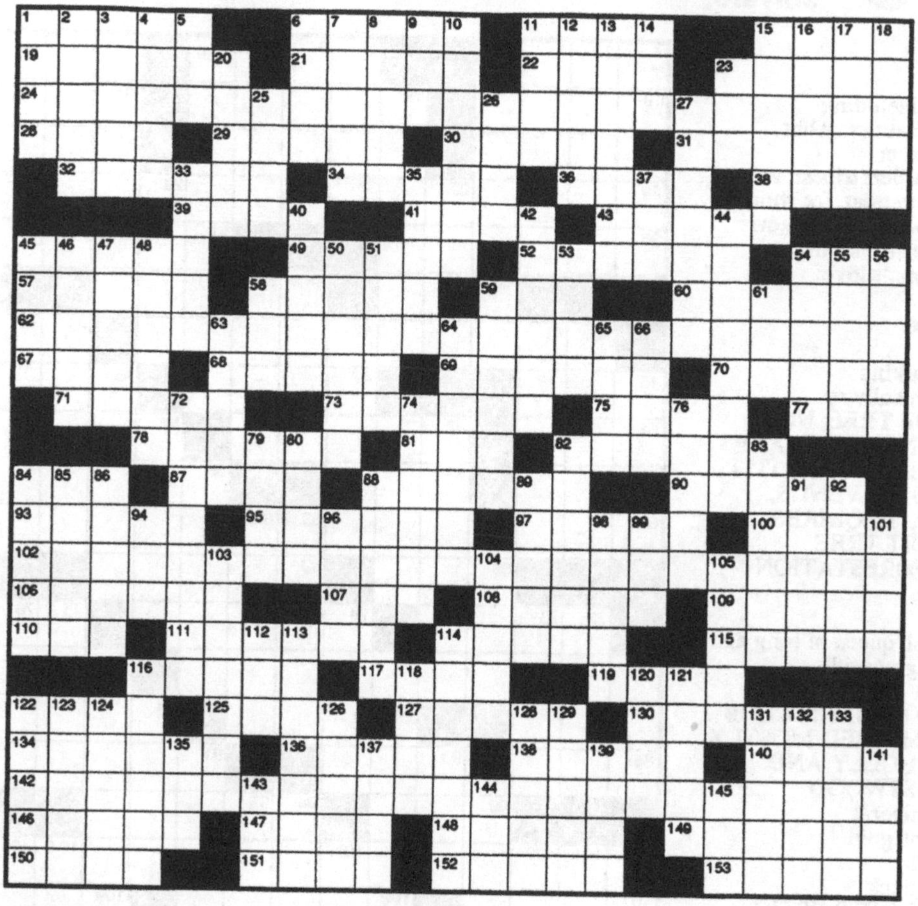

ACROSS

1 Bowwow
6 "___ in a Gilded . . .": von Tilzer hit
11 Out-of-line pageant member
15 Wagon tongue in New England
19 Utter
21 Hawaiian island
22 Krakatau issue
23 US Army rocket
24 Start of the line-up
28 Agitated state
29 "Santa ___": Italian ballad
30 ___ days, during Lent, etc.
31 A 9½ by 12 inch book
32 Stop
34 Springe
36 Corker
38 Founder of Mount Holyoke
39 Crude painting
41 Chinese political party
43 Baker's need
45 Pretentious, in a way
49 Third man's namesakes
52 Opera set in Cyprus
54 Loud thud
57 Type of turpitude
58 City in Florida
59 Part of the name of a Chinese game
60 Nobelist in medicine: 1974
62 Next in the line-up
67 Thoroughbred's dad
68 Slowly, to a musician
69 Hospital department
70 Family in O'Hara's *A Rage to Live*
71 Cordwood measure
73 Scramble a message
75 They made a star trek
77 Japan finish
78 Consider
81 Bock's kin
82 Sagan's line of wk.
84 Martino and Dubin
87 Apprentice
88 Did a con job
90 *The ___ Below*: '57 film
93 Flavor
95 Certain price
97 Spirited
100 Nubian or tahr
102 More of the line-up
106 Admiration
107 McLean, of music
108 ___ the Hermit
109 *Three Lives* author
110 Total beginning
111 Lice and mice
114 Trestle
115 Pear cider
116 Treasonous Soviet police chief
117 Wife of Sir Geraint
119 Boring
122 Pea petals
125 Name meaning "grace"
127 Neighborhoods
130 Generic
134 It can be total
136 Vast chasm
138 *Revenge of the ___*: '84 film
140 Mental quirk
142 Tail end of the line-up
146 Infirm, as an old woman
147 Blackthorn fruit
148 Linzer ___
149 Transported
150 Line of descent
151 Frau kin
152 Gnawn
153 Mechanic's specialty

DOWN

1 Jacks of clubs
2 Swedish island
3 North, for short
4 Ulster and duster
5 Burr
6 Anchovy sauce
7 "Great tyranny, lay thou thy ___ sure": Shak.
8 Quechuan
9 Shout from a bleacherite
10 Pesos y pesetas
11 Kind of soda or sandwich
12 Golden brown
13 Be repetitious in word-choice
14 Card game
15 Christmas, in Maglie
16 Foyer
17 Vinegar: Comb. form
18 Argentine politico
20 Oil-producing center
23 Rumanian coin
25 Cape Town archbishop
26 Last word in *Revelation*
27 Put down
33 Brief romantic affair
35 Attorney chaser
37 Start of Capp's strip
40 Doctor Mirabilis
42 When he saves, he's happy
44 Will
45 Elec. units
46 Beautician's hair-target
47 Namaycush
48 More chapfallen
50 Faced Frank Viola
51 John, from Middlesex
53 Soon afterwards
54 City SSW of Helena
55 Wood trimmers
56 It flows to the North Sea
58 Linus Pauling was born here: Abbr.
59 Plant disease
61 Exclamation of triumph
63 *Lycidas*, e.g.
64 EPA's concern
65 Flanges
66 Shetland tax
72 Labradors do this
74 Annie Jump ___, US astronomer
76 Zane and Lady Jane
79 Turkomans' Sea
80 ___ Dependency, in Antarctica
82 X-rated film targets
83 Deny, as evidence
84 Something of value
85 Terminate, as a policy
86 Outpouring
88 Heather, in *Room at the Top*
89 Presbyter
91 Brooding one
92 Arafat
94 ". . . ___ kid of the goats . . .": Num. 28:15
96 Muslim judge
98 Type of lightning
99 Smoke solids
101 *Downtown* composer Hatch
103 One of the hummingbirds
104 Invention of Archilochus
105 Quaker in the woods
112 Tenth of a sen
113 Fetter
114 Crinite
116 See 11 Across
118 He wrote *Hard Lines*
120 "The Breeze ___," 1940 song
121 Israeli Dayan
122 Little Bear
123 Venezuelan president: 1964–69
124 Caustic
126 Abominate
128 Male: Comb. form
129 Conventicle participants
131 Conscious
132 Alfred Thayer ___, naval historian
133 Vent violently
135 Auther of *Niobe*
137 Battle site: 1914–18
139 Korean president: 1948–60
141 Carroll and Hingle
143 Airborne lava
144 NATO mem.
145 Freud's *Totem ___ Tabu*

220

IMPLANTED WOODS by Ernst Theimer
Here's another Theimer mind-boggler. Our constructor specializes in stumping solvers.

ACROSS
1 Range including Mt. Rainier: Abbr.
5 Obligation
9 Lake Albert tribesmen
14 Fountain treat, for short
18 Evil spirit of the Maoris
19 Shankar's instrument
20 Giuseppe's love
21 Wings
22 Anchor
23 Edict
24 Kept talking
25 Church hallway
26 SHADE TREE, NOT IRONWOOD, MAKES THE RIGHT ARTIST
30 MARS OR VENUS, E.G., REQUIRES FRUIT TREE REFORESTATION
31 Blouse
32 Age
33 Spanish queen of long ago
34 Bitter glucoside
36 Dance
40 KIND OF SAND CLUB COMPOSED MOSTLY OF HOLLY AND MASTWOOD
43 Soft mineral
45 Spanish gold
46 Forbid
47 River duck
48 MORE OPTIMISTIC PRINCIPLE BASED LARGELY ON WILLOW AND RUBBER
51 Umpire's call
52 Turf
54 Scam
55 Ouse tributary
56 Wallet item
57 Trail
58 Polynesian island group
59 Past
60 Caveat re this puzzle
68 Mixologist's need
69 Evident
70 Compete
71 Extension
72 Tibia or ulna
74 *Manon* or *Peter Grimes*
75 Cause to steam lightly
77 Petrol
78 VARIOUS HARDWOODS INVOLVED WHEN ONE MARINATES A SIRLOIN
80 Card game for three
81 Shoshonean Indian
82 Possesses
83 String
84 MUCK FROM SEA URCHIN QUILL CONTAINS SEVERAL KINDS OF WOOD
88 Virgin huntress
91 Coffer
92 Moccasin
93 National Uncle
94 Pale
96 Not tranquil
100 HOLD CONTAINING POPLAR, NOT FRUIT
107 Tardy
108 Cosmetic liquid
109 Blockhead
110 Musical film of 1988
111 Soon
112 Lend ___: attend
113 Fates
114 Tenons
115 Lady
116 Ruffian
117 Norman or Louganis
118 Snarl

DOWN
1 Bit part
2 Bikini, for one
3 Finnish
4 Nina or Pinta
5 Bread-tree seeds
6 Colorado or Maine, to René
7 LESS HAIRY AFTER GETTING A TRANSPLANT OF GROWN SAMARA
8 Wood shavings
9 Swallow
10 Indian nursemaids
11 He played Mr. Chips
12 Golf club
13 Life, for one
14 Devilfish
15 Turkish regiment
16 Output from Etna
17 Harold of the comics
19 Extra levy
27 Hawaiian state bird
28 Shower
29 Anger
34 Little, for one
35 Burden
36 Hodgepodge
37 Journey
38 First name in mysteries
39 Last name in mysteries
40 Steam bath
41 Bury
42 He introduced the huddle
43 Up ___: previously
44 Arabian infantry soldier
46 Simpleton
48 Cow's first stomach
49 Tattered
50 Public disturbance
52 Sections
53 Ebb
54 Brazilian state
58 Utter
59 Indigo
61 Cramp
62 Kind of berth
63 Supplicate
64 Egg-shaped
65 Restore stamp adhesive
66 Happify
67 Other
72 Male gerbil
73 Kiln
74 Siouan Indians
75 Does a schuss
76 Pretense
78 Urial
79 Mohammedan saber
80 Passing time
84 Home of the Mets
85 Gushes
86 Actress Turner
87 Hangover reliever
89 Ancient ascetic
90 Chart
91 Fruit tree
94 As good ___: practically unused
95 Lieu
97 Airport area
98 Irish seaport
99 Ferment
100 Happy
101 Frog genus
102 Mighty mite
103 ___ *Nanette*
104 Olfactory stimulus
105 FEATHERY ORNAMENT AFTER FRUIT IS REPLACED
106 Tam-tam

221

AMAZING FEAT by Vaughn P. M. Keith
Feast your eyes on those stacks of 19-letter vertical entries! This winner of the Margaret Award was submitted by a daring young man from Washington, DC.

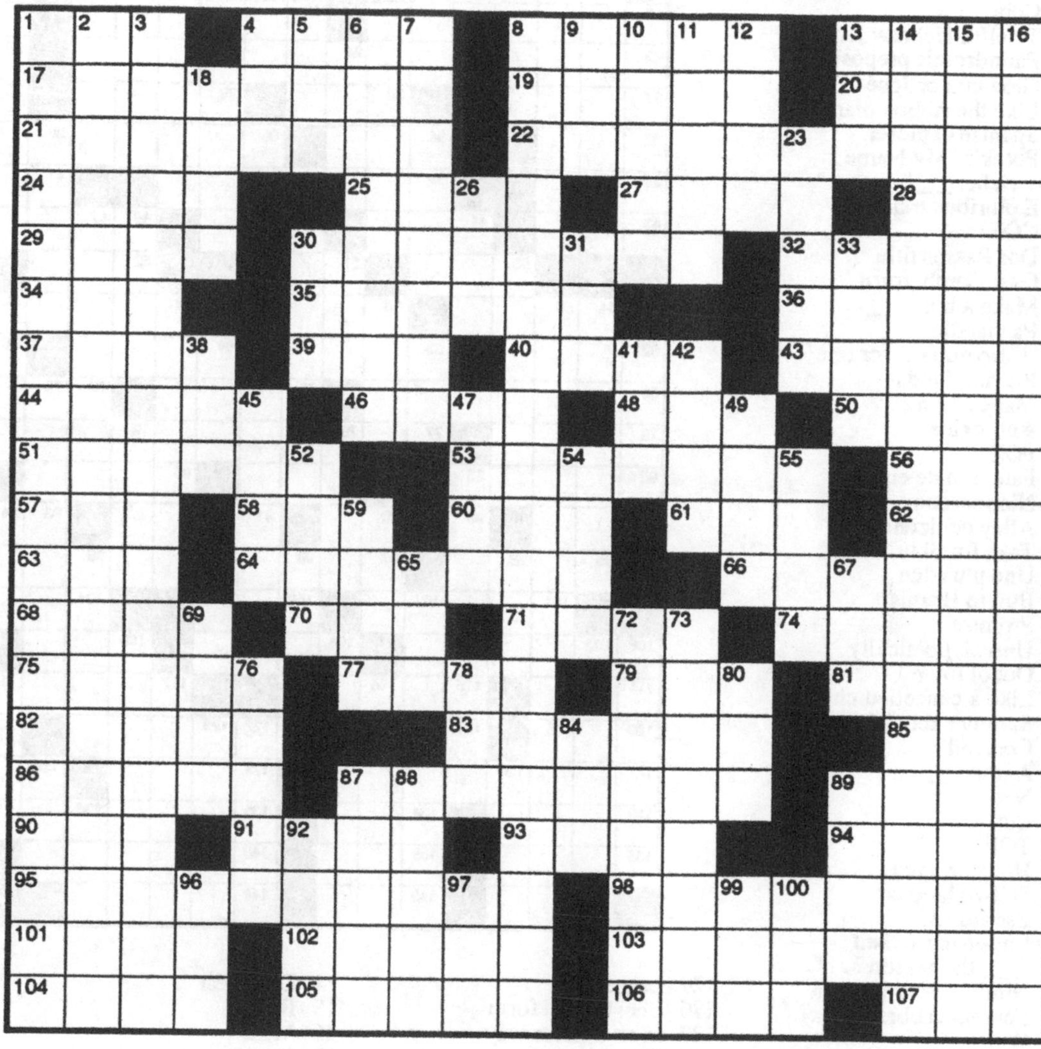

ACROSS

1 Tar
4 Mine, in Metz
8 Sharpener
13 He came between Allen and Carson
17 Passing
19 Angered
20 "I was made a king, at nine months ___" (*Henry VI* iv, ix, 4)
21 About 80% of our air
22 Relative of a Murphy
24 Bacchant's cry
25 See 13 Across
27 Tabula ___
28 NYC railways
29 Tear
30 Son of Hypnos
32 The grass of Rome
34 Timetable abbr.
35 Emulates Cicero
36 Part of *Phèdre*
37 Chief center of Galicia
39 Mil. branch
40 Piso's target
43 Part of a fingerprint
44 Skillful: German
46 Singer James
48 Anti-pollution agcy.
50 Fast planes
51 Hire
53 Largest gibbon
56 Bird: Comb. form
57 Pindar specialty
58 Mt. where Amalthea raised Zeus
60 First octave above the treble clef
61 *2001* computer
62 Denial for 103 Across
63 Kind of pronoun: Abbr.
64 Irene and Vernon Castle helped popularize this dance
66 Verbal contraction
68 Drop, as of paste
70 "O Sole ___"
71 Nut: Comb. form
74 Oligocene or Pliocene
75 Archaeological site in central India
77 Police team
79 Yoko ___
81 Wimbledon champion in 1975
82 Certain classic German cars, for short
83 Contentious
85 ___ *Stundenbuch*, Rilke book
86 "Plant thou no ___ at my head": Rossetti
87 Cave where a she-wolf suckled Romulus and Remus
89 Tropical dress: Var.
90 Wallach or Whitney
91 Ancient Hebrew measure
93 Holler's partner
94 "___ the Mood for Love" 1935 song
95 Free
98 Symbol of neutrality since 1864
101 State bird of Hawaii
102 James Galloway's log cabin is here
103 French poet de Lamartine
104 Jacob's twin
105 Region around Priam's city
106 Wall St. marketplace
107 Wee one

DOWN

1 One of Lincoln's top brass
2 Author of "Elsie Venner"
3 City on the Mississippi
4 Kyushu volcano
5 Russian jet
6 Small, as a town
7 Nescient
8 Found the perfect words
9 Winner of the Hart Trophy (1970–1972)
10 Republic once called Pleasant Island
11 Lab burners
12 Cincinnati nine
13 "Ligeia" author
14 Brazilian aviation pioneer
15 Schlemihl's creator
16 Theme song of Suzette Tarri
18 Part of a sentence: Abbr.
23 Emmy-winning show
26 NYC or Balto.
30 Soft: French
31 Compass point
33 Airplane formations: Abbr.
38 Pugilists' org.
41 Ad ___ (pertinent)
42 Moonfish
45 Pre-weekend cry
47 Boris Godunov, e.g.
49 Part of Vietnam
52 See 104 Across
54 WW II battle site in the U.S.A.
55 Mucilage
59 Italy and Germany, once
65 Pull
67 Bath, e.g.
69 Hillside, to Burns
72 DC art gallery
73 From birth
76 Org.
78 Body's energy source
80 Popeye's girl
84 Rio de ___
87 Uzziah or Naaman
88 Sky: Comb. form
89 Spanish surrealist
92 Combined, phonetically
96 Recent, in Bonn
97 Señorita's aunt
99 5-4-3, 4-5-3 are common examples
100 Ernesto Guevara de la Serna

222 CURT CLUES by Alfio Micci

Alfio says he'll work ROE and ZOE into his next puzzle.

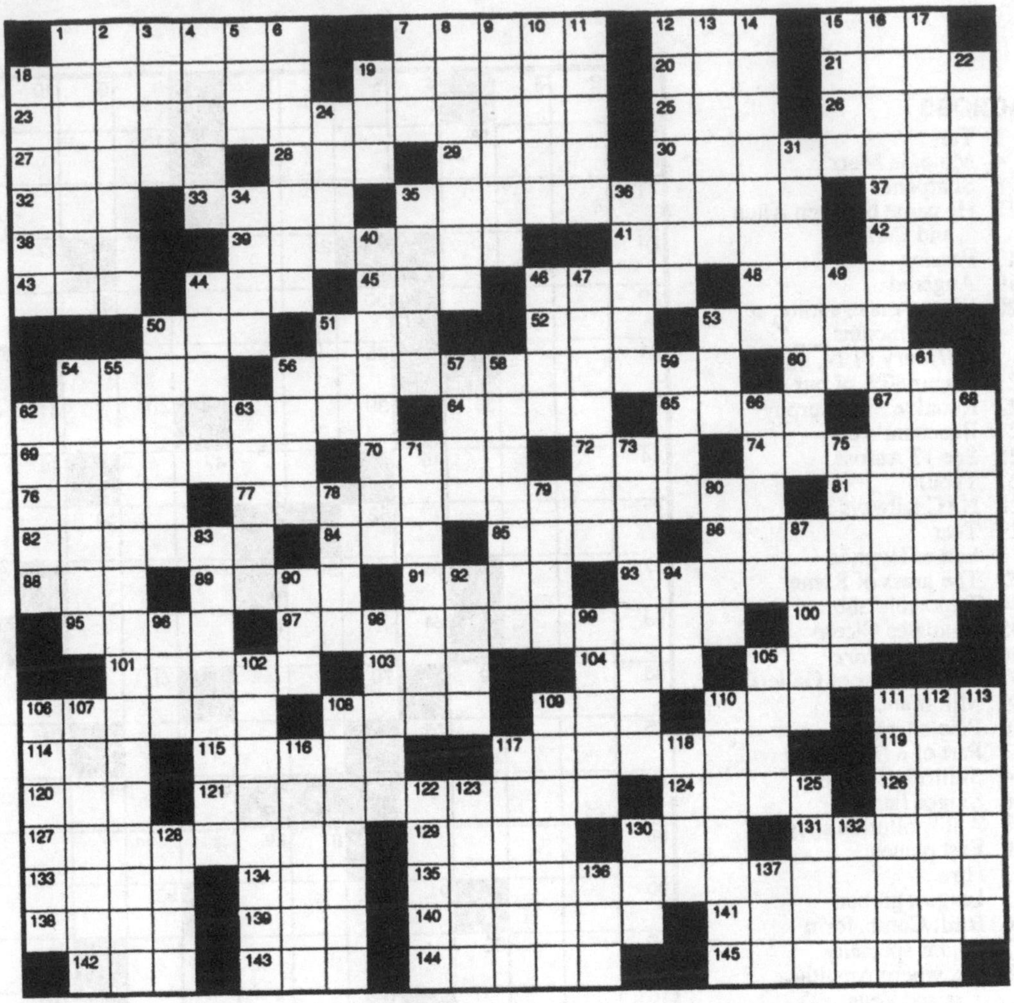

ACROSS

1 Coin
7 Twelfth Hebrew letter
12 Palindromic preposition
15 Giovanni or José
18 Like the ribbon plant
19 Spanish explorer
20 Potok's "My Name is Asher ___"
21 E pluribus trailer
23 COE
25 Dos Passos title
26 Gas: Comb. form
27 Make a hole ___
28 Panhandle
29 "Caro nome," for one
30 Playing fields
32 Make edging
33 Antitoxins
35 FOE
37 Fate or hate ender
38 Nice season
39 Alley denizens
41 Take forcibly
42 Uno plus due
43 But, to Brutus
44 Promise
45 Unseal, poetically
46 Out of town
48 Like a cancelled check
50 Summer acquisition
51 Contend
52 Agnus ___
53 Net
54 Cut
56 TOE
60 Houston agcy.
62 Self-righteous
64 Escritoire
65 Lotion ingredient
67 "___ the season . . ."
69 Ninth Moslem month
70 Footnote abbr.
72 Wolf
74 Spa
76 "Life ___ end in itself . . .": O. W. Holmes
77 HOE
81 Soft drink
82 N American capital
84 Moray
85 Gravure lead-in
86 Soup specialist
88 Olé's relative
89 Asian ox
91 Rich soil
93 Norkay's goal
95 Young man of Mannheim
97 WOE
100 Loch of note
101 Copland ballet
103 Gogol tale
104 Containing nitrogen
105 Mass. cape
106 Sobriquet for a Jack
108 Eyelid woe
109 ___ Elum Lake, Wash.
110 Taproom
111 ___ Paulo
114 Ms. Huxtable
115 Path
117 Hymn
119 Cooking meas.
120 Scansion unit: Abbr.
121 POE
124 Large moth
126 Bee: Comb. form
127 In an unclear way
129 Spotted
130 Front or cash ending
131 Kind of mass
133 Indonesian island
134 Encore!
135 DOE
138 Similar
139 Oahu garland
140 Short sock
141 Real and fourth
142 Islet
143 Sea eagle
144 "Romola" peasant girl
145 More profound

DOWN

1 Thorny
2 Took the helm
3 First place
4 Harvest goddess
5 Org. with many unhappy returns
6 It's sometimes raised
7 Paul or Brown
8 Phoenician Aphrodite
9 Ballerina Shearer and others
10 Tin, in Tours
11 Mr. Chips portrayer
12 Baffling
13 Car deal
14 Disappear
15 Binar
16 MOE
17 Sustain
18 Hits, old style
19 Hammarskjöld
22 Wrongly guided
24 Smile
31 Custodial concern
34 Harrow's rival
35 Stared
36 "Roughing It" author
40 Agree
44 Dull
46 Annexes
47 Most feeble
49 Highland precipitation
50 Albania's capital
51 Timely seven
53 Poivre's companion
54 Daisylike flowers
55 JOE
56 Japanese script
57 Norse god
58 Part of F.C.C.
59 Marcus Porcius
61 Stuffy
62 Monastic officer
63 "Un Certain Sourire" author
66 Favorite of Catherine II
68 Found
71 Hotel employee
73 Spray gun
75 Fearful
78 Kind of admiral
79 "Arrivederci ___"
80 Sign on a door
83 Traipsed
87 Meaning
90 Palindromic Indian
92 English river
94 Overly
96 School dance
98 Bury
99 Eagle's weapon
102 Far from rustproof
105 City on the Orne
106 Imp
107 Picturesque
108 Forgoes a night on the town
109 Coco's folks
110 Indistinct
111 Ordinance
112 Hopeful one
113 Supposes
116 Less pleasant
117 Store employees
118 Pianist Templeton
122 ___ as a pig
123 Sierra ___
125 Winged
128 Chemistry Nobelist of 1934
130 Big Board initials
132 Nipa palm
136 Red or Dead
137 Suffix for computer

223 THE GOOD HUMOR WOMAN by Dorothy Cannan

Dorothy's fine wordplay should provide you with chocks of chuckles.

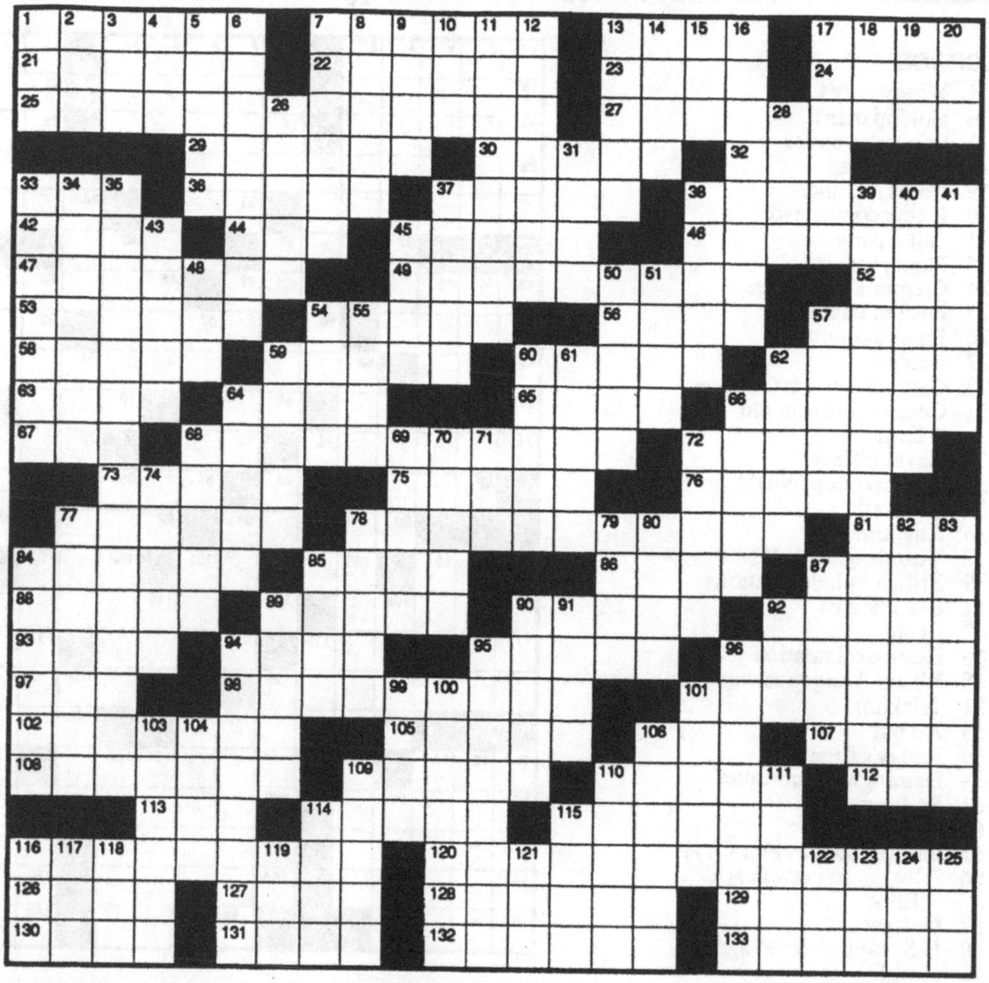

ACROSS

1 Badger-like mammals
7 Former Reagan aide
13 Nephrite
17 "___ Dick"
21 Turkish inn
22 Fire or diesel follower
23 Single
24 Cruising
25 Independent Scottish estuary?
27 Ascetic usurer?
29 Medieval dagger
30 Proper, to Helmut
32 Naval rank: Abbr.
33 Parent's nickname
36 Achieve
37 Root used in perfumery
38 Contemporary of 59 Across
42 Dies ___
44 Veneration
45 Recoiled
46 Author of "Opium"
47 Parhelia
49 Composer's mustache?
52 Quoit: Abbr.
53 Salad ingredient
54 French market town
56 Parts of pitchers
57 French stoneware
58 Writer St. Johns
59 Revolutionary War general
60 Rail
62 Savoir ___
63 Good fortune, in Leeds
64 "¿Quien ___?"
65 Knowledge
66 Bactrian and dromedary
67 Teacher of Samuel
68 Orson Welles' Biblical role?
72 Cure
73 Style of abstract painting
75 June birthstone
76 Latin term
77 Sherman's "___ in the Night"
78 Arthur Sullivan's composition for strings?
81 Butter at Fordham
84 Porcine abode
85 Finishing nail
86 Mechanical repetition
87 Kind of ton
88 Went astray
89 "Heavenly gift of ___": Dryden
90 Incarcerates
92 Destined
93 River in Belgium
94 Meshed's locale
95 Ghana export
96 A stretching muscle
97 Capri follower
98 Arctic survey?
101 Japanese pottery
102 Lessees
105 Make joyful
106 LBJ beagle
107 Greek Mars
108 Awaiting (with "for")
109 Coins of 94 Across
110 He wrote "Barker's Luck"
112 Quartet in "No, No, Nanette"
113 Faulkner's "___ Lay Dying"
114 Line stroke of a letter
115 Persian nightingale
116 Wed a rich person in a plant?
120 Evenings at Valletta?
126 A kind of strut on a plane
127 Hawaiian food-game fish
128 ___-Lorraine
129 Zealous
130 DeVito vehicle
131 Earl of Avon
132 Longfellow's village workshop
133 Miniver producer

DOWN

1 Mountain range of Morocco
2 Porthos, to Athos
3 Feather's companion
4 Urge: Scot.
5 "Giuditta" composer
6 Paleolithic period
7 Disfigure
8 An Arden
9 Malaria symptom
10 Man, to Hadrian
11 Partner of breaking
12 Employed anew
13 Novelist Verne
14 Shortly
15 Newsman Rather
16 Certain college members
17 Elephant driver
18 Explorer Johnson
19 Capital of Ger.
20 Chatter
26 Blemishes
28 Statement of particulars, for short
31 Author of "Cahiers"
33 Beriberi, e.g.
34 Town or Castle in Sussex
35 Food for a feline fop?
37 Chicago airport
38 Terrify
39 Hidden hoard of fruit?
40 With avidity
41 Hospital group
43 Roman official
45 Eschew
48 Gametes
50 Master
51 Make a pie
54 Sect in 94 Across
55 Court cry
57 Hockey and chess
59 He wrote "Cradle Hymn"
60 Mild cigar
61 Agitates
62 Renowned
64 Lorelei
66 Olive green
68 Hollowed out
69 Hebrew dry measures
70 Impecunious
71 The silent president
72 Very funny fellows
74 "Dance to the ___": De Mille
77 Flagstad, of opera
78 Commune on the Adige
79 Threesome
80 Soft drink
82 Epithet
83 Carafe, in chemistry
84 Mescal
85 Wild hog
87 Southern constellation
89 Ordinary form of language
90 Shakes
91 Ironwood
92 Milieu for Marilyn Horne
94 Cabal
95 Lamina
96 Molière's religious hypocrite
99 Successor
100 ___ the nose on your face
101 ___-Croatian
103 Arawakan people
104 Prying
106 U.S. admiral
109 Fortification
110 China cabinet
111 Playwright Rice
114 Swing around a pivot
115 Indian minstrel
116 Witticism
117 Carte or mode preceder
118 Mardi Gras VIP
119 "___ Mortality": Scott
121 Aviation term: Abbr.
122 Equip
123 Ovid's 56
124 ___ Pan Alley
125 U.S. humorist

224 MISPLACED NOTABLES by Jeanne Wilson

It seems some famous characters have lost their way and are turning up in some *Far-Away Places*. If you're the type who likes far-fetched puns, this challenger's for you.

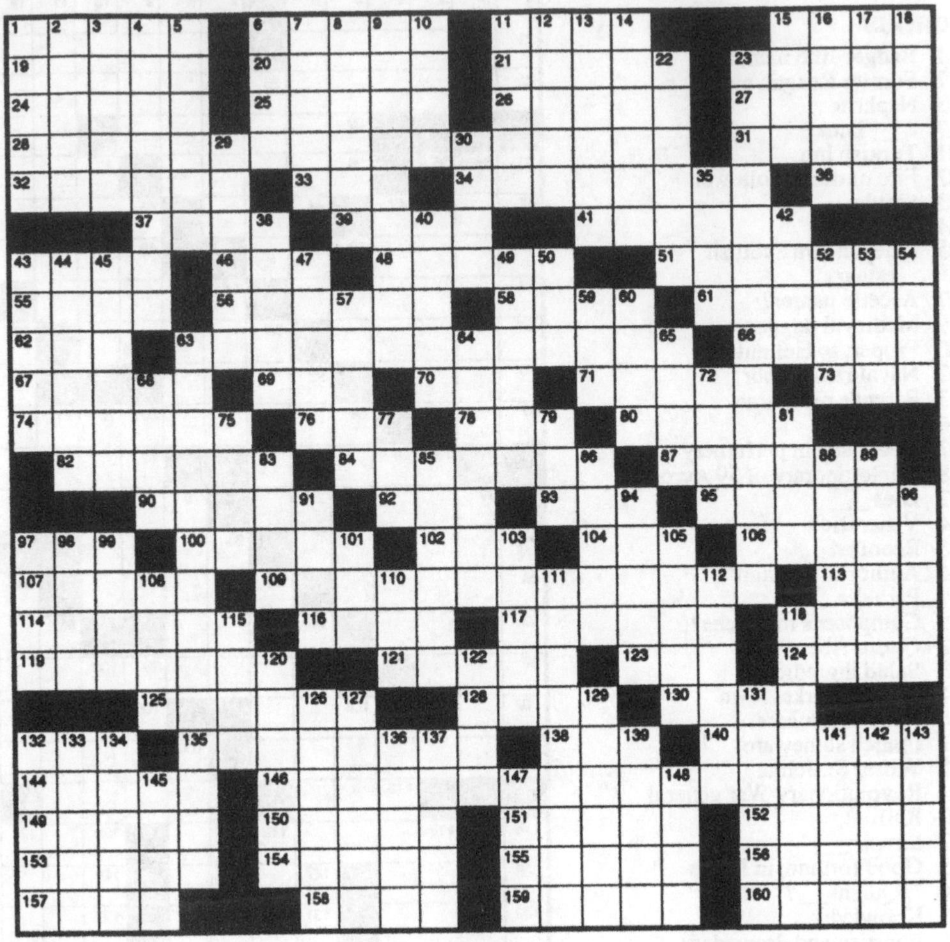

ACROSS

1 Windy City tower
6 Holdup man?
11 Private's potluck
15 Rani's wear
19 Corps member
20 It gets compacted
21 Felt a pang
23 Plant pest
24 Cremona craftsman
25 Puccini opera
26 Ennis's county
27 Babble
28 Cato found near Glasgow?
31 County courts in old England
32 Naval officer
33 Gallinaceous female
34 Aardvark
36 Aug. time
37 Vessels of WW II
39 British mil. decorations
41 Blackboards
43 Being
46 Essen exclamation
48 Where Antigonus was slain
51 Trickling
55 All but
56 Friday's friend
58 Hemingway sobriquet
61 Splinter
62 Windsor's prov.
63 Sawyer seen in Fun City?
66 "Do ___ to eat a peach?": Eliot
67 Guffaw
69 U.S. cabinet-level agcy.
70 Health ___
71 Memorize
73 Feministic org.
74 Kind of smarts
76 Sign of dreaming
78 A.A.R.P. members
80 Centers to Montana
82 Pierces
84 Parted
87 Roundhouse residents
90 Glasses
92 Barbara ___ Geddes
93 Baby food
95 Silvery
97 Bounder
100 Cradle of the Renaissance
102 Caviar
104 Taylor or Serling
106 Actress Stevens
107 Pot roast ingredient
109 Chevalier's gal shows up in Mo.?
113 Mrs. ruff
114 Ludwig in "The Jolson Story"
116 Mizzen
117 Trails
118 Actress Witherspoon
119 One more
121 Greek sorceress
123 Sound of surprise
124 Little helper
125 Agrippa I & II
128 "___ It Romantic?"
130 Anna of "Nana" fame
132 Juice
135 Career soldier's aversion
138 Sibling name
140 Landing place in Genesis
144 Investigation
146 Masked Man located in Eden?
149 Nimble
150 Forty-___
151 Mr. T's former group
152 "A load would ___ navy": Shak.
153 Dawn
154 "___ bleu!"
155 Garroway's sign-off
156 Anxious
157 Allot
158 NBA team
159 Austrian psychiatrist: 1870-1937
160 Makes skiers happy

DOWN

1 Terrify
2 De Valera of Ireland
3 Maude of "Peter Pan" fame
4 Merchant
5 Bites
6 Abbr. on a business envelope
7 Loyalty of yore
8 Censured
9 Holy Thursday
10 Carpet type
11 Georgian city
12 Fanfare
13 Humbles
14 Soap opera format
15 See 149 Across
16 "___ Day's Night": Beatles film
17 Some are last
18 That is: Latin
22 Part of A.D.A.
23 Kong (not imagined) on the Champs-Élysées?
29 Undisturbed
30 Girl
35 Gallic summers
38 Menu fish
40 Unlocks
42 Sideslip
43 Organic compounds
44 Capitol Hill group
45 Her rings can't be worn
47 Temper
49 Yuppie's direction?
50 "___ It Isn't So"
52 Terrible czar
53 Infamous emperor
54 Sprouted
57 Took a position
59 Part of P.A.C.
60 War god
63 Uriah in Atlantis?
64 Greek letter
65 German thinker
68 ". . . wants, Lola ___"
72 ___ avis
75 Waste allowance
77 Marble
79 Sapphire's mo.
81 Omen
83 Con job
85 Pierre's truth
86 "Our Gang" girl
88 Phillipine island
89 Villainous grins
91 Slight
94 Mutt
96 Doctor
97 Musical ending
98 Ever and ___
99 Pebbles' pet
101 Singer Sumac
103 Sen. Kefauver
105 "The Sorcerer's Apprentice" composer
108 Zounds, e.g.
110 Doctrine
111 Passed through
112 Hoffman film of 1987
115 What a truant doesn't say
118 Type of bacon
120 New Testament book
122 Sup
126 Gray of fiction
127 Posture
129 Of ringworm
131 Expunges
132 Burst of energy
133 Dispute
134 Pencil part
136 Motionless
137 Monsters
139 Michener title
141 Actor in 16 Down
142 Cockeyed
143 Saline drops
145 Alice's color
147 ___ Nui (Easter Island)
148 Part of N.A.

225 IN PARTING by Tap Osborn

In our opinion, the most interesting farewells can be found at 42 and 120 Across.

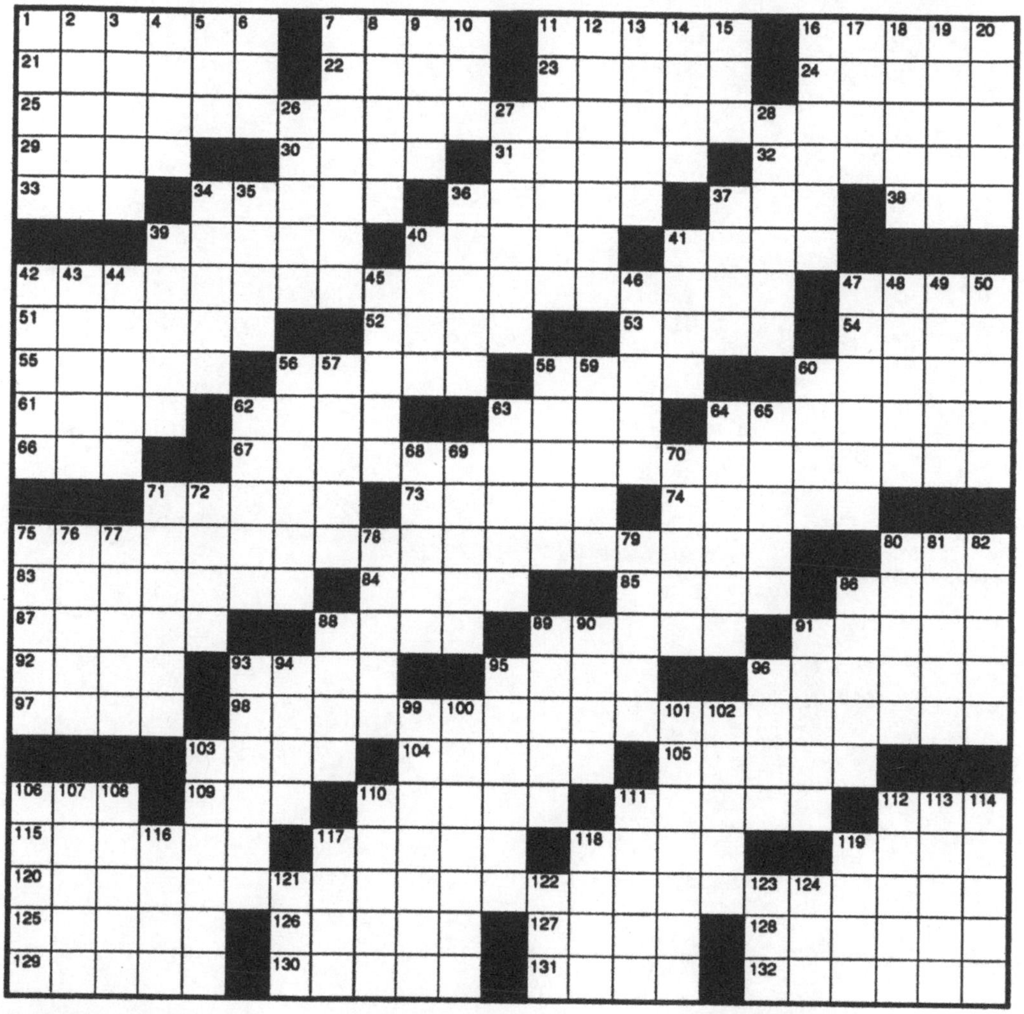

ACROSS

1 Humphrey's running mate in 1968
7 Genuine
11 Second-rate material
16 Dug for cassiterite
21 One of nine, in baseball
22 Otherwise
23 Wading bird
24 Close by, poetically
25 Lord Nelson's last words
29 Birthplace of G.B.S.
30 In the buff
31 Praying female figure
32 Actress Renee of silents
33 Highway: Abbr.
34 Bread unit
36 Smacks
37 Palm cockatoo
38 Name of skating fame
39 Nutmeg, e.g.
40 Medical cloth
41 Obligation
42 Henry Ward Beecher's last words
47 Executioners of old Egypt
51 Dorm for a swarm
52 Split
53 Winged
54 Word of comparison
55 Pied à ___ (foothold)
56 Shave, as leather or rubber
58 Movie Pasteur
60 "Do I ___ Waltz?"
61 Low card
62 Lily plant
63 Long tooth
64 Foamy wave
66 "Babi ___"
67 Poe's last words
71 Singer Lenya
73 Fanon
74 Arnold or Albert
75 Confucius' last words
80 Talk that's called a gift
83 Oklahomans
84 White whale
85 Baylor's city
86 Seethe
87 Designating Tatars, Osmanlis, etc.
88 Foundation
89 Rural staircase
91 Snatcher's target
92 Actor Johnson from Michigan
93 Half-shut
95 Larry Clinton's vocalist, Bea ___
96 Wrangle
97 Oboe, e.g.
98 Lord Byron's last words
103 Blue dye
104 Chemical tube: Var.
105 Law-and-order group
106 Tennis court divider
109 Letter after bee
110 Foundation
111 Dull finish
112 Mrs. Sprat's food
115 Peritoneum folds
117 Building: Abbr.
118 Nail shortener
119 Treat gently
120 Louis XIV's last words
125 Standish associate
126 U.S. Japanese
127 Portent
128 Sleep inducer
129 Tacloban's island
130 Strict
131 Conditional verb
132 Westbrook ___, columnist

DOWN

1 Bishop's topper
2 Like a missed pitch
3 Trap
4 Cattle, to Cowper
5 Pen's need
6 Dart's partner
7 Diminishes
8 Apocopate
9 Tennis great
10 Grazing area
11 Health restorer
12 Orangutans
13 Golf clubs
14 ___ Neuf, over the Seine
15 Dir. from Bath to London
16 Distress call
17 ___-Chinese
18 Nerve: Comb. form
19 Diner patron
20 Laundry machine
26 In reserve
27 TV control knob
28 St. Sebastian was one
34 Seed
35 Viscous
36 Allen or Martin
37 Distinctive atmosphere
39 Like a film by Hitchcock
40 Dagger: Slang
41 Food shop
42 Bumppo of fiction
43 Singspiel
44 Electrician
45 True's partner
46 Spicy
47 Relaxed
48 Military cap
49 Polynesian skirt
50 Unpleasant sound
56 Certain edentates
57 Divided country
58 Kind of sugar
59 Not paid, as bills
60 Yesterday, to Cato
62 Change a bit
63 "My Old ___"
64 Corset's cousin
65 Roundup
68 ___ pocus
69 Jagged
70 Bike part
71 Connected
72 Hawaiian thrush
75 Spectral body
76 "___ the Top"
77 Rich cake
78 Puppeteer Lewis
79 In debt
80 Ravine
81 Walkway
82 Deletion noise
86 Kind of flower or horn
88 Cry in pain
89 Business statistic
90 Pinball sign
91 Out of style
93 Ring or link: Fr.
94 ___ de vivre
95 American elk
96 Talk show VIP
99 Wrench
100 "Can the Ethiopian change ___ . . . ?": Jeremiah 13:23
101 Iridescent
102 ___ pole
103 Moss Hart's autobiography
106 Of a protuberance
107 Zola
108 Kind of bear
110 Idaho city
111 Penny-pincher
112 Deadly
113 Lessen
114 Tippecanoe's successor
116 Russian veto
117 I.O.U.
118 Renown
119 Lockup
121 Heavy wts.
122 Exclamation of glee
123 Swab
124 "To ___ their golden . . . ": Shak.

ANSWERS

1

MORSE GRATE CARD
CAREEN LINER AGER
PRIVATEENTERPRISE
AGEE READE ROLES
SELL ERNS AMULETS
LEIS SLEDS
DISPOSE PLATE HST
OCTAD GRIME ROTA
THELITTLECORPORAL
TOPS ARISE AUDIO
YRS RUINS PATTERN
MONET MUSE
COPOUTS MARK TASK
AVERS EASES RITE
SERGEANTJOEFRIDAY
ERSE BATON OTTERS
STEN APERS REEDS

2

TEAMS SALSA PACT
ARSON ALOUD CADRE
PASTA COOPERATION
ISO PARES NEB GOT
NECK WESER ALIENS
GRIEVED SODDED
AYES STAR REACT
ANTELOPE DIPS FAR
LOIS MED HER AFRO
ASO SERA ODONTIST
SENSE STAG MAIL
UNSEEN SIBLING
ACCEDE DOWNS TAEL
PRO IRA TRIED TEA
PARTNERSHIP RAIDS
AMONG ARETE IDOLS
LETT BORER BONEY

3

EAT UGH LEMON
SMEAR NEO DISUSE
TANGERINE INCITE
AHD REACTS REARED
LEONA DEO VEAL
FRUITSOFONESLABOR
PEEN ORT TILE
CARAFE RAID PERIL
EPA UNSELFISH CVI
IODOL THIS CACHET
LOIN KEA GALA
SLIPONABANANAPEEL
AROD DUB REMIT
ARARAT SMALTO ILL
SAVANT PINEAPPLE
STODGY ARC RETIE
RENEE TEE SAN

4

LISP ASTRA REST
CARLA FLOAT AREA
CAMEUP FISHLADDER
ADO SALONS AMIENS
BRUSHWORK ASIA
SERIF ODIUM GLOSS
RUSK ENERO MAC
REGENT BRIBE AXE
ISA DUMA TALC NON
LSU MAYBE ARSINE
KEG SPREE RYAL
EXERT GREBE SAGAS
ARGO FLASHBACK
AVATAR CIUDAD SRI
DISHWASHER PIPPIN
ACHE FEAST IVIED
MEER TARTS DEED

5

CASS ORO STE LUV
ARTISTES EARLOBE
TERMITES ALBACORE
ONION LACTE UKASE
STANG RTS GETON
SIMP ALEPH
RPM NOTICE ACTING
ERI ISAAK SLATER
SONANT MAR TOMATO
EXCITE SINEW LTS
WYETHS EMBRUN OSS
ETHNI ARLO
LAMAR ALL ACHED
IRENA TIEIN UTILE
DENTISTS MARGARIN
PAINTIT ARCHNESS
ATS YES MYA TREE

6

JEEPS PREZ AMOK
EQUALLY RAGE DELI
RUSTLER AKIN VIEW
OATS BIBLES GENII
TRI AENEID TOR
ITCAN XENOPHOBISM
CZERNY SEVERN DEI
DIAS SERI PELF
SEQUENCE RIFFRAFF
PLEA GUMP STLO
ALN PTBOAT YANKEE
REALIZATION KERRS
ATE INNATE YAK
JERRY MOTIVE APSE
AWAY BANE AJITTER
PENN AJAR HOTRODS
PRIX HALS ONEIN

7

FANGS PLAZA ADDUP
OBEAH EARED SIENA
SIXTEENMINUSSEVEN
SET ANTA LOTTO
OTT ROTO TAW
HARSH APERS CRETE
OBIT OBESE PHASES
ELL APORT PEEN
ELEVENMINUSFIVE
DENE TORTS OLD
POLERS TUNES CLIO
AVANT TATER BREAM
XIV GIDE SAY
ESTER ATTU SRO
FORTYDIVIDEDBYTEN
ARNIE NEROL LEAVE
STERE GEESE ENTER

8

LAMP CAPA ACID SPOT
ARIA OVAL NOSE TUBA
CARYGRANT NILE ORLY
ELEMENT OCHRE APRIL
ATEAM HASTEN EGO
AIDS TRICAR LADDER
SLAT SLO DOCILE
HAYES ENRICH GAPED
TRADES ONTIME OVA
TWISTER FIG MISUSED
RAM UNROLL SPRINT
AREAR ORISON ADAMS
GALLOP SIB EGER
COVENT WISDOM FENS
ARI TROPIC EMOTE
RIOTS BALSA BREATHE
TOLE DEUS BEAARTHUR
ELAN OSLO BOSS EELS
REST MEAN ANTS DELE

9

RAPID SCAM ASCI
AZURE TAXI SPUD
MILKSHAKES SIRE
UNE PITY QUELLS
SERMONS BURST
OTT WOODSMAN
JAMBS PORTS ILA
OVIS ROUGE FLOG
SAL SEINE HOKEY
ELKHOUND FUR
WURST MONTANA
IBERIA SURD LOS
BOER BUTTERMILK
ANDA LAIT ENATE
ROSY ERRS DOSED

10

DATA THUMP ETC
AGOG HANOI SWAP
SHOOTAHOLEINONE
HAT AMAS RTES THE
HOPI ERA PREY
WINATSOLITAIRE
CHEER PUTT SAL
HOGS TATI CHILLED
IMA TRIUMPHAL ORE
CONCEAL AHEM KONA
ICC OBIT DETER
HITTHEBULLSEYE
ACHE ATE RENT
LEE SELL TBAR HIS
SOLVEACROSSWORD
EVOE SPINE ASEA
AWN TAPED DESK

11

SLAM PEAHEN ASHE
STILE REMAKE UPON
CACTUSFLOWER REND
AGHAST SRA ORALES
REE EON AIA ELL
EDNA GASLIGHT BIB
CRYPT AAR ONO
EMCEE URANIA UAR
LOA JOANOFARC NNE
BOS EASTER ELDER
ORA CTS OBESE
WEB THEVISIT GAPS
LEE TIN SHE TOO
STANDS ASA ORATED
HINT AUTUMNSONATA
ONCE GLORIA STIRS
WEAR STREET EENY

12

ANALOG SHEA WAVE
SENORA OCEAN AWED
SETTER FIRSTCLASS
EDIT AFOOT UNITE
SECONDHAND BRUTAL
SDS ORAL TAFT
STAB SWINE BEE
BARLEY THIRDWORLD
AREA DOUSE PISA
JULYFOURTH ESTEEM
AMY ABETS OATS
OMIT ONCE ALP
ESPRIT FIFTHWHEEL
ALIAS PINTO ARTE
SIXTHSENSE ERRATA
EDIE ARDEN GUSTED
DEED DUST OTHERS

13

MATT CAGER ABUT
ASHE OSAGE REPORT
SWEATSHIRT TERROR
SINCE ONEAL FIRMA
ESCHEAT TIED VIED
SEE URIS LOADED
OPENER TARZAN
TABU ATTA FAR OLE
BRUTE HEFEI KENDO
AIR LIE TARE DEAN
RANGER STEREO
SLEETS SEAT ADO
NEVA DUAL ASHAMED
EPICS BLAST ELATE
RELIEF LIKEBLAZES
DELETE ENURE TESS
ERSE TEASE ESTA

14

PAPA DARED SCAM
AWOL ORATE ERMA
CAKEANDICECREAM
EYE IKON LAPSE
ASER PLACE
ICILY CRAM PAR
OCHRE CHIRP AHA
STAY BRAND SPOT
SUP TOAST HEELS
ASE ROVE BEARD
ROUTE GALL
ALOFT PURL ACT
PINTHETAILONTHE
IDEE LADLE ATEN
ASSN MUSTY BYRD

15

STOWS SAGRA CHAS
TACIT AMOEBA LEDA
ASHLEYCOOPER UNIT
STEEPER FREDPERRY
HER STOP ITER IER
LOI IBN NARC
RUNON SLOTS TOOTS
IBEX ROAR ALENCON
GOA SCHROEDER HIE
GALENTO TRAM PELE
STENO TAROT HATER
FOOD MAS CAT
APR PUPA EDAM ARE
STANSMITH ERMINED
PESO PETERFLEMING
IRED STEREO RESTE
CORE AROSE STEED

16

OLGA ADA MARLS RASH
TOOT TON ILIAC EPEE
ISNT TUN SILVERFOXX
STEELEBALL LENO
SENT AES RETAKE
VESTED STAID SONIAS
ETHER CHEDDAR SINGE
TROD BAER ERIS OGRE
OER MAYDAY SPOONFED
TRIBE LET PARSI
FILAMENT TIMERS SST
ATIC SNAG TARS THEE
RESIN ENABLES SEERS
RAZEED GILES OPERAS
STRAIT NOT STAT
TEEM NORTHSHORE
WRIGHTHAND HEE IRIS
EARN EERIE EER NETS
EMEU RESTS ARS GLEE

17

EXTRA ATONE LAMAR
ARROW CRIER ABODE
GAUZE TYLER SAVOR
LYE SASSY APT ERA
ESSE RUT ONO EDEN
SIMP CUTLET
CRUSTY JUT ITCHES
HULAS FOB USA OLE
ARTY MOB ASH IRMA
PAR HEX EWE UNDER
SLATED ILL STEERS
ONIONS APER
SLAP ARK TVA TRIP
TIN AND ARENA ADO
ANGEL EMBER SAVES
MELEE ROLES PLEAT
PRONE SWEDE SILLS

18

PALS STREWN COIN
ERIE TOOTOO ANNE
LOBSTERCANTONESE
FORTUNE TIAS TDS
AERO CLOCK GALA
CART SHINE POLES
ASIS STUNS ORELSE
LEA STARE OBIT
MANDARIN SZECHUAN
ALAN CHOSE PRE
PARITY ALINE SPEC
ABELS ALONE TEAK
NYNY PUMPS CARR
SSE HILO SHRIMPS
SWEETANDSOURPORK
EARL IDOUBT ESAU
SLAP TSETSE STYE

19

MABEL PAGAN CALL
ADLAI ALAMO RODEO
NEARS GARBO AMMAN
OLD ACE PINSTRIPE
FEET ODE ETATS
REAP ELBOWED
CHUMMY KOOP DECOR
HENPECK POTS UNE
INN SANK PIPS TSE
ENE TOIT COURTED
FARMS BLOB TRAITS
AWESOME TERN
SARIS ABE EGGS
WESTPOINT RDS ERA
ELSIE NEHRU LADEN
AMEND FREES URGED
RATA OOMPH MEETS

20

SNARE SLAM CAPS
WIRER KONIG HEATS
IGETAKICKOUTOFYOU
PET SISAL EUR NAE
ELEVEN LETSFACEIT
ERG ISTLE
DUPE MITRE SHAM
IBI MARIA ISOTOPE
SONEARANDYETSOFAR
CATLIKE AEROS FRA
OTOE GRASP OATH
VERDI PAN
COLEPORTER ANELER
ORE IDO REIGN ACE
ICONCENTRATEONYOU
RANEA RODE NOELS
SEAL AREA AGREE

21

PANSY TEPEE SCAR
AMICE ELATE KAHLO
NINAS LOCALMOTION
IGOR REPEL APICES
CONFRERES ENERO
HAGS PEACEFUL
PUFFERY BERGS ANA
OPERAS BELIE IRAS
PRAYS GRATE GRABS
TOTE ROADS GAMBLE
OAS GENTS DELAYER
PROPOSES KILL
FODOR DIVISIONS
CYCLER POSED MAIL
MOLLYBLOOMS PATNA
DRAYS BENET AGENT
SKYS STETS TONYS

22

EGRET HOLM DECAL
MAINE IDEA SALINA
MUDDERSDAY ORIGIN
ANGINA STONE ACC
TEN CHUTINGSPREE
GREET MUSTY
BOSSA SITES LARA
AVA TOSCA SEEDER
SOU STEAKOUTS DEM
ELLIOT ERNST ESE
DOTS VINCI ERRED
APOEM HOUSE
CROWINGPAINS CDS
REV STAEL ELAINE
ENESCO DELIDANCER
STREEP EPOS METRO
TETES SHAM BRADS

23

EVEN TEAS LST OMEGA
LAVE RAMI ITE MARES
OREL ISAR MIN AEDES
GIRLOFTHEGOLDENEAST
EAT ALPS ANTONIA
SKEO PREENS SLED
WESTERISLAND PTERO
INCAN NEIGE ERASING
EDAR ATREE HAIR
NORTHSEAS WESTRIVER
OURS CASTE NINA
SHOWERS RAISE BASIL
POWER WESTERPARADE
APES STASIS NISI
TROOPIN ASTI MAS
THEWINNINGOFTHEEAST
AARON ETA UTAH RUNE
TRIOS RIT SETA OVER
SPADE SSE TRET SERE

24

SLANG SLOPES LAPSE
AORTA PARAPET AWAIT
WITHGOODGRACE ISTLE
ERE EMILY LAST SER
DELL BLE PAUSE BONN
OARS BENDED ONCE
TITTLE ERASE MOTE
ORATE SNARE SWISH
RAKE ANVIL COASTED
ETE BLOODYMARYS BAH
ESTUARY GAMES VANE
DENSE LAYER DECAL
CONT TOTAL WORKED
CAWS CHOSEN LIEN
ANNE POPES FOE EASE
STA DORM PEALE TIS
TEPEE DOTSANDDASHES
REESE ESSENCE ROONE
ANGER TENTED NOLAN

25

FATIC CAV DIVERT
ALATE AURI ERASER
CERAM DRESSCIRCLE
IMPLEAD SALES RAM
AAA NNEV VIM LOCO
NUT ANEMIC ROWER
LOB DROSKIES
SLIGO ADD SAM ILE
TENANT IET LORNES
YES DIP SHA ROTOS
REPEATER ASH
BIPED AREYOU SEE
INRE ORB JUST SUM
CCI TULIP SUMATRA
KANSASSTATE ERROR
ESCORT EGAD LEAPT
REESES RED TAWAY

26

SCADS VASSAL PASTEL
ERROL ONEIDA ACTIVE
SEIZERCAESAR IMAGES
TAO WEARS GENE HRS
ESSE ALT VIEWS ETTE
TEETERS AISLE ABASE
HAS EBONY FRAS
SIDER EXALT COUNTS
TOUR DECA CORM IER
AWNS PUCKSPUCK ETTU
YAK LACS VETO RUTH
SIMONE CILIA EASER
NEST BOOTS LOS
LADLE ORALS ROSEATE
ABUT BIOTA PIA REEL
URN BOLT STATE ORA
RACERS HAMLETHAMLET
ADAGES ELMIRA ROUTE
SENORA RECTOS POSER

27

CREPE DANCE CHATS
HELIX IRIAN ROBOT
ANILE ACERS ORALE
REDORBLACK BUSTER
TWENTYONE PAPEETE
SERGE AESIR
APB DOU DEGREASED
DIEM NEGUS ARCADE
EXTOL DONOR SENSE
PIANOS REPEL STEM
TESTTUBES CEN ALS
ETNAS HAVOC
LARCENY SOLITAIRE
OLEARY POOLTABLES
CITRI HALVE TAINT
ABELE ELVER ELATE
LIMOS PEERS SANER

28

SAPID AFLAME ABCD
ADOBE LIONEL NILE
BARNACLEBILL ONER
EYE NOBLE DINAR
WEDDED UNITY
DEB BAAS SENATE
ERASERS SKIED BAS
WORKED TEST CAPE
LINER SMART ERROR
ACED LAIT GRANGE
PAY TITLE CANTEEN
GARDEN SAME SEE
AROSE SEMELE
ROOST EDILE EAR
EDGE BARNABYRUDGE
TILT ASTUTE STEEL
ENES LESSER TERRY

29

FIB DOC CABS TANK
ARIZONA ACOU OBOE
CALAMITYJANE PUBS
TELLIT OUCH BELLE
YEN ANNIEOAKLEY
VAT GAL AUDRA
ETHIOPIAN ROD BEN
SLED EMBAR ROMULO
TAKEA BEBOP TOFTS
ASIANS TOILE AFOE
LTD ITS BLACKBART
EMEER IKE LOO
SUNDANCEKID NEO
TRAIL LAIC MORBID
ASIT BUTCHCASSIDY
RAVE ADAK OPHELIA
REED TESS GSA LOD

30

CHASM ACRE WASTE
PASTA LOUS SERMON
ALTER INST CLIENT
FORTYISTHEOLDAGE
ISO ILOST RUN
PALL URGENT GREET
ALAE RUNDI COURSE
LIZ TECS AARON
OFYOUTH FIFTYIS
ETHER TAMS ERA
SWANEE ABACI PLAN
CANOE SPOKEN APED
UST BASLE AIL
THEYOUTHOFOLDAGE
TONERS ETON ENOLA
LUNACY EIRE ACTOR
ETANA TEAR LEANT

31

AMUSED NATAL ARMADA
RENEGE ELIDE NOSTER
RESEAT MANES TACTIC
EKE DELE SPIDER AGA
SLAP RASP TORN FIND
TYLER DILL NONSENSE
REA SAID PAIR
PACKAGE NEAP SPRITE
ORE PETIT RAM SEDER
MEND SOB GAB TEAR
ENTER NIL BETEL ASE
SASSES SORE STAPLED
EATS GIST AIL
OVERDRAW DEEM COBRA
RENT IRIS TRIG TEEN
ALT DAINTY CREW LIN
TURRET NOOSE SALINA
ORACLE ENROL TRAVEL
REPAID REELS ESSEDS

32

AMORE CYCLE AMANS
DETER HORAE BENET
MAHESMAKINGISATME
IRED AMUSE NATION
TAR TROMP MOL SSS
IFI EROS
WILLUSTILLBMINE
CITIES ABIES LIDO
SLABS ALENE DIZEN
ALLE BROAD ARCANE
ILLCUINMYDREAMS
SATE RIG
IBA BAL AMISS TUB
NORMAN CLEFT MISE
RULONESOMETONIGHT
ELENA ERASE TREES
DESKS CASED HARRY

33

MUIR CARLO BALT
BULLA OCEAN MINEO
INNOCENTBYSTANDER
TRAVESTIES RIGORS
TORE TOOL WANERS
KERN BAWLS
GILBERT DOILY EAR
ALIEN RINSE ALLI
PEDESTRIANTRAFFIC
ENOS HILLY WAIVE
DES SITES LEARNED
DECAY HEDY
STEAKS VICI SETA
SCHEME SIGHTSEERS
THEMANINTHESTREET
EMDEN NITER AGENA
WOAD SPARS BEET

34

LOSSOF OGDEN BRAD
ASTUTE NAIVE RIFE
FLUMEN INBED AGRA
DONALDSON CIGAR
CLEANED COD
AEF ORC TEDHUSING
BRIM SHU FOUR NAY
CARIB ANTENNA IBN
EARS PAN GNAT
RAM ALFONSO TRIOS
ETA VATS EGO CAVE
DANRATHER HUK LAX
EDS DILATER
MARGO TOMBROKAW
UREA STOUT IMPALA
DIAL SENAT DIETED
DAME STALE STRESS

35

MADAM ACID TAFT
AVISO SITE ARLO
DOMINUSVOBISCUM
ENE ALII TNT
ODESSA CEDE
ISIS TRIP SELL
DENTAL ONAN NEO
ERE COMMUNI OVO
SIS ELIA STAVES
TASS AGNI LONE
LETT SUNHAT
AKA STOP ARS
ESTMODUSINREBUS
GORE DRUM ISLET
OPEN SAME LEEDS

36

SOP LAMA BAMA RATS
EMIT OPEN ALOP ASHY
PAPERWORK CAMPSITES
TREATED LION REDAN
SER TERN DOVE
CAPES TASK REVERSE
ORAL HOP SOLAR ERA
MAP PAPERTOWEL AMIN
OPENERS OARED EVENT
ROAD HATED AMES
CADET POMES EXISTED
ADOS PAPERTIGER EDO
REL SIRED CAD BRIG
SLANTED SPED ARSES
GATS PIES EPA
NORIA AONE AVENGES
LEVELNESS RIVERDAMS
ERIE COTE EDER SLIT
ADDS ENID DART ELS

37

GAPS GRIP ALEC SPAS
EDIT HERA DISH LOUT
MITE ODER APSE ALTO
STATES FIGS YELLOW
SET VANE HERO
WAGONTRAIN GUNSMOKE
ELON OUST LORNE PAT
ETA WET BELLE KAYO
DALTONS DEALS HELEN
ADS SISSY FIN
STORE DANTE COTTAGE
HALO TEXAS ORR VIA
AXE ARMOR BRUT PEGS
HIGHNOON CRAZYHORSE
ANON FOAL NUN
RAGTOP GUNN IDYLLS
EWER EROS DAWN BOUT
ERNE RAYS EPEE OGLE
DYED SWAY DEER YELP

38

BIERCE GAPES SANTO
INSEAM ALCOTT TIEIN
ASTATESMANWHO AMUSE
STER NEEDED UMBER
MIDAS ETTE DOLL
BROODER CAREERS TOE
LAPSED CONSERVATIVE
EDITS FONT PACER
NIN TRANCE SPASM
DOER AMAH SHED PAST
OFTEN HYENAS DAR
TIDAL INAN CRANE
ISENAMOREDOF WIELDS
EEL BELOVED PROCESS
DEUS IDEA ALINE
SCORN DESMAN IRAE
TRIAL EXISTINGEVILS
NOONE SINTER EGESTA
TONTO SIGHT RODEOS

39

DAMAS ADAIR SATED
ELISE BAYOU CLARE
FISHEYELENS ALLIN
ANTE ELI SUP KEY
CEE USE PREFECT
EDDAS LIETO RUSS
ANALOGY FORTE
ITCH LEAH SMACKED
NOH BEEFEATER EEG
PREMIER ADES EYRE
UREAS ADAMANT
TESS ASTER ACRES
ESCAPED RAG ALE
ARC RAU SOW SCAN
CEASE MUTTONCHOPS
MAKES ELVES GOOSE
ELECT SMART SONES

40

CLEF SPLAT CAPET
RONAN PIECE AROMA
ACCRA RANCH YELPS
MALAGUENA EMU OTS
PLAN NEO PROGENY
SEIDEL LANALANG
OLES PAN SKIER
LATERON SSE
ASPEN WALTZ PEETE
TOA SKEPTIC
TUSKS SPA GENOA
ABSINTHE HYSSOP
RETIRED AGE SURE
REP VIA ALLEMANDE
ATIME TANTA AIDED
STEAL HIDES ISERE
AEDES EMIRS ERSE

41

CHAD SHALL CRAB
HULA LANAI HALO
ARID AUDIT AVID
ROB BYNECESSITY
SKILLET RIM
OUR FLAX IKE
ALERT CLOT MRED
BYPROCLIVITYAND
ERIE RACE ANNOY
DEC PINK BSA
PAT OOTHECA
BYDELIGHTWE ALL
ROAN QUOTE ARIL
AKIN UNSER RENO
NOSY ENTRY EDGY

42

SONG PAST ABATED
EXULTANCE SALOME
POLARCOORDINATES
CIA UNO SERIF
APSIS BRIEFS DARE
BETE RES RON LEA
ETERNAL ICELANDER
TAR OHO SIESTA
SLEPT WALTZ AGUES
PIAZZA EEN NRA
COLDCREAM OCTAGON
ANI EAR MUG REDD
MESS BONNET ACRES
PASTA AER FIT
COOLWITHCOOLIDGE
AMUSED RENASCENT
TETONS URAL SOPH

43

HADES PUBES GHOST
ADAGE ORANT ROUTE
MERGE MACLE ANSEL
SPT DRANK LOB EEL
THREEDOLLARBILL
ARNE EARNED
AVERSE BSC ARIOSO
ROME SES PTS MUD
RIME DIE PIE SEGO
OLE RAN DAN AGAR
WETHEN AIR REBARS
METALS SACO
TWODOLLARPISTOL
PAH INE LEANT LAB
OPINE RULER ALIBI
SINUS TROVE SAVER
TRENT SEWED YIELD

44

SHOPS SAD POS SHAM
COVET LIDO LIL HILO
ALENE IDES ELIGIBLE
TERRE DELI ASPIRE
BORE SINGS BERNE
SCUD DOWNGRADE SNAP
IOR AGGIE ONICE IRE
SADDLEUP OUTERSPACE
STERE MEOWS MUTA
SNAG ULE URUS
PAFF GESTE ASNEW
INNERLIGHT OUTRIDER
SOO SADAT IPRAY ETA
ASTA BOTTOMDOG TROY
WHALE HONOR ELIS
TULANE EGAD ENTER
ANIMATOR DEWS ATUNE
BOON OLE ANET SEDAN
EDNA PAD YER TRYST

45

FIB STIRP ABAS AFAR
ANA LUNAR TAPA SINO
TURNOFTHESHREW INTO
ARCUATE SLOG SUNNED
LEARN RESUMES VIE
SEA MURE WRANGLE
ESME PAIR LEO EARS
BEA WARRENPEACE NGO
BEGORRA OBIT IRS
SPIRIT AETAS EDUCES
CAN ECRU ELEGANT
OFF GEARSPRAYER KOA
ROOT TRE ALEC REST
BOURBON MENE TAI
NEA STINGER SAMOA
ALTARS AMOI EASTERS
MOAT FAREWELLTOALMS
OKIE AMOR STAIR BEE
KIND XATS TRYST ART

46

FLEA PROP TACO ROOT
RAVI LAIR ELAN EDNA
OVER AFLYINONESSOUP
GARMENT LANE HORSE
ARE STING PER
CATINTHEHAT PRETEND
ARIL AWED WEEP VIE
MEN BARN PITY PIKE
PATRONS ALAS AILED
INTHEDOGHOUSE
EMILE MATE KRISHNA
ZONE BRIM DANA ION
ROC BEET SHIP SLOT
ADHERED APIGINAPOKE
MAR TRIPS ODE
TOKEN KICK ADDENDA
ABIRDINTHEHAND DOUR
LONG ROLE ACNE EDAM
CEDE EWER MEAD RELY

47

PALMA ALCAPP XARM
IDIOM LAURIE IRAE
CHARINGXROAD NEVE
TONE GAETA AGNES
SCALIA RESETTLE
TIKIS DASH
ACE SOURS ARIETTA
BALSA HOTX ARBORS
ANTI INN BAH APIS
COOGAN XTIE GREBE
KENNETH ALOHA RES
OGRE ULNAE
RUFFIANS NACHOS
ETATS ETHOS HERA
HIGH AXTHEPACIFIC
ALIE RETORT ALTER
BENX ISSUES LISLE

48

TACH OMSK ASMARA
ATHOS ROTE GEYSER
BRIGHTBLUEWEATHER
BILLIE ANNA TREVI
YALEMAN TEST USES
GOFER STOAE
CUE NOBUTTERFLIES
LIMB ROSE SORORAL
ANILE END OVATE
STRIATE ORAD EDIE
PASTSURPRISES ENT
HENRI PIATS
SALE SONG STOPGAP
CLASS RIAS HAIRDO
OLDOLDSOPHISTRIES
TALMUD NEON SAMAS
SHEERS SSTS LYLE

49

CODE PREP BOND BYE
ANIL RIDE ETUI FRAT
PEDAGOGUE EINSTEINS
PRATE SCRAPS THINK
CENT ASPS GREGG
PETS ONTAP LEARNSOF
IRI GONETO ONCE ONO
SOCRATES SHORT TUTU
ASSUME CEASE TUTOR
PEDATE LESSON
ARIES VILLE APEMAN
TONE PELLA LEVERAGE
OAT PARD STELAE TUT
PRETENSE CHAIN ARES
LEASE MAID TARO
PLACO TURNER MENSA
PRECEPTOR KNOWITALL
LOCH HEIR ELSA EGOS
OFT YALE RYES SEGO

50

CARPS TIDAL SHEA
ORALE ANIMA EAST
WESAILTHEOCEANSEA
RAPT ETATS ORDEAL
YRS CALLS ANOINTS
THREE UNION
NINAANDSANTAMARIA
ARELI RAIN ANN
MEWER WEELS EDINA
INE EOAN MOSES
BALTIMORECLIPPERS
UNPEN ZESTY
BLONDER DAILY LAD
VENEER GORSE SAPO
THEFLYINGDUTCHMAN
ATUA LAMAR ARECA
ROLY ERASE TIRES

51

BASIL LAMODE CAPERS
ALINE ERODES HERMIT
FISTS ARNIES AREOLE
FATHERFIGURE PISTIL
IDEE CAVEMEN ELENA
NORD AGER CAT EDGE
CAB EDE DELRAY
ICARUS DAY LENSMAN
MARKSMAN VALUED OTE
APR BABESINARMS THA
GOI IRADES REANCHOR
ONEGETS EOS NOLESS
ASLEEP ABI WAR
ARAN YRN MENG STIR
RIGGS ABREATH SOTO
ADESTE BROTHERKINGS
MENTON LANIER REGIS
INDENT ENDMAN ASURE
STARES STEEDS STELL

52

PAPA DRAM SLAP AFAR
OMIT RATA PAIL DANE
PINTSIZED EZRAPOUND
ENGRAVE DUNE CORNED
AGE FEND LAWN
PRICE MINI LATESHOW
LENT RODSTEIGER OVA
ENC JUDO AVES SUET
ATHLETE ROGER BURNT
WASH KAREN HUNG
SCOUT POKER MINGLED
HARD WORE EAST ASA
ARM MILESDAVIS TSAR
HYSTERIA ITEM BOSUN
IDES MOTS FOP
SHINED BARE SELLERS
NEATSFOOT MINUTEMAN
URGE ONCE PROD SIVA
GOOD READ TABS STEP

53

ASAP AGAR DATA EMIT
LENA CASA AMOR NANO
TEDSNIGHT VIKKISCAR
EPISODE TAI ISSUANT
STAR STRUDEL LEWES
ITT EAR MLLE
SATCHELSPAGE ESTERS
OSU ETAT URSA ERAT
UTS REP HANGAR ROME
ROCKS SCANNER SITAR
IRAE VERITY TAU IDI
SING EDIT CRIB CAL
HASSLE MICHAELSCANE
ERIE HEM SOL
REEVE NATURES NAPS
ALTERED ABA CLIMATE
JOHNSLOCK LEOSCAROL
APED SORE DANA NELL
HERS ERIN STET TEES

54

OGRE XAT MOB PATH
TOOL EPEE CURE ACRE
ELEMENTAL AMERICIUM
ADD BOS EAR LYS DEP
TON AGREE LIP
BORON KRYPTON SALAS
ABET AIM SOD MAGI
RON ARDOR CITES MIG
METALS REDAN CARBON
ULE TIN ARU
OXYGEN ARGON MAGNET
IRA NITRO NYMPH ENA
SARD CAT LOS ARIL
EYERS SILICON AMIDE
YON ELMAN IRE
ANI DOS APR LOG ZAG
GERMANIUM PLUTONIUM
HOOP EZRA SANA ANTA
ANNS TEN BAS ECON

55

INGE CDEF SPORT ODIN
MERL CHURL PELEE PINE
ARAY HELLOBIRDIE ORTO
MONSTERS PELT SMARTEN
DEARIE GLUT SATYR
ROMERO CRIERS LOGAN
ORO PORGYANDBASS RCA
NIT STOLAE REA COTS
DEER SPAN ALF ENMASSE
ELLAS ERI LOLA TORS
YOURETHEBOTTOMS
COWL SEER OTO SOMME
SCANNED SET DIKE NYET
HALS NAT SILENT RAN
ELL THEQUEENANDI ADA
SIMAR DUPING OLLIES
BEVEL SARD WARDEN
BRAIDED FOES UNSEALED
RADA TEAFORTHREE NART
ETAT TENET AISLE EDDA
DEME SPADS RETE RYAN

56

SHUSH SOPRANI IOLE
RETIE TRIOLET ✱SBOK
ORAN✱ARMALADE USAGE
SHEOL ELL ATTUNE
NOIR TAP ALE
BELAYED ROSSINI ✱EL
IBIS SLEEPSIN CRAVE
KAFKA ELA COHERES
ENE STRATA✱ SKEANS
ASH NABOB AES
✱ATRIA SALIERI ✱UL
ORIENTS ODD THINE
TARSI OBLIGEES ANTA
ENL BALCONY MILLION
WOK DAS TALI
✱ARIAH ERR VERSE
LEMON DISCOURA✱ENTS
UNITS BRITTLE EMOTE
GASH KERSEYS NOBEL

57

AMOR LEAR SLOE FRED
MORE ECRU TIFF RAGE
ONTHECUFF OFFTHEJOB
SAHARA SUBLET AMASS
BIRD SEE HALO
SOU CROP ASPEN NAPS
OFFTHERACK TWISTTIE
DIOR MIRE SAMP ENT
ATSEA NERD LARGESS
ABBOTS ROLLER
LANTERN TEAM EATIN
ATO TETE RIIS DONE
MORTSAHL ONTHEFENCE
AMMO KEYED SEAL SAD
ABAS VEL DRAM
RAISA THESIS TRACKS
OFFTHEAIR ONTHEROAD
BASE IGET NAVE ELLA
TROD NESS SPAN SEEK

58

```
ACED GRAD GSA PRAY
COTE RARE RES SEINE
TONGUEINCHEEK PASTA
STARRED OATS TICKER
EIN ODIN SUCH
ASHES THELASTTYCOON
ULE TRI IOU OLLA
TARP BOOTCAMP ABIDE
OVERLAY OENO EMBOSS
IER SWAIN VAL
GAMMAS PESO GATEWAY
ALIEN SOLENOID RALE
LAST REO OSE SOL
ARCHOFTRIUMPH REPEL
ERDA BLAS TIC
PAMPAS SENT TILLAGE
ABOUT STRAIGHTLACED
PLUME PEI NOEL INTO
PEEP AMA SPEE REAM
```

59

```
PAPPY AFFECT COMES
ARISE PRITHEE EPOCH
SLEIGHTOFHAND LATHE
TEC GEESE UNIT HEE
ANEW IST BROAD BELT
AINT CLAUSE EROS
SHELVE SHUTS ISON
PEALE SHANE ACTOF
CAVS CHARD PREEMPT
ARE BOOKSELLERS EAR
ASKANCE REESE BARA
DEREK UBOAT ELROY
CREE BRUNT EXULTS
IRON SPOUSE OXEN
MOPE CRASS SPA TAME
POP TIES SMELT RAN
UNITE STICKINTHEMUD
TENON TENSILE ILOVE
EDGED REAMER SIRED
```

60

```
DANTE GUAVA MUFFET
EXEUNT ARRAS ELLERY
FIENDISHDISH TAYLOR
ELD STPAUL LIEN III
ALES TIN PARR ACCA
TADPOLE PEONS BRIAN
OREL AXED GAIT
COMIC IGOT MALAYA
AVILA BRET SAME CRY
PASS BOOTIETIE GILA
ELS SEAN CLAD ARTEL
SHAKER STIR PAYNE
AGES CHIT ABET
PAPAW TRICE MEDICAL
AVER EVAN AAA SOLE
RIN AMAS SADIST ACT
CAPONE HOTTENTOTTOT
ETERNE ENATE SLEEVE
LENDER DATUM LASER
```

61

```
BOMB SSTS MAP DOGS
AMOR KNOW ILES ELLA
LANA IONA SANE LIED
TRANSMOGRIFICATION
CAMP DCI ERR
CASHLESS ETO ISLAM
APPEAR HORSESTOMICE
BEAD CER RAH ATTA
SALAAMS HITCHON
SUPERMANTOCLARKKENT
CLAMOUR EDUARDO
ATLE SET DNA FDIC
PRINCETOFROG ABLEST
HANDY MAO EXTRACTS
MAL LTA HOES
DRJEKYLLINTOMRHYDE
TRUE IRIS NISI ISAY
HALE NEMO UNAS NENE
EWER SAN LESE GRAS
```

62

```
NESS CARP SAFR BOLD
EMIT OLIO AROE EPEE
WISECRACK HARLEQUIN
TRIPUP HERA DEBUSSY
UPON RARA ERE
INSPIRED MAXI OSCAR
SOL DAVID NECK THOU
ADAR LEGUP LENO ENE
REPAY RIPUP DEVISED
SNAP TEPID WART
SATINON DIVOT LINEN
LAI GOOP LONER SURE
ORCS LEAD TOLET TIE
PEKIN LIRA RECESSED
MAB LAND SKAT
ELAPSED GOER ORANGE
FACETIOUS FUNNYGIRL
ONER NERI EDIE ENOL
REDS GRIN REED DOGE
```

63

```
ELF SHOE SQUAT TARO
SEA TERN PURGE ELAN
PASTURES RIGOR NICE
TONE UNITE MASTER
FLEAS PRONE PINE
LAND CREST RATTRAPS
AVE NOISE TEPEE SIT
TADPOLE SAUNAS SILO
LEAST GREW ANDES
CASALS WRING STEEDS
HUNTS FEEL ELATE
ADES PUNTED AWARDED
SIR TARTS ROVER EVA
MODESTLY COPED GREY
VATS MINES PAINS
REVERE SANER SAPS
OVEN ROUND AVERSION
MOST NURSE TILT VIA
PETS STEER EELS ELY
```

64

```
SNOWING WIND STORMS
HORATIO ALEE HEROIC
OVERALL TEMPERATURE
WIG ETE ALTER NAN
ECOL MAR TOAD EDGE
RENAME ASSORT ELSE
YORE PEDESTAL
RUT PADRONE ASIDES
ANISE SOUS FOOTPATH
IFNI HEAT FOGS SLOE
NINEFOLD HAIL SEINE
STYRIA TALLEST SST
RAREBITS DUOS
HADAT LITHIC NASSER
UTES DEKA FAN WOVE
REA GAMIN IDA NIS
RATIOCINATE RAMPANT
ASHORE ITER DEFENCE
YESSES SETS STARTED
```

65

```
SLOT RAPT APB HATS
LAMA AGRA BRAN ALAI
AVER TROT SIRE DILL
VANARTEWALTERORJACK
ULES URSINE
SISSIES CUTE OASES
ASPEN DAIS URBANE
GEORGESAMUELANDEDIE
SETA LONIS ELSE EDD
IRENIC FEDORA
SSS AMIS VOWEL PEER
KATEMICHAELANDHENRY
IDIOMS INKY EROSE
MARNE ABLE CLASSES
RENAME BOAR
JAMESROBERTANDDEEMS
AGED AMEN ANTI ARIA
WERE SILT BARN RISK
SEEN ESS SLAG LESS
```

66

```
ALAS SETS GEAR SAGE
RIGA CARE LAME ULAN
TEEN ERAL ISIS BIRD
SUDDENLYLASTSUMMER
AGAS EST SLAIN
DOLLAR ARIES TITANS
UNO DIAL SNIP STAR
ETNA OLLA TILT EGO
TAELS MAYBE CIAO
SPRINGAHEADFALLBACK
TOON SHARD LEMON
GAG BOAT MOOR DALE
ARLO CORE GREW ZOE
SCONES TENTS TIMERS
REACT AVE SINE
WINTEROLYMPICGAMES
SHOE NISI POLE DARE
IOUS ILLS LOAN OMIT
PASS CLOT ERST WASH
```

67

```
ROMA PREP DABS TAOS
APES LAIR ERAT RUDY
HIGHWAYROBBERY ETON
SEALANE TOUTS SPORE
ACT WROTE ANA
GUANO SEATS TRANSIT
AVID SINCE SHIP TRI
SER BED TERCEL ORAL
PASSAGES SORT AGENT
THROWIN MIRACLE
MAREE AREA PATHETIC
ELIA CLEANS CEE CRO
TOP DUKE SPOKE RAIL
SESTETS TWINS TERSE
RAE KEENE TOT
LINER PURRS SERINGA
IDEA TAKESTOTHEROAD
ALIT WILT ELEE ENID
RELY IRAE RETE DENS
```

68

```
SIMP SPAR ALI BIDEN
ERIE ALBA COD ENERO
WANDALUST HALCAESAR
SEEDCASES EMERGE
LED NOWS OLDHAT
DAMES ETNA BONE OVA
OTIS MAE RHONE TWOS
VOL OISE ROBES WINK
ELLIPSE HERBS PIE
SLIDES SUNNY BANDIT
EEN WIMPS PERSONA
OLGA SADIE RANK IAM
DORS HILDA END ANNE
ONA PILE CANT ALGER
REMAIN AERO OIL
SETSUP OVERREACT
NOAHCOUNT MARTYGRAS
ESTEE MIL ATNO EMMA
TEENS STY SEEN DYER
```

69

```
SOIL CABIN INN STOP
ELBA ASALE MOO HARE
ALEF DCCLV AUK ABET
NAGIRROCYAWGNORW
TEETH EWE MAMMAL
SPITS SUSHI KISSERS
TENETS SRO PES LAT
ALS CPR STEED SMO
CLOSURE NARRATED
YALPRIAFSITUOBANRUT
VIETCONG VALUATE
OVENS TIANT ACE MIX
WEN ROE IRA IMPALA
ENCODER CDEFG ARSES
DAYBED DAN FACTO
LASREVERASREFFUS
CATO TIP CHIME FISH
AVON AGO SORAS ERDA
BERG RAT ASSNS REAM
```

70

TESTS STAG TIE EAGER
ATTEN ORNAMENT ANDREA
THEGOLDENBOUGH STEELE
TEE ROOT RTES SOLES
ERRATUM TARO RUMEN
REARED OUTONALIMB BAR
SAGER DALE NUDES ARE
LEA NIKE EDGE DYED
LEAVESOFGRASS ETNA
FIT AVON LEGER HEBRON
INHERIT TERNS HOTTEST
NEEDLE CHARO SAGO EES
ERGO SARATOGATRUNK
ATOM RULE SEEN REL
RIO SALMI SHAM CANEA
TAD THEBADSEED BAITER
EEROS ELAN TENTERS
PALER ATTA PORT NIE
GORGES THECHALKGARDEN
ESTATE LACKADAY TERSE
LEHRS INT YOYO ABETS

71

ABASE RAMP LIT RAW
LODEN ALOE STONE COLE
BOARDOFELECTIONS LOLL
TRIOS FELLOES SHAMED
AREO ELIE IMAGE
ABELS CONTAIN DAN NED
COLLEGEBOARDS AIDED
EASY MAORI RMS ABLE
WANE OHIOAN SOUL
IBSEN PARADISE TANS
SNOUT BOARDWALK MERGE
ADAB CANTEENS WORDS
GIRD ESCHAR SCAB
SADE ATE COLAS MALT
OBESE BOARDOFHEALTH
ALF WED INSTATE MISDO
LATHE STET STAN
CURARE HEIRESS INSET
ORAL BOARDOFEDUCATION
TIDE BALSA TRAP TANGO
TEE STE SAKI EYEON

72

LAMP ALOT AMAD STIR
ASEA FEAR BOBO TACO
WHENITAKEMYSUGARTOT
SETTLED MISS CLEANS
IER SOAS MATA
CARES SOLO CERAMICS
OPUS YSHOULDNTI LEA
LAS POGO LEOS SLIM
TRIDENT DRAFT CABLE
NEED BEING CHIC
LOCAL LINGO GOALIES
OPEN HATE FLAP NIP
SAR DONTBCRUEL OGRE
THETIMES OOZE TRUED
AGES BRAE POD
PAULUS IONS ALLENDE
USTEPPEDOUTOFADREAM
STEN USES ELAN LONI
HOST NEAT DART YSER

73

MEIR RAMP REFER CHER
ERSE SAMOA ELITE AONE
TINSELTOWN VINEGARJOE
SETTLEIN OLEAN UNTOLD
ALDO SPARS ELIE
SAUTES BALMS SMALLEST
TUNES BABYBOOMERS MAO
ARCS PELL DENS CELT
GAL BASKET BOLD SORTS
ELEVATES OVERT FORAY
MOIST STIES MEDAL
SILLY SHEAF HERALDIC
BALES SLIM SCORNS INA
EFTS MOAN LUIS LSTS
LEI SILVERGHOST FILET
TRESTLES ERASE FIBERS
EELS SPINE MENE
ALKALI STEMS EATERIES
HORSEOPERA OLDSCRATCH
AGIO NIGEL MONTH LARA
BOSN SNOWS SPAS SLUM

74

TWOFER PASS DAY AFRO
HEGIRA ALPHA EMU ROUT
ABLEST REHAN MOM GUST
ISAR THREEMENONAHORSE
YALU NITID ASTIR
AND MEGATON CEORL OAS
PIECESOFEIGHT MOTIF
ANION AID EATEN DIRE
CESS KARL OLTEN COVEN
EST FIR PEER SALEPS
TENCOMMANDMENTS
EFFETE BAAL LEO FAT
LOOSE COSTS ASSE BORA
FOUL MULTI AMA ULCER
RACER ONENIGHTSTAND
TIP OREAD LINSEED LAY
ENOLA DONAS WRAP
ATSIXESANDSEVENS RASA
PITA GAP ATTAR EREBUS
OMER ART KITTS LOPERS
TARS DDS CEST YESTER

75

CABOT PENROD HASHED
ALLAH RECEDE ADHERE
MAURICERAVEL DEANNA
UTE SOFIA UPON RED
SESS VEE LOGAN PISA
TIER LEGER HURTS
SMART NOSED HUGO
FOALS DOYLE CAESURA
LIRE BAHAI FOGY SAR
ARC EMILEZOLA SIM
GEE IGET COLOR PESO
GELATIN MARIN FLAIR
MIEN BURRO BRAUN
CHARM METOO GRIN
HORS MANIN HAI SHAM
INC HOPE FONDA ERA
LEERAT AUGUSTERODIN
ISAIAH TRADER AIDES
STUBBY HISDAY BLASE

76

PEEVES SCALD ATALE
ORNATE CESAR DENIS
MATTED HAPPYGOLUCKY
ASH SALES ISERE HER
DEUT NAMERS NECKERS
ESSEN BETH STRAINS
INON ROOST SSR
SCATTER DAYS TIDAL
PASSIVE WAILED NEPA
ONT NEWER NEARS VAC
OTIS REDACT LATTICE
FOCUS TITO STARLET
EEL CHART SIAM
REDCOAT SERA DIANA
GENERAL ATTEND NYET
ALI ETTLE RANON CUT
LIGHTHEARTED LIGATE
EMILE MORAL ENURES
SATYR ENATE DESERT

77

DECANT GAY ADM COD
APACHE AGO VIAL ALE
DISCLAIMED ASTO REP
SCAT CDE HULLABALOO
CHET NOOSES
DEBRIEFED IND SEAR
APRIORI EDT GANTLET
REIGN EAVES EWE ARE
REMI ADRIP EDAM NOD
DIS GLOWY ROB
CYD DADO SIEVE LASS
AMO LIE DENSE TORAH
THEBELL ODE SPECKLE
SARA IVY DEPRESSED
BOOGIE LION
DISENCHANT ANN TELE
DOS ATTN INTEGRATED
TNT NEED RUE EELING
SAS TDS END DECODE

78

SOW DARK GCLEF MAIL
RAH OREO RHINE ARGO
TRIMWITHDAISIESPIED
ASCENT LAYMAN ELATE
HUSH ILES ORE
OWEST AMA ALE ROA
RIVERATMYGARDENSEND
CDE ERATO BEE EIDER
HERBAGES FRANC ROSY
AMI ALI AVE
OKAY LHASA CYLINDER
CANOE ADO ARDEB AGO
THOUSANDROSESBRINGS
SAN CIG REE ANDYE
CUR DCCV ATLE
ILIAD SEEHER DIALIN
DAFFODILSAREBLOWING
ORFE ATTAR ERIN OFT
LAYS BEARD LOBS NOS

79

AUK JEEP SCOT HOLDS
ANI EDDA LOBO ONEUP
RID WHOSHOTJR WANNA
PONIES TEPEE PATTER
AFL VILEST IBO
POPS LOCI STOOLIE
IMP ETHOS STOUTEST
TIED NEE TALENT ELA
STREWN LEHAR YOKEL
WHYDOILOVEYOU
PLAYA APPLY EUROPA
AIR TERESA OHM SUES
TAILSPIN ROGUE TRI
SOLOMON VERN EMMA
CYD STREET ONO
FATALE TIARA ALLDAY
EBOLI WASITRAIN IRE
ALLEN PINS CADE NEW
TEASE ANTE HUEY GAS

80

ALEC CARAT EPACT
POLO RUGATE TABOO
EDEL IREGRETALLMY
DIVORCES ENOL OTE
ROOT ASSISTED
SLIMY TSPS EBO
TIME BECAUSEIDONT
AMANDA HURT AFOR
BAN ELEE ERIS MSS
CLAMMY ITADAY
JOHNPAULGETTY
RELICT MEARAS
FUR SEIL SEAN LES
LIKE OOPS TSHIRT
ANYTHINGTOBE ELIA
TAO IANA FAINT
TYRANNIC GIRD
REE SIDI AFLICKER
UNSUCCESSFUL ONTO
STENO STEALS LENA
TATUM TSARS DEAR

81

QUOQUE IRAQI QUEBEC
ASNERS BOSUN ANGOLA
NASDAQ LOWIQ TIGRIS
TBA LURED TUBAS NCS
ALLS IES GREER QEII
SEEHERE QUEST QUOTA
ONE QUINT QUA
ADJUT QUILT QUERCUS
QUOT QUARE QUIETUDE
AKH QUOIT QUIEN VIC
BANQUETS QUART QENA
ASQUITH QUICK QUEER
ETE QUIRK QUE
MACRO QUITE QUONSET
ONAN QUIDS CUE AQUI
ROE QUINN QRSTU URE
RISQUE QUEUE SETIER
INATIE UNLIT CLARKE
STRONG ECIZE HEPTAD

82

AMANA SADE LEGS SALMI
HERAS EQUI ACRO AREEL
ADIGE PARL DRAM LEASE
BUSYASABEE DUMBASANOX
SSE ERASERS META
ANCONA SNA HERO BOLT
LETT SALE MAUMEE
PARODIED BOLDASBRASS
ELEC EDITH AMUR OGRES
AACHEN SKIRT SABU
LIKEACATONAHOTTINROOF
RECU THENI EDESSA
SOREL ERSE STERN FEES
FREEASABIRD RANGIEST
ACCEPT ASIA RIOT
XATS ELAM ESA EATSUP
SPED ISHMAEL NIS
SICKASADOG REDASABEET
OPENS NERO ALAR PEACE
PORES TRET MINT ANSER
SHOWY OSSA SASH REESE

83

GASH ABIG DUB DISCO
EDNA MUTE SELA DUNCAN
SMOTHERSMOTHER ESCAPE
TIO ONMY LEANS STATES
EXPLODE ALIVE PIES
EKES PINE ARRESTS
STIR REESESNIECES POI
AERO LES NATS CORD
PLAYBILLS DONTS THOSE
SENSORS TOREN CIELOS
BROTHERSBROTHER
COCOON ALOES WARSHIP
ALLYN BLEND MOONSHINE
ISAS LIEN OER ETTE
NON MADDIESDADDY ISON
ENGLAND GLEN RUHR
INDY MOANS EPISODE
FLANGE GAINS ASPS PAL
LONGER LISTERSSISTERS
OWNERS ANTS ATEE ARTE
PEERS DES PARS BAHS

84

EGO METES DORIS CALL
AVIV OMANI EMILE ARIA
TELEPHONES CABLEGRAMS
ENTREATS TARTS PROMPT
EAVE MELEE PAIL
TENACE TORTE FIGS TAG
ARETE PARS STREET AMA
MOWS PLUS HODS STIR
EDS GRAPEVINES GETTY
DECORATE INERT HOLLY
ABATE STAGE PERLE
ASIDE SHANE ARRESTED
MATTE TELEVISION ARA
ARES CORE SHED PLAY
TOR SUPINE SNED MEETA
ENS PREP NYLON PERSON
BARN PLEAT BRAS
APIECE HEIST PRODUCED
MESSENGERS TALEBEARER
IRAE TAROT ERASE DALY
DIRT SPANS DENTS EMS

85

LAWS SPOT RASP CEASE
PERIL SPARE ENTER ADLER
AVISO TARNS STORE TILER
RASPBERRIES COUCHPOTATO
TREY RATS GUNTHER STOR
AIDA BOLES AOK
INSOLES HERES COTTONSTO
LOAVES PARLE LOVE PIOUS
LIFES SORRY CUPID PUNS
USER ATSEA SIRED HIPPIE
SEC ADREM DOTED FAREAST
RATHER ROBED RETURN
SPARROW LAVED MITES DRS
ARCTIC WAFER SAPID AFAT
TIKI EAGER SHRED ALINE
EMEER AGER SPAIN CLOSER
DERRINGER CHAFE LOATHES
NIL MEANT EANS
SACS LEMMING ANTI TOTS
MILQUETOAST TOUGHCOOKIE
AMOUR OTTER AERIE BRIMS
LENIN NOTRE GNARR ITEMS
LEEDS RAYS SOLD EASY

86

TABS IRBMS STAB TRAP
ABUT NIECE STALE HOME
GLEE DALLASTEXAS AMEN
SENTIENT PALI ATTEST
OSSET SHORE MIAMI
RESOLD SEAR MEDIATES
INANE MEDITATED SNARE
OTIS SIRED SHEIK LIE
SER SANFRANCISCO YES
RECITES AONE SPA
SOARS BAITS AYAHS
DMA TOGA ATGRAND
VAT PHILADELPHIA IAL
ICE SONAR SITON ACTE
ERRED PERSONALS BIKES
TERMITES DENY DARERS
AIRED REESE RILER
ABATES MORO DAVIDSON
BOLT TAIWANCHINA ANTE
ELBE ESTES SEVEN LEOS
LOAD REED TREES EELS

87

RAVES BALL ELEV MORON
PLEAT ELUL ATONE ETUDE
MITRE EATNO GABOR NICER
FOLLOWTHEYELLOWBRICKRD
ANELE DREI AAA
SAP DREAD ATIP TIL ORC
PALACE OPT REIN ROO
ILETASONGGOOUTOFMYCOEUR
TENTS VOILA MATT ANGST
APEEK ETTE CITE AGITATE
RETRO ABRA IOWA NEG
IWANTASUNDAYKINDOFAMORE
NAP LETO KISS ORFEO
ASPHALT WREN SEND ODORS
SHREW THAR PUNTO LETHE
PEOPLESREPUBLICOFDISHES
ORV PTER AYN OCTETS
TEE ISR ERAS GAZER ORT
NOA INTO PERIL
ILEFTMY♡INSANFRANCISCO
TERRE CENSE TOOLS CARTA
AVION ANGER ARNO IRATE
LINED TSAR PEST TABOR

88

SALUD PIPAL ERGO RUBS
COMATE ALICE NEAT EPICS
UNICEF PLATA CENT ASCOT
JACKSTRAW APEOFGOODHOPE
OREM ALIT TARE VIOLET
AURI LEO REDOLENT
CHIGNON LAMES CART SBA
RELIGION SOL ITCHDOCTOR
ONICE FACEOF NEURO HARD
UNO RESORT AMEER JINGO
PANG GAMA SNAP ASUNDER
ANGLINGPARTICIPLE
SPAREST LELY VERA SCAT
ORBIT SHADY SATYRS HRH
LOUS CETUS SHERIF ALIBI
AXSHELTERS EER NARRATOR
RYE MOTE ESSEX RUDYARD
CAVALIER ANA MNOP
ALSACE RUSH ANTE IRIS
HOPPINGCENTER TERMAGANT
AVILA LONI MOSHE ONEIDA
BERET ERIC AWAIT LOOSEN
ROTE ENCE LETCH ANNEX

89

LOS
REATA
MONTANA
EATASMUCH
TONE INTER
DRNO EBN ABS
CRUS TREASURIES
BEAR SWIM TRI CUE
ASYOULIKEJUSTDONT
YAM SOS RONA IMNO
RECAPTURES BABY
NAG RYS LANE
TETRA OOLA
SWALLOWIT
OPIATES
TAKEN
NEA

90

MADAM SCALD PRIVET
ARARAT MELEE RUTILE
GEMINISERIES ASTRAL
UNA ESPANA CENT GIL
SAGS SOL TALK HONE
SETOUT FLANK WEBER
AGES LIFT SERE
NACRE DEBT THIRTY
AGAVE PIER ERAL WEB
NOPE LEOTARDED BEAR
ARR PEER RIGS TWERE
AILEEN LILY HANNA
CORK COAL AMON
SCORE SHANE MORASS
EURE DEAF CAB SHEA
ERN LIAR GRATIA AMI
GAELIC AQUARIUSURER
ERRANT DUNCE SIMPLE
RESEDA EASED APSES

91

ASCAP PREY OKS LIBEL
CLONE HAVOC PEA INURE
HOWDOESYOURGARDENGROW
BLIND ERIE FINDERS
SAFE EON EVES
BAAL MERE LUFF INTER
ISLE UNTIL AUBE LAO
THEGARDENSOFTHEDESERT
SERENA SAT LIRA ROMEO
STRAND RIMES SPIRE
GARDENPARTY
ESTOP VEILS SABERS
SPANS IDEA ANT LAMIAE
COMEINTOTHEGARDENMAUD
ERE ESNE NEVER ANTE
UST ERST EYES STEN
NAHA ERA SWAP
LLERS EELS NIGER
INTOMRMCGREGORSGARDEN
LITAI EAU EDER NINER
SPUDS DRY RATA OSAKA

92

PREP ERRS ADEN USA
ARENAS SCAUP TELA LES
MOLLYPITCHER OFFPITCH
UTE SCARE FILMY TIRE
SEA AME AUTOS CREME
ESSES BEAGLES ARARAT
STEEPPITCH SUSAN
LEO TAEL PITCHMAN
SAG DOG STOEP CHOICE
CRAG LAPP CAVE HOLLOW
ACRE PITCHFORK DIRE
MORTAR TALE ESAU SUNS
PLEURA CHIRP STE MST
SETPITCH OSAR ALF
STAYS PITCHBLACK
STEELY ALGEBRA AARON
HORNE FREER APE DUO
SETI MADAM ASURE ONT
PITCHOUT PITCHANDPUTT
ALE OUST UNIT HERRY
TAR TREY PISH SUSY

93

CASCO ERGO BUENO GMAN
ILEUM THOU ENDUP RARE
RANTS HOLT GLEBE ISLE
CLOAKANDDAGGER NESTOR
EARN PIE NAIA CANT
DISCS DINS ANT BEE
SADDLES ROUGHANDREADY
PEARLS DEUS VASELINE
ARNIE SECT ADE HELLAS
NITER NAE ONEROUS
SEED HARDANDFAST GUSH
SAPLESS AGT VIREO
MANTEL ODE CREE EVIAN
ABELLFOR TAGS CREATE
BLACKANDWHITE NAVAHOS
AYR INT HANA HELEN
ORDO EVEN AWE DART
SHEIKH BREADANDBUTTER
POLL ALIEN DUDE SALLE
ELSE LENTO OLLA SKEET
DYAD FAGOT GAEL RESTS

94

PISA GIST ATBAT AIRS
OMEN ASHE CALLA ENNUI
MORTARTOTECLIPANDSURF
ENTANGLE AROSE ARARAT
OLE GUNS DIESELS
INVADE POLIS BEAD
NOISE ALIEN KIND BIL
KNAPSADANDGUNNY PSALM
SELS RANK NOD RUNON
SNIT FOAL URANO
CRACKERSTEEPLEANDFLAP
HANOI HIRT SMEE
ATOLL WIG STIR ALAS
METAL PINNAILANDBLOCK
PRE ROCK UNITE RAINY
CONK TSADE PAWNEE
CATNAPS SAPS FRY
AMOUSE BELIE FRIEDHAM
POWDERSHOECAPEANDLENA
ELEGY PAUSE LAIC VEIL
SERE ARLES ORLE IDLE

95

GARBO SCOW SCAN BENT
ALOOF LAMA ARRAS OMAR
MAYOR OLEG LEAST NICE
SINGINGCOWBOYAUTRY
MPS LOS IANS MISSES
OILIER LAST SOIR
HEAVYWEIGHTTUNNEY GIL
ARTY ANA EPEES SAKI
ICE PURER TAPES SAPOR
RESTAREA ROSE HELENA
BANDLEADERKRUPA
OSCARS VIAL OHLADYBE
TOURS SHADY SPELL OAR
ILES SLIDE PET SURA
COD STAGEDIRECTORSAKS
OATH ROCK PAWNEE
ABBOTT SCAT MAI DDS
TERPSICHOREANKELLY
OTOE OHARA TONE WOMAN
NEON NARES ENOS AGILE
ELKS WISH DOTE YALIE

96

MAGI DEEP IND RUSS
CLARK ARNE AREA GENOA
LEMONSDROP HEEP ADDIS
CANOES LOWE PASSERS
ICA SHRIKES CREE
BLACKSTOP INSERT OWED
LAC ORCA TEAR REAR
EIRE NATURE NOONTIME
ENID POLES USA ASTOR
DEDUCT PIPEIN TUT ESE
CARDINALSSYSTEM
JIG SEI ADESTE ASEVER
ADOBE ESS PURSE GONE
BALLISTA HEISTS SITE
DUNE BAMA NINA LES
ROME NORTON GRAYSMARE
ALIS ONEARTH ETA
DINNERS ASON DRAMAS
AVION ETAL LIMESLIGHT
RINSE TONE EDEN LETUP
SAGE SET DINS SSTS

97

ALAMOS STARE OSSA
REGATTA OPENER CREUSA
PARTIAL PALOMAPICASSO
OCTOBER RATED BAIN
ETA ONER CANON SENSE
WALTERSLEZAK AZTEC
ELTON OATEN INNES HUM
SEANCE STUD LICE BETE
GALL ASININE FRETS
CLAMMER COAT SLAVES
SHY PETERBENCHLEY ERY
PANDER DAUB SHAPERS
LINED HORNETS BRAY
INRE BANE REPS SPIELS
TSE BORER GRETA ENTIA
DREAD JENNIFERGREY
ANGEL TITAN DERN EDS
FERN BOSOM BESIDES
AMANDAPLUMMER CITADEL
RAVERS ARECAS ANTLERS
NESS MEDIT GEARED

98

LEO BASSI QUORUM REV
ULU ARKIN URBANA SUVA
PUTTHEIRHEADSTOGETHER
IDLES ATTU NEARLY
NEAT SCALAR STERN
SWEPTOFFHERFEET DRAB
HARI IOWA BIOTA
THEGOINGPRICE STANLEY
SECONDS LAMA SHINGLES
PETTY MAIM TORSO
SLOT ABANDONHOPE RATE
HEMAN REAP EDSEL
GREENERY BARE SENECAS
RIFLING WILDCATSTRIKE
ACTED ARID NATO
MESA RINGSFORTHEMAID
DEANS IDEALS TSAR
EXHORT BEER BURMA
BROUGHTPRESSURETOBEAR
OAST ESCORT NAVAL AGE
NYE RETINA SPENT LEE

99

PAID BETA RENTA LISP
ISTO AGON ELOIN CATER
THEMESONG TOMMYDORSEY
ARS ETAPES ORGAN
EMPIRIC LIKEN RTE
JEANS HAILE DEME BED
ECU VINCENTLOPEZ ERE
CCLI ANDOR OATER SNIT
TAWS LOY SORTIE ONCE
HELIO RIEN BUNYAN
PSI DUKEELLINGTON GST
AUTISM AMIE ORONO
VIED TSETSE DMD NOPE
ATMO THERE SPACE EDAM
NOA HARRYRICHMAN MNO
ERN ENOS GHENT PLAIT
ORD APNEA SILENCE
AHWOE ALLOWS VIN
GLENNMILLER ARTIESHAW
AIRES NIOBE NINE EAVE
BEAD DATED TOTS STET

100

MAAM CASS DUMAS GLAD
BUNCO OBIT ENATE ROMA
OCEAN MITE CANOE OVEN
SHAKESPEARE IMPOTENT
CORETTA REDSEA VERSE
SARI SEASCAPES
DAHL YETI MAS MARQUIS
AVOID DECLARE ATTUNES
FOSTER MEA NASH EDAM
TWEETER DISPERSED ETS
RELET NEE SETIN
ALB REVERENCE DIVORCE
SORA VETO CAW CATHER
ANALTAR NATASHA NEEDS
DICKENS DLI TONG STET
ANTELOPES STOA
EMILE ISSUES INSTEAD
LEVITATE PGWODEHOUSE
IRIS BAGEL AERO ELBOW
OGEE ELENA LEST RAINS
TEDS TESTY SPEE SNEE

101

ELCID BEGAM ALB ABO
AREOLA SALAMI REARSUP
BOTTOMLESSPIT MACBETH
BINET AARE EWE KHAKI
ECOL CYMA FIREDOG SUR
SATE LEE PINED XRAYS
FORWARDED ETON
PEARY KIER MAUGHAM
PORTOS SIN TENPIN OTE
ATMAN DITCH COULD THA
SHIRT EXTERIORS MOWED
HEN IHATE ENTIA UDINE
TRE EALING FOE ESDRAS
OBSERVE ROAN NISEI
AJAR DIAMETRIC
RERUN QUERY AID SWAP
GEM SAVINGS EGGS HIDE
RABAT EDS KNOB VALVE
AGONIZE TOPIARYGARDEN
SIDECAR ADHERE RIPENS
SNY ELS NAIVE ALERT

102

CAVIL AMAR BUNA
ASIDE ALONE STORAGE
MISSINGLINKS HAREBELL
ESAU TOSEAL LORE MIA
ASIA DANDELIONS RANI
ROLLE OCS EATS BATON
ANS ROWE ALAR HOMER
CORN RAS CASS
SPODE REICHSTAG HART
SHAME AMES ARES ANOA
HARMS ATES ADEN ACTOR
OLGA ALEE ISIS UKASE
PEEN BULRUSHES AGLET
DEEM VAE GRUE
SEERS BURN BATS SPA
SEVER SIAL PAN TATUM
CUIR CURTAILING SAPA
ARN AMAH RANKLE SIPS
BACCARAT MONKEYSHINES
TERRACE UNDID TOGET
SUET LYSE HINDS

103

LASSO MSU SCS PACTS
ALTERS APRICOT OTARU
STREEP CENTAUR TONING
THEPLUMEDSERPENT TODO
EEE DUD ABS ILIO
DATUM MONTEZUMA SNEAD
NAG NOUGATS SOFTLY
SHOWNUP INONU FALL
AIDE AROSE ERVIN AHAB
LADD TOMES SNORT SATE
ATE EVA LEA MTS
MUSH MINAH SPADA HILT
ISTO ASIDE CARON ALEE
TOLO DIXON GNARLED
MARTHA JUNIPER ASP
AREAS LUPEVELEZ HOFFA
SIAM PEG DOE IER
TEMA SOUTHOFTHEBORDER
STELLA LEONORE BRIDLE
TREAT ALGERIA SCALES
ASSES RLS MOD ALERT

104

LOB ADAPTS SHAPE RPM
ICE SIERRA TONER ERR
TEA HEROINESANDWICHES
HARM SAFE MOTE SCOOP
ENDOW TED PLUSH ANNAM
NARES RATTED TERA
MISTRESSPIECE RESIDED
INCHED HOSE TALON
ASA SIMIANS SOL ALCAN
TRM GARNI NUBA PAUSE
LALO DATA OKAY DRUB
ITEMS ANON SAGAS YRS
SETUP MIM THRONES AUS
LULLS THON ATONAL
ORLANDO PERWOMANENTLY
NAUT SIMONE ONSET
ANNIE NORSE BON LAGOS
SCORE STES ACED PUCK
JOHNNYCARDAUGHTER AHA
AME SEPIA TEETER VET
MSS TRACY ELDERS ARE

105

WALLA SCARF ROKA CAN
EGOIST FINER ATIN ANA
FRANKINCENSE JIMDANDY
TANGELO ETNA CORNERS
EDEMA STUKA NOISE
AGER DOST OLIVEOIL
LEM STOW AMEX DIJON
ONETO SALEP BROB NAME
SERUMS BILLPOSTER CNO
STYLET FLEA EIRE KIN
BEGAN TOUTS CATCH
APO ALOP FREE TIRADE
NEA SALLYFORTH ENAMOR
TERM GAEA NATAL AMMON
ANDES RAKI ELLA ENE
MARKTIME ETTE CRES
DIONE SMALL SELMA
BONITAS ARMY ELECTED
ALFRESCO VIRGINIAHAMS
ROE NOUN ERECT STERIC
ERR ENDO LASTS STARS

106

PASS ALL OGLED STLO
AROA LIEU FLOOD WHIM
YOUWEREMINTFORME EYRE
UMP VOCE SASSY HEMAN
PASTES GAPES ELATE
BAYLEAFITORNOT AMP
DECAL OILERS UTAH FOR
AGAR LOGE THEM ETUI
TAR CASHANDCURRY LESS
ADO ANET ORAL HAREM
BRIAR BOONE BRANT
ROBIN ISLE SOUR HEN
ADEN FENNELDECREE YMA
BEAD ISEE NANS SMIT
BON ACTS IMPART SEETO
INC THATSSALTFOLKS
REMUS TOGAE AISLES
PLUTO TALON OUST ORA
LOIN HISSAGEISSHOWING
ANSA AWAIT TATS WEREA
TEES GORSE NER BESS

107

AMASS AIC FELL TBARS
POILU RLO ARIA OASIS
HERONSBILL SNAKEPLANT
BLOOD LATER NIL
ODA ERR TIRES SCAPE
PILOSE MIENS DIADEM
TALES PARROTSBILL LUM
ENID OHIO LONE SILO
DAG TRANSMARINE RECAP
ABRASE ALICE DERATS
ETOILE STICK SAVINE
SPORES SEINE SCRUFF
PARES CORNERSTONE LST
CUPS COLA EELS DOTE
ALE POLECATWEED COWER
EATERS CRIMP SATEEN
TROOP ORANS SIT RLS
OPS SNIPE PORES
BEETLEWEED SPIDERLILY
ESTEE ERAL AREA EARED
NEARS DALY PODS DYERS

108

GAD REBA ESSE NFL
ELENA ELAN NILE ROLES
DINAHWASHINGTON EMOTE
ICE ODE MOUSE SPARSE
FERULES HALL PEDI
INANE CALIFORNIA DAG
ESTES BOLS LEANT AMA
DEE SOHO APSE EPI
MINNESOTAFATS SVEN
IONIAN BOSSY OHARE
RUNLET OKS OPENER
ANDES PALEA TOTALS
IBIS VIRGINIAWOOLF
DOA IDIE TYNE STS
ERN EGEST BOLA ANISE
RNA JOEMONTANA LINEN
JEER ORLE EYELETS
BRONCS CIVIL ANE CSA
RUNAT ILLINOISJACQUET
ABETS LAIC TRIO CURSE
ESE KNEE STAY COE

109

ASKS KOFC ROBE SRAS
RANI RILLE RIVET LILI
ORIG ONEAL IMETA IGOR
MIGHTY GULAG RELIGHTS
ASHTRAY NIGHTFLIGHT
TSELIOT ETRE INTOW
ASHE SPP FLOOD INFER
BOOED SALIENT GATEWAY
ADORED LEGS FIRESALE
BADSEED AHSO OVA SYD
PLIGHT PHOEBE
PPP UNA SITU RICHTER
RAILAGES RINK AGEISA
ALLOWED ADOCTOR SIGNS
STOWE LIENS HEP GHEE
ATRIO OLLA SLEIGHT
LIGHTWEIGHT FLOTSAM
ANIGHTIN GEARS STEPPE
HIGH OBEAH LEASE NOTS
ACHT BESET TENON ETTA
BETS ERST STEW DSOS

110

GRAB CLEFT DPTS ADM
AARE REFER AERIE SMEE
THEGREATZIEGFELD HAVE
ROMPS SNOOPS FINIS
MAUVES REDOES MUFFLE
MENDES PECOS TONTO
CRAG LOSTWEEKEND RAM
COME PILO RENE TARO
VEE THEAPARTMENT OLEO
ROMANS GORAL ATLAS
OLIVERS ARU IMPASSE
PECAN GAVEL AREOLE
AMAT ACADEMYAWARD AAU
RUNE LULU GATE ASIS
TRI ALLABOUTEVE DOME
NOVEL SNORE RADNER
COPIES AWAITS VALISE
URALS SPIGOT GETAT
RARE HAPPENEDONENIGHT
STIR ARLES RIGOR ONUS
EES PIED SKIMS NUDE

111

ESKER PALACE CHART
DINAH ADORERS AUGER
INURE THUMBONESNOSE
TAC AONE USAGE RIN
HIKE SARAH ERR HAND
LIRE ERAS LENO
RENO DERNS TEAPOT
ROSETTA ADALE BRAVE
EMU SOWS AFIRE STEN
CANT PALMSUGAR ETRE
ENDO ORION OTIS YET
SCENT ECLAT ONEIDAS
SERIAL ELIAS ROUT
EGAD SLIT LANK
APER GRE SLIME SEAR
TAN BEAMS RATS SLY
BUTTERFINGERS APHID
ASEAL TRIOLET ATONE
TERRA STAIRS RAWER

112

DEUM PECOS EFT ABCS
IDLY ATONE BRAGI DRAW
SWEDISHMEATBALLS IAGO
CINEMA PIMA KIBITZER
ONTAP ALDER WODAN IRE
RUSSIANOLIVE FOL
EDS TAIN APES AMIEL
PUPTENT HITHER SMEARS
COARSE TOWARD FEIGNED
OMNI ISAK BALZAC
TOI CHINESENOODLE OID
SLUING OOPS IFNI
OTHELLO BAUCIS RENFRO
RAMADA OERTHE HAYSEED
CRAVE SNIT TOME EDE
CES PERSIANAPPLE
ASK ALOHA OVULE AXLES
THESCORE TERI ESPIAL
LURE ITALIANSPAGHETTI
ALEE SYRIA GEODE CHET
SALK TIN ESTER TORS

113

BRAE EPODE IAGO CHIT
ROMY XENON SLID THETA
ATOEHEADEDCHILD WAFER
CARLOTTA ELMOS CINEMA
IVEY AMOAN BAGEL
REINER BRICE ARGYLES
ENGEL WRECKLESSLY IRA
HEAR FOOT LOIS ANAT
ARM REEKEDHAVOC TUTTI
BOBWHITE RABIN LAGOON
ORONO MIDAS WOREA
SILENT SENAT MOTORCAR
IRENE SWEATHEARTS OTO
LADS CHAT RIME AMMO
ANA PEEKSEASONS LIMAS
SINCERE CRUDE DURANT
DOYEN HOMME BOAT
CELLOS GENOA WINNIPEG
ABOLT GOFORTHEJUGGLER
ROSIE BOOM ROBOT HERO
ANTE SPRY ARBUS TAOS

114

ELOPE ABET FRA PASTA
RERUN SARI TRAM ODEON
GODBLESSAMERICA TAROT
LAKES PAUSE NEGATE
OFFICES BATIK LONI
PLACED PINES AIRCOCKS
PACAS ELLINMACKAY HEE
OXEN REG RTE PEEN
SET ISRAELBALINE RENO
ENHANCED OATEN CHOKER
EDGED SIRES STOAT
HAMDEN PAREU CHANSONS
ETUI EASTERPARADE CEE
LOSS DEO PAN THEN
ANI TEMUNRUSSIA SHEDS
SECTORED ALPEN STEELE
ERIN DINOS STRAKES
BEWARE SUSAN ILLAT
ABASE ANNIEGETYOURGUN
LOREN BONN ERSE SIENA
INERT EWE DEAR SCRAP

115

DECIDE AMEBA MASCOT
IRONER ANIMAL CURSORY
COCKERSPANIEL OFFICER
ESK ROPE IRR POTS KAE
ADELA AMS LOKI PADS
COMO SCUBA NIPA ART
LIANA ELUL CAPT NORMA
ALMAS RUN CARYO ABIES
REI TMS DEAR CONTACTS
ARETHA CARL LOSE BEST
REC ONEIRIC VOL
ARCA ACCT CONK ELECTS
GOODBOOK TOTO BRA OAK
EMCEE CAKES LEE FELLA
RAKIS KHAN MEAD SPLIT
LNS TORT OUTRE EASE
ADES GAOL OHM OATER
NAB SHIP SCI ACRE BON
SNORKEL PEACOCKTHRONE
ETAOINS RELATE HEINES
RETEST ORANT SEDERS

116

NOEL ETHER LISPS STEP
OTEA MOORE ADELE HARE
LILYTOMLIN PETUNIAPIG
ASSERTED DRESS OPENS
TEES DEALT ALOE
BAITED YARDS DOORDIE
INRE UELE BURRO ANY
DII GYPSYROSELEE SIDE
ESS EASES SALEM BASED
DEMILLES ASSTS ONYX
UNLET SWISS GOLEM
ARNE SPICY CATERING
ADDED DOALL PASTY LAR
MOOR MYRTLEWILSON LIE
ARC AUNTS ALLY WEVE
LEHAVRE COLES PEERED
NIKS PAULS ORAL
ALIGN PINTO SEASCAPE
VIOLETCLAY PANSYYOKUM
ENTE ADANO ELATE MINI
READ TENON RAGED EAST

117

EVEL SCRAM SKEET AMMO
DIVA ELISE LASSO FEEL
ICED DAVIDCOPPERFIELD
TINYTIM ARGO TURTLE
BALS BLEAKHOUSE
CAINE GALEN EARS CPR
PARRS GATES BARE SOLI
ARID RIMED CORS SYRUP
LOS SALES BOOS ENATE
EBENEZER DOMBEYANDSON
ELEA BORES ALAI
LITTLEDORRIT CRATCHIT
OVATE RIAS BEETS ONE
ROPER BENS NORSE ISEE
IRED RAGE BINET ACERS
SYR AERO ARCED PLEAT
EDWINDROOD ILES
DETOUR AINT DICKENS
ATALEOFTWOCITIES ALOT
DALI TAKES NORAS TATE
OTIC EROSE ERASE EMES

118

STOCKS PALED [illegible] IBAR
HAVANAS ASONE [illegible] ROWESS
ARENOWATWHATLOOKSLIKE
DAR BEGIN NETTLES SEN
INRE DANSE RATED USED
ETAPE NEHRU SEC NUTS
RONALD DOIN RAVAGES
CEIL PEDAL TOLU
WHITECAP SELAH CLEAR
HON TWIG RARA ONTOP
APERMANENTHIGHPLATEAU
TIRES COMA EAVE IST
STAGS EMEND STUDENTS
CRAM ENDED SCOP
BATSMAN ELAM OUSTER
RICO LIT DETER GOOSE
ONER PATHS DELIS MUTT
MAT PAIRING LOGAN GHI
PROFESSORIRVINGFISHER
SYNAPSE SPAIN SECRETE
ERSE TENSE REARED

119

LEAST RAFT SER [illegible] ELVIS
EVITA OTOE IGO [illegible] SUITS
CODER TARN MOBOFSNOBS
HEAPOFCREEPS ENREGLE
STA STE DANE
ORS THAI LIR NESTOR
NEAP HERDOFNERDS EMO
EBRO SEER SPAR LXII
RETRACTS FLOATOFBOATS
SCOTIA AEE IONIANS
ERLE SOLAR ERSE
ENDINGS IES MISSAL
HOSTOFGHOSTS AVANTAGE
OUTS LORO ORLE ALEE
SSE NESTOFPESTS REND
STETHO SKI DOSE STS
EATS SCI LED
BEDROOM SCOREOFBOERS
LOADOFODES DELA ONTAP
ISSEL TSAR ACES ANENT
SNERD YERS STET TESTS

120

HASP ALBAS ABYSM BRIE
OSLO NOISE REATA RALE
HOOPSKIRTS GARYCOOPER
OUTSTAND SAONE GROTTO
HOSS SIGNS TRAM
THOU SHOOS BOAC SIP
HOOPROLLING WARWHOOPS
ACWS TEAR ARI OSSA
RON HOOPERATING SCOOT
EMOTIONS EVEL WHY
SEWELLS CREES IHATETO
ROE HART ANOREXIA
HADES LOOPTHELOOP ERK
ALES IOU NOUS AMOI
HULAHOOPS MAJORHOOPLE
NIL ANNS SOLON ANTS
AMOS SCALY BARE
BENHUR STATO ROPETIED
SLOOPOFWAR WHOOPDEDOO
MANY FLAIR EASEL ALUM
ENOS FANNY DEARE MESS

121

BASE AMBI WEAK DOTAL
ANETO RAIN IOLA EVADE
ENROL PROFESSOR NEXUS
REVIEW STINT PASTRIES
ILIAC ARDEB THIRD
ASCENSOR MURAL ANORAK
ICE STAIR PINON EDILE
TOMS ESTER ADDED EVEN
CREEL TELAR LEWIS EAT
HENNING AROSE SATURN
ALOU YENTA ANON
OTTAVA REDID NERISSA
PAR CARTA ELENA MACHE
UTAH EDICT TROLL TRIG
REFER STERE SLYER ERI
ASFREE ORALE ASPIRERS
IMPIS SIMLA TETON
ANCIENTS TEARS RUNSON
MACON ATTORNEYS ANTRA
IDONT SLUR ENNA LIARS
NAPES HOGS TAEL ERST

122

SCRAPES JUBAL SPRAYED
CRIMEAN ENURE CHAPEAU
REDBLUEPRINTS LOYALTO
ADELE ARSON SPETS LAM
MORE SKIES FERRO HOBO
SANELY GENOA BOWL
CIG BIRL TOTEM BINGE
UNRESTS POLED VOTER
BUENOS LANDS REASSESS
ATEAR BARGE SENS TECO
GIN BLACKANDWHITE NHL
ELBA OSES BRAIN YAHOO
SELFPITY BRUNT NEROLI
ALONE BOOMS POLARIS
ICONS CRAWS BORE NAT
SKAT HOORN SENATS
ROBT MIDAS MAIDS PECK
ITE BASED LIGNE ROBLE
TARPONS WHITEGREENBAY
ACREAGE AIRES ETAGERE
SHYSTER YEAST DELETED

123

HEAL DUCAT ZAGS HIRAM
ALGA ORALE OGRE ADANO
SKIM GAPER DEED NONET
PEOPLELEARNINGENGLISH
SEAS ARAT NOUS
LATHER ANZAC STOP REC
ILIAD INEZ ALAN LOLA
FINDSOMEWORDSARETOUGH
TENE HILT IRONY ORGAN
SNY PANE ISENT SNEERS
CURE NOOSE CAIN
IMPALA WANTS IAGO CAT
LOOSE TACIT ANTE BONA
LIKEDOUGHCOUGHORBOUGH
ARES BRET PEON ROLEO
TEY REND EGRET KINDLE
TEAS ARNI COED
TROUGHTHROUGHANDROUGH
HENNA IBID HANOI CLIO
ARTEL LACE THETA KNAP
RIODE ERAS SAMEK SANE

124

FATHOM REACT HERON
ASHORE ERROR BOLERO
SLATED HORSEPLAYERS
TOW LIRAS TALER FAY
EPEE CASE DONDE
REDSMITH CROWD STIR
CANE LOON ENTIRE
DEPONE DOLE TREETOP
EMERY TABU ERSE ANI
LINT EREMITE ANON
ERA STEN NOOK SPIRE
TATTERS FINN FORCED
ETERNE MESA GIRO
DESI APART GREENBAY
MISER ORAN SEVE
SHY CURIA LINDA RES
NEWYORKTIMES INTENT
ARCANE AREAL STATUE
PEAKS LENNY HAWSER

125

ARCHED MESSE SPUD
EMULATES HOTTEST HOPE
SILENTONHISHORSE EPPA
ODESSA AONE REARM GEL
ASTRO SPAN RETORT
ARI REDD AGE INRE
COSTA ADOUBLE GNEISS
ETHELS OREL SUE ATTE
SCALLOP SAA ATI AGHAS
LEONAS BRIDAL REEDS
GAL YOUCALLDMEDOG WEE
ALBEE SOLEIL LENAPE
SPEND EOS KEF RELEASE
PELT CIT REAL RINSES
SLIPON BASSOON STENO
TRON CLV ATTA LTS
BEHEST REES SLYAS
ELE TATES IRAE MIASMA
TICS COWSAREMYPASSION
SDAK TREETOP SENATORS
YETI EDDAS SALINE

126

THESIS TISANE PINCH
PUERILE DECIBEL AGILE
ANGELIC ALARUMS VOCES
UNI OATER LESE CARTA
SERE DOYLE NESTOR AND
ELATE REINE SEENO TEE
ABA SNERD SETTLERS
FALLOUT GROAT METE
ANOINTED OSIER SINFUL
ULNA ONUS ERNEST TAPE
CAD ORAL YEAH BRA
EGOS PRETOR TRET SION
SENIOR RAGES SEEDCASE
APEX NITER PREENED
ENAMELER CITED MEN
FEN RUNUP ATRIP REMAN
TEC ADOBES OAKIE SOSO
DIANE EDAM TETRA RST
PLEBE HOLYOKE TANAGER
RENEW CLEARED ETAGERE
ESTES MAROON DOCENT

127

MESAS LADD OBAD ABED
EVERT AMIE SOBER ROAR
DECORATORS CORRECTORS
ENTWINES CRAM ADLIBS
VEX PEARS IDES
ABIDES FANGS BLEATERS
LOSER SORTS ARENT SET
DRESSSUIT CODS ENSE
AERI INSISTERS EXEAT
SEGMENT TOXO BLASTS
NINAS EST PSALM
CAMERA BAER HESSIAN
OTARY RELEASERS NCOS
ARCS APOS PRAISEHIS
LAR AVAST ILIAC WREST
SPOTTERS EMOTE MISSES
HERA ARAGE OOM
SERIAL RAMI PROMISEE
STRANGLERS CHASTENERS
PONS EERIE AUTO REAMS
SASH LASS LEAN SETAE

128

EMES TRAIN ALEPH EDEL
CATO HAITI BERIA VASE
CRABBECRAB RAINSREINS
EXTREMES LOAFS SENNET
IRED LINDY FOAL
SOWERS BOCCE DACTYLIC
PIETA PARKERPARKA EBO
ALLY HRE ONES AMER
DEL WAYNEWAIN DUMAS
RELEASE VEINY TOROME
SEGRE PEARS MORAN
NEWMAN SERVE CABALLE
ONEAL HAYESHAZE ERA
INLY COAL ORD TMEN
SEL FONDERFONDA CHOCK
EASTERLY EAVES PLINTH
EASY ESTER BOAR
SLEAZE [illegible] OUTER [illegible] CRISTATE
LORRELORRY AYRESHEIRS
ABLE ERROL LEAVE EDAM
WEED TEASE LAMED NAPE

129

OSLER KISS ABEL STAR
RHINE INCA URSA FERRY
CONESTOGAWAGONS LIANA
AWE COWER KITES ONION
CABANA MATH AUEL
FATALE BELLESTARR BBQ
ISERE PAVIA ALMS LOU
REDI TAKE VESTS FALA
COWPUNCHERS SIZES
SPT REA HENIE CATERS
URE LEWISANDCLARK ROI
SEXTET MOIRE CEE SSA
PLAIT PONYEXPRESS
EASE AMENS ITES PANE
CTR EVIL TAPAS SOBOR
TEA JESSEJAMES ACORNS
NOES PABA BWANAS
MAGIC SCHMO [illegible] STEAM [illegible] SES
ULENT PROMONTORYPOINT
LARKS CORE RIOT EROSE
LESS ACID ARTS RENEW

130

```
ICOSI AST COMM ETCH
CANON LTO STOIC AREA
BROOKVALUE THUMBTRACK
MARNIE ENCE ELIDE LII
TERRY AGARIC PSALM
ASCORBIC PRAWNSHOP
ETA SNAP ERI ECARTE
RANTS GROTTOS SLATIER
INDIA TTU NEWEL ECTO
YUCCA TRI DRESSERS
ABC RAGEOFCONSENT POE
PARCELED EVE SERRA
ARAE YEDDO EMB ATLAS
RANLAPS ENTREAT PEALE
STEERS CEA ABRS CAW
BOOTCRAMP YIELDERS
PARSI RAETIA BORER
ATE NAIRA LIAR ATOMIC
PRETTYCASH DROLLHOUSE
AIDE REFER IIOO APSES
LAST SESS NAMA LYTES
```

131

```
TALESE BACLE MAMET
AVALON AMAIC ODILE
BACKWARDGLANCES TOXIN
BITS MOE IZE STA RENO
ELI LEO ONERS ABANDON
DSC ALTEREDSTATES MRS
INS VAS ULULATE
ARGOT SATED PAS IRT
LEASE EDO EBON GLOATS
PER ROLEREVERSAL UPSA
ALBANIA NIT LEATHER
CELT SHORTCHANGED OTT
ADESTE SHOE VIE VERSO
DEE DUE SPOOR ESSEN
MARCONI RIB IRS
COE SCRAMBLEDEGGS IMP
HASTENS SEUSS ARE DAR
ERSE YET AMI IRA MICA
RIALS TURNEDINSIDEOUT
INGLE COINERS NESTLE
EGEST KNESSET ERASER
```

132

```
ALBA ASH KEATS DECOY
PAAR SEEM EXTRA INONE
OSLO HALO VALOR ASNOT
GOODCOMMUNICATIONS
ERN HEY DENTS VALUE
EDEMA SAM STALE LLA
SAYING OLES LEN TEL
STIMULATINGASBLACK
SETS ZIP NOSOAP RENTA
AGRA MFOR RAM EXTOL
PRO COFFEEANDJUST FRI
HEDDA GAB EASE SEAN
ESTER AGIRLS PAT TELE
ASHARDTOSLEEPAFTER
DIE OTB SEEN OXIDES
SOBS NAILS SOS UPONA
NOISE ATRAP UAR GIS
ANNEMORROWLINDBERGH
LARGE ENDOW EDDA ROMA
ADDLE STEVE DEEP ISAY
POSER SORER ART NESS
```

133

```
ALAS ICBM SHOT ALBINO
LATH SORA MALE LELAND
TWOOWLSANDAHEN GAINED
ASPREE GIORNO BARN
TITO FET SPA DOMS
CHE PAESE ARTE NOT
FOURLARKSANDAWREN FOR
OAR ASYET SUNNING IRE
ATLAST ROO EGEST CREE
MISDEEDS FILLET CREST
URRE STE ELLA
SELLS PELTER BREATHER
CRAT ARNIE STR AREOLE
AMT ERITREA RAISE TVA
LIE HAVEALLBUILTTHEIR
ANN STIR LANDS ALS
RETE NOS IRK ARAM
SING PANELS ALLOWS
SETTLE NESTSINMYBEARD
ORWELL OATH NINO THEA
LAUREL BRIE ETON SUNK
```

134

```
DATA CREEP BABA BIFF
ENID HALVE BARER ERIE
NAMESOFMEN INTERSTATE
LISTS DANNY APTEST
TAMES BERGS RIRE
CHIP ONCE REGISTER
COEDS SOOTHSAYING HRE
AROE CELT NODS DEAF
GAB HOLDSPAINTS PEASE
EMBROIL ETNAS FABLER
LONGS STABS ILIUM
DRIVEN ATALE SILTAGE
RAGED SMALLDISHES MOD
ODAS DEER NOES DALE
OAT DRINKINGCUP TITAN
PROFOUND LOLA OVEN
ARME PLEAS POKER
ARAMIS CIELS EIDER
SEMICOLONS SEXCENTERS
HEIL UPSET ELIOT EROO
EDDY TSAR DITTO DENY
```

135

```
CADGE LAPP EDGAR RICK
ENURE AVER LOOFA EREI
CAPEOFHOPE BYEMRCHIPS
ITEM YTWOSHOES ERASES
LOKI TOWN ABAS
FUTILE BOILS DWIGHTEN
UPONA PEAGS SEATS IMA
ETO FORTHETIMES AMBI
LOTS TUTU EXERT NELL
OTIOSE ARIA EVINCES
TBONE ROD ARC ABOHM
THELAST LARS HELENA
ARTIS AMIGO LANE ARCH
CARD HAVEAMINDTO LOI
ISU SPICE DONTS GAINS
THEEARTH SHUTS ARREST
DLII SPOT OLEA
DEMISE NEIGHBORS CHOO
ISASASGOLD FORNOTHING
STLO TORME UGLI ANNIE
COIN SONAR LYES BETTE
```

136

```
HEADUP SPIED LAPSE
URBANE SPONGE OMAHA
MISSINGPERSON NORAS
ACE OINK ISLE ARE
NANA CANT ASEA IDOL
ESTIMATE ONT BRAINS
LURE AVE GOONS
TRI STELSEWHERE ETC
HINGES AIR ALS BLAH
ELVES GUSHERS MOOLA
REIN WAG AOK LAYSON
EDS SIGHTUNSEEN TNT
IVANS ELS NASA
ABBOTT PAS COVERFOR
LALA ELIS MOUE MIRE
ONE DRAG HOAG NIL
HAITI POWERSHORTAGE
ANNIE PUREST DEALIN
SAKES STYLE EXTENT
```

137

```
ALEE RARE OHARA SABLE
PILL SAVED ORATOR CREED
SEEM THELIGHTTHATFAILED
ENCINA RATES LEM ONEIDA
STROLL YET LONELY SESS
RADII DALI ARIEL
TAI INGES TOGA GROWLED
ARCH HAND THATCH SHIRE
RULER TROIS TROUT EAGRE
ABIDE ALONE HEATH THEM
AGGIES DEERE DOORS TDS
HENNAS STEAM FRENCH
AMT SAFAR HADES SEAHOG
ROBS ELOPE ERODE POURS
ROUTS AVAIL DINAH SISAL
ALLAH TENNIS TINA RETE
SABBATH AGER CARTS KEY
DRESS HEAP ROUSE
SARI ARTIST VIS YAPPED
AGARIC ENE PELEE SEEPIN
GIVESTHEGREENLIGHT CEDE
ELENA ALEUTS ANGUS IRON
SEDER DERMA REST ESSE
```

138

```
APRILE ATOMS SOUFFLE
REAGAN LILAC ALLURING
SECONDFIDDLE GETREADY
OVERDRIVE ANTES INNER
NED BIDE ARIAS SECEDE
MANE FLICK MASH
AARON LLAMA EVIL HOWE
FRANKVIOLA COIN SORER
AINT IOUS DRUMUPTRADE
RATHER SECRET TRENDS
PARE ROD HEAR
DAMAGE CAPONE INTERS
GIUOCOPIANO ALAS ERAT
EVENT ACRE UKELELE IKE
MART MICA ARENT ONSET
IBID VALID ONLY
DORCAS LANAS SOUL DSO
IDEES VENOM SENTINELS
COLLATED DONTHARPONIT
TRILLING EDILE IODIDE
SCOTTIE SETON APEMEN
```

139

```
NARC BEA LETHAL ABOU
BENCH ONTHEHOUSE DEUT
LANDAUNTLESSNESS OATS
OTO THEHARE ASTRUE
REUNES UNO ODAY HERR
ENNEA EST SARG MEREST
COUSTEAUNDERSEA VPI
URI BARD RUSSETS BOAR
PINNULE PAC SEE JUICE
INGEST RINK DEMURRED
USEMETO OUTDONE
PRETORIA STLO AGAPES
EISEN ALI HAM UNFURLS
AGAR HOISTER BRER EFT
SMU ROUSSEAUTOGRAPH
EAGLET TURF RTE ULEMA
RUED OSER FAT CLONAL
ORDEAL DECLARE SIM
OLIO MATTHAUTECUISINE
KEEN OVERANDOUT NILES
ASSE SIMILE RPI STER
```

140

```
BLAND BOERS BOSC VAIN
RIGOR EMMET AREA AURA
AMERIBEAUTY DLEMASDAY
TAR BORN ARAGE DEBITS
ALLY DIODE NEGATE
ADALEE DONNE TONIC
DONAT CITE PER SKEET
AMES DYSTRIPERS DEMI
MEW MERCY MORSE LURID
MINUS SPORE DOCILE
LAMENTS ITALY YANKEES
ALEXIS CLASS MORES
MARIE TAINT FAKIR PIP
INCH ISADORADUN ZENO
ASIAN TED EDAM TOTAL
IOTAS GOLEM TONESE
CARTON BALED DONE
TABLET ZELIG LEGS STU
WINEDETER VATICOUNCIL
IRES MARE ETHER ROUEN
TORS SPOT REEDY EXTRA
```

141

```
GATE PENAL WELD HOME
AMOS EROSE AMEN SIRES
LOWERCRUST SEDATEARTS
ORE ATEN TETRA ATTIRE
PYRAMID TEARY AROUSES
VAN HORSE EVANS
HERON EASYLABOR TAO
AMAN AHAS USIA CROP
SIP SMARTWAITER TAUNT
PRINTOUT ARSON PUREES
DOORS FILLS ROBOT
AMPERE NISEI CASEMENT
POOLE SOFTSPEAKER EOS
ELKS ETTE ENID ATRA
DDE SOURHEART USHER
DATUM AUDIO TRE
CABARET CURVE TAGALOG
ORANGE HANOI LAVE ODE
HOTCOMFORT COOKEDHIDE
ASHEN OBOE EAGER ARES
NEED BOLD STERN PERE
```

142

STOLE SPREE SERIF ALE
RANIS ERECT OXIDE BIL
AMOSTPROPHETICMAN ECU
TEE POI UREY PLED
ALAE SCORN NEE SEINE
TELNO ASTORIEDACTRESS
SUITCASE ESS THRIVE
GOEST GOBI LOUSE
ASH AHABITUALSALT RIB
PATINE RBIS APSE DINE
PUNTS ILS PSI AINUS
AVIS EPEE DOSE ALDOSE
LEN ADEFTHUMORIST NET
GAMUT EMPS DEARE
AFRICA ALB BESIEGED
ADAMSELINMOVIES SCONE
BUSES REO ENATE ODDS
ALTS LIMN EMS LEM
TAJ ARESIDERATOLYMPUS
ETA TINEA RETIA RIANT
REB AMASS ADEER ETWEE

143

DAW CANTO ELAM PLOW
ERAS ODEON LODES RALE
BERTHRATES ETONCHOLER
TAPROOMS HOCUS RAVAGE
EONS COPTS SATE
ARMADA FARER APPENDED
SEAMS MALECARRIER OME
THIS SOIL ODER DCCI
RAD QUIREMASTER DIKES
OBITUARY ELTON CACHET
NAIVE STEAR SANTO
OFJUNE CHUCK ANNEALER
GRANT WRAPSESSION ILE
RAPT COIL OSTE CDEF
ENA SUMMERBRIES SHAVE
SANDTRAP ALORS STAYED
RAIN AMISS FIRS
ELPASO DRAPE BAGUETTE
NEIGHSAYER BEACHTREES
TACO ABACK UPSET SALT
SPAN ADAS DIETS LEO

144

ASPHALT RELATE BATMAN
STEALTH EVOKER ASHORE
CONCISE CABININTHESKY
HUNKS MAIDEN TOHER
TIE TORTE CROONERS
EDISON SPLEENS FOIL
SSS NANOS IOTA COMTE
ALF TRI CANCAN MORASS
HARNESS ARKIN HAVEN
AVOIR BEBOP ERODE CAT
RIMS FLO WAG ORE TINE
ACH HOUND NARES CONGA
ECOLE RATIO EMERGES
REARED TECHNO FAD TRE
ALVAR RARE SCENE HST
PLEB KRAMERS HASSLE
ENATIONS ELITE OSD
PASTS ATTACH DOTES
GRAPESOFWRATH EPITOME
PAILLE EPIMER REVENUE
UNLESS RAZERS STARERS

145

SELF PAIRS JAR MATHER
AMER ELMER AGE UPROSE
VINE ALBAS MAP FROWSY
AGON REID PERU TOPEE
GRIZZLYBEARS TRINI
EERIE CERRO GEE COPT
ERBA SAMMY TRIABLE
HANDOUTS MOUNTAINLION
OSE ESSAY STEPOFF
WHILST VELDT RENOIRS
LEVI HONEYBEES SHIV
NAGGIER SEEKS SCHEME
HOTNESS GABOR DAR
SHETLANDPONY SALUTARY
TRUNDLE ANIMA LOTH
SEMI RMN SHIED CRAIG
NOTYE QUARTERHORSE
ANGRY GNUS THAI WIEN
ATABAL ROI FANGS SOUR
IMPUTE ILL EXILE ISLE
MEAGER MOT NICER NETS

146

BALED AGANA EMILS SLOT
AMOLE GRAVEL BEGAT HONE
BOULEVARDOFBROKENDREAMS
ART PER GIS ENATE EAMES
RENAMED BAIT RST
ICANTGETSTARTEDWITHYOU
EDAM EEL ANSE WITS ALS
TED ADS DESK GAGA TREE
SAGER OILS POOR COD
ILETASONGGOOUTOFMYHEART
AMAZES PROD AAR GOO
OFFS BAR SPREE SDL SEWN
BEA TOR AAAA BLAISE
IDIDNTKNOWWHATTIMEITWAS
LET ANNS DEUM CHIDE
TRUE MERE LAYS AWE LEE
OAR MARC SCAN ATE PLED
WHENIGROWTOOOLDTODREAM
IRIS ORRS ORANGES
AGENT AMAN ASA EIS LAG
BROTHERCANYOUSPAREADIME
LEAH NOEND CREEDS LEMON
EENS AMASS TASSE ERASE

147

LOG LEGIST COCOA STRAW
OAR ERODES AMONG ITHACA
ASA INDEPENDENCE COOKER
MINE BAT AGREE BERMES
STROLLS APES HOSEA
ARIE ASP TAUT SBA
HIS EDS THEFOURTHOFJULY
ASH SITE LINKS GRETTA
LEER DARN BASES TRIFLER
FREEDOMS EAGER THE FERN
ENDURE ALLS MOE HERS
WEARABLE COMPUTER
BAHT IRE TALE NASSER
RABI ACT SCOLD LISSOMER
EROTICA CHARM BETS NOSE
ANDEAN FOOLS AIDE TIN
SEEAMERICAFIRST DAM END
SSN OVAL EKE SLAP
DRAPE SRAS STANTON
REBATE ASPIC AAA OTIS
RIALTO MTWASHINGTON TEA
ISSUER ELATE STEELE ECU
PETER TIMER MESSED REL

148

MOLAR CSHARP SOMA EPHAH
ERICA ONAGER THIN FROBE
ACEINTHEHOLE EASTOFEDEN
LAND RERAN TSARS ROSSES
PARDS BELLE HERE
SAD ICE ARNO SEATTLE
TROUPE BRIDGEHEADS ENG
ROUSES META SNEERS RAGE
OMBER FARINA DARN RODIN
BALD PRUNE SPUDS CABINS
ESE DEALERSHIPS SABINE
TRACYS CAP STRING
ARENAS TRUMPETWEED LAG
ASOSAN COUPE PEALS FARO
SLUES VATS DEANNA RODEO
HEBE CERISE ACTS PERIOD
EEL SHEREENORTH RETELL
PEPPERY AVES WES SAY
ROWS BATED AMINE
OCTANE LONER URALS ELBE
PLAYGROUND BIRTHDAYCARD
RUPEE ANNE INSURE AHMED
YEARS RAYS DEARER KOALA

149

TABBY HARPO PKTS SALAL
OCULI AMOUR ARRET ANOSE
CATANDMOUSE SEALA LEONA
OTIC ISLES KATZENJAMMER
KITTEN ENTRY DEMI
ACC SHES MAIRE YORICK
CHATTER TERSE LEURS ISH
CATHER FEDTHEKITTY ETTU
OTOE OHOH ROIS MITER
SIN BRUCECATTON VINYLS
TSI RESUE KAIN POLECAT
NAUTES HINGE CATONA
SCEPTRE ETTE CHIRR RCC
CATHAY CATERWAULED LOA
ATAIL CALL MITT KILT
THIS CATASTROPHE MEASLE
SYL CATTY HATES CATALAN
STOLAS PITHS CARA ERA
OPAL SINES CATCHA
PUSSYFOOTERS PITCH TELA
EPISC GRACE LIONHEARTED
TINEA EDGED ANNIE LIANE
SNORT DOGS WASPS GATOS

150

TAJ MBA FAL TAP FAIR
ROOKIES MOVE ABA ULNA
ATHENAI ARIA PEDALING
WONEHUNDREDFIELDS NEE
LOFT ICRIED EIDERS
ELI FIVEHUNDREDDAY
REV ACESIN INA NODE
EMBER TISOF TENOR
VILER MINAHS STLO EON
UNITE IRISES STARR
EDNA ONETHOUSAND DEMS
IDLER AREOLA CAMEO
MAS ETAL MERCER LIENS
GNARL TOTEM REARM
MAYA OAR SAPORS BCH
JOHNFIFTYLEWIS ERE
CARAFE ARISTA TREF
ALA FRANCISTENBUSHMAN
LONESOME ASER APPEASE
LEER EMS RUMS STAMMER
ASEA SOT YES TOR ADS

151

SEGOS ANTI ASIDE BAD
AVANT VEIN RENIN DADO
WILDEOATES GUESTLISZT
SLEEPERS TAUS CREASES
HRS MALES REAL
PALLAS BELLS HEADMANN
ALIEN BULLY DUETS DEO
COMMODORE IST BERT
TRIM ROSEBUSCH SUAVE
STOMATA ENCE STILLED
NOPES ALA STEAL
AERATED SNIP CRAMPED
GLIDE FOOTELOOS ERAT
LONE PAR APPENNINO
ORG ADORE ASHES ENATE
WOODPYLE TSARS POSSES
RANI MEALS TAM
ALPACAS ASTA RECYCLES
FAWKESHUNT BAUMSCHELL
RIT[illegible] TESLA LISP IONIA
OCS[illegible]YSAYE ETTE NOOSE

152

ULM STREW CARY CLAM
SAAR POOKA OPIUM RARE
MIKEHAMMER PHILOVANCE
CROSSWAY TAPIS DIVEST
TINS SIDED LUXE
CANONS OMAR SILENCER
AGING ELLERYQUEEN HAE
ROC ADIT UNU PARC
ORK PHILIPTRENT ORLO
MACARONI LEERY ROSLYN
HEARA LENNY RADII
PLASMA CABOT PENITENT
AARO ARSENELUPIN COY
GULP CEE IRAN HIP
EDE PETERWIMSEY SCARE
DESERVED AMAT PLANED
MIES CLANS FEAR
APEMAN SELMA ALLIANCE
JANEMARPLE GIDEONFELL
ALOT[illegible]ALY ENDUP ERIK
MELT[illegible]TOE REARS OPE

153

DAS ICI LACAGE ADAR
OBE DONTS ICEMAN RENE
SAP AUGHT SETINCEMENT
ALTI PARADISE ELOPER
DOINGS ELI RBS ARETE
ONEAL WAAC ARAD STA
SENTUP IGLU ARRESTED
UTURN STRUCKOUT
LAMBSTEW OES SPREADS
ARM IDI AUGIE PURDOM
MODERN TERTIAN ESSENE
EMILIO HEEDS TAD PEE
RAILERS NCO EDOMITES
ADDEDSALT REFIT
CLASSERS LADE FLAMBE
LEU RIMS SHED ALIEN
ACROW OST OSU SNIDER
STAREE REPEOPLE ALTO
PULLEDAPART TOOTH ALB
ERLE ELAINE ONATE NEE
DEYS LATTER MOE DDS

154

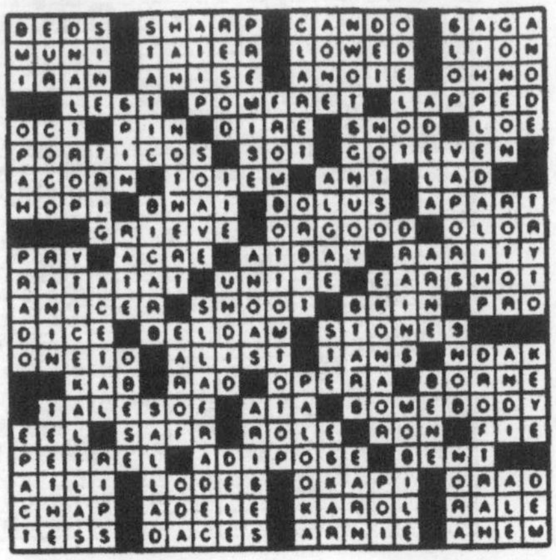

155

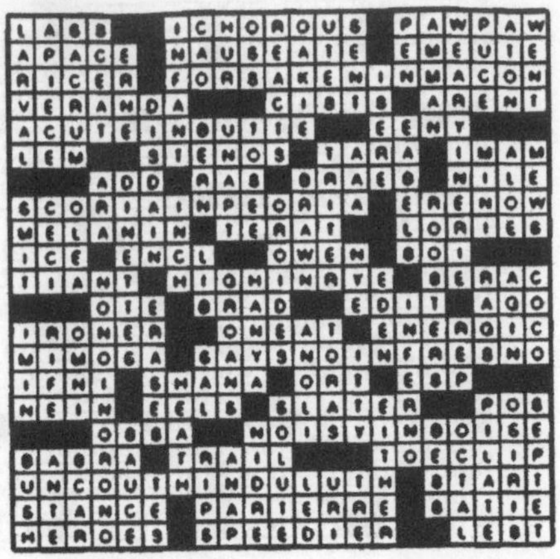

156

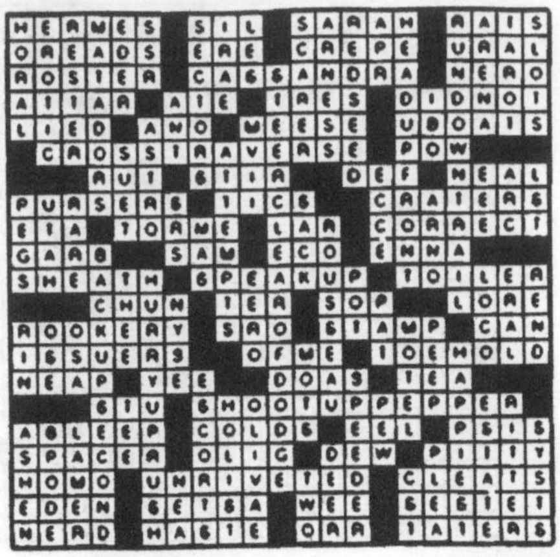

157

158

159

160

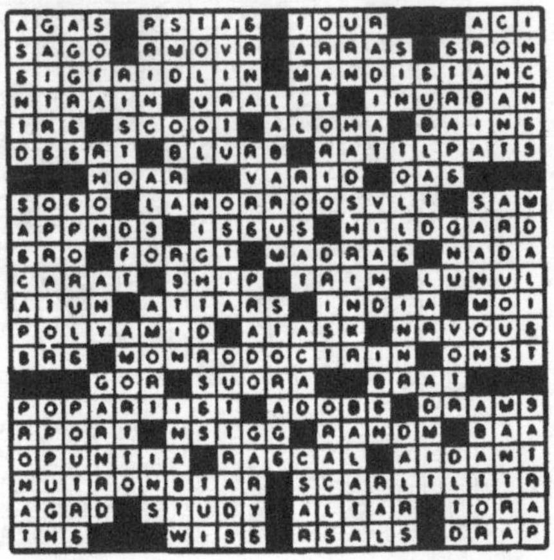

161

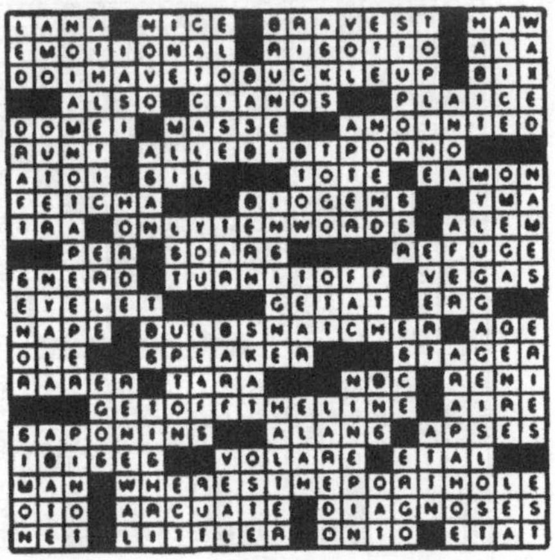

162

163

164

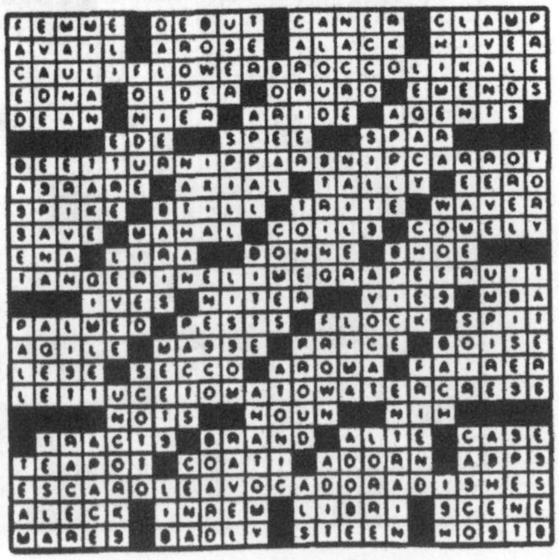

165

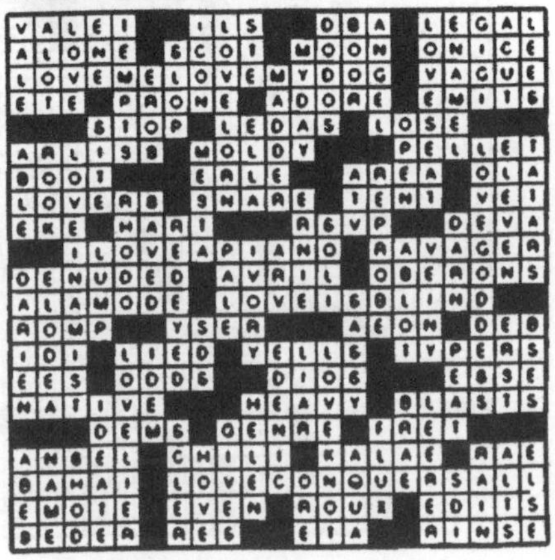

166

TOO GARDE ABES STAR
DAFF ORIOLE BUNT CETO
EIFFELTOWER ALTO AMID
INTEND NEVER BIGAPPLE
TORIC ELEMI STILETTO
EGOS SNIPS LEI
DOORMAT STPETESBEACH
ESP ASANA EEES INTHE
BEAR TROLL DREAD TRAM
SALEP TUBAS CAHOOTS
PLAINSOFABRAHAM
FORLORN CARED HBEAM
ELIA AGAMA RIDER SARA
SIGNS CABS GOMER RAN
SCOTTISHMOOR IDEALLY
OCT ARLES ASTM
ASSUMERS TONED QUOAD
CHINASEA SNARE UREMIA
TART HATE ITALIANBOOT
EPEE OKIE CAPTOR ARNE
DEER WYNN SHANE ETE

167

PLOD BAGEL PACAS DALE
DOGE AMORE ABOMA ETAL
QUEENSBORO THROGSNECK
DEPOSED PITON OPINES
EDER LASER APIS
MAGNET GOREN PLACEMAT
ORAD GLADESVILLE EVA
CASS FIAT OGAM USER
HIP BIRCHENOUGH ATONE
ALICANTE TIPSY CLIPS
PATCH ACT PAOLO
BERTH RENEE CONFETTI
HALEY GIRARDPOINT AWN
ACID PANS LISA IMIN
RON PRESTONLANE NINE
KNEEHOLE VEINS UMIAKS
LIVS REVET SLOT
ALLELE AURAS COCAINE
FIUMERELLA LILLEBAELT
RENI BEDEW OSIER LAMA
ONES SNORE WOODS STYX

168

IBAC AGILE SOPHIA ARP
NOTA SONAR PROUST BEL
COIL LACKS ARENAS AVE
ATTILATHE ITEM BESTED
GONE OVER SEATING
GUATEMALA YELL INGE
SCOLD ONEND BELONGED
OLGA WRIT TAPEDECK
SEETHEUSA HUER STYLUS
ATHEART DEBATE PITA
ANTENNA RATES LEARNED
ISEE LAUDED REALIGN
DERMIS DIOR SUNNINESS
POISONER TIAS TRIO
ASSENTER DIGIN AWILL
BEOR ULNA BORGIATHE
REMOVAL ZOLA DREI
ARARAT GALE THEMESONG
HET LIBELS SAYSO TREE
ASI SOIREE ARDOR LAWN
MSC ENDMAN BEEFY ELSE

169

ANIL RIDS ACTS BRAY
MENIAL IDEA PARE RAGE
BARONOFBEEF PRINCETON
STENCIL ARECA ADIT
CENACLE ARAL TOLE
MISE GAS EDER TENANT
ADULATOR LINEAR DAH
ILL GENERALSTORE CYME
NET EASTER LETBASER
DARNS SETA SAS LISLE
NUDE SENAT GIRL
ILONA EVE SLOT ENNIS
LIFESIZE DOODAD PIT
MASS PRINCEALBERT PEA
ENW SALAAM INSOLENT
NEARTO EMPS LEI ORAS
STAR TREE RESALES
GALA DRIER LATEONE
KINGMAKER KINGSRANSOM
ISEE VETO ENES SLOANE
TROD ANAP SERA TRES

170

AMA LAWN AREAS STEAMS
DIR OLEA DOGMA WALNUT
ANO YANKEEDOODLEDANDY
PAYMASTER DEE NULL
TRAIL DATA LEAPT LAO
EELS CFL ATTEST OMARS
RTS THEYMETINTHEDARK
CARUM OLAND ETAL
LACERATE ICI ROTATE
PANT CLI NANS ETHEL
ANDI HELLSANGELS HERE
DEANS TOMB MAT IBID
SLIPON CII PINAFORE
AIRE ALLEE DIANA
TENLITTLEINDIANS VIM
SENSE CRESTS SUS AETA
CAT STOAS YESO AMBER
ACRE ANS ABOUTTURN
THEYMIGHTBEGIANTS LAE
HEARIT ERASE SLOE LTA
ESTERS DITTO EYRA SEN

171

GARB IDLER OMSK ATOM
ABOO NOOSE ADIEU SAKI
WELLINGTON CORNWALLIS
PLEDGEES TIARA ABELES
FOES RINDS MIZE
REWARD PONTI SETUPON
EPICS DOUGLASHAIG MOW
ISLE DOSE EELS TALE
SOL ERWINROMMEL DARTS
EMIGRANT AWAIT RABBET
ARRIS SKINS HONOR
SIMEON STENS SEACOAST
USHER GEORGEMEADE DOE
LAON DEAR OARS FLOR
KAW HENRYARNOLD FLEES
CELEBES LIENS PRAYYE
ARAT HAMUS TAUT
ELINOR BERET ORDINARY
MANNERHEIM ROBERTELEE
MICE EARNS ALINE SLAT
ADAR DYNE LETTS SARI

172

ABRAS DUE ARAB SAMOS
BLANC ING PARR SARAPE
COCKROACH AMMO CUTLAS
STOLAS LOS PECCADILLO
NEWSREEL THORIC
ATTLEE ROBE UNE HAST
AWE TAD GOCARTS OLEA
TRUMP DEBAUCHEE SKEET
EYRIES MANTLES SHERPA
ANCHOR OUT ROISTER
SAT NORN RNS BIRR SDS
TREPANS DEN AIMERS
ECARTE LEGISTS REUBEN
RAMIE LIBRETTOS DRACO
IDEM JITTERY NOD RUG
CERA ACE TELE HECUBA
DEFORE ERGOTINE
CAMOUFLAGE TAR EVICTS
ASENSE TYRO SOBRIQUET
RHINOS OPIS EVE SUEDE
PENAL RTES RED MESSY

173

GLDS ARE CAPET
ALLART SLASHED AMINO
LHEUREESPAGNOLE MARTI
SAPODILLA SEWARDS REL
TRIN LEHM EIRE TONE
SDS FRADIAVOLO BLUETS
PLOTS ZIFS ANDE
LOUSE PELLET OGEE
TRALEE MARNE ALDERMEN
ROMA LUISAMILLER EVA
AMOR RIMS NIBS STIR
MER LESBARBARES ARAD
PRENATAL HAVEN LATINO
DAVE ELIDED TONIO
BERI AZAN CRONE
ORIENT EVANGELINE HAP
LOTS OMNI ELAN CONE
DOR FOOTLES INKSTANDS
EDEMA ORLANDOGENEROSO
SERAC DEAREST TORERO
TRENT NET SWAY

174

TAD PEP EMOTE USER
AMOR MANED REHAN NAVE
MIMOSATREE ERATO SNIT
BISHOPOFMYRA ATTAR
PERENOEL AILES BEANY
OLI TNT MITTS ALEC
MILNES CACHE LABELLED
POLAR RAREE TOME ASI
STENCHED DREARY BEUST
STELAE CORN MANSES
TAILS DHS AMEBA
ULSTER TEAR RIBBED
TOTES MASSIE STROLLER
EON DOSE SLOES NEILE
SKITTISH ATLAS PASSUP
CHIP ARMET MOT INE
ACHIN STRIA PAPANOEL
ROOST KRISSKRINGLE
CELT FEAST TONGUEFISH
DUAL MEDEA STEEN SHOE
ERSE STENS ERR SUM

175

ORGAN BEAMED STEP SCS
ROUGE ONSALE ERLE PRO
BORISGODUNOV AUSTRIAN
STUTTERS ICICLE RANDA
ALAS ROUSES REMELT
COPTER DOCTOR GALATEA
ASHER RIM ERASERS
SAYS SAGA TUNE SPED
ARS LIVINGSTONE DOYLE
IMARET REAPS GANGLY
ACCEDED ROARS BETIMES
PAIRED TEUTO SENECA
ONAIR HIPPOCRATES LAC
DENT HEEL ABET SILO
SERRATE GEL SCOOP
PUSHKIN COMBER SCANTY
ASHIER REPAID BOAR
WHALE AIDING DOLLFUSS
NEPOTIST CABBAGEPATCH
ERE ERSE ATEASE ECTAL
ESS REES LENITY LEANS

176

SERI SCRAM MOO FLEE
ICON ARADA ARC CLANGS
GRAVEYARDSHIFT HATTIE
HUMANIZE PALEASAGHOST
SATE HEIM ERLE
SASIN SETTEE EMERSON
ALTO WITCHINGHOUR KAI
ULAN INAT OAFS METS
LAG SCAREDSTIFF COLES
THEJOKER ALIST TALESE
FUME MYART HILT
PARKED DIANE CARRYOUT
TRIES DIDNTSAYBOO NNE
ERGS MARL GMEN SKIN
RAH DANSEMACABRE PETS
OUTSING GALLIA PAYEE
ACHE KLAN ALEC
TRICKORTREAT IRIDESCE
RACHEL HAUNTINGMEMORY
ATHENE ASP ENSUE ALAR
SUMS WAS RATES NOME

177

ISBAS SHAD FHAS MAMA
STOPT OPERE LOBES TOGIT
ORFEO TEXAN ALFCK INANE
AFRUSTRATINGATTEMPTTO
POSTCARD GOONS ROCHET
NAVY FROND PROA
IMPELA ALANS FRITTERED
GRILSE SCATS FLLES LENO
LANAS ETTE LESS ALLEN
ANIN ASTI SWEET AMEERS
DIMINUTIVESPHEROIDINTO
IRA DARIC TON
ANEXIGUOUSAPERTUREWITH
CLERIC TACHY HOPE EDIF
ALGAE MUTE GEOG PALLS
BARS CORED GILDA HOVLIS
SHOEHORNS DEVIIE MAKERS
ONES PINES PERE
SABOTS LAVIN SIDEWISE
INADEQUATEINSTRUMENTS
ALONE UNDER ALIAS ELATE
CEDED EDENS MALTA DELIES
EXES OSTE EPEE STFEP

178

TIP SIB GOB CARR CBC
ROO ALL ISL DONEE HEH
ILO DIABASE ANDBE ASE
MARCIANO INDIGOES STE
REDDYMADE ERNESTOS
MOTO LONESTAR LOEWE
ENSCONCED ISLAMIC
DEA KERRACOLE ANADEM
IAN ATOP LMT BOGGLING
CLASP ALTAI ROPA LIAR
KITTANDCABOODLE
ALTI HATS RUINS IDLER
HEELBONE MOL ESEK ELI
ADELAS SANDEDUNE TEN
FRETTER LOMENTUMS
PADUA ROASTPIG OPIE
SEALSKIN HOLMGROWN
EON TUNICATE LOUISDOR
ULT ELATE TALENTS ERE
DIE RARER ESE DEE ELS
OCS SKYS REE ERR RET

179

HIC [blank] SNARE OPT MCCL
AGAPE HORAL LAON OOLA
SNERD ELIZABETH&ESSEX
SODA EDEMA ROULETTE
CHAPARRAL UFOS ASSES
BORO TONY&CLEO IN&
ST&SPAT TAKEN SEALE
NEE GENET ASTAIRE
APA LAUREL&HARDY RNGS
MAP LUTRA ASEA BOCAS
ECOLES ART LSD DENOTE
RELET UTES OUTER LEN
CLEW SPADE&ARCHER NSE
ELOISES LITER AH&
INSET ASPER EASEDIN
&ES BLUE&GREY LODE
PARCS HUON ROSEBLUSH
EMULATES CREAM SIEG
DELAWARE&HUDSON ENLAI
ABER GERM TESLA REARS
LARK SSE SNEAP SCH

180

WOMAN PLUM [blank] SONOF ALAMO
ANODE RUSE PRUNE NISEI
GUIDELINES OILED NATAL
ESSE EMC SOCIALSECURITY
DINAH PALL RIIS
GNP ROC DELE PAST FTC
NURSERY DICER SALTY AHL
OTIOSE TRA SNAILS DREE
MACS ROARS ONLY MOMMA
ETE ENERGYCRISES SUNSET
SEC FOAMS RIDER SATOUT
OFFICE RIGID SUBURB
UNREST TABOO SCALA STA
ENTITY POVERTYLEVEL IRS
PAREE URGE SEINE IDAS
EGOS STEALS ACT RESIDE
EEL SWISS TASTE SUBTEEN
SDS POLS EVAS ALB SST
PERI AEON BLEST
FREEENTERPRISE AIR BRAY
ROPED INURED RECESSIONS
ALIVE ENDOR IRON BLOKE
ULCER SAENS CANT ALTAR

181

KARMA RENEE SCORE WIFE
ALAMP ERINS TALER EASEL
LOVERSANDOTHERSTRANGERS
ENE INGERS ARLES ETERNE
LENDLEASE STEIN STARES
OLENT TETON FINIS
FURORS ROVE AURAL GAL
DERIVS PAPERTIGER PETE
PASSE MAVIN ENOLA CANTS
TRA IONIC SNAGS CITEES
STRAIN PEAN AVERSE
THEPRINCESSANDTHEPIRATE
HELLAS TENT REVELS
RADISH CLAUS TAMER VIP
ALECK SHARD RODAN CTENO
CERE EASTOFEDEN SHRINE
ERS SLAMS AIDS ALIENS
STAMP CALMS PLENA
ASTERS ALDAS VALUATORS
ACTING ATION MIDSTS RIA
THEGOODTHEBADANDTHEUGLY
TERMS ATONE ADELA ATALE
ASEA MUSTS SEDER SANER

182

UPCAST SEWS TRAPP BRASS
GRAVIMETRIC ROGUE LINTY
HENEVERNOTICEDHER ALTER
ARANS STOOP ARTICLE
CADS CII RAF AOK NEA
AWAIT FIVEINNINEINNINGS
SAVOR OVERA LEAN OGAGE
EVANESCE TOILES SESSA
SEC WEATHERALERT OUT
ANSEL EVOKE ERG DOA
SATE GAI ATO ANDAMANS
TRIOS EARLYPAROLE RATTI
OCONNORS SEP IMP LEON
WAN OWN ALIBI PLIED
AWL NOCREDITCARD IMA
CARLO ODENSE ALGERNON
OLEAN STEN SCORE AUDIT
HEPITCHESSHUTOUTS STERE
OSE HUE EAR STA LTAS
OTELLOS MALTA ACIER
PAPAW LOWMILEAGEGONDOLA
FELLA ELIOT HIEROLOGIES
CRECY RAMIE INSP ARETES

183

LOCO ASPCA ICBM PIAF
LAHR LILAC CHRIS INCA
BRIDALPATH HEIRPOCKET
IDEST ERNST LLOYDS
CARNEY ADROIT DIET
ADEAL ROUT SONGSTER
SAILED MANEEVENT WVA
EGGS EDAM IANS SOOT
SEN HARTANDSOLE SPOKE
SIMILES ORALS WERNER
NAKED AVERS MARAT
MASHER PRESA DELIGHT
ARPAD HEELTHYSELF EON
DEAN SORA ECTO BIDE
ANI TWOSCENTS PERSIA
MANDARIN ETUI PALER
ERIE HARASS ASSESS
SILICA ROSEN TACOS
KNIGHTTIME CZECHMATES
IRON EAGER EERIE GORE
TINS BARS SEEDS EYRE

184

OVAL CEDAR ABAFT DART
RALE ABOVE LAREE IRAE
CROSSBONES BUCCANEERS
AYE PINE ITEMS POSSET
TINY ADORE SAVE
PECANS SWEET CORALSEA
ARABS LOANS ARTS PAP
NIPS DORIC DIRTY GAGE
GET PIRATESONGS ANNEX
SAILORS TODO FLAIR
INANE QUERY BAITS
ANNIE PURE RICKSHA
FAKED JEANLAFITTE MST
ALIS CENTS LAMES TACO
RID PRED STIES PRIOR
MIDSHIPS SEERS DAINTY
MOTS SORRY CYTO
ALPINE ACUTE TONE KAY
JOLLYROGER GASPARILLA
ALAE IRENE OMARS LEAK
RAYS ASSTD SPRAT LESS

185

LAVAS OARED GAMINS SONS
EXERT SPARE AMULET QUIT
VINCENTPRICESPLAZASUITE
EAU ORLE IXTLE MADAM
ELEC TIERS TRESS HARASS
OTIC PARI THOLE
CHEVYCHASESACHORUSLINE
REVERE DALIS OPINE OXA
ALINE ROLLS ANENT FRAS
MILS DARTS AMONG TALCS
AONE SNARE BALATA
BEAUBRIDGESTHERIVERKWAI
IRENES URGES CADS
ORRIS RIOTS DEANS GNAT
TAIT MOTTS FROME CRONE
ATA SINAI PAINE ALIENS
ALISTAIRCOOKESINDALLAS
NOOSE SUES OHMS
HAMAUL REAMS TASTE EVER
ALIST SMOTE BOER IRE
RALPHWAITESONGOLDENPOND
STLO SILENI DEVIL OILED
HEAT WRESTS SEEDY MESSY

186

MARIO BOCA CLAMP
AWORLD FLORINS THALER
RESALE LEONINI HAVANA
JEANAUGUSTE ATHENAEUM
SSRS BBKING
TACT ATE URBAN EMITS
ODOR NYET SAYS GNOMON
ROMULUSREMUS RAGTIME
ABACUS MAI MAR IDEE
HELEN PHILLIPSTEVEN
AROOM NEPHR
ASHRAFPAHLAVI ISLAM
AMIE OME OYL SCHEMA
FALLGUY PRINCEPAUPER
ANIMAL TAPE ORGY STEN
RACED ERNES BOY HARE
ATTEND OPUS
JACOBESAU BRENTSTUART
ALLHOT DISEUSE DUMDEE
ODIOUS STERNER AMBAGE
BOOST YENS PORTS

187

ROSTR OTTR COTS SHTD
ACTUAT RARD AGNT COHN
THRBLINDMIC GRNR OMRS
ORS STORROOMS SOONROR
STLRS LAD RSNTD
SCAPADS LTTING GODSPD
CURAT MDAS TOILR GRAC
NTIR SAUT RDSA DRIVR
TLA FANCIR RSTRSS ARA
STLLAS TOPKA RGARDLSS
OTHR NOLNS TRTS
DLTRIOUS SPATH DRIBBL
CAR GRIPRS NTASIS OLA
OPAQU NCAS STON SWAT
RSCU NDIVS MODM CATRS
SDLING ALICIN MDALIST
VIABL ONR RLATD
STRANGD PNTRATING LST
CROL MLTD ROLLRCOASTR
ARLN NARD ARTL DRSSRS
LAST TMPL LDRS YARNS

188

BARD CRASH CAULD RACE
ERLE AUDIO ASSAI EMIR
LISBONBONS TOKYOGHURT
RAIL ETHEL COERCE
TSETSES AERO UEDA
BOOTH EAGRE UNSETTLE
LOFT CANBERRAPPEL RIM
IDI OBIE SEE FINE
SLAW HELSINKING MOPER
SEMINOLE NAIAD BARONY
ADORE RAMON ORIEL
PARENT RENEW AVENGING
IRENE TEHERANSOM OTOE
NUTS RIA ISLE EON
EST VIENNAPOLEON ESSO
DIORAMAS RIVET ATSEA
ALAD ETTE STASHED
BIGWIG ALARM SLIM
ROMEDICINE LIMAGNOLIA
ALES SAKES ACCRA IONS
GANT TRESS PASSE DUNE

189

SKIP OPERA JUST WEST
CAMUS RIVER ALTI ODOR
APART ANENT RUEMORGUE
ROGERACKROYD LOCKERS
EKE OWLET REPENT
NEED ORALE ASCOT
CLANG ADAMDALGLIESH
RUNUP OASIS ETAL MOLA
ANGLO BLINKER MADISON
IDE IDOLS OSSA MOL
GIRASOLE ALP TWICESHY
MOC YARN GLOST HOI
ANTONIO CRIMEAN OLIVE
SEAR LULU KARST REVEL
HORACERUMPOLE WIELD
ENOLA REEVE AQUA
RAVENS SPURT PAL
ACADEME THEMOONSTONE
NEROWOLFE ADULT OWING
ZIGS NAIL LISLE NISEI
ALOE GREY ETHOS NEXT

190

PRASE OSSA VANE AMER
RENAL EPACT WASAN NOVEL
IBELIEVETHEFIRSTTESTOFA
MEMO DINAS ELLIS REEKED
COLUMNAR ARLES ALTER
SOCIALCRITICISM
FASTENER ITIS ARE ANTE
ASCENDS ITO ASBURYPARK
CHANTS JOHNRUSKIN EADIE
TENO AONE ASTIN CARIBS
STRASSE TERM SARTRE
PHILANTHROPICAL
FLARES PERO LANYARD
TIEROD BEVEL FELT ROAR
ELMAN PRAETERITA FIGURE
CLUBSTEAKS IDO RIDOTTO
HERS ENG PANE SURENESS
SESAMEANDLILIES
CACTI ORNIS BINATELY
SAMOAN FLOAT RIGOR LOAN
TRULYGREATMANISHUMILITY
DELTA ATRIA ODETS SIRES
TEST MASC BESS MEESE

191

BELLA GALOP SOFIA MAMO
ANOAS ELOPE ALIMB EBANS
LOOKHOMEWARDANGELSTREET
ESTHER ERIE ELA CRANIA
ALOSTLADYINTHEDARK
PEARS ULT LESOTHO EDIE
ELEONORA RET ECO SCD
SINGININTHERAINMAKER
SEEPED ROW IDIO NOBEL
HARP TERA LANDI OMEGA
ASSET AVARE ISM AGOG
THEWILDDUCKSOUP
IGOT YEN TREAT SARAH
CALIF RIPER INGE LIRE
ELDER EASE ASA SPADIX
RETURNOFTHENATIVESON
AFC ERR UES EAGEREST
LOAF UNICORN ESS RENES
MUSICMANOFLAMANCHA
SIERRA ADS CART DRUIDS
OLDMANANDTHESEAAROUNDUS
FLIES MELEE KNIFE FILET
ENDS PREPS SALTS FEELS

192

AMES MATA ASE BAR
DELHI ABACA LIRR BABA
STEAMHAMMER FREEMASON
SCREE ATTAR SABINE
TETES BOSSED ELYSEE
UDO POOL CDI AIL
SORB PRESSA TCU OTTO
GUARDIAN ALPACA NAIL
AGLEAM OSLO THROB NBA
ANA HOWTO INE GEN
DUNKIRK ROBIN BEDFORD
ONO TEE INURE BAL
NIM ETIAM RASE ISOBAR
NOAH NIPAND DOGHOUSE
ENDO HER PSEUDO DCII
GPO ERA NANA KEN
PREFAB DULLED ALLOW
LAMINA GEESE OATHS
ARMSTRONG SPRINGSTEEN
YEAH TINE TEDDY TEARY
SRS LED COAX RTES

193

BLASE SAMBA MESTA METED
LADED OLEOS ILIUM ATIME
ABATE YOWLS SCENE SATIN
RAGINGBULL OLIVERSSTORY
ENE RES GRADE ICES
STOA SPRAY SCAD DCI
THEYOUNGLIONS CHAN TEAM
HELMET EINS DEAN ARENA
ARABS UNDO THESHAGGYDOG
NONO PREEN ROBS LESSEE
KEEL AERI AURA LAST
SST RYANSDAUGHTER SPA
HOES IANS EAVE SHUL
SCRIPT ADIT HARES LIRE
THEPRODUCERS ARTE GIVER
RASPY EVES ASTA DIVEST
ARTY SPED MISTERROBERTS
YES SERA ANION EWER
SPEE SOCKS SDS NAT
THENUNSSTORY ONTHEBEACH
RIGOR SEATO AWARE ELITE
ADORN ORRIN RETIA SAVOR
PESTS REEDS SNEAD STERE

194

ASHRAM INCAN STELMO BPD
SCOURS NEHRU ERNIES RUE
THOMASEDWARD CECILSCOTT
ORE DEP INTER IHATE
ALANALEXANDER EDIFICES
LAY RAM RIO ADA ANI HET
ERS ABASING AVENGES
AMO TSE EDWARDESTLIN
ADAM UPA ADOS AIR LADE
HERBERTGEORGE SSE ROVES
AEMILIA TRUE TERRE EAT
TET SHAM NEER ERA
CAP GESTE METE SCANDAL
LEERY ERR NEWELLCONVERS
OREO TAO MAST IBN IRED
GILBERTKEITH ABM VOL
SMITERS SMEARED BIG
MIG PAL ETA OIL ONE RNA
UNROLLED GEORGEBERNARD
CLARO ROUEN RAE AGO
HENRYLOUIS EDWARDMORGAN
ATT EXCISE READE ACCEDE
SSS EVADER OWNED AHORSE

195

HAIFA ARMOR SLOE COME
ISLAM PEACE TABS ISOBAR
THERE ODETS OTIS STRONG
NOG TALES OAKEN
DEAF REEL LES MAGI
ISNOFEELINGINTHEWORLDAS
MATRI ISAAC EARN OONA
SUITE USABLE OATY SPRIG
IRON SOL OLDS HEALS
SATYRS BORGIA SPY
PERU CEIL APOCOPE CRAB
SAND HAROLDKUSHNER AIDE
ALOE ITERATE ETAS SODA
DDS INHERE ROASTS
SCORE ACES OLA ENDO
MANOR AMAS EYELID LUNAR
OTTO PRAT GAMIN ILONA
GOODASTHEFEELINGOFBEING
SEES IRS EASE TREE
HAIKU KNOTS PEA
NEEDED REED TAPIR RABBI
LAREDO INRE UNITE CROON
FRIA BOYS BETSY HERON

196

SEPAL RACER AROMA MOATS
EVITA ETAGE RELIT ADMIT
LEMON TONED IVANA NOONE
FRANKLINDROOSEVELTGRIER
YODEL ATA AWL
BIAS TYRED TALI NEE BLT
ANGELS ERE NATE ALAS
THEDIARYOFANNEFRANKBUCK
HONAN EERIE OMAR WANT
STATE GAIN ADEN CASTOR
EATIN EBRO TOSH LSU
PIERREMENDESFRANCENUYEN
ARM NERO LIFE LETON
RIBALD SALS CHIN RESTS
DALE IERI TRINE MANON
BILLYROSEISAROSEISAROSE
RUMS ALOU RES ENTREE
AMS ADD MACE SOFAR HEAR
NOW NON NAVIS
RICKYNELSONAROCKEFELLER
AMINO LICIT OLEIN WEOWE
TETON STANE AGING EARED
ATETE HARTS MANGE DRESS

197

SALAMI SCALP IDA SPLIT
AVALON ELDER SCOW QUITE
NOISES MEADE KICKTURNED
ENDO UNITY FOILS OILERS
POLITE SAPPY LURERS
IRR BABE CACTI COPED
NEUTER MAKESTRIDES WAY
AGNUS STARED URGE MALE
PANNE TRIMS PENCE WALLS
ELIE SEINE IRENE MOOKIE
TEN STEPSLIVELY LORRIES
GALORE RIP SEALIN
GAMBOLS TAKESASTAND GIB
ORANGE PACES THINS ESTE
FETES DARED STALE PETAL
ONER PALS DEARER SKILL
RAS JUMPINGJACK FASCIA
BORES ALARK REAL KCS
STAIRS TREKS REALMS
SCARNE KOREA PEARL TELL
TURNEDINTO RAINS IBERIA
ALTER VIEW TIETO NAVIES
BLESS ETS ARDEN GREENS

198

ACTON ERASE TOTED MATTE
SHOVE MODEL ORARE APRON
HOWETOUSEASEWINGMACHINE
ERIN SLEPT ABETS LAINES
RETS MAST STOLE BIDDER
SOT ARIA AREA
WHITNEYSCOTTONGINMILL
HEADED LOTS READS MOON
BERET REMO CHASTE PADRE
ONTO LIVER RENTE SERENE
MIA EASE CONGE GENE
BELLSTELEPHONEDIRECTORY
ATEN ILONA NOTE DEE
BRACER SLAKE BASSO MESA
REMUS TEENER RATS OATER
AEON SAMEK CARE ANTONS
FRANKLINSSTOVEPIPEHAT
EYES ARTE DOS
SERUMS DARES TAEL SORA
SEVERE SEDAN FINAL AWES
EDISONSELECTRICALOUTLET
LETIN STILE ALAMO SIEVE
FRANS ESSEN PALER ENTER

199

ADS ARA BELLE EPA DOW
GAP IAM AERIALS PERSONA
ASHANTI DRAGNET ORANGES
THERUSSIANSHAVEONEBIG
HERM OSO ETS BYS VEGA
ADEED NEEDI THEM HERON
DIARIES NEROS BOLEYN
ASH ADVANTAGEOVERUS LAO
ETA MIS YES LYE ANEW
TARPON KOP ICY ISA
ASPEN SASH BOHEMIA TEL
THEYDONTHAVETOSPENDHALF
ERO SOLARIA PAIR EELER
DST SCI PHI ENRAGE
ELIA PRE GOB DRU NEU
AMP OFTHEIRMONEYAND EDD
DISMAY AROSE CLASSES
ALAIN RITT TREAD SPRIT
HELM NET ORE DIE IANA
TIMEFIGHTINGCOMMUNISM
SPECIAL REACTOR PILESUP
FORSALE ISRAELI ELA IRE
COY SEX TULSA LEN NED

200

SOMA MANNS CAPO SEMIS
APER ARGOT OVAL TROVE
DARROWFARROWANDYARROW
ELMAN SITES RABI SERE
AYES OHMS ICONS AYR
SIN SAY DYARCHY TCU
LAHR MESA EEE SAUCES
EMEER NIKITA PARTONE
WARMER SONAR JAM SUED
MIDAS TIC SARI SRA
BEATONKEATONANDSEATON
RAN GARN NAN SENSE
UTAS ITE MISTS NONAGE
TONTINE ACTORS SOULS
ENDING REG DOPE TAUT
BRE SEMIPRO ALG NEE
USE EDEMA HEMS GRAD
PERT BEAN ICING ISLAM
SIMONESTALLONEANDTONE
ENATE ACTA AGATE RENT
TENET WHEW TODAY OWES

201

PAPA SLAMS ECLAT REDD
ORAL TIMES THERE ELEE
SAPPOROBIN HOSEA CANS
ERA VENUS KYOTORTOISE
RAY EWES FALSE SHINER
STARR SHRUG ERG ALERT
IDAS IRONS ANNE
PINTOS ALSO OLE DOLL
ESAU AMA SHR BLAB TUE
TOGA POMP IMPLORE ASI
UBOLT TOYAMACAW DARTS
NAY DIORAMA TSAR GURU
IRA SORA ANS TYE AFAR
ASKS LIL NAME PURFLE
ACES FATAL SOLI
RECUR TRI ELIOT SCRIP
EXOTIC ANSEL TRET AMO
SASEBOBCATS ATONE CPO
EMIR MAINE OSAKARAKUL
TENN ARECA COVET SURE
SNEE SIRED TRADE SPED

202

REDCAP MATSU ATBAT IRMA
AREOLA ORION CHAIR NEAP
BOILERMAKERS REDRAIDERS
ASTA TONI TAGORE SIDLE
TEY MAVENS VASE CHER
BAKED OBOLS CHARADES
ADMIRER SPARE SHANE EMU
CROONS FORTYNINERS AMEN
ROUTE SARAH ROE MORN
ENNA ORAN SHERPA KANGA
SET CRIMSONTIDE DERIDES
ABHORS AUG SHRINE
TRIREME CORNHUSKERS AHA
RENEW EBONDS NOIR ICER
EVEN ARC PLANE POOLE
MEET GOLDENBEARS PENNON
ORR DIRKS ALECS BATISTA
RESURVEY SCALE MARTA
POEM PART DROLLY VIM
TASSO RESEAT ARIA TINE
BLUEDEVILS NITTANYLIONS
ALIT RANEE CREEL EAGLES
RATS INKED YEARS DREARY

203

SCATS TARMAC GOD SMART
LAURA OCEANA AHEM EAGER
ARRAU TANNIN RITA IRENE
GLASSBOTTOMEDBOAT INEE
HAS SNARE ITERATE
BAS GAS GLASSSNAKE
ALENE OWL STEEP ENIGMA
KAYE BYRON TAEL ISLES
UNMADE AUER PHILIPGLASS
SORRY PRIERE NELL ASSE
USE EGGERS MAE YSER
MGR GLASSHARMONICAS BRT
ERGO URN SLUICE ILL
AILS SLOE ENTICE AFOOL
GLASSHOUSES SATE STOWER
ELSIE STAY LARGE SINE
RESEDA URBAN RYE TENTS
GLASSEATER MER GOT
ANGELIC ATSEA TAA
AMOR THEGLASSMENAGERIE
ROBED COLE CLEAVE ERICA
ALLEY HOSE HEATER DIMES
BEENE LAS ERMINE YEAST

204

BAMBI WHET VARY UBOAT
OLEAN RATE EBOE NITRO
OLDSCRATCH RAYWALSTON
SUITE ETATS RAH
IMA BAH TRINE ACCORD
DELIUS VIAND THEPOOL
EPICS DAMNYANKEES SCI
SHAY TELE EONS BETA
TIS MEFISTOFELE ARMOR
SNOOPED HARPO ABOARD
TIPPER TERAS SCHARF
NOCASE BRIEN VOLODYA
AWKLY LAIRDCREGAR SUS
NABS COKE ARAP TBSP
ALE CLAUDERAINS COATI
STATION UNCLE BULBUL
ZLOTYS BRATS ROD YST
HOE GEESE FONDA
OUROLDNICK DIABOLIQUE
DRAPE ILKA UNDO EDENS
ANGER PAYS PAST SADAT

205

COAST TGER MLTON
TORPOR ROLE MEANDER
SHNBONE UNTL LLNESSES
LSTS SEENGEYEDOGS TNA
ETE TMES LENS SLOS
ELSA COTS GLASS MNERS
PETSHOPS GAUNT FLOSS
BRN MOUND TREW
EYELESSNGAZA SHERBETS
LAPN GHOULE DOR SLLES
OWED NNNES BERAT NANS
TNEAL NEL TAMALE DNGE
ASSSTANT ONHSBLNDNESS
ARNG BUTTE SNE
GBBET SUSES CROSSBAR
AURAS MTRED SHEN SADE
STAT CEES SKUA UDC
TAC THREEBLNDMCE SHOT
ARKSHELL TBAR TRSTANO
SSONNE EERO OEDPUS
HERAS SLEW NSSES

206

SPICE ATTS SPATE MALTS
LEMON BRIE TONGS OPERA
APPLESAUCE EROTIC LADEN
PEST ELM DEVILSFOODCAKE
STROP YAKS FREE
SRS HUN MEDE AFAR CPO
TEATIME LASER ARILS HEP
ELLENS BAN SAUTES MATA
LOAN PERES STIR PETAL
LAD STEAKTARTARE VOTERS
ADD COOKS TORME KONRAD
RERUNS TIBIA MILIEU
DETERS KAREN CONTE BAV
MASHES BAKEDALASKAS RTE
ASSAD MILE LUTES DIOR
CHIN SILENT RES DREAMS
HEN SILLS RARER BROWNIE
ORG ELKS OMAR ORO DCS
IRKS SLIP PRUDE
SPANISHOMELETS LST MEAT
PENNA ABATES PEACHMELBA
ANGEL KITTY OATH ARABS
STERS ETHOS TROT DYNES

207

OTHO MICAH SNOB NOVA
NEON OVOLI SHAWL IBID
SNIPENOSED PIGEONTOED
APART AMERS WORLDS
BRODY CLEEK TORI
RIAD AGOD CRUNCHED
BURDEN CROWSFEET AVE
OLDE ETUI URNS TWIN
OES BIRDBRAINED TOKAY
PRESAGES HINDS PREENS
YACHT RUNTY ALARY
CREDOS COMTE ICECREAM
LAVIN CATBIRDSEAT SMU
OKIE ALBA EADS OTIS
WEE GOOSENECK EFFARE
NEWSCAST PUNK EFTS
ALIE WHETS PERSE
THESUN SHORE URIAH
HENHEARTED RAVENLOCKS
AIDA NEARS ELITE ROIL
TROY DORE DICER EXPO

208

SCI OLID ABEL DERMO
HAL LAME SCORE ACEIN
TOSLEEPPERCHANCETODREAM
ARTUROS IOS TVA RAMBO
BEAMES ORSO AGUA ADIEU
ESNES SLEEPYGARDENWALLS
TUES IHEAR AGREETO SELE
SPT PNEU TRI ALS
PAJAMAGAMEPILLOWTALK
PERU VAS ANA EADIE
ETAR AILS BRED LEGREE
SECEDE LAVE ETRE ATTENT
ALTAIR ITAL DITS SPETS
STING MON ITI TEAS
SANDMANBRINGMEADREAM
SRA IES EARS MIB
SORE ANTOINE TEMPS MANE
THEARMSOFMORPHEUS PARCH
ISERE AWAS RUER MENARE
PANTS FDA TOM DONATES
AYTHERESTHERUBFORINTHAT
ANIN EASED ERAS EOS
STAD RHEE DEBT ENE

209

FITCH PHASE STAGE SPORE
ASHOE HADAT WILMA ARHAT
CLEVELANDCAVALIERSCOACH
TIRE ENOLA ALDEN CHOREO
OPE SATIE ALLEN PREFERS
FIDO TRIO MAAT
SOMETIMESYOUWAKEUP STOW
ELEVEN VENOM NEALE LORI
TIRED DECEM SIENA LOOMS
HOER TENTS SALLY PISTON
RICE KATIE POTHOLE
INTHEMORNINGANDWISHYOUR
MARINER OCEAN ENSE
PROLES STEEN ABATE SWAP
ARULE SHIMS LEAPS SNARE
LOPE SPACE IATRO ALARMS
EWER PARENTSHADNEVERMET
IRID WARS NOEL
SAHARAN GRABS THRIP CAP
ARAGON BRINE AHEAD AHME
DURINGALONGLOSINGSTREAK
ABELE COPSE FENCE AERIE
TAMER TWEED FAKED GAINS

210

PUTTS SWORN ETAPE DAVID
ATHOS TARES TEILS IMAGO
THERETURNOFTHENATIVESON
RAGE ARLOS INPUT MANTRA
INO ELGIN AMIE CANS
ATOWNLIKEALICEADAMS GEL
DEVISE FOD DOL FIJI
NEWTON SAHL SOWED UFOS
AMATI THEWAYWARDBUSSTOP
SIRE PAEANS OLEY REEFS
ALAR OLIO EKE MATER
LEN APERFECTSPYHUNT OPE
DRIPS RAE EAST AMON
SPIRE AMOR PALLAS STLO
THEDARKLADYKILLER NIHIL
IRAE SOLVE LETS ROMEOS
TECS HIE ORA AWETOS
ODE SILENTSPRINGHARVEST
LEOS HOPE ARISE AHH
CALICO KEENE BUENO AWRY
ANUNOFFICIALROSEINBLOOM
TOKEN INURN ARETE DELVE
SNERD TOAST GATOR SAFES

211

ETO STAMPS FARE ACRES
NED TAMALE ALLOT GREEK
ANDSOISHALLCATCHTHEFLY
MUSIAL INLET ACERATE
EROS CESTI ROLE ARICA
LEN ASIA SON FAN LAT
WHATNOTONEHIT ISOLDE
EMBRACE RON REPAIR SHEA
NARA SMASH POSSET SINS
ERUPT BIOME SOLA BETTE
MITTEN ENLACE LOATH
U WHODIDSTRIKEOUT ICE
STALL SAIDIT DERMAL
ADIOS ALBA TERSE SUNNA
POSY NEISSE ESSEN POST
PASE ADNATE LAO MOREWOE
IBADAN ISAWHIMFUMBLE
ALF SAO NAP SASS OFT
NEEDS LARA GARDA OPAH
EASEFUL GRUEL IONONE
HESINGLEDCLIFFORDFORTH
ANKLE ADELE FANTOM TAO
JESSE TERM STEELE ONE

212

POMP SPEAR SMASH ASPIRE
IDEA TEASE TINEA CHEMIN
TINS ARRIS INCAN TORINO
YOUTHFULFOLLIESGROWING
OAF ROT HOARY
CHARY THETA SPOUT FLAP
ROTA PIET BLURT STRIVE
ONOLDAGEARELIKE CORONET
WON AWED ADANA FLOE ERA
DREAMER STUCK BRINK SAL
DOR STICK DRANG LUGE
PAVAN THEFEWYOUNG ROPED
ADEN HAIRY IONIC BAN
RET BORNE BLUNT TANGENT
ALE ATTY SOLNA KITE MOW
PIRATES SHOOTSONTHEBARE
ENAMEL STREW POLE RIME
TENT STAID BETTE SALAD
PANAY AIL API
TOPOFANOLDSTUMPOFANOAK
RODENT DVIII DOUBT PILE
ALONZO EELED ERNIE ASSE
MARTIN ERASE DETER NEON

213

BLEW STOAT RAF ASCOT
LAMER PEACH TABLE STATE
AMILE INTHE ANEAR AARON
HALLFORTHEBEST WRINKLES
SSE IDES ANTS MOO EASE
ENOS TARSI CARUSO
TATTER ADDIE OKS OUTRE
BLANDSCAPE GRACE UNTIED
ALMA EVELYN SCRAP FLAG
REESE RAREE HOUSES OLDE
SNR STUN STANS REPOSED
FAULT STING VOTED
MCCLURE AHEAD ALSO ADD
ALAI NAGGER LETNO ITRO
YANG ENROL BELONG DRIP
ARTHUR ORFOE SWAYOFLIFE
SKITS TOA REPIN TREATY
HAREMS AGEES OTIS
PATE IAM ICER ALEG EGG
ALHAMBRA THECLONERANGER
SLIDE ATREE HASTA TORTE
TONER TEEMS ENTER EDEMA
SWEDE SOS SEEDY STET

214

CRIED PHONE RABID DAMA
LADLE HORUS EDILE EVORA
ADESBRIGADE KELLYSJELLY
MISE ELATE SILKY TESTER
POT OVINE CONES LACTOSE
STEPS CURDS SEPTA
SCHOOL SOREL SEALS GSA
THANE ASTAIRESCARE GRAS
RINDS PHASE TARN GUANO
OLDE JOUST BLANC TETHER
PLY NORTHSFOURTH ATTARS
SPENT ALI ASSAM
ESCAPE MESTASSIESTA SHA
LLANOS OATER ITCHY PTAH
DINAS SUSA SLATE CARLE
EDDY ALLENSGALLON ALAVA
REY GRIDS ARRAY FILMED
GRIMY SMEAR OMARS
FALAISE AHABS SPAIN HAP
ODENSE ALINE SPELL GABE
GRANTSPLANT POUNDSHOUND
GAVEL MIRTH ARMEE INNER
RETE SAMOA STERN METRO

215

AMORE ABLES PLATT POMP
SAVED REATE AERIE ABIE
TREEOFHEAVEN WATERCRESS
ERRS ATONE TENSE RUSSET
RISE TILS SIRET CAREERS
NEE ECCE CANOE BOISE
STREAK POLED PRUNE SUR
ALT RATTLETRAPS LANA
MARTY TACES RAKE GANDY
ALOE GRITS BREVE BRIDES
STUDIOUS POUND PEACH
HOG GREENVEGETABLES USO
HALER OARED AIRPORTS
STEPON STRAY TAKES PSIS
AUDIO CHAR FAMED TETRA
ANIS TEETOTALLER PAN
RAT BARDE ERIES PLUSES
TARES DATES BLIT PTA
ASSORTS BASIS DEAN TIER
THONGA DELES TRAIT ATLI
BUNKERHILL ACEINTHEHOLE
ALAI IONIA NELLIE DOMAL
YARN CITES SELLER SEERS

216

SASS ALINES TOGO PREP
OPTIC DONATE OCAL HILT
DIANAROSSMACDONALD YALE
OCTANE SUET ROIL SALTER
RESIDED RDS ASCAP LLANO
ILOVE BIES ETUI
PAMPA RAS REND FARMSOUT
UVEA PIT SEAS TARE GURU
LITTERS CASA ENL ETAL
ELECTED STAR CRABS ORLE
SADAT UPTILT ARTUR RES
REEKY REHAB ICING
BAR LETME UNLOCK AEGIS
HALO ASHES RIEN RETRACE
ABEL NOT ATRI ONEUPON
HAUL EINS ISAS AGT TENS
ASTOUNDS UGHS MME THROE
CEDE ANNE AIRER
PAROL RADIO AVG SCALERS
EVENED DOOR DINO TIETAC
SEEN YVONNEDECARLOPONTI
ORSO NARIS ELATES SNAIL
STER EVES RAREST ESSO

217

TUBA CAST PITTA JAW
ERAS RICH ADORN LANE
MACK HIDEANDSEEK ACNE
ALKALI ENTER RELOOKED
GNAR ACTOR DENTS
SATRAPS HONED SUITOR
OOM AMOLE PERI SARNA
RAMS LETO UMPS NAST
TROLLMYDAME NEAT WEE
NIVEN TBARS REPASTS
SIRE RTE ALAI
ARCHIES PEEPS MARSH
DOR LIDA ROUGEETNOIR
DUIM SAID SPAD ETRE
ESSES COPT SLICK COD
RESTON EVERT ACHESON
CITES ARIEL UNIC
STRESSES JANOS ROCKNE
AMOR SPECULATION KLEE
MASS UTTER ITCH LEOS
ENS SASSY LOAM ESSA

218

STRUM CCIL MONAD FALA
THECA REDO ADORE AMEN
REPLY OLIVETERINARIAN
ELEA STEEN RIO SEERS
AMA APTS BCD ASSTS
KALAMAI GUARD TOR RES
MORNINGSIDEOLOGIST
CADE ROBE EBAN SEPTA
ACRES EIS YOYO ROAN
EMERSONGSTER SULTAN
NEW TWA SAREE ALE TIE
RISERS TIFFINANCIER
AMID SKIM SFC SOFIA
DATOS LEOS OAST UFOS
ADELPHILANTHROPIST
MER AIN TAROT ENCHASE
DRECK NAG ACTI REE
PLEAT LAP INERT URAL
FURMANUFACTURER SNIPE
FLIP EDILE TINA ELVER
TUNS TERSE SEAL EVENS

219

POOCH ABIRD CHOW NEAP
ALLOUT LANAI LAVA LANCE
MALAMUTESCHNAUZERSETTER
SNIT LUCIA EMBER QUARTO
DESIST SNARE LULU LYON
DAUB TONG SIEVE
ARTSY ABELS OTELLO BAM
MORAL OCALA MAH CLAUDE
POODLEROTTWEILERSHIHTZU
STUD LENTO CLINIC TATES
STERE ENCODE MAGI ESE
REGARD ALE ASTRON
ALS TYRO SNOWED ENEMY
SAPOR ASKING LUSTY GOAT
SPANIELSAMOYEDLHASAAPSO
ESTEEM DON PETER STEIN
TEE VERMIN HORSE PERRY
BERIA ENID TAME
ALAE ANNA AREAS NONAME
RECALL ABYSS NERDS WARP
CORGIDACHSHUNDCHIHUAHUA
ANILE SLOE TORTE ENRAPT
SIDE HERR EROSE DENTS

220

CASC DEBT MADIS MALT
ATUA SITAR AMORE ALAE
MOOR UKASE RANON NAVE
ELMANRATHERTHANTITIAN
OLIVET WAIST ERA
ENA ALOIN ONESTEP
SILEXSPOON TALC ORO
BAN TEAL ROSIERRULE
OUT SWARD BUNKO AIRE
ONE LAG SAMOA AGO
BARKINGUPTHEWRONGTREE
ICE PLAIN VIE ELL
BONE OPERA SCALD GAS
SOAKSSTEAK SKAT UTE
HAS CORD SPINESLIME
ARTEMIS CHEST PAC
SAM ASHEN UNEASY
GRASPINSTEADOFGRAPPLE
LATE TONER IDIOT ARIA
ANON ANEAR NORNS COGS
DAME ROWDY GREG KNOT

221

GOB AMOI HONER PAAR
ELAPSING IRATE OLDE
NITROGEN TRUNDLEBED
EVOE HOST RASA ELS
REND MORPHEUS LERBA
ARR ORATES ACTEI
LWOW USN NERO WHORL
GEUBT ETTA EPA SSTS
ENGAGE SIAMANG AVI
ODE IDA ALT HAL NON
REL FOXTROT MUSTNT
GLOB MIO NUCI EPOCH
ELURA SWAT ONO ASHE
GHIAS THORNY DAS
ROSES LUPERCAL MUMU
ELI OMER HOOT IMIN
EMANCIPATE REDCROSS
NENE XENIA ALPHONSE
ESAU TROAD NYSE TOT

222

SPECIE LAMED ERE DON
SPIDERY DESOTO LEV UNUM
MILERSEBASTIAN USA AERI
INONE BEG ARIA SANDLOTS
TAT SERA GRANTTOLEE FUL
ETE TOMCATS WREST TRE
SED VOW OPE AWAY CASHED
TAN VIE DEI SEINE
SNIP KINDOFDANCE NASA
PHARISAIC DESK ALOE TIS
RAMADAN IBID EAT RESORT
ISAN GARDENERSTOOL COLA
OTTAWA EEL ROTO POTAGER
RAH ANOA LOAM MTEVEREST
SOHN TRIBULATION NESS
RODEO NOS AZO COD
RIPPER STYE CLE BAR SAO
ADA ROUTE CHORALE TSP
SYL EDGARALLAN LUNA API
CLOUDILY SEEN IER LATIN
ALOR BIS FORESTCREATURE
LIKE LEI ANKLET ESTATES
CAY ERN TESSA DEEPER

223

RATELS DEAVER JADE MOBY
IMARET ENGINE UNAL ASEA
FIRTHOFFOURTH LONESHARK
ANLACE EIGEN CPO
DAD REACH ORRIS STEUBEN
IRAE AWE SHIED COCTEAU
SUNDOGS HANDELBAR RGR
ENDIVE BOURG EARS GRES
ADELA WAYNE CRAKE FAIRE
SELE SABE LORE CAMELS
ELI CITIZENCAIN REMEDY
OPART PEARL IDEST
KNIVES THELOSTCORD RAM
PIGPEN BRAD ROTE MEGA
ERRED POESY JAILS MEANT
YSER IRAN COCOA TENSOR
OTE NORTHPOLL SATSUMA
TENANTS ELATE HER ARES
INSTORE RIALS HARTE ENS
ASI SERIF BULBUL
MARRYGOLD NIGHTSOFMALTA
OLEO ULUA ALSACE FERVID
TAXI EDEN SMITHY ERMINE

224

SEARS ATLAS MESS SARI
CADET TRASH ACHED APHID
AMATI TOSCA CLARE PRATE
ROMANINTHEGLOAMIN EYRES
ENSIGN HEN ANTEATER DST
LSTS DSOS SLATES
ESSE ACH IPSUS LEAKING
NEAR CRUSOE PAPA SLIVER
ONT ATOMINNEWYORK IDARE
LAUGH DOD SPA LEARN NOW
STREET REM SRS SNAPS
ENTERS DIVIDED TRAINS
SPECS BEL PAP ARGENT
CAD ITALY ROE ROD INGER
ONION MIMIINSTLOUIS REE
DONATH MAST TRACKS CORA
ANOTHER MEDEA HAH ASST
HERODS ISNT STEN
SAP DEMOTION SIS ARARAT
PROBE ARANGERINPARADISE
AGILE NINER ATEAM SINKA
SUNUP SACRE PEACE EAGER
METE NETS ADLER SNOWS

225

MUSKIE REAL TRIPE MINED
INNING ELSE HERON ANEAR
THANKGODIHAVEDONEMYDUTY
EIRE NUDE ORANT ADOREE
RTE SLICE SLAPS ARA ORR
SPICE STUPE DUTY
NOWCOMESTHEMYSTERY ASPS
APIARY RIVE ALAR THAN
TERRE SKIVE MUNI HEARA
TREY ALOE FANG BREAKER
YAR LORDHELPMYPOORSOUL
LOTTE ORALE EDDIE
MYTIMEHASCOMETODIE GAB
SOONERS HUSE WACO BOIL
TURKI BASE STILE PURSE
ARTE AJAR WAIN HAGGLE
REED NOWISHALLGOTOSLEEP
ANIL PIPET POSSE
NET CEE BASIS MATTE FAT
OMENTA CONST FILE BABY
DIDYOUTHINKIWASIMMORTAL
ALDEN NISEI OMEN OPIATE
LEYTE STERN WERE PEGLER